Philosophy and Contemporary Issues

Brian Cross

—72

The Macmillan Company   New York

P9-DEZ-562

The Macmillan Company
866 Third Avenue, New York, New York 10022
Collier-Macmillan Canada, Ltd., Toronto, Ontario

Library of Congress catalog card
number: 76-152869

First Printing

Preface

The editors of this anthology of readings showing the illumination philosophy can bring in advancing the resolution of some of the important issues troubling contemporary man seriously intend it to be an introductory one. Unfortunately, many introductory texts in philosophy are flawed by one of two major defects: (1) they are too difficult for the beginning student or (2) they are too simple for the beginning student. Some introductory philosophy texts are introductory in name only because they demand of the philosophically innocent student a mastery of technical philosophical language and a knowledge of the history of philosophy one could reasonably expect only from a professional philosopher. No wonder students struggling to understand such books become convinced of the truth of the popular view that philosophy is a subject wholly unintelligible to all except a few compulsive adepts and completely irrelevant to life outside of the classroom. On the other hand, in an attempt to eliminate excessive philosophical sophistication, other introductory philosophy texts are philosophical in name only because they contain no technical philosophy. Not surprisingly students reading such books in order to learn about philosophy as a distinct discipline find them hollow and conclude philosophy is not worth serious study.

In designing the structure of this book, in selecting the readings, in writing the introductions to the various parts, and in choosing the books to be listed in the bibliographies, the editors have striven to produce a work avoiding both defective extremes. Throughout, the guiding aim has been to make philosophy interesting and intelligible to students undertaking their first sustained study of the subject and, above all, to encourage them to engage in philosophizing themselves. To achieve this end, each part of this volume contains pro and con articles on provocative contemporary issues, which in turn raise fundamental philosophical issues. In addition to the material dealing directly with contemporary issues, each part includes other selections discussing at length and in depth some of the philosophical problems raised by the contemporary controversies. Therefore, each part forms a coherent unit of mutually relevant sections rather than a miscellaneous grouping. Every effort has been made to pick readings for their substance, their intelligibility, and their freshness for the beginning student of philosophy. Since the editors planned a single volume and not a library, not all philosophical issues, positions, movements, and methods could be included. It should also be pointed out that the readings in one part often will throw light on the material dealt with in other parts. Of course, the decisions as to what material is covered in his course and in what order it is taken up are those of the individual instructor. Nothing is implied by the order in which the parts of this book are arranged.

This introductory text in philosophy is a mutual enterprise, each editor sharing equally in the work of its production and benefiting from the comments and suggestions of his colleague. However, primary responsibility for Parts One, Two, Three, and Four was that of Milton Goldinger and the General Introduction, Parts Five and Six, and the Epilogue that of John R. Burr.

We wish to thank Charles E. Smith, Philosophy Editor of The Macmillan Company, the Oshkosh Public Library, the Wisconsin State University–Oshkosh Library, and Mrs. Nathalie Moore for their help.

J. R. B.
M. G.

Contents

**Three:
Morality and Society**   173

General Introduction

Many university or college students take their academic courses as travelers visit Eufaula, Alabama; Sweetgrass, Montana; or Passadumkeag, Maine. They simply pass through and go on their way. After a short passage of time, memory fades out and the experience leaves no detectable trace. Obviously, in such cases the students have wasted their time in class and the professor has squandered his. On the contrary, if a course of study is to be worthwhile, the subject matter must be assimilated by the student. Worthwhile philosophy courses provide no counterinstances to this generalization.

This process of assimilating a subject means more than diligently and doggedly memorizing names, dates, and definitions—more than the accumulating of inert information long enough to pass examinations and then allowing it to scatter and soon be lost. A student who truly assimilates a subject finds himself changed in significant ways at the conclusion of his philosophy course. In this respect, taking a philosophy course should be analogous to undergoing battle in war, getting married, or giving birth to a child. At least some of the beliefs, values, methods of thinking, and general attitudes of the students should be altered.

But altered in what way? The editors of this volume think the change should be from less to more intellectual independence on the part of the student. An introductory philosophy course cannot transform a neophyte into a professional philosopher, a sophomore into a profound thinker. Still, it can strengthen students' courage and skill in thinking for themselves. An introductory philosophy course can advance the enlightenment of students. Immanuel Kant, one of the great philosophers, wrote an essay entitled "What Is Enlightenment," in which he defined *Enlightenment* in the following words:

> Enlightenment is the emergence of man from the immaturity for which he is himself responsible. Immaturity is the inability to use one's understanding without the guidance of another. Man is responsible for his own immaturity, when it is caused, by lack not of understanding, but of the resolution and the courage to use it without the guidance of another. *Sapere aude!* Have the courage to use your own reason! is the slogan of the Enlightenment.

Of course, Kant was trying to articulate the spirit of the eighteenth-century Enlightenment. Nevertheless, such "enlightenment" is not something appropriate only to a past historical period. It must be renewed in every age, particularly in our own, which the classical scholar Gilbert Murray dubbed an "age of lying." And we must remember that in the story it was a youngster who dared to say out loud that the Emperor was wearing no clothes. Often young people have not become hopelessly habituated to hypocrisy and intellectual conformity as have their elders. Many university or college students have not degenerated as yet to the state of the average American who reacts to new ideas much as he does to the onset of Asian flu and who denounces all critical thinking concerning fundamental assumptions as sheer cynicism. The youth of students, in short, argues a certain plasticity, a willingness to change. At least occasionally many students, however vaguely, recognize their immaturity in Kant's sense of the term. They know they possess the understanding but need the courage and resolution to use their reason "without the guidance of another."

Students tend to distrust authority, be it political, moral, aesthetic, scientific, religious, parental, academic, or that of the adolescent herd. Chaotic visions and confused indignations afflict them. However dimly and erratically, students want "enlightenment," intellectual independence; at least the best among them in their best moments desire to be bold and skeptical, not timid and believing. Therefore, however unconsciously, they desire to philosophize, to clarify and criticize basic assumptions in all fields, to free themselves from conventional pictures of reality by constructing new ones and defending them by argument.

Philosophy has performed many functions down the centuries. Certainly not the least of these in importance has been the encouragement of intellectual independence. That philosophers have been thought worth executing, exiling, or imprisoning shows this. The ancient Greeks invented philosophy, as they invented so many cultural enterprises. The ancient Greeks also were typical of "good" citizens everywhere and at all times. They distrusted their best men as subversive, persecuted them, exiled them, executed them. All decently educated people know the fate of Socrates, who questioned the soundness of customary morality; ironically exposed the "wisdom" of politicians, priests, and prominent citizens in the community as a sham; and cast doubt on the superior virtue of democracy. Socrates attempted to substitute the authority of reason or intelligence for that of custom, tradition, superstition, myth, art, religion, government by majority, and the general torpid circulation of clichés constituting most of the intellectual life of any community.

We today have not completed that substitution. Contemporary "good" citizens closely resemble those of ancient Athens in their distrust of unconventional ideas and their opposition to the assertion of intellectual independence. A prominent American educator recently declared:

> There seems to be nothing in the study of chemistry that makes you feel like a superior order of being, but you study Plato and you begin to believe you're a philosopher—and a philosopher should be king. This is a dangerous trend, and it jeopardizes the democratic principles on which this country was founded.[1]

In the *Apology,* Plato represents his teacher, Socrates, defending himself against the charges of corrupting the youth and introducing strange gods by saying:

> Men of Athens, I honor and love you; but I shall obey God rather than you, and while I have life and strength I shall never cease from the practice and teaching of philosophy, exhorting anyone whom I meet and saying to him after my manner: You, my friend,—a citizen of the great and mighty and wise city of Athens,—are you not ashamed of heaping up the greatest amount of money and honor and reputation, and caring so little about wisdom and truth and the greatest improvement of the soul, which you never regard or heed at all?

This is the most fundamental contemporary issue confronting every thinking individual personally: Are you on the side of Socrates or on that of his accusers?

The argument against the development of intellectual independence claims that it will result in anarchy, destroying law and order. Socrates, on the contrary, contended that a society where reason is sovereign will be more stable and just than any other because such a rational collective life will rest on knowledge, not on ignorance, fear, fraud, and force. Socrates further seemed to hold that truth is consistent and unchanging. Therefore, to the extent that men know the truth, they will agree. Men disagree through ignorance. Hence, the ideal or "real" community, being based on full knowledge of all the truth, would be free of internal dissension and perfectly stable, having taken on the characteristics of truth. The hegemony of reason will produce the only enduring social unity and harmony, the only "real" law and order. Appeal to authorities other than reason produces only a temporary and therefore illusory simulacrum of social order and harmony. Socrates was tried and condemned to death for introducing strange gods and corrupting the youth. He was found guilty by a jury of his peers and probably rightly so. Reason is a strange god and corrupts provincial ignorance and complacency.

---

[1] Dr. Samuel I. Hayakawa, "The Playboy Panel: Student Revolt," *Playboy,* September 1969, p. 98. Reprinted by permission of *Playboy.*

This book of introductory readings in philosophy now in your hands has been designed in the spirit of Socrates. The readings have been selected and arranged in order to encourage the student to use his own reason. Socrates counted men and women truly his followers, not because they agreed with his conclusions, but because they dared to "follow the argument wherever it may lead." The son of a father who was a stonecutter and of a mother who practiced the trade of a midwife, Socrates neglected stonecutting, in which he had been trained, and in a sense adopted the vocation of his mother. Socrates called himself an intellectual midwife, helping others to give birth to the new ideas with which their minds already were pregnant. Nearly every day Socrates could be found in the busy public square of ancient Athens, where all day long he buttonholed the rich politicians, poets, generals, businessmen, actors, philosophers, and all the Rotarians and intellectuals and "beautiful people," all the shrewd old men of power and the clever young men of ambition of his time, and asked them searching questions about what they were doing, what they wanted, what they believed and why they were doing, wanting, believing it. As the great and powerful, the talented, the learned, the old, and the young passed by, Socrates asked them: What do you really want? Riches, power, happiness, knowledge? Is the Good pleasure and Evil pain? Does might really make right? What is love and what is worthy of love? Should children always obey their parents? How do you know your teacher really is wise? What can be taught and learned and what not? Can anything be taught? Who should rule the city: politicians, wealthy families, soldiers, intellectuals, artists? Do the gods really exist? Is there a life after death? Or is religion a confidence game perpetrated by clever priests? Who knows the truth: philosophers, inspired artists, men of practical experience, or drug-crazed oracles? And what is "truth"? In short, Socrates put the questions asked by intelligent, sensitive, civilized people—the questions that always occur to young people—indeed, many of the questions no doubt formulated at one time or another by you, the reader of these lines.

It has been well said that philosophy begins in the conflict of opinions. Each Part of this book contains a section of readings dealing with certain contemporary issues, with some of the questions asked and discussed in the public life of America today: Can men be made happy by science? Is anyone ever responsible for his acts and deserving of punishment? Should obscene art be censored? Do we live forever or rot when dead? Do we need religion to lead a meaningful life? Do some people possess unusual psychic powers, such as the ability to foretell the future or communicate with the dead? Are men merely complex machines? Can we have a sound sexual morality? Is civil disobedience ever justified?

The selections chosen for each contemporary issue clearly conflict with one another. Both affirmative and negative sides of the debate are pre-

sented on each issue, and every effort has been made by the editors to
find equally powerful and persuasive statements both *pro* and *con.*

Yet whatever the issue, as men reflect and by argument are driven back to
question their fundamental assumptions, as the protagonists discover they
were ignorant of their own ignorance, as they realize they know least about
that of which they talk most, then debate and discussion mature into philosophical inquiry. Etymologically, *philosophy* means "love of wisdom." This
definition may satisfy the beginning student temporarily. However, more
probing queries soon come to mind. What is love? What is wisdom? Does
Jean-Paul Sartre really love wisdom? Was William James really wise?
Traditionally, philosophy has been surveyed into such general fields as
Ethics, Metaphysics, Logic, Epistemology, and, more recently, Aesthetics
or Philosophy of Art. Library catalogues still divide philosophy in this
manner. Yet this approach with its dry and abstract schematism sheds little
illumination for the unskilled in philosophy. The editors judge that students
will derive the most enlightenment from first encountering philosophy as a
congeries of problems or issues invariably met by men when they no longer
are content to reflect superficially on human life. As long as men are certain
their fundamental assumptions in morality, politics, religion, art, science,
and other cultural enterprises are true and complete, they do not philosophize. If they argue, it is only over matters of detail, over the application
to particular cases of commonly accepted principles. In our revolutionary
era, no such complacency remains honorable for intelligent and informed
people. The Contemporary Issues sections in each Part of the book show
men being led to question their fundamental assumptions. Grouped with
the Contemporary Issues selections are readings scrutinizing some of the
relevant philosophical issues all too often left implicit. One cannot sensibly
discuss whether or not religion is necessary to a meaningful life until he
has settled for himself the question of whether or not religion is an illusion.
How can men be praised or blamed if they are not morally responsible but
are complex machines? Why censor art if it produces no effect on human
conduct? Why should we elect car salesmen, country lawyers, chicken
farmers, real estate agents, and other such people ignorant of science to
the United States Congress if all genuine knowledge comes from science?
Faced with questions like these, one may ignore them, play bridge or golf,
make money, watch television—in short, act the typical Americano, be
sentimental, fatuous, go-getting, unthinking, a zero. However, a quite different reaction is possible. A man may pluck up his courage and think for
himself, follow his own reason, philosophize.

Intellectual independence does not necessitate the repudiation of all tradition. Ample and venerable precedent exists for inaugurating a new enterprise with ten commandments. Here are ten commandments for beginning

philosophizers written down by the late Bertrand Russell, one of the most intellectually independent men of our day:

1   Do not feel certain of anything.

2   Do not think it worthwhile to produce belief by concealing evidence, for the evidence is sure to come to light.

3   Never try to discourage thinking, for you are sure to succeed.

4   When met with opposition, even if it should be from your husband or your children, endeavour to overcome it by argument and not by authority, for a victory dependent upon authority is unreal and illusory.

5   Have no respect for the authority of others, for there are always contrary authorities to be found.

6   Do not use power to suppress opinions you think pernicious, for if you do the opinions will suppress you.

7   Do not fear to be eccentric in opinion, for every opinion now accepted was once eccentric.

8   Find more pleasure in intelligent dissents than in passive agreement, for, if you value intelligence as you should, the former implies a deeper agreement than the latter.

9   Be scrupulously truthful, even when truth is inconvenient, for it is more inconvenient when you try to conceal it.

10   Do not feel envious of the happiness of those who live in a fool's paradise, for only a fool will think that it is happiness.[2]

[2] Bertrand Russell, *The Independent,* June 1965, p. 4. Reprinted by permission of *The Independent.*

One:
Freedom
or Determinism

Introduction

As currently discussed, the issue of whether man's behavior is free or determined has been generated by the development of the natural sciences since the sixteenth century. A basic assumption of the evolving sciences was universal causation, i.e., that every event has a cause. Further it was thought that events occurred in orderly patterns, which could be formulated as causal or natural laws. On the basis of these laws and knowledge of the actual causes at work, accurate predictions would be made. In principle, any event could be predicted; it was only the lack of knowledge of the laws or the present causes that limited prediction. The theory asserting universal causation and total predictability traditionally has been called *determinism.*

For the determinist, human actions are events as predictable as any other type of event. Just as the behavior of water heated to 212 degrees can be predicted, so, in principle, can the behavior of a person given a million dollars. The determinist would admit that, at the moment, the latter sort of prediction cannot be made reliably because we lack the necessary exact laws of human behavior. Someday, however, the social sciences may find such laws, and correct predictions will become possible.

Determinism is rejected by a group of theorists holding a position called *libertarianism.* Although libertarians present a number of specific criticisms of determinism, most of these objections are concerned primarily with what appears to be a consequence of that position. Libertarians contend that if all actions are the result of causes (and those causes of other causes, and so on), then no actions are ones for which anyone can be held morally responsible. The robber sticking up a bank today does so as a result of a series of causes which can be traced back prior to his birth. His behavior results from such factors as his education, a lack of parental love, and the nutritional quality of the food he ate as a child. In turn, these causes flow from the kind of education his parents received, their lack of parental love, and other such elements. How can the robber justifiably be held responsible or blamed for his behavior? He could not help the way his parents treated him nor the manner in which they were educated. For the libertarian, to be considered responsible for an act is to be free to have acted otherwise; but such freedom apparently cannot exist when all human actions are the predictable outcome of various causes. In "Freedom of Choice and Human Responsibility," Corliss Lamont presents a detailed defense of libertarianism. He maintains that we have an immediate, powerful, common-sense intuition that we are free. While such an intuition could be false, it puts the burden of proving that it is so on the determinists. Also, Lamont maintains that determinism must be considered false because if it were true it would imply that all deliberation is illusory since one never can choose. To maintain that all our deliberation never results in any real choice seems, to Lamont, absurd.

Not all philosophers have been willing to accept the libertarian claim that determinism erases moral responsibility. Some, defending *soft determinism,* maintain that people can be morally responsible even though their behavior is determined. One argument soft determinists frequently use holds that a person's behavior is free if it is not the result of any compulsion. If you go to the movies because you wish to and are not pressured or coerced by anyone to do so, then your action ordinarily would be called a free one. Of course your wish is the result of numerous causes swarming in your background. Thus, we have an action which is determined and yet called "free." The soundness of this soft determinist argument depends on the cogency of the analysis of the meaning of "free." W. T. Stace defends soft determinism in his article "The Problem of Free Will."

Hard determinism consists in accepting the rejection of moral responsibility as an undeniable consequence of determinism. In fact, hard determinists often maintain that knowledge that no one is morally responsible provides the basis for a satisfactory personal life as well as the ground for a more rational and humane system of interpersonal relationships. For them, the realization that man is completely determined produces a liberating cessation of worry about the future (since it is out of one's control) and the fortitude to accept whatever befalls one. In dealing with others, one realizes the irrationality of concern about blame, merit, or retribution. In his article "The Delusion of Free Will," Robert Blatchford presents the hard determinists' position. He argues both that there is no free will and that the traditional notions of responsibility are unacceptable. All human actions are ruled by heredity and environment; and, since we are not responsible for either of these, all blame is unjust. Blatchford argues that if the will were free, prediction on the basis of environment and training would be impossible. But since in many cases we can make very reliable predictions about future behavior, free will cannot be true. Blatchford also doubts that most supporters of free will really believe it. If they did, would they try so hard to secure a good environment for their children? The concern for the child's environment indicates a belief that it is of great importance in molding the man.

Sometimes confused with hard determinism, *fatalism,* as usually held, asserts that events are bound to occur regardless of what we do. The hard determinist, as distinguished from the fatalist, claims that events occur because of antecedent causes and that our own behavior constitutes one of those causal factors. *Predestination* offers a version of fatalism that asserts that certain events must occur because they have been willed by God. The early Calvinists, who espoused this doctrine, declared that all men were predestined to be saved or damned according to the will of God. The defenses of fatalism and predestination generally depend on various theological or metaphysical positions whose consideration would take us too far from the context of the current discussions of free will and determinism.

A number of important issues have arisen as a result of different views regarding determinism. One often debated issue concerns the control of human behavior. Determinists see enormous possibilities in directing the development of man through the study of the hereditary and environmental factors influencing behavior. Many look forward to the day when the various social sciences will have formulated laws which allow us to produce happier and "better" people. The selections from B. F. Skinner's *Walden Two* give us a famous psychologist's view of an ideal society possibly resulting from a greater knowledge of human conditioning. Skinner argues that through the application of various conditioning and reinforcement techniques, we can produce people who have those psychological characteristics necessary for a productive and viable society. In the selection, he shows how children might be conditioned to have self-control and a large degree of tolerance to annoying situations. It should be kept in mind that Skinner does not desire to manipulate men otherwise free; rather, he wants to change present causal determinants for ones productive of more capable and happy human beings.

Libertarians maintain that precise laws of human behavior will always elude investigators because such behavior, being undetermined, is unpredictable. Other philosophers think human behavior may be controllable someday, but they fear the manner in which such power might be used. In "Ignoble Utopias," Joseph Wood Krutch argues that even if a society like Walden Two were possible, it would be morally unpalatable because such a community would end in a dictatorship capable of manipulating men in any way the rulers desired. He feels that before any techniques are tried, there should first be some agreement on the goals sought. But perhaps more worrisome to Krutch is the conviction that, if conditioning procedures are successful, all human thinking as we have known it will come to an end. Unlike Thomas Huxley, whom he quotes, Krutch is appalled at the prospect that man might be turned into a robot. Skinner attempts to answer Krutch's charges in "The Control of Human Behavior." He argues that Krutch is inconsistent because the latter claims that man is not determined and yet admits that scientific developments may eliminate freedom. If behavior is not determined, then conditioning techniques should not be effective. Skinner, who feels that Krutch is really fearful of new scientific developments, sees no virtue in ignorance. New scientific knowledge can help us better understand man and design a world that satisfies man's needs. Rejection of science would mean the end of our only hope to build a better world.

A second frequently debated problem arising from the conflict between determinists and libertarians involves the proper treatment of criminals. Hard determinists argue that any punishment resting on notions of moral blame, retribution, and desert should be replaced by a treatment of criminals that recognizes their lack of responsibility. Thus, such advocates often defend the rehabilitation of criminals rather than any sort of traditional punishment. In "The Criminal Law System," Karl Menninger attacks the traditional views of punishment, which consider men as responsible for their behavior and, as a result, deserving of punishment for their crimes. Judgments that criminals are vicious or greedy result from an archaic view, which he wishes to see replaced by a scientific one. The criminal, instead of going to prison to serve some specific sentence, should go to an institution where he can be treated for as long as necessary to change his behavior and so make him a valuable citizen. Menninger is convinced that psychiatrists have the knowledge to discern the causes of criminal behavior and, through the application of appropriate techniques, bring about the desired rehabilitation.

C. S. Lewis, in his article "The Humanitarian Theory of Punishment," is concerned that the psychological methods used in rehabilitation will be as harsh and inhuman as many traditional penalties have been in the past. The young delinquent who cannot convince his psychiatrist that he is well may spend the rest of his life in a mental institution. Lewis also attacks the use of punishment as a device to deter potential criminals. He fears that to lower the crime rate officials might proclaim innocent men guilty and punish them. He champions punishment on the basis of desert because only this position preserves the criminal's dignity as a responsible agent.

Libertarianism

Freedom of Choice and Human Responsibility   Corliss Lamont

Corliss Lamont (1902–   ) is an American philosopher whose philosophical defense of Humanism has been combined with active participation in human affairs. Secretary-Treasurer of the *Journal of Philosophy,* he is also Chairman of the National Emergency Civil Liberties Committee.

It is my thesis that a man who is convinced he possesses freedom of choice or free will has a greater sense of responsibility than a person who thinks that total determinism rules the universe and human life. Determinism in the classic sense means that the flow of history, including all human choices and actions, is completely predetermined from the beginning of time. He who believes that "whatever is, was to be" can try to escape moral responsibility for wrongdoing by claiming that he was compelled to act as he did because it was predestined by the iron laws of cause and effect.

But if free choice truly exists at the moment of choosing, men clearly have full moral responsibility in deciding between two or more genuine alternatives, and the deterministic alibi has no weight. The heart of our discussion, then, lies in the question of whether free choice or universal determinism represents the truth. I shall try to summarize briefly the main reasons that point to the existence of free will.

First, there is the immediate, powerful, common-sense intuition shared by virtually all human beings that freedom of choice is real. This intuition seems as strong to me as the sensation of pleasure or pain; and the attempt of the determinists to explain the intuition away is as artificial as the Christian Scientist claim that pain is not real. The intuition of free choice does not, of course, in itself prove that such freedom exists, but that intuition is so strong that the burden of proof is on the determinists to show that it is based on an illusion.

Second, we can defuse the determinist argument by admitting and indeed insisting that a great deal of determinism exists in the world. Determinism in the form of if-then causal laws governs much of the human body's functioning and much of the universe as a whole. We can be glad that the autonomic system of breathing, digestion, circulation of the blood and beating of the heart operate deterministically—until

Reprinted from *Religious Humanism,* Vol. III, No. 3, Summer 1969. This paper was followed by a discussion by Professors Van Meter Ames, Robert Atkins, John Herman Randall, Williard Enteman, James Gould, Milic Capek, and Sterling Lamprecht. A copy of these papers can be obtained for 50¢ from the Fellowship of Religious Humanists, Yellow Springs, Ohio.

they get out of order. Determinism *versus* free choice is a false issue; what we always have is *relative* determinism and *relative* free choice. Free will is ever limited by the past and by the vast range of if-then laws. At the same time human beings utilize free choice to take advantage of those deterministic laws embodied in science and man-made machines. Most of us drive cars, but it is we and not the autos that decide when and where they are to go. Determinism wisely used and controlled—which is by no means always the case—can make us freer and happier.

Third, determinism is a relative thing not only because human free choice exists, but also because contingency or chance is an ultimate trait of the cosmos. Contingency is best seen in the intersection of mutually independent event-streams between which there was no previous causal connection. My favorite example here is the collision of the steamship *Titanic* with an iceberg off Newfoundland in the middle of the night on April 14, 1912. It was a terrible accident, with more than 1500 persons lost. The drifting of the iceberg down from the north and the steaming of the *Titanic* west from England clearly represented two causal streams independent of each other.

Even if a team of scientific experts had been able, *per impossible,* to trace back the two causal streams and ascertain that the catastrophe had been predestined from the moment the steamship left Southampton, that would not upset my thesis. For the space-time relation of the iceberg and the *Titanic,* as the ship started on its voyage, would have been itself a matter of contingency, since there was no relevant cause to account for that precise relation.

The pervasive presence of contingency in the world is also proved by the fact that all natural laws, as I have observed, take the form of if-then sequences or relations. The *if* factor is obviously conditional and demonstrates the continual co-existence of contingency with determinism. The actuality of contingency negates the idea of total and all-inclusive necessity operating throughout the universe. As regards human choice, contingency ensures that at the outset the alternatives one faces are indeterminate in relation to the act of choosing, which proceeds to make one of them determinate.

My fourth point is that the accepted meaning of potentiality, namely, that every object and event in the cosmos possesses plural possibilities of behavior, interaction and development, knocks out the determinist thesis. From the determinist viewpoint multiple potentialities are an illusion. If you want to take a vacation trip next summer, you will no doubt think over a number of possibilities before you make a final decision. Determinism logically implies that such deliberation is mere playacting, because you were destined all the time to choose the trip you did choose. When we relate the causal pattern to potentiality, we find that causation as mediated through free choice can have its appropriate effect in the actualization of any one of various possibilities.

Fifth, the normal processes of human thought are tied in with potentiality as I have just described it and likewise tend to show that freedom of choice is real. Thinking constantly involves general conceptions, universals or abstractions under which are classified many varying particulars. In the case that I discussed under my fourth point, "vacation travel" was the general conception and the different places that might be visited were the particulars, the alternatives, the potentialities, among which one could freely choose. Unless there is free choice, the function of human thought in solving problems becomes superfluous and a mask of make-believe.

Sixth, it is clarifying for the problem of free choice to realize that only the present exists and that it is always some present activity that builds up the past, as a skier leaves a trail behind him in the snow as he weaves down a hill. Everything that exists—the whole vast aggregate of inanimate matter, the swarming profusion of earthly life, man in his every aspect—exists only as an event or events taking place at this instant moment which is now. The past is dead and gone; it is efficacious only as it is embodied in present structures and activities.

The activity of former presents establishes the foundations upon which the immediate present operates. What happened in the past creates both limitations and potentialities, always conditioning the present. But conditioning in this sense is not the same as determining; and each day sweeps onward under its own momentum, actualizing fresh patterns of existence, maintaining other patterns and destroying still others. Thus a man choosing and acting in the present is not wholly controlled by the past, but is part of the unending forward surge of cosmic power. He is an active, initiating agent, riding the wave of the present, as it were, and deliberating among open alternatives to reach decisions regarding the many different phases of his life.

My seventh point is that the doctrine of universal and eternal determinism is seen to be self-refuting when we work out its full implications in the cases of *reductio ad absurdum* implied. If our choices and actions today were all predestined yesterday, then they were equally predestined yesteryear, at the day of our birth and at the birth of our solar system and earth some five billion years ago. To take another instance, for determinism the so-called "irresistible impulse" that the law recognizes in assessing crimes by the insane must hold with equal force for the actions of the sane and virtuous. In the determinist philosophy the good man has an irresistible impulse to tell the truth, to be kind to animals and to expose the graft in City Hall.

Eighth, in the novel dialect of determinism many words lose their normal meaning. I refer to such words as *refraining, forbearance, self-restraint,* and *regret.* If determinism turns out to be true, we shall have to scrap a great deal in existing dictionaries and do a vast amount of redefining. What meaning, for example, is to be assigned to *forbearance* when it is determined in advance that you are going to refuse that second Martini cocktail? You can truly forbear only when you refrain from doing something that it is possible for you to do. But under the determinist dispensation it is not possible for you to accept the second cocktail because fate has already dictated your "No." I am not saying that nature necessarily conforms to our linguistic usages, but human language habits that have evolved over aeons of time cannot be neglected in the analysis of free choice and determinism.

Finally, I do not think that the term *moral responsibility* can retain its traditional meaning unless freedom of choice exists. From the viewpoint of ethics, law and criminal law, it is difficult to understand how a consistent determinist would have a sufficient sense of personal responsibility for the development of decent ethical standards. But the question remains whether there have ever been or can be any consistent determinists or whether free choice runs so deep in human nature as an innate characteristic that, as Jean-Paul Sartre suggests, "We are not free to cease being free."

Soft Determinism

The Problem of Free Will   W. T. Stace

Walter Terence Stace (1886–   ) was born in Britain and served in the British
Civil Service in Ceylon before coming to the United States to teach at Princeton
in 1932. He has written widely acclaimed books in many areas of philosophy.

[A] great problem which the rise of scientific naturalism has created
for the modern mind concerns the foundations of morality. The old
religious foundations have largely crumbled away, and it may well be
thought that the edifice built upon them by generations of men is in
danger of collapse. A total collapse of moral behavior is, as I pointed
out before, very unlikely. For a society in which this occurred could
not survive. Nevertheless the danger to moral standards inherent in the
virtual disappearance of their old religious foundations is not illusory.

I shall first discuss the problem of free will, for it is certain that if
there is no free will there can be no morality. Morality is concerned
with what men ought and ought not to do. But if a man has no freedom
to choose what he will do, if whatever he does is done under compulsion,
then it does not make sense to tell him that he ought not to have done
what he did and that he ought to do something different. All moral
precepts would in such case be meaningless. Also if he acts always under
compulsion, how can he be held morally responsible for his actions?
How can he, for example, be punished for what he could not help doing?

It is to be observed that those learned professors of philosophy or
psychology who deny the existence of free will do so only in their professional moments and in their studies and lecture rooms. For when it
comes to doing anything practical, even of the most trivial kind, they
invariably behave as if they and others were free. They inquire from
you at dinner whether you will choose this dish or that dish. They will
ask a child why he told a lie, and will punish him for not having
chosen the way of truthfulness. All of which is inconsistent with a disbe-
lief in free will. This should cause us to suspect that the problem is not
a real one; and this, I believe, is the case. The dispute is merely verbal,
and is due to nothing but a confusion about the meanings of words. It
is what is now fashionably called a semantic problem.

How does a verbal dispute arise? Let us consider a case which, although it is absurd in the sense that no one would ever make the
mistake which is involved in it, yet illustrates the principle which we

shall have to use in the solution of the problem. Suppose that someone believed that the word "man" means a certain sort of five-legged animal; in short that "five-legged animal" is the correct *definition* of man. He might then look around the world, and rightly observing that there are no five-legged animals in it, he might proceed to deny the existence of men. This preposterous conclusion would have been reached because he was using an incorrect definition of "man." All you would have to do to show him his mistake would be to give him the correct definition; or at least to show him that his definition was wrong. Both the problem and its solution would, of course, be entirely verbal. The problem of free will, and its solution, I shall maintain, is verbal in exactly the same way. The problem has been created by the fact that learned men, especially philosophers, have assumed an incorrect definition of free will, and then finding that there is nothing in the world which answers to their definition, have denied its existence. As far as logic is concerned, their conclusion is just as absurd as that of the man who denies the existence of men. The only difference is that the mistake in the latter case is obvious and crude, while the mistake which the deniers of free will have made is rather subtle and difficult to detect.

Throughout the modern period, until quite recently, it was assumed, both by the philosophers who denied free will and by those who defended it, that *determinism is inconsistent with free will*. If a man's actions were wholly determined by chains of causes stretching back into the remote past, so that they could be predicted beforehand by a mind which knew all the causes, it was assumed that they could not in that case be free. This implies that a certain definition of actions done from free will was assumed, namely that they are actions *not* wholly determined by causes or predictable beforehand. Let us shorten this by saying that free will was defined as meaning indeterminism. This is the incorrect definition which has led to the denial of free will. As soon as we see what the true definition is we shall find that the question whether the world is deterministic, as Newtonian science implied, or in a measure indeterministic, as current physics teaches, is wholly irrelevant to the problem.

Of course there is a sense in which one can define a word arbitrarily in any way one pleases. But a definition may nevertheless be called correct or incorrect. It is correct if it accords with a *common usage* of the word defined. It is incorrect if it does not. And if you give an incorrect definition, absurd and untrue results are likely to follow. For instance, there is nothing to prevent you from arbitrarily defining a man as a five-legged animal, but this is incorrect in the sense that it does not accord with the ordinary meaning of the word. Also it has the absurd result of leading to a denial of the existence of men. This shows that *common usage is the criterion for deciding whether a definition is correct or not*. And this is the principle which I shall apply to free will. I shall show that indeterminism is not what is meant by the phrase "free will" *as it is commonly used*. And I shall attempt to discover the correct definition by inquiring how the phrase is used in ordinary conversation.

Here are a few samples of how the phrase might be used in ordinary conversation. It will be noticed that they include cases in which the question whether a man acted with free will is asked in order to determine whether he was morally and legally responsible for his acts.

Jones   I once went without food for a week.
Smith   Did you do that of your own free will?
Jones   No. I did it because I was lost in a desert and could find no food.

But suppose that the man who had fasted was Mahatma Gandhi. The conversation might then have gone:

Gandhi   I once fasted for a week.
Smith   Did you do that of your own free will?
Gandhi   Yes. I did it because I wanted to compel the British Government to give India its independence.

Take another case. Suppose that I had stolen some bread, but that I was as truthful as George Washington. Then, if I were charged with the crime in court, some exchange of the following sort might take place:

Judge   Did you steal the bread of your own free will?
Stace   Yes. I stole it because I was hungry.

Or in different circumstances the conversation might run:

Judge   Did you steal of your own free will?
Stace   No. I stole because my employer threatened to beat me if I did not.

At a recent murder trial in Trenton some of the accused had signed confessions, but afterwards asserted that they had done so under police duress. The following exchange might have occurred:

Judge   Did you sign this confession of your own free will?
Prisoner   No. I signed it because the police beat me up.

Now suppose that a philosopher had been a member of the jury. We could imagine this conversation taking place in the jury room.

Foreman of the Jury   The prisoner says he signed the confession because he was beaten, and not of his own free will.
Philosopher   This is quite irrelevant to the case. There is no such thing as free will.
Foreman   Do you mean to say that it makes no difference whether he signed because his conscience made him want to tell the truth or because he was beaten?
Philosopher   None at all. Whether he was caused to sign by a beating or by some desire of his own—the desire to tell the truth, for example—in either case his signing was causally determined, and therefore in neither case did he act of his own free will. Since there is no such thing as free will, the question whether he signed of his own free will ought not to be discussed by us.

The foreman and the rest of the jury would rightly conclude that the philosopher must be making some mistake. What sort of a mistake could it be? There is only one possible answer. The philosopher must be using the phrase "free will" in some peculiar way of his own which is not the way in which men usually use it when they wish to determine a question of moral responsibility. That is, he must be using an incorrect definition of it as implying action not determined by causes.

Suppose a man left his office at noon, and were questioned about it. Then we might hear this:

Jones   Did you go out of your own free will?
Smith   Yes. I went out to get my lunch.

But we might hear:

Jones   Did you leave your office of your own free will?
Smith   No. I was forcibly removed by the police.

We have now collected a number of cases of actions which, in the ordinary usage of the English language, would be called cases in which people have acted of their own free will. We should also say in all these cases that they *chose* to act as they did. We should also say that they could have acted otherwise, if they had chosen. For instance, Mahatma Gandhi was not compelled to fast; he chose to do so. He could have eaten if he had wanted to. When Smith went out to get his lunch, he chose to do so. He could have stayed and done some more work, if he had wanted to. We have also collected a number of cases of the opposite kind. They are cases in which men were not able to exercise their free will. They had no choice. They were compelled to do as they did. The man in the desert did not fast of his own free will. He had no choice in the matter. He was compelled to fast because there was nothing for him to eat. And so with the other cases. It ought to be quite easy, by an inspection of these cases, to tell what we ordinarily mean when we say that a man did or did not exercise free will. We ought therefore to be able to extract from them the proper definition of the term. Let us put the cases in a table:

Free Acts	Unfree Acts
Gandhi fasting because he wanted to free India.	The man fasting in the desert because there was no food.
Stealing bread because one is hungry.	Stealing because one's employer threatened to beat one.
Signing a confession because one wanted to tell the truth.	Signing because the police beat one.
Leaving the office because one wanted one's lunch.	Leaving because forcibly removed.

It is obvious that to find the correct definition of free acts we must discover what characteristic is common to all the acts in the left-hand column, and is, at the same time, absent from all the acts in the right-hand column. This characteristic which all free acts have, and which no unfree acts have, will be the defining characteristic of free will.

Is being uncaused, or not being determined by causes, the characteristic of which we are in search? It cannot be, because although it is true that all the acts in the right-hand column have causes, such as the beating by the police or the absence of food in the desert, so also do the acts in the left-hand column. Mr. Gandhi's fasting was caused by his desire to free India, the man leaving his office by his hunger, and so on. Moreover there is no reason to doubt that these causes of the free acts were in turn caused by prior conditions, and that these were again the results of causes, and so on back indefinitely into the past. Any physiologist can tell us the causes of hunger. What caused Mr. Gandhi's tremendously powerful desire to free India is no doubt more difficult to discover. But it must have had causes. Some of them may have lain in peculiarities of his glands or brain, others in his past experiences, others in his heredity, others in his education. Defenders of free will have usually tended to deny such facts. But to do so is plainly a case of special pleading, which is unsupported by any scrap of evidence. The only reasonable view is that all human actions, both those which are freely done and those which are not, are either wholly determined by causes, or at least as much determined as other events in nature. It may be true, as the physicists tell us, that nature is not as deterministic as was once thought. But whatever degree of determinism prevails in the world, human actions appear to be as much determined as anything else. And if this is so, it cannot be the case that what distinguishes actions freely chosen from those which are not free is that the latter are determined by causes while the former are not. Therefore, being uncaused or being undetermined by causes, must be an incorrect definition of free will.

What, then, is the difference between acts which are freely done and those which are not? What is the characteristic which is present to all the acts in the left-hand column and absent from all those in the right-hand column? Is it not obvious that, although both sets of actions have causes, the causes of those in the left-hand column are *of a different kind* from the causes of those in the right-hand column? The free acts are all caused by desires, or motives, or by some sort of internal psychological states of the agent's mind. The unfree acts, on the other hand, are all caused by physical forces or physical conditions, outside the agent. Police arrest means physical force exerted from the outside; the absence of food in the desert is a physical condition of the outside world. We may therefore frame the following rough definitions. *Acts freely done are those whose immediate causes are psychological states in the agent. Acts not freely done are those whose immediate causes are states of affairs external to the agent.*

It is plain that if we define free will in this way, then free will certainly exists, and the philosopher's denial of its existence is seen to be what it is—nonsense. For it is obvious that all those actions of men which we should ordinarily attribute to the exercise of their free will, or of which we should say that they freely chose to do them, are in fact actions which have been caused by their own desires, wishes, thoughts, emotions, impulses, or other psychological states.

In applying our definition we shall find that it usually works well, but that there are some puzzling cases which it does not seem exactly to fit. These puzzles can always be solved by paying careful attention to the ways in which words are used, and remembering that they are not always used consistently. I have space for only one example. Suppose that a thug threatens to shoot you unless you give him your wallet, and suppose that you do so. Do you, in giving him your wallet, do so of your own free will or not? If we apply our definition, we find that you acted freely, since the immediate cause of the action was not an actual outside force but the fear of death, which is a psychological cause. Most people, however, would say that you did not act of your own free will but under compulsion. Does this show that our definition is wrong? I do not think so. Aristotle, who gave a solution of the problem of free will substantially the same as ours (though he did not use the term "free will") admitted that there are what he called "mixed" or borderline cases in which it is difficult to know whether we ought to call the acts free or compelled. In the case under discussion, though no actual force was used, the gun at your forehead so nearly approximated to actual force that we tend to say the case was one of compulsion. It is a borderline case.

Here is what may seem like another kind of puzzle. According to our view an action may be free though it could have been predicted beforehand with certainty. But suppose you told a lie, and it was certain beforehand that you would tell it. How could one then say, "You could have told the truth"? The answer is that it is perfectly true that you could have told the truth *if* you had wanted to. In fact you would have done so, for in that case the causes producing your action, namely your desires, would have been different, and would therefore have produced different effects. It is a delusion that predictability and free will are incompatible. This agrees with common sense. For if, knowing your character, I predict that you will act honorably, no one would say when you do act honorably, that this shows you did not do so of your own free will.

Since free will is a condition of moral responsibility, we must be sure that our theory of free will gives a sufficient basis for it. To be held morally responsible for one's actions means that one may be justly punished or rewarded, blamed or praised, for them. But it is not just to punish a man for what he cannot help doing. How can it be just to punish him for an action which it was certain beforehand that he would do? We have not attempted to decide whether, as a matter of fact, all events, including human actions, are completely determined. For that question is irrelevant to the problem of free will. But if we assume for the purposes of argument that complete determinism is true, but that we are nevertheless free, it may then be asked whether such a deterministic free will is compatible with moral responsibility. For it may seem unjust to punish a man for an action which it could have been predicted with certainty beforehand that he would do.

But that determinism is incompatible with moral responsibility is as much a delusion as that it is incompatible with free will. You do not excuse a man for doing a wrong act because, knowing his character, you felt certain beforehand that he would do it. Nor do you deprive a man of a reward or prize because, knowing his goodness or his capabilities, you felt certain beforehand that he would win it.

Volumes have been written on the justification of punishment. But so far as it affects the question of free will, the essential principles involved are quite simple. The punishment of a man for doing a wrong act is justified, either on the ground that it will correct his own character, or that it will deter other people from doing similar acts. The instrument of punishment has been in the past, and no doubt still is, often unwisely used; so that it may often have done more harm than good. But that is not relevant to our present problem. Punishment, if and when it is justified, is justified only on one or both of the grounds just mentioned. The question then is how, if we assume determinism, punishment can correct character or deter people from evil actions.

Suppose that your child develops a habit of telling lies. You give him a mild beating. Why? Because you believe that his personality is such that the usual motives for telling the truth do not cause him to do so. You therefore supply the missing cause, or motive, in the shape of pain and the fear of future pain if he repeats his untruthful behavior. And you hope that a few treatments of this kind will condition him to the habit of truth-telling, so that he will come to tell the truth without the infliction of pain. You assume that his actions are determined by causes, but that the usual causes of truth-telling do not in him produce their usual effects. You therefore supply him with an artificially injected motive, pain and fear, which you think will in the future cause him to speak truthfully.

The principle is exactly the same where you hope, by punishing one man, to deter others from wrong actions. You believe that the fear of punishment will cause those who might otherwise do evil to do well.

We act on the same principle with non-human, and even with inanimate, things, if they do not behave in the way we think they ought to behave. The rose bushes in the garden produce only small and poor blooms, whereas we want large and rich ones. We supply a cause which will produce large blooms, namely fertilizer. Our automobile does not go properly. We supply a cause which will make it go better, namely oil in the works. The punishment for the man, the fertilizer for the plant, and the oil for the car, are all justified by the same principle and in the same way. The only difference is that different kinds of things require different kinds of causes to make them do what they should. Pain may be the appropriate remedy to apply, in certain cases, to human beings, and oil to the machine. It is, of course, of no use to inject motor oil into the boy or to beat the machine.

Thus we see that moral responsibility is not only consistent with determinism, but requires it. The assumption on which punishment is based is that human behavior is causally determined. If pain could not be a cause of truth-telling there would be no justification at all for punishing lies. If human actions and volitions were uncaused, it would be useless either to punish or reward, or indeed to do anything else to correct people's bad behavior. For nothing that you could do would in any way influence them. Thus moral responsibility would entirely disappear. If there were no determinism of human beings at all, their actions would be completely unpredictable and capricious, and therefore irresponsible. And this is in itself a strong argument against the common view of philosophers that free will means being undetermined by causes.

Hard Determinism

The Delusion of Free Will   Robert Blatchford

Robert Blatchford (1851–1943) was an English determinist, agnostic, socialist, and crusading social reformer, whose writings exerted great influence and were translated into many languages.

The free will delusion has been a stumbling block in the way of human thought for thousands of years. Let us try whether common sense and common knowledge cannot remove it.

Free will is a subject of great importance to us in this case; and it is one we must come to with our eyes wide open and our wits wide awake; not because it is very difficult, but because it has been tied and twisted into a tangle of Gordian knots by twenty centuries full of wordy but unsuccessful philosophers.

The free will party claim that man is responsible for his acts, because his will is free to choose between right and wrong.

We reply that the will is not free, and that if it were free man could not know right from wrong until he was taught.

As to the knowledge of good and evil the free will party will claim that conscience is an unerring guide. But I have already proved that conscience does not and cannot tell us what is right and what is wrong: it only reminds us of the lessons we have learnt as to right and wrong.

The "still small voice" is not the voice of God: it is the voice of heredity and environment.

And now to the freedom of the will.

When a man says his will is free, he means that it is free of all control or interference: that it can over-rule heredity and environment.

We reply that the will is ruled by heredity and environment.

The cause of all the confusion on this subject may be shown in a few words.

When the free will party say that man has a free will, they mean that he is free to act as he chooses to act.

There is no need to deny that. *But what causes him to choose?*

That is the pivot upon which the whole discussion turns.

The free will party seem to think of the will as something independent of the man, as something outside him. They seem to think that the will decides without the control of the man's reason.

If that were so, it would not prove the man responsible. "The will"

From *Not Guilty* by Robert Blatchford, Albert and Charles Boni, Inc., 1913. Reprinted by permission of Albert and Charles Boni, Inc.

would be responsible, and not the man. It would be as foolish to blame a man for the act of a "free" will, as to blame a horse for the action of its rider.

But I am going to prove to my readers, by appeals to their common sense and common knowledge, that the will is not free; and that it is ruled by heredity and environment.

To begin with, the average man will be against me. He knows that he chooses between two courses every hour, and often every minute, and he thinks his choice is free. But that is a delusion: his choice is not free. He can choose, and does choose. But he can only choose as his heredity and his environment cause him to choose. He never did choose and never will choose except as his heredity and his environment—his temperament and his training—cause him to choose. And his heredity and his environment have fixed his choice before he makes it.

The average man says "I know that I can act as I wish to act." But what causes him to wish?

The free will party say, "We know that a man can and does choose between two acts." But what settles the choice?

There is a cause for every wish, a cause for every choice; and every cause of every wish and choice arises from heredity, or from environment.

For a man acts always from temperament, which is heredity, or from training, which is environment.

And in cases where a man hesitates in his choice between two acts, the hesitation is due to a conflict between his temperament and his training, or, as some would express it, "between his desire and his conscience."

A man is practising at a target with a gun, when a rabbit crosses his line of fire. The man has his eye and his sights on the rabbit, and his finger on the trigger. The man's will is free. If he press the trigger the rabbit will be killed.

Now, how does the man decide whether or not he shall fire? He decides by feeling, and by reason.

He would like to fire, just to make sure that he could hit the mark. He would like to fire, because he would like to have the rabbit for supper. He would like to fire, because there is in him the old, old hunting instinct, to kill.

But the rabbit does not belong to him. He is not sure that he will not get into trouble if he kills it. Perhaps—if he is a very uncommon kind of man—he feels that it would be cruel and cowardly to shoot a helpless rabbit.

Well. The man's will is free. He can fire if he likes: he can let the rabbit go if he likes. How will he decide? On what does his decision depend?

His decision depends upon the relative strength of his desire to kill the rabbit, and of his scruples about cruelty, and the law.

Not only that, but, if we knew the man fairly well, we could guess how his free will would act before it acted. The average sporting Briton would kill the rabbit. But we know that there are men who would on no account shoot any harmless wild creature.

Broadly put, we may say that the sportsman would will to fire, and that the humanitarian would not will to fire.

Now, as both their wills are free, it must be something outside the wills that makes the difference.

Well. The sportsman will kill, because he is a sportsman: the humanitarian will not kill, because he is a humanitarian.

And what makes one man a sportsman and another a humanitarian? Heredity and environment: temperament and training.

One man is merciful, another cruel, by nature; or one is thoughtful and the other thoughtless, by nature. That is a difference of heredity.

One may have been taught all his life that to kill wild things is "sport"; the other may have been taught that it is inhuman and wrong: that is a difference of environment.

Now, the man by nature cruel or thoughtless, who has been trained to think of killing animals as sport, becomes what we call a sportsman, because heredity and environment have made him a sportsman.

The other man's heredity and environment have made him a humanitarian.

The sportsman kills the rabbit, because he is a sportsman, and he is a sportsman because heredity and environment have made him one.

That is to say the "free will" is really controlled by heredity and environment.

Allow me to give a case in point. A man who had never done any fishing was taken out by a fisherman. He liked the sport, and for some months followed it eagerly. But one day an accident brought home to his mind the cruelty of catching fish with a hook, and he instantly laid down his rod, and never fished again.

Before the change he was always eager to go fishing if invited: after the change he could not be persuaded to touch a line. His will was free all the while. How was it that his will to fish changed to his will not to fish? It was the result of environment. He had learnt that fishing was cruel. This knowledge controlled his will.

But, it may be asked, how do you account for a man doing the thing he does not wish to do?

No man ever did a thing he did not wish to do. When there are two wishes the stronger rules.

Let us suppose a case. A young woman gets two letters by the same post; one is an invitation to go with her lover to a concert, the other is a request that she will visit a sick child in the slums. The girl is very fond of music, and is rather afraid of the slums. She wishes to go to the concert, and to be with her lover; she dreads the foul street and the dirty home, and shrinks from the risk of measles or fever. But she goes to the sick child, and she foregoes the concert. Why?

Because her sense of duty is stronger than her self-love.

Now, her sense of duty is partly due to her nature—that is, to her heredity—but it is chiefly due to environment. Like all of us, this girl was born without any kind of knowledge, and with only the rudiments of a conscience. But she has been well taught, and the teaching is part of her environment.

We may say that the girl is free to act as she chooses, but she *does* act as she has been *taught* that she *ought* to act. This teaching, which is part of her environment, controls her will.

We may say that a man is free to act as he chooses. He is free to act as *he* chooses, but *he* will choose as heredity and environment cause *him* to choose. For heredity and environment have made him that which he is.

A man is said to be free to decide between two courses. But really he is only free to decide in accordance with his temperament and training. . . .

Macbeth was ambitious; but he had a conscience. He wanted Duncan's crown; but he shrank from treason and ingratitude. Ambition pulled him one way, honour pulled him the other way. The opposing forces were so evenly balanced that he seemed unable to decide. Was Macbeth free to choose? To what extent was he free? He was so free that he could arrive at no decision, and it was the influence of his wife that turned the scale to crime.

Was Lady Macbeth free to choose? She did not hesitate. Because her ambition was so much stronger than her conscience that she never was in doubt. She chose as her over-powering ambition compelled her to choose.

And most of us in our decisions resemble either Macbeth or his wife. Either our nature is so much stronger than our training, or our training is so much stronger than our nature, that we decide for good or evil as promptly as a stream decides to run down hill; or our nature and our training are so nearly balanced that we can hardly decide at all.

In Macbeth's case the contest is quite clear and easy to follow. He was ambitious, and his environment had taught him to regard the crown as a glorious and desirable possession. But environment had also taught him that murder, and treason, and ingratitude were wicked and disgraceful.

Had he never been taught these lessons, or had he been taught that gratitude was folly, that honour was weakness, and murder excusable when it led to power, he would not have hesitated at all. It was his environment that hampered his will. . . .

In all cases the action of the will depends upon the relative strength of two or more motives. The stronger motive decides the will; just as the heavier weight decides the balance of a pair of scales. . . .

How, then, can we believe that free will is outside and superior to heredity and environment? . . .

"What! Cannot a man be honest if he choose?" Yes, if he choose. But that is only another way of saying that he can be honest if his nature and his training lead him to choose honesty.

"What! Cannot I please myself whether I drink or refrain from drinking?" Yes. But that is only to say you will not drink because it pleases *you* to be sober. But it pleases another man to drink, because his desire for drink is strong, or because his self-respect is weak.

And you decide as you decide, and he decides as he decides, because you are *you,* and he is *he;* and heredity and environment made you both that which you are.

And the sober man may fall upon evil days, and may lose his self-respect, or find the burden of his trouble greater than he can bear, and may fly to drink for comfort, or oblivion, and may become a drunkard. Has it not been often so?

And the drunkard may, by some shock, or some disaster, or some passion, or some persuasion, regain his self-respect, and may renounce drink, and lead a sober and useful life. Has it not been often so?

And in both cases the freedom of the will is untouched: it is the change in the environment that lifts the fallen up, and beats the upright down.

We might say that a woman's will is free, and that she could, if she wished, jump off a bridge and drown herself. But she cannot *wish*. She is happy, and loves life, and dreads the cold and crawling river. And yet, by some cruel turn of fortune's wheel, she may become destitute and miserable; so miserable that she hates life and longs for death, and *then* she can jump into the dreadful river and die.

Her will was free at one time as at another. It is the environment that has wrought the change. Once she could not wish to die: now she cannot wish to live.

The apostles of free will believe that all men's wills are free. But a man can only will that which he is able to will. And one man is able to will that which another man is unable to will. To deny this is to deny the commonest and most obvious facts of life. . . .

We all know that we can foretell the action of certain men in certain cases, because we know the men.

We know that under the same conditions Jack Sheppard would steal and Cardinal Manning would not steal. We know that under the same conditions the sailor would flirt with the waitress, and the priest would not; that the drunkard would get drunk, and the abstainer would remain sober. We know that Wellington would refuse a bribe, that Nelson would not run away, that Buonaparte would grasp at power, that Abraham Lincoln would be loyal to his country, that Torquemada would not spare a heretic. Why? If the will is free, how can we be sure, before a test arises, how the will must act?

Simply because we know that heredity and environment have so formed and moulded men and women that under certain circumstances the action of their wills is certain.

Heredity and environment having made a man a thief, he will steal. Heredity and environment having made a man honest, he will not steal.

That is to say, heredity and environment have decided the action of the will, before the time has come for the will to act.

This being so—and we all know that it is so—what becomes of the sovereignty of the will?

Let any man that believes that he can "do as he likes" ask himself *why* he *likes*, and he will see the error of the theory of free will, and will understand why the will is the servant and not the master of the man: for the man is the product of heredity and environment, and these control the will.

As we want to get this subject as clear as we can, let us take one or two familiar examples of the action of the will.

Jones and Robinson meet and have a glass of whisky. Jones asks Robinson to have another. Robinson says, "no thank you, one is enough." Jones says, "all right: have another cigarette." Robinson takes the cigarette. Now, here we have a case where a man refuses a second drink, but takes a second smoke. Is it because he would like another cigarette, but would not like another glass of whisky? No. It is because he knows that it is *safer* not to take another glass of whisky.

How does he know that whisky is dangerous? He has learnt it—from his environment.

"But he *could* have taken another glass if he wished."

But he could not wish to take another, because there was something he wished more strongly—to be safe.

And why did he want to be safe? Because he had learnt—from his environment—that it was unhealthy, unprofitable, and shameful to get drunk. Because he had learnt—from his environment—that it is easier to avoid forming a bad habit than to break a bad habit when formed. Because he valued the good opinion of his neighbours, and also his position and prospects.

These feelings and this knowledge ruled his will, and caused him to refuse the second glass.

But there was no sense of danger, no well-learned lesson of risk to check his will to smoke another cigarette. Heredity and environment did not warn him against that. So, to please his friend, and himself, he accepted.

Now suppose Smith asks Williams to have another glass. Williams takes it, takes several, finally goes home—as he often goes home. Why?

Largely because drinking is a habit with him. And not only does the mind instinctively repeat an action, but, in the case of drink, a physical craving is set up, and the brain is weakened. It is easier to refuse the first glass than the second; easier to refuse the second than the third; and it is very much harder for a man to keep sober who has frequently got drunk.

So, when poor Williams has to make his choice, he has habit against him, he has a physical craving against him, and he has a weakened brain to think with.

"But. Williams could have refused the first glass."

No. Because in his case the desire to drink, or to please a friend, was stronger than his fear of the danger. Or he may not have been so conscious of the danger as Robinson was. He may not have been so well taught, or he may not have been so sensible, or he may not have been so cautious. So that his heredity and environment, his temperament and training, led him to take the drink, as surely as Robinson's heredity and environment led him to refuse it.

And now, it is my turn to ask a question. If the will is "free," if conscience is a sure guide, how is it that the free will and the conscience of Robinson caused him to keep sober, while the free will and the conscience of Williams caused him to get drunk?

Robinson's will was curbed by certain feelings which failed to curb the will of Williams. Because in the case of Williams the feelings were stronger on the other side.

It was the nature and the training of Robinson which made him refuse the second glass, and it was the nature and the training of Williams which made him drink the second glass.

What had free will to do with it?

We are told that *every* man has a free will, and a conscience.

Now, if Williams had been Robinson, that is to say if his heredity and his environment had been exactly like Robinson's, he would have done exactly as Robinson did.

It was because his heredity and environment were not the same that his act was not the same.

Both men had free wills. What made one do what the other refused to do?

Heredity and environment. To reverse their conduct we should have to reverse their heredity and environment. . . .

Two boys work at a hard and disagreeable trade. One leaves it, finds other work, "gets on," is praised for getting on. The other stays at the trade all his life, works hard all his life, is poor all his life, and is respected as an honest and humble working man; that is to say, he is regarded by society as Mr. Dorgan was regarded by Mr. Dooley—"he is a fine man, and I despise him."

What causes these two free wills to will so differently? One boy knew more than the other boy. He "knew better." All knowledge is environment. Both boys had free wills. It was in knowledge they differed: environment!

Those who exalt the power of the will, and belittle the power of environment, belie their words by their deeds.

For they would not send their children amongst bad companions or allow them to read bad books. They would not say the children have free will and therefore have power to take the good and leave the bad.

They know very well that evil environment has power to pervert the will, and that good environment has power to direct it properly.

They know that children may be made good or bad by good or evil training, and that the will follows the training.

That being so, they must also admit that the children of other people may be good or bad by training.

And if a child gets bad training, how can free will save it? Or how can it be blamed for being bad? It never had a chance to be good. That they know this is proved by their carefulness in providing their own children with better environment.

As I have said before, every church, every school, every moral lesson is a proof that preachers and teachers trust to good environment, and not to free will, to make children good.

In this, as in so many other matters, actions speak louder than words.

That, I hope, disentangles the many knots into which thousands of learned men have tied the simple subject of free will; and disposes of the claim that man is responsible because his will is free. But there is one other cause of error, akin to the subject, on which I should like to say a few words.

We often hear it said that a man is to blame for his conduct because "he knows better."

It is true that men do wrong when they know better. Macbeth "knew better" when he murdered Duncan. But it is true, also, that we often think a man "knows better," when he does not know better.

For a man cannot be said to know a thing until he believes it. If I am told that the moon is made of green cheese, it cannot be said that I *know* it to be made of green cheese.

Many moralists seem to confuse the words "to know" with the words "to hear."

Jones reads novels and plays opera music on Sunday. The Puritan says Jones "knows better," when he means that Jones has been told that it is wrong to do those things.

But Jones does not know that it is wrong. He has heard someone say that it is wrong, but does not believe it. Therefore it is not correct to say that he knows it.

And, again, as to that matter of belief. Some moralists hold that it is wicked not to believe certain things, and that men who do not believe those things will be punished.

But a man cannot believe a thing he is told to believe: he can only believe a thing which he *can* believe; and he can only believe that which his own reason tells him is true.

It would be no use asking Sir Roger Ball to believe that the earth is flat. He *could not* believe it.

It is no use asking an agnostic to believe the story of Jonah and the whale. He *could not* believe it. He might pretend to believe it. He might try to believe it. But his reason would not allow him to believe it.

Therefore it is a mistake to say that a man "knows better," when the fact is that he has been told "better" and cannot believe what he has been told.

That is a simple matter, and looks quite trivial; but how much ill-will, how much intolerance, how much violence, persecution, and murder have been caused by the strange idea that a man is wicked because *his* reason *cannot* believe that which to another man's reason [is] quite true.

Free will has no power over a man's belief. A man cannot believe by will, but only by conviction. A man cannot be forced to believe. You may threaten him, wound him, beat him, burn him; and he may be frightened, or angered, or pained; but he cannot *believe,* nor can he be made to believe. Until he is convinced.

Now, truism as it may seem, I think it necessary to say here that a man cannot be convinced by abuse, nor by punishment. He can only be convinced by *reason.*

Yes. If we wish a man to believe a thing, we shall find a few words of reason more powerful than a million curses, or a million bayonets. To burn a man alive for failing to believe that the sun goes round the world is not to convince him. The fire is searching, but it does not seem to him to be relevant to the issue. He never doubted that fire would burn; but perchance his dying eyes may see the sun sinking down into the west, as the world rolls on its axis. He dies in his belief. And knows no "better."

Contemporary Issues

The Control of Men

Walden Two: Selections   B. F. Skinner

Burrhus Frederic Skinner (1904–   ), professor of psychology at Harvard University, is one of America's most prominent psychologists. He is known both for his defense of behaviorism and his experimentation with modern teaching devices.

The participants of the following discussion are Frazier, the founder of Walden Two; Castle, a philosopher who is skeptical of the society's achievements and purposes; and Professor Burris, the narrator of the discussion, who is trying objectively to evaluate Frazier's new society.

"Each of us," Frazier began, "is engaged in a pitched battle with the rest of mankind."

"A curious premise for a Utopia," said Castle. "Even a pessimist like myself takes a more hopeful view than that."

"You do, you do," said Frazier. "But let's be realistic. Each of us has interests which conflict with the interests of everybody else. That's our original sin, and it can't be helped. Now, 'everybody else' we call 'society.' It's a powerful opponent, and it always wins. Oh, here and there an individual prevails for a while and gets what he wants. Sometimes he storms the culture of a society and changes it slightly to his own advantage. But society wins in the long run, for it has the advantage of numbers and of age. Many prevail against one, and men against a baby. Society attacks early, when the individual is helpless. It enslaves him almost before he has tasted freedom. The 'ologies' will tell you how it's done. Theology calls it building a conscience or developing a spirit of selflessness. Psychology calls it the growth of the super-ego.

"Considering how long society has been at it, you'd expect a better job. But the campaigns have been badly planned and the victory has never been secure. The behavior of the individual has been shaped according to revelations of 'good conduct,' never as the result of experimental study. But why not experiment? The questions are simple enough. What's the best behavior for the individual so far as the group is concerned? And how can the individual be induced to behave in that way? Why not explore these questions in a scientific spirit?

"We could do just that in Walden Two. We had already worked out a code of conduct—subject, of course, to experimental modification. The code would keep things running smoothly if everybody lived up to it. Our job was to see that everybody did. Now, you can't get people to follow a useful code by making them into so many jacks-in-the-box. You can't foresee all future circumstances, and you can't specify adequate future conduct. You don't know what will be required. Instead you have to set up certain behavioral processes which will lead the individual to design his own 'good' conduct when the time comes. We call that sort of thing 'self-control.' But don't be misled, the control always rests in the last analysis in the hands of society.

"One of our Planners, a young man named Simmons, worked with me. It was the first time in history that the matter was approached in an experimental way. Do you question that statement, Mr. Castle?"

"I'm not sure I know what you are talking about," said Castle.

"Then let me go on. Simmons and I began by studying the great works on morals and ethics—Plato, Aristotle, Confucius, the New Testament, the Puritan divines, Machiavelli, Chesterfield, Freud—there were scores of them. We were looking for any and every method of shaping human behavior by imparting techniques of self-control. Some techniques were obvious enough, for they had marked turning points in human history. 'Love your enemies' is an example—a psychological invention for easing the lot of an oppressed people. The severest trial of oppression is the constant rage which one suffers at the thought of the oppressor. What Jesus discovered was how to avoid these inner devastations. His technique was to *practice the opposite emotion*. If a man can succeed in 'loving his enemies' and 'taking no thought for the morrow,' he will no longer be assailed by hatred of the oppressor or rage at the loss of his freedom or possessions. He may not get his freedom or possessions back, but he's less miserable. It's a difficult lesson. It comes late in our program."

"I thought you were opposed to modifying emotions and instincts until the world was ready for it," said Castle. "According to you, the principle of 'love your enemies' should have been suicidal."

"It would have been suicidal, except for an entirely unforeseen consequence. Jesus must have been quite astonished at the effect of his discovery. We are only just beginning to understand the power of love because we are just beginning to understand the weakness of force and aggression. But the science of behavior is clear about all that now. Recent discoveries in the analysis of punishment—but I am falling into one digression after another. Let me save my explanation of why the Christian virtues—and I mean merely the Christian techniques of self-control—have not disappeared from the face of the earth, with due recognition of the fact that they suffered a narrow squeak within recent memory.

"When Simmons and I had collected our techniques of control, we had to discover how to teach them. That was more difficult. Current educational practices were of little value, and religious practices scarcely any better. Promising paradise or threatening hell-fire is, we assumed, generally admitted to be unproductive. It is based upon a fundamental fraud which, when discovered, turns the individual against society and nourishes the very thing it tries to stamp out. What Jesus offered in return for loving one's enemies was heaven *on earth,* better known as peace of mind.

"We found a few suggestions worth following in the practices of the clinical psychologist. We undertook to build a tolerance for annoying experiences. The sunshine of midday is extremely painful if you come from a dark room, but take it in easy stages and you can avoid pain altogether. The analogy can be misleading, but in much the same way it's possible to build a tolerance to painful or distasteful stimuli, or to frustration, or to situations which arouse fear, anger or rage. Society and nature throw these annoyances at the individual with no regard for the development of tolerances. Some achieve tolerances, most fail. Where would the science of immunization be if it followed a schedule of accidental dosages?

"Take the principle of 'Get thee behind me, Satan,' for example," Frazier continued. "It's a special case of self-control by altering the environment. Subclass A 3, I believe. We give each child a lollipop which has been dipped in powdered sugar so that a single touch of the tongue can be detected. We tell him he may eat the lollipop later in the day, provided it hasn't already been licked. Since the child is only three or four, it is a fairly diff—"

"Three or four!" Castle exclaimed.

"All our ethical training is completed by the age of six," said Frazier quietly. "A simple principle like putting temptation out of sight would be acquired before four. But at such an early age the problem of not licking the lollipop isn't easy. Now, what would you do, Mr. Castle, in a similar situation?"

"Put the lollipop out of sight as quickly as possible."

"Exactly. I can see you've been well trained. Or perhaps you discovered the principle for yourself. We're in favor of original inquiry wherever possible, but in this case we have a more important goal and we don't hesitate to give verbal help. First of all, the children are urged to examine their own behavior while looking at the lollipops. This helps them to recognize the need for self-control. Then the lollipops are concealed, and the children are asked to notice any gain in happiness or any reduction in tension. Then a strong distraction is arranged—say, an interesting game. Later the children are reminded of the candy and encouraged to examine their reaction. The value of the distraction is generally obvious. Well, need I go on? When the experiment is repeated a day or so later, the children all run with the lollipops to their lockers and do exactly what Mr. Castle would do—a sufficient indication of the success of our training."

"I wish to report an objective observation of my reaction to your story," said Castle, controlling his voice with great precision. "I find myself revolted by this display of sadistic tyranny."

"I don't wish to deny you the exercise of an emotion which you seem to find enjoyable," said Frazier. "So let me go on. Concealing a tempting but forbidden object is a crude solution. For one thing, it's not always feasible. We want a sort of psychological concealment—covering up the

candy by paying no attention. In a later experiment the children wear
their lollipops like crucifixes for a few hours."

" 'Instead of the cross, the lollipop,
About my neck was hung,' "

said Castle. . . .

"How do you build up a tolerance to an annoying situation?" I said.

"Oh, for example, by having the children 'take' a more and more painful shock, or drink cocoa with less and less sugar in it until a bitter con-
coction can be savored without a bitter face."

"But jealousy or envy—you can't administer them in graded doses," I
said.

"And why not? Remember, we control the social environment, too, at
this age. That's why we get our ethical training in early. Take this case. A
group of children arrive home after a long walk tired and hungry. They're
expecting supper; they find, instead, that it's time for a lesson in self-
control: they must stand for five minutes in front of steaming bowls of
soup.

"The assignment is accepted like a problem in arithmetic. Any groan-
ing or complaining is a wrong answer. Instead, the children begin at once
to work upon themselves to avoid any unhappiness during the delay. One
of them may make a joke of it. We encourage a sense of humor as a good
way of not taking an annoyance seriously. The joke won't be much, according to adult standards—perhaps the child will simply pretend to empty
the bowl of soup into his upturned mouth. Another may start a song with
many verses. The rest join in at once, for they've learned that it's a good
way to make time pass."

Frazier glanced uneasily at Castle, who was not to be appeased.

"That also strikes you as a form of torture, Mr. Castle?" he asked.

"I'd rather be put on the rack," said Castle.

"Then you have by no means had the thorough training I supposed.
You can't imagine how lightly the children take such an experience. It's
a rather severe biological frustration, for the children are tired and hungry and they must stand and look at food; but it's passed off as lightly
as a five-minute delay at curtain time. We regard it as a fairly elementary
test. Much more difficult problems follow."

"I suspected as much," muttered Castle.

"In a later stage we forbid all social devices. No songs, no jokes—
merely silence. Each child is forced back upon his own resources—a very
important step."

"I should think so," I said. "And how do you know it's successful? You
might produce a lot of silently resentful children. It's certainly a dangerous stage."

"It is, and we follow each child carefully. If he hasn't picked up the
necessary techniques, we start back a little. A still more advanced stage"
—Frazier glanced again at Castle, who stirred uneasily—"brings me to my
point. When it's time to sit down to the soup, the children count off—
heads and tails. Then a coin is tossed and if it comes up heads, the 'heads'
sit down and eat. The 'tails' remain standing for another five minutes."

Castle groaned.

"And you call that envy?" I asked.

"Perhaps not exactly," said Frazier. "At least there's seldom any aggression against the lucky ones. The emotion, if any, is directed against Lady Luck herself, against the toss of the coin. That, in itself, is a lesson worth learning, for it's the only direction in which emotion has a surviving chance to be useful. And resentment toward things in general, while perhaps just as silly as personal aggression, is more easily controlled. Its expression is not socially objectionable." . . .

"May you not inadvertently teach your children some of the very emotions you're trying to eliminate?" I said. "What's the effect, for example, of finding the anticipation of a warm supper suddenly thwarted? Doesn't that eventually lead to feelings of uncertainty, or even anxiety?"

"It might. We had to discover how often our lessons could be safely administered. But all our schedules are worked out experimentally. We watch for undesired consequences just as any scientist watches for disrupting factors in his experiments.

"After all, it's a simple and sensible program," he went on in a tone of appeasement. "We set up a system of gradually increasing annoyances and frustrations against a background of complete serenity. An easy environment is made more and more difficult as the children acquire the capacity to adjust."

"But *why?*" said Castle. "Why these deliberate unpleasantnesses—to put it mildly? I must say I think you and your friend Simmons are really very subtle sadists."

"You've reversed your position, Mr. Castle," said Frazier in a sudden flash of anger with which I rather sympathized. Castle was calling names, and he was also being unaccountably and perhaps intentionally obtuse. "A while ago you accused me of breeding a race of softies," Frazier continued. "Now you object to toughening them up. But what you don't understand is that these potentially unhappy situations are never very annoying. Our schedules make sure of that. You wouldn't understand, however, because you're not so far advanced as our children."

Castle grew black.

"But what do your children get out of it?" he insisted, apparently trying to press some vague advantage in Frazier's anger.

"What do they get out of it!" exclaimed Frazier, his eyes flashing with a sort of helpless contempt. His lips curled and he dropped his head to look at his fingers, which were crushing a few blades of grass.

"They must get happiness and freedom and strength," I said, putting myself in a ridiculous position in attempting to make peace.

"They don't sound happy or free to me, standing in front of bowls of Forbidden Soup," said Castle, answering me parenthetically while continuing to stare at Frazier.

"If I must spell it out," Frazier began with a deep sigh, "what they get is escape from the petty emotions which eat the heart out of the unprepared. They get the satisfaction of pleasant and profitable social relations on a scale almost undreamed of in the world at large. They get immeasurably increased efficiency, because they can stick to a job without suffering the aches and pains which soon beset most of us. They get new horizons, for they are spared the emotions characteristic of frustration and failure. They get—" His eyes searched the branches of the trees. "Is that enough?" he said at last.

"And the community must gain their loyalty," I said, "when they discover the fears and jealousies and diffidences in the world at large."

"I'm glad you put it that way," said Frazier. "You might have said that they must feel superior to the miserable products of our public schools. But we're at pains to keep any feeling of superiority or contempt under control, too. Having suffered most acutely from it myself, I put the subject first on our agenda. We carefully avoid any joy in a personal triumph which means the personal failure of somebody else. We take no pleasure in the sophistical, the disputative, the dialectical." He threw a vicious glance at Castle. "We don't use the motive of domination, because we are always thinking of the whole group. We could motivate a few geniuses that way—it was certainly my own motivation—but we'd sacrifice some of the happiness of everyone else. Triumph over nature and over oneself, yes. But over others, never."

"You've taken the mainspring out of the watch," said Castle flatly.

"That's an experimental question, Mr. Castle, and you have the wrong answer." ...

"Are your techniques really so very new?" I said hurriedly. "What about the primitive practice of submitting a boy to various tortures before granting him a place among adults? What about the disciplinary techniques of Puritanism? Or of the modern school, for that matter?"

"In one sense you're right," said Frazier. "And I think you've nicely answered Mr. Castle's tender concern for our little ones. The unhappinesses we deliberately impose are far milder than the normal unhappinesses from which we offer protection. Even at the height of our ethical training, the unhappiness is ridiculously trivial—to the well-trained child.

"But there's a world of difference in the way we use these annoyances," he continued. "For one thing, we don't punish. We never administer an unpleasantness in the hope of repressing or eliminating undesirable behavior. But there's another difference. In most cultures the child meets up with annoyances and reverses of uncontrolled magnitude. Some are imposed in the name of discipline by persons in authority. Some, like hazings, are condoned though not authorized. Others are merely accidental. No one cares to, or is able to, prevent them.

"We all know what happens. A few hardy children emerge, particularly those who have got their unhappiness in doses that could be swallowed. They become brave men. Others become sadists or masochists of varying degrees of pathology. Not having conquered a painful environment, they become preoccupied with pain and make a devious art of it. Others submit—and hope to inherit the earth. The rest—the cravens, the cowards—live in fear for the rest of their lives. And that's only a single field—the reaction to pain. I could cite a dozen parallel cases. The optimist and the pessimist, the contented and the disgruntled, the loved and the unloved, the ambitious and the discouraged—these are only the extreme products of a miserable system.

"Traditional practices are admittedly better than nothing," Frazier went on. "Spartan or Puritan—no one can question the occasional happy result. But the whole system rests upon the wasteful principle of selection. The English public school of the nineteenth century produced brave men—by setting up almost insurmountable barriers and making the most of the few who came over. But selection isn't education. Its crops of brave men will always be small, and the waste enormous. Like all primitive principles, selection serves in place of education only through a profligate use of material. Multiply extravagantly and select with rigor. It's the philosophy of the 'big litter' as an alternative to good child hygiene.

"In Walden Two we have a different objective. We make every man a brave man. They all come over the barriers. Some require more preparation than others, but they all come over. The traditional use of adversity is to select the strong. We control adversity to build strength. And we do it deliberately, no matter how sadistic Mr. Castle may think us, in order to prepare for adversities which are beyond control. Our children eventually experience the 'heartache and the thousand natural shocks that flesh is heir to.' It would be the cruelest possible practice to protect them as long as possible, especially when we *could* protect them so well."

Frazier held out his hands in an exaggerated gesture of appeal.

"What alternative *had* we?" he said, as if he were in pain. "What else could we do? For four or five years we could provide a life in which no important need would go unsatisfied, a life practically free of anxiety or frustration or annoyance. What would *you* do? Would you let the child enjoy this paradise with no thought for the future—like an idolatrous and pampering mother? Or would you relax control of the environment and let the child meet accidental frustrations? *But what is the virtue of accident?* No, there was only one course open to us. We had to *design* a series of adversities, so that the child would develop the greatest possible self-control. Call it deliberate, if you like, and accuse us of sadism; there was no other course." . . .

"A modern, mechanized, managerial Machiavelli—that is my final estimate of you, Mr. Frazier," he [Castle] said, with the same challenging stare.

"It must be gratifying to know that one has reached a 'final estimate,' " said Frazier.

"An artist in power," Castle continued, "whose greatest art is to conceal art. The silent despot."

"Since we are dealing in 'M's,' why not sum it all up and say 'Mephistophelian'?" said Frazier, curiously reviving my fears of the preceding afternoon.

"I'm willing to do that!" said Castle. "And unless God is very sure of himself, I suspect He's by no means easy about this latest turn in the war of the angels. So far as I can see, you've blocked every path through which man was to struggle upward toward salvation. Intelligence, initiative—you have filled their places with a sort of degraded instinct, engineered compulsion. Walden Two is a marvel of efficient coordination—as efficient as an anthill!"

"Replacing intelligence with instinct—" muttered Frazier. "I had never thought of that. It's an interesting possibility. How's it done?" It was a crude maneuver. The question was a digression, intended to spoil Castle's timing and to direct our attention to practical affairs in which Frazier was more at home.

"The behavior of your members is carefully shaped in advance by a Plan," said Castle, not to be taken in, "and it's shaped to perpetuate that Plan. Intellectually Walden Two is quite as incapable of a spontaneous change of course as the life within a beehive."

"I see what you mean," said Frazier distantly. But he returned to his strategy. "And have you discovered the machinery of my power?"

"I have, indeed. We were looking in the wrong place. There's no *current* contact between you and the members of Walden Two. You threw us off the track very skillfully on that point last night. But you were behaving as a despot when you first laid your plans—when you designed the social structure and drew up the contract between community and member, when you worked out your educational practices and your guarantees against despotism—What a joke! Don't tell me you weren't in control *then!* Burris saw the point. What about your career as organizer? *There* was leadership! And the most damnable leadership in history, because you were setting the stage for the withdrawal of yourself as a personal force, knowing full well that everything that happened would still be your doing. Hundreds—you predicted millions—of unsuspecting souls were to fall within the scope of your ambitious scheme."

Castle was driving his argument home with great excitement, but Frazier was lying in exaggerated relaxation, staring at the ceiling, his hands cupped behind his head.

"Very good, Mr. Castle," he said softly. "I gave you the clue, of course, when we parted last night."

"You did, indeed. And I've wondered why. Were you led into that fatal error by your conceit? Perhaps that's the ultimate answer to your form of despotism. No one could enjoy the power you have seized without wishing to display it from time to time."

"I've admitted neither power nor despotism. But you're quite right in saying that I've exerted an influence and in one sense will continue to exert it forever. I believe you called me a *primum mobile*—not quite correctly, as I found upon looking the term up last night. But I did plan Walden Two—not as an architect plans a building, but as a scientist plans a long-term experiment, uncertain of the conditions he will meet but knowing how he will deal with them when they arise. In a sense, Walden Two is predetermined, but not as the behavior of a beehive is determined. Intelligence, no matter how much it may be shaped and extended by our educational system, will still function as intelligence. It will be used to puzzle out solutions to problems to which a beehive would quickly succumb. What the plan does is to keep intelligence on the right track, for the good of society rather than of the intelligent individual—or for the eventual rather than the immediate good of the individual. It does this by making sure that the individual will not forget his personal stake in the welfare of society."

"But you are forestalling many possibly useful acts of intelligence which aren't encompassed by your plan. You have ruled out points of view which may be more productive. You are implying that T. E. Frazier, looking at the world from the middle of the twentieth century, understands the best course for mankind forever."

"Yes, I suppose I do."

"But that's absurd!"

"Not at all. I don't say I foresee the course man will take a hundred years hence, let alone forever, but I know which he should take now."

"How can you be sure of it? It's certainly not a question you have answered experimentally."

"I think we're in the course of answering it," said Frazier. "But that's beside the point. There's no alternative. We must take that course."

"But that's fantastic. You who are taking it are in a small minority."

Frazier sat up.

"And the majority are in a big quandary," he said. "They're not on the road at all, or they're scrambling back toward their starting point, or sidling from one side of the road to the other like so many crabs. What do you think two world wars have been about? Something as simple as boundaries or trade? Nonsense. The world is trying to adjust to a new conception of man in relation to men."

"Perhaps it's merely trying to adjust to despots whose ideas are incompatible with the real nature of man."

"Mr. Castle," said Frazier very earnestly, "let me ask you a question. I warn you, it will be the most terrifying question of your life. *What would you do if you found yourself in possession of an effective science of behavior?* Suppose you suddenly found it possible to control the behavior of men as you wished. What would you do?"

"That's an assumption?"

"Take it as one if you like. *I* take it as a fact. And apparently you accept it as a fact too. I can hardly be as despotic as you claim unless I hold the key to an extensive practical control."

"What would I do?" said Castle thoughtfully. "I think I would dump your science of behavior in the ocean."

"And deny men all the help you could otherwise give them?"

"And give them the freedom they would otherwise lose forever!"

"How could you give them freedom?"

"By refusing to control them!"

"But you would only be leaving the control in other hands."

"Whose?"

"The charlatan, the demagogue, the salesman, the ward heeler, the bully, the cheat, the educator, the priest—all who are now in possession of the techniques of behavioral engineering."

"A pretty good share of the control would remain in the hands of the individual himself."

"That's an assumption, too, and it's your only hope. It's your only possible chance to avoid the implications of a science of behavior. If man is free, then a technology of behavior is impossible. But I'm asking you to consider the other case."

"Then my answer is that your assumption is contrary to fact and any further consideration idle."

"And your accusations—?"

"—were in terms of intention, not of possible achievement."

Frazier sighed dramatically.

"It's a little late to be proving that a behavioral technology is well advanced. How can you deny it? Many of its methods and techniques are really as old as the hills. Look at their frightful misuse in the hands of the Nazis! And what about the techniques of the psychological clinic? What about education? Or religion? Or practical politics? Or advertising and salesmanship? Bring them all together and you have a sort of rule-of-thumb technology of vast power. No, Mr. Castle, the science is there for the asking. But its techniques and methods are in the wrong hands—they are used for personal aggrandizement in a competitive world or, in the case of the psychologist and educator, for futilely corrective purposes. My question is, have you the courage to take up and wield the science of behavior for the good of mankind? You answer that you would dump it in the ocean!"

"I'd want to take it out of the hands of the politicians and advertisers and salesmen, too."

"And the psychologists and educators? You see, Mr. Castle, you can't have that kind of cake. The fact is, we not only *can* control human behavior, we *must*. But who's to do it, and what's to be done?"

"So long as a trace of personal freedom survives, I'll stick to my position," said Castle, very much out of countenance.

"Isn't it time we talked about freedom?" I said. "We parted a day or so ago on an agreement to let the question of freedom ring. It's time to answer, don't you think?"

"My answer is simple enough," said Frazier. "I deny that freedom exists at all. I must deny it—or my program would be absurd. You can't have a science about a subject matter which hops capriciously about. Perhaps we can never *prove* that man isn't free; it's an assumption. But the increasing success of a science of behavior makes it more and more plausible."

"On the contrary, a simple personal experience makes it untenable," said Castle. "The experience of freedom. I *know* that I'm free."

"It must be quite consoling," said Frazier.

"And what's more—you do, too," said Castle hotly. "When you deny your own freedom for the sake of playing with a science of behavior, you're acting in plain bad faith. That's the only way I can explain it." He tried to recover himself and shrugged his shoulders. "At least you'll grant that you *feel* free."

"The 'feeling of freedom' should deceive no one," said Frazier. "Give me a concrete case."

"Well, right now," Castle said. He picked up a book of matches. "I'm free to hold or drop these matches."

"You will, of course, do one or the other," said Frazier. "Linguistically or logically there seem to be two possibilities, but I submit that there's only one in fact. The determining forces may be subtle but they are inexorable. I suggest that as an orderly person you will probably hold—ah! you drop them! Well, you see, that's all part of your behavior with respect to me. You couldn't resist the temptation to prove me wrong. It was all lawful. You had no choice. The deciding factor entered rather late, and naturally you couldn't foresee the result when you first held them up. There was no strong likelihood that you would act in either direction, and so you said you were free."

"That's entirely too glib," said Castle. "It's easy to argue lawfulness after the fact. But let's see you predict what I will do in advance. Then I'll agree there's law."

"I didn't say that behavior is always predictable, any more than the weather is always predictable. There are often too many factors to be taken into account. We can't measure them all accurately, and we couldn't perform the mathematical operations needed to make a prediction if we had the measurements. The legality is usually an assumption—but none the less important in judging the issue at hand."

"Take a case where there's no choice, then," said Castle. "Certainly a man in jail isn't free in the sense in which I am free now."

"Good! That's an excellent start. Let us classify the kinds of determiners of human behavior. One class, as you suggest, is physical restraint—handcuffs, iron bars, forcible coercion. These are ways in which we shape human behavior according to our wishes. They're crude, and they sacrifice the affection of the controllee, but they often work. Now, what other ways are there of limiting freedom?"

Frazier had adopted a professorial tone and Castle refused to answer.

"The threat of force would be one," I said.

"Right. And here again we shan't encourage any loyalty on the part of the controllee. He has perhaps a shade more of the feeling of freedom, since he can always 'choose to act and accept the consequences,' but he doesn't feel exactly free. He knows his behavior is being coerced. Now what else?"

I had no answer.

"Force or the threat of force—I see no other possibility," said Castle after a moment.

"Precisely," said Frazier.

"But certainly a large part of my behavior has no connection with force at all. There's my freedom!" said Castle.

"I wasn't agreeing that there was no other possibility—merely that *you* could see no other. Not being a good behaviorist—or a good Christian, for that matter—you have no feeling for a tremendous power of a different sort."

"What's that?"

"I shall have to be technical," said Frazier. "But only for a moment. It's what the science of behavior calls 'reinforcement theory.' The things that can happen to us fall into three classes. To some things we are indifferent. Other things we like—we want them to happen, and we take steps to make them happen again. Still other things we don't like—we don't want them to happen and we take steps to get rid of them or keep them from happening again.

"*Now,*" Frazier continued earnestly, "if it's in our power to create any of the situations which a person likes or to remove any situation he doesn't like, we can control his behavior. When he behaves as we want him to behave, we simply create a situation he likes, or remove one he doesn't like. As a result, the probability that he will behave that way again goes up, which is what we want. Technically it's called 'positive reinforcement.'

"The old school made the amazing mistake of supposing that the reverse was true, that by removing a situation a person likes or setting up one he doesn't like—in other words by punishing him—it was possible to *reduce* the probability that he would behave in a given way again. That simply doesn't hold. It has been established beyond question. What is emerging at this critical stage in the evolution of society is a behavioral and cultural technology based on positive reinforcement alone. We are gradually discovering—at an untold cost in human suffering—that in the long run punishment doesn't reduce the probability that an act will occur. We have been so preoccupied with the contrary that we always take 'force' to mean punishment. We don't say we're using force when we send shiploads of food into a starving country, though we're displaying quite as much *power* as if we were sending troops and guns."

"I'm certainly not an advocate of force," said Castle. "But I can't agree that it's not effective."

"It's *temporarily* effective, that's the worst of it. That explains several thousand years of bloodshed. Even nature has been fooled. We 'instinctively' punish a person who doesn't behave as we like—we spank him if he's a child or strike him if he's a man. A nice distinction! The immediate effect of the blow teaches us to strike again. Retribution and revenge are the most natural things on earth. But in the long run the man we strike is no less likely to repeat his act."

"But he won't repeat it if we hit him hard enough," said Castle.

"He'll still *tend* to repeat it. He'll *want* to repeat it. We haven't really altered his potential behavior at all. That's the pity of it. If he doesn't repeat it in our presence, he will in the presence of someone else. Or it will be repeated in the disguise of a neurotic symptom. If we hit hard enough, we clear a little place for ourselves in the wilderness of civilization, but we make the rest of the wilderness still more terrible.

"Now, early forms of government are naturally based on punishment. It's the obvious technique when the physically strong control the weak. But we're in the throes of a great change to positive reinforcement—from a competitive society in which one man's reward is another man's punishment, to a cooperative society in which no one gains at the expense of anyone else.

"The change is slow and painful because the immediate, temporary effect of punishment overshadows the eventual advantage of positive reinforcement. We've all seen countless instances of the temporary effect of force, but clear evidence of the effect of not using force is rare. That's why I insist that Jesus, who was apparently the first to discover the power of refusing to punish, must have hit upon the principle by accident. He certainly had none of the experimental evidence which is available to us today, and I can't conceive that it was possible, no matter what the man's genius, to have discovered the principle from casual observation."

"A touch of revelation, perhaps?" said Castle.

"No, accident. Jesus discovered one principle because it had immediate consequences, and he got another thrown in for good measure."

I began to see light.

"You mean the principle of 'love your enemies'?" I said.

"Exactly! To 'do good to those who despitefully use you' has two unrelated consequences. You gain the peace of mind we talked about the
other day. Let the stronger man push you around—at least you avoid the
torture of your own rage. *That's* the immediate consequence. What an
astonishing discovery it must have been to find that in the long run you
could *control the stronger man* in the same way!"

"It's generous of you to give so much credit to your early colleague,"
said Castle, "but why are we still in the throes of so much misery? Twenty
centuries should have been enough for one piece of behavioral engineering."

"The conditions which made the principle difficult to discover made
it difficult to teach. The history of the Christian Church doesn't reveal
many cases of doing good to one's enemies. To inoffensive heathens,
perhaps, but not enemies. One must look outside the field of organized
religion to find the principle in practice at all. Church governments are
devotees of *power,* both temporal and bogus."

"But what has all this got to do with freedom?" I said hastily.

Frazier took time to reorganize his behavior. He looked steadily
toward the window, against which the rain was beating heavily.

"Now that we *know* how positive reinforcement works and why negative doesn't," he said at last, "we can be more deliberate, and hence
more successful, in our cultural design. We can achieve a sort of control
under which the controlled, though they are following a code much more
scrupulously than was ever the case under the old system, nevertheless
feel free. They are doing what they want to do, not what they are forced
to do. That's the source of the tremendous power of positive reinforcement—there's no restraint and no revolt. By a careful cultural design,
we control not the final behavior, but the *inclination* to behave—the motives, the desires, the wishes.

"The curious thing is that in that case *the question of freedom never
arises.* Mr. Castle was free to drop the matchbook in the sense that
nothing was preventing him. If it had been securely bound to his hand
he wouldn't have been free. Nor would he have been quite free if I'd
covered him with a gun and threatened to shoot him if he let it fall. The
question of freedom arises when there is restraint—either physical or
psychological.

"But restraint is only one sort of control, and absence of restraint
isn't freedom. It's not control that's lacking when one feels 'free,' but
the objectionable control of force. Mr. Castle felt free to hold or drop
the matches in the sense that he felt no restraint—no threat of punishment in taking either course of action. He neglected to examine his positive reasons for holding or letting go, in spite of the fact that these were
more compelling in this instance than any threat of force.

"We have no vocabulary of freedom in dealing with what we want to do," Frazier went on. "The question never arises. When men strike for freedom, they strike against jails and the police, or the threat of them—against oppression. They never strike against forces which make them want to act the way they do. Yet, it seems to be understood that governments will operate only through force or the threat of force, and that all other principles of control will be left to education, religion, and commerce. If this continues to be the case, we may as well give up. A government can never create a free people with the techniques now allotted to it.

"The question is: Can men live in freedom and peace? And the answer is: Yes, if we can build a social structure which will satisfy the needs of everyone and in which everyone will want to observe the supporting code. But so far this has been achieved only in Walden Two. Your ruthless accusations to the contrary, Mr. Castle, this is the freest place on earth. And it is free precisely because we make no use of force or the threat of force. Every bit of our research, from the nursery through the psychological management of our adult membership, is directed toward that end—to exploit every alternative to forcible control. By skillful planning, by a wise choice of techniques we *increase* the feeling of freedom.

"It's not planning which infringes upon freedom, but planning which uses force. A sense of freedom was practically unknown in the planned society of Nazi Germany, because the planners made a fantastic use of force and the threat of force.

"No, Mr. Castle, when a science of behavior has once been achieved, there's no alternative to a planned society. We can't leave mankind to an accidental or biased control. But by using the principle of positive reinforcement—carefully avoiding force or the threat of force—we can preserve a personal sense of freedom."

Ignoble Utopias   Joseph Wood Krutch

Joseph Wood Krutch (1893–1970) was a philosopher, essayist, and naturalist. He taught English at Columbia until the early 1950's when he moved to the Arizona desert. *The Measure of Man* is generally considered his most important philosophical work.

Walden Two is a utopian community created by an experimental psychologist named Frazier who has learned the techniques for controlling thought with precision and who has conditioned his subjects to be happy, obedient and incapable of antisocial behavior. Universal benevolence and large tolerance of individual differences reign—not because it is assumed, as the founders of such utopias generally do assume, that they are natural to all innocent men uncorrupted by society—but because an experimental scientist, having at last mastered the "scientific ability to control men's thoughts with precision," has caused them to think benevolently and tolerantly.

An appeal to reason in contradistinction to passion, habit, or mere custom has been the usual basis of utopias from Plato to Sir Thomas More and even down to Samuel Butler. Mr. Skinner's is, on the other hand, distinctly modern in that it puts its faith in the conditioned reflex instead, and proposes to perfect mankind by making individual men incapable of anything except habit and prejudice. At Walden Two men behave in a fashion we are accustomed to call "reasonable," not because they reason, but because they do not; because "right responses" are automatic. At the very beginning of the story we are shown a flock of sheep confined to the area reserved for them by a single thread which long ago replaced the electric fence once employed to condition them not to wander. As predicted in official Communist theory, the State—represented here by electricity—has "withered away" and no actual restraint is necessary to control creatures in whom obedience has become automatic. Obviously the assumption is that what will work with sheep will work with men.

Now though men can reason, they are not exclusively reasoning creatures. None, therefore, of the classic utopias could be realized because each is based on the assumption that reason alone can be made to guide human behavior. Moreover—and what is perhaps more important —few people have ever seriously wished to be exclusively rational. The good life which most desire is a life warmed by passions and touched with that ceremonial grace which is impossible without some affectionate loyalty to traditional forms and ceremonies. Many have, nevertheless, been very willing to grant that a little more reason in the conduct of private and public affairs would not be amiss. That is why, as fantasies, the utopias of Plato and Sir Thomas More have seemed interesting, instructive, even inspiring. But who really wants, even in fancy, to be, as Walden Two would make him, more unthinking, more nearly automatic than he now is? Who, even in his imagination, would like to live in a community where, instead of thinking part of the time, one never found it possible to think at all?

Is it not meaningful to say that whereas Plato's Republic and More's Utopia are noble absurdities, Walden Two is an ignoble one; that the first two ask men to be more than human, while the second urges them to be less? When, in the present world, men behave well, that is no doubt sometimes because they are creatures of habit as well as, sometimes, because they are reasonable. But if one proposes to change Man as Professor Skinner and so many other cheerful mechanists propose, is it really so evident that he should be changed in the direction they advocate? Is he something which, in Nietzsche's phrase, "must be surpassed," or is he a creature to whom the best advice one can give is the advice to retreat—away from such reasoned behavior as he may be capable of and toward that automatism of which he is also capable.

Obviously Walden Two represents—glorified, perfected, and curiously modernized—that ideal of a "cloistered virtue" which European man has tended to find not only unsatisfactory as an ideal but almost meaningless in terms of his doubtless conflicting aspirations. Nevertheless it must be admitted that Thomas Henry Huxley, a protomodern, once admitted in an often quoted passage that "if some great power would agree to make me always think what is true and do what is right, on condition of being turned into a sort of clock and wound up every morning before I got out of bed, I should instantly close with the offer." And what a Huxley would have agreed to, prospective candidates for admission into Walden Two might also find acceptable.

Frazier himself is compelled to make a significant confession: the motives which led him to undertake his successful experiment included a certain desire to exercise power over his fellows. That is not admirable in itself and is obviously not without its dangers. But he insists that the danger will disappear with him because those who succeed to his authority and inherit his techniques will have enjoyed, as he did not, the advantages of a scientific conditioning process and that therefore such potentially antisocial impulses as his will no longer exist. In other words, though the benevolent dictator is a rare phenomenon today, the happy chance which produced this one will not have to be relied on in the future. Walden Two will automatically produce the dictators necessary to carry it on.

Nevertheless and even if the skeptical reader will grant for the sake of argument that automatic virtue represents an ideal completely satisfactory, a multitude of other doubts and fears are likely to arise in his mind. He will remember of course that Brook Farm and the rest failed promptly and decisively. Perhaps he will remember also that Russian communism achieved at least some degree of permanence only by rejecting, more and more completely, everything which in any way parallels the mildness, the gentleness, and the avoidance of all direct restraints and pressures which is characteristic of Walden Two; that the makers of Soviet policy came to denounce and repress even that somewhat paradoxical enthusiasm for the culture of a different world which was as much encouraged in the earliest days of the experiment as it is at Walden Two.

Hence, if a Walden Two is possible it obviously has become so only because—and this is a point which presumably Mr. Skinner himself wishes to emphasize—it differs in several respects from all superficially similar projects. Like the Russian experiment it assumes that, for all practical purposes, man is merely the product of society; but it also assumes a situation which did not exist when the Communist state was set up: namely one in which "the scientific ability to control men's thoughts with precision" has fully matured.

Thus if the man upon whom the experiment is performed is nothing but the limitlessly plastic product of external processes operating upon him and is, by definition, incapable of any significant autonomous activity, he is also, in this case, a creature who has fallen into the hands of an ideally competent dictator. His desires, tastes, convictions and ideals are precisely what the experimenter wants to make them. He is the repository of no potentialities which can ever develop except as they are called forth by circumstances over which he has no control. Finally, of course, his happy condition is the result of the fortunate accident which determined that the "engineer" who created him and, indirectly, will create all of his progeny, was an experimenter whose own random conditioning happened to produce, not the monster who might just as likely have been the first to seize the power that science offered, but a genuinely benevolent dictator instead.

À propos this last premise it might, in passing, be remarked as a curious fact that though scientific method abhors the accidental, the uncontrollable and the unpredicted; though Mr. Skinner's own ideal seems to be to remove forever any possible future intrusion of it into human affairs; yet the successful establishment of the first utopia depended ultimately on the decisive effect of just such an accident as will henceforth be impossible.

Critics of the assumption that technological advance is the true key to human progress have often urged that new powers are dangerous rather than beneficial unless the question of how they should be used is at least opened before the powers become available. With more than usual anxiety they might contemplate the situation in which we are now placed if it is true that only chance will answer the question by whom and in the interest of what "our approaching scientific ability to control men's thoughts with precision" is to be used. But this is only one of several desperate questions which the premises of *Walden Two* provoke. Most of them can also be related to points made by Mr. Skinner in less fanciful contexts and to one or two of them we may turn in connection with a more general consideration of problems raised if we are ready to assume that we actually do stand at the threshold of a world in which men's thoughts will be controlled scientifically and as a matter of course.

To begin with, we must, of course, abandon the old platitude, "You can't change human nature," and accept its opposite, "You can change human nature as much and in whatever direction you wish"—because "human nature" does not exist in the sense which the phrase implies. Whatever desires, tastes, preferences, and tendencies have been so general and so persistent as to create the assumption that they are innate or "natural" must be, as a matter of fact, merely the most ancient and deeply graven of the conditionings to which the human animal has been subjected. As Pascal—an odd thinker to be invoked in defense of a mechanistic and completely relativist ethic—once exclaimed in one of those terrifying speculations of which, no doubt, his own conditioning made him capable: "They say that habit is Second Nature; but perhaps Nature is only First Habit."

By eager reformers "You can't change human nature" has often been denounced as both a counsel of despair and a convenient excuse for lazy indifference in the face of the world's ills. Yet the fact or alleged fact which the phrase attempts to state has also its positive aspect. To say that human nature cannot be changed means that human nature is something in itself and there is at least the possibility that part of this something is valuable. If we say that it cannot be changed we are also saying that it cannot be completely corrupted; that it cannot be transformed into something which we would not recognize as human at all. This is what the eighteenth century allowed Pope to say for it, and as long as one holds the doctrine that the term Nature actually describes some enduring set of possibilities and values, then some limit is set, not only to human perfectibility, but also, and more encouragingly, to things which it can become or be made.

But once this view of "Nature" has been dismissed as an illusion and even what appear to be the most persistent of its traits are thought of as merely the result of conditioning, then there is no limit to the extent to which men may become different from what they now are. There is nothing against which it may be assumed that human nature will revolt. Only by a temporarily established convention is any kind of vice a "creature of so frightful mien." Anything can be made to seem "natural." Cruelty, treachery, slander and deceit might come generally to seem not frightful but beautiful. And if it be said that the successful putting into practice of certain recent political philosophies supports the contention of determinists that man may, indeed, be taught to believe precisely this, it must be added that something more is also implied: namely that we must abandon—along with the conviction that human nature cannot be changed—all the hopes expressed in such phrases as "human nature will in the end revolt against" this or that.

Since no human nature capable of revolting against anything is now presumed to exist, then some other experimenter—conditioned perhaps as the son of the commandant of a Nazi labor camp—might decide to develop a race of men who found nothing more, delightful than the infliction of suffering, and to establish for them a colony to be called Walden Three. By what standards could the dictator of Walden Two presume to judge that his utopia was any more desirable than its new rival? He could not appeal to God's revealed word; to the inner light of conscience; or to that eighteenth-century stand-by, the voice of Nature. He could say only that the accidents of his previous existence in a world where accident still played its part in determining how an individual should be conditioned had conditioned him to prefer what he would, in full realization of the unjustifiability of the metaphor, call "light rather than darkness." The life in Walden Two appears to him as "good" but the adjective would, of course, have no meaning in relation to anything outside himself.

In the light of such possibilities those who have not yet been molded by either Walden Two or Walden Three will tend to feel that before the "scientific ability to control men's thoughts with precision" has been fully utilized by whoever may seize the limitless power it will confer, we had better take a last look around—if not for that way of escape which may not exist, then at least in order to grasp certain implications and possible consequences as they appear to the minds of men who are still "free"—free at least in the limited sense that they are the product of conditions which were brought about, in part, through the presence of random factors destined to play a smaller and smaller part in determining human personality. That second generation of dictators to whom the dictator of Walden Two expects to pass on the control of affairs will be conditioners who have themselves been conditioned. The circle of cause and effect will have been closed and no man will ever again be anything which his predecessor has not consciously willed him to be.

According to the mechanist's own theories, everything which happened in the universe from its beginning down, at least until yesterday, was the result of chance. The chemical molecule didn't "want" or "plan" to grow more complex until it was a protein; the protein did not plan to become protoplasm; and the amoeba did not plan to become man. As a matter of fact, a theory very popular at the moment explains the fact that life seems to have arisen on our earth but once in all the billions of years of the planet's existence by saying that it could arise only as the result of a combination of circumstances so fantastically improbable that they have never occurred again. Yet though they owe to chance both their very existence and all progress from the protozoan to civilization, they are eager to take a step which would make it forever impossible for the unexpected and the unplanned to erupt again into the scheme which will pass completely under their own control.

No doubt many practical-minded people will object that such speculations as these are a waste of time. After all, they will say, even Walden Two does not exist except in fancy and no one has yet claimed that the "approaching scientific ability to control men's thoughts with precision" has already arrived. Logical dilemmas and metaphysical difficulties are cobwebs which will not entangle those who refuse to take seriously their gossamer threads. We have work to do and practical problems to solve.

But to all such it may be replied that practical problems and the metaphysical forms to which they may be reduced are not so unrelated as they may think, and that the logical extreme sometimes serves to make clear the real nature of a purely practical problem. It is true that no man has yet established a Walden Two or Walden Three, and that neither has any man yet controlled *with precision* men's thoughts. But it is also true that there has been a movement in a direction which suggests Walden Two as an ideal. Moreover, statesmen, educators and publicists have already achieved considerable success in their frankly admitted attempts to use the techniques already developed to control and condition large sections of the public and have increasingly declared their faith in the desirability and practicality of such methods in contradistinction to what used to be called education, on the one hand, and appeals to the enlightened understanding of the public, on the other. Already it has quite seriously and without any conviction of cynicism been proposed that the advertisers' principle, "say a thing often enough and it will be believed," be utilized by those who have what they regard as "correct" or "healthy" or "socially useful" ideas to sell. Every time it is proposed that schools should develop certain attitudes in their pupils or that the government should undertake propaganda along a certain line, the question of the difficult distinction between education in some old-fashioned sense and "conditioning" definitely arises.

Moreover, it is because the techniques of the social scientist and the experimental psychologists do to some extent work that some attempt must be made to understand their implications. By their methods many men may be made to do and think many things. Already in the relatively simple case of education versus "useful conditioning," the difficult distinction ceases to be difficult once a border line has been definitely crossed. Writing to George Washington not long after our particular democracy had been founded, Thomas Jefferson remarked, "It is an axiom in my mind that our liberty can never be safe but in the hands of the people themselves, and that, too, of the people with a certain degree of instruction." What would Jefferson have thought of the suggestion that "a certain degree of instruction" be interpreted to mean "a certain degree of conditioning"? Would he not have pointed out that the distinction between the two is clear and fundamental; that "conditioning" is achieved by methods which by-pass or, as it were, short-circuit those very reasoning faculties which education proposes to cultivate and exercise? And would he not have added that democracy can have no meaning or no function unless it is assumed that these faculties do lie within a realm of freedom where the sanctions of democracy arise?

Thus the whole future of mankind may well depend not only on the question whether man is entirely or only in part the product of conditionings, but also on the extent to which he is treated as though he were. Will we come ultimately to base what we call "education," in and out of schools, on the assumption that conditioning by propaganda as well as other methods is the most effective, even if it is not the only, method of influencing human beings.

To all such questions an answer in pragmatic terms has already been given at least positively enough to make it very pertinent to ask into whose hands the power already being exercised is to fall; to ask who is to decide in what direction the citizen is to be conditioned, and on the bases of what standards of value those decisions are to be made. That is simply the practical aspect of the theoretical question, "Who shall be master of Walden Two?"

In the totalitarian countries, where deterministic theories have been accepted in their most unqualified form and the techniques of control most systematically practiced, the question just posed has been answered in the simplest possible manner, and very much in the same way that it was answered at Walden Two. Power is exercised by those who seized it and, theoretically at least, this seizure was the last event which could "happen" because henceforward human destiny will be in the hands of those who are now in a position to control it. The question whether they ought to have done so and whether it is well for humanity that they did was either always meaningless or soon to become so since all the value judgments made in the future will be made by those who have been conditioned to approve what has happened to them.

One result of all this is that during the transition period while there are still survivors from the age when men's minds had not yet been controlled with precision and a conflict of wills is still possible—*i.e.,* under the conditions prevailing in the totalitarian states as they actually exist —a sharp distinction has to be made between those in possession of the power which they have seized and those who are subject to their manipulations. As a catchword the old term "classless society" may be used, but it is evident that no two classes could be more widely separated than the class of those who decide what shall be done and the class of those who are conditioned and controlled.

Obviously such a situation cannot arise either in Germany, Russia or Walden Two until the seizure of power has actually occurred and the power seized must include not only the classic essential, "the instruments of production," but also those "instruments of thought control" which seem to be assuming a more crucial importance than Marx assigned them.

No less obviously this seizure has not yet been made in the countries still called "democratic." Power may be drifting into the hands of certain groups but most of the members of these groups are not quite so completely committed as the totalitarian leaders were to the theories by which they justified their acts and are therefore not so ready to assume the dictatorship which may possibly be already within their reach. In such countries it is, therefore, still possible to consider certain questions, both practical and metaphysical, which even those still capable of considering them are forbidden to raise publicly in totalitarian states. We can still think—or at least go through those mental motions which were formerly called thinking—about the direction in which our own society seems to be moving, about certain large questions of values and ethics, even about the possibilities that under certain conditions men may not be the automata they are more and more assumed to be and that therefore their thoughts never can be controlled either completely or "with precision." Even more specifically we may ask whether totalitarianism on either the model of Soviet Russia or Walden Two is what we wish for or must inevitably accept.

It has sometimes been said that the totalitarian state is merely what democracy must in time become. Enthusiastically in the one case, reluctantly in the other, the same premises lead to the same methods and the same methods to the same results. What one proclaims definitively as dogma is the same as what the other drifts toward and this distinction is the only one which can be made, no matter where we attempt to draw it. In this view a "people's democracy" is only a "welfare state" which has fully accepted its implications. In theory as well as in practice the difference is always merely in the degree to which the logic of any position has been followed to its ultimate conclusion.

No doubt reality is much less simple. But after this large proviso has been accepted much can be said to support the contention that what we of the democracies toy with and lean toward are the same scientific hypotheses and the same philosophical notions that totalitarians proclaim as truths it is forbidden to question.

Roman Catholic doctrine makes the useful distinction between those beliefs which are *de fide* and those which are no more than *pia sententia*. The one must be accepted without dispute by all who wish to remain within the fold; the other, though part of commonly held opinion, have the weight of no authority behind them. In many cases the distinction between what the Communist state proclaims concerning the real nature of man and the proper methods of dealing with it differs from what many of our own psychologists and sociologists tend to assume only as an article of belief which has been proclaimed *de fide* differs from *pia sententia*. What we may tend to deduce from, say, the Pavlovian experiments does not differ too significantly from what an orthodox Russian scientist would say that these same experiments have proved with ultimate finality.

In what the sociologist previously quoted was pleased to call "today's thinking" man tends to appear very much what the Russian version of Marxist science would make him and those who follow such lines of thought are inevitably led to the same next step. If man is the product of the conditioning to which chance has subjected him, why should we not make him what we would like him to be?

We have, it is said, already effectively asserted our control over nature, animate and inanimate. Technology has already entered its mature phase and biology is entering it. We have mastered the atom; we have also learned how both to breed and to train animals. Since man is part of nature he also should be subject to control and no more should be necessary to make him so than easy extensions of the methods already successfully applied. We boast that we have mastered nature but that mastery can hardly be called complete until human nature is at least as completely under our control as the other phenomena of animate nature have become.

Perhaps the most general aspect of this subtle but inclusive shift of emphasis is revealed in the almost unconscious substitution of one term for another when the characteristics of a good social order are discussed. At the beginning of the democratic movement the watchword was "opportunity." Social and political evils were thought of as impediments to the free development of aspirations and abilities. But because "opportunity" as an ideal implies faith in the autonomous powers of the individual it has given way to others embodied in words which suggest in one way or another, not what men may be permitted to do for themselves, but what with benevolent intentions of course may be done to them.

The most brutally frank of such words is of course "control" but it is used most freely by those who have come frankly to accept a barely disguised totalitarian ideal. In those who wish still to pay lip service at least to some sort of faith in democracy and freedom the preferred words are "education," "adjustment" and, with a closer approach to frankness, "conditioning." But the difference is one of degree, not in the fundamental assumption which is that men should not be left to develop but must have their characters and temperaments, as well as their daily lives, somehow "planned" for them. The most benign aspect of this assumption is revealed in the desire for a "welfare state" which will assure the physical well-being of its citizens. The most sinister aspect is that more fully revealed in the speculations of the most advanced and theoretical social psychologists who have passed on, as the author of *Walden Two* has, to consider how the character, opinions and tastes of the individual may also be "planned" for him.

No doubt many of those who agree with that Dean of the Humanities to whose happy phrase we find ourselves again and again recurring would speak with the customary horror of the frankly totalitarian states which have, to date, achieved the greatest success in controlling men's thoughts with precision. They would carefully avoid such frank terms as "brain washing" which the Communists use to state clearly their intentions. But it is difficult to see what difference there is except the difference between a philosophy which is still tentative and somewhat reluctant to admit its ultimate implications and one which, facing those implications, proceeds confidently to put into practice the techniques which it has found effective. If "adjustment" is not to become "control" and "conditioning" is to stop short of "brain washing," some limits must be set which are not defined or even hinted at in such statements as those made by some psychologists.

Even those of us whose convictions permit us to doubt that men's thoughts will ever be completely controlled with absolute "precision" must realize, nevertheless, that the "scientific ability" to control them to some considerable degree has been growing and that in all probability it will grow still further. The terrifying extent to which many (if not all) the individuals in a group may be made to act and think in ways which we would once have thought inconceivable is already all too evident. Hence the question of how that power, whether it be limited or unlimited, will be used in our own society is of immediate as well as remote importance. It is no longer merely a metaphysical one.

It does no good to say that the democracy to which we assure ourselves we are committed safeguards us against the arbitrary use of that power. To say anything of the sort is merely to beg the question because an essential part of the question has to do with the reasonable doubt whether what we call democracy can survive the maturing techniques for determining in advance what "the voice of the people" will say. "Democracy," as the West defined it and in contradistinction to the new definition which totalitarianism has attempted to formulate, is meaningless except on the assumption that the individual man's thoughts and desires are to some extent uncontrollable and unpredictable. There can be no possible reason for taking a vote if the results can either be determined or even predicted in advance. In a society which assures, rightly or wrongly, that events are predictably determined, elections can be no more than those rituals with only a formal, ceremonial significance which, in Soviet Russia and Nazi Germany, they actually became.

In Walden Two this fact is tacitly recognized. Its founding dictator expects authority to "wither away" at the time of his death if not before, precisely as, in Communist theory, the dictatorship of the party will some day wither. But before withering away has occurred, the whole future history of mankind will have been set in a pattern which can never suffer any fundamental change because it must correspond to the pattern of conditionings which are self-perpetuating once they have been firmly and universally established. It is hard to see how we can accept even pragmatically the convictions and ideals of Walden Two without incurring consequences which correspond in the realm of the actual to the theoretical consequences of its theoretical premises. The question whether our own society is in the process of turning itself into some sort of Walden Two is far from being merely fantastic.

The Control of Human Behavior   B. F. Skinner

We are seldom willing to admit that we are engaged in controlling the behavior of other people. The commonest techniques of control use force or the threat of force and are objectionable to the controllee and have come to be censured by society. But the condoned techniques of education, persuasion, and moral discourse differ only in the behavioral processes through which they operate and in the minimizing of certain side effects. They are still devices through which one man controls the behavior of another in some measure. Cajolery, seduction, incitement, and the various forms of what biographers call "influence" suggest other techniques.

Familiar rules of thumb in controlling men are embedded in folk wisdom and in many great works of literature. This prescientific technology is rapidly being extended by the scientific study of human behavior (there are those who refuse to admit even the possibility of such a science, but I am speaking here to those who are not only aware of the science but share a deep concern for its consequences). In civilized countries, the more powerful controlling techniques have eventually been contained by a sort of ethical counter-control, which prevents exploitation by those in a position to use them. There is a real danger, however, that the rapid development of new techniques will outstrip appropriate measures of counter-control, with devastating results.

We can see how counter-control originates in the case of force or the threat of force. In primitive literature, the hero is often the man who can whip everyone else in the group in open combat. He controls with the techniques of the bully. The relevant processes have been analyzed in the scientific study of behavior under the headings of avoidance and escape. We see these techniques exemplified today in the government of conquered peoples, in despotic governments of all sorts, by religious agencies which lean heavily on the threat of punishment, by many parents in the control of their children, and by most teachers. The tech-

From *Transactions*, Vol. 17, No. 7, B. F. Skinner, pp. 547–551. © The New York Academy of Sciences 1955. Reprinted by permission.

nique is psychologically and biologically harmful to the controllee and, for this reason, has generated counter-control. The weak are, at least, more numerous, and we now generally hold it to be "wrong" to control through the use of force or the threat of force (although an impartial observer might not come to this conclusion). Formalized governmental and religious precepts support this containment of the techniques of the bully. The result is called peace—a condition in which men are not permitted to use force in controlling each other.

A later type of popular hero is the cheat, who outwits the strong man by misrepresentation and deceit (in a technical analysis, the relevant processes would be classified under the extinction of conditioned reflexes). But the cheat, eventually, is almost as objectionable as the bully, and ethical control accordingly arises. It is held to be "wrong" to lie, cheat, or cry "Wolf" for one's amusement.

There are techniques which may be as effective as these but may not lead so directly to counter-control. These techniques are becoming more powerful as their processes are better understood. A few examples follow.

1. *Emotional Conditioning.* Aldous Huxley, in *Brave New World,* describes a perfectly plausible process through which certain inferior types of citizens are permanently dissuaded from wasting time on books and the beauties of nature. Babies are allowed to crawl toward books and flowers but receive electric shocks just as they touch them. The example appears to be borrowed, not from the science of conditioned reflexes, but from certain forms of moral education in which, for example, a child is spanked for taking an interest in parts of his own body. The same principle is used to generate strong reactions of rage and aggression toward the enemy in preparaing servicemen for combat. It is the basis of advertising which shows a product being used by or otherwise associated with pretty girls or admired public figures. The controllee is not likely to revolt against such control, and he may carry the resulting prejudices contentedly to his grave.

2. *Motivational Control.* Crude instances, such as the starving of a whole people so that food may be used to reinforce those who begin to support the government, bring their own eventual containment, but the exploitation of prevailing deprivations may be more subtle and possibly equally effective. The deliberate design of art and literature (as in the movies and "comics") to appeal to people with sadistic tendencies is easily detected, but the subtle design of an automobile so that riding in it is in some measure a sexual experience is not so easily spotted. Neither practice may meet any objection from the people so controlled.

3. *Positive Reinforcement.* Wages, bribes, and tips suggest a classical pattern in which we generate behavior in others through reinforcement or reward. Better ways of using reinforcement in shaping up new behavior and in maintaining the condition called interest, or enthusiasm, have been recently discovered. The reinforcing effect of personal attention and affection is coming to be better understood, especially by clinical psychologists. Lord Chesterfield and Dale Carnegie have recommended the use of feigned attention in influencing people.

4. *Drugs.* We are entering the age of the chemical control of human

behavior. Drugs have been used for this purpose ever since the first man was deliberately made drunk. But better drugs are now available, not only for allaying anxiety but for other purposes of control. Our government would probably not hesitate to use a drug which, taken by servicemen before combat, would eliminate all signs of fear, thus depriving the individual of the protective reflexes which man has acquired through a long process of evolution. In the not-too-distant future, the motivational and emotional conditions of normal daily life will probably be maintained in any desired state through the use of drugs.

5. *Knowledge of the Individual.* Techniques of control can be effective only when certain facts about the controllee are known. Gathering information through eavesdropping, employing spies and informers, opening mail, and wiretapping has, from time to time, come under ethical counter-control, though the present state of this in our culture is uncertain. Meanwhile, new techniques have been developed. Something like the projective tests of clinical psychology, combined with the technique of the political trial balloon, might make it possible to discover information about an individual or a whole people, not only without the knowledge of the controllee but with respect to matters of which the controllee himself has no clear understanding.

The doctrine that there is an absolute moral law applicable to all conditions of human life discourages the analysis of controlling practices and obscures our understanding of the need for counter-control. The methods by which men alter the behavior of other men change, and changing ethical measures are required. A technique need not be immediately objectionable to the controllee to engender counter-control. The gambler, for instance, is possibly the last person to ask for legal or moral restrictions on gambling enterprises. The alcoholic does not usually advocate the control of alcoholic beverages. Few workers object to being paid, even for kinds of work or according to pay schedules which society proscribes. It is the rare man who objects to the tyranny of the beautiful woman. In all these cases, society appeals to long-term consequences to justify measures of counter-control. Unfortunately, such consequences do not supply any hard-and-fast rule. We must continue to experiment in cultural design, as nature has already experimented, testing the consequences as we go. We may deal with cultural practices as a whole, as in "utopian" thinking, or piecemeal by changing one counter-controlling technique at a time. Eventually, the practices which make for the greatest biological and psychological strength of the group will presumably survive, as will the group which adopts them. Survival is not a criterion which we are free to accept or reject, but it is, nevertheless, the one according to which our current decisions will eventually be tested. It is less clear-cut than some absolute criterion of right and wrong, but it is more reassuring in its recognition of the changing needs of society.

Such an experimental attitude is sometimes criticized by those who want to defend some principle appropriate to an earlier stage of our cultural history. An example is the recent book by Joseph Wood Krutch, *The Measure of Man,* which is in considerable part an attack on my utopian novel, *Walden Two.* While arguing that the notion of behavioral engineering is ultimately faulty, because man is in some sense free and hence may escape control, Krutch admits that human freedom is under attack and that, if science is not checked, freedom may vanish altogether. Krutch argues that unless we put a stop to the machinations of scientists, "we may never really be able to think again." By freedom, Krutch seems to mean merely a lack of order. The virtues of the prescientific era were the virtues of accident. The great crime of the founder of Walden Two, according to Krutch, was the destruction of the possibility of the happy chance—even such as that which gave rise to the founder himself, before "men's thoughts were controlled with precision." On the same grounds, we might object to the synthetic fibre industry for circumventing the accidental evolutionary processes which produced cotton and wool. If we can arrange better conditions of human life and growth, why should we wait for the happy accident, even if past accidents have brought us to this very point of power?

Krutch's answer is essentially a mystical one: some vague power or faculty has permitted man to transcend his chaotic environment, and this cannot continue to function in less chaotic circumstances. But the existence of such powers or faculties grows more doubtful as man's actual achievements come to be analyzed. Nothing will be lost if science is applied to education or moral discourse. A better way of teaching a child to spell words meets the objection that he is not taught something called "spelling," just as better moral and ethical training meets the objection that the child no longer "has" to be good. In the past, it was natural that some special honor should accrue to the individual who rises above his faulty intellectual and ethical training and is wise and good in spite of it. Men have been at times almost entirely occupied in deciding what is right, intellectually and morally. A world in which education is so successful that one is naturally right in both these senses is criticized because it provides for no heroism in transcending an inadequate environment. One might as well criticize fireproof buildings because the world is thus deprived of brave firemen.

It is easy to object to the control of human behavior by applying the slogans of democracy. But the democratic revolution in government and religion was directed against a certain type of control only. Men were freed from autocratic rulers employing techniques based upon force or the threat of force. It does not follow that men were thus freed of all control, and it is precisely the other forms of control which we must now learn to contain and to which the pattern of the democratic revolution is inappropriate. The democratic concept of "freedom" is no longer effective in international politics because it has lost its point. All major governments profess to be governing *for* the people, and no government will bear close scrutiny of its actual practices. A new conception of the function and practice of government is needed in dealing with the counter-control of techniques against which there is no revolt.

Mr. Krutch is justifiably concerned lest a new type of despotism arise which utilizes the more effective techniques of control provided by the science of human behavior. But his suggestion that we deny the possibility of such a science, or that we abandon it, would deprive us of important help in building adequate safeguards against its misuse. Science poses problems, but it also suggests solutions. In contending that the founder of Walden Two could as easily have been a monster, instead of the fairly benevolent figure he seems to be, Krutch misses the point that, in the long run, the strength of any government depends upon the strength of the governed. Under present conditions of competition, it is unlikely that a government can survive which does not govern in the best interests of everyone.

Unless there is some unseen virtue in ignorance, our growing understanding of human behavior will make it all the more feasible to design a world adequate to the needs of men. But we cannot gain this advantage if we are to waste time defending outworn conceptions of human nature, conceptions which have long since served their original purpose of justifying special philosophies of government. A rejection of science at this time, in a desperate attempt to preserve a loved but inaccurate conception of man, would represent an unworthy retreat in man's continuing effort to build a better world.

The Responsibility of Criminals

The Criminal Law System   Karl Menninger

Karl Menninger (1893–   ), a psychiatrist, is chief of staff of Menninger Clinic and dean of the Menninger School of Psychiatry. He has written widely on the treatment of criminals and in 1968 published *The Crime of Punishment,* which attacks traditional penal methods.

Our highly civilized nation has the most crime of any country in the world. Our beloved President was only recently assassinated by a nonentity who was himself assassinated before a trial could be held. Our jails are full, our court dockets are jammed. Every state is enlarging its prison "facilities" at the very moment that all progressive states are reducing the capacities and populations of their state hospitals. While four-fifths of the patients in our state hospitals are now discharged within a few months of their admission, seventy per cent of the people in jail receiving the standard *penological* "treatment" have been there longer, and have been there before. They have already *had* our idea of treatment once or twice or thrice. And over and beyond all the felons who are locked up and re-locked up, released and rearrested, retried and re-sentenced (at great and wasteful expense to the body politic) there is the much larger number who are never detected, never convicted, never serve a sentence. Crime is costing us twenty-eight billion dollars

Reprinted from *The Tasks of Penology* edited by Harvey S. Perlman and Thomas B. Allington by permission of University of Nebraska Press. Copyright 1969 by University of Nebraska Press.

per year in this country, and a pall of darkness extends over the entire administration of criminal justice.

Many people are distressed about this situation. Many are alarmed and say so publicly. And, let it be said in fairness, many are trying to remedy it—either by piecemeal changes in the process here and there— improved police science, for example—or by more radical proposals.

I. The Role of the Psychiatrist

What can the field of psychiatry, a branch of medical science, contribute to the improvement of the situation? What can the psychiatrist do—or refrain from doing—that would help? Often the psychiatrist seems to merely add confusion and subterfuge rather than clarification.

I submit that our negative help, made with the best of intentions, stems from our being in the wrong place, offering our help at the wrong time. A psychiatrist is out of place in the courtroom, because he does not speak the language used there or understand the principles in operation in the courtroom nor concur with the method of finding truth to which the law is committed. The psychiatrist enters the courtroom—by invitation, remember—to be exploited by someone, either by the prosecution or by the defense, usually the latter. He is introduced to utter a few magic words, to say that the individual who has been accused is or was bewitched. If he is bewitched then of course he is not responsible for the crime he committed; the witch is responsible. In the older days the prisoner could be executed for that—or someone else could be—but we have grown more humane. Since we cannot execute the witch we do not execute anyone.

Modern psychiatrists do not use the term "bewitched." They use an equally fantastic, meaningless term, "responsible." This is not their word; it is a legal word. They really do not know what it means. Nevertheless, the court asks them if the prisoner has it. If the prisoner is behaving in a way which psychiatrists regard as ill, they assume this to be what the lawyers call "irresponsibility." And so, the psychiatrists answer "yes" or "no."

Psychiatrists are inclined to doubt that *anyone* is completely irresponsible for anything about his life except his own birth. In everything in which he participates a human being has a share of responsibility, as we interpret the word. Do not talk about what fate has done to you, said Freud in essence; look rather at what you have done with your fate. Someone asked Freud if people were responsible even for their dreams, and he replied dryly, that if the dreamer were not responsible, who indeed is?

Whatever the quality of legal responsibility, it is nothing which psychiatrists have been trained to identify. On the other hand, since it is a human opinion about a course of treatment which psychiatrists do not use, namely, punishment, it is up to the judge or the jury, certainly not the psychiatrist, to say whether or not the man should receive this treatment. If the psychiatrist must testify in the courtroom he can say whether or not a man is deluded or hallucinated or how he is in contact with reality; these are behavior patterns which he has learned to detect. The judge can then decide from this information whether it fits his notion of punishability, which is to say responsibility.

It is a real blessing that in the majority of cases psychiatrists are not called to testify in court. But it is a great tragedy that in all cases psychiatrists are not available to judges *after* the guilt has been established to advise them regarding disposition, as was recommended by the Wickersham report in 1927, by the section on criminal law of the American Bar Association the same year, by the National Crime Commission the following year, and by the American Medical Association and the American Psychiatric Association in succeeding years. It would be a great step forward if the judge could obtain psychiatric, social and educational evaluation of the offender by a board of experts. We shall discuss this further, shortly.

II. The Role of the Judge

As it is, in most instances, a man convicted of having broken the law is for the time being at the mercy of the judge, who must decide without any information where the convicted man goes next, what he does next, what roundabout route he follows in his temporary removal and slow return to society.

Does the judge order the offender to make restitution in kind to the person injured? No. Does he draw any conclusions about the unhealthy neighborhood or precinct in which the crime committed by this man seems to be endemic? No.

Will the judge investigate the personality, the character, the strengths and weaknesses of the offender? Will he be guided in making his decision (the offender's social treatment) by any hint that the criminal needs counsel or crutches or a confessor? Most probably not. The judge is not a doctor; he is not a sociologist; he is not a policeman; he is not a welfare man; he is a judge. He must act for the state in balancing the offense committed with the corresponding offensiveness on the part of the state. The offender may have been ruthless; he may have committed his crime without finesse, but he will receive his repayment with formality and dignity. The judge will consult the statute books and read the prescription.

Let us not be too hard on the judge. Most of the improvements that have been brought about in recent times have come because some judge could not take it any more. He is really in a dreadful position because he is expected to do the impossible. He is expected to know in advance just how much frustration and humiliation it is going to require to change the convicted offender into something better—or something worse. There is usually nobody to help him, and in many instances he has only a few minutes to decide each case. And he has very few alternatives; things are pretty well specified in the books.

If he is a very enlightened judge operating in a very enlightened state where something like the enlightened Model Penal Code is in effect, he may venture to suggest that the case be studied impartially by scientific experts and the recommendation made to him as to where the man might be sent for some kind of social handling which would effect a change in his behavior patterns. At least it could be determined whether he was sick or senile, feeble minded or frantic, meretricious or merely fatuous. Such a judge might allow himself to assume that if a man has done something wrong, there may be something wrong with that man or with the situation in which that man operates. He might assume a capacity for receiving help which could at least be explored.

But in a vast majority of instances the judge may not assume that and does not proceed accordingly. He assumes that the man who has been convicted of crime is mentally and physically healthy, and is moreover willful and perverse, such that he did defiantly, aggressively, knowingly and impudently violate the laws of our state. By due process of law, this individual is convicted.

For such persons there is a stipulated remedy. It has been established by law. Regardless of other factors relevant to the single act which has been pronounced criminal, there must now be an official ordering of punishment and subsequent infliction of this punishment. The punishment must fit the crime, not the criminal, and the legislature long ago decided how that fit was to be measured.

This is one place where the psychiatrist could and should come in. The facts have been decided. The guilt has been established. Now the question is, what can be done with this man? What is wrong with him? What is wrong with the environment in which he lives? What is it that is overtaxing him? Why can not he behave like the rest of us? Why does he want to make everyone mad, at such great expense to himself as well as to us? Is he feeble minded? Is he moronic? Is he blind with rage, and if so what about? Is there a nail in his shoe or a tumor in his brain?

It is often easy to dismiss such cases by saying, "Oh, he is just a greedy fellow who wanted to make money," or "a vicious fellow who wanted to see blood." But these are not scientific judgments. These are primitive judgments. These are the kinds of judgments about human behavior which gave rise to our now archaic system.

Following the trial the psychiatrist could be very useful. He could be part of a team which might have sixty days, for example, in which to study the offender and offense or offenses which he has committed. They could evaluate his educational level, his peculiar emotional constitution, his physical status, his talents if any, his proficiencies and also his deficiencies.

As a result of such a diagnostic study the psychiatrist and his associates could say to the judge, "This man, who does such bad things, is driven in this direction by forces that unaided he cannot control. He was beaten daily by his father for the first ten years of his life. And in his blind rage he keeps wanting to beat back. It will take him a long time to learn that there is a different kind of human relationship, and he is not likely to learn it unless he can be in a place for awhile in which he can re-learn his living habits and the ways of relating himself to other human beings."

Or the clinic may say to the judge, "This man does bad things because he has a very bad head. The poor fellow has the intelligence level of a nine-year-old child and yet he is expected to live and cooperate with people as if he were at least half his real age, which is thirty. He can't do it. Society must temper the winds to the shorn lamb, or they will have a continuously erring or straying member."

Or the clinic might say to the judge, "This man did commit a criminal act and under circumstances which made it the only possible thing he could do. It was the lesser of two evils and in a certain sense he did wisely. The chances are a hundred to one that he will not do anything like this again and he should return immediately to his work and report to the judge periodically."

Or the clinic might say, "This man is possessed of delusions and hallucinations to the extent that he has no idea of the real nature of what he does or what the court intends to do to him. We should recommend his immediate treatment in a hospital."

Just such recommendations as these are made daily by such diagnostic centers as are provided by the laws of the State of Kansas and the State of California. Theoretically all offenders are supposed to have such examinations and their judges given such reports before a sentence goes into effect. Practically, the demand for such services has been so great that in Kansas at least all the psychiatrists we can muster cannot keep up with the job.

III. The Role of the Prison

The recommendations of any scientific clinic are going to disregard the assumption that the prisoner has to be punished. Just being mean to a person because he has been mean to society does no good. But treatment people must take for any condition is going to have its unpleasant aspects and perhaps seem to them to be punishment. If you doubt this, make an appointment with the dentist to have your tooth pulled. Treatment is never a pleasure.

The whole idea of punishment is so inextricably wrapped up with law, tradition, morality of various versions, childhood recollections, sentimental identifications, fear, resentment and other emotions that it is extremely difficult to speak about it or write about it objectively. Our statutes themselves contain prohibitions against cruel and unusual punishments, indicating that in some way or other the hurting done by the state must be a familiar and garden variety of hurting and not something unexpected. To deprive a man of decent social relationships, palatable food, normal sexual relations, friendships and constructive communication does not strike the law or the lawyers or even the public conscience as being cruel or unusual.

It is really hard for a scientist to find any justification for punishment as the law interprets it. The general idea seems to be that since the man has offended society, society must now officially offend him. It must deliver him a "tit" for the "tat" that *he* delivered. So this must not be impulsive retaliation; it must not be mob action. It must be done by agency, by stipulation and by statute. It must be something that will make him sorry for what he did; if he is already sorry, then it must be something that makes him sorrier. The fact that he is more apt to be sorry that he let himself be caught does not enter into the formula.

Furthermore, the "tit" that we inflict upon him, must be different from the "tat" that he inflicted upon us. He may have murdered or robbed or cheated or seduced; we—society, the law, the prison—do not do any of those terrible things. But we will take him out of his ordinary walks of life, out of his vocation, if any, out of his family, out of his community, out of the world of free human beings. He will be transferred to a housed colony of strangers with whom he has nothing in common for the most part except that like himself they have been caught at something illegal, could not escape from the "system" and hence are now being given the treatment. These others have also been sentenced to undergo this public, official revenge for their offenses, including this reduction to a state of humiliation, anonymity, idleness and futility.

In this state of quarantine and degradation, the offender will meditate upon his evil deeds, his stupidity in having permitted himself to get caught in what "everybody was doing," and upon the generosity of the state and of society in providing him with a living free of charge.

He will be assigned a number and a uniform, and he will be maintained at public expense in the most drab and dreary environment conceivable, for a period of time which becomes the subject of complicated methodological recalculation based on the number of years defined as minimum, the number of times the prisoner is caught whispering or smuggling "contraband" into his cell, the number of auto tags manufactured, and other criteria of good and bad behavior.

IV. The Role of the Parole Board

When the minimum prescribed "time" has been served, the prisoner may go before the parole board. He lives the last months of the period in an agony of mixed fear, uncertainty and anticipation. On the day appointed he dresses in his best overalls. He may be allowed to have his shabby old out-of-style coat brought from the locker room and draped over his shoulders. Wistful, frightened, suspicious—sometimes sullen, but always apprehensive—he sits at the long table before the warden and the chief guard and the solemn members of the parole board. His record is read; abstracts of his "case" lie before each member of the board. This includes his prison record, which usually tells how many times he has been punished for talking in ranks, for buying smuggled tobacco, for replying to an officer, or for quarreling with another prisoner. If his record is not too bad, if the deputy warden can say a few good words for him, if his legal time minus his gained time fits the formula decided by the judge long, long ago, he is "eligible." He is then asked a few questions.

I have heard some of these questions: "Do you think you have learned your lesson?" "Do you intend to go straight now?" "Will you behave yourself?" "Can you keep out of trouble?" "Are you sorry for what you did?" "Have you been treated fairly here?" "Do you have a job?" "Will you join the church?"

Questions even sillier than these are fired at a fellow who would answer affirmatively any question in the world if he thought it would get him out of the torture of his imprisonment. Sometimes, of course, members of parole boards ask very intelligent questions, but most of them realize that the answers given under such circumstances are not very credible. The great deformity of this man's personality (if there is one) is never examined, and of course could not be under these circumstances. For all its strength and growth, psychiatry has not yet been able to convince the parole boards, the lawyers, judges, or even the general public that there can be a useful, systematic, scientific investigation of the motives, feelings, fears, sorrows, hates and loves, delusions, and phobias of individuals who will cooperate. But these private inner secrets cannot be elicited in a public situation.

I do not criticize the board members for the questions they ask. I criticize them for asking any questions at all, under the circumstances. The best interviewer in the world would probably fail to elicit any useful information out of an examination like this made under these conditions in front of these jurymen. But the right kind of an examination *could* be made and reported.

But the tragedy of it is that as a rule there is not much scientific data to go by. There has been no psychiatric examination. There has been no case study. There has been no objective personality inventory. Frequently, if not usually, there has been no social worker investigation of the family, the neighborhood, the sociological surroundings of the crime. Furthermore, most parole boards have under their jurisdiction too small a number of parole officers; often extremely conscientious and capable individuals but often insufficiently trained and inadequately supervised, and usually underpaid.

Thus whether the parole board is perspicacious and conscientious as I know some to be, or stupid and unscrupulous as I have known others to be, the fate of the prisoner is a toss-up. He may be remanded back to prison for a little more penitence and reflection—at state expense, of course. Or he may be dumped back upon society to sink or swim, blessed only with the expensive education he has had in concealing bitterness and fury. In some states, such as my own, he will not be released, no matter how good his record or how long his service, until he or someone else has obtained for him some sort of employment prospect. Many are kept waiting to serve a post graduate term in prison while presumably more meritorious and virtuous (at least more fortunate) people on the outside take the available jobs. But if there are any jobs that no one wants, prisoners, *i.e.* ex-prisoners, may have a chance at them.

V. The Role of the Public

The ex-prisoner thus re-enters a world no longer like the one he left some years before, and certainly nothing like the one he has been living in. In the new world, aside from a few uneasy relatives and uncertain friends, the prisoner is surrounded by hostility, suspicion, distrust and dislike. Complex social and economic situations which were already too much for him have grown no simpler. The unequal tussle with a smarter, "nicer" and more successful people begins again. The ex-prisoner is thus proscribed from employment by most concerns, and usually unable to find new friends and ways of living, and above all is forced to survive, without any further help except an occasional warning from a watchful parole officer.

His chief occupation for awhile will be the search for an occupation, accompanied by innumerable rebuffs, suspicious glances, discouragements and hostile encounters and of course inevitably, temptations. Aside from that of his parole officer, toward whom he may not always feel kindly, the first friendly face that such an individual is likely to see is that of some crony of the old days who has been waiting for a little help to do a little job.

Remember, we are talking about a human being, a handicapped one at that, one who needs all the things the rest of us do—something to do, something to eat, someone to talk to, and a little bit more! You and I can get along without committing crimes (most of the time). But obviously the criminal cannot, or at least does not. The fellow who has been in jail not only has what made him commit the crime, but he has what the jail did to him. Like the rest of us he is inevitably attracted to other people, but it is a lot harder for him after discharge to get to those other people, and the people he is finally able to get to are often poorly equipped to help him, to love him, or even to like him.

Do the churches reach out to take him in? Do business firms recruit him? Do the unions quickly take him in and find him a job? Does the country club give him a locker? Does any but the lowest class restaurant or rooming house welcome so unprepossessing, shabbily dressed and often ill favored individual?

Does anyone know or care if he is depressed, desperate, deluded, hallucinated, delirious, suffused with ideas that he is being persecuted or convinced that he is an avenging angel who must slay the enemies of white supremacy? Does anyone ask whether he might still be dangerous? Does anyone ask what useful things this man might do, what values he might render to society in exchange for the offenses he perpetrated upon it? Does anyone ask what might have been done to deter him from continuing as he was obviously going? Does anyone ask what might be done to redirect him?

No, certainly not. That is not in the book. Criminals are not to be "helped." Criminals are to be *held,* and hurt, threatened and warned, pushed and punished, released and paroled. But "helped"—for heaven's sake! Soft-headed sentimentalism, liberalism, egg-head stuff, practically communistic. These men are toughs; they are dangerous; they are vicious; they are enemies of society. Do not pity them; pity their poor victims. They owe a debt to society. They should pay for their crimes. And keep paying.

If there were ten times as many parole officers as there are, and if they were all as good as a few of our parole officers are, and if they

could carry ten times the load these men and women are now carrying
—which is already too great—and if these parole officers could have just
a little more training and occasionally a little encouragement from the
judges, a little assistance from psychiatric clinics or other behavioral
scientists, above all if they could have a little more appreciation from
the public for what they do—well, this is one of the biggest combinations
of "ifs" imaginable. But if all these "ifs" could be, these indefatigable
but inconspicuous friends and guides of former prisoners might turn the
tide. But at the present time they are swamped.

VI. Conclusions

The Seven Steps-Freedom House plan tries to enlist former prisoners
to help one another and also to win the support and sponsorship of Big
Brother friends in the outside world. The idea of helping one another
is based on the similar principle in Alcoholics Anonymous, which has
been so successful. I think it will be successful here too.

The rapid growth of the Freedom House idea and the Seven Steps
Program—which is only one of several projects having a similar aim
—is an indication of the great need for proper post-prison support
of these men whom we have ruined—perhaps not quite ruined, but
severely damaged. For the prison is not merely inefficient and vastly
expensive, not merely a source of a false sense of reassurance to the
public—it is a vicious, degrading, destroying, expensive juggernaut which
society keeps in its back yard like some extravagant Roman nobleman
keeping pet lions to harass his "lazy" slaves.

The architects of the prevailing system knew nothing about modern
science; their notion of controlling human behavior was based entirely
on various forms and degrees of force. They did not think in terms of
changing the individual but only in terms of intimidating him and—if
necessary—making good the official threats of retaliating harm. But science
has uncovered facts not known to our ancestors—the authors of this
system. We know better. And so, again, why do we continue this obsolete
system? Does not the public care—even the intelligent public?

Time and time and time again somebody shouts about our present
sorry system and its failures, just as I am shouting now. The President
shouts. J. Edgar Hoover shouts. The magazines shout. The newspapers
shout. They shout that the situation is bad, bad, bad and getting worse,
that we should replace obsolete procedures with scientific methods. But
do we?

It is not just psychiatrists who have thus cried in the wilderness,
unheeded. The voices of progressive penologists have been loud and clear.
Leading jurists, wardens, psychologists, sociologists, intelligent police
chiefs are speaking out, and begging for better tools and methods. Even
occasional governors and mayors and congressmen are to be heard. And
recently the President of the United States, in his message to Congress on
March 8, 1965, suggested four measures which might help to curb the
increasing incidence of crime.

Associate Justice Brennan of the United States Supreme Court does not shout. He is encouraged by something he sees. Recently he said quietly, "we may be at the threshold of a major re-examination of the premises which underlie our system for the administration of criminal justice."

Let us hope he is right.

The Humanitarian Theory of Punishment   C. S. Lewis

Clive Staples Lewis (1898–1963) was professor of Medieval and Renaissance English at Cambridge University from 1954 until his death. He is most famous for his numerous books and essays that defend various aspects of Christianity.

In England we have lately had a controversy about Capital Punishment. I do not know whether a murderer is more likely to repent and make a good end on the gallows a few weeks after his trial or in the prison infirmary thirty years later. I do not know whether the fear of death is an indispensable deterrent. I need not, for the purpose of this article, decide whether it is a morally permissible deterrent. Those are questions which I propose to leave untouched. My subject is not Capital Punishment in particular, but that theory of punishment in general which the controversy showed to be almost universal among my fellow-countrymen. It may be called the Humanitarian Theory. Those who hold it think that it is mild and merciful. In this I believe that they are seriously mistaken. I believe that the "Humanity" which it claims is a dangerous illusion and disguises the possibility of cruelty and injustice without end. I urge a return to the traditional or Retributive theory not solely, nor even primarily, in the interests of society but in the interests of the criminal.

According to the Humanitarian theory, to punish a man because he deserves it, and as much as he deserves, is mere revenge, and, therefore, barbarous and immoral. It is maintained that the only legitimate motives for punishing are the desire to deter others by example or to mend the criminal. When this theory is combined, as frequently happens, with the belief that all crime is more or less pathological, the idea of mending tails off into that of healing or curing and punishment becomes therapeutic. Thus it appears at first sight that we have passed from the harsh and self-righteous notion of giving the wicked their deserts to the charitable and enlightened one of tending the psychologically sick. What could be more amiable? One little point which is taken for granted in this theory needs, however, to be made explicit. The things done to the criminal, even if they are called cures, will be just as compulsory as they were in the old days when we called them punishments. If a tendency

From *Res Judicatae*, June 1953. Reprinted with permission of the Melbourne University Law Review and the Trustee of the C. S. Lewis estate.

to steal can be cured by psychotherapy, the thief will no doubt be forced to undergo the treatment. Otherwise, society cannot continue.

My contention is that this doctrine, merciful though it appears, really means that each one of us, from the moment he breaks the law, is deprived of the rights of a human being.

The reason is this. The Humanitarian theory removes from Punishment the concept of Desert. But the concept of Desert is the only connecting link between punishment and justice. It is only as deserved or undeserved that a sentence can be just or unjust. I do not here contend that the question "Is it deserved?" is the only one we can reasonably ask about a punishment. We may very properly ask whether it is likely to deter others and to reform the criminal. But neither of these two last questions is a question about justice. There is no sense in talking about a "just deterrent" or a "just cure." We demand of a deterrent not whether it is just but whether it will deter. We demand of a cure not whether it is just but whether it succeeds. Thus when we cease to consider what the criminal deserves and consider only what will cure him or deter others, we have tacitly removed him from the sphere of justice altogether; instead of a person, a subject of rights, we now have a mere object, a patient, a "case."

The distinction will become clearer if we ask who will be qualified to determine sentences when sentences are no longer held to derive their propriety from the criminal's deservings. On the old view the problem of fixing the right sentence was a moral problem. Accordingly, the judge who did it was a person trained in jurisprudence; trained, that is, in a science which deals with rights and duties, and which, in origin at least, was consciously accepting guidance from the Law of Nature, and from Scripture. We must admit that in the actual penal code of most countries at most times these high originals were so much modified by local custom, class interests, and utilitarian concessions, as to be very imperfectly recognizable. But the code was never in principle, and not always in fact, beyond the control of the conscience of the society. And when (say, in Eighteenth Century England) actual punishments conflicted too violently with the moral sense of the community, juries refused to convict and reform was finally brought about. This was possible because, so long as we are thinking in terms of Desert, the propriety of the penal code, being a moral question, is a question on which every man has the right to an opinion, not because he follows this or that profession, but because he is simply a man, a rational animal enjoying the Natural Light. But all this is changed when we drop the concept of Desert. The only two questions we may now ask about a punishment are whether it deters and whether it cures. But these are not questions on which anyone is entitled to have an opinion simply because he is a man. He is not entitled to an opinion even if, in addition to being a man, he should happen also to be a jurist, a Christian, and a moral theologian. For they are not questions about principle but about matter of fact; and for such *cuiquam in sua arte credendum*.* Only the expert "penologist" (let

* ["experts must be believed."—ed.]

barbarous things have barbarous names), in the light of previous experiment, can tell us what is likely to deter: only the psychotherapist can tell us what is likely to cure. It will be in vain for the rest of us, speaking simply as men, to say, "but this punishment is hideously unjust, hideously disproportionate to the criminal's deserts." The experts with perfect logic will reply, "but nobody was talking about deserts. No one was talking about *punishment* in your archaic vindictive sense of the word. Here are the statistics proving that this treatment deters. Here are the statistics proving that this other treatment cures. What is your trouble?"

The Humanitarian theory, then, removes sentences from the hands of jurists whom the public conscience is entitled to criticize and places them in the hands of technical experts whose special sciences do not even employ such categories as Rights or Justice. It might be argued that since this transference results from an abandonment of the old idea of punishment, and, therefore, of all vindictive motives, it will be safe to leave our criminals in such hands. I will not pause to comment on the simple minded view of fallen human nature which such a belief implies. Let us rather remember that the "cure" of criminals is to be compulsory; and let us then watch how the theory actually works in the mind of the Humanitarian. The immediate starting point of this article was a letter I read in one of our Leftist weeklies. The author was pleading that a certain sin, now treated by our Laws as a crime, should henceforward be treated as a disease. And he complained that under the present system the offender, after a term in gaol, was simply let out to return to his original environment where he would probably relapse. What he complained of was not the shutting up but the letting out. On his remedial view of punishment the offender should, of course, be detained until he was cured. And of course the official straighteners are the only people who can say when that is. The first result of the Humanitarian theory is, therefore, to substitute for a definite sentence (reflecting to some extent the community's moral judgement on the degree of ill-desert involved) an indefinite sentence terminable only by the word of those experts—and they are not experts in moral theology nor even in the Law of Nature—who inflict it. Which of us, if he stood in the dock, would not prefer to be tried by the old system?

It may be said that by the continued use of the word Punishment and the use of the verb "inflict" I am misrepresenting the Humanitarians. They are not punishing, not inflicting, only healing. But do not let us be deceived by a name. To be taken without consent from my home and friends; to lose my liberty; to undergo all those assaults on my personality which modern psychotherapy knows how to deliver; to be remade after some pattern of "normality" hatched in a Viennese laboratory to which I never professed allegiance; to know that this process will never end until either my captors have succeeded or I grown wise enough to cheat them with apparent success—who cares whether this is called Punishment or not? That it includes most of the elements for which any punishment is feared—shame, exile, bondage, and years eaten by the locust—is obvious. Only enormous ill-desert could justify it; but ill-desert is the very conception which the Humanitarian theory has thrown overboard.

If we turn from the curative to the deterrent justification of punishment we shall find the new theory even more alarming. When you punish a man *in terrorem,* make of him an "example" to others, you are admittedly using him as a means to an end; someone else's end. This, in itself, would be a very wicked thing to do. On the classical theory of Punishment it was of course justified on the ground that the man deserved it. That was assumed to be established before any question of "making him an example" arose. You then, as the saying is, killed two birds with one stone; in the process of giving him what he deserved you set an example to others. But take away desert and the whole morality of the punishment disappears. Why, in Heaven's name, am I to be sacrificed to the good of society in this way?—unless, of course, I deserve it.

But that is not the worst. If the justification of exemplary punishment is not to be based on desert but solely on its efficacy as a deterrent, it is not absolutely necessary that the man we punish should even have committed the crime. The deterrent effect demands that the public should draw the moral, "If we do such an act we shall suffer like that man." The punishment of a man actually guilty whom the public think innocent will not have the desired effect; the punishment of a man actually innocent will, provided the public think him guilty. But every modern State has powers which make it easy to fake a trial. When a victim is urgently needed for exemplary purposes and a guilty victim cannot be found, all the purposes of deterrence will be equally served by the punishment (call it "cure" if you prefer) of an innocent victim, provided that the public can be cheated into thinking him guilty. It is no use to ask me why I assume that our rulers will be so wicked. The punishment of an innocent, that is, and undeserving, man is wicked only if we grant the traditional view that righteous punishment means deserved punishment. Once we have abandoned that criterion, all punishments have to be justified, if at all, on other grounds that have nothing to do with desert. Where the punishment of the innocent can be justified on those grounds (and it could in some cases be justified as a deterrent) it will be no less moral than any other punishment. Any distaste for it on the part of a Humanitarian will be merely a hang-over from the Retributive theory.

It is, indeed, important to notice that my argument so far supposes no evil intentions on the part of the Humanitarian and considers only what is involved in the logic of his position. My contention is that good men (not bad men) consistently acting upon that position would act as cruelly and unjustly as the greatest tyrants. They might in some respects act even worse. Of all tyrannies a tyranny sincerely exercised for the good of its victims may be the most oppressive. It may be better to live under robber barons than under omnipotent moral busybodies. The robber baron's cruelty may sometimes sleep, his cupidity may at some point be satiated; but those who torment us for our own good will torment us without end for they do so with the approval of their own conscience. They may be more likely to go to Heaven yet at the same time likelier to make a Hell of earth. Their very kindness stings with intolerable insult.

To be "cured" against one's will and cured of states which we may not regard as disease is to be put on a level with those who have not yet reached the age of reason or those who never will; to be classed with infants, imbeciles, and domestic animals. But to be punished, however severely, because we have deserved it, because we "ought to have known better," is to be treated as a human person made in God's image.

In reality, however, we must face the possibility of bad rulers armed with a Humanitarian theory of punishment. A great many popular blue prints for a Christian society are merely what the Elizabethans called "eggs in moonshine" because they assume that the whole society is Christian or that the Christians are in control. This is not so in most contemporary States. Even if it were, our rulers would still be fallen men, and, therefore, neither very wise nor very good. As it is, they will usually be unbelievers. And since wisdom and virtue are not the only or the commonest qualifications for a place in the government, they will not often be even the best unbelievers. The practical problem of Christian politics is not that of drawing up schemes for a Christian society, but that of living as innocently as we can with unbelieving fellow-subjects under unbelieving rulers who will never be perfectly wise and good and who will sometimes be very wicked and very foolish. And when they are wicked the Humanitarian theory of Punishment will put in their hands a finer instrument of tyranny than wickedness ever had before. For if crime and disease are to be regarded as the same thing, it follows that any state of mind which our masters choose to call "disease" can be treated as crime; and compulsorily cured. It will be vain to plead that states of mind which displease government need not always involve moral turpitude and do not therefore always deserve forfeiture of liberty. For our masters will not be using the concepts of Desert and Punishment but those of disease and cure. We know that one school of psychology already regards religion as a neurosis. When this particular neurosis becomes inconvenient to government what is to hinder government from proceeding to "cure" it? Such "cure" will, of course, be compulsory; but under the Humanitarian theory it will not be called by the shocking name of Persecution. No one will blame us for being Christians, no one will hate us, no one will revile us. The new Nero will approach us with the silky manners of a doctor, and though all will be in fact as compulsory as the *tunica molesta* or Smithfield or Tyburn, all will go on within the unemotional therapeutic sphere where words like "right" and "wrong" or "freedom" and "slavery" are never heard. And thus when the command is given every prominent Christian in the land may vanish overnight into Institutions for the Treatment of the Ideologically Unsound, and it will rest with the expert gaolers to say when (if ever) they are to re-emerge. But it will not be persecution. Even if the treatment is painful, even if it is life-long, even if it is fatal, that will be only a regrettable accident; the intention was purely therapeutic. Even in ordinary medicine there were painful operations and fatal operations; so in this. But because they are "treatment," not punishment, they can be criticized only by fellow-experts and on technical grounds, never by men as men and on grounds of justice.

This is why I think it essential to oppose the Humanitarian theory of Punishment, root and branch, wherever we encounter it. It carries on its front a semblance of Mercy which is wholly false. That is how it can deceive men of good will. The error began, perhaps, with Shelley's statement that the distinction between Mercy and Justice was invented in the courts of tyrants. It sounds noble, and was indeed the error of a noble mind. But the distinction is essential. The older view was that Mercy "tempered" Justice, or (on the highest level of all) that Mercy and Justice had met and kissed. The essential act of Mercy was to pardon; and pardon in its very essence involves the recognition of guilt and ill-desert in the recipient. If crime is only a disease which needs cure, not sin which deserves punishment, it cannot be pardoned. How can you pardon a man for having a gum-boil or a club foot? But the Humanitarian theory wants simply to abolish Justice and substitute Mercy for it. This means that you start being "kind" to people before you have considered their rights, and then force upon them supposed kindnesses which they in fact had a right to refuse, and finally kindnesses which no one but you will recognize as kindnesses and which the recipient will feel as abominable cruelties. You have overshot the mark. Mercy, detached from Justice, grows unmerciful. That is the important paradox. As there are plants which will flourish only in mountain soil, so it appears that Mercy will flower only when it grows in the crannies of the rock of Justice: transplanted to the marshlands of mere Humanitarianism, it becomes a man-eating weed, all the more dangerous because it is still called by the same name as the mountain variety. But we ought long ago to have learned our lesson. We should be too old now to be deceived by those humane pretensions which have served to usher in every cruelty of the revolutionary period in which we live. These are the "precious balms" which will "break our heads."

There is a fine sentence in Bunyan: "It came burning hot into my mind, whatever he said, and however he flattered, when he got me home to his house, he would sell me for a slave." There is a fine couplet, too, in John Ball:

> Be ware ere ye be wo.
> Know your friend from your foe.

One last word. You may ask why I send this to an Australian periodical. The reason is simple and perhaps worth recording; I can get no hearing for it in England.

Suggestions for Further Reading

Anthologies

Enteman, Willard F. (ed.). *The Problem of Free Will.* New York: Scribner, 1967. A collection of important articles on various aspects of the free will–determinism controversy. Since most of the articles are easily readable, this is a good book for the beginning student to turn to for additional reading.

Hook, Sidney (ed.). *Determinism and Freedom in the Age of Modern Science.* New York: New York U.P., 1958. A collection of twenty-seven articles that analyze the concepts of determinism and freedom and the significance of these concepts in physics, law, and ethics. Most of the articles will be difficult for the beginning student.

Individual Works

Clemens, Samuel. "What Is Man?" in *What Is Man? and Other Essays.* New York: Harper, 1917. An interesting and amusing statement of the determinist position by a famous writer.

Cranston, Maurice. *Freedom: A New Analysis.* London: Longmans, 1953. The latter half of this book is a good discussion of the main positions and a defense of libertarianism.

D'Angelo, Edward. *The Problem of Freedom and Determinism.* Columbia, Mo.: University of Missouri Press, 1968. A good, clear discussion of the three major positions.

Darrow, Clarence. *Crime: Its Cause and Treatment.* New York: Crowell, 1922. A famous discussion of criminal treatment from the hard determinist viewpoint.

Matson, Floyd W. *The Broken Image.* New York: George Braziller, 1964. A good discussion of how the hard determinist position has affected man's image of himself. There is also an examination of Skinner and other behaviorists in this connection.

Schopenhauer, Arthur. "Free-Will and Fatalism" in *The Pessimist's Handbook* (*Parerga und Paralipomena*). Translated by T. Bailey Saunders, edited by Hazel E. Barnes. Lincoln: University of Nebraska Press, 1964. A concise and forceful defense of fatalism. Schopenhauer, a clear stylist, uses many illustrations drawn from everyday human behavior and world literature in this essay intended for the general reading public.

———. *Essay on the Freedom of the Will.* Translated by K. Kolenda. Indianapolis: The Liberal Arts Press, The Library of Liberal Arts, 1960. A defense of fatalism in terms of Schopenhauer's voluntaristic metaphysics. The beginning student would do well to start with the essay "Free-Will and Fatalism" and then turn to this more extensive and demanding essay.

Taylor, Richard. *Metaphysics.* Englewood Cliffs, N.J.: Prentice-Hall, 1963. Chapter Four contains a clearly written attack on hard and soft determinism and a defense of a version of libertarianism.

Encyclopedia of Philosophy. Paul Edwards, editor-in-chief. New York: Macmillan, 1967. The student will find many worthwhile articles on the subject treated in this Part, and excellent bibliographies.

Two: God and Religion

Introduction

A question troubling many students is whether they should believe in religion. One reason for their hesitation simply to follow in the paths of their parents in this matter is their conviction that religion has failed to bring about a better world for mankind. Perhaps an even more important reason is that there appears to be no scientific manner by which the basic religious tenets can be established. The desire that one's beliefs be supported by science has its roots in the movement of Western civilization away from a religious view of the world to a scientific one. The great success of science has led many to the view that we should believe only those things that can be established in a proper scientific manner. Further, the advance of science has certainly tended to undermine any simplistic acceptance of religious doctrines and writings. The scientifically trained no longer accept, for example, the biblical accounts of creation and the garden of Eden as literally true. Thus, it is easy to understand why so many of today's students are dubious about accepting traditional orthodox religion. In the light of modern science it appears to be a remnant of ancient superstition that will one day be completely replaced by a scientific view of the world.

Contemporary religious thinkers generally deplore the tendency to view science and religion as competing views of the world. For them, religion and science are concerned with different issues. Science is concerned to discover the laws that are operative in the physical universe, whereas religion is concerned with issues beyond the scope of science, such as the reason for the existence of the universe, the existence of a God, and the purpose of man's life. Since the issues with which religion is concerned are not within the scope of science, it is held to be inappropriate to demand that religious beliefs should be substantiated by scientific facts.

Must religious beliefs be supported by scientific evidence, or is it acceptable to believe without proof? Do the discoveries of modern science show that the views of the major religions are untenable? Such are some of the questions that the philosopher seeks to answer about religion. The philosopher's interest in such questions arises out of the fact that religion gives answers to many of man's most fundamental questions about himself and his place in the world. The philosopher wants to know if the answers are true. Thus, in examining religious views, the philosopher is concerned with their accurate assessment rather than their defense or destruction. The readings in this section will show that there exists a great diversity of opinion among philosophers regarding the truth and value of religion. Some hold that only in a religious framework can a foundation for morality and a meaning to life be found. Others see various religious views as not only false but a great detriment to man's happiness. The student's job is to assess carefully the various positions and arguments to determine which, if any, is sound.

The basic tenet of the major Western religions is that there exists a supernatural being called "God." God is defined as being an all-good, all-knowing, all-powerful creator of the universe. God is viewed as concerned with our affairs rather than being withdrawn and aloof. For the most part, religious believers are convinced that such a God exists without inquiring into the question of scientific or rational proofs for their conviction. Yet many religious theorists believe it important to show, if possible, that the existence of God can be proven or at least shown to be probable on the basis of scientific evidence or other rational arguments. If God's existence could be proven, not only could the skeptics and atheists be converted, but many who believe would feel more confident in their belief.

Numerous proofs have been offered for the existence of God. Most are of little interest to philosophers since they are clearly unsound. Typical of these widely used but unsound arguments are the argument from agreement and the argument from Scripture. *The argument from agreement* consists in attempting to show that God exists on the basis of the fact that so many people throughout the world have believed in the existence of God. It is claimed that such a widespread belief cannot be explained on any other basis than the actual existence of God. One problem with arguing in this manner is that it makes the majority opinion the basis of truth; but it is certainly well known that large majorities have been wrong. At one time there was widespread agreement that the earth was flat. Another difficulty with this argument is that the widespread belief in God can perhaps be explained as the result of superstition, wishful thinking, or fear. If so, the belief in God would not indicate his existence but the psychological characteristics or the lack of scientific knowledge of the majority of mankind. *The argument from Scripture* attempts to prove God's existence on the basis of the fact that we have some writings (Old Testament, New Testament, Koran, and so on) which tell of God. These writings are assumed to be inspired by God and therefore reliable. The obvious difficulty with attempting to prove God in this manner is that the events recorded in the writings must be proved to be accurate and such proof seems impossible to get. Those who doubt the existence of God will also be doubtful that the Bible was inspired by God and that the events given there are accurately reported.

In the readings which follow, some of the arguments that philosophers have considered more plausible are presented. The one that will probably be most familiar to the student is the *argument from design.* According to this argument the world is so intricately put together to maintain the existence of various types of life that it must have been designed by an extremely rational being. This argument is presented in a simple, straightforward manner by A. Cressy Morrison, a highly respected American scientist. Morrison argues that life could not possibly exist by chance since the probability of all the necessary factors existing in the proper relationships would be too great. Also, he claims that the fact that nature is so balanced that no species can conquer all the others indicates that some great Intelligence planned the world. The soundness of the argument is attacked by Clarence Darrow, who argues that the universe shows no clear order or design. He goes on to say that even if it did, it was apparently not designed for human life since we could easily imagine ways in which the world could have been made to provide a better habitation for human beings.

Another frequently encountered argument, *the argument from religious experience,* is presented by James Bisset Pratt. Pratt maintains that belief in God can be upheld by mystical experiences that supporters of various religions have had. The main problem that he feels stands in the way of acceptance of such experiences as evidence of God is the naturalistic explanation of them given by psychologists. It would seem that if such experiences could be accounted for as the result of unusual psychological states, then they could not be considered as evidence of God's existence. Pratt argues, however, that such psychological interpretations are not necessarily incompatible with a religious interpretation of the same phenomena. The student should consider whether Pratt has shown merely that certain experiences could be given a religious interpretation, or whether he has shown that such experiences must be given a religious interpretation and thus are good evidence of God's existence.

In "The Basis of the Moral Law," C. S. Lewis presents a version of the *moral argument* for God. He maintains that men have a sense of moral obligation, which they feel as a claim coming from outside themselves. No naturalistic account of this sense of obligation in terms of human needs or interests satisfactorily explains it. It can only be explained, Lewis argues, by assuming the existence of a lawgiver outside the universe. The crucial issue in assessing this argument is whether he is correct in denying that the sense of obligation can be given an alternative explanation.

Many of the arguments for the existence of God, including the argument from design, are discussed by Bertrand Russell. Russell maintains that none of the arguments for God are convincing. Further, he attacks all religions, not just Christianity, on several grounds. Religion, he maintains, is born of fear and a desire to have a protector. We must not give in to such feelings but must learn to stand on our own feet and conquer the world by intelligence. Further, the various organized religions have hindered progress by defending a morality which is not conducive to human happiness. To improve human institutions and allow for moral progress, the morality of the churches must be opposed.

Some philosophers have maintained that not only is God's existence unprovable, but that we can show that God does not exist. The main attempt to show that an all-good, all-powerful God does not exist arises from a consideration of the evil that exists in the world. It seems undeniably true that bad or evil things happen. Hurricanes and floods destroy houses and crops, children are born crippled or deformed, and murderers and thieves plague our cities. The question that must be answered is this: Why does a God who has the power to eliminate such evils allow them to occur? If God is indifferent to or powerless to prevent such evils, then he is not the kind of good and all-powerful being that Western religions worship. Many theologians have argued that all of the things we call evils are allowed to occur by God for some good purpose. For this view to be defended, it must be shown that God could not have produced equally good results without this evil or at least with less of it.

The existence of evil and its bearing on God's existence is discussed by John Hick and H. J. McCloskey. John Hick argues that evil is allowed to exist because God's purpose for man in this world is not to provide him with a carefree, happy existence but to continue the process of "soul-making." To achieve full development, man must experience and learn to overcome the problems that exist in this world. McCloskey argues that the problem of evil cannot be overcome. He surveys and rejects many of the proposed solutions. He maintains that man does not have to experience evil to achieve a better soul or be allowed to commit evil because he has a free will. He argues that since God is a being who is free and yet never inclined to commit evil, then men could have been created with the same freedom and disinclination to sin.

When confronted with the difficulty of proving the existence of God, many philosophers and theologians fall back on faith as the basis for religious belief. Faith is usually thought of as belief unsupported by evidence. The claim that it is acceptable to believe in religion on faith has not gone unchallenged. In "Reason and Faith" Richard Robinson argues that religion, insofar as it encourages belief on faith, is supporting an irrational approach to the world. Believing in anything without evidence produces bad mental habits. Our beliefs should be determined by an assessment of the evidence and probabilities involved, not by unfounded hopes and wishes. In contrast to this view of the value of faith, William James argues that belief without evidence is sometimes justified. James is careful to point out, however, that such belief is justified only in certain types of situations. He does not want to encourage the holding of unsupported beliefs in every instance where evidence is not available. Ultimately, James believes that to withhold belief on an important matter like religion just because there is insufficient evidence of God's existence would be too cautious. Since withholding belief might cut one off from God's grace, he believes that one should run the risk of error in hopes one's belief may be true. In considering James's position, the student should consider whether it rests on a conception of God as a wrathful being. Would James's argument be correct if God would not punish those who do not believe without evidence? Also, it is interesting to decide if there are any areas outside of religion where one should believe without evidence.

It is frequently claimed that religion is necessary to give life any meaning or purpose. It is held that unless there is a future life, then it is pointless to live. Not only would we have no goal to strive for, but the pains and sorrows we endure in this world make life on balance more trouble than it's worth. Others have claimed that religion is necessary to give a foundation to morality and to guide man's behavior. The selection from Dostoevsky's novel *The Brothers Karamazov* brings out this view of the need of religion for man. In the selection, Christ has returned to earth and been arrested by the Grand Inquisitor of Seville. The Inquisitor argues that Christ's actual teachings, which stress human freedom, would not be acceptable to most men. What they need is a belief that there is something in the future to live for. They cannot stand the idea that there may be no God and that they are free to make their own choices about how they should live. What they desire is some authority to control them and take the burden of decision-making from them.

The claim that religion is necessary to give meaning and value to life is rejected by Kurt Baier. Baier argues that his life has been improperly assessed when it is called a "vale of tears." It is true that when compared to a heaven of constant bliss our life seems poor, but heaven is too high a standard with which to compare it. Further, Baier admits that there is no final purpose for life as a whole, but that does not mean that people cannot set goals to achieve within their lives and, thereby, live a meaningful life.

Does God Exist?

Seven Reasons Why a Scientist Believes in God
A. Cressy Morrison

A. Cressy Morrison (1884–1951) was an astronomer and president of the New York Academy of Sciences, 1938–39. He wrote a number of books on scientific topics, as well as *Man Does Not Stand Alone*, from which the article below was condensed.

We are still in the dawn of the scientific age and every increase of light reveals more brightly the handiwork of an intelligent Creator. In the 90 years since Darwin we have made stupendous discoveries; with a spirit of scientific humility and of faith grounded in knowledge we are approaching even nearer to an awareness of God.

For myself, I count seven reasons for my faith:

First: *By unwavering mathematical law we can prove that our universe was designed and executed by a great engineering Intelligence.*

Suppose you put ten pennies, marked from one to ten, into your pocket and give them a good shuffle. Now try to take them out in sequence from one to ten, putting back the coin each time and shaking them all again. Mathematically we know that your chance of first drawing number one is one to ten; of drawing one and two in succession, one to 100; of drawing one, two and three in succession, one in a thousand, and so on; your chance of drawing them all, from number one to number ten in succession, would reach the unbelievable figure of one chance in ten billion.

By the same reasoning, so many exacting conditions are necessary for life on the earth that they could not possibly exist in proper relationship by chance. The earth rotates on its axis one thousand miles an hour; if it turned at one hundred miles an hour, our days and nights would be ten times as long as now, and the hot sun would then burn up our vegetation each long day while in the long night any surviving sprout would freeze.

Again, the sun, source of our life, has a surface temperature of 12,000 degrees Fahrenheit, and our earth is just far enough away so that this "eternal fire" warms us *just enough and not too much!* If the sun gave off only one half its present radiation, we would freeze and if it gave half as much more, we would roast.

The slant of the earth, tilted at an angle of 23 degrees, gives us our seasons; if it had not been so tilted, vapors from the ocean would move north and south, piling up for us continents of ice. If our moon was, say, only 50 thousand miles away instead of its actual distance, our tides would be so enormous that twice a day all continents would be submerged; even the mountains would soon be eroded away. If the crust of the earth had been only ten feet thicker, there would be no oxygen, without which animal life must die. Had the ocean been a few feet deeper, carbon dioxide and oxygen would have been absorbed and no vegetable life could exist. Or if our atmosphere had been much thinner, some of the meteors, now burned in space by the millions every day, would be striking all parts of the earth, setting fires everywhere.

Because of these and a host of other examples, there is not one chance in millions that life on our planet is an accident.

Second: *The resourcefulness of life to accomplish its purpose is a manifestation of all-pervading Intelligence.*

What life itself is, no man has fathomed. It has neither weight nor dimensions, but it does have force; a growing root will crack a rock. Life has conquered water, land and air, mastering the elements, compelling them to dissolve and reform their combinations.

Life, the sculptor, shapes all living things; an artist, it designs every leaf of every tree, and colors every flower. Life is a musician and has taught each bird to sing its love songs, the insects to call each other in the music of their multitudinous sounds. Life is a sublime chemist, giving taste to fruits and spices, and perfume to the rose, changing water and carbonic acid into sugar and wood, and, in so doing, releasing oxygen that animals may have the breath of life.

Behold an almost invisible drop of protoplasm, transparent, jellylike, capable of motion, drawing energy from the sun. This single cell, this transparent mistlike droplet, holds within itself the germ of life, and has the power to distribute this life to every living thing, great and small. The powers of this droplet are greater than our vegetation and animals and people, for all life came from it. Nature did not create life; fire-blistered rocks and a saltless sea could not meet the necessary requirements.

Who, then, has put it here?

Third: *Animal wisdom speaks irresistibly of a good Creator who infused instinct into otherwise helpless little creatures.*

The young salmon spends years at sea, then comes back to his own river, and travels up the very side of the river into which flows the tributary where he was born. What brings him back so precisely? If you transfer him to another tributary he will know at once that he is off his course and he will fight his way down and back to the main stream and then turn up against the current to finish his destiny accurately.

Even more difficult to solve is the mystery of eels. These amazing creatures migrate at maturity from all ponds and rivers everywhere—those from Europe across thousands of miles of ocean—all bound for the same abysmal deeps near Bermuda. There they breed and die. The little ones, with no apparent means of knowing anything except that they are in a wilderness of water, nevertheless start back and find their way not

[handwritten margin notes: "moon was there before we were? any life."; "what?"; "is God in nature; nature is life; nature is life; life is God"; "can't say who, only what"]

only to the very shore from which their parents came but thence to the rivers, lakes or little ponds—so that each body of water is always populated with eels. No American eel has ever been caught in Europe, no European eel in American waters. Nature has even delayed the maturity of the European eel by a year or more to make up for its longer journey. Where does the directing impulse originate? *eel is nature*

A wasp will overpower a grasshopper, dig a hole in the earth, sting the grasshopper in exactly the right place so that he does not die but becomes unconscious and lives on as a form of preserved meat. Then the wasp will lay her eggs handily so that her children when they hatch can nibble without killing the insect on which they feed; to them dead meat would be fatal. The mother then flies away and dies; she never sees her young. Surely the wasp must have done all this right the first time and every time, else there would be no wasps. Such mysterious techniques cannot be explained by adaptation; they were bestowed.

Fourth: *Man has something more than animal instinct—the power of reason.*

No other animal has ever left a record of its ability to count ten, or even to understand the meaning of ten. Where instinct is like a single note of a flute, beautiful but limited, the human brain contains all the notes of all the instruments in the orchestra. No need to belabor this fourth point; thanks to human reason we can contemplate the possibility that we are what we are only because we have received a spark of Universal Intelligence.

Fifth: *Provision for all living is revealed in phenomena which we know today but which Darwin did not know—such as the wonders of genes.*

So unspeakably tiny are these genes that, if all of them responsible for all living people in the world could be put in one place, there would be less than a thimbleful. Yet these ultramicroscopic genes and their companions, the chromosomes, inhabit every living cell and are the absolute keys to all human, animal and vegetable characteristics. A thimble is a small place in which to put all the individual characteristics of two billions of human beings. However, the facts are beyond question. Well, then—how do genes lock up all the normal heredity of a multitude of ancestors and preserve the psychology of each in such an infinitely small space?

Here evolution really begins—at the cell, the entity which holds and carries the genes. How a few million atoms, locked up as an ultramicroscopic gene, can absolutely rule all life on earth is an example of profound cunning and provision that could emanate only from a Creative Intelligence; no other hypothesis will serve.

Sixth: *By the economy of nature, we are forced to realize that only infinite wisdom could have foreseen and prepared with such astute husbandry.*

Many years ago a species of cactus was planted in Australia as a protective fence. Having no insect enemies in Australia the cactus soon began a prodigious growth; the alarming abundance persisted until the plants covered an area as long and wide as England, crowding inhabitants out of the towns and villages, and destroying their farms. Seeking a defense, the entomologists scoured the world; finally they turned up an insect which lived exclusively on cactus, and would eat nothing else. It would breed freely, too; and it had no enemies in Australia. So animal soon conquered vegetable and today the cactus pest has retreated, and with it all but a small protective residue of the insects, enough to hold the cactus in check forever.

Such checks and balances have been universally provided. Why have not fast-breeding insects dominated the earth? Because they have no lungs such as man possesses; they breathe through tubes. But when insects grow large, their tubes do not grow in ratio to the increasing size of the body. Hence there never has been an insect of great size; this limitation on growth has held them all in check. If this physical check had not been provided, man could not exist. Imagine meeting a hornet as big as a lion!

Seventh: *The fact that man can conceive the idea of God is in itself a unique proof.*

The conception of God rises from a divine faculty of man, unshared with the rest of our world—the faculty we call imagination. By its power, man and man alone can find the evidence of things unseen. The vista that power opens up is unbounded; indeed, as man's perfected imagination becomes a spiritual reality, he may discern in all the evidences of design and purpose the great truth that heaven is wherever and whatever; that God is everywhere and in everything but nowhere so close as in our hearts.

It is scientifically as well as imaginatively true, as the Psalmist said: *The heavens declare the glory of God and the firmament showeth His handiwork.*

The Delusion of Design and Purpose   Clarence Darrow

Clarence Seward Darrow (1857–1938) was one of America's outstanding criminal and trial lawyers. Among his famous cases were the Leopold and Loeb murder trial and the Scopes's evolution trial in Tennessee. He was an outspoken agnostic and an opponent of traditional penal practices.

Seldom do the believers in mysticism fail to talk about the evidence of purpose and design shown in the universe itself. This idea runs back at least one hundred and five years, to Paley's "Natural Theology." There was a time when this book was a part of the regular course in all schools of higher learning, which then included theology; but the book is now more likely to be found in museums.

Paley points out that if a man travelling over the heath should find a watch and commence examining it he would soon discover in the watch itself abundant evidence of purpose and design. He would observe the wheels that fit into each other and turn the hour hand and the minute hand, the crystal made to fit over the face, etc., etc.

What the hypothetical man would observe and conclude would depend on the man. Most men that we know would think that the watch showed a design to accomplish a certain purpose, and therefore must have had a maker. They would reach that conclusion because they are familiar with tools and their use by man. But, suppose the watch had been picked up by a bushman or some other savage or an ape? None of them would draw an inference, for the article would be new to them. Supposing, instead of a man, a coyote or wolf came upon the watch, turned it over and examined it, would the animal read or sense any design? Most assuredly not. Suppose the civilized man should pick up an unfamiliar object, a stone, or a piece of quartz; he might view it and examine it, but it would never enter his head that it was designed, and yet on close inspection and careful study the stone or quartz is just as marvellous as the watch.

Paley passes from the watch to the human structure and shows how the mouth and teeth are adjusted to prepare the food for man's digestion, and how his stomach is formed to digest it; how the eye and ear were made to carry sensations to the brain, etc. Many of the clergy say the same thing to-day, in spite of the fact that the organs of man were never made for any such purpose. In fact, man never was made. He was evolved from the lowest form of life. His ancestors in the sea slowly threw its jellylike structure around something that nourished it and absorbed it. Slowly through ages of continued development and change and mutations the present man was evolved, and with him the more perfect and adaptable and specialized structure, with which he sees and hears and takes his food, and digests it and assimilates it to his structure. The stomach was not made first, and then food created for its use. The food came first, and certain forms of life slowly developed an organ that would absorb food to be utilized in the process of growth. By degrees, through the survival of the construction most fitted for life, the stomach and digestive apparatus for men and other animals gradually grew and unfolded in endless time.

To discover that certain forms and formations are adjusted for certain action has nothing to do with design. None of these developments are perfect, or anywhere near so. All of them, including the eye, are botchwork that any good mechanic would be ashamed to make. All of them need constant readjustment, are always out of order, and are entirely too complicated for dependable work. They are not made for any purpose; they simply grew out of needs and adaptations; in other words, they happened. Just as God must have happened, if he exists at all.

Turning from Paley and his wornout watch to the universe and the physical world in general, is there any more evidence here? First, the "design and order" sharks ought to tell what they mean by their terms, and how they find out what they think they understand. To say that a certain scheme or process shows order or system, one must have some norm or pattern by which to determine whether the matter concerned shows any design or order. We have a norm, a pattern, and that is the universe itself, from which we fashion our ideas. We have observed this universe and its operation and we call it order. To say that the universe is patterned on order is to say that the universe is patterned on the universe. It can mean nothing else.

The earth revolves around the sun in a long curve not far from a circle. Does that show order? Let us suppose that instead of going in a circle it formed a rectangle. Would this not have been accepted as order? Suppose it were a triangle, or any other figure. Suppose it took a tooth-like course, would that, then, be considered order? As a matter of fact, the earth does not go regularly in the same path around the sun; it is drawn out into the universe with the whole solar system, and never travels the same course twice. The solar system really has an isolated place in space. The sun furnishes light and heat to nine different planets, of which the earth is one of the smallest and most insignificant. The earth has one satellite, the moon. Saturn and Jupiter have eight moons each, and, besides that, Saturn has a ring that looks very beautiful from here, running all around the planet. We do know that all the planets of the solar system, and the sun as well, are made of the same stuff. It is most likely that every moving thing in the universe has the same constituents as the earth. What is the plan that gave Jupiter eight moons, while only one was lavished upon the earth, supposed to be the special masterpiece of the Almighty, and for whose benefit all the hosts of the heavens were made? Jupiter is three hundred and seventeen times the weight of the earth, and it takes four years for it to go around the sun. Perhaps the universe was made for inhabitants that will one day live on Jupiter.

It is senseless to talk about order and system and design in the universe. Sir James Jeans' book, published in 1931, "The Stars in Their Course," tells us his theory of the origin of our solar system, which is of more interest to us than the Milky Way. The theory of Jeans, and most of the other astronomers, is that there was a time when all the planets of the solar system were a part of the sun, and that some wandering star in its course across the heavens entered the sphere of the sun and dragged after it the planets and moons that make up the solar system by the power of gravitation. This is the planetismal theory, postulated by Professors Chamberlain and Moulton, of the University of Chicago. These mighty chunks of matter drawn from the sun rushed on through space at a terrific speed, and each was caught by gravitation and revolved around the sun. Their distance from the sun depended largely upon their size before gravitation held them in its grasp.

There is nothing in the solar system that could be called design and order. It came from a catastrophe of whose immensity no one could even dream. Religionists have pointed to the ability of an astronomer to fix the time of an eclipse as evidence of system. There are only a few heavenly bodies involved in an eclipse of the sun or moon, from the standpoint of the earth. The motions and positions of all these bodies are well known, and from this the passage of another heavenly planet or the moon between the earth and the sun can be easily determined. It matters not whether the date of an eclipse is far-off or near-by, the method is the same. To an astronomer the computation is as simple as the question propounded to the first-grade pupil: "If John had three apples and James gave him two more, how many apples would John then have?"

We know that gravitation caught the various planets at a certain point as they sped across space, and that these accidents of colliding bodies are very rare; the reason is that regardless of what seems to be the distance between the stars, they are so far apart that it is almost impossible for them ever to meet. To quote from Jeans': "For the most part, each voyage is in splendid isolation, like a ship on the ocean. In a scale model in which the stars are ships, the average ship will be well over a million miles from its neighbor."

Still, catastrophes have occurred and do occur. Our solar system was probably born from one. The moon was thrown from the earth by some pull of gravitation. The heavens are replete with dark planets, and parts of planets, and meteors hurrying through space. Now and then one drops onto the earth, and is preserved in some park or museum; so that in various parts of the world numerous specimens exist. If there was any purpose in the creation of the universe, or any part of it, what was it? Would any mortal dare to guess?

Our solar system is one of the smallest of the endless systems of which we have any knowledge. Our earth is eight thousand miles in diameter. The star, Betelgeuse, is so large that it would fill all the space occupied in the heavens in the whole orbit made by the earth going around the sun. There are many stars known to be much larger than Betelgeuse. The diameter of this sun is thirty-seven thousand times that of our little earth, for which all the universe is supposed to have been made, and whose inhabitants are endowed with everlasting life.

When the telescope is turned toward the heavens we learn another story. Leaving the sparsely settled section of eternity in which we live forever, and going out into the real main universe, we find worlds on worlds, systems upon systems, and nebula after nebula. No one can possibly imagine the dimensions of endless space. The great Nebula M. 31 in Andromeda is so far away from the earth that it takes light nine hundred thousand millions of years to reach our planet. The nebula itself is so vast that it takes fifty thousand years for light to cross it. To make it still more simple I have taken the pains to figure the distance of this nebula from our important planet, called the earth, which boasts of a diameter of eight thousand miles. This nebula is 5,279,126,400,000,-000,000 miles away from us, if my computations are right. I would not positively guarantee the correctness of the answer, but I think it is all right, although I did it by hand. I have gone over the figures three times, and got a different result each time, so I think the answer can be pretty well depended upon. I cannot help feeling sorry for the residents of Nebula M. 31 in Andromeda, when I think what a great deprivation they must suffer through living so far away from our glorious planet, which Mark Twain named "the wart," but which theology has placed at the centre of the universe and as the sole concern of gods and men.

What lies beyond Andromeda? No one can answer that question. And still there is every reason to believe that other worlds and systems and nebulae reach out into stellar space, without end. It is obvious that no one can form a conception of the extent of space or the infinite number of suns and planets with which the limitless sky is strewn. No one can vision a beginning or an end. If it were possible for any fertile mind to imagine a conception of the end of space, then we should wonder what lies beyond that limit. We cannot attain the slightest comprehension of the extent of our pigmy solar system, much less any of the greater ones. The planet which is the farthest from our sun is Pluto, one of the smallest in our system. The diameter of Pluto's orbit around the sun is only about 7,360,000,000 miles. This may be taken as the extent of our solar system. This can be compared with the distance to the nebula in Andromeda, which I hesitate to record again, showing the trifling importance of our whole solar system in so much of the universe as we can scan.

When the new telescope is completed and mounted on the top of Mount Wilson, it is hoped that we can produce figures of distance that are real figures.

Among the endless number of stars that whirl in the fastnesses of illimitable space, how many millions of billions of planets are likely to be in existence? How many of these may possibly have as much special and historical importance as the tiny globe to which we so frantically cling? To find that number, go and count the grains of sand on all the coasts of all the waters of the earth, and then think of the catastrophe that would result to the coasts if one grain were shattered or lost.

In spite of the countless numbers of bodies moving about in limitless space, and the distances between them so great that they seldom clash, still they do sometimes clash. What is our solar system in comparison with the great nebula out there in the beginning, or end, or middle stretch of real space? Compared with that part of the heavens the density of the steller population of our solar system is like the prairies of Kansas compared with the city of New York. Can anything be inferred about the origin or arrangement of all this, so far as man can tell, except that it is the outcome of the merest, wildest chance?

But let us try to clear the cobwebs from our brains, and the dizziness from our stomachs, and come back to earth, as it were. Let us talk of something where we can deal with what at least approaches facts. Does the earth show design, and order, and system, and purpose? Again, it would be well for the designers to tell what the scheme really is. If the plan is so clear as to justify the belief in a master designer, then it must be plain that the believers should be able to give the world some idea of the purpose of it all. Knowing winks and Delphic utterances and cryptic insinuations are not enough. Was the earth ever designed for the home of man? Sir James Jeans, in his admirable book on astronomy, shows us in no uncertain way that it evidently was not; that the human race has made the most of a bad environment and a most unfortunate habitation. Strange that the high-priests of superstition should so convulsively clutch Jeans and Eddington; neither one believes in a future life of the individual; neither one believes in the God of the theologians; neither believes in a special revelation, although Jeans does manage to say that Venus is the planet that the religionists thought was the star that led the camels over the desert to the stable where Jesus was born. Is this science or religion?—this bit of hearsay.

Even had this planet been meant for life, it plainly was not meant for human life. Three-fourths of the surface is covered with water, which would show that if it was ever designed for life it was designed for fishes and not for men. But what about the dry land? Two-thirds of this is not fitted for human beings. Both the polar zones are too cold for the abode of man. The equatorial regions are too hot. Vast deserts are spread out in various sections, and impassable and invincible mountain ranges make human habitation and the production of food impossible over immense areas. The earth is small enough, to begin with; the great seas, the wide useless stretches of land and the hostile climates have shrunk the livable portion almost to the vanishing point, and it is continually shrinking day by day. The human race is here because it is here, and it clings to the soil because there is nowhere else to go.

Even a human being of very limited capacity could think of countless ways in which the earth could be improved as the home of man, and from the earliest time the race has been using all sorts of efforts and resources to make it more suitable for its abode. Admitting that the earth is a fit place for life, and certainly every place in the universe where life exists is fitted for life, then what sort of life was this planet designed to support? There are some millions of different species of animals on this earth, and one-half of these are insects. In numbers, and perhaps in other ways, man is in a great minority. If the land of the earth was made for life, it seems as if it was intended for insect life, which can exist almost anywhere. If no other available place can be found they can live by the million on man, and inside of him. They generally succeed in destroying his life, and, if they have a chance, wind up by eating his body.

Aside from the insects, all sorts of life infest the earth and sea and air. In large portions of the earth man can make no headway against the rank growths of jungles and the teeming millions of animals that are seeking his death. He may escape the larger and most important of these only to be imperilled and probably eaten by the microbes, which seem instinctively to have their own idea of the worth and purpose of man's existence. If it were of any importance, we might view man from the standpoint of the microbe and consider his utility as the microbe's "meal-ticket." Can any one find any reason for claiming that the earth was meant for man, any more than for any other form of life that is spawned from land and sea and air?

But, how well is the earth itself adapted to human life? Even in the best parts of this world, speaking from the standpoint of man, one-fourth of the time it is too cold and another fourth of the seasons it is too hot, leaving little time for the comfort and pleasure of the worthiest product of the universe, or, that small fraction of it that we have some limited knowledge about.

Passing up the manifold difficulties that confront man and his brief life and career upon this mundane sphere, let us look at the world itself. It is a very wobbly place. Every year, upon the surface of this globe, and in the seas that cover such a major part of it, there are ten thousand earthquakes, ranging from light shocks to the total destruction of large areas of territory and the annihilation of great numbers of human lives. Were these, too, designed? Then, there is no such meaning as is usually applied to the word "design." What "design" was there in the earthquake that destroyed Lisbon in 1755? The entire city was blotted out, together with the destruction of thirty thousand to forty thousand human beings. This earthquake occurred on a Sunday which was also a saint's day, and a large number were killed in a cathedral, which was also destroyed. And yet people talk about design and purpose and order and system as though they knew the meaning of the words.

Let us look at the earth as it exists to-day. It is not the same earth that came into some sort of separate existence millions of years ago. It has not only experienced vast and comparatively sudden changes, like the throwing up of mountain ranges in the cooling and contracting processes, but other changes not so sudden and acute have worked their way through ages of time, and changes are still going on all the time all over the earth. New lands keep rising, others sinking away. Volcanoes are sending out millions of tons of matter each year, new islands are rising above the surface of the sea, while other islands are lowered beneath the waves. Continents are divided by internal forces and the ruthless powers of the sea.

Great Britain was cut off from the mainland not so very long ago, according to geological time. The shores of America and Africa were once connected, as seems evident from looking at the maps, and countless other geological shiftings have happened all over the surface and inside the earth, so that the world was no more made as it is now than was man created as we find him to-day. The destruction of the island of Martinique, the Mont Pelée disaster, the earthquake of San Francisco, are all within the memory of many now living. Active volcanoes are continuously pouring solid matter into the waters and slowly or rapidly building up new land where once was only sea.

The various archipelagoes are instances of this formation of fairly recent times. The Allegheny Mountains were once thirty thousand feet high. The crevices of their rocks have been penetrated by rain, split by frost and ice, pulverized by friction, and every minute are moving off toward the Gulf of Mexico. This range of mountains, which once reached an altitude of thirty thousand feet at the highest point, now has its highest peak but six thousand feet above the sea. These mountains have been worn down day after day, and the Ohio and Tennessee and Mississippi Rivers, carrying off the sediment, are building up the delta on the Louisiana coast. The earth and its seas were never made; they are in constant flux, moved by cold and heat and rain, and with no design or purpose that can be fathomed by the wit of man.

The delta of the Nile has through the long ages been carried down in mud and sand and silt from two thousand miles away and deposited in the open sea; and this is also called design by those who look for things they wish to find.

Nature brings hordes of insects that settle over the land and destroy the farmers' crops. Who are the objects of the glorious design: the farmers who so patiently and laboriously raise the crops or the grasshoppers that devour them? It must be the insects, because the farmers hold prayer meetings and implore their God to kill the bugs, but the pests go on with their deadly work unmolested. Man prates glibly about design, but Nature furnishes not a single example or fact as proof. Perhaps the microbe who bores a hole into the vitals of man and brings him down to his death may believe in a Providence and a design. How else could he live so royally on the vitals of one of the lords of creation?

All that we know is that we were born on this little grain of sand we call the earth. We know that it is one of the smallest bits of matter that floats in the great shoreless sea of space, and we have every reason to believe that it is as inconsequential in every other respect. On board the same craft, sailing the same seas, are all sorts of living things, fighting each other, and us, that each may survive. Most of these specimens are living on the carcasses of the dead. The strongest instinct of most of our crew is to stay here and live. The strongest in intellect and prowess live the longest. Nature, in all her manifestations, is at war with life, and sooner or later will doubtless have her way. No one can give a reason for any or all of the manifestations which we call life. We are like a body of shipwrecked sailors clutching to a raft and desperately engaged in holding on.

Men have built faith from hopes. They have struggled and fought in despair. They have frantically clung to life because of the will to live. The best that we can do is to be kindly and helpful toward our friends and fellow passengers who are clinging to the same speck of dirt while we are drifting side by side to our common doom.

Religious Knowledge and Mystical Experience   James Bisset Pratt

James Bisset Pratt (1875–1944) was a prominent American philosopher, who wrote widely on the philosophy of religion and metaphysics.

In spite of innumerable differences between the experiences of individual Christians, the general sense of some kind of divine presence . . . is common to a surprisingly large number. For that matter, it is very like the mystical experiences found in some of the non-Christian religions. Naturally it has been differently nurtured and differently expressed in the various religious cultures within which it has arisen. It has had a prominent place in the faith and worship of every Christian generation. In our time it has received, and is receiving, unusual stress. This for two reasons. One is the interest which our time feels in psychology, and the interest which our psychologists have come to feel in religion. The other reason is of a theological sort. As we have seen, various influences have united, during the last half-century, to diminish the prestige of the historical arguments for the existence of God and to reduce almost to the vanishing point the old confidence in the literal inspiration of the Scriptures. As a result the defenders of the Christian belief have evacuated one position after another, and many of them are today concentrating their strength within the fortifications of what they sometimes call the "inner experience."

At the close of the last century the psychologists awoke to the fact that religion was interesting, and began to take the lead in studying it. The first results of this serious work of psychologists upon religion were heartening in the extreme. The theologians were assured by their technical colleagues of the reality and the depth of the religious life. The next step to be taken by the psychologists was not quite so reassuring, namely, the description and analysis of the experience. The third step was frankly disquieting, though inevitable—the attempt, namely, not only to describe but to explain. Once more it seemed that the Ark of the Lord had fallen into the hands of the Philistines. For if the religious experience could be explained, set within the nexus of scientific laws, it seemed to be in effect explained away; not indeed denied, but put in a position where it could no longer be used as an empirical argument for the existence of God.

In view of this situation the attempt has been made to take back the religious experience from psychology to theology, so to speak, by insisting that theology is an empirical science and that "God" is as objective a fact as are the objects of the physical sciences. Thus it is said that in the experience of moral regeneration and in the mystics' apprehension of the Divine, God is directly presented as a scientific fact and not merely as a hypothesis for the explanation of other facts. In other words, that the religious experience is an experience of God and that this proposition is neither a philosophical hypothesis nor a matter of faith and hope, but a plain fact of science.

In making up our minds as to the tenability of this view we should first ask ourselves what we mean by a fact of science. As was pointed out in a previous paragraph, a little reflection will show that a scientific fact, as distinguished from a private and individual experience, must have the characteristics of being repeatable and verifiable. The experiences of the isolated individual may be as real as you like, but they cannot possess the social authority of a scientific fact unless they are describable in terms capable of communication to all rational beings and verifiable by all properly equipped observers. The question now is: Can God, even in the vaguest sense, as a Source of Power not identical with our empirical selves, be truly said to be a directly experienced fact in this scientific sense? Is He a verifiable object in the sense of being directly presented to the experience of all normal or standardized and properly equipped observers? For my part, I cannot honestly answer this question in the affirmative. The experience of moral regeneration through religious influence may give us reasons to infer the influence of a Power not ourselves; but God, if reached in this way, would be an inference (as logical as you like, but still an inference, a hypothesis) and not an empirical fact. The mystical experience is on a different footing from moral regeneration, for it purports to be an immediate apprehension of the Divine as a directly felt object. But while it is conceivable that God for the mystic may be no hypothesis but a fact, can we honestly say He is even here a *scientific* fact? I judge we cannot. For a scientific fact, let me repeat, must be verifiable by all standardized observers with suitable training. And very few would maintain that the God of the mystics is verifiable in this fashion; and certainly He is, at all events, very far from having been thus scientifically verified. The man who doubts the existence of X-rays can be put in a position where he can perceive them; but there is no laboratory in which the mystics' God can be exhibited to the nonmystical. Nor is it an answer to assert that the mystics' God is verifiable by anyone with the proper psychical make-up; for while this is doubtless true, it really is merely a tautologous assertion to the effect that all mystics can perceive what all mystics can perceive. As much could be said of the hallucinatory objects commonly seen under the influence of nitrous oxide. And as a fact, those most eloquent in their assertions that only a few can apprehend God in the mystic fashion are just the mystics themselves. If not all, at any rate a very large portion of them assert that no amount of training, no amount of effort will enable one to attain to the mystic apprehension. It is like the wind which bloweth where it listeth. What need we any further witness? With mystics and nonmystics agreeing almost universally that God as an object of direct apprehension is not verifiable, it would seem to follow inevitably that God is not a scientific fact and that therefore theology cannot be regarded as an empirical science.

Hence we are back again with the religious experience in the hands of the psychologists, and faced with the question: Has the psychological description and explanation of this experience made it valueless in the attempt to give a spiritual interpretation to the universe? Students of the psychology of religion are often tempted to say that it is valueless; and it is, I think, their scientific duty to point out all that can be said to justify this negative interpretation. To put the psychologist's position in summary fashion, one may maintain that since the religious experience is experience, the interpretation of it belongs solely to psychology; and that the question whether the religious experience proves the existence and presence of God is an empirical and scientific question, and one with which, therefore, not the theologian but only the psychologist is qualified to deal. If now the religious experience can be explained in purely naturalistic fashion, it is said, we are not warranted in looking for any divine explanation or in using it as evidence for the existence of God. Can the religious experience be so explained?

With this problem in mind the psychologist proceeds to an elaborate description and analysis of the religious—and especially of the mystical—consciousness; and he comes to the conclusion that the religious experience is essentially of the same sort as nonreligious experience, having the same character and the same causation. Thus there would seem to be nothing in it to indicate that the mystic or the religious person has come in touch with God in any peculiar sense. It is in content and character on a par with nonreligious experience. What *appears* to be more is a matter not of actual experience but of interpretation. It may be the philosopher can show that all experience points to God, or somehow implies the Absolute; but the psychologist is very doubtful whether the religious or mystical experience implies God any more directly or obviously or in any other way than the most commonplace experience of sense perception.

The psychologist, moreover, has another argument against what I might call the religious interpretation of the religious experience. Not only does psychological analysis show that the religious experience is like other experience in quality; it also shows that its occurrence, its rise, intensity, and decline may be explained by the same general psychological laws that account for the various changes in the nonreligious consciousness. This, to be sure, is not yet fully proved. The situation is complex; many factors, some of them quite obscure, are involved, and no one could seriously claim that all the factors of the religious experience are known. But many of them are known, and it is the necessary hypothesis of psychology that the unknown factors must be of the same general type as the known ones. This position of the psychologist is, in a sense, a matter of faith rather than of demonstration, but it is for him a necessary faith; for unless he make the postulate that psychological laws can explain all the facts of human psychosis, he would have to give up his claim that psychology is a complete science.

A good deal has been done to substantiate the first of the two arguments referred to above, by which psychology throws doubt on the significance of mysticism: a large part of religious experience turns out on analysis to be of the same sort as nonreligious experience. Even the more striking phenomena of ecstasy can largely be paralleled by the effects of drugs and of Yoga training. Personally I am not convinced that the peculiar joy of religion, or what Otto calls numinous feeling, is really to be paralleled outside of religion. And so far as I can judge, the central thing in the religious experience—the sense of immediate contact with some being other than, though possibly inclusive of, oneself—is strictly unique. This sense of presence differentiates the religious experience pretty sharply from the various forms of drug ecstasy, and also from the usual results of Yoga. I think it is safe to say that when Yoga brings an intuition of the Absolute as present and directly known, some other factor is at work besides the Yoga methods. In other words, the sort of experience brought about by controllable physical and psychological means lacks the one characteristic that is essential to the religious experience.

It may indeed be argued that what has been added in this experience is easily explained by the rationalizing interpretation of the mystic, on the basis of his already accepted belief in the supernatural. We must distinguish, it is frequently and properly pointed out, between what the mystic actually experiences and his interpretation of it. No one will doubt that he has the sensations which he reports; but interpretation is not the product of psychological introspection but of philosophical theory. It does not grow out of the experience, or at any rate, not out of it alone. As Professor J. M. Moore points out, "our categories and established modes of reaction are present before any particular experience, and condition the form which the experience takes. The relation of experience and interpretation is reciprocal and complex rather than being a simple one-way relation of dependence."[1]

There is much truth in this criticism of mystic pronouncements. When the Salvation Army lassie tells us she has seen Christ, when Suzo asserts that he has communed with the Madonna, when the Hindu Vaishnavite recounts his immediate apprehension of Sri Krishna, very few of us will doubt that rationalistic interpretation has been busy, and that what we are given is not a description of actually experienced fact, but an interpretation of some simpler experience, formulated on the plan of some familiar creed. There is a line, however, beyond which this distinction of immediate sense data and interpretation cannot profitably and truthfully be carried. For the simplest elements of actual adult experience are seldom if ever sensations, but what John Laird significantly calls "sign facts."[2] A pure sensation is something that few of us who have passed infancy any longer experience. Our simplest forms of perceptual activity are drenched with meaning. The immediately given is already significant; it is never a mere sense datum, but a sense datum that means more than it is. And this is as true of the religious man's sense of presence as of any other form of experience. What he tells us of the further nature of the being he experiences is doubtless a matter of interpretation, but his immediate awareness that he is in the presence of an Other is hardly to be analyzed further without altering it into something very different from what it really is. This awareness of an Other, stripped of its creedal interpretation, differs, so the mystic asserts, *toto coelo* from a mere belief. It comes with all the immediacy of sense perception. It has, of course, sensuous elements, as every percept has; but to identify it with any collection of mere sense data is to mutilate it beyond recognition. It is, in short, if we may trust the mystics' introspective description (not their interpretation), a sign fact.

In saying this I have not forgotten Professor Leuba's artificial production of the sense of presence in the laboratory.[3] But it is well to remind ourselves in passing that Professor Leuba did not produce the *religious* sense of presence in his laboratory. His experiments were not dealing with that directly. What his experiments showed was that a sense of presence in general may be induced without anyone actually being present. The subject, that is, may be fooled. In short, like other forms of cognitive experience, the sense of presence may be illusory. But surely we did not need experimental evidence to show us this. Occasionally any of us may be mistaken about the presence of a human

---

[1] J. M. Moore, *Theories of Religious Experience,* p. 187.

[2] See John Laird, *A Study of Realism,* chaps. ii, v.

[3] See Leuba, *The Psychology of Religious Mysticism,* pp. 283–286.

fellow. We may suppose ourselves not alone in the room and discover that we are. When in doubt about the matter we put the thing to a test, using various methods to find out. The fact that sometimes we are mistaken does not prove to us that we are always mistaken. Each case must stand on its own merits and be judged by its own evidence. As a fact, the cases of mistake are so small a fraction of the total, and the cases in which we are correct form so large a majority, that in normal human experience this sense of another's presence carries with it a strong a priori probability of its own validity.

Now there is no doubt that the mystic may be mistaken like other people. As Professor James pointed out, his emotion of conviction as to the validity of his experience of presence may be authoritative for him, but it is not for anyone else. It is quite possible that various causes, known or unknown, may have united to delude him. His own certainty is no guarantee of the truth of his assertion. But the fact that he *may be* mistaken does not prove that he *is* mistaken. The fact—if it be a fact—that he is *sometimes* mistaken does not prove that he is *always* mistaken. Here as elsewhere each case must be judged on its merits. Nor can we say that there is so much uncertainty about the cause of this experience that the assertion of the religious man is entirely negligible. The matter is not left as if nothing had happened. Certainly the mystic's evidence is not as good as the ordinary evidence of eye and ear, for we have a means of testing the validity of these instruments of knowledge, and in the vast majority of cases they prove trustworthy. The mystic's assertion does not carry with it the same weight of a priori probability as does the more common conviction that someone we do not see is in the room with us. But the assertion of the mystic is not entirely worthless as evidence. It at least sets us a problem of further investigation; and if such investigation can produce no complete explanation for the mystic's experience, the experience must be set down at least tentatively as having a certain minimal evidential value in favor of the truth of the mystic's assertion. The strength of this evidence will be increased with every demonstration that the religious sense of presence, its joy and its other by-products, are different in quality from the corresponding experiences of the nonreligious life.

The claim to evidential validity on the part of the religious sense of presence is the more difficult wholly to deny because of the immense number of witnesses that might be called upon to give confirmatory testimony. A student of the history of religions can hardly fail to be struck with the ubiquity of this experience. The way it springs up, spontaneously and independently in remotely separated lands, among peoples of unrelated races, in nearly all the ages and in all the religions with which we are acquainted, is at least an impressive fact. Indeed, one might argue that if any evidential value whatever is to be granted the religious experience, one will have to go on and grant it a good deal, because of the cumulative nature of its testimony.

Whether it has any evidential value is, of course, just the question we are discussing. It will be recalled that there are two principal arguments for the naturalistic interpretation of the religious experience. The one based on the similarity between religious and nonreligious experiences we have discussed. The other argument—which indeed is so closely related to the first as to be hardly separable except for purposes of exposition—consists in pointing out that the same psychological laws obtain among religious facts as those which govern the whole mental life of man. In other words, it is the aim of this argument to show that the various experiences of the religious life follow laws of definite and regular sequence, and are therefore susceptible of purely psychological explanation. Since they can be explained psychologically, the argument continues, they need no other explanation, and hence cannot be used as evidence for anything beyond the human mind with its human contents and its human ways of working.

As I have already pointed out, psychology has not yet been fully successful in making out these laws of regular sequence between religious phenomena and various psychophysical conditions; they represent rather a program and ideal than an actual achievement. Much successful work toward this ideal has been done and more may be expected. The psychologist, I think, is justified in making a working hypothesis of this ideal of complete psychological explanation for all mental facts. In a sense it is a necessary hypothesis, for his claim that psychology is at least potentially a science capable of giving complete explanation and prediction depends upon it. Unfortunately many psychologists often forget that this hypothesis is as yet only a hypothesis and is very far indeed from having been empirically verified. The truth is, we cannot as yet explain all the facts of human experience and of mental activity by psychological laws. To assert in the present state of our ignorance that we can because we must—which means because we want to—is not science but dogma and the will to make believe.

It is, however, perfectly conceivable that some day all the activities of the human mind, including the religious experience, will be explicable in psychological fashion; in other words, that we shall be able to show how, say, the mystical experience follows invariably upon certain definable conditions, and that by going through certain psychophysical processes one may induce it. This possibility opens up a rather interesting logical question. For if this situation should ever be reached, how would it, and how should it be interpreted? The interpretation that would be given it by most psychologists is obvious enough: they would say that the religious experience was thereby shown to be, like any other conscious state, producible by certain definite conditions, and therefore no more significant of objective reality than dreams or hypnosis. But there would be an equally obvious interpretation open to the mystics. It will be recalled that in our discussion of the claims of theology to rank as an empirical science, I argued that this was not admissible because the mystic fact is not a scientific fact; and that it is not a scientific fact because it is not verifiable by all normal or standardized human beings—that is to say, not reproducible at will within the field of awareness. But on the hypothesis we have now set up of the future perfecting of psychology, the mystic experience is to be reproducible at will. We can therefore picture the mystics, or their philosophical defenders, turning the tables on the psychologists by saying: you told us our apprehension of the Divine was not a scientific fact because not verifiable in the sense of being reproducible. Now, thanks to your kind of researches, it is reproducible and verifiable. Is not our apprehension of the Divine, therefore, a fact, and a scientific fact? Is it not a scientific fact in the same sense as your apprehension of brain cells; and immeasurably more scientific than the physicist's apprehension of the invisible electrons? Instead of interpreting it as you do dreams and illusions, should you not rather, on your own showing, interpret it as you do veridical perception?

The situation is sufficiently bewildering. Plainly it will hardly do to argue: mysticism is illusory because its cognitive states are *not* reproducible; and with the next breath to argue, mysticism is illusory because its cognitive states *are* reproducible. To do that would be to blow hot and cold, to play fast and loose with nature. Either the religious experience is reproducible, given certain conditions, or it is not; and from both these opposites we can hardly draw the same conclusion. If it is incumbent upon us to give the devil his due, surely it is only fair to give the Lord a chance!

How, then, should we construe this rather puzzling situation? A good deal, I think, would depend on the actual details of the actual facts which, by hypothesis, psychology shall one day discover. If, for example, it were found that the religious experience, in all its fullness and with its cognizable quality, could be reproduced by a dose of some newly discovered drug, and that it never arose except under psychophysical conditions which were, in the last analysis, identical with those induced by this drug; it would then follow—that the new-found drug was an excellent means for bringing about the psychophysical conditions requisite for the religious experience! It would prove nothing more; and it would still be open to anyone who wished to do so to assert that these identical psychophysical conditions might be produced by the direct action of God. It is unlikely, however, that many would make such an assertion; and probably not only the psychologists but most of us would agree that the religious experience was a symptom of certain physical conditions but without further objective or cosmic significance. We may, however, picture other results from the scientific investigation of the religious consciousness and its "causes." We may well imagine that psychology might discover that the religious experience followed regularly upon a long process of purifying the heart and concentrating the mind, by proper means, upon the thought of the Divine. Now if this were true, if it were a verifiable scientific fact that the experience of the Divine Presence, the immediate and undoubtable sense of the numinous at hand, sufficiently different from every other sort of experience to be distinguishable and recognizable, and having the same compelling objectivity that visual and tactual experiences possess—if this form of cognitive consciousness, I say, were found to follow invariably upon a definable process of heart purification and mind concentration, how should we interpret the logic of the situation?

I think it is perfectly plain that there would be two answers. The conscientious psychologist *as psychologist* would say: The religious consciousness is now fully explained in psychological terms. I leave to the philosopher the explanation of the cosmos, but I have shown that no reference to anything supernatural, to anything outside of human nature, is needed to explain the sense of divine presence and its various by-products. It follows regularly upon definable and predictable psychophysical conditions by laws of regular and invariable sequence. On the other hand, the mystic would say: the direct apprehension of God is now become a verifiable fact. If you doubt my word, put yourself through the long course of mental and spiritual training which the psychologist and I can plan out for you, and you shall see for yourself. If any man will follow the religious life in the light of modern science, he shall know of the doctrine. For it is God who will be working in you, God who will be revealing Himself to you, who can now be *counted on* to reveal Himself to you, through the working of the laws of the human mind which He Himself made. The religious experience is now a scientific fact, and is to be explained by the actual presence of the Divine before the eyes of the soul.

Of these two interpretations which would be correct? By hypothesis all the relevant facts would be in, and further empirical evidence would be unnecessary. The question would be purely a matter of logic. Plainly it would be exceedingly difficult to prove either of the rival interpretations wrong. And I want to suggest that they might *both* be right.

For what, after all, is a psychological explanation? It consists (in logical outline) in tracing laws of regular sequence between the psychosis to be explained and certain definable conditions, either within the psychophysical mechanism of the subject or within so much of the environment as natural science is able to define, understand, and for experimental purposes, control. Psychological explanation is therefore a form of description and generalization. It does not pretend to point out ultimate or original causes. Psychology is not interested in ultimate or original causes. Its explanation is complete if it has constructed a formula of sequence among scientific, i.e., verifiable facts, and on the basis of this sequence is able without failure to predict the psychosis in question on the appearance of the facts with which the formula connects it. Now there is nothing in the actuality of this kind of an explanation inconsistent with the religious interpretation of the situation. The mystic is not interested in denying the validity of the psychologist's explanation, but he is interested in something more. To him explanation means something different from a generalized description of regular sequences. He is interested in ultimate and original causes. And provided we are willing to relieve the concept of the Divine from the attribute of arbitrariness, there is nothing to prevent our supposing that the steady action of the Divine upon the soul is the ultimate cause of the religious experience, and that what the psychologist describes is the regular process by which the soul may be exposed to this Divine influence. The white radiance of eternity, we may suppose, steadily beats upon us, but only in certain conditions of body and mind can we become sensitive to its light. If this were so, it would be quite within the province of psychology to describe exactly and completely what these conditions are, and on the basis of them to predict and "explain" the rise of the religious experience. To do so, and to do it without any reference to the ultimate source of the inflowing Light, would be to give a complete and exhaustive psychological explanation. Yet it would be equally true that religious experience was exactly what the religious man insists that it is—an immediate awareness of a Divine Other.

By making these suggestions I do not mean that God is to be taken as filling the gaps which science leaves, nor that He is to be proved by miraculous interventions. As I have said, it is quite likely that all religious experience will some day be found to have its scientific explanation—in the sense I have indicated. The Unity of the World is not destroyed. God must be conceived as existing in and expressing Himself through all reality. Yet owing to the finiteness of our human nature and our very limited and partial insight, it may be true—and I think it is true—that most of us apprehend the universal Divine more readily and clearly in some parts of our experience than in others. To the angel's vision God may be "as full, as perfect, in a hair as hart." Yet so long as man remains a little lower than the angels it is probable that he will realize God more fully and perfectly in the religious experience than anywhere else. My aim in this chapter has been, not to attack science nor to defend a view of supernatural divine interventions, but to show that something may be said for the faith of the religious man that, in what he knows as his most religious moments, it is God with whom he comes in touch. Later on he may learn that he is in touch with God always and everywhere; but it is in the mystic experience that he first and most fully *recognizes* God.

Possibly we can make a little plainer to ourselves the contribution made by mysticism to the religious view of the world if we put to ourselves one further question. Let us suppose that in all the world's history there had been no mystics, and no suggestion in any mind of an immediate apprehension of the Divine. Would not, I ask, a religious view of the world under those circumstances have been much less probable, much harder to believe, than it is today? Would not many people, would not most people, on hearing a religious philosophy propounded, have asked the question: "Why, if there be a Divine, has it never come in touch with any human mind?" In other words, if there be a God, would you not naturally expect mystics? The facts of mysticism do not indeed prove the existence of God; but the fact of mysticism makes the existence of God considerably more probable.

Thus, I believe, a psychological study of the mystical states combined with a philosophical interpretation of the nature of science may make a distinct contribution to the religious view of reality. But if this is to be done, religion, I trust, will make fewer demands of a specific nature than it has been accustomed to make as to the interpretation of the Divine. It will be content to *believe* in God without *defining* Him. More in particular, it will lay less stress than formerly upon the anthropomorphic and excessively personal aspects of the Divine. It will have nothing to say of specific answer to prayer or of Divine interventions. And in place of the dogmatic view of the older theology, it will adopt a more empirical attitude toward the universe, and while less eager to tell who and what God is, it will be more ready to learn.

We come back, then, after our long discussion, to the question: Is the religious experience such as to furnish any relevant empirical evidence on the ultimate religious problems of our time? The answer would seem to be emphatically in the affirmative. A chastened theology may appeal to the facts of the religious life with a certain justifiable confidence. The testimony of the religious consciousness through thirty centuries is not without cosmic significance.

The Basis of the Moral Law   C. S. Lewis

I now go back to what I said . . . that there were two odd things about the human race. First, that they were haunted by the idea of a sort of behaviour they ought to practise, what you might call fair play, or decency, or morality, or the Law of Nature. Second, that they did not in fact do so. Now some of you may wonder why I called this odd. It may seem to you the most natural thing in the world. In particular, you may have thought I was rather hard on the human race. After all, you may say, what I call breaking the Law of Right and Wrong or of Nature, only means that people are not perfect. And why on earth should I expect them to be? That would be a good answer if what I was trying to do was to fix the exact amount of blame which is due to us for not behaving as we expect others to behave. But that is not my job at all. I am not concerned at present with blame; I am trying to find out truth. And from that point of view the very idea of something being imperfect, of its not being what it ought to be, has certain consequences.

If you take a thing like a stone or a tree, it is what it is and there seems no sense in saying it ought to have been otherwise. Of course you may say a stone is "the wrong shape" if you want to use it for a rockery, or that a tree is a bad tree because it does not give you as much shade as you expected. But all you mean is that the stone or tree does not happen to be convenient for some purpose of your own. You are not, except as a joke, blaming them for that. You really know, that, given the weather and the soil, the tree could not have been any different. What we, from our point of view, call a "bad" tree is obeying the laws of its nature just as much as a "good" one.

Now have you noticed what follows? It follows that what we usually call the laws of nature—the way weather works on a tree for example—may not really be *laws* in the strict sense, but only in a manner of speaking. When you say that falling stones always obey the law of gravitation, is not this much the same as saying that the law only means "what stones always do"? You do not really think that when a stone is let go, it suddenly remembers that it is under orders to fall to the ground. You only mean that, in fact, it does fall. In other words, you cannot be sure that there is anything over and above the facts themselves, any law about what ought to happen, as distinct from what does happen. The laws of nature, as applied to stones or trees, may only mean "what Nature, in fact, does." But if you turn to the Law of Human Nature, the Law of Decent Behaviour, it is a different matter. That law certainly does not mean "what human beings, in fact, do"; for as I said before, many of them do not obey this law at all, and none of them obey it completely. The law of gravity tells you what stones do if you drop them; but the Law of Human Nature tells you what human beings ought to do and do not. In other words, when you are dealing with humans, something else comes in above and beyond the actual facts. You have the facts (how men do behave) and you also have something else (how they ought to behave). In the rest of the universe there need not be anything but the facts. Electrons and molecules behave in a certain way, and certain results follow, and that may be the whole story. But men behave in a certain way and that is not the whole story, for all the time you know that they ought to behave differently.

Now this is really so peculiar that one is tempted to try to explain it away. For instance, we might try to make out that when you say a man ought not to act as he does, you only mean the same as when you say that a stone is the wrong shape; namely, that what he is doing happens to be inconvenient to you. But that is simply untrue. A man occupying the corner seat in the train because he got there first, and a man who slipped into it while my back was turned and removed my bag, are both equally inconvenient. But I blame the second man and do not blame the first. I am not angry—except perhaps for a moment before I come to my senses—with a man who trips me up by accident; I am angry with a man who tries to trip me up even if he does not succeed. Yet the first has hurt me and the second has not. Sometimes the behaviour which I call bad is not inconvenient to me at all, but the very opposite. In war, each side may find a traitor on the other side very useful. But though they use him and pay him they regard him as human vermin. So you cannot say that what we call decent behaviour in others is simply the behaviour that happens to be useful to us. And as for decent behaviour in ourselves, I suppose it is pretty obvious that it does not mean the behaviour that pays. It means things like being content with thirty shillings when you might have got three pounds, doing school work honestly when it would be easy to cheat, leaving a girl alone when you would like to make love to her, staying in dangerous places when you could go somewhere safer, keeping promises you would rather not keep, and telling the truth even when it makes you look a fool.

Some people say that though decent conduct does not mean what pays each particular person at a particular moment, still, it means what pays the human race as a whole; and that consequently there is no mystery about it. Human beings, after all, have some sense; they see that you cannot have real safety or happiness except in a society where every one plays fair, and it is because they see this that they try to behave decently. Now, of course, it is perfectly true that safety and happiness can only come from individuals, classes, and nations being honest and fair and kind to each other. It is one of the most important truths in the world. But as an explanation of why we feel as we do about Right and Wrong it just misses the point. If we ask: "Why ought I to be unselfish?" and you reply "Because it is good for society," we may then ask, "Why should I care what's good for society except when it happens to pay *me* personally?" and then you will have to say, "Because you ought to be unselfish"—which simply brings us back to where we started. You are saying what is true, but you are not getting any further. If a man asked what was the point of playing football, it would not be much good saying "in order to score goals," for trying to score goals is the game itself, not the reason for the game, and you would really only be saying that football was football—which is true, but not worth saying. In the same way, if a man asks what is the point of behaving decently, it is no good replying, "in order to benefit society," for trying to benefit society, in other words being unselfish (for "society" after all only means "other people"), is one of the things decent behaviour consists in; all you are really saying is that decent behaviour is decent behaviour. You would have said just as much if you had stopped at the statement, "Men ought to be unselfish."

And that is where I do stop. Men ought to be unselfish, ought to be fair. Not that men are unselfish, nor that they like being unselfish, but that they ought to be. The Moral Law, or Law of Human Nature, is not simply a fact about human behaviour in the same way as the Law of Gravitation is, or may be, simply a fact about how heavy objects behave. On the other hand, it is not a mere fancy, for we cannot get rid of the idea, and most of the things we say and think about men would be reduced to nonsense if we did. And it is not simply a statement about how we should like men to behave for our own convenience; for the behaviour we call bad or unfair is not exactly the same as the behaviour we find inconvenient, and may even be the opposite. Consequently, this Rule of Right and Wrong, or Law of Human Nature, or whatever you call it, must somehow or other be a real thing—a thing that is really there, not made up by ourselves. And yet it is not a fact in the ordinary sense, in the same way as our actual behaviour is a fact. It begins to look as if we shall have to admit that there is more than one kind of realty; that, in this particular case, there is something above and beyond the ordinary facts of men's behaviour, and yet quite definitely real—a real law, which none of us made, but which we find pressing on us.

Let us sum up what we have reached so far. In the case of stones and trees and things of that sort, what we call the Laws of Nature may not be anything except a way of speaking. When you say that nature is governed by certain laws, this may only mean that nature does, in fact, behave in a certain way. The so-called laws may not be anything real—anything above and beyond the actual facts which we observe. But in the case of Man, we saw that this will not do. The Law of Human Nature, or of Right and Wrong, must be something above and beyond the actual facts of human behaviour. In this case, besides the actual facts, you have something else—a real law which we did not invent and which we know we ought to obey.

I now want to consider what this tells us about the universe we live in. Ever since men were able to think, they have been wondering what this universe really is and how it came to be there. And, very roughly, two views have been held. First, there is what is called the materialist view. People who take that view think that matter and space just happen to exist, and always have existed, nobody knows why; and that the matter, behaving in certain fixed ways, has just happened, by a sort of fluke, to produce creatures like ourselves who are able to think. By one chance in a thousand something hit our sun and made it produce the planets; and by another thousandth chance the chemicals necessary for life, and the right temperature, occurred on one of these planets, and so some of the matter on this earth came alive; and then, by a very long series of chances, the living creatures developed into things like us. The other view is the religious view. According to it, what is behind the universe is more like a mind than it is like anything else we know. That is to say, it is conscious, and has purposes, and prefers one thing to another. And on this view it made the universe, partly for purposes we do not know, but partly, at any rate, in order to produce creatures like itself—I mean, like itself to the extent of having minds. Please do not think that one of these views was held a long time ago and that the other has gradually taken its place. Wherever there have been thinking men both views turn up. And note this too. You cannot find out which view is the right one by science in the ordinary sense. Science works by experiments. It watches how things behave. Every scientific statement in the long run, however complicated it looks, really means something like, "I pointed the telescope to such and such a part of the sky at 2:20 A.M. on January 15th and saw so-and-so," or, "I put some of this stuff in a pot and heated it to such-and-such a temperature and it did so-and-so." Do not think I am saying anything against science: I am only saying what its job is. And the more scientific a man is, the more (I believe) he would agree with me that this is the job of science—and a very useful and necessary job it is too. But why anything comes to be there at all, and whether there is anything behind the things science observes—something of a different kind—this is not a scientific question. If there is "Something Behind," then either it will have to remain altogether unknown to men or else make itself known in some different way. The statement that there is any such thing, and the statement that there is no such thing, are neither of them statements that science can make. And real scientists do not usually make them. It is usually the journalists and popular novelists who have picked up a few odds and ends of half-baked science from textbooks who go in for them. After all, it is really a matter of common sense. Supposing science ever became complete so that it knew every single thing in the whole universe. Is it not plain that the questions, "Why is there a universe?" "Why does it go on as it does?" "Has it any meaning?" would remain just as they were?

Now the position would be quite hopeless but for this. There is one thing, and only one, in the whole universe which we know more about than we could learn from external observation. That one thing is Man. We do not merely observe men, we *are* men. In this case we have, so to speak, inside information; we are in the know. And because of that, we know that men find themselves under a moral law, which they did not make, and cannot quite forget even when they try, and which they know they ought to obey. Notice the following point. Anyone studying Man from the outside as we study electricity or cabbages, not knowing our language and consequently not able to get any inside knowledge from us, but merely observing what we did, would never get the slightest evidence that we had this moral law. How could he? for his observations would only show what we did, and the moral law is about what we ought to do. In the same way, if there were anything above or behind the observed facts in the case of stones or the weather, we, by studying them from outside, could never hope to discover it.

The position of the question, then, is like this. We want to know whether the universe simply happens to be what it is for no reason or whether there is a power behind it that makes it what it is. Since that power, if it exists, would be not one of the observed facts but a reality which makes them, no mere observation of the facts can find it. There is only one case in which we can know whether there is anything more, namely our own case. And in that one case we find there is. Or put it the other way round. If there was a controlling power outside the universe, it could not show itself to us as one of the facts inside the universe—no more than the architect of a house could actually be a wall or staircase or fireplace in that house. The only way in which we could expect it to show itself would be inside ourselves as an influence or a command trying to get us to behave in a certain way. And that is just what we do find inside ourselves. Surely this ought to arouse our suspicions? In the only case where you can expect to get an answer, the answer turns out to be Yes; and in the other cases, where you do not get an answer, you see why you do not. Suppose someone asked me, when I see a man in a blue uniform going down the street leaving little paper packets at each house, why I suppose that they contain letters? I should reply, "Because whenever he leaves a similar little packet for me I find it does contain a letter." And if he then objected, "But you've never seen all these letters which you think the other people are getting," I should say, "Of course not, and I shouldn't expect to, because they're not addressed to me. I'm explaining the packets I'm not allowed to open by the ones I am allowed to open." It is the same about this question. The only packet I am allowed to open is Man. When I do, especially when I open that particular man called Myself, I find that I do not exist on my own, that I am under a law; that somebody or something wants me to behave in a certain way. I do not, of course, think that if I could get inside a stone or a tree I should find exactly the same thing, just as I do not think all the other people in the street get the same letters as I do. I should expect, for instance, to find that the stone had to obey the law of gravity —that whereas the sender of the letters merely tells me to obey the law of my human nature, He compels the stone to obey the laws of its stony nature. But I should expect to find that there was, so to speak, a sender of letters in both cases, a Power behind the facts, a Director, a Guide.

Do not think I am going faster than I really am. I am not yet within a hundred miles of the God of Christian theology. All I have got to is a Something which is directing the universe, and which appears in me as a law urging me to do right and making me feel responsible and uncomfortable when I do wrong. I think we have to assume it is more like a mind than it is like anything else we know—because after all the only other thing we know is matter and you can hardly imagine a bit of matter giving instructions. But, of course, it need not be very like a mind, still less like a person. . . .

Why I Am Not a Christian   Bertrand Russell

> Bertrand Russell (1872–1970) was one of the most prominent philosophers of
> the twentieth century. He is the author of numerous books on a wide variety
> of philosophical and social issues. He was known to the general public for
> his outspoken stands on religion, marriage, the banning of the nuclear bomb.
> In 1950 he was awarded the Nobel Prize for Literature.

As your Chairman has told you, the subject about which I am going to speak to you tonight is "Why I Am Not a Christian." Perhaps it would be as well, first of all, to try to make out what one means by the word *Christian*. It is used these days in a very loose sense by a great many people. Some people mean no more by it than a person who attempts to live a good life. In that sense I suppose there would be Christians in all sects and creeds; but I do not think that that is the proper sense of the word, if only because it would imply that all the people who are not Christians—all the Buddhists, Confucians, Mohammedans, and so on—are not trying to live a good life. I do not mean by a Christian any person who tries to live decently according to his lights. I think that you must have a certain amount of definite belief before you have a right to call yourself a Christian. The word does not have quite such a full-blooded meaning now as it had in the times of St. Augustine and St. Thomas Aquinas. In those days, if a man said that he was a Christian it was known what he meant. You accepted a whole collection of creeds which were set out with great precision, and every single syllable of those creeds you believed with the whole strength of your convictions.

What Is a Christian?

Nowadays it is not quite that. We have to be a little more vague in our meaning of Christianity. I think, however, that there are two different items which are quite essential to anybody calling himself a Christian. The first is one of a dogmatic nature—namely, that you must believe in God and immortality. If you do not believe in those two things, I do not think that you can properly call yourself a Christian. Then, further than that, as the name implies, you must have some kind of belief about Christ. The Mohammedans, for instance, also believe in God and in immortality, and yet they would not call themselves Christians. I think you must have at the very lowest the belief that Christ was, if not divine, at least the best and wisest of men. If you are not going to believe that much about Christ, I do not think you have any right to call yourself a Christian. Of course, there is another sense, which you find in *Whitaker's Almanack* and in geography books, where the population of the world is said to be divided into Christians, Mohammedans, Buddhists, fetish worshipers, and so on; and in that sense we are all Christians. The geography books count us all in, but that is a purely geographical sense, which I suppose we can ignore. Therefore I take it that when I tell you why I am not a Christian I have to tell you two different things: first, why I do not believe in God and in immortality; and, secondly, why I do not think that Christ was the best and wisest of men, although I grant him a very high degree of moral goodness.

But for the successful efforts of unbelievers in the past, I could not take so elastic a definition of Christianity as that. As I said before, in olden days it had a much more full-blooded sense. For instance, it included the belief in hell. Belief in eternal hell-fire was an essential item of Christian belief until pretty recent times. In this country, as you know, it ceased to be an essential item because of a decision of the Privy Council, and from that decision the Archbishop of Canterbury and the Archbishop of York dissented; but in this country our religion is settled by Act of Parliament, and therefore the Privy Council was able to override their Graces and hell was no longer necessary to a Christian. Consequently I shall not insist that a Christian must believe in hell.

The Existence of God

To come to this question of the existence of God: it is a large and serious question, and if I were to attempt to deal with it in any adequate manner I should have to keep you here until Kingdom Come, so that you will have to excuse me if I deal with it in a somewhat summary fashion. You know, of course, that the Catholic Church has laid it down as a dogma that the existence of God can be proved by the unaided reason. That is a somewhat curious dogma, but it is one of their dogmas. They had to introduce it because at one time the freethinkers adopted the habit of saying that there were such and such arguments which mere reason might urge against the existence of God, but of course they knew as a matter of faith that God did exist. The arguments and the reasons were set out at great length, and the Catholic Church felt that they must stop it. Therefore they laid it down that the existence of God can be proved by the unaided reason and they have had to set up what they considered were arguments to prove it. There are, of course, a number of them, but I shall take only a few.

The First-Cause Argument

Perhaps the simplest and easiest to understand is the argument of the First Cause. (It is maintained that everything we see in this world has a cause, and as you go back in the chain of causes further and further you must come to a First Cause, and to that First Cause you give the name of God.) That argument, I suppose, does not carry very much weight nowadays, because, in the first place, cause is not quite what it used to be. The philosophers and the men of science have got going on cause, and it has not anything like the vitality it used to have; but, apart from that, you can see that the argument that there must be a First Cause is one that cannot have any validity. I may say that when I was a young man and was debating these questions very seriously in my mind, I for a long time accepted the argument of the First Cause, until one day, at the age of eighteen, I read John Stuart Mill's Autobiography, and I there found this sentence: "My father taught me that the question 'Who made me?' cannot be answered, since it immediately suggests the further question 'Who made God?' " That very simple sentence showed me, as I still think, the fallacy in the argument of the First Cause. If everything must have a cause, then God must have a cause. If there can be anything without a cause, it may just as well be the world as God, so that there cannot be any validity in that argument. It is exactly of the same nature as the Hindu's view, that the world rested upon an elephant and the elephant rested upon a tortoise; and when they said, "How about the tortoise?" the Indian said, "Suppose we change the subject." The argument is really no better than that. There is no reason why the world could not have come into being without a cause; nor, on the other hand, is there any reason why it should not have always existed. There is no reason to suppose that the world had a beginning at all. The idea that things must have a beginning is really due to the poverty of our imagination. Therefore, perhaps, I need not waste any more time upon the argument about the First Cause.

The Natural-Law Argument

Then there is a very common argument from natural law. That was a favorite argument all through the eighteenth century, especially under the influence of Sir Isaac Newton and his cosmogony. People observed the planets going around the sun according to the law of gravitation, and they thought that God had given a behest to these planets to move in that particular fashion, and that was why they did so. That was, of course, a convenient and simple explanation that saved them the trouble of looking any further for explanations of the law of gravitation. Nowadays we explain the law of gravitation in a somewhat complicated fashion that Einstein has introduced. I do not propose to give you a lecture on the law of gravitation, as interpreted by Einstein, because that again would take some time; at any rate, you no longer have the sort of natural law that you had in the Newtonian system, where, for some reason that nobody could understand, nature behaved in a uniform fashion. We now find that a great many things we thought were natural laws are really human conventions. You know that even in the remotest depths of stellar space there are still three feet to a yard. That is, no doubt, a very remarkable fact, but you would hardly call it a law of nature. And a great many things that have been regarded as laws of nature are of that kind. On the other hand, where you can get down to any knowledge of what atoms actually do, you will find they are much less subject to law than people thought, and that the laws at which you arrive are statistical averages of just the sort that would emerge from chance. There is, as we all know, a law that if you throw dice you will get double sixes only about once in thirty-six times, and we do not regard that as evidence that the fall of the dice is regulated by design; on the contrary, if the double sixes came every time we should think that there was design. The laws of nature are of that sort as regards a great many of them. They are statistical averages such as would emerge from the laws of chance; and that makes this whole business of natural law much less impressive than it formerly was. Quite apart from that, which represents the momentary state of science that may change tomorrow, the whole idea that natural laws imply a lawgiver is due to a confusion between natural and human laws. Human laws are behests commanding you to behave a certain way, in which way you may choose to behave, or you may choose not to behave; but natural laws are a description of how things do in fact behave, and being a mere description of what they in fact do, you cannot argue that there must be somebody who told them to do that, because even supposing that there were, you are then faced with the question "Why did God issue just those natural laws and no others?" If you say that he did it simply from his own good pleasure, and without any reason, you then find that there is something which is not subject to law, and so your train of natural law is interrupted. If you say, as more orthodox theologians do, that in all the laws which God issues he had a reason for giving those laws rather than others—the reason, of course, being to create the best universe, although you would never think it to look at it—if there were a reason for the laws which God gave, then God himself was subject to law, and therefore you do not get any advantage by introducing God as an intermediary. You have really a law outside and anterior to the divine edicts, and God does not serve your purpose, because he is not the ultimate lawgiver. In short, this whole argument about natural law no longer has anything like the strength that it used to have. I am traveling on in time in my review of the arguments. The arguments that are used for the existence of God change their character as time goes on. They were at first hard intellectual arguments embodying certain quite definite fallacies. As we come to modern times they become less respectable intellectually and more and more affected by a kind of moralizing vagueness.

The Argument from Design

The next step in this process brings us to the argument from design. You all know the argument from design: everything in the world is made just so that we can manage to live in the world, and if the world was ever so little different, we could not manage to live in it. That is the argument from design. It sometimes takes a rather curious form; for instance, it is argued that rabbits have white tails in order to be easy to shoot. I do not know how rabbits would view that application. It is an easy argument to parody. You all know Voltaire's remark, that obviously the nose was designed to be such as to fit spectacles. That sort of parody has turned out to be not nearly so wide of the mark as it might have seemed in the eighteenth century, because since the time of Darwin we understand much better why living creatures are adapted to their environment. It is not that their environment was made to be suitable to them but that they grew to be suitable to it, and that is the basis of adaptation. There is no evidence of design about it.

When you come to look into this argument from design, it is a most astonishing thing that people can believe that this world, with all the things that are in it, with all its defects, should be the best that omnipotence and omniscience have been able to produce in millions of years. I really cannot believe it. Do you think that, if you were granted omnipotence and omniscience and millions of years in which to perfect your world, you could produce nothing better than the Ku Klux Klan or the Fascists? Moreover, if you accept the ordinary laws of science, you have to suppose that human life and life in general on this planet will die out in due course: it is a stage in the decay of the solar system; at a certain stage of decay you get the sort of conditions of temperature and so forth which are suitable to protoplasm, and there is life for a short time in the life of the whole solar system. You see in the moon the sort of thing to which the earth is tending—something dead, cold, and lifeless.

I am told that that sort of view is depressing, and people will sometimes tell you that if they believed that, they would not be able to go on living. Do not believe it; it is all nonsense. Nobody really worries much about what is going to happen millions of years hence. Even if they think they are worrying much about that, they are really deceiving themselves. They are worried about something much more mundane, or it may merely be a bad digestion; but nobody is really seriously rendered unhappy by the thought of something that is going to happen to this world millions and millions of years hence. Therefore, although it is of course a gloomy view to suppose that life will die out—at least I suppose we may say so, although sometimes when I contemplate the things that people do with their lives I think it is almost a consolation—it is not such as to render life miserable. It merely makes you turn your attention to other things.

The Moral Arguments for Deity

Now we reach one stage further in what I shall call the intellectual descent that the Theists have made in their argumentations, and we come to what are called the moral arguments for the existence of God. You all know, of course, that there used to be in the old days three intellectual arguments for the existence of God, all of which were disposed of by Immanuel Kant in the *Critique of Pure Reason;* but no sooner had he disposed of those arguments than he invented a new one, a moral argument, and that quite convinced him. He was like many people: in intellectual matters he was skeptical, but in moral matters he believed implicitly in the maxims that he had imbibed at his mother's knee. That illustrates what the psychoanalysts so much emphasize—the immensely stronger hold upon us that our very early associations have than those of later times.

Kant, as I say, invented a new moral argument for the existence of God, and that in varying forms was extremely popular during the nineteenth century. It has all sorts of forms. One form is to say that there would be no right or wrong unless God existed. I am not for the moment concerned with whether there is a difference between right and wrong, or whether there is not: that is another question. The point I am concerned with is that, if you are quite sure there is a difference between right and wrong, you are then in this situation: Is that difference due to God's fiat or is it not? If it is due to God's fiat, then for God himself there is no difference between right and wrong, and it is no longer a significant statement to say that God is good. If you are going to say, as theologians do, that God is good, you must then say that right and wrong have some meaning which is independent of God's fiat, because God's fiats are good and not bad independently of the mere fact that he made them. If you are going to say that, you will then have to say that it is not only through God that right and wrong came into being, but that they are in their essence logically anterior to God. You could, of course, if you liked, say that there was a superior deity who gave orders to the God who made this world, or could take up the line that some of the gnostics took up— a line which I often thought was a very plausible one—that as a matter of fact this world that we know was made by the devil at a moment when God was not looking. There is a good deal to be said for that, and I am not concerned to refute it.

The Argument for the Remedying of Injustice

Then there is another very curious form of moral argument, which is this: they say that the existence of God is required in order to bring justice into the world. In the part of this universe that we know there is great injustice, and often the good suffer, and often the wicked prosper, and one hardly knows which of those is the more annoying; but if you are going to have justice in the universe as a whole you have to suppose a future life to redress the balance of life here on earth. So they say that there must be a God, and there must be heaven and hell in order that in the long run there may be justice. That is a very curious argument. If you looked at the matter from a scientific point of view, you would say, "After all, I know only this world. I do not know about the rest of the universe, but so far as one can argue at all on probabilities one would say that probably this world is a fair sample, and if there is injustice here the odds are that there is injustice elsewhere also." Supposing you got a crate of oranges that you opened, and you found all the top layer of oranges bad, you would not argue, "The underneath ones must be good, so as to redress the balance." You would say, "Probably the whole lot is a bad consignment"; and that is really what a scientific person would argue about the universe. He would say, "Here we find in this world a great deal of injustice, and so far as that goes that is a reason for supposing that justice does not rule in the world; and therefore so far as it goes it affords a moral argument against deity and not in favor of one." Of course I know that the sort of intellectual arguments that I have been talking to you about are not what really moves people. What really moves people to believe in God is not any intellectual argument at all. Most people believe in God because they have been taught from early infancy to do it, and that is the main reason.

Then I think that the next most powerful reason is the wish for safety, a sort of feeling that there is a big brother who will look after you. That plays a very profound part in influencing people's desire for a belief in God.

The Character of Christ

I now want to say a few words upon a topic which I often think is not quite sufficiently dealt with by Rationalists, and that is the question whether Christ was the best and the wisest of men. It is generally taken for granted that we should all agree that that was so. I do not myself. I think that there are a good many points upon which I agree with Christ a great deal more than the professing Christians do. I do not know that I could go with Him all the way, but I could go with Him much further than most professing Christians can. You will remember that He said, "Resist not evil: but whosoever shall smite thee on thy right cheek, turn to him the other also." That is not a new precept or a new principle. It was used by Lao-tse and Buddha some 500 or 600 years before Christ, but it is not a principle which as a matter of fact Christians accept. I have no doubt that the present Prime Minister,[1] for instance, is a most sincere Christian, but I should not advise any of you to go and smite him on one cheek. I think you might find that he thought this text was intended in a figurative sense.

Then there is another point which I consider excellent. You will remember that Christ said, "Judge not lest ye be judged." That principle I do not think you would find was popular in the law courts of Christian countries. I have known in my time quite a number of judges who were very earnest Christians, and none of them felt that they were acting contrary to Christian principles in what they did. Then Christ says, "Give to him that asketh of thee, and from him that would borrow of thee turn not thou away." That is a very good principle. Your Chairman has reminded you that we are not here to talk politics, but I cannot help observing that the last general election was fought on the question of how desirable it was to turn away from him that would borrow of thee, so that one must assume that the Liberals and Conservatives of this country are composed

[1] Stanley Baldwin.

of people who do not agree with the teaching of Christ, because they certainly did very emphatically turn away on that occasion.

Then there is one other maxim of Christ which I think has a great deal in it, but I do not find that it is very popular among some of our Christian friends. He says, "If thou wilt be perfect, go and sell that which thou hast, and give to the poor." That is a very excellent maxim, but, as I say, it is not much practiced. All these, I think, are good maxims, although they are a little difficult to live up to. I do not profess to live up to them myself; but then, after all, it is not quite the same thing as for a Christian.

Defects in Christ's Teaching

Having granted the excellence of these maxims, I come to certain points in which I do not believe that one can grant either the superlative wisdom or the superlative goodness of Christ as depicted in the Gospels; and here I may say that one is not concerned with the historical question. Historically it is quite doubtful whether Christ ever existed at all, and if He did we do not know anything about Him, so that I am not concerned with the historical question, which is a very difficult one. I am concerned with Christ as He appears in the Gospels, taking the Gospel narrative as it stands, and there one does find some things that do not seem to be very wise. For one thing, He certainly thought that His second coming would occur in clouds of glory before the death of all the people who were living at that time. There are a great many texts that prove that. He says, for instance, "Ye shall not have gone over the cities of Israel till the Son of Man be come." Then He says, "There are some standing here which shall not taste death till the Son of Man comes into His kingdom"; and there are a lot of places where it is quite clear that He believed that His second coming would happen during the lifetime of many then living. That was the belief of His earlier followers, and it was the basis of a good deal of His moral teaching. When He said, "Take no thought for the morrow," and things of that sort, it was very largely because He thought that the second coming was going to be very soon, and that all ordinary mundane affairs did not count. I have, as a matter of fact, known some Christians who did believe that the second coming was imminent. I knew a parson who frightened his congregation terribly by telling them that the second coming was very imminent indeed, but they were much consoled when they found that he was planting trees in his garden. The early Christians did really believe it, and they did abstain from such things as planting trees in their gardens, because they did accept from Christ the belief that the second coming was imminent. In that respect, clearly He was not so wise as some other people have been, and He was certainly not superlatively wise.

The Moral Problem

Then you come to moral questions. There is one very serious defect to my mind in Christ's moral character, and that is that He believed in hell. I do not myself feel that any person who is really profoundly humane can believe in everlasting punishment. Christ certainly as depicted in the Gospels did believe in everlasting punishment, and one does find repeatedly a vindictive fury against those people who would not listen to His preaching—an attitude which is not uncommon with preachers, but which does somewhat detract from superlative excellence. You do not, for instance, find that attitude in Socrates. You find him quite bland and urbane toward the people who would not listen to him; and it is, to my mind, far more worthy of a sage to take that line than to take the line of indignation. You probably all remember the sort of things that Socrates was saying when he was dying, and the sort of things that he generally did say to people who did not agree with him.

You will find that in the Gospels Christ said, "Ye serpents, ye generation of vipers, how can ye escape the damnation of hell." That was said to people who did not like His preaching. It is not really to my mind quite the best tone, and there are a great many of these things about hell. There is, of course, the familiar text about the sin against the Holy Ghost: "Whosoever speaketh against the Holy Ghost it shall not be forgiven him neither in this World nor in the world to come." That text has caused an unspeakable amount of misery in the world, for all sorts of people have imagined that they have committed the sin against the Holy Ghost, and thought that it would not be forgiven them either in this world or in the world to come. I really do not think that a person with a proper degree of kindliness in his nature would have put fears and terrors of that sort into the world.

Then Christ says, "The Son of Man shall send forth His angels, and they shall gather out of His kingdom all things that offend, and them which do iniquity, and shall cast them into a furnace of fire; there shall be wailing and gnashing of teeth"; and He goes on about the wailing and gnashing of teeth. It comes in one verse after another, and it is quite manifest to the reader that there is a certain pleasure in contemplating wailing and gnashing of teeth, or else it would not occur so often. Then you all, of course, remember about the sheep and the goats; how at the second coming He is going to divide the sheep from the goats, and He is going to say to the goats, "Depart from me, ye cursed, into everlasting fire." He continues, "And these shall go away into everlasting fire." Then He says again, "If thy hand offend thee, cut it off; it is better for thee to enter into life maimed, than having two hands to go into hell, into the fire that never shall be quenched; where the worm dieth not and the fire is not quenched." He repeats that again and again also. I must say that I think all this doctrine, that hell-fire is a punishment for sin, is a doctrine of cruelty. It is a doctrine that put cruelty into the world and gave the world generations of cruel torture; and the Christ of the Gospels, if you could take Him as His chroniclers represent Him, would certainly have to be considered partly responsible for that.

There are other things of less importance. There is the instance of the Gadarene swine, where it certainly was not very kind to the pigs to put the devils into them and make them rush down the hill to the sea. You must remember that He was omnipotent, and He could have made the devils simply go away; but He chose to send them into the pigs. Then there is the curious story of the fig tree, which always rather puzzled me. You remember what happened about the fig tree. "He was hungry; and seeing a fig tree afar off having leaves, He came if haply He might find anything thereon; and when He came to it He found nothing but leaves, for the time of figs was not yet. And Jesus answered and said unto it: 'No man eat fruit of thee hereafter for ever' . . . and Peter . . . saith unto Him: 'Master, behold the fig tree which thou cursedst is withered away.' " This is a very curious story, because it was not the right time of year for figs, and you really could not blame the tree. I cannot myself feel that either in the matter of wisdom or in the matter of virtue Christ stands quite as high as some other people known to history. I think I should put Buddha and Socrates above Him in those respects.

The Emotional Factor

As I said before, I do not think that the real reason why people accept religion has anything to do with argumentation. They accept religion on emotional grounds. One is often told that it is a very wrong thing to attack religion, because religion makes men virtuous. So I am told; I have not noticed it. You know, of course, the parody of that argument in Samuel Butler's book, *Erewhon Revisited*. You will remember that in *Erewhon* there is a certain Higgs who arrives in a remote country, and after spending some time there he escapes from that country in a balloon. Twenty years later he comes back to that country and finds a new religion in which he is worshiped under the name of the "Sun Child," and it is said that he ascended into heaven. He finds that the Feast of the Ascension is about to be celebrated, and he hears Professors Hanky and Panky say to each other that they never set eyes on the man Higgs, and they hope they never will; but they are the high priests of the religion of the Sun Child. He is very indignant, and he comes up to them, and he says, "I am going to expose all this humbug and tell the people of Erewhon that it was only I, the man Higgs, and I went up in a balloon." He was told, "You must not do that, because all the morals of this country are bound round this myth, and if they once know that you did not ascend into heaven they will all become wicked"; and so he is persuaded of that and he goes quietly away.

That is the idea—that we should all be wicked if we did not hold to the Christian religion. It seems to me that the people who have held to it have been for the most part extremely wicked. You find this curious fact, that the more intense has been the religion of any period and the more profound has been the dogmatic belief, the greater has been the cruelty and the worse has been the state of affairs. In the so-called ages of faith, when men really did believe the Christian religion in all its completeness, there was the Inquisition, with its tortures; there were millions of unfortunate women burned as witches; and there was every kind of cruelty practiced upon all sorts of people in the name of religion.

You find as you look around the world that every single bit of progress in humane feeling, every improvement in the criminal law, every step toward the diminution of war, every step toward better treatment of the colored races, or every mitigation of slavery, every moral progress that there has been in the world, has been consistently opposed by the organized churches of the world. I say quite deliberately that the Christian religion, as organized in its churches, has been and still is the principal enemy of moral progress in the world.

How the Churches Have Retarded Progress

You may think that I am going too far when I say that that is still so. I do not think that I am. Take one fact. You will bear with me if I mention it. It is not a pleasant fact, but the churches compel one to mention facts that are not pleasant. Supposing that in this world that we live in today an inexperienced girl is married to a syphilitic man; in that case the Catholic Church says, "This is an indissoluble sacrament. You must endure celibacy or stay together. And if you stay together, you must not use birth control to prevent the birth of syphilitic children." Nobody whose natural sympathies have not been warped by dogma, or whose moral nature was not absolutely dead to all sense of suffering, could maintain that it is right and proper that that state of things should continue.

That is only an example. There are a great many ways in which, at the present moment, the church, by its insistence upon what it chooses to call morality, inflicts upon all sorts of people undeserved and unnecessary suffering. And of course, as we know, it is in its major part an opponent still of progress and of improvement in all the ways that diminish suffering in the world, because it has chosen to label as morality a certain narrow set of rules of conduct which have nothing to do with human happiness; and when you say that this or that ought to be done because it would make for human happiness, they think that has nothing to do with the matter at all. "What has human happiness to do with morals? The object of morals is not to make people happy."

Fear, the Foundation of Religion

Religion is based, I think, primarily and mainly upon fear. It is partly the terror of the unknown and partly, as I have said, the wish to feel that you have a kind of elder brother who will stand by you in all our troubles and disputes. Fear is the basis of the whole thing —fear of the mysterious, fear of defeat, fear of death. Fear is the parent of cruelty, and therefore it is no wonder if cruelty and religion have gone hand in hand. It is because fear is at the basis of those two things. In this world we can now begin a little to understand things, and a little to master them by help of science, which has forced its way step by step against the Christian religion, against the churches, and against the opposition of all the old precepts. Science can help us to get over this craven fear in which mankind has lived for so many generations. Science can teach us, and I think our own hearts can teach us, no longer to look around for imaginary supports, no longer to invent allies in the sky, but rather to look to our own efforts here below to make this world a fit place to live in, instead of the sort of place that the churches in all these centuries have made it.

What We Must Do

We want to stand upon our own feet and look fair and square at the world—its good facts, its bad facts, its beauties, and its ugliness; see the world as it is and be not afraid of it. Conquer the world by intelligence and not merely by being slavishly subdued by the terror that comes from it. The whole conception of God is a conception derived from the ancient Oriental despotisms. It is a conception quite unworthy of free men. When you hear people in church debasing themselves and saying that they are miserable sinners, and all the rest of it, it seems contemptible and not worthy of self-respecting human beings. We ought to stand up and look the world frankly in the face. We ought to make the best we can of the world, and if it is not so good as we wish, after all it will still be better than what these others have made of it in all these ages. A good world needs knowledge, kindliness, and courage; it does not need a regretful hankering after the past or a fettering of the free intelligence by the words uttered long ago by ignorant men. It needs a fearless outlook and a free intelligence. It needs hope for the future, not looking back all the time toward a past that is dead, which we trust will be far surpassed by the future that our intelligence can create.

The Problem of Evil

The Problem of Evil John Hick

John Hick (1922–   ) is lecturer in Divinity at Cambridge University in
England. He is the author of several books on the philosophy of religion.

To many, the most powerful positive objection to belief in God is
the fact of evil. Probably for most agnostics it is the appalling depth
and extent of human suffering, more than anything else, that makes the
idea of a loving Creator seem so implausible and disposes them toward
one or another of the various naturalistic theories of religion.

As a challenge to theism, the problem of evil has traditionally been
posed in the form of a dilemma: if God is perfectly loving, he must
wish to abolish evil; and if he is all-powerful, he must be able to
abolish evil. But evil exists; therefore God cannot be both omnipotent
and perfectly loving.

Certain solutions, which at once suggest themselves, have to be ruled
out so far as the Judaic-Christian faith is concerned.

To say, for example (with contemporary Christian Science), that
evil is an illusion of the human mind, is impossible within a religion
based upon the stark realism of the Bible. Its pages faithfully reflect
the characteristic mixture of good and evil in human experience. They
record every kind of sorrow and suffering, every mode of man's inhumanity to man and of his painfully insecure existence in the world. There
is no attempt to regard evil as anything but dark, menacingly ugly,
heart-rending, and crushing. In the Christian scriptures, the climax of
this history of evil is the crucifixion of Jesus, which is presented not
only as a case of utterly unjust suffering, but as the violent and murder-
ous rejection of God's Messiah. There can be no doubt, then, that for
biblical faith, evil is unambiguously evil, and stands in direct opposition
to God's will.

Again, to solve the problem of evil by means of the theory (sponsored,
for example, by the Boston "Personalist" School) of a finite deity who
does the best he can with a material, intractable and coeternal with
himself, is to have abandoned the basic premise of Hebrew-Christian
monotheism; for the theory amounts to rejecting belief in the infinity and
sovereignty of God.

Indeed, any theory which would avoid the problem of the origin of
evil by depicting it as an ultimate constituent of the universe, coordinate

with good, has been repudiated in advance by the classic Christian teaching, first developed by Augustine, that evil represents the going wrong of something which in itself is good. Augustine holds firmly to the Hebrew-Christian conviction that the universe is *good*—that is to say, it is the creation of a good God for a good purpose. He completely rejects the ancient prejudice, widespread in his day, that matter is evil. There are, according to Augustine, higher and lower, greater and lesser goods in immense abundance and variety; but everything which has being is good in its own way and degree, except in so far as it may have become spoiled or corrupted. Evil—whether it be an evil will, an instance of pain, or some disorder or decay in nature—has not been set there by God, but represents the distortion of something that is inherently valuable. Whatever exists is, as such, and in its proper place, good; evil is essentially parasitic upon good, being disorder and perversion in a fundamentally good creation. This understanding of evil as something negative means that it is not willed and created by God; but it does not mean (as some have supposed) that evil is unreal and can be disregarded. On the contrary, the first effect of this doctrine is to accentuate even more the question of the origin of evil.

Theodicy,[1] as many modern Christian thinkers see it, is a modest enterprise, negative rather than positive in its conclusions. It does not claim to explain, nor to explain away, every instance of evil in human experience, but only to point to certain considerations which prevent the fact of evil (largely incomprehensible though it remains) from constituting a final and insuperable bar to rational belief in God.

In indicating these considerations it will be useful to follow the traditional division of the subject. There is the problem of *moral evil* or wickedness: why does an all-good and all-powerful God permit this? And there is the problem of the *non-moral evil* of suffering or pain, both physical and mental: why has an all-good and all-powerful God created a world in which this occurs?

Christian thought has always considered moral evil in its relation to human freedom and responsibility. To be a person is to be a finite center of freedom, a (relatively) free and self-directing agent responsible for one's own decisions. This involves being free to act wrongly as well as to act rightly. The idea of a person who can be infallibly guaranteed always to act rightly is self-contradictory. There can be no guarantee in advance that a genuinely free moral agent will never choose amiss. Consequently, the possibility of wrongdoing or sin is logically inseparable from the creation of finite persons, and to say that God should not have created beings who might sin amounts to saying that he should not have created people.

This thesis has been challenged in some recent philosophical discussions of the problem of evil, in which it is claimed that no contradiction is involved in saying that God might have made people who would

---

[1] The word "theodicy," from the Greek *theos* (God) and *dike* (righteous), means the justification of God's goodness in the face of the fact of evil.

be genuinely free and who could yet be guaranteed always to act rightly. A quote from one of these discussions follows:

> If there is no logical impossibility in a man's freely choosing the good on one, or on several occasions, there cannot be a logical impossibility in his freely choosing the good on every occasion. God was not, then, faced with a choice between making innocent automata and making beings who, in acting freely, would sometimes go wrong: there was open to him the obviously better possibility of making beings who would act freely but always go right. Clearly, his failure to avail himself of this possibility is inconsistent with his being both omnipotent and wholly good.[2]

A reply to this argument is suggested in another recent contribution to the discussion.[3] If by a free action we mean an action which is not externally compelled but which flows from the nature of the agent as he reacts to the circumstances in which he finds himself, there is, indeed, no contradiction between our being free and our actions being "caused" (by our own nature) and therefore being in principle predictable. There is a contradiction, however, in saying that God is the cause of our acting as we do but that we are free beings in relation to God. There is, in other words, a contradiction in saying that God has made us so that we shall of necessity act in a certain way, and that we are genuinely independent persons in relation to him. If all our thoughts and actions are divinely predestined, however free and morally responsible we may seem to be to ourselves, we cannot be free and morally responsible in the sight of God, but must instead be his helpless puppets. Such "freedom" is like that of a patient acting out a series of post-hypnotic suggestions: he appears, even to himself, to be free, but his volitions have actually been pre-determined by another will, that of the hypnotist, in relation to whom the patient is not a free agent.

A different objector might raise the question of whether or not we deny God's omnipotence if we admit that he is unable to create persons who are free from the risks inherent in personal freedom. The answer that has always been given is that to create such beings is logically impossible. It is no limitation upon God's power that he cannot accomplish the logically impossible, since there is nothing here to accomplish, but only a meaningless conjunction of words—in this case "person who is not a person." God is able to create beings of any and every conceivable kind; but creatures who lack moral freedom, however superior they might be to human beings in other respects, would not be what we mean by persons. They would constitute a different form of life which God might have brought into existence instead of persons. When we ask why God did not create such beings in place of persons, the traditional answer is that only persons could, in any meaningful sense, become "children of God," capable of entering into a personal relationship with their Creator by a free and uncompelled response to his love.

When we turn from the possibility of moral evil as a correlate of

[2] J. L. Mackie, "Evil and Omnipotence," *Mind* (April, 1955), 209.

[3] Flew, in *New Essays in Philosophical Theology.*

man's personal freedom to its actuality, we face something which must remain inexplicable even when it can be seen to be possible. For we can never provide a complete causal explanation of a free act; if we could, it would not be a free act. The origin of moral evil lies forever concealed within the mystery of human freedom.

The necessary connection between moral freedom and the possibility, now actualized, of sin throws light upon a great deal of the suffering which afflicts mankind. For an enormous amount of human pain arises either from the inhumanity or the culpable incompetence of mankind. This includes such major scourges as poverty, oppression and persecution, war, and all the injustice, indignity, and inequity which occur even in the most advanced societies. These evils are manifestations of human sin. Even disease is fostered to an extent, the limits of which have not yet been determined by psychosomatic medicine, by moral and emotional factors seated both in the individual and in his social environment. To the extent that all of these evils stem from human failures and wrong decisions, their possibility is inherent in the creation of free persons inhabiting a world which presents them with real choices which are followed by real consequences.

We may now turn more directly to the problem of suffering. Even though the major bulk of actual human pain is traceable to man's misused freedom as a sole or part cause, there remain other sources of pain which are entirely independent of the human will, for example, earthquake, hurricane, storm, flood, drought, and blight. In practice it is often impossible to trace a boundary between the suffering which results from human wickedness and folly and that which falls upon mankind from without. Both kinds of suffering are inextricably mingled together in human experience. For our present purpose, however, it is important to note that the latter category does exist and that it seems to be built into the very structure of our world. In response to it, theodicy, if it is wisely conducted, follows a negative path. It is not possible to show positively that each item of human pain serves the divine purpose of good; but, on the other hand, it does seem possible to show that the divine purpose as it is understood in Judaism and Christianity could not be forwarded in a world which was designed as a permanent hedonistic paradise.

An essential premise of this argument concerns the nature of the divine purpose in creating the world. The skeptic's assumption is that man is to be viewed as a completed creation and that God's purpose in making the world was to provide a suitable dwelling-place for this fully-formed creature. Since God is good and loving, the environment which he has created for human life to inhabit is naturally as pleasant and comfortable as possible. The problem is essentially similar to that of a man who builds a cage for some pet animal. Since our world, in fact, contains sources of hardship, inconvenience, and danger of innumerable kinds, the conclusion follows that this world cannot have been created by a perfectly benevolent and all-powerful deity.

Christianity, however, has never supposed that God's purpose in the creation of the world was to construct a paradise whose inhabitants would experience a maximum of pleasure and a minimum of pain. The world is seen, instead, as a place of "soul-making" in which free beings, grappling with the tasks and challenges of their existence in a common environment, may become "children of God" and "heirs of eternal life." A way of thinking theologically of God's continuing creative purpose for man was suggested by some of the early Hellenistic Fathers of the Christian Church, especially Irenaeus. Following hints from St. Paul, Irenaeus taught that man has been made as a person in the image of God but has not yet been brought as a free and responsible agent into the finite likeness of God, which is revealed in Christ. Our world, with all its rough edges, is the sphere in which this second and harder stage of the creative process is taking place.

This conception of the world (whether or not set in Irenaeus' theological framework) can be supported by the method of negative theodicy. Suppose, contrary to fact, that this world were a paradise from which all possibility of pain and suffering were excluded. The consequences would be very far-reaching. For example, no one could ever injure anyone else: the murderer's knife would turn to paper or his bullets to thin air; the bank safe, robbed of a million dollars, would miraculously become filled with another million dollars (without this device, on however large a scale, proving inflationary); fraud, deceit, conspiracy, and treason would somehow always leave the fabric of society undamaged. Again, no one would ever be injured by accident: the mountain-climber, steeplejack, or playing child falling from a height would float unharmed to the ground; the reckless driver would never meet with disaster. There would be no need to work, since no harm could result from avoiding work; there would be no call to be concerned for others in time of need or danger, for in such a world there could be no real needs or dangers.

To make possible this continual series of individual adjustments, nature would have to work by "special providences" instead of running according to general laws which men must learn to respect on penalty of pain or death. The laws of nature would have to be extremely flexible: sometimes gravity would operate, sometimes not; sometimes an object would be hard and solid, sometimes soft. There could be no sciences, for there would be no enduring world structure to investigate. In eliminating the problems and hardships of an objective environment, with its own laws, life would become like a dream in which, delightfully but aimlessly, we would float and drift at ease.

One can at least begin to imagine such a world. It is evident that our present ethical concepts would have no meaning in it. If, for example, the notion of harming someone is an essential element in the concept of a wrong action, in our hedonistic paradise there could be no wrong actions—nor any right actions in distinction from wrong. Courage and fortitude would have no point in an environment in which there is, by definition, no danger or difficulty. Generosity, kindness, the *agape* aspect of love, prudence, unselfishness, and all other ethical notions which presuppose life in a stable environment, could not even be formed. Consequently, such a world, however well it might promote pleasure, would be very ill adapted for the development of the moral qualities of human personality. In relation to this purpose it would be the worst of all possible worlds.

It would seem, then, that an environment intended to make possible the growth in free beings of the finest characteristics of personal life, must have a good deal in common with our present world. It must operate according to general and dependable laws; and it must involve real dangers, difficulties, problems, obstacles, and possibilities of pain, failure, sorrow, frustration, and defeat. If it did not contain the particular trials and perils which—subtracting man's own very considerable contribution —our world contains, it would have to contain others instead.

To realize this is not, by any means, to be in possession of a detailed theodicy. It is to understand that this world, with all its "heartaches and the thousand natural shocks that flesh is heir to," an environment so manifestly not designed for the maximization of human pleasure and the minimization of human pain, may be rather well adapted to the quite different purpose of "soul-making."

On Being an Atheist   H. J. McCloskey

H. J. McCloskey (1925–   ) is a professor of philosophy at La Trobe University in Melbourne, Australia. He has written numerous articles on a variety of philosophical issues.

In this article I wish to remind fellow atheists of the grounds upon which theists base their belief in God, of the inadequacy of these grounds, why we believe that there is no God, and then I shall look at the claim that theists commonly make that atheism is a cold, comfortless position, that, as one Christian recently put it to me, 'It's harder if you don't believe in God.' I shall offer reasons why I believe that atheism is a much more comfortable belief than theism, and why theists should be miserable just because they are theists. I shall therefore be making points familiar to most thoughtful atheists, but I make no apology for doing so, as it is useful for us to remind ourselves of the reasons for and virtues of our belief. This is especially true in respect of the superiority of atheism to theism as a source of strength, for the theist's claim that theism gives benefits which do not come with atheism is gravely false, yet atheists are not uncommonly deceived by it. I shall not attempt to consider all the benefits theists claim to come with belief in God. For example, I recently heard a Christian seriously commending Jesus Christ as the supreme tranquillizer, as being better for one's nerves than any tonic or

From *Question #1*, February 1968. Reprinted by permission of the Pemberton Publishing Company.

tranquillizer. Such claims are so absurd and so disrespectful of thoughtful religious belief, it would be discourteous to serious theists to consider them.

A Christian colleague and friend has often observed to me that our philospher colleagues attribute too much importance to the role of the proofs of the existence of God as a basis for religious belief, that most theists do not come to believe in God as a result of reflecting on the proofs, but come to religion as a result of other reasons and factors. This is probably true of most proofs, especially those which so occupy the attention of philosophers. Proofs such as the ontological proof carry no weight with the ordinary theist. And while such proofs may confirm a doubting theist in his belief if he accepts them as sound, they seem not to be causes of the initial religious belief, even in those who take them seriously. I shall therefore pass over these more exotic proofs. There are, however, three proofs which do seem to me to move ordinary theists to their theism, and indeed, to constitute major motivations towards a belief in God, namely the cosmological proof, the teleological proof, and the argument from design. (The latter are distinct, although they are commonly confused and advanced in conjunction as one proof. Because they have similar defects, I shall discuss them together.)

People are moved to a general, if vague, theism by reflection on the cause of it all. They feel that there must be a first cause, a creator, who brought everything into being, and who now 'holds the whole world in his hands.' They do not think far enough nor hard enough about the problem of an uncaused cause, who must be a necessarily existing being, to see that this argument is less conclusive than it seems at first sight. And people are, to my mind, even more frequently moved to a belief in God by what they take to be evidence of design and purpose in the world. One is constantly hearing theists, the parson more perhaps than the theologian, alluding to design and purpose as facts which necessitate a belief in God. It is not surprising that this is so. If one knows nothing about evolution it is easy to fall into the error of seeing adaption to environment as evidence of design and purpose. I shall therefore briefly remind my readers of the defects of these arguments, as they bear on why I think theism to be a comfortless, spine-chilling doctrine.

I propose to treat *the cosmological argument* as being the argument its name suggests it to be, namely an argument from the existence of the world as we know it, and not as it is often set out as simply an argument from the existence of something. The defects of this argument are many. There is the difficulty already alluded to, that the first cause must be explained as an uncaused cause, otherwise we are left with an infinite regress of causes, gods in this case, the very sort of regress this argument seeks to avoid. This means that the first cause must be explained as being a necessarily existing being, one who cannot not exist. The mere existence of the world constitutes no reason for believing in the existence of such a being. If we use the causal argument at all, all we are entitled to infer is the existence of a cause commensurate with the effect to be explained, the universe, and this does not entitle us to postulate an all-powerful, all-perfect, uncaused cause. The most it would entitle one to conclude is that the cause is powerful enough and imperfect enough to have created the sort of world we know.

The world we know does not reveal itself to us as the handiwork of an omnipotent, all-perfect being. This objection is one way of putting Kant's criticism that the cosmological proof involves the ontological proof. Other difficulties, for instance, that it is illicit to extend the causal argument in this way, for after all, why must we postulate some ultimate cause, might be pressed here. However, I shall pass them over and note a related objection to that which has just been discussed. It is that the world we know is a world containing a great deal of evil, in particular, avoidable suffering endured by innocent human beings and animals. If we argue from the existence of this world to its creator, we must endow this creator with attributes which explain how he came to create such a world. We must conclude that he is either a malevolent powerful being or that he is a well-intentioned muddler, that the creator and ruler of the universe is either not a god but an evil spirit or a well-intentioned finite being whose limitations result in very disastrous consequences. A belief in the existence of either is hardly a source of strength and security.

The teleological argument and the argument from design are no more satisfactory, and for exactly the same reason as the last noted above, and for many other reasons as well. One can reject the argument from design by rejecting its premise, that there is evidence of design and purpose. So many things which were, before the theory of evolution, construed as evidence of design and purpose, are now seen to be nothing of the sort. To get the proof going, genuine indisputable examples of design or purpose are needed. There are no such indisputable examples, so the proof does not get going at all. However, disregarding this very conclusive objection, we may note how our last objection to the cosmological arises equally fatally for the teleological argument and argument from design. One cannot legitimately argue, as do the exponents of this argument, from there being some sort of evidence of purpose or design to there being an all-powerful, all-perfect planner or designer. Even if we uncritically accepted the examples of purpose and design pointed to by exponents of this argument, all we should be entitled to conclude was that there was a powerful, malevolent, or imperfect planner or designer.

The problem of evil is a real and persistent problem for the theist. Even theists who use this argument and treat it as a conclusive one worry about the solution to the problem posed by the existence of evil. Yet, when formulating this argument they carry on as if the existence of evil in the world did not seriously tell against the perfection of the divine design or divine purpose as revealed in the world. We must look at the world as it is, and if we argue from what apparent design and purpose there is, the most we could legitimately conclude is that there is a supreme malevolent designer, or a supreme, well-intentioned, bungling, or finite designer, who muddles along with the best of intentions and the most unhappy results.

Thus I suggest that two considerations which lead theists to a belief in God provide no grounds for such a belief. Even if a number of important, valid, conclusive objections are ignored, they then at most would suggest the existence of beings, the existence of which would be a source of concern, dismay, and anxiety rather than of comfort and security.

Other theists come to their belief in God through what they call 'faith'. Tillich speaks of faith as the state of being ultimately concerned, as claiming truth for its concern, and as involving commitment, courage, and the taking of a risk. It does involve taking a risk, a reckless, irrational risk. The theist suggests that to have faith in the existence and goodness of God is like having faith in the goodness of a friend one has known to be a man of honour and integrity all his life and against whom there is now circumstantial evidence that he is a criminal. To have faith in one's friend on the basis of past knowledge is reasonable, even though it may involve a risk of error. However, the situation with God is not like that at all. There is not the past knowledge of a good and perfect being. All we know of God is through his alleged works; and his alleged works are such that we cannot conclude from them that he is all-perfect. Rather, we must conclude that if there were a god he would be seriously imperfect. To have faith in his existence and perfection in the face of the existence of evil is to be irrational and foolish. Hence it is that faith cannot provide grounds for rational belief in God.

In bringing out the weakness of these arguments and the appeal to faith, I have stressed the fact of *the existence of evil*. This is a fact it is vitally important to stress. There is physical evil, such as pain, privations of appropriate goods, and the like, and there is moral evil, as evinced by people such as Hitler and Eichmann on a grand scale and by most of us in more modest forms. It is because evil exists that we believe God does not exist. No being who was perfect could have created a world in which there was avoidable suffering or in which his creations would (and who could have been created so as not to) engage in morally evil acts, acts which very often result in injury to innocent persons. Theists seek to solve the problem these facts pose in a wide variety of ingenious ways. Their 'solutions' are discussed at some length by me elsewhere. (See *God and Evil*, edited by N. Pike, Prentice-Hall, Ch. 6, pp. 61–84; also 'The Problem of Evil', *Journal of Bible and Religion*, 1962.) Here it is sufficient simply to note some of the more common of these 'solutions' to see how threadbare they are.

We are told by some that pain is unreal, by others that it is not a positive evil, but simply a privation of a proper good, that it is God's punishment for sin (even of the 'sins' of animals and newly born children, presumably), that animals and young children who are innocent of sin do not really experience pain, that pain is God's way of reminding men of his existence and of warning them to mend their ways (suggesting a bungling God, for he in fact thereby leads many to deny his existence, for they cannot reconcile the evil they see with his alleged goodness), that pain makes the world a better world, being like an ugly element which contributes to the overall beauty of the painting, that pain is a means to higher goods such as courage and benevolence (and hence, presumably, that we act immorally in using anaesthetics and in combating disease), that pain results from the operation of natural laws which are the best

God could devise and which lead to greater good over all (as if a God who is all-perfect could not have devised a world in which the operation of the natural laws resulted in less suffering), and many other stories are offered.

And of moral evil the usual story is in terms of free will (or free will and the goods free will makes to be possible), that God in conferring free will could not guarantee that we abstain from evil, for to do so would be to limit freedom. But have we free will? And if we have, is it so valuable as to justify all the evil caused by men's morally evil acts, i.e. would it really be a worse total state of affairs for us to be rational automata? More basically, is it not the case that complete virtue is compatible with the possession of free will, might not God have very easily so have arranged the world and biased man to virtue that men always freely chose what is right? Clearly theists cannot consistently argue that free will and necessitation to virtue are incompatible, for they represent God himself as possessing a free will and as being incapable of acting immorally. If this can be the case with God, why can it not be so with all free agents?

The existence of evil is therefore fatal to the claims that there is a Supreme Being who is perfect in every respect, i.e. the fact of evil is fatal to the claims of orthodox Roman Catholics, who postulate such a God. Protestants sometimes seek to solve the problem by explaining God as a finite being who is all-good but not all-powerful, who does the best he can and who needs our help because his best is often disastrous. The fact that the proofs provide no reasons for believing in the existence of such a god, and that there are positive reasons which it is not convenient to go into here for disbelieving in such a being, and even more for not worshipping, holding in awe, and generally treating such a being as a god, makes this view one which merits little attention (see my 'Would Any Being Merit Worship?', *Southern Journal of Philosophy*, 1964). However, it is none the less worth reflecting on whether one would feel very happy and secure in the thought, as the song puts it, that such a being 'holds the whole world in his hands'.

Let us now consider more explicitly whether belief in God would bring comfort and security of which a denial of the existence of such a God would deprive us.

What are the occasions on which we are told that religion is a great source of comfort? Most of us accept the loss of our loved ones after a long and full life if their deaths do not involve suffering; and we feel the same about our own deaths. The occasions upon which we need strength and comfort are when we or our loved ones are jolted by 'acts of God'. They are occasions such as when we lose a loved one as a result of a natural disaster, flood, fire, famine, earthquake, storm, or, as is more commonly the case, as a result of a disease. Or we may need comfort and support when our near and dear to us is smitten by a grave disease, a paralysing stroke, a coronary, cancer, rheumatoid arthritis, meningitis, encephalitis, or the like. Or we may need strength and help if we are parents to a gravely defective, newly born child, or if we find our son is going blind and there is nothing that can be done for him, or if our child or spouse or friend goes insane. We typically feel the need for comfort and support when we or our loved ones are victims of these evils which are commonly, and for the theist accurately, called 'acts of God'. It is true that morally evil acts and accidents may hurt us or our loved ones, and render us in need of comfort and support, but since, for the reasons alluded to earlier, God must be held ultimately responsible for these too, it is better to concentrate on those blows of fate which render us in need of comfort and which are so properly described by theists on the basis of their beliefs as evils resulting from acts of God.

If one's loved one or oneself were smitten by 'an act of God', if for example, one's daughter at the age of two months falls victim of meningitis, and suffers permanent impairment for the rest of her life, would and ought one to be comforted to believe that there is a God who caused your daughter's condition? Would and ought you to be comforted to think that this God—and here I remind you of theists' accounts of evil—thought your daughter so evil as to deserve such severe punishment, or that he simply chose to allow the world to be governed by inferior laws of nature which he, being omniscient, foresaw would have this precise effect? Would you be cheered to think that God had arbitrarily chosen your daughter as his vehicle to remind the world of his existence and of their duty to worship him? Would the thought that your daughter's suffering was an evil, ugly component which heightened and increased the beauty and goodness of the overall plan reconcile you to her suffering? And would you accept her suffering more happily because it provided you and others with opportunities to engage in acts of higher virtue, and thereby to promote more total good? I suggest that a belief in God in such a situation would and should be a source of great distress and worry. A man could not reasonably be happier for thinking that God had knowingly brought about the harm to his daughter.

Consider alternatively if you were the victim, if you suffered a stroke which deprived you of all power of movement and even of speech while leaving your mind unaffected, would and ought you to gain comfort and strength from the thought that your condition was a deliberate foreseen result of God's will? I myself should be utterly dispirited by the thought; and if I saw it as my duty to respect God's wishes I would decline medical aid in so far as my condition allowed me to do so, as being something which would frustrate God's will. Allusion to an immortal existence would not help here, as a God who so arranges things in this world can hardly be counted on to arrange things better in the next; and many theists in any case offer us reasons for believing that for most of us things will be much worse in the next life. The suggestion that God is all-good but imperfect, that he does not deliberately bring about these evils, that he is doing his best and cannot prevent them, is scarcely more comforting than the view that he deliberately arranges things so that these evil effects occur as part of his divine plan.

Clearly, in the examples cited above, whether one be the father of the victim or the victim himself, one must feel much happier in the knowledge that there is no God, that God had nothing to do with the blow one had suffered. And instead of cold comfort in religious belief, the atheist in such a situation would seek and receive strength and comfort where it is available, from those able to give it, his friends and men of good will. If I were the father of the afflicted daughter, as an atheist I should exert myself rationally, seeking for her the best help mankind could provide, instead of piously telling her to seek comfort from God, who brought about her unhappy condition. And, knowing that there is no God, I should and do support the efforts of mankind to reduce the occasions on which such comfort is needed. It is at least in a large part because there have been atheists who have opposed reactionary and conservative religious influences which have resisted the use of anaesthetics, vaccinations, enlightened treatment of the insane, acceptance of abortion to save a mother's life or to prevent a defective child being born, the use of effective methods of birth control for the same reasons, voluntary euthanasia and suicide, there are now fewer occasions on which people need the comfort and help of others than in former times. Atheism, adopted by a thoughtful and sensitive person, leads to a spirit of self-reliance, to a self-respect which demands that we comfort and help those who need such support, and to a furthering and supporting of all measures which will reduce or moderate the blows of fate.

Contemporary Issues

Should We Believe in God Without Evidence?

Reason and Faith   Richard Robinson

Richard Robinson (1902–   ), who is a Fellow of Oriel College at Oxford University, has written numerous books and articles on a variety of philosophical issues.

Religion and Reason

I come now to something commonly accepted as a great good which I reject, namely religion.

Religion has held a big place in the thoughts and feelings of most of the human beings who have yet lived; and, though some have found it an inescapable evil, most have found it a great good. The founder of the Gifford lectures said that 'religion is of all things the most excellent and precious' (according to Sherrington, *Man on his Nature,* p. 360).

The religious man feels that his god is the supreme good, and the worship of him is the supreme good for man; and he obtains an immense satisfaction in worship and obedience. His creed gives him the feeling that the universe is important and that he has his own humble but important part in it. 'God is working his purpose out, as year succeeds to year'; and in this august enterprise the believer has an assured place. When he says that 'man cannot be at ease in the world unless he has a faith to sustain him', the faith he is thinking of is in part that there is something extremely important to do. Thus his religion lays that spectre of futility and meaninglessness, which man's selfconsciousness and thoughtfulness are always liable to raise. The convert says to himself, in the words at the end of Tolstoy's *Anna Karenina:* 'My whole life, every moment of my life, will be, not meaningless as before, but full of deep meaning, which I shall have power to impress on every action.' The great comfort of such a belief is obvious.

But this is still less than half of the comfort religion can give. For it is not yet an answer to man's greatest horror, the death of his loved ones and himself. If his religion also makes him believe that death is not the end of life, that on the contrary he and his loved ones will live for ever in perfect justice and happiness, this more than doubles his feeling of comfort and security. This doctrine of the happy survival of death is the chief attraction of the Christian religion to most of its adherents; and their first profound religious belief comes to them as a reassurance after their first realization that they are going to die. It is an easy defensive re-

From *An Atheist's Values* by Richard Robinson. Reprinted by permission of the Clarendon Press, Oxford.

action against this terrible discovery. (This point is well put by Bergson in *Les Deux Sources*, &c., e.g. p. 137.)

Such is the enormous comfort that religion can give. Because of it a man who deprives the people of the comfort of believing 'in the final proportions of eternal justice' is often regarded as a 'cruel oppressor, the merciless enemy of the poor and wretched' (Edmund Burke, 'Reflections on the French Revolution', *Works*, v. 432).

But is it a cruel oppression to preach atheism? There is a sinister suggestion in this idea, namely the suggestion that we ought to preach religion whether or not it is true, and that we ought not to estimate rationally whether it is true, which implies that truth is below comfort in value.

It seems to me that religion buys its benefits at too high a price, namely at the price of abandoning the ideal of truth and shackling and perverting man's reason. The religious man refuses to be guided by reason and evidence in a certain field, the theory of the gods, theology. He does not say: 'I believe that there is a god, but I am willing to listen to argument that I am mistaken, and I shall be glad to learn better.' He does not seek to find and adopt the more probable of the two contradictories, 'there is a god' and 'there is no god'. On the contrary, he makes his choice between those two propositions once for all. He is determined never to revise his choice, but to believe that there is a god no matter what the evidence. The secretary of the Christian Evidence Society wrote to *The Times* (19 March 1953) and said: 'When demand is made upon devout Christians to produce evidence in justification of their intense faith in God they are apt to feel surprised, pained, and even disgusted that any such evidence should be considered necessary.' That is true. Christians do not take the attitude of reasonable inquiry towards the proposition that there is a god. If they engage in discussion on the matter at all, they seek more often to intimidate their opponent by expressing shock or disgust at his opinion, or disapproval of his character. They take the view that to hold the negative one of these two contradictories is a moral crime. They make certain beliefs wicked as such, without reference to the question whether the man has reached them sincerely and responsibly. This view, that certain beliefs are as such wicked, is implied in these two sentences in John's gospel (xvi. 8–9 and xx. 29): 'He will reprove the world of sin ... because they believe not on me', and 'Blessed are they that have not seen, and yet have believed'. There is an extensive example of this attitude in Newman's fifteenth sermon.

Along with the view that certain beliefs are as such wicked there often goes, naturally, the view that it is wicked to try to persuade a person to hold certan beliefs. The believer's complaint, 'you are undermining my faith', implies that it is wrong as such to try to convince a man that there is no god. It implies that whether one believes the proposition or not, and whether one has a good reason to believe it or not, are irrelevant, because it is just wrong in itself to recommend this proposition. This view is contrary to the search for truth and the reasonable attitude of listening to argument and guiding oneself thereby.

If theology were a part of reasonable inquiry, there would be no objection to an atheist's being a professor of theology. That a man's being an atheist is an absolute bar to his occupying a chair of theology proves that theology is not an open-minded and reasonable inquiry. Someone may object that a professor should be interested in his subject and an atheist cannot be interested in theology. But a man who maintains that there is no god must think it a sensible and interesting question to ask whether there is a god; and in fact we find that many atheists are interested in theology. Professor H. D. Lewis tells (*Philosophy*, 1952, p. 347) that an old lady asked him what philosophy is, and, when he had given an answer, she said: 'O I see, theology.' She was nearly right, for theology and philosophy have the same subject-matter. The difference is that in philosophy you are allowed to come out with whichever answer seems to you the more likely.

In most universities the title of theology includes a lot of perfectly good science which is not theory of god, and which I do not reject, I mean the scientific study of the history of the Jews and their languages and their religious books. All that can be reasonable study, and usually is so. But it is a hindrance to the progress of knowledge that we are largely organized for research in such a way that a man cannot be officially paid to engage in these branches of research unless he officially maintains that there is a god. It is as if a man could not be a professor of Greek unless he believed in Zeus and Apollo.

Religious persons often consider gambling to be a bad thing. It certainly causes a great deal of misery. But much of the badness of gambling consists in its refusal to face the probabilities and be guided by them; and in the matter of refusing to face the probabilities religion is a worse offender than gambling, and does more harm to the habits of reason. Religious belief is, in fact, a form of gambling, as Pascal saw. It does more harm to reason than ordinary gambling does, however, because it is more in earnest.

It has been said that the physicist has just as closed a mind about cause as the Christian has about god. The physicist assumes through thick and thin that everything happens according to causal laws. He presupposes cause, just as the Christian presupposes god.

But the physicist does not *assume* that there is a reign of law; he *hopes* that there is. He looks for laws; but, whenever a possible law occurs to him, he conscientiously tries to disprove it by all reasonable tests. He asserts at any time only such laws as seem at that time to have passed all reasonable tests, and he remains always prepared to hear of new evidence throwing doubt on those laws. This is far from the Christian attitude about god. The Christian does not merely hope that there is a god and maintain only such gods as the best tests have shown to be more probable than improbable.

The main irrationality of religion is preferring comfort to truth; and it is this that makes religion a very harmful thing on balance, a sort of endemic disease that has so far prevented human life from reaching its full stature. For the sake of comfort and security religion is prepared to sophisticate thought and language to any degree. For the sake of comfort and security there pours out daily, from pulpit and press, a sort of propaganda which, if it were put out for a non-religious purpose, would be seen by everyone to be cynical and immoral. We are perpetually being urged to adopt the Christian creed not because it is true but because it is beneficial, or to hold that it must be true just because belief in it is beneficial. 'The Christian faith', we are assured, 'is a necessity for a fully adjusted personality' (a psychiatrist in the *Radio Times* for 20 March 1953, p. 33). Hardly a week passes without someone recommending theism on the ground that if it were believed there would be much less crime; and this is a grossly immoral argument. Hardly a week passes without someone recommending theism on the ground that unless it is believed the free nations will succumb to the Communists; and that is the same grossly immoral argument. It is always wicked to recommend anybody to believe anything on the ground that he or anybody else will feel better or be more moral or successful for doing so, or on any ground whatever except that the available considerations indicate that it is probably true. The pragmatic suggestion, that we had better teach the Christian religion whether it is true or not, because people will be much less criminal if they believe it, is disgusting and degrading; but it is being made to us all the time, and it is a natural consequence of the fundamental religious attitude that comfort and security must always prevail over rational inquiry.

This pragmatic fallacy is not the only fallacy into which religion is frequently led by preferring comfortingness to truth, though it is the main one. The religious impulse encourages all the fallacies. It encourages the argument *ad hominem,* that is the argument that my adversary's view must be false because he is a wicked man: the atheist is impious, therefore he is wicked, therefore his view is false. Religion encourages also the argument from ignorance: instead of rejecting a proposition if it is probably false, the religious man thinks himself entitled to accept it because it is not certainly false. Biased selection of the instances is also very common in religious language. Any case of a man getting his wish after praying for it, or being struck by lightning after doing something mean, is taken as good evidence that there is a god who gives and punishes. Contrary cases are not looked for; and if they obtrude themselves they are dealt with by the further hypothesis that 'God's ways are inscrutable'. Religious arguments even exhibit, very often, what seems the most fallacious possible fallacy, namely inferring a theory from something that contradicts the theory. Thus we often find: 'since no explanation is final, God is the final explanation'; and 'since everybody believes in God, you are wrong not to believe in God'.

I have been saying that religion is gravely infected with intellectual dishonesty. You may find this very unlikely for a general reason. You may think it very unlikely that such widespread dishonesty would go unnoticed. I do not think so. I think, on the contrary, that it is quite common for a moral defect to pervade a certain sphere and yet escape notice in that sphere, although the people concerned are wide awake to its presence in other places. I think there are plenty of other cases of this. One of them is that the English, who are great haters of the bully and the might-is-right man, nevertheless bully and intimidate each other when driving a motor-car. They know that power does not confer any right, but they assume that horse-power does. Life is full of such inconsistencies, because we can never see all the implications and applications of our principles. In religion it is particularly easy for intellectual dishonesty to escape notice, because of the common assumption that all honesty flows from religion and religion is necessarily honest whatever it does.

Faith

According to Christianity one of the great virtues is faith. Paul gave faith a commanding position in the Christian scheme of values, along with hope and love, in the famous thirteenth chapter of his first letter to the Corinthians. Thomas Aquinas held that infidelity is a very great sin, that infidels should be compelled to believe, that heretics should not be tolerated, and that heretics who revert to the true doctrine and then relapse again should be received into penitence, but killed (*Summa Theologica*, 2-2.11.4).

According to me this is a terrible mistake, and faith is not a virtue but a positive vice. More precisely, there is, indeed, a virtue often called faith, but that is not the faith which the Christians make much of. The true virtue of faith is faith as opposed to faithlessness, that is, keeping faith and promises and being loyal. Christian faith, however, is not opposed to faithlessness but to unbelief. It is faith as some opposite of unbelief that I declare to be a vice.

When we investigate what Christians mean by their peculiar use of the word 'faith', I think we come to the remarkable conclusion that all their accounts of it are either unintelligible or false. Their most famous account is that in Heb. xi. 1: 'Faith is the substance of things hoped for, the evidence of things not seen.' This is obviously unintelligible. In any case, it does not make faith a virtue, since neither a substance nor an evidence can be a virtue. A virtue is a praiseworthy habit of choice, and neither a substance nor an evidence can be a habit of choice. When a Christian gives an intelligible account of faith, I think you will find that it is false. I mean that it is not a true dictionary report of how he and other Christians actually use the word. For example, Augustine asked: 'What is faith but believing what you do not see?' (*Joannis Evang. Tract.*, c. 40, § 8). But Christians do not use the word 'faith' in the sense of believing what you do not see. You do not see thunder; but you cannot say in the Christian sense 'have faith that it is thundering', or 'I have faith that it has thundered in the past and will again in the future'. You do not see mathematical truths; but you cannot say in the Christian sense 'have faith that there is no greatest number'. If we take Augustine's 'see' to stand here for 'know', still it is false that Christians use the word 'faith' to mean believing what you do not know, for they would never call it faith if anyone believed that the sun converts hydrogen into helium, although he did not know it.

A good hint of what Christians really mean by their word 'faith' can be got by considering the proposition: 'Tom Paine had faith that there is no god.' Is this a possible remark, in the Christian sense of the word 'faith'? No, it is an impossible remark, because it is self-contradictory, because part of what Christians mean by 'faith' is belief that there *is* a god.

There is more to it than this. Christian faith is not merely believing that there is a god. It is believing that there is a god no matter what the evidence on the question may be. 'Have faith', in the Christian sense, means 'make yourself believe that there is a god without regard to evidence.' Christian faith is a habit of flouting reason in forming and maintaining one's answer to the question whether there is a god. Its essence is the determination to believe that there is a god no matter what the evidence may be.

No wonder that there is no true and intelligible account of faith in Christian literature. What they mean is too shocking to survive exposure. Faith is a great vice, an example of obstinately refusing to listen to reason, something irrational and undesirable, a form of self-hypnotism. Newman wrote that 'if we but obey God strictly, in time (through His blessing) faith will become like sight' (*Sermon* XV). This is no better than if he had said: 'Keep on telling yourself that there is a god until you believe it. Hypnotize yourself into this belief.'

It follows that, far from its being wicked to undermine faith, it is a duty to do so. We ought to do what we can towards eradicating the evil habit of believing without regard to evidence.

The usual way of recommending faith is to point out that belief and trust are often rational or necessary attitudes. Here is an example of this from Newman: 'To hear some men speak, (I mean men who scoff at religion), it might be thought we never acted on Faith or Trust, except in religious matters; whereas we are acting on trust every hour of our lives. ... We trust our *memory* ... the general soundness of our reasoning powers. ... Faith in [the] sense of *reliance on the words of another* as opposed to trust in oneself ... is the common meaning of the word' (*Sermon* XV).

The value of this sort of argument is as follows. It is certainly true that belief and trust are often rational. But it is also certainly true that belief and trust are often irrational. We have to decide in each case by rational considerations whether to believe and trust or not. Sometimes we correctly decide *not* to trust our memory on some point, but to look the matter up in a book. Sometimes even we correctly decide not to trust our own reason, like poor Castlereagh deciding he was mad because the Duke of Wellington told him he was. But Christian faith is essentially a case of irrational belief and trust and decision, because it consists in deciding to believe and trust the proposition that there is a god no matter what the evidence may be.

Another common way to defend Christian faith is to point out that we are often obliged to act on something less than knowledge and proof. For example, Newman writes: 'Life is not long enough for a religion of inferences; we shall never have done beginning if we determine to begin with proof. Life is for action. If we insist on proof for everything, we shall never come to action; to act you must assume, and that assumption is faith' (*Assent,* p. 92).

The value of this argument is as follows. It is true that we are often unable to obtain knowledge and proof. But it does not follow that we must act on faith, for faith is belief reckless of evidence and probability. It follows only that we must act on some belief that does not amount to knowledge. This being so, we ought to assume, as our basis for action, those beliefs which are more probable than their contradictories in the light of the available evidence. We ought not to act on faith, for faith is assuming a certain belief without reference to its probability.

There is an ambiguity in the phrase 'have faith in' that helps to make faith look respectable. When a man says that he has faith in the president he is assuming that it is obvious and known to everybody that there is a president, that the president exists, and he is asserting his confidence that the president will do good work on the whole. But, if a man says he has faith in telepathy, he does not mean that he is confident that telepathy will do good work on the whole, but that he believes that telepathy really occurs sometimes, that telepathy exists. Thus the phrase 'to have faith in x' sometimes means to be confident that good work will be done by x, who is assumed or known to exist, but at other times means to believe that x exists. Which does it mean in the phrase 'have faith in God'? It means ambiguously both; and the selfevidence of what it means in the one sense recommends what it means in the other sense. If there is a perfectly powerful and good god it is selfevidently reasonable to believe that he will do good. In this sense 'have faith in God' is a reasonable exhortation. But it insinuates the other sense, namely 'believe that there is a perfectly powerful and good god, no matter what the evidence'. Thus the reasonableness of trusting God if he exists is used to make it seem also reasonable to believe that he exists.

It is well to remark here that a god who wished us to decide certain questions without regard to the evidence would definitely *not* be a perfectly good god.

Even when a person is aware that faith is belief without regard to evidence, he may be led to hold faith respectable by the consideration that we sometimes think it good for a man to believe in his friend's honesty in spite of strong evidence to the contrary, or for a woman to believe in her son's innocence in spite of strong evidence to the contrary. But, while we admire and love the love that leads the friend or parent to this view, we do not adopt or admire his conclusion unless we believe that he has private evidence of his own, gained by his long and intimate association, to outweigh the public evidence on the other side. Usually we suppose that his love has led him into an error of judgment, which both love and hate are prone to do.

This does not imply that we should never act on a man's word if we think he is deceiving us. Sometimes we ought to act on a man's word although we privately think he is probably lying. For the act required may be unimportant, whereas accusing a man of lying is always important. But there is no argument from this to faith. We cannot say that sometimes we ought to believe a proposition although we think it is false!

So I conclude that faith is a vice and to be condemned. As Plato said, 'It is unholy to abandon the probably true' (*Rp.* 607 c). Out of Paul's 'faith, hope, and love' I emphatically accept love and reject faith. As to hope, it is more respectable than faith. While we ought not to believe against the probabilities, we are permitted to hope against them. But still the Christian overtones of hope are otherworldly and unrealistic. It is better to take a virtue that avoids that. Instead of faith, hope, and love, let us hymn reason, love, and joy.

What is the application of this to the common phrase 'a faith to live by'? A faith to live by is not necessarily a set of beliefs or valuations maintained without regard to evidence in an irrational way. The phrase can well cover also a criticized and rational choice of values. To decide, for example, that the pursuit of love is better than the pursuit of power, in view of the probable effects of each on human happiness and misery, and to guide one's actions accordingly, is a rational procedure, and is sometimes called and may well be called 'a faith to live by'. In this case a faith to live by is a choice of values, a decision as to great goods and evils, and is what I am doing in these lectures. On the other hand, many 'faiths to live by' are irrational and bad. Some people will not count anything as a faith to live by unless it deliberately ignores rational considerations; so that what they will consent to call a faith to live by must always be something that is bad according to me. Other people refuse to count anything as a faith to live by unless it includes a belief that the big battalions are on their side, so that according to them a man who rationally concludes that he is not the darling of any god by definition has no faith to live by.

The Will to Believe   William James

William James (1842–1910) is considered one of America's greatest philosophers. He attended Harvard Medical School and later taught anatomy and physiology at Harvard. Later his interests were primarily in the fields of psychology and philosophy. He is considered one of the main developers of pragmatism.

... I have long defended to my own students the lawfulness of voluntarily adopted faith; but as soon as they have got well imbued with the logical spirit, they have as a rule refused to admit my contention to be lawful philosophically, even though in point of fact they were personally all the time chock-full of some faith or other themselves. I am all the while, however, so profoundly convinced that my own position is correct, that your invitation has seemed to me a good occasion to make my statements more clear. Perhaps your minds will be more open than those with which I have hitherto had to deal. I will be as little technical as I can, though I must begin by setting up some technical distinctions that will help us in the end.

Let us give the name of *hypothesis* to anything that may be proposed to our belief; and just as the electricians speak of live and dead wires, let us

From William James, *The Will to Believe*. Reprinted from the Dover Publications, edition published in 1960.

speak of any hypothesis as either *live* or *dead*. A live hypothesis is one which appeals as a real possibility to him to whom it is proposed. If I ask you to believe in the Mahdi, the notion makes no electric connection with your nature,—it refuses to scintillate with any credibility at all. As an hypothesis it is completely dead. To an Arab, however (even if he be not one of the Mahdi's followers), the hypothesis is among the mind's possibilities: it is alive. This shows that deadness and liveness in an hypothesis are not intrinsic properties, but relations to the individual thinker. They are measured by his willingness to act. The maximum of liveness in an hypothesis means willingness to act irrevocably. Practically, that means belief; but there is some believing tendency wherever there is willingness to act at all.

Next, let us call the decision between two hypotheses an *option*. Options may be of several kinds. They may be—1, *living* or *dead*; 2, *forced* or *avoidable*; 3, *momentous* or *trivial*; and for our purposes we may call an option a *genuine* option when it is of the forced, living, and momentous kind.

1. A living option is one in which both hypotheses are live ones. If I say to you: "Be a theosophist or be a Mohammedan," it is probably a dead option, because for you neither hypothesis is likely to be alive. But if I say: "Be an agnostic or be a Christian," it is otherwise: trained as you are, each hypothesis makes some appeal, however small, to your belief.

2. Next, if I say to you: "Choose between going out with your umbrella or without it," I do not offer you a genuine option, for it is not forced. You can easily avoid it by not going out at all. Similarly, if I say, "Either love me or hate me," "Either call my theory true or call it false," your option is avoidable. You may remain indifferent to me, neither loving nor hating, and you may decline to offer any judgment as to my theory. But if I say, "Either accept this truth or go without it," I put on you a forced option, for there is no standing place outside of the alternative. Every dilemma based on a complete logical disjunction, with no possibility of not choosing, is an option of this forced kind.

3. Finally, if I were Dr. Nansen and proposed to you to join my North Pole expedition, your option would be momentous; for this would probably be your only similar opportunity, and your choice now would either exclude you from the North Pole sort of immortality altogether or put at least the chance of it into your hands. He who refuses to embrace a unique opportunity loses the prize as surely as if he tried and failed. *Per contra*, the option is trivial when the opportunity is not unique, when the stake is insignificant, or when the decision is reversible if it later prove unwise. Such trivial options abound in the scientific life. A chemist finds an hypothesis live enough to spend a year in its verification: he believes in it to that extent. But if his experiments prove inconclusive either way, he is quit for his loss of time, no vital harm being done.

It will facilitate our discussion if we keep all these distinctions well in mind. . . .

The thesis I defend is, briefly stated, this: *Our passional nature not only lawfully may, but must, decide an option between propositions, whenever it is a genuine option that cannot by its nature be decided on*

intellectual grounds; for to say, under such circumstances, "Do not de-
cide, but leave the question open," is itself a passional decision,—just like
deciding yes or no,—and is attended with the same risk of losing the
truth. . . .

Wherever the option between losing truth and gaining it is not momentous, we can throw the chance of *gaining truth* away, and at any rate
save ourselves from any chance of *believing falsehood,* by not making up
our minds at all till objective evidence has come. In scientific questions,
this is almost always the case; and even in human affairs in general, the
need of acting is seldom so urgent that a false belief to act on is better
than no belief at all. Law courts, indeed, have to decide on the best evidence attainable for the moment, because a judge's duty is to make law
as well as to ascertain it, and (as a learned judge once said to me) few
cases are worth spending much time over: the great thing is to have them
decided on *any* acceptable principle, and got out of the way. But in our
dealings with objective nature we obviously are recorders, not makers,
of the truth; and decisions for the mere sake of deciding promptly
and getting on to the next business would be wholly out of place.
Throughout the breadth of physical nature facts are what they are
quite independently of us, and seldom is there any such hurry about
them that the risks of being duped by believing a premature theory need
be faced. The questions here are always trivial options, the hypotheses are
hardly living (at any rate not living for us spectators), the choice between
believing truth or falsehood is seldom forced. The attitude of sceptical
balance is therefore the absolutely wise one if we would escape mistakes.
What difference, indeed, does it make to most of us whether we have or
have not a theory of the Röntgen rays, whether we believe or not in
mind-stuff, or have a conviction about the causality of conscious states? It
makes no difference. Such options are not forced on us. On every account
it is better not to make them, but still keep weighing reasons *pro et*
contra with an indifferent hand.

I speak, of course, here of the purely judging mind. For purposes of
discovery such indifference is to be less highly recommended, and science
would be far less advanced than she is if the passionate desires of individuals to get their own faiths confirmed had been kept out of the game.
. . . On the other hand, if you want an absolute duffer in an investigation,
you must, after all, take the man who has no interest whatever in its
results: he is the warranted incapable, the positive fool. The most useful
investigator, because the most sensitive observer, is always he whose
eager interest in one side of the question is balanced by an equally keen
nervousness lest he become deceived. Science has organized this nervousness into a regular *technique,* her so-called method of verification; and
she has fallen so deeply in love with the method that one may even say
she has ceased to care for truth by itself at all. It is only truth as technically verified that interests her. The truth of truths might come in
merely affirmative form, and she would decline to touch it. Such truth as
that, she might repeat with Clifford, would be stolen in defiance of her
duty to mankind. Human passions, however, are stronger than technical
rules. "Le coeur a ses raisons," as Pascal says, "que la raison ne connaît

pas";* and however indifferent to all but the bare rules of the game the umpire, the abstract intellect, may be, the concrete players who furnish him the materials to judge of are usually, each one of them, in love with some pet 'live hypothesis' of his own. Let us agree, however, that wherever there is no forced option, the dispassionately judicial intellect with no pet hypothesis, saving us, as it does, from dupery at any rate, ought to be our ideal.

The question next arises: Are there not somewhere forced options in our speculative questions, and can we (as men who may be interested at least as much in positively gaining truth as in merely escaping dupery) always wait with impunity till the coercive evidence shall have arrived? It seems *a priori* improbable that the truth should be so nicely adjusted to our needs and powers as that. In the great boarding-house of nature, the cakes and the butter and the syrup seldom come out so even and leave the plates so clean. Indeed, we should view them with scientific suspicion if they did.

Moral questions immediately present themselves as questions whose solution cannot wait for sensible proof. A moral question is a question not of what sensibly exists, but of what is good, or would be good if it did exist. Science can tell us what exists; but to compare the *worths,* both of what exists and of what does not exist, we must consult not science, but what Pascal calls our heart. Science herself consults her heart when she lays it down that the infinite ascertainment of fact and correction of false belief are the supreme goods for man. Challenge the statement, and science can only repeat it oracularly, or else prove it by showing that such ascertainment and correction bring man all sorts of other goods which man's heart in turn declares. The question of having moral beliefs at all or not having them is decided by our will. Are our moral preferences true or false, or are they only odd biological phenomena, making things good or bad for *us,* but in themselves indifferent? How can your pure intellect decide? If your heart does not *want* a world of moral reality, your head will assuredly never make you believe in one. Mephistophelian scepticism, indeed, will satisfy the head's play-instincts much better than any rigorous idealism can. Some men (even at the student age) are so naturally cool-hearted that the moralistic hypothesis never has for them any pungent life, and in their supercilious presence the hot young moralist always feels strangely ill at ease. The appearance of knowingness is on their side, of *naïveté* and gullibility on his. Yet, in the inarticulate heart of him, he clings to it that he is not a dupe, and that there is a realm in which (as Emerson says) all their wit and intellectual superiority is no better than the cunning of a fox. Moral scepticism can no more be refuted or proved by logic than intellectual scepticism can. When we stick to it that there *is* truth (be it of either kind), we do so with our whole nature, and resolve to stand or fall by the resuls. The sceptic with his whole nature adopts the doubting attitude; but which of us is the wiser, Omniscience only knows.

Turn now from these wide questions of good to a certain class of

* [The heart has its reasons that reason does not know.—ed.]

questions of fact, questions concerning personal relations, states of mind between one man and another. *Do you like me or not?*—for example. Whether you do or not depends, in countless instances, on whether I meet you half-way, am willing to assume that you must like me, and show you trust and expectation. The previous faith on my part in your liking's existence is in such cases what makes your liking come. But if I stand aloof, and refuse to budge an inch until I have objective evidence, until you shall have done something apt, as the absolutists say, *ad extorquendum assensum meum,* ten to one your liking never comes. How many women's hearts are vanquished by the mere sanguine insistence of some man that they *must* love him! he will not consent to the hypothesis that they cannot. The desire for a certain kind of truth here brings about that special truth's existence; and so it is in innumerable cases of other sorts. Who gains promotions, boons, appointments, but the man in whose life they are seen to play the part of live hypotheses, who discounts them, sacrifices other things for their sake before they have come, and takes risks for them in advance? His faith acts on the powers above him as a claim, and creates its own verification.

A social organism of any sort whatever, large or small, is what it is because each member proceeds to his own duty with a trust that the other members will simultaneously do theirs. Wherever a desired result is achieved by the co-operation of many independent persons, its existence as a fact is a pure consequence of the precursive faith in one another of those immediately concerned. A government, an army, a commercial system, a ship, a college, an athletic team, all exist on this condition, without which not only is nothing achieved, but nothing is even attempted. A whole train of passengers (individually brave enough) will be looted by a few highwaymen, simply because the latter can count on one another, while each passenger fears that if he makes a movement of resistance, he will be shot before any one else backs him up. If we believed that the whole car-full would rise at once with us, we should each severally rise, and train-robbing would never even be attempted. There are, then, cases where a fact cannot come at all unless a preliminary faith exists in its coming. *And where faith in a fact can help create the fact,* that would be an insane logic which should say that faith running ahead of scientific evidence is the 'lowest kind of immorality' into which a thinking being can fall. Yet such is the logic by which our scientific absolutists pretend to regulate our lives!

In truths dependent on our personal action, then, faith based on desire is certainly a lawful and possibly an indispensable thing.

But now, it will be said, these are all childish human cases, and have nothing to do with great cosmical matters, like the question of religious faith. Let us then pass on to that. Religions differ so much in their accidents that in discussing the religious question we must make it very generic and broad. What then do we now mean by the religious hypothesis? Science says things are; morality says some things are better than other things; and religion says essentially two things.

First, she says that the best things are the more eternal things, the overlapping things, the things in the universe that throw the last stone, so to speak, and say the final word. "Perfection is eternal,"—this phrase of Charles Secrétan seems a good way of putting his first affirmation of religion, an affirmation which obviously cannot yet be verified scientifically at all.

The second affirmation of religion is that we are better off even now if we believe her first affirmation to be true.

Now, let us consider what the logical elements of this situation are *in case the religious hypothesis in both its branches be really true.* (Of course, we must admit that possibility at the outset. If we are to discuss the question at all, it must involve a living option. If for any of you religion be a hypothesis that cannot, by any living possibility be true, then you need go no farther. I speak to the 'saving remnant' alone.) So proceeding, we see, first, that religion offers itself as a *momentous* option. We are supposed to gain, even now, by our belief, and to lose by our nonbelief, a certain vital good. Secondly, religion is a *forced* option, so far as that good goes. We cannot escape the issue by remaining sceptical and waiting for more light, because, although we do avoid error in that way *if religion be untrue,* we lose the good, *if it be true,* just as certainly as if we positively chose to disbelieve. It is as if a man should hesitate indefinitely to ask a certain woman to marry him because he was not perfectly sure that she would prove an angel after he brought her home. Would he not cut himself off from that particular angel-possibility as decisively as if he went and married some one else? Scepticism, then, is not avoidance of option; it is option of a certain particular kind of risk. *Better risk loss of truth than chance of error,*—that is your faith-vetoer's exact position. He is actively playing his stake as much as the believer is; he is backing the field against the religious hypothesis, just as the believer is backing the religious hypothesis against the field. To preach scepticism to us as a duty until 'sufficient evidence' for religion be found, is tantamount therefore to telling us, when in presence of the religious hypothesis, that to yield to our fear of its being error is wiser and better than to yield to our hope that it may be true. It is not intellect against all passions, then; it is only intellect with one passion laying down its law. And by what, forsooth, is the supreme wisdom of this passion warranted? Dupery for dupery, what proof is there that dupery through hope is so much worse than dupery through fear? I, for one, can see no proof; and I simply refuse obedience to the scientist's command to imitate his kind of option, in a case where my own stake is important enough to give me the right to choose my own form of risk. If religion be true and the evidence for it be still insufficient, I do not wish, by putting your extinguisher upon my nature (which feels to me as if it had after all some business in this matter), to forfeit my sole chance in life of getting upon the winning side,—that chance depending, of course, on my willingness to run the risk of acting as if my passional need of taking the world religiously might be prophetic and right.

All this is on the supposition that it really may be prophetic and right, and that, even to us who are discussing the matter, religion is a live hypothesis which may be true. Now, to most of us religion comes in a still further way that makes a veto on our active faith even more illogical. The more perfect and more eternal aspect of the universe is represented in our religions as having personal form. The universe is no longer a mere *It* to us, but a *Thou*, if we are religious; and any relation that may be possible from person to person might be possible here. For instance, although in one sense we are passive portions of the universe, in another we show a curious autonomy, as if we were small active centres on our own account. We feel, too, as if the appeal of religion to us were made to our own active good-will, as if evidence might be forever withheld from us unless we met the hypothesis half-way. To take a trivial illustration: just as a man who in a company of gentlemen made no advances, asked a warrant for every concession, and believed no one's word without proof, would cut himself off by such churlishness from all the social rewards that a more trusting spirit would earn,—so here, one who should shut himself up in snarling logicality and try to make the gods extort his recognition willy-nilly, or not get it at all, might cut himself off forever from his only opportunity of making the gods' acquaintance. This feeling, forced on us we know not whence, that by obstinately believing that there are gods (although not to do so would be so easy both for our logic and our life) we are doing the universe the deepest service we can, seems part of the living essence of the religious hypothesis. If the hypothesis *were* true in all its parts, including this one, then pure intellectualism, with its veto on our making willing advances, would be an absurdity; and some participation of our sympathetic nature would be logically required. I, therefore, for one, cannot see my way to accepting the agnostic rules for truth-seeking, or wilfully agree to keep my willing nature out of the game. I cannot do so for this plain reason, that *a rule of thinking which would absolutely prevent me from acknowledging certain kinds of truth if those kinds of truth were really there, would be an irrational rule.* That for me is the long and short of the formal logic of the situation, no matter what the kinds of truth might materially be.

I confess I do not see how this logic can be escaped. But sad experience makes me fear that some of you may still shrink from radically saying with me, *in abstracto,* that we have the right to believe at our own risk any hypothesis that is live enough to tempt our will. I suspect, however, that if this is so, it is because you have got away from the abstract logical point of view altogether, and are thinking (perhaps without realizing it) of some particular religious hypothesis which for you is dead. The freedom to 'believe what we will' you apply to the case of some patent superstition; and the faith you think of is the faith defined by the schoolboy when he said, "Faith is when you believe something that you know ain't true." I can only repeat that this is misapprehension. *In concreto,* the freedom to believe can only cover living options which the intellect of the individual cannot by itself resolve; and living options never seem absurdities to him who has them to consider. When I look at the religious question as it really puts itself to concrete men, and when I think of all the possibilities which both practically and theoretically it involves, then this command that we shall put a stopper on our heart, instincts, and courage, and *wait*—acting of course meanwhile more or less as if religion were *not* true—till doomsday, or till such time as our intellect and senses working together may have raked in evidence enough,—

this command, I say, seems to me the queerest idol ever manufactured in the philosophic cave. Were we scholastic absolutists, there might be more excuse. If we had an infallible intellect with its objective certitudes, we might feel ourselves disloyal to such a perfect organ of knowledge in not trusting to it exclusively, in not waiting for its releasing word. But if we are empiricists, if we believe that no bell in us tolls to let us know for certain when truth is in our grasp, then it seems a piece of idle fantasticality to preach so solemnly our duty of waiting for the bell. Indeed we *may* wait if we will,—I hope you do not think that I am denying that, —but if we do so, we do so at our peril as much as if we believed. In either case we *act,* taking our life in our hands. No one of us ought to issue vetoes to the other, nor should we bandy words of abuse. We ought, on the contrary, delicately and profoundly to respect one another's mental freedom: then only shall we bring about the intellectual republic; then only shall we have that spirit of inner tolerance without which all our outer tolerance is soulless, and which is empiricism's glory; then only shall we live and let live, in speculative as well as in practical things. . . .

Is Religion Necessary to Give Meaning to Life?

The Grand Inquisitor   Fyodor Dostoevsky

Fyodor Mikhailovich Dostoevsky (1821–1881), a Russian, is generally considered one of the world's greatest novelists. His most famous novels are *Crime and Punishment* and *The Brothers Karamazov.*

"My story is laid in Spain, in Seville, in the most terrible time of the Inquisition, when fires were lighted every day to the glory of God, and 'in the splendid *auto da fé* the wicked heretics were burnt.' Oh, of course, this was not the coming in which He will appear according to His promise at the end of time in all His heavenly glory, and which will be sudden 'as lightning flashing from east to west.' No, He visited His children only for a moment, and there where the flames were crackling round the heretics. In His infinite mercy He came once more among men in that human shape in which He walked among men for three years fifteen centuries ago. He came down to the 'hot pavement' of the southern town in which on the day before almost a hundred heretics had, *ad majorem gloriam Dei,* been burnt by the cardinal, the Grand Inquisitor, in a magnificent *auto da fé,* in the presence of the king, the court, the knights, the cardinals, the most charming ladies of the court, and the whole population of Seville.

"He came softly, unobserved, and yet, strange to say, every one

From *The Brothers Karamazov,* translated by Constance Garnett. Published by the Modern Library, 1937. Reprinted by permission of Random House, Inc.

recognised Him. That might be one of the best passages in the poem. I mean, why they recognised Him. The people are irresistibly drawn to Him, they surround Him, they flock about Him, follow Him. He moves silently in their midst with a gentle smile of infinite compassion. The sun of love burns in His heart, light and power shine from His eyes, and their radiance, shed on the people, stirs their hearts with responsive love. He holds out His hands to them, blesses them, and a healing virtue comes from contact with Him, even with His garments. An old man in the crowd, blind from childhood, cries out, 'O Lord, heal me and I shall see Thee!' and, as it were, scales fall from his eyes and the blind man sees Him. The crowd weeps and kisses the earth under His feet. Children throw flowers before Him, sing, and cry hosannah. 'It is He—it is He!' all repeat. 'It must be He, it can be no one but Him!' He stops at the steps of the Seville cathedral at the moment when the weeping mourners are bringing in a little open white coffin. In it lies a child of seven, the only daughter of a prominent citizen. The dead child lies hidden in flowers. 'He will raise your child,' the crowd shouts to the weeping mother. The priest, coming to meet the coffin, looks perplexed, and frowns, but the mother of the dead child throws herself at His feet with a wail. 'If it is Thou, raise my child!' she cries, holding out her hands to Him. The procession halts, the coffin is laid on the steps at His feet. He looks with compassion, and His lips once more softly pronounce, 'Maiden, arise!' and the maiden arises. The little girl sits up in the coffin and looks round, smiling with wide-open wondering eyes, holding a bunch of white roses they had put in her hand.

"There are cries, sobs, confusion among the people, and at that moment the cardinal himself, the Grand Inquisitor, passes by the cathedral. He is an old man, almost ninety, tall and erect, with a withered face and sunken eyes, in which there is still a gleam of light. He is not dressed in his gorgeous cardinal's robes, as he was the day before, when he was burning the enemies of the Roman Church—at that moment he was wearing his coarse, old, monk's cassock. At a distance behind him come his gloomy assistants and slaves and the 'holy guard.' He stops at the sight of the crowd and watches it from a distance. He sees everything; he sees them set the coffin down at His feet, sees the child rise up, and his face darkens. He knits his thick grey brows and his eyes gleam with a sinister fire. He holds out his finger and bids the guards take Him. And such is his power, so completely are the people cowed into submission and trembling obedience to him, that the crowd immediately make way for the guards, and in the midst of deathlike silence they lay hands on Him and lead Him away. The crowd instantly bows down to the earth, like one man, before the old inquisitor. He blesses the people in silence and passes on. The guards lead their prisoner to the close, gloomy vaulted prison in the ancient palace of the Holy Inquisition and shut Him in it. The day passes and is followed by the dark, burning 'breathless' night of Seville. The air is 'fragrant with laurel and lemon.' In the pitch darkness the iron door of the prison is suddenly opened and the Grand Inquisitor himself comes in with a light in his hand. He is alone; the door is closed at once behind him. He stands in the doorway and for a minute or two gazes into His face. At last he goes up slowly, sets the light on the table and speaks.

" 'Is it Thou? Thou?' but receiving no answer, he adds at once, 'Don't answer, be silent. What canst Thou say, indeed? I know too well what Thou wouldst say. And Thou hast no right to add anything to what Thou hadst said of old. Why, then, art Thou come to hinder us? For Thou hast come to hinder us, and Thou knowest that. But dost Thou know what will be to-morrow? I know not who Thou art and care not to know whether it is Thou or only a semblance of Him, but to-morrow I shall condemn Thee and burn Thee at the stake as the worst of heretics. And the very people who have to-day kissed Thy feet, to-morrow at the faintest sign from me will rush to heap up the embers of Thy fire. Knowest Thou that? Yes, maybe Thou knowest it,' he added with thoughtful penetration, never for a moment taking his eyes off the Prisoner."

"I don't quite understand, Ivan. What does it mean?" Alyosha, who had been listening in silence, said with a smile. "Is it simply a wild fantasy, or a mistake on the part of the old man—some impossible *qui pro quo?*"

"Take it as the last," said Ivan, laughing, "if you are so corrupted by modern realism and can't stand anything fantastic. If you like it to be a case of mistaken identity, let it be so. It is true," he went on, laughing, "the old man was ninety, and he might well be crazy over his set idea. He might have been struck by the appearance of the Prisoner. It might, in fact, be simply his ravings, the delusion of an old man of ninety, over-excited by the *auto da fé* of a hundred heretics the day before. But does it matter to us after all whether it was a mistake of identity or a wild fantasy? All that matters is that the old man should speak out, should speak openly of what he has thought in silence for ninety years."

"And the Prisoner too is silent? Does He look at him and not say a word?"

"That's inevitable in any case," Ivan laughed again. "The old man has told Him He hasn't the right to add anything to what He has said of old. One may say it is the most fundamental feature of Roman Catholicism, in my opinion at least. 'All has been given by Thee to the Pope,' they say, 'and all, therefore, is still in the Pope's hands, and there is no need for Thee to come now at all. Thou must not meddle for the time, at least.' That's how they speak and write too—the Jesuits, at any rate. I have read it myself in the works of their theologians. 'Hast Thou the right to reveal to us one of the mysteries of that world from which Thou hast come?' my old man asks Him, and answers the question for Him. 'No, Thou hast not; that Thou mayest not add to what has been said of old, and mayest not take from men the freedom which Thou didst exalt when Thou wast on earth. Whatsoever Thou revealest anew will encroach on men's freedom of faith; for it will be manifest as a miracle, and the freedom of their faith was dearer to Thee than anything in those days fifteen hundred years ago. Didst Thou not often say then, "I will make you free"? But now Thou has seen these "free" men,' the old man adds suddenly, with a pensive smile. 'Yes, we've paid dearly for it,' he goes on, looking sternly at Him, 'but at last we have completed that work in Thy name. For fifteen centuries we have been wrestling with Thy freedom, but now it is ended and over for good. Dost Thou not believe that it's over for good? Thou lookest meekly at me and deignest not even to be wroth with me. But let me tell Thee that now, to-day, people are more persuaded than ever that they have perfect freedom, yet they have brought their freedom to us and laid it humbly at our feet. But that has been our doing. Was this what Thou didst? Was this Thy freedom?' "

"I don't understand again," Alyosha broke in. "Is he ironical, is he jesting?"

"Not a bit of it! He claims it as a merit for himself and his Church that at last they have vanquished freedom and have done so to make men happy. 'For now' (he is speaking of the Inquisition, of course) 'for the first time it has become possible to think of the happiness of men. Man was created a rebel; and how can rebels be happy? Thou wast warned,' he says to Him. 'Thou hast had no lack of admonitions and warnings, but Thou didst not listen to those warnings; Thou didst reject the only way by which men might be made happy. But, fortunately, departing Thou didst hand on the work to us. Thou has promised, Thou hast established by Thy word, Thou hast given to us the right to bind and to unbind, and now, of course, Thou canst not think of taking it away. Why, then, hast Thou come to hinder us?' "

"And what's the meaning of 'no lack of admonitions and warnings'?" asked Alyosha.

"Why, that's the chief part of what the old man must say."

" 'The wise and dread Spirit, the spirit of self-destruction and non-existence,' the old man goes on, 'the great spirit talked with Thee in the wilderness, and we are told in the books that he "tempted" Thee. Is that so? And could anything truer be said than what he revealed to Thee in three questions and what Thou didst reject, and what in the books is called "the temptation"? And yet if there has ever been on earth a real stupendous miracle, it took place on that day, on the day of the three temptations. The statement of those three questions was itself the miracle. If it were possible to imagine simply for the sake of argument that those three questions of the dread spirit had perished utterly from the books, and that we had to restore them and to invent them anew, and to do so had gathered together all the wise men of the earth—rulers, chief priests, learned men, philosophers, poets—and had set them the task to invent three questions, such as would not only fit the occasion, but express in three words, three human phrases, the whole future history of the world and of humanity—dost Thou believe that all the wisdom of the earth united could have invented anything in depth and force equal to the three questions which were actually put to Thee then by the wise and mighty spirit in the wilderness? From those questions alone, from the miracle of their statement, we can see that we have here to do not with the fleeting human intelligence, but with the absolute and eternal. For in those three questions the whole subsequent history of mankind is, as it were, brought together into one whole, and foretold, and in them are united all the unsolved historical contradictions of human nature. At the time it could not be so clear, since the future was unknown; but now that fifteen hundred years have passed, we see that everything in those three questions was so justly divined and foretold, and has been so truly fulfilled, that nothing can be added to them or taken from them.

" 'Judge Thyself who was right—Thou or he who questioned Thee then? Remember the first question; its meaning, in other words, was this: "Thou wouldst go into the world, and art going with empty hands, with some promise of freedom which men in their simplicity and their natural unruliness cannot even understand, which they fear and dread— for nothing has ever been more insupportable for a man and a human society than freedom. But seest Thou these stones in this parched and barren wilderness? Turn them into bread, and mankind will run after Thee like a flock of sheep, grateful and obedient, though for ever trembling, lest Thou withdraw Thy hand and deny them Thy bread." But Thou wouldst not deprive man of freedom and didst reject the offer, thinking, what is that freedom worth, if obedience is bought with bread? Thou didst reply that man lives not by bread alone. But dost Thou know that for the sake of that earthly bread the spirit of the earth will rise up against Thee and will strive with Thee and overcome Thee, and all will follow him, crying, "Who can compare with this beast? He has given us fire from heaven!" Dost Thou know that the ages will pass, and humanity will proclaim by the lips of their sages that there is no crime, and therefore no sin; there is only hunger? "Feed men, and then ask of them virtue!" that's what they'll write on the banner, which they will raise against Thee, and with which they will destroy Thy temple. Where Thy temple stood will rise a new building; the terrible tower of Babel will be built again, and though, like the one of old, it will not be finished, yet Thou mightest have prevented that new tower and have cut short the sufferings of men for a thousand years; for they will come back to us after a thousand years of agony with their tower. They will seek us again, hidden underground in the catacombs, for we shall be again persecuted and tortured. They will find us and cry to us, "Feed us, for those who have promised us fire from heaven haven't given it!" And then we shall finish building their tower, for he finishes the building who feeds them. And we alone shall feed them in Thy name, declaring falsely that it is in Thy name. Oh, never, never can they feed themselves without us! No science will give them bread so long as they remain free. In the end they will lay their freedom at our feet, and say to us, "Make us your slaves, but feed us." They will understand themselves, at last, that freedom and bread enough for all are inconceivable together, for never, never will they be able to share between them! They will be convinced, too, that they can never be free, for they are weak, vicious, worthless and rebellious. Thou didst promise them the bread of Heaven, but, I repeat again, can it compare with earthly bread in the eyes of the weak, ever sinful and ignoble race of man? And if for the sake of the bread of Heaven thousands and tens of thousands shall follow Thee, what is to become of the millions and tens of thousands of millions of creatures who will not have the strength to forego the earthly bread for the sake of the heavenly? Or dost Thou care only for the tens of thousands of the great and strong, while the millions, numerous as the sands of the sea, who are weak but love Thee, must exist only for the sake of the great and strong? No, we care for the weak too. They are sinful and rebellious, but in the end they too will become obedient. They will marvel at us and look on us as gods, because we are ready to endure the freedom which they have found so dreadful and to rule over them—so awful it will seem to them to be free. But we shall tell them that we are Thy servants and rule them in Thy name. We shall deceive them again, for we will not let Thee come to us again. That deception will be our suffering, for we shall be forced to lie.

" 'This is the significance of the first question in the wilderness, and this is what Thou hast rejected for the sake of that freedom which Thou hast exalted above everything. Yet in this question lies hid the great secret of this world. Choosing "bread," Thou wouldst have satisfied the universal and everlasting craving of humanity—to find some one to worship. So long as man remains free he strives for nothing so incessantly and so painfully as to find some one to worship. But man seeks to worship what is established beyond dispute, so that all men would agree at once to worship it. For these pitiful creatures are concerned not only to find what one or the other can worship, but to find something that all would believe in and worship; what is essential is that all may be *together* in it. This craving for *community* of worship is the chief misery of every man individually and of all humanity from the beginning of time. For the sake of common worship they've slain each other with the sword. They have set up gods and challenged one another, "Put away your gods and come and worship ours, or we will kill you and your gods!" And so it will be to the end of the world, even when gods disappear from the earth; they will fall down before idols just the same. Thou didst know, Thou couldst not but have known, this fundamental secret of human nature, but Thou didst reject the one infallible banner which was offered Thee to make all men bow down to Thee alone—the banner of earthly bread; and Thou hast rejected it for the sake of freedom and the bread of Heaven. Behold what Thou didst further. And all again in the name of freedom! I tell Thee that man is tormented by no greater anxiety than to find some one quickly to whom he can hand over that gift of freedom with which the ill-fated creature is born. But only one who can appease their conscience can take over their freedom. In bread there was offered Thee an invincible banner; give bread, and man will worship Thee, for nothing is more certain than bread. But if some one else gains possession of his conscience —oh! then he will cast away Thy bread and follow after him who has ensnared his conscience. In that Thou wast right. For the secret of man's being is not only to live but to have something to live for. Without a stable conception of the object of life, man would not consent to go on living, and would rather destroy himself than remain on earth, though he had bread in abundance. That is true. But what happened? Instead of taking men's freedom from them, Thou didst make it greater than ever! Didst Thou forget that man prefers peace, and even death, to freedom of choice in the knowledge of good and evil? Nothing is more seductive for man than his freedom of conscience, but nothing is a greater cause of suffering. And behold, instead of giving a firm foundation for setting the conscience of man at rest for ever, Thou didst choose all that is exceptional, vague and enigmatic; Thou didst choose what was utterly beyond the strength of men, acting as though Thou didst not love them at all—Thou who didst come to give Thy life for them! Instead of taking possession of men's freedom, Thou didst increase it, and burdened the spiritual kingdom of mankind with its sufferings for ever. Thou didst desire man's free love, that he should follow Thee freely, enticed and taken captive by Thee. In place of the rigid ancient law, man must hereafter with free heart decide for himself what is good and what is evil, having only Thy image before him as his guide. But didst Thou not know he would at last reject even Thy image and Thy truth, if he is weighed down with the fearful burden of free choice? They will cry aloud at last that the truth is not in Thee, for they could not have been left in greater confusion and suffering than Thou hast caused, laying upon them so many cares and unanswerable problems.

" 'So that, in truth, Thou didst Thyself lay the foundation for the destruction of Thy kingdom, and no one is more to blame for it. Yet what was offered Thee? There are three powers, three powers alone, able to conquer and to hold captive for ever the conscience of these impotent rebels for their happiness—those forces are miracle, mystery and authority. Thou hast rejected all three and hast set the example for doing so. When the wise and dread spirit set Thee on the pinnacle of the temple and said to Thee, "If Thou wouldst know whether Thou art the Son of God then cast Thyself down, for it is written: the angels shall hold him up lest he fall and bruise himself, and Thou shalt know then whether Thou art the Son of God and shalt prove then how great is Thy faith in Thy Father." But Thou didst refuse and wouldst not cast Thyself down. Oh! of course, Thou didst proudly and well like God; but the weak, unruly race of men, are they gods? Oh, Thou didst know then that in taking one step, in making one movement to cast Thyself down, Thou wouldst be tempting God and have lost all Thy faith in Him, and wouldst have been dashed to pieces against that earth which Thou didst come to save. And the wise spirit that tempted Thee would have rejoiced. But I ask again, are there many like Thee? And couldst Thou believe for one moment that men, too, could face such a temptation? Is the nature of men such, that they can reject miracle, and at the great moments of their life, the moments of their deepest, most agonising spiritual difficulties, cling only to the free verdict of the heart? Oh, Thou didst know that Thy deed would be recorded in books, would be handed down to remote times and the utmost ends of the earth, and Thou didst hope that man, following Thee, would cling to God and not ask for a miracle. But Thou didst not know that when man rejects miracle he rejects God too; for man seeks not so much God as the miraculous. And as man cannot bear to be without the miraculous, he will create new miracles of his own for himself, and will worship deeds of sorcery and witchcraft, though he might be a hundred times over a rebel, heretic and infidel. Thou didst not come down from the Cross when they shouted to Thee, mocking and reviling Thee, "Come down from the cross and we will believe that Thou art He." Thou didst not come down, for again Thou wouldst not enslave man by a miracle, and didst crave faith given freely, not based on miracle. Thou didst crave for free love and not the base raptures of the slave before the might that has overawed him for ever. But Thou didst think too highly of men therein, for they are slaves, of course, though rebellious by nature. Look round and judge; fifteen centuries have passed, look upon them. Whom hast Thou raised up to Thyself? I swear, man is weaker and baser by nature than Thou hast believed him! Can he, can he do what Thou didst? By showing him so much respect, Thou didst, as it were, cease to feel for him, for Thou didst ask far too much from him—Thou who hast loved him more than Thyself! Respecting him less, Thou wouldst have asked less of him. That would have been more like love, for his burden would have been lighter. He is weak and vile. What though he is everywhere now rebelling against our power, and proud of his rebellion? It is the pride of a child and a schoolboy. They are little children rioting and barring out the teacher at school. But their childish delight will end; it will cost them dear. They will cast down temples and drench the earth with blood. But they will see at last, the foolish children, that, though they are rebels, they are impotent rebels, unable to keep up their own rebellion. Bathed in their foolish tears, they will recognise at last that He who created them rebels must have meant to mock at them. They will say this in despair, and their utterance will be a blasphemy which will make them more unhappy still, for man's nature cannot bear blasphemy, and in the end always avenges it on itself. And so unrest, confusion and unhappiness— that is the present lot of man after Thou didst bear so much for their freedom! Thy great prophet tells in vision and in image, that he saw all those who took part in the first resurrection and that there were of each tribe twelve thousand. But if there were so many of them, they must have been not men but gods. They had borne Thy cross, they had endured scores of years in the barren, hungry wilderness, living upon locusts and roots—and Thou mayest indeed point with pride at those children of freedom, of free love, of free and splendid sacrifice for Thy name. But remember that they were only some thousands; and what of the rest? And how are the other weak ones to blame, because they could not endure what the strong have endured? How is the weak soul to blame that it is unable to receive such terrible gifts? Canst Thou have simply come to the elect and for the elect? But if so, it is a mystery and we cannot understand it. And if it is a mystery, we too have a right to preach a mystery, and to teach them that it's not the free judgment of their hearts, not love that matters, but a mystery which they must follow blindly, even against their conscience. So we have done. We have corrected Thy work and have founded it upon *miracle, mystery* and *authority*. And men rejoiced that they were again led like sheep, and that the terrible gift that had brought them such suffering, was, at last, lifted from their hearts. Were we right teaching them this? Speak! Did we not love mankind, so meekly acknowledging their feebleness, lovingly lightening their burden, and permitting their weak nature even sin with our sanction? Why hast Thou come now to hinder us? And why dost Thou look silently and searchingly at me with Thy mild eyes? Be angry. I don't want Thy love, for I love Thee not. And what use is it for me to hide anything from Thee? Don't I know to Whom I am speaking? All that I can say is known to Thee already. And is it for me to conceal from Thee our mystery? Perhaps it is Thy will to hear it from my lips. Listen, then. We are not working with Thee, but with *him*—that is our mystery. It's long—eight centuries—since we have been on *his* side and not on Thine. Just eight centuries ago, we took from him what Thou didst reject with scorn, that last gift he offered Thee, showing Thee all the kingdoms of the earth. We took from him Rome and the sword of Caesar, and proclaimed ourselves sole rulers of the earth, though hitherto we have not been able to complete our work. But whose fault is that? Oh, the work is only beginning, but it has begun. It has long to await completion and the earth has yet much to suffer, but we shall triumph and shall be Caesars, and then we shall plan the universal happiness of man. But Thou mightest have taken even then the sword of Caesar. Why didst Thou reject that last gift? Hadst Thou accepted that last counsel of the mighty spirit, Thou wouldst have accomplished all that man seeks on earth—that is, some one to worship, some one to keep his conscience, and some means of uniting all in one unanimous and harmonious ant-heap, for the craving for universal unity is the third and last anguish of men. Mankind as a whole has always striven to organise a universal state. There have been many great nations with great histories, but the more highly they were developed the more unhappy they were, for they felt more acutely than other people the craving for worldwide union. The great conquerors, Timours and Ghenghis-Khans, whirled like hurricanes over the face of the earth striving to subdue its people, and they too were but the unconscious expression of the same craving for universal unity. Hadst Thou taken the world and Caesar's purple, Thou wouldst have founded the universal state and have given universal peace. For who can rule men if not he who holds their conscience and their bread in his hands. We have taken the sword of Caesar, and in taking it, of course, have rejected Thee and followed *him*. Oh, ages are yet to come of the confusion of free thought, of their science and cannibalism. For having begun to build their tower of Babel without us, they will end, of course, with cannibalism. But then the beast will crawl to us and lick our feet and spatter them with tears of blood. And we shall sit upon the beast and raise the cup, and on it will be written, "Mystery." But then, and only then, the reign of peace and happiness will come for men. Thou art proud of Thine elect, but Thou hast only the elect, while we give rest to all. And besides, how many of those elect, those mighty ones who could become elect, have grown weary waiting for Thee, and have transferred and will transfer the powers of their spirit and the warmth of their heart to the other camp, and end by raising their *free* banner against Thee. Thou didst Thyself lift up that banner. But with us all will be happy and will no more rebel nor destroy one another as under Thy freedom. Oh, we shall persuade them that they will only become free when they renounce their freedom to us and submit to us. And shall we be right or shall we be lying? They will be convinced that we are right, for they will remember the horrors of slavery and confusion to which Thy freedom brought them. Freedom, free thought and science, will lead them into such straits and will bring them face to face with such marvels and insoluble mysteries, that some of them, the fierce and rebellious, will destroy themselves, others, rebellious but weak, will destroy one another, while the rest, weak and unhappy, will crawl fawning to our feet and whine to us: "Yes, you were right, you alone possess His mystery, and we come back to you, save us from ourselves!"

" 'Receiving bread from us, they will see clearly that we take the bread made by their hands from them, to give it to them, without any miracle. They will see that we do not change the stones to bread, but in truth they will be more thankful for taking it from our hands than for the bread itself! For they will remember only too well that in old days, without our help, even the bread they made turned to stones in their hands, while since they have come back to us, the very stones have turned to bread in their hands. Too, too well they know the value of complete submission! And until men know that, they will be unhappy. Who is most to blame for their not knowing it, speak? Who scattered the flock and sent it astray on unknown paths? But the flock will come together again and will submit once more, and then it will be once for all. Then we shall give them the quiet humble happiness of weak creatures such as they are by nature. Oh, we shall persuade them at last not to be proud, for Thou didst lift them up and thereby taught them to be proud. We shall show them that they are weak, that they are only pitiful children, but that childlike happiness is the sweetest of all. They will become timid and will look to us and huddle close to us in fear, as chicks to the hen. They will marvel at us and will be awestricken before us, and will be proud at our being so powerful and clever, that we have been able to subdue such a turbulent flock of thousands of millions. They will tremble impotently before our wrath, their minds will grow fearful, they will be quick to shed tears like women and children, but they will be just as ready at a sign from us to pass to laughter and rejoicing, to happy mirth and childish song. Yes, we shall set them to work, but in their leisure hours we shall make their life like a child's game, with children's songs and innocent dance. Oh, we shall allow them even sin, they are weak and helpless, and they will love us like children because we allow them to sin. We shall tell them that every sin will be expiated, if it is done with our permission, that we allow them to sin because we love them, and the punishment for these sins we take upon ourselves. And we shall take it upon ourselves, and they will adore us as their saviour who have taken on themselves their sins before God. And they will have no secrets from us. We shall allow or forbid them to live with their wives and mistresses, to have or not to have children—according to whether they have been obedient or disobedient—and they will submit to us gladly and cheerfully. The most painful secrets of their conscience, all, all they will bring to us, and we shall have an answer for all. And they will be glad to believe our answer, for it will save them from the great anxiety and terrible agony they endure at present in making a free decision for themselves. And all will be happy, all the millions of creatures except the hundred thousand who rule over them. For only we, we who guard the mystery, shall be unhappy. There will be thousands of millions of happy babes, and a hundred thousand sufferers who have taken upon themselves the curse of the knowledge of good and evil. Peacefully they will die, peacefully they will expire in Thy name, and beyond the grave they will find nothing but death. But we shall keep the secret, and for their happiness we shall allure them with the reward of heaven and eternity. Though if there were anything in the other world, it certainly would not be for such as they. It is prophesied that Thou wilt come again in victory, Thou wilt come with Thy chosen, the proud and strong, but we will say that they have only saved themselves, but we have saved all. We are told that the harlot who sits upon the beast, and holds in her hands the *mystery,* shall be put to shame, that the weak will rise up again, and will rend her royal purple and will strip naked her loathsome body. But then I will stand up and point out to Thee the thousand millions of happy children who have known no sin. And we who have taken their sins upon us for their happiness will stand up before Thee and say: "Judge us if Thou canst and darest." Know that I fear Thee not. Know that I too have been in the wilderness, I too have lived on roots and locusts, I too prized the freedom with which Thou hast blessed men, and I too was striving to stand among Thy elect, among the strong and powerful, thirsting "to make up the number." But I awakened and would not serve madness. I turned back and joined the ranks of those *who have corrected Thy work.* I left the proud and went back to the humble, for the happiness of the humble. What I say to Thee will come to pass, and our dominion will be built up. I repeat, to-morrow Thou shalt see that obedient flock who at a sign from me will hasten to heap up the hot cinders about the pile on which I shall burn Thee for coming to hinder us. For if any one has ever deserved our fires, it is Thou. To-morrow I shall burn Thee. Dixi.' " . . .

"When the Inquisitor ceased speaking he waited some time for his Prisoner to answer him. His silence weighed down upon him. He saw that the Prisoner had listened intently all the time, looking gently in his face and evidently not wishing to reply. The old man longed for Him to say something, however bitter and terrible. But He suddenly approached the old man in silence and softly kissed him on his bloodless aged lips. That was all his answer. The old man shuddered. His lips moved. He went to the door, opened it, and said to Him: 'Go, and come no more. . . . Come not at all, never, never!' And he let Him out into the dark alleys of the town. The Prisoner went away."

"And the old man?"

"The kiss glows in his heart, but the old man adheres to his idea."

The Meaning of Life   Kurt Baier

Kurt Baier (1917–   ) is professor of philosophy at the University of Pittsburgh. He is the author of a highly acclaimed book on ethics, *The Moral Point of View*, as well as many articles.

Tolstoy, in his autobiographical work, "A Confession", reports how, when he was fifty and at the height of his literary success, he came to be obsessed by the fear that life was meaningless.

> At first I experienced moments of perplexity and arrest of life, as though I did not know what to do or how to live; and I felt lost and became dejected. But this passed, and I went on living as before. Then these moments of perplexity began to recur oftener and oftener, and always in the same form. They were always expressed by the questions: What is it for? What does it lead to? At first it seemed to me that these were aimless and irrelevant questions. I thought that it was all well known, and that if I should ever wish to deal with the solution it would not cost me much effort; just at present I had no time for it, but when I wanted to, I should be able to find the answer. The questions however began to repeat themselves frequently, and to demand replies more and more insistently; and like drops of ink always falling on one place they ran together into one black blot.[1]

A Christian living in the Middle Ages would not have felt any serious doubts about Tolstoy's questions. To him it would have seemed quite certain that life had a meaning and quite clear what it was. The medieval Christian world picture assigned to man a highly significant, indeed the central part in the grand scheme of things. The universe was made for the express purpose of providing a stage on which to enact a drama starring Man in the title role.

To be exact, the world was created by God in the year 4004 B.C. Man was the last and the crown of this creation, made in the likeness of God, placed in the Garden of Eden on earth, the fixed centre of the universe, round which revolved the nine heavens of the sun, the moon, the planets and the fixed stars, producing as they revolved in their orbits the heavenly harmony of the spheres. And this gigantic universe was created for the enjoyment of man, who was originally put in control of it. Pain and death were unknown in paradise. But this state of bliss was not to last. Adam and Eve ate of the forbidden tree of knowledge, and life on this earth turned into a death-march through a vale of tears. Then, with the

From *The Meaning of Life* by Kurt Baier, the Inaugural Lecture delivered at the Canberra University College (1957). Reprinted by permission of the Registrar, The Australian National University, and the author.

[1] Count Leo Tolstoy, "A Confession", reprinted in *A Confession, The Gospel in Brief, and What I Believe*, No. 229, The World's Classics (London: Geoffrey Cumberlege, 1940).

birth of Jesus, new hope came into the world. After He had died on the cross, it became at least possible to wash away with the purifying water of baptism some of the effects of Original Sin and to achieve salvation. That is to say, on condition of obedience to the law of God, man could now enter heaven and regain the state of everlasting, deathless bliss, from which he had been excluded because of the sin of Adam and Eve.

To the medieval Christian the meaning of human life was therefore perfectly clear. The stretch on earth is only a short interlude, a temporary incarceration of the soul in the prison of the body, a brief trial and test, fated to end in death, the release from pain and suffering. What really matters, is the life after the death of the body. One's existence acquires meaning not by gaining what this life can offer but by saving one's immortal soul from death and eternal torture, by gaining eternal life and everlasting bliss.

The scientific world picture which has found ever more general acceptance from the beginning of the modern era onwards is in profound conflict with all this. At first, the Christian conception of the world was discovered to be erroneous in various important details. The Copernican theory showed up the earth as merely one of several planets revolving round the sun, and the sun itself was later seen to be merely one of many fixed stars each of which is itself the nucleus of a solar system similar to our own. Man, instead of occupying the centre of creation, proved to be merely the inhabitant of a celestial body no different from millions of others. Furthermore, geological investigations revealed that the universe was not created a few thousand years ago, but was probably millions of years old.

Disagreements over details of the world picture, however, are only superficial aspects of a much deeper conflict. The appropriateness of the whole Christian outlook is at issue. For Christianity, the world must be regarded as the "creation" of a kind of Superman, a person possessing all the human excellences to an infinite degree and none of the human weaknesses, Who has made man in His image, a feeble, mortal, foolish copy of Himself. In creating the universe, God acts as a sort of playwright-cum-legislator-cum-judge-cum-executioner. In the capacity of playwright, He creates the historical world process, including man. He erects the stage and writes, in outline, the plot. He creates the *dramatis personae* and watches over them with the eye partly of a father, partly of the law. While on stage, the actors are free to extemporise, but if they infringe the divine commandments, they are later dealt with by their creator in His capacity of judge and executioner.

Within such a framework, the Christian attitudes towards the world are natural and sound: it is natural and sound to think that all is arranged for the best even if appearances belie it; to resign oneself cheerfully to one's lot; to be filled with awe and veneration in regard to anything and everything that happens; to want to fall on one's knees and worship and praise the Lord. These are wholly fitting attitudes within the framework of the world view just outlined. And this world view must have seemed wholly sound and acceptable because it offered the best explanation which was then available of all the observed phenomena of nature.

As the natural sciences developed, however, more and more things in the universe came to be explained without the assumption of a super-natural creator. Science, moreover, could explain them better, that is, more accurately and more reliably. The Christian hypothesis of a super-natural maker, whatever other needs it was capable of satisfying, was at any rate no longer indispensable for the purpose of explaining the exist-ence or occurrence of anything. In fact, scientific explanations do not seem to leave any room for this hypothesis. The scientific approach demands that we look for a natural explanation of anything and everything. The scientific way of looking at and explaining things has yielded an im-mensely greater measure of understanding of, and control over, the uni-verse than any other way. And when one looks at the world in this scien-tific way, there seems to be no room for a personal relationship between human beings and a supernatural perfect being ruling and guiding men. Hence many scientists and educated men have come to feel that the Christian attitudes towards the world and human existence are inap-propriate. They have become convinced that the universe and human existence in it are without a purpose and therefore devoid of meaning. . . .

The Purpose of Man's Existence

. . . There are two quite different senses of "purpose". Which one is meant? Has science deprived human life of purpose in both senses? And if not, is it a harmless sense, in which human existence has been robbed of purpose? Could human existence still have meaning if it did not have a purpose in that sense?

What are the two senses? In the first and basic sense, purpose is nor-mally attributed only to persons or their behaviour as in "Did you have a purpose in leaving the ignition on?" In the second sense, purpose is normally attributed only to things, as in "What is the purpose of that gadget you installed in the workshop?" The two uses are intimately con-nected. We cannot attribute a purpose to a thing without implying that someone did something, in the doing of which he had some purpose, namely, to bring about the thing with the purpose. Of course, *his* pur-pose is not identical with *its* purpose. In hiring labourers and engineers and buying materials and a site for a factory and the like, the entre-preneur's purpose, let us say, is to manufacture cars, but the purpose of cars is to serve as a means of transportation.

There are many things that a man may do, such as buying and sell-ing, hiring labourers, ploughing, felling trees, and the like, which it is foolish, pointless, silly, perhaps crazy, to do if one has no purpose in doing them. A man who does these things without a purpose is engaging in inane, futile pursuits. Lives crammed full with such activities devoid of purpose are pointless, futile, worthless. Such lives may indeed be dis-missed as meaningless. But it should also be perfectly clear that accept-ance of the scientific world picture does not force us to regard our lives as being without a purpose in this sense. Science has not only not robbed us of any purpose which we had before, but it has furnished us with enormously greater power to achieve these purposes. Instead of praying for rain or a good harvest or offspring, we now use ice pellets, artificial manure, or artificial insemination.

By contrast, having or not having a purpose, in the other sense, is value neutral. We do not think more or less highly of a thing for having or not having a purpose. "Having a purpose", in this sense, confers no kudos, "being purposeless" carries no stigma. A row of trees growing near a farm may or may not have a purpose: it may or may not be a windbreak, may or may not have been planted or deliberately left standing there in order to prevent the wind from sweeping across the fields. We do not in any way disparage the trees if we say they have no purpose, but have just grown that way. They are as beautiful, made of as good wood, as valuable, as if they had a purpose. And, of course, they break the wind just as well. The same is true of living creatures. We do not disparage a dog when we say that it has no purpose, is not a sheep dog or a watch dog or a rabbiting dog, but just a dog that hangs around the house and is fed by us.

Man is in a different category, however. To attribute to a human being a purpose in that sense is not neutral, let alone complimentary: it is offensive. It is degrading for a man to be regarded as merely serving a purpose. If, at a garden party, I ask a man in livery, "What is your purpose?" I am insulting him. I might as well have asked, "What are you *for?*" Such questions reduce him to the level of a gadget, a domestic animal, or perhaps a slave. I imply that *we* allot to *him* the tasks, the goals, the aims which he is to pursue; that *his* wishes and desires and aspirations and purposes are to count for little or nothing. We are treating him, in Kant's phrase, merely as a means to our ends, not as an end in himself.

The Christian and the scientific world pictures do indeed differ fundamentally on this point. The latter robs man of a purpose in this sense. It sees him as a being with no purpose allotted to him by anyone but himself. It robs him of any goal, purpose, or destiny appointed for him by any outside agency. The Christian world picture, on the other hand, sees man as a creature, a divine artefact, something halfway between a robot (manufactured) and an animal (alive), a homunculus, or perhaps Frankenstein, made in God's laboratory, with a purpose or task assigned him by his Maker.

However, lack of purpose in this sense does not in any way detract from the meaningfulness of life. I suspect that many who reject the scientific outlook because it involves the loss of purpose of life, and therefore meaning, are guilty of a confusion between the two senses of "purpose" just distinguished. They confusedly think that if the scientific world picture is true, then their lives must be futile because that picture implies that man has no purpose given him from without. But this is muddled thinking, for, as has already been shown, pointlessness is implied only by purposelessness in the other sense, which is not at all implied by the scientific picture of the world. These people mistakenly conclude that there can be no purpose *in* life because there is no purpose *of* life; that *men* cannot themselves adopt and achieve purposes because *man*, unlike a robot or a watchdog, is not a creature with a purpose.[2] . . .

The Meaning of Life

. . . To many people the crux of the matter seems as follows. How can there be any meaning in our life if it ends in death? What meaning can there be in it that our inevitable death does not destroy? How can our existence be meaningful if there is no after-life in which perfect justice is meted out? How can life have any meaning if all it holds out to us are a few miserable earthly pleasures and even these to be enjoyed only rarely and for such a piteously short time?

I believe this is the point which exercises most people most deeply. Kirilov, in Dostoevsky's novel, *The Possessed,* claims, just before committing suicide, that as soon as we realize that there is no God, we cannot live any longer, we must put an end to our lives. One of the reasons which he gives is that when we discover that there is no paradise, we have nothing to live for.

". . . there was a day on earth, and in the middle of the earth were three crosses. One on the cross had such faith that He said to another, 'To-day thou shalt be with me in paradise'. The day came to an end, both died, and they went, but they found neither paradise nor resurrection. The saying did not come true. Listen: that man was the highest of all on earth . . . There has never been any one like Him before or since, and never will be . . . And if that is so, if the laws of Nature did not spare even *Him,* and made even Him live in the midst of lies and die for a lie, then the whole planet is a lie and is based on a lie and a stupid mockery. So the very laws of the planet are a lie and a farce of the devil. What, then, is there to live for?"[3] And Tolstoy, too, was nearly driven to suicide when he came to doubt the existence of God and an after-life.[4] And this is true of many.

What, then, is it that inclines us to think that if life is to have a meaning, there would have to be an after-life? It is this. The Christian world view contains the following three propositions. The first is that since the Fall, God's curse of Adam and Eve, and the expulsion from Paradise, life on earth for mankind has not been worthwhile, but a vale of tears, one long chain of misery, suffering, unhappiness, and injustice. The second is that a perfect after-life is awaiting us after the death of the body. The third is that we can enter this perfect life only on certain conditions, among which is also the condition of enduring our earthly existence to its bitter end. In this way, our earthly existence which, in itself, would not (at least for many people if not all) be worth living, acquires meaning and

---

[2] See e.g. "Is Life Worth Living?" B.B.C. Talk by the Rev. John Sutherland Bonnell in *Asking Them Questions,* Third Series, ed. by R. S. Wright (London: Geoffrey Cumberlege, 1950).

[3] Fyodor Dostoevsky, *The Devils* (London: The Penguin Classics, 1953), pp. 613–614.

[4] Leo Tolstoy, *A Confession, The Gospel in Brief, and What I Believe,* The World's Classics, p. 24.

significance: only if we endure it, can we gain admission to the realm of the blessed.

It might be doubted whether this view is still held to-day. However, there can be no doubt that even to-day we all imbibe a good deal of this view with our earliest education. In sermons, the contrast between the perfect life of the blessed and our life of sorrow and drudgery is frequently driven home and we hear it again and again that Christianity has a message of hope and consolation for all those "who are weary and heavy laden".

It is not surprising, then, that when the implications of the scientific world picture begin to sink in, when we come to have doubts about the existence of God and another life, we are bitterly disappointed. For if there is no after-life, then all we are left is our earthly life which we have come to regard as a necessary evil, the painful fee of admission to the land of eternal bliss. But if there is no eternal bliss to come and if this hell on earth is all, why hang on till the horrible end?

Our disappointment therefore arises out of these two propositions, that the earthly life is not worth living, and that there is another perfect life of eternal happiness and joy which we may enter upon if we satisfy certain conditions. We can regard our lives as meaningful, if we believe both. We cannot regard them as meaningful if we believe merely in the first and not the second. It seems to me inevitable that people who are taught something of the history of science, will have serious doubts about the second. If they cannot overcome these, as many will be unable to do, then they must either accept the sad view that their life is meaningless or they must abandon the first proposition: that this earthly life is not worth living. They must find the meaning of their life in this earthly existence. But is this possible?

A moment's examination will show us that the Christian evaluation of our earthly life as worthless, which we accept in our moments of pessimism and dissatisfaction, is not one that we normally accept. Consider only the question of murder and suicide. On the Christian view, other things being equal, the most kindly thing to do would be for everyone of us to kill as many of our friends and dear ones as still have the misfortune to be alive, and then to commit suicide without delay, for every moment spent in this life is wasted. On the Christian view, God has not made it that easy for us. He has forbidden us to hasten others or ourselves into the next life. Our bodies are his private property and must be allowed to wear themselves out in the way decided by Him, however painful and horrible that may be. We are, as it were, driving a burning car. There is only one way out, to jump clear and let it hurtle to destruction. But the owner of the car has forbidden it on pain of eternal tortures worse than burning. And so we do better to burn to death inside.

On this view, murder is a less serious wrong than suicide. For murder can always be confessed and repented and therefore forgiven, suicide cannot—unless we allow the ingenious way out chosen by the heroine of Graham Greene's play, *The Living Room,* who swallows a slow but deadly poison and, while awaiting its taking effect, repents having taken it. Murder, on the other hand, is not so serious because, in the first place, it need not rob the victim of anything but the last lap of his march in the vale of tears, and, in the second place, it can always be forgiven. Hamlet, it will be remembered, refrains from killing his uncle during the latter's prayers because, as a true Christian, he believes that killing his uncle at that point, when the latter has purified his soul by repentance, would merely be doing him a good turn, for murder at such a time would simply dispatch him to undeserved and everlasting happiness.

These views strike us as odd, to say the least. They are the logical consequence of the official medieval evaluation of this our earthly existence. If this life is not worth living, then taking it is not robbing the person concerned of much. The only thing wrong with it is the damage to God's property, which is the same both in the case of murder and suicide. We do not take this view at all. Our view, on the contrary, is that murder is the most serious wrong because it consists in taking away from some one else against his will his most precious possession, his life. For this reason, when a person suffering from an incurable disease asks to be killed, the mercy killing of such a person is regarded as a much less serious crime than murder because, in such a case, the killer is not robbing the other of a good against his will. Suicide is not regarded as a real crime at all, for we take the view that a person can do with his own possessions what he likes.

However, from the fact that these are our normal opinions, we can infer nothing about their truth. After all, we could easily be mistaken. Whether life is or is not worthwhile, is a value judgment. Perhaps all this is merely a matter of opinion or taste. Perhaps no objective answer can be given. Fortunately, we need not enter deeply into these difficult and controversial questions. It is quite easy to show that the medieval evaluation of earthly life is based on a misguided procedure.

Let us remind ourselves briefly of how we arrive at our value judgments. When we determine the merits of students, meals, tennis players, bulls, or bathing belles, we do so on the basis of some criteria and some standard or norm. Criteria and standards notoriously vary from field to field and even from case to case. But that does not mean that we have *no* idea about what are the appropriate criteria or standards to use. It would not be fitting to apply the criteria for judging bulls to the judgment of students or bathing belles. They score on quite different points. And even where the same criteria are appropriate as in the judgment of students enrolled in different schools and universities, the standards will vary from one institution to another. Pupils who would only just pass in one, would perhaps obtain honours in another. The higher the standard applied, the lower the marks, that is, the merit conceded to the candidate.

The same procedure is applicable also in the evaluation of a life. We examine it on the basis of certain criteria and standards. The medieval Christian view uses the criteria of the ordinary man: a life is judged by what the person concerned can get out of it: the balance of happiness over unhappiness, pleasure over pain, bliss over suffering. Our earthly life is judged not worthwhile because it contains much unhappiness, pain, and suffering, little happiness, pleasure, and bliss. The next life is judged worthwhile because it provides eternal bliss and no suffering.

Armed with these criteria, we can compare the life of this man and that, and judge which is more worthwhile, which has a greater balance of bliss over suffering. But criteria alone enable us merely to make comparative judgments of value, not absolute ones. We can say which is more and which is less worthwhile, but we cannot say which is worthwhile and which is not. In order to determine the latter, we must introduce a standard. But what standard ought we to choose?

Ordinarily, the standard we employ is the average of the kind. We call a man and a tree tall if they are well above the average of their kind. We do not say that Jones is a short man because he is shorter than a tree. We do not judge a boy a bad student because his answer to a question in the Leaving Examination is much worse than that given in reply to the same question by a young man sitting for his finals for the Bachelor's degree.

The same principles must apply to judging lives. When we ask whether a given life was or was not worthwhile, then we must take into consideration the range of worthwhileness which ordinary lives normally cover. Our end poles of the scale must be the best possible and the worst possible life that one finds. A good and worthwhile life is one that is well above average. A bad one is one well below.

The Christian evaluation of earthly lives is misguided because it adopts a quite unjustifiably high standard. Christianity singles out the major shortcomings of our earthly existence: there is not enough happiness; there is too much suffering; the good and bad points are quite unequally and unfairly distributed; the underprivileged and underendowed do not get adequate compensation; it lasts only a short time. It then quite accurately depicts the perfect or ideal life as that which does not have any of these shortcomings. Its next step is to promise the believer that he will be able to enjoy this perfect life later on. And then it adopts as its standard of judgment the perfect life, dismissing as inadequate anything that falls short of it. Having dismissed earthly life as miserable, it further damns it by characterizing most of the pleasures of which earthly existence allows as bestial, gross, vile, and sinful, or alternatively as not really pleasurable.

This procedure is as illegitimate as if I were to refuse to call anything tall unless it is infinitely tall, or anything beautiful unless it is perfectly flawless, or any one strong unless he is omnipotent. Even if it were true that there is available to us an after-life which is flawless and perfect, it would still not be legitimate to judge earthly lives by this standard. We do not fail every candidate who is not an Einstein. And if we do not believe in an after-life, we must of course use ordinary earthly standards.

I have so far only spoken of the worthwhileness, only of what a person can get out of a life. There are other kinds of appraisal. Clearly, we evaluate people's lives not merely from the point of view of what they yield to the persons that lead them, but also from that of other men on whom these lives have impinged. We judge a life more significant if the person has contributed to the happiness of others, whether directly by what he did for others, or by the plans, discoveries, inventions, and work he performed. Many lives that hold little in the way of pleasure or happiness for its owner are highly significant and valuable, deserve admiration and respect on account of the contributions made.

It is now quite clear that death is simply irrelevant. If life can be worthwhile at all, then it can be so even though it be short. And if it is not worthwhile at all, then an eternity of it is simply a nightmare. It may be sad that we have to leave this beautiful world, but it is so only if and because it is beautiful. And it is no less beautiful for coming to an end. I rather suspect that an eternity of it might make us less appreciative, and in the end it would be tedious.

It will perhaps be objected now that I have not really demonstrated that life has a meaning, but merely that it can be worthwhile or have value. It must be admitted that there is a perfectly natural interpretation of the question, "What is the meaning of life?" on which my view actually proves that life has no meaning. I mean the interpretation discussed in section 2 of this lecture [omitted here, ed.], where I attempted to show that, if we accept the explanations of natural science, we cannot believe that living organisms have appeared on earth in accordance with the deliberate plan of some intelligent being. Hence, on this view, life cannot be said to have a purpose, in the sense in which man-made things have a purpose. Hence it cannot be said to have a meaning or significance in that sense.

However, this conclusion is innocuous. People are disconcerted by the thought that *life as such* has no meaning in that sense only because they very naturally think it entails that no individual life can have meaning either. They naturally assume that *this* life or *that* can have meaning only if *life as such* has meaning. But it should by now be clear that your life and mine may or may not have meaning (in one sense) even if life as such has none (in the other). Of course, it follows from this that your life may have meaning while mine has not. The Christian view guarantees a meaning (in one sense) to every life, the scientific view does not (in any sense). By relating the question of the meaningfulness of life to the particular circumstances of an individual's existence, the scientific view leaves it an open question whether an individual's life has meaning or not. It is, however, clear that the latter is the important sense of "having a meaning." Christians, too, must feel that their life is wasted and meaningless if they have not achieved salvation. To know that even such lost lives have a meaning in another sense is no consolation to them. What matters is not that life should have a guaranteed meaning, whatever happens here or here-after, but that, by luck (Grace) or the right temperament and attitude (Faith) or a judicious life (Works) a person should make the most of his life.

"But here lies the rub," it will be said. "Surely, it makes all the difference whether there is an after-life. This is where morality comes in." It would be a mistake to believe that. Morality is not the meting out of punishment and reward. To be moral is to refrain from doing to others what, if they followed reason, they would not do to themselves, and to do for others what, if they followed reason, they would want to have done. It is, roughly speaking, to recognize that others, too, have a right to a worthwhile life. Being moral does not make one's own life worthwhile, it helps others to make theirs so. . . .

Suggestions
for Further Reading

Anthologies

Flew, Anthony and MacIntyre, Alasdair (eds.). *New Essays in Philosophical Theology.* London: SCM Press, 1955. A collection of important writings on various aspects of the philosophy of religion. Many of these articles will be difficult for the beginning student.

Hick, John (ed.). *The Existence of God.* New York: Macmillan, 1964. A good collection of classical and contemporary writings on the major arguments for the existence of God.

Kaufmann, Walter (ed.). *Religion from Tolstoy to Camus.* New York: Harper, 1961. A collection of some of the most important writings on the philosophy of religion.

Pike, Nelson (ed.). *God and Evil.* Englewood Cliffs, N.J.: Prentice-Hall, 1964. A collection of opposing views and arguments about the problem of evil. There is a good bibliography for the student who wishes to read further on this topic.

Individual Works

Collins, John. *God in Modern Philosophy.* Chicago: Regnery, 1959. A survey of many of the major issues in the philosophy of religion from a Catholic point of view.

Du Noüy, Lecompte. *Human Destiny.* New York: Longmans, 1947. A version of the argument from design. Du Noüy argues that the facts of biology cannot be adequately explained unless the existence of a Designer is accepted.

Hick, John. *Philosophy of Religion.* Englewood Cliffs, N.J.: Prentice-Hall, 1965. An excellent brief introduction to the philosophy of religion. The student will find this a valuable guide in organizing the issues raised by the readings in his text.

Hume, David. *Dialogues on Natural Religion,* edited by Norman Kemp Smith. Indianapolis: Bobbs, 1947. A classic discussion of the argument from design. The beginning student will find this difficult but very rewarding.

Matson, Wallace I. *The Existence of God.* Ithaca, N.Y.: Cornell University Press, 1965. An excellent, detailed analysis of the major arguments for the existence of God.

Paley, William. *Natural Theology: Selections,* edited by Frederick Ferre. Indianapolis: Bobbs, 1963. The classic statement of the argument from design.

Scriven, Michael. *Primary Philosophy.* New York: McGraw-Hill, 1966. Chapter Four presents an interesting and detailed defense of atheism.

Encyclopedia of Philosophy. Paul Edwards, editor-in-chief. New York: Macmillan, 1967. The beginning student will find many worthwhile articles on the subjects treated in this Part, and excellent bibliographies.

Three: Morality and Society

Introduction

Just about everyone seeks to distinguish right behavior from wrong and to determine what is worthwhile in life. In our society we frequently encounter discussions about the morality of the death penalty, the decline in current moral values, and the injustice done to minority groups. Also, at times, we are faced with personal moral decisions: Should we lie to get out of an unpleasant situation? Should we fight in a war if we think it unjust? Should we cheat on our income tax if we are sure we will not get caught? It is these kinds of questions that produce philosophical speculations about the basis of morality and the good life.

While the philosopher is concerned with the kinds of moral problems we face in daily life, he believes that his primary concern should be given to a number of very basic problems that must be answered before it is possible to give a reasoned answer to any other moral issues. *Ethics* is that branch of philosophy that is concerned with finding answers to these basic problems. Some of the problems most often discussed in the study of ethics are: Is there a basis for deciding whether any act is right? How can we prove or disprove that there is such a basis? What kinds of things are most worth attaining? When does a person deserve to be praised or blamed? In answering these kinds of questions, the philosopher does not merely give his opinion or list a variety of opinions on the subject, but rather attempts to find reasons that will show that a certain answer is correct. The student, if he is to get much out of the readings, must pay close attention to reasons that are offered and attempt to decide which philosopher, if any, has proven his case.

Many students approach ethics with the belief that there is little to be gained from the investigation because they believe that moral standards or principles are merely products of the society in which one lives. They believe that the moral views of people in other societies, no matter how much they differ from one's own, are correct for the people in those societies. Such a view is called *relativism.*

Two kinds of relativism, sociological and ethical, must be distinguished and defined before the topic can be clearly discussed. *Sociological relativism* is the name given to the factual claim that societies sometimes have different ultimate principles. An ultimate principle is one that is used as a basis for defending all other moral judgments and principles. It seems evident that societies do have different moral principles regarding a variety of matters such as marriage, raising the young, and the treatment of women. The crucial point, however, is whether societies that obviously differ in their moral practices also differ on their view of the correct ultimate principle. The observed differences may not indicate differences in ultimate principles but merely the necessity of different behavior to satisfy the same principle. For example, a society with insufficient food to feed everyone might kill the elderly when they are no longer productive in order to save the young. A society with abundant means to care for the elderly would probably consider killing them abhorrent. Yet if the latter society were suddenly to find its means reduced to that of the former, it too might well consider the killing of the elderly as a necessity because, like the first society, it too wants to insure survival of the group.

The belief in sociological relativism has been of great significance because for many it justifies ethical relativism. *Ethical relativism* is the view that there are different but equally correct ultimate principles. This position is opposed to that of *ethical absolutism,* a theory which holds that there is only one correct ultimate principle or set of principles. The conflict between the ethical absolutist and relativist is of crucial importance. If the relativist is right, it would be necessary to give up the criticism of other societies', and possibly each individual's ultimate moral principles, although one still could criticize the application of these principles.

W. T. Stace presents the arguments for and against both ethical relativism and absolutism. He shows that sociological relativism, even if true, would not require a belief in ethical relativism; for the absolutist could claim that those ultimate moral principles contrary to the "true" one were merely mistaken. Further, Stace argues that the consequences of ethical relativism are unacceptable and that absolutism, despite the difficulty of establishing the correct moral principle, is preferable. In his discussion of relativism, Paul Taylor considers some recent suggestions by social scientists to the effect that there are certain basic cultural factors that are similar in all societies, and the inference that ethical relativism must be false. Taylor argues that any facts about cultural similarities would be as irrelevant in establishing the falsity of ethical relativism as facts about cultural differences would be in establishing its truth.

Philosophers have presented a number of theories concerning the correct ultimate moral principles. Two prominent views are ultilitarianism and formalism. *Utilitarianism* is a moral theory that holds that right acts are acts producing the greatest happiness. In deciding which acts are right, a utilitarian considers the consequences of all the acts open to him and performs the one that would produce the best consequences for everybody concerned. While many would agree that this is generally a proper procedure, sometimes there is dissatisfaction with some kinds of acts that might turn out to be right on this basis. For example, if it would produce the best results for all concerned, then it would be right to lie, steal, and even murder. Jeremy Bentham presents a clear statement of the utilitarian position and attempts to work out some of the details required for its implementation. He maintains that in assessing the consequences of various possible acts, we should be concerned with the amounts of pleasure and pain produced and perform only those acts resulting in the most pleasure or the least pain. Bentham believed that the only thing ultimately worthwhile in life is pleasure. Such a view that the good is pleasure is called *hedonism.* The student should realize, however, that a utilitarian need not be a hedonist. He could believe that many things besides pleasure, such as intellectual growth, beauty, and integrity, are worthwhile and these should be considered in assessing possible actions.

Unlike egoists and utilitarians, some moral theorists maintain that the rightness or wrongness of actions is not determined by the consequences produced. Such a view is called *formalism* in ethical theory. The kinds of ultimate principles that formalists have held have varied widely. One formalist principle that has had great appeal is the golden rule, "Do unto others as you would have others do unto you." R. M. MacIver defends this rule as the only one which can bring agreement out of the conflicting moral viewpoints because it lays down a procedure to follow in determining proper behavior rather than stating final goals and values. A problem for the student in considering MacIver's view is to decide on what basis the golden rule is being defended. Is MacIver appealing to the utility of accepting it or is there some other basis of appeal?

One moral issue much debated at present is whether or not men should disobey those laws of their society they believe immoral. In the twentieth century, many countries have experienced mass civil disobedience to laws thought immoral. The United States has certainly had its share, as attested by the refusal of many to obey Southern laws requiring separate seating in buses and lunch counters and by the resistance of large numbers to the draft. Some theorists hold that we have an obligation to disobey any law that would require us to act contrary to our moral beliefs. Others, at the opposite extreme, claim that we should always obey the law and use only legal means to try to change it. The readings on this topic should help the student understand the reasons for the various stands taken and help him to assess their adequacy.

Henry David Thoreau, a famous nineteenth-century American essayist and philosopher, maintained that men should disobey their government when it pursues actions or enforces laws they think unconscionable. He was opposed to the government in his day because it was waging a war, the Mexican War, that he thought immoral. To show his dissatisfaction, he refused to pay his taxes and, as a result, was sent to jail. Jail, he maintained, was where all good men belonged until the government changed its policies. Thoreau explicitly rejects a utilitarian approach to the issue of whether or not we should disobey the law. He believes that there are certain principles of justice and morality that men should always obey regardless of the consequences. In this, Thoreau holds a formalist moral position.

While defending the right of civil disobedience in extreme cases, Sidney Hook, a contemporary American philosopher, thinks that there are certain limits to the justification of disobedience. Further, he distrusts the claim that the voice of one's conscience is sufficient grounds for opposing the law since its deliverances are not a good guide to truth and proper conduct. On the basis of conscience one is justified in launching legitimate social protest but not in attempting to obstruct the democratic process.

A recurring area of controversy in democratic countries concerns the relation that should exist between law and morality. Should there be laws that require people to act in the way that the majority of society thinks moral, or should the legislation of laws be restricted only to certain very important matters, such as the protection of rights and defense of one's person against physical harm? Should there be laws that prevent storeowners from opening on Sunday or laws against the possession of pornographic literature? Many people, perhaps a majority, think suicide and sexual intercourse outside marriage are immoral. Should there be laws against them?

Sir Patrick Devlin, a prominent English judge, considers this problem in the light of a recommendation by a government committee to eliminate any laws against homosexuality among consenting adults. He believes that such a change in the law would weaken public morality and thereby add to those pressures that could lead to the disintegration of the society. For him, "the suppression of vice is as much the law's business as the suppression of subversive activities." H. L. A. Hart opposes such a view. Although he agrees that a stable society needs some moral cohesion, he doubts that every moral matter is of equal importance to society. Surely society will not disintegrate if some activities of which it disapproves are left open to the individual. Hart fears that Sir Patrick Devlin's approach to the problem might result in giving legal sanction to the public's moral whims no matter how irrational.

Are Ethical Values Relative?

Ethical Relativism   W. T. Stace

Any ethical position which denies that there is a single moral standard which is equally applicable to all men at all times may fairly be called a species of ethical relativity. There is not, the relativist asserts, merely one moral law, one code, one standard. There are many moral laws, codes, standards. What morality ordains in one place or age may be quite different from what morality ordains in another place or age. The moral code of Chinamen is quite different from that of Europeans, that of African savages quite different from both. Any morality, therefore, is relative to the age, the place, and the circumstances in which it is found. It is in no sense absolute.

This does not mean merely—as one might at first sight be inclined to suppose—that the very same kind of action which is *thought* right in one country and period may be *thought* wrong in another. This would be a mere platitude, the truth of which everyone would have to admit. Even the absolutist would admit this—would even wish to emphasize it—since he is well aware that different people have different sets of moral ideas, and his whole point is that some of these sets of ideas are false. What the relativist means to assert is, not this platitude, but that the very same kind of action which *is* right in one country and period may *be* wrong in another. And this, far from being a platitude, is a very startling assertion.

It is very important to grasp thoroughly the difference between the two ideas. For there is reason to think that many minds tend to find ethical relativity attractive because they fail to keep them clearly apart. It is so very obvious that moral ideas differ from country to country and from age to age. And it is so very easy, if you are mentally lazy, to suppose that to say this means the same as to say that no universal moral standard exists,—or in other words that it implies ethical relativity. We fail to see that the word "standard" is used in two different senses. It is perfectly true that, in one sense, there are many variable moral standards. We speak of judging a man by the standard of his time. And this implies that different times have different standards. And this, of course, is quite true. But when the word "standard" is used in this sense it means simply the set of moral ideas current during the period in question. It means what people *think* right, whether as a matter of fact it *is* right or not. On the other hand when the absolutist asserts that there exists a single universal moral "standard," he is not using the word in this sense at all. He means by "standard" what *is* right as distinct from what people merely think right. His point is that although what people think right varies in different countries and periods, yet what actually is right is everywhere and always the same. And it follows that when the ethical relativist disputes the position of the absolutist and denies that any universal moral standard exists he too means by "standard" what actually is right. But it is exceedingly easy, if we are not careful, to slip loosely from using the word in the first sense to using it in the second sense; and to suppose that the variability of moral beliefs is the same thing as the variability of what really is moral. And unless we keep the two senses of the word "standard" distinct, we are likely to think the creed of ethical relativity much more plausible than it actually is.

The genuine relativist, then, does not merely mean that Chinamen may think right what Frenchmen think wrong. He means that what *is* wrong for the Frenchman may *be* right for the Chinaman. And if one enquires how, in those circumstances, one is to know what actually is right in China or in France, the answer comes quite glibly. What is right in China is the same as what people think right in China; and what is right in France is the same as what people think right in France. So that, if you want to know what is moral in any particular country or age all you have to do is to ascertain what are the moral ideas current in that age or country. Those ideas are, *for that age or country,* right. Thus what is morally right is identified with what is thought to be morally right, and the distinction which we made above between these two is simply denied. To put the same thing in another way, it is denied that there can be or ought to be any distinction between the two senses of the word "standard." There is only one kind of standard of right and wrong, namely, the moral ideas current in any particular age or country.

Moral right *means* what people think morally right. It has no other meaning. What Frenchmen think right is, therefore, right *for Frenchmen.* And evidently one must conclude—though I am not aware that relativists are anxious to draw one's attention to such unsavoury but yet absolutely necessary conclusions from their creed—that cannibalism is right for people who believe in it, that human sacrifice is right for those races which practice it, and that burning widows alive was right for Hindus until the British stepped in and compelled the Hindus to behave immorally by allowing their widows to remain alive.

When it is said that, according to the ethical relativist, what is thought right in any social group is right for that group, one must be careful not to misinterpret this. The relativist does not, of course, mean that there actually is an objective moral standard in France and a different objective standard in England, and that French and British opinions respectively give us correct information about these different standards. His point is rather that there are no objectively true moral standards at all. There is no single universal objective standard. Nor are there a variety of local objective standards. All standards are subjective. People's subjective feelings about morality are the only standards which exist.

To sum up. The ethical relativist consistently denies, it would seem, whatever the ethical absolutist asserts. For the absolutist there is a single universal moral standard. For the relativist there is no such standard. There are only local, ephemeral, and variable standards. For the absolutist there are two senses of the word "standard." Standards in the sense of sets of current moral ideas are relative and changeable. But the standard in the sense of what is actually morally right is absolute and unchanging. For the relativist no such distinction can be made. There is only one meaning of the word standard, namely, that which refers to local and variable sets of moral ideas. Or if it is insisted that the word must be allowed two meanings, then the relativist will say that there is at any rate no actual example of a standard in the absolute sense, and that the word as thus used is an empty name to which nothing in reality corresponds; so that the distinction between the two meanings becomes empty and useless. Finally—though this is merely saying the same thing in another way—the absolutist makes a distinction between what actually is right and what is thought right. The relativist rejects this distinction and identifies what is moral with what is thought moral by certain human beings or groups of human beings. . . .

I shall now proceed to consider, first, the main arguments which can be urged in favour of ethical relativity; and secondly, the arguments which can be urged against it. . . . The first is that which relies upon the actual varieties of moral "standards" found in the world. It was easy enough to believe in a single absolute morality in older times when there was no anthropology, when all humanity was divided clearly into two groups, Christian peoples and the "heathen." Christian peoples knew and possessed the one true morality. The rest were savages whose moral ideas could be ignored. But all this is changed. Greater knowledge has brought greater tolerance. We can no longer exalt our own morality as alone true, while dismissing all other moralities as false or inferior. The investigations of anthropologists have shown that there exist side by side in the world a bewildering variety of moral codes. On this topic endless volumes have been written, masses of evidence piled up. Anthropologists have ransacked the Melanesian Islands, the jungles of New Guinea, the steppes of Siberia, the deserts of Australia, the forests of central Africa, and have brought back with them countless examples of weird, extravagant, and fantastic "moral" customs with which to confound us. We learn that all kinds of horrible practices are, in this, that, or the other place, regarded as essential to virtue. We find that there is nothing, or next to nothing, which has always and everywhere been regarded as morally good by all men. Where then is our universal morality? Can we, in face of all this evidence, deny that it is nothing but an empty dream?

This argument, taken by itself, is a very weak one. It relies upon a single set of facts—the variable moral customs of the world. But this variability of moral ideas is admitted by both parties to the dispute, and is capable of ready explanation upon the hypothesis of either party. The relativist says that the facts are to be explained by the non-existence of any absolute moral standard. The absolutist says that they are to be explained by human ignorance of what the absolute moral standard is.

And he can truly point out that men have differed widely in their opinions about all manner of topics including the subject-matters of the physical sciences—just as much as they differ about morals. And if the various different opinions which men have held about the shape of the earth do not prove that it has no one real shape, neither do the various opinions which they have held about morality prove that there is no one true morality.

Thus the facts can be explained equally plausibly on either hypothesis. There is nothing in the facts themselves which compels us to prefer the relativistic hypothesis to that of the absolutist. And therefore the argument fails to prove the relativist conclusion. If that conclusion is to be established, it must be by means of other considerations.

This is the essential point. But I will add some supplementary remarks. The work of the anthropologists, upon which ethical relativists seem to rely so heavily, has as a matter of fact added absolutely nothing *in principle* to what has always been known about the variability of moral ideas. Educated people have known all along that the Greeks tolerated sodomy, which in modern times has been regarded in some countries as an abominable crime; that the Hindus thought it a sacred duty to burn their widows; that trickery, now thought despicable, was once believed to be a virtue; that terrible torture was thought by our own ancestors only a few centuries ago to be a justifiable weapon of justice; that it was only yesterday that western peoples came to believe that slavery is immoral. Even the ancients knew very well that moral customs and ideas vary—witness the writings of Herodotus. Thus the principle of the variability of moral ideas was well understood long before modern anthropology was ever heard of. Anthropology has added nothing to the knowledge of this principle except a mass of new and extreme examples of it drawn from very remote sources. But to multiply examples of a principle already well known and universally admitted adds nothing to the argument which is built upon that principle. The discoveries of the anthropologists have no doubt been of the highest importance in their own sphere. But in my considered opinion they have thrown no new light upon the special problems of the moral philosopher.

Although the multiplication of examples has no logical bearing on the argument, it does have an immense *psychological* effect upon people's minds. These masses of anthropological learning are impressive. They are propounded in the sacred name of "science." If they are quoted in support of ethical relativity—as they often are—people *think* that they must prove something important. They bewilder and over-awe the simple-minded, batter down their resistance, make them ready to receive humbly the doctrine of ethical relativity from those who have acquired a reputation by their immense learning and their claims to be "scientific." Perhaps this is why so much ado is made by ethical relativists regarding the anthropological evidence. But we must refuse to be impressed. We must discount all this mass of evidence about the extraordinary moral customs of remote peoples. Once we have admitted—as everyone who is instructed must have admitted these last two thousand years without any anthropology at all—the principle that moral ideas vary, all this new evidence adds nothing to the argument. And the argument itself proves nothing for the reasons already given. . . .

The second argument in favour of ethical relativity is also a very strong one. And it does not suffer from the disadvantage that it is dependent upon the acceptance of any particular philosophy such as radical empiricism. It makes its appeal to considerations of a quite general character. It consists in alleging that no one has ever been able to discover upon what foundation an absolute morality could rest, or from what source a universally binding moral code could derive its authority.

If, for example, it is an absolute and unalterable moral rule that all men ought to be unselfish, from whence does this *command* issue? For a command it certainly is, phrase it how you please. There is no difference in meaning between the sentence "You ought to be unselfish" and the sentence "Be unselfish." Now a command implies a commander. An obligation implies some authority which obliges. Who is this commander, what this authority? Thus the vastly difficult question is raised of *the basis of moral obligation*. Now the argument of the relativist would be that it is impossible to find any basis for a universally binding moral law; but that it is quite easy to discover a basis for morality if moral codes are admitted to be variable, ephemeral, and relative to time, place, and circumstance.

In this book I am assuming that it is no longer possible to solve this difficulty by saying naïvely that the universal moral law is based upon the uniform commands of God to all men. There will be many, no doubt, who will dispute this. But I am not writing for them. I am writing for those who feel the necessity of finding for morality a basis independent of particular religious dogmas. And I shall therefore make no attempt to argue the matter.

The problem which the absolutist has to face, then, is this. The religious basis of the one absolute morality having disappeared, can there be found for it any other, any secular, basis? If not, then it would seem that we cannot any longer believe in absolutism. We shall have to fall back upon belief in a variety of perhaps mutually inconsistent moral codes operating over restricted areas and limited periods. No one of these will be better, or more true, than any other. Each will be good and true for those living in those areas and periods. We shall have to fall back, in a word, on ethical relativity.

For there is no great difficulty in discovering the foundations of morality, or rather of moralities, if we adopt the relativistic hypothesis. Even if we cannot be quite certain *precisely* what these foundations are—and relativists themselves are not entirely agreed about them—we can at least see in a general way the *sort* of foundations they must have. We can see that the question on this basis is not in principle impossible of answer—although the details may be obscure; while, if we adopt the absolutist hypothesis—so the argument runs—no kind of answer is conceivable at all. . . .

This argument is undoubtedly very strong. It *is* absolutely essential to solve the problem of the basis of moral obligation if we are to believe in any kind of moral standards other than those provided by mere custom or by irrational emotions. It is idle to talk about a universal morality unless we can point to the source of its authority—or at least to do so is to indulge in a faith which is without rational ground. To cherish a blind faith in morality may be, for the average man whose business is primarily to live aright and not to theorize, sufficient. Perhaps it is his wisest course. But it will not do for the philosopher. His function, or at least one of his functions, is precisely to discover the rational grounds of our everyday beliefs—if they have any. Philosophically and intellectually, then, we cannot accept belief in a universally binding morality unless we can discover upon what foundation its obligatory character rests.

But in spite of the strength of the argument thus posed in favour of ethical relativity, it is not impregnable. For it leaves open one loop-hole. It is always possible that some theory, not yet examined, may provide a basis for a universal moral obligation. The argument rests upon the negative proposition that *there is no theory which can provide a basis for a universal morality*. But it is notoriously difficult to prove a negative. How can you prove that there are no green swans? All you can show is that none have been found so far. And then it is always possible that one will be found tomorrow. . . .

It is time that we turned our attention from the case in favour of ethical relativity to the case against it. Now the case against it consists, to a very large extent, in urging that, if taken seriously and pressed to its logical conclusion, ethical relativity can only end in destroying the conception of morality altogether, in undermining its practical efficacy, in rendering meaningless many almost universally accepted truths about human affairs, in robbing human beings of any incentive to strive for a better world, in taking the life-blood out of every ideal and every aspiration which has ever ennobled the life of man. . . .

First of all, then, ethical relativity, in asserting that the moral standards of particular social groups are the only standards which exist, renders meaningless all propositions which attempt to compare these standards with one another in respect of their moral worth. And this is a very serious matter indeed. We are accustomed to think that the moral ideas of one nation or social group may be "higher" or "lower" than those of another. We believe, for example, that Christian ethical ideals are nobler than those of the savage races of central Africa. Probably most of us would think that the Chinese moral standards are higher than those of the inhabitants of New Guinea. In short we habitually compare one civilization with another and judge the sets of ethical ideas to be found in them to be some better, some worse. The fact that such judgments are very difficult to make with any justice, and that they are frequently made on very superficial and prejudiced grounds, has no bearing on the question now at issue. The question is whether such judgments have any *meaning*. We habitually assume that they have.

But on the basis of ethical relativity they can have none whatever. For the relativist must hold that there is no *common* standard which can be applied to the various civilizations judged. Any such comparison of moral standards implies the existence of some superior standard which is applicable to both. And the existence of any such standard is precisely what the relativist denies. According to him the Christian standard is applicable only to Christians, the Chinese standard only to Chinese, the New Guinea standard only to the inhabitants of New Guinea.

What is true of comparisons between the moral standards of different races will also be true of comparisons between those of different ages. It is not unusual to ask such questions as whether the standard of our own day is superior to that which existed among our ancestors five hundred years ago. And when we remember that our ancestors employed slaves, practiced barbaric physical tortures, and burnt people alive, we may be inclined to think that it is. At any rate we assume that the question is one which has meaning and is capable of rational discussion. But if the ethical relativist is right, whatever we assert on this subject must be totally meaningless. For here again there is no common standard which could form the basis of any such judgments.

This in its turn implies that the whole notion of moral *progress* is a sheer delusion. Progress means an advance from lower to higher, from worse to better. But on the basis of ethical relativity it has no meaning to say that the standards of this age are better (or worse) than those of a previous age. For there is no common standard by which both can be measured. Thus it is nonsense to say that the morality of the New Testament is higher than that of the Old. And Jesus Christ, if he imagined that he was introducing into the world a higher ethical standard than existed before his time, was merely deluded. . . .

I come now to a second point. Up to the present I have allowed it to be taken tacitly for granted that, though judgments comparing different races and ages in respect of the worth of their moral codes are impossible for the ethical relativist, yet judgments of comparison between individuals living within the same social group would be quite possible. For individuals living within the some social group would presumably be subject to the same moral code, that of their group, and this would therefore constitute, as between these individuals, a common standard by which they could both be measured. We have not here, as we had in the other case, the difficulty of the absence of any common standard of comparison. It should therefore be possible for the ethical relativist to say quite meaningfully that President Lincoln was a better man than some criminal or moral imbecile of his own time and country, or that Jesus was a better man than Judas Iscariot.

But is even this minimum of moral judgment really possible on relativist grounds? It seems to me that it is not. For when once the whole of humanity is abandoned as the area covered by a single moral standard, what smaller areas are to be adopted as the *loci* of different standards? Where are we to draw the lines of demarcation? We can split up humanity, perhaps,—though the procedure will be very arbitrary—into races, races into nations, nations into tribes, tribes into families, families into individuals. Where are we going to draw the *moral* boundaries? Does the *locus* of a particular moral standard reside in a race, a nation, a tribe, a family, or an individual? Perhaps the blessed phrase "social group" will be dragged in to save the situation. Each such group, we shall be told, has its own moral code which is, for it, right. But what *is* a "group"? Can any one define it or give its boundaries? This is the seat of that ambiguity in the theory of ethical relativity to which reference was made on an earlier page.

The difficulty is not, as might be thought, merely an academic difficulty of logical definition. If that were all, I should not press the point. But the ambiguity has practical consequences which are disastrous for morality. No one is likely to say that moral codes are confined within the arbitrary limits of the geographical divisions of countries. Nor are the notions of race, nation, or political state likely to help us. To bring out the essentially practical character of the difficulty let us put it in the form of concrete questions. Does the American nation constitute a "group" having a single moral standard? Or does the standard of what I ought to do change continuously as I cross the continent in a railway train? Do different States of the Union have different moral codes? Perhaps every town and village has its own peculiar standard. This may at first sight seem reasonable enough. "In Rome do as Rome does" may seem as good a rule in morals as it is in etiquette. But can we stop there? Within the village are numerous cliques each having its own set of ideas. Why should not each of these claim to be bound only by its own special and peculiar moral standards? And if it comes to that, why should not the gangsters of Chicago claim to constitute a group having its own morality, so that its murders and debaucheries must be viewed as "right" by the only standard which can legitimately be applied to it? And if it be answered that the nation will not tolerate this, that may be so. But this is to put the foundation of right simply in the superior force of the majority. In that case whoever is stronger will be right, however monstrous his ideas and actions. And if we cannot deny to any set of people the right to have its own morality, is it not clear that, in the end, we cannot even deny this right to the individual? Every individual man and woman can put up, on this view, an irrefutable claim to be judged by no standard except his or her own.

If these arguments are valid, the ethical relativist cannot really maintain that there is anywhere to be found a moral standard binding upon anybody against his will. And he cannot maintain that, even within the social group, there is a common standard as between individuals. And if that is so, then even judgments to the effect that one man is morally better than another become meaningless. All moral valuation thus vanishes. There is nothing to prevent each man from being a rule unto himself. The result will be moral chaos and the collapse of all effective standards. . . .

But even if we assume that the difficulty about defining moral groups has been surmounted, a further difficulty presents itself. Suppose that we have now definitely decided what are the exact boundaries of the social group within which a moral standard is to be operative. And we will assume—as is invariably done by relativists themselves—that this group is to be some actually existing social community such as a tribe or nation. How are we to know, even then, what actually *is* the moral standard within that group? How is anyone to know? How is even a member of the group to know? For there are certain to be within the group—at least this will be true among advanced peoples—wide differences of opinion as to what is right, what wrong. Whose opinion, then, is to be taken as representing *the* moral standard of the group? Either we must take the opinion of the majority within the group, or the opinion of some minority. If we rely upon the ideas of the majority, the results will be disastrous. Wherever there is found among a people a small band of select spirits, or perhaps one man, working for the establishment of higher and nobler ideals than those commonly accepted by the group, we shall be compelled to hold that, for that people at that time, the majority are right, and that the reformers are wrong and are preaching what is immoral. We shall have to maintain, for example, that Jesus was preaching immoral doctrines to the Jews. Moral goodness will have to be equated always with the mediocre and sometimes with the definitely base and ignoble. If on the other hand we said that the moral standard of the group is to be identified with the moral opinions of some minority, then what minority is this to be? We cannot answer that it is to be the minority composed of the best and most enlightened individuals of the group. This would involve us in a palpably vicious circle. For by what standard are these individuals to be judged the best and the most enlightened? There is no principle by which we could select the right minority. And therefore we should have to consider every minority as good as every other. And this means that we should have no logical right whatever to resist the claim of the gangsters of Chicago—if such a claim were made—that their practices represent the highest standards of American morality. It means in the end that every individual is to be bound by no standard save his own.

The ethical relativists are great empiricists. *What* is the actually moral standard of any group can only be discovered, they tell us, by an examination on the ground of the moral opinions and customs of that group. But will they tell us how they propose to decide, when they get to the ground, which of the many moral opinions they are sure to find there is *the* right one in that group? To some extent they will be able to do this for the Melanesian Islanders—from whom apparently all lessons in the nature of morality are in future to be taken. But it is certain that they cannot do it for advanced peoples whose members have learnt to think for themselves and to entertain among themselves a wide variety of opinions. They cannot do it unless they accept the calamitous view that the ethical opinion of the majority is always right. We are left therefore once more with the conclusion that, even within a particular social group, anybody's moral opinion is as good as anybody else's, and that every man is entitled to be judged by his own standards.

Finally, not only is ethical relativity disastrous in its consequences for moral theory. It cannot be doubted that it must tend to be equally disastrous in its impact upon practical conduct. If men come really to believe that one moral standard is as good as another, they will conclude that their own moral standard has nothing special to recommend it. They might as well then slip down to some lower and easier standard. It is true that, for a time, it may be possible to hold one view in theory and to act practically upon another. But ideas, even philosophical ideas, are not so ineffectual that they can remain for ever idle in the upper chambers of the intellect. In the end they seep down to the level of practice. They get themselves acted on.

Social Science and Ethical Relativism   Paul Taylor

Paul Taylor (1923–   ) is professor of philosophy at Brooklyn College. He has written widely in the field of ethics.

As a participant in the American Philosophical Association (Eastern Division) symposium on "Ethical Relativity in the Light of Recent Developments in Social Science," Professor Clyde Kluckhohn published a summary or recent studies in anthropology, sociology, and psychology concerning universal elements to be found in all human cultures.[1] "For at least a generation," he says, "American anthropology (and to a considerable degree, anthropology in the world in general) concentrated its attention upon the differences between peoples, neglecting the similarities. Recently, the balance has been righted somewhat."[2] He then goes on to give an account of these similarities as they have been set forth in recent published work by psychologists and sociologists as well as by anthropologists. Throughout this discussion Professor Kluckhohn appears to believe that such universal elements or similarities among different cultures are evidence against, or somehow provide the basis for an argument against, or at least justify a qualification of, ethical relativism. (By "ethical relativism" he means, and I shall mean, the assertion that two people or groups of people may hold contradictory ethical views without either being mistaken.[3]) I want to argue that these recent findings of the social scientists do not disprove or provide evidence against ethical relativism, and that they are not even relevant to the relativism-absolution controversy in ethics.

It has long been the opinion of moral philosophers that the facts about the *differences* among the ethical judgments of different societies do not give support to ethical relativism. A person who denies relativism and claims that moral standards validly apply to all men everywhere and in every age may accept the scientific evidence of the contradictions

From *The Journal of Philosophy*, Vol. LV, No. 1 (January 2, 1958). Reprinted with permission of the author and *The Journal of Philosophy*.

[1] Clyde Kluckhohn, "Ethical Relativity: Sic et Non," this JOURNAL, Vol. LII (Nov. 10, 1955), pp. 663–677.

[2] *Ibid.*, p. 664.

[3] If "holding contradictory ethical views" is interpreted as "disagreement in attitude" and not as a contradiction in the usual sense, then relativism is the view that there are no better reasons for taking one attitude rather than another, while absolutism is the view that such reasons can be given.

among moral opinions of different cultures. He simply says some opinions are true (i.e., good reasons can be given for them) and some opinions are false (i.e., good reasons can be given against them). He might not know which are true and which are false. It might be *empirically* impossible for him at the time to give good reasons for or against certain opinions. But he believes that at least it makes sense to say that some are true and others are false, which is precisely what the ethical relativist denies. The ethical relativist claims it is *logically* impossible to give good reasons (reasons which are not culture-bound) for or against moral judgments.

Now just as the facts of cultural differences do not argue for ethical relativism, so the facts of cultural similarities do not argue against ethical relativism. Let us first examine the principle behind this statement and then consider the particular facts of cultural similarities pointed out by Professor Kluckhohn and see why they do not affect the argument for or against ethical relativism. Suppose that there were no differences in the ethical views of different societies. Indeed we can imagine without very much difficulty that a totalitarian power has conquered the world and has subjected everyone to a particular ethical code. By means of indoctrination, propaganda, censorship, brainwashing, and other techniques, the totalitarian power has made everyone in the world come to accept identical moral views. Would this make those moral views true? Of course not. Would this universal concurrence of moral opinion have any bearing on whether any moral view was true or false? I think we must again answer in the negative. Whether a given moral opinion is true or false depends not on who believes it or how many believe it, but on whether reasons can be given to justify it. And such reasons will not include counting the number of people who believe it. One can say that it is true if *rational* people believe it. But again what makes a person rational has nothing to do with how many people he agrees with in his moral opinions. Therefore, even if there were universal concurrence of moral opinion throughout the world, the ethical relativist would not be refuted and the ethical absolutist would not be vindicated. For the relativist would simply say: What is right in such a world is right because people believe it is right, or because they approve of it. If in another world, or in some future age, people (even one person) came to believe otherwise, then that which is right now, for everyone, would become wrong for those who disagreed. And neither person or group could be said to have a more valid opinion than the other. The absolutist would say: The fact that all people now agree about what is right and wrong does not make their beliefs true. They may be correct or they may be mistaken. To decide this we must examine their beliefs to see whether good reasons can be given for or against them.

But it may still be objected that the universal concurrence of moral opinion was imagined to be artificially forced on people, and this is what makes it irrelevant to the relativism-absolutism controversy. If everyone in the world came to have the same opinion naturally, without any interference from despots or thought controllers, then the relativist's position would be invalidated. The crux of this argument lies in the meaning of the word "naturally." If this means spontaneously and emotionally, without the discipline of rational thought, then relativism remains untouched. But if "naturally" means by the free exercise of reason and intelligence, then relativism would indeed be invalidated, but it would not be invalidated just because everyone agreed about morals.

If people came to agree about moral matters spontaneously and emotionally, the relativist would point out that a person's emotional life is conditioned in part by his social environment, and therefore whatever ethical opinions he arrived at through the spontaneous expression and development of his emotions would be relative to his social conditioning. And the fact that everyone had similar emotional reactions in ethical matters would merely imply that they had been subjected to similar environmental conditioning (though a conditioning which had not been deliberately controlled by human agents). Furthermore he would infer that *if* people had been subjected to *other* conditioning their moral opinions would be just as valid as the opinions of those who all agree under the same conditioning.

If, on the other hand, we accept the second meaning of "naturally," then relativism would be disproved and absolutism proved. For in this case rational beings would come to agree about what is right and wrong, and their opinions would be morally justifiable. But what would justify them is not their agreement but their rationality. (Being rational *means* being able to justify, to give good reasons for, one's opinions.) Even if rational beings did not agree, ethical relativism would not by that fact be shown to be true. For this would be a case of honest disagreement among enlightened and competent judges, whose disagreement must leave the correct moral judgment in doubt until further enlightenment brings about agreement. Ethical relativism would be proven only if two or more completely rational and enlightened judges disagreed. We cannot be sure that such a hypothetical eventuality would not happen, of course, and this is one of the reasons why we cannot be sure that ethical relativism is a mistaken view. But whether relativism or absolutism be true, it is sufficient for our argument that this question is not settled by pointing out either that everyone agrees or that no one agrees in their ethical judgments.

Let us now turn to Professor Kluckhohn's exposition of the specific findings of social scientists concerning the similarities among different societies, and let us see if anything can be inferred from them as to whether ethical relativism or ethical absolutism is true. Although Professor Kluckhohn does not classify the findings he discusses, I think they can be arranged into five major groups, according to the kind of factor whose universality is asserted: (1) the universality of morality in general, (2) the universality of certain human needs, (3) the universality of certain human capacities, (4) the universality of "basic field conditions," of social structures and psychological functions, and (5) the universality of certain sentiments, emotions, and attitudes.

(1) Professor Kluckhohn refers to "the universality of moral standards in general,"[4] and to the fact that even very different types of society

---

[4] Kluckhohn, *loc. cit.*, p. 671.

"affirm the same moral value: allegiance to the norms of one's culture."[5] Examples given for universal moral standards in general are: a concept of murder as distinguished from "justifiable homicides," regulations upon sexual behavior, prohibitions upon untruth, and mutual obligations between parents and children. Variation occurs, however, "as to details of prescribed behavior, instrumentalities, and sanctions."[6] And at one point Professor Kluckhohn declares: "To be sure, there must be room left for relativity as regards specific moral rules."[7]

Now let us grant that in every culture there is a set of moral principles of rules of conduct to which the members of the society owe allegiance. If these principles or rules differ on such matters as what types of homicide are justified and what are to be considered murder, what types of sexual behavior are permissible, what circumstances exempt a person from the obligation to tell the truth, and what kinds of acts are obligatory with regard to one's parents or one's children, this variation will make almost all moral judgments culture-bound. What an ethical absolutist wants to know is not so much whether morality in general is good for society, but whether it is right to let a person die of neglect when he can no longer contribute to a society's economic production, whether it is right to kill unwanted infants, whether monogamy is the best sexual institution, whether a person ought to tell the truth under specified circumstances, and so on. No justification, however valid, of morality in general will be relevant to his problem. . . .

• • • • •

(2) After presenting certain recent findings in psychology, Professor Kluckhohn concludes that there is a "growing trend toward agreement" that "there are pan-human universals as regards needs and capacities that shape, or could rightly shape, at least the broad outlines of a morality that transcends cultural difference."[8] I wish to distinguish "needs" and "capacities," so I shall discuss only the former at this point. No doubt it is the case that human beings have certain fundamental needs which are present no matter what kind of society exists. But two ethical questions must be asked with reference to these needs: (1) Why ought these needs to be satisfied? (2) If some needs are not inborn (unlearned) and depend for their emergence and development on a certain type of physical and social environment, it is then at least theoretically within human capacity to control their emergence and development, and one must ask, What needs ought to be allowed to emerge and develop? Neither of these questions can be answered by indicating the universality of a certain number of needs in all existing cultures. One might say that at least the needs for survival of the individual ought to be satisfied. But this is to assume that survival is desirable, and there is not universal agreement on this, as the existence of people who want to commit suicide testifies. The relativist claims that no arguments can be given to show that com-

[5] *Ibid.*, p. 673.
[6] *Ibid.*, p. 672.
[7] *Ibid,* p. 673.
[8] *Ibid.*, p. 666.

mitting suicide is wrong (or right), while the absolutist says there are such arguments. But their dispute clearly will not be resolved by pointing out universal or near-universal needs for the preservation of life, unless it is also shown why such needs ought to be fulfilled.

If reference is made to universal "drives," "motives," or "dynamic forces" among all men, the same reasoning applies, since the question to be answered is: *Ought* these drives or motives or dynamic forces to be satisfied, to be allowed to guide human behavior, whether in a pure or in a "sublimated" form? Professor Kluckhohn quotes Franz Boas: "The dynamic forces that mould social life are the same now as those that moulded life thousands of years ago."[9] But this common element cannot provide a basis for ethical absolutism unless reasons are given which justify the channeling of these dynamic forces in particular ways, rather than trying to repress, frustrate, or block them to whatever degree man is capable.

(3) The appeal to universal human capacities or potentialities in support of ethical absolutism is certainly not new with Professor Kluckhohn. It is becoming a very widespread idea among contemporary social scientists and psychologists who are interested in ethics. Perhaps the most prominent example is Erich Fromm, who in *Man for Himself* interprets human existence as "the unfolding of the specific powers of an organism."[10] He goes on to say that "all organisms have an inherent tendency to actualize their specific potentialities. *The aim of man's life,* therefore, is to be understood as *the unfolding of his powers according to the laws of his nature.*"[11] At another point he states, "There is no meaning to life except the meaning man gives his life by the unfolding of his powers, by living productively."[12] Now it has often been said that man is potentially anything he can become. He has the potentiality for sainthood or sadism, for benevolence or bigotry. The ethical question, of course, is concerned with *which* potentialities ought to be actualized. Fromm's answer to this is that those potentialities ought to be actualized which are peculiarly human.[13] But certainly there are many ways of behaving, thinking, and feeling which only man is capable of, yet which no psychologist or social scientist would want to judge as morally right. Fromm himself recognizes this difficulty and tries to get around it by making a distinction between "primary" and "secondary" potentialities. The former are actualized if "proper" or "normal" conditions are present, the latter are actualized under "abnormal, pathogenic" conditions which are "in contrast to existential needs."[14] It is clear that this distinction assumes the moral criterion which, according to Fromm, the "science of man" is supposed to provide. Suppose someone wishes to

[9] *Ibid.,* p. 669.

[10] Erich Fromm, *Man for Himself* (New York, 1947), p. 19.

[11] *Ibid.,* p. 20. Italics are Fromm's.

[12] *Ibid.,* p. 45.

[13] *Ibid.,* p. 45.

[14] *Ibid.,* p. 218.

actualize his "secondary" potentialities. To claim he is making a mistake or is doing what is morally wrong requires a justification on grounds other than the pointing out of other potentialities the person is capable of realizing, and other than asserting that his life is "abnormal" or "pathogenic." And clearly the fact that certain potentialities are common to all men, in all cultures, is not a good reason for the ethical judgment that they are the potentialities which ought to be actualized. For this is simply to say that a person ought to do what other people can do, given the environmental conditions of their cultures. This rule is ambiguous, since part of man's potentiality is the ability to change his culture and this rule gives no guidance as to the morally proper or obligatory direction of change. Enough has been said, I think, to show that no reasonable or intelligent person would accept such a rule, and that the relativist and absolutist positions regarding moral standards are not affected by citing universal potentialities in man.

(4) The fourth category of universal elements which Professor Kluckhohn discusses includes a rather wide variety of "formal similarities" which may be suggested by the following very incomplete list: "basic field conditions" such as society, culture, and symbolic interaction (p. 666); "the experience of intimate association with the 'primary group' upon whom [the individual] was emotionally and otherwise dependent" (p. 667); having two parents of opposite sex and facing the emotional problems of being in competition with one's siblings (p. 668); possessing basically similar neurological mechanisms for dealing with problems (p. 668); the existence of music, graphic arts, dancing, parallels in linguistic standards of personal excellence, kinship terminology, and age grading (p. 670); such "cultural constants" as family, religion, war, and communication (p. 670); "the notion of integration of individual to the group" (p. 671); and "the fundamental idea of reciprocity" (p. 671). These relationships, social structures, psychological functions, environmental conditions, etc., which are common to all human societies are no more relevant to the issue between relativism and absolutism in ethics than are the previous types of universals we have considered. To give evidence that everyone competes with his siblings or that everyone grows up in intimate association with two parents of opposite sex is not to give evidence that any particular set of family relations is better than any other. Nor is it to give evidence that one can or cannot make reasonable judgments about the proper way of living with one's siblings, parents, or children. Similarly, that there are such "cultural constants" as war and religion does not imply that wars are ethically right or that religion ought to continue to be a part of human culture. Of course if one has already given reasons for adopting a set of moral rules or for seeking a set of ideals in life, and if it is then demonstrated that wars violate these rules and prevent the realization of these ideals, and that religion gives dramatic symbolization of and emotional orientation toward the rules and ideals, then one may deduce the wrongness of war and the rightness of religion. But the relativist and absolutist are disputing over the first point: whether reasons can be given for adopting a set of moral rules or for seeking certain ideals in life, and whether, if such reasons can

be found, those reasons are not entirely culture-bound. And this dispute cannot be resolved by pointing out cultural universals of the sort mentioned above.

(5) The last group of universals are sentiments, emotions, and attitudes common to all human beings in all societies. Professor Kluckhohn speaks of the "universal sentiments" of "love, jealousy, respect, need for respect, and the like." Even if we expand this to include a wide range of emotions and attitudes, which I think Professor Kluckhohn and many other social scientists would be willing to do, the relativism-absolutism controversy is not logically involved. For the ethical issues concern such questions as, Whom ought we to love, and in what way? Under what circumstances, if any, is it proper or permissible to feel jealousy? Why should a person respect others? To acknowledge the universality of love, jealousy, and respect has nothing to do with answering these questions. It may be thought, however, that under the "emotive" theory of ethics, according to which ethical terms are expressive of attitudes (liking, disliking, approval, disapproval, etc.), these facts about the universality of certain attitudes would become relevant. But I do not think this is so, since the beliefs about which the relativist and absolutist disagree are concerned with what ought to be the objects of positive attitudes and what ought to be the objects of negative attitudes, as well as with what reasons, if any, can be cited to justify the taking of one attitude rather than another about a given object. It may be the case that in all human societies people have the experience of approving and disapproving of different things, but if they do not agree on what to approve of and what to disapprove of, the mere fact that they all have the experience of approving and disapproving is of no consequence for the truth or falsity, verifiability or unverifiability, reasonableness or unreasonableness, of moral utterances.

.   .   .   .   .

... What social scientists and psychologists can do in the attempt to work out a rationally justifiable decision or judgment concerning rules of conduct, objectives worth striving for, etc., is (1) to give us facts to help us to predict with greater probability the consequences of adopting various rules or objectives; (2) to widen our horizon of knowledge so that we can envisage alternatives we might not have thought of before; (3) to show us the origin of our attitudes and customs, their causes and effects in social history and in the individual psyche, so that we may understand how they influence our present judgments and how they might be changed; and (4) in general to make us well informed about all empirical knowledge that bears on the situation of choice or judgment. Now the pointing out of universal elements in all cultures will be relevant only so far as the knowledge of such universals contributes to these four tasks. But there would be nothing special about the fact that pan-human universals rather than peculiarities of societies were being pointed out. They would simply comprise further facts which, in the forming of a rational decision or judgment, would be helpful in varying degrees according to the situation.

How Should We Behave?

Utilitarianism   Jeremy Bentham

Jeremy Bentham (1748–1832), the English philosopher and political theorist,
developed the utilitarian theory as a basis for political and legal reform.

Of the Principle of Utility

I. Nature has placed mankind under the governance of two sovereign
masters, *pain* and *pleasure*. It is for them alone to point out what we
ought to do, as well as to determine what we shall do. On the one hand
the standard of right and wrong, on the other the chain of causes and
effects, are fastened to their throne. They govern us in all we do, in all
we say, in all we think: every effort we can make to throw off our subjection, will serve but to demonstrate and confirm it. In words a man may
pretend to abjure their empire: but in reality he will remain subject
to it all the while. The *principle of utility* recognises this subjection, and
assumes it for the foundation of that system, the object of which is to
rear the fabric of felicity by the hands of reason and of law. Systems
which attempt to question it, deal in sounds instead of sense, in caprice
instead of reason, in darkness instead of light.

But enough of metaphor and declamation: it is not by such means
that moral science is to be improved.

II. The principle of utility is the foundation of the present work: it
will be proper therefore at the outset to give an explicit and determinate
account of what is meant by it. By the principle of utility is meant that
principle which approves or disapproves of every action whatsoever, according to the tendency which it appears to have to augment or diminish
the happiness of the party whose interest is in question: or, what is the
same thing in other words, to promote or to oppose that happiness. I
say of every action whatsoever; and therefore not only of every action of
a private individual, but of every measure of government.

III. By utility is meant that property in any object, whereby it tends
to produce benefit, advantage, pleasure, good, or happiness (all this in
the present case comes to the same thing) or (what comes again to the
same thing) to prevent the happening of mischief, pain, evil, or unhappiness to the party whose interest is considered: if that party be the community in general, then the happiness of the community: if a particular
individual, then the happiness of that individual.

IV. The interest of the community is one of the most general expressions that can occur in the phraseology of morals: no wonder that the

From *An Introduction to the Principles of Morals and Legislation* by Jeremy Bentham. Reprinted by permission of Clarendon Press, Oxford.

meaning of it is often lost. When it has a meaning, it is this. The community is a fictitious *body*, composed of the individual persons who are considered as constituting as it were its *members*. The interest of the community then is, what?—the sum of the interests of the several members who compose it.

V. It is in vain to talk of the interest of the community, without understanding what is the interest of the individual. A thing is said to promote the interest, or to be *for* the interest, of an individual, when it tends to add to the sum total of his pleasures: or, what comes to the same thing, to diminish the sum total of his pains.

VI. An action then may be said to be conformable to the principle of utility, or, for shortness sake, to utility, (meaning with respect to the community at large) when the tendency it has to augment the happiness of the community is greater than any it has to diminish it.

VII. A measure of government (which is but a particular kind of action, performed by a particular person or persons) may be said to be conformable to or dictated by the principle of utility, when in like manner the tendency which it has to augment the happiness of the community is greater than any which it has to diminish it.

VIII. When an action, or in particular a measure of government, is supposed by a man to be conformable to the principle of utility, it may be convenient, for the purposes of discourse, to imagine a kind of law or dictate, called a law or dictate of utility: and to speak of the action in question, as being conformable to such law or dictate.

IX. A man may be said to be a partisan of the principle of utility, when the approbation or disapprobation he annexes to any action, or to any measure, is determined by and proportioned to the tendency which he conceives it to have to augment or to diminish the happiness of the community: or in other words, to its conformity or unconformity to the laws or dictates of utility.

X. Of an action that is conformable to the principle of utility one may always say either that it is one that ought to be done, or at least that it is not one that ought not to be done. One may say also, that it is right it should be done; at least that it is not wrong it should be done: that it is a right action; at least that it is not a wrong action. When thus interpreted, the words *ought,* and *right* and *wrong,* and others of that stamp, have a meaning: when otherwise, they have none.

XI. Has the rectitude of this principle been ever formally contested? It should seem that it had, by those who have not known what they have been meaning. Is it susceptible of any direct proof? it should seem not: for that which is used to prove everything else, cannot itself be proved: a chain of proofs must have their commencement somewhere. To give such proof is as impossible as it is needless.

XII. Not that there is or ever has been that human creature breathing, however stupid or perverse, who has not on many, perhaps on most occasions of his life, deferred to it. By the natural constitution of the human frame, on most occasions of their lives men in general embrace this principle, without thinking of it: if not for the ordering of their own actions, yet for the trying of their own actions, as well as of those of other men. There have been, at the same time, not many, perhaps, even of the most intelligent, who have been disposed to embrace it purely and without reserve. There are even few who have not taken some occasion or other to quarrel with it, either on account of their not understanding always how to apply it, or on account of some prejudice or other which they were afraid to examine into, or could not bear to part with. For such is the stuff that man is made of: in principle and in practice, in a right track and in a wrong one, the rarest of all human qualities is consistency.

XIII. When a man attempts to combat the principle of utility, it is with reasons drawn, without his being aware of it, from that very principle itself. His arguments, if they prove any thing, prove not that the principle is *wrong*, but that, according to the applications he supposes to be made of it, it is *misapplied*. Is it possible for a man to move the earth? Yes; but he must first find out another earth to stand upon.

Of Principles Adverse to That of Utility

I. If the principle of utility be a right principle to be governed by, and that in all cases, it follows from what has been just observed, that whatever principle differs from it in any case must necessarily be a wrong one. To prove any other principle, therefore, to be a wrong one, there needs no more than just to show it to be what it is, a principle of which the dictates are in some point or other different from those of the principle of utility: to state it is to confute it.

II. A principle may be different from that of utility in two ways: 1. By being constantly opposed to it: this is the case with a principle which may be termed the principle of *asceticism*. 2. By being sometimes opposed to it, and sometimes not, as it may happen: this is the case with another, which may be termed the principle of *sympathy* and *antipathy*.

III. By the principle of asceticism I mean that principle, which, like the principle of utility, approves or disapproves of any action, according to the tendency which it appears to have to augment or diminish the happiness of the party whose interest is in question; but in an inverse manner: approving of actions in as far as they tend to diminish his happiness; disapproving of them in as far as they tend to augment it.

IV. It is evident that any one who reprobates any the least particle of pleasure, as such, from whatever source derived, is *pro tanto* a partisan of the principle of asceticism. It is only upon that principle, and not from the principle of utility, that the most abominable pleasure which the vilest of malefactors ever reaped from his crime would be to be reprobated, if it stood alone. The case is, that it never does stand alone; but is necessarily followed by such a quality of pain (or, what comes to the same thing, such a chance for a certain quantity of pain) that the pleasure in comparison of it, is as nothing: and this is the true and sole, but perfectly sufficient, reason for making it a ground for punishment. . . .

X. The principle of utility is capable of being consistently pursued; and it is but tautology to say, that the more consistently it is pursued, the better it must ever be for humankind. The principle of asceticism never was, nor ever can be, consistently pursued by any living creature.

Let but one tenth part of the inhabitants of this earth pursue it consistently, and in a day's time they will have turned it into a hell.

XI. Among principles adverse to that of utility, that which at this day seems to have most influence in matters of government, is what may be called the principle of sympathy and antipathy. By the principle of sympathy and antipathy, I mean that principle which approves or disapproves of certain actions, not on account of their tending to augment the happiness, nor yet on account of their tending to diminish the happiness of the party whose interest is in question, but merely because a man finds himself disposed to approve or disapprove of them: holding up that approbation or disapprobation as a sufficient reason for itself, and disclaiming the necessity of looking out for any extrinsic ground. Thus far in the general department of morals: and in the particular department of politics, measuring out the quantum (as well as determining the ground) of punishment, by the degree of the disapprobation.

XII. It is manifest, that this is rather a principle in name than in reality: it is not a positive principle of itself, so much as a term employed to signify the negation of all principle. What one expects to find in a principle is something that points out some external consideration, as a means of warranting and guiding the internal sentiments of approbation and disapprobation: this expectation is but ill fulfilled by a proposition, which does neither more nor less than hold up each of those sentiments as a ground and standard for itself.

XIII. In looking over the catalogue of human actions (says a partisan of this principle) in order to determine which of them are to be marked with the seal of disapprobation, you need but to take counsel of your own feelings: whatever you find in yourself a propensity to condemn, is wrong for that very reason. For the same reason it is also meet for punishment: in what proportion it is adverse to utility, or whether it be adverse to utility at all, is a matter that makes no difference. In that same *proportion* also is it meet for punishment: if you hate much, punish much: if you hate little, punish little: punish as you hate. If you hate not at all, punish not at all: the fine feelings of the soul are not to be overborne and tyrannized by the harsh and rugged dictates of political utility....

XV. It is manifest, that the dictates of this principle will frequently coincide with those of utility, though perhaps without intending any such thing. Probably more frequently than not: and hence it is that the business of penal justice is carried on upon that tolerable sort of footing upon which we see it carried on in common at this day. For what more natural or more general ground of hatred to a practice can there be, than the mischievousness of such practice? What all men are exposed to suffer by, all men will be disposed to hate. It is far yet, however, from being a constant ground: for when a man suffers, it is not always that he knows what it is he suffers by. A man may suffer grievously, for instance, by a new tax, without being able to trace up the cause of his sufferings to the injustice of some neighbour, who has eluded the payment of an old one.

XVI. The principle of sympathy and antipathy is most apt to err on the side of severity. It is for applying punishment in many cases which deserve none: in many cases which deserve some, it is for applying more than they deserve. There is no incident imaginable, be it ever so trivial, and so remote from mischief, from which this principle may not extract a ground of punishment. Any difference in taste: any difference in opinion: upon one subject as well as upon another. No disagreement so trifling which perseverance and altercation will not render serious. Each becomes in the other's eyes an enemy, and, if laws permit, a criminal. This is one of the circumstances by which the human race is distinguished (not much indeed to its advantage) from the brute creation. . . .

XIX. There are two things which are very apt to be confounded, but which it imports us carefully to distinguish:—the motive or cause, which, by operating on the mind of an individual, is productive of any act: and the ground or reason which warrants a legislator, or other by-stander, in regarding that act with an eye of approbation. When the act happens, in the particular instance in question, to be productive of effects which we approve of, much more if we happen to observe that the same motive may frequently be productive, in other instances, of the like effects, we are apt to transfer our approbation to the motive itself, and to assume, as the just ground for the approbation we bestow on the act, the circumstance of its originating from that motive. It is in this way that the sentiment of antipathy has often been considered as a just ground of action. Antipathy, for instance, in such or such a case, is the cause of an action which is attended with good effects: but this does not make it a right ground of action in that case, any more than in any other. Still farther. Not only the effects are good, but the agent sees beforehand that they will be so. This may make the action indeed a perfectly right action: but it does not make antipathy a right ground of action. For the same sentiment of antipathy, if implicitly deferred to, may be, and very frequently is, productive of the very worst effects. Antipathy, therefore, can never be a right ground of action. No more, therefore, can resentment, which, as will be seen more particularly hereafter, is but a modification of antipathy. The only right ground of action, that can possibly subsist, is, after all, the consideration of utility, which, if it is a right principle of action, and of approbation, in any one case, is so in every other. Other principles in abundance, that is, other motives, may be the reasons why such and such an act *has* been done: that is, the reasons or causes of its being done: but it is this alone that can be the reason why it might or ought to have been done. Antipathy or resentment requires always to be regulated, to prevent its doing mischief: to be regulated by what? always by the principle of utility. The principle of utility neither requires nor admits of any other regulator than itself.

Value of a Lot of Pleasure or Pain, How to Be Measured

I. Pleasures then, and the avoidance of pains, are the *ends* which the legislator has in view: it behooves him therefore to understand their *value.* Pleasures and pains are the *instruments* he has to work with: it behoves him therefore to understand their force, which is again, in other words, their value.

II. To a person considered *by himself,* the value of a pleasure or pain considered *by itself,* will be greater or less, according to the four following circumstances:

1. Its *intensity.*
2. Its *duration.*
3. Its *certainty* or *uncertainty.*
4. Its *propinquity* or *remoteness.*

III. These are the circumstances which are to be considered in estimating a pleasure or a pain considered each of them by itself. But when the value of any pleasure or pain is considered for the purpose of estimating the tendency of any *act* by which it is produced, there are two other circumstances to be taken into the account; these are,

5. Its *fecundity,* or the chance it has of being followed by sensations of the *same* kind: that is, pleasures, if it be a pleasure: pains, if it be a pain.

6. Its *purity,* or the chance it has of *not* being followed by sensations of the *opposite* kind: that is, pains, if it be a pleasure: pleasures, if it be a pain.

These two last, however, are in strictness scarcely to be deemed properties of the pleasure or the pain itself; they are not, therefore, in strictness to be taken into the account of the value of that pleasure or that pain. They are in strictness to be deemed properties only of the act, or other event, by which such pleasure or pain has been produced; and accordingly are only to be taken into the account of the tendency of such act or such event.

IV. To a *number* of persons, with reference to each of whom the value of a pleasure or a pain is considered, it will be greater or less, according to seven circumstances: to wit, the six preceding ones; *viz.*

1. Its *intensity.*
2. Its *duration.*
3. Its *certainty* or *uncertainty.*
4. Its *propinquity* or *remoteness.*
5. Its *fecundity.*
6. Its *purity.*

And one other; to wit:

7. Its *extent;* that is, the number of persons to whom it *extends;* or (in other words) who are affected by it.

V. To take an exact account then of the general tendency of any act, by which the interests of a community are affected, proceed as follows. Begin with any one person of those whose interests seem most immediately to be affected by it: and take an account,

1. Of the value of each distinguishable *pleasure* which appears to be produced by it in the *first* instance.

2. Of the value of each *pain* which appears to be produced by it in the *first* instance.

3. Of the value of each pleasure which appears to be produced by it

after the first. This constitutes the *fecundity* of the first *pleasure* and the *impurity* of the first *pain*.

4. Of the value of each *pain* which appears to be produced by it after the first. This constitutes the *fecundity* of the first *pain,* and the *impurity* of the first pleasure.

5. Sum up all the values of all the *pleasures* on the one side, and those of all the pains on the other. The balance, if it be on the side of pleasure, will give the *good* tendency of the act upon the whole, with respect to the interests of that *individual* person; if on the side of pain, the *bad* tendency of it upon the whole.

6. Take an account of the *number* of persons whose interests appear to be concerned; and repeat the above process with respect to each. *Sum up* the numbers expressive of the degrees of *good* tendency, which the act has, with respect to each individual, in regard to whom the tendency of it is *good* upon the whole: do this again with respect to each individual, in regard to whom the tendency of it is *good* upon the whole: do this again with respect to each individual, in regard to whom the tendency of it is *bad* upon the whole. Take the *balance;* which, if on the side of *pleasure,* will give the general *good tendency* of the act, with respect to the total number or community of individuals concerned; if on the side of pain, the general *evil tendency,* with respect to the same community.

VI. It is not to be expected that this process should be strictly pursued previously to every moral judgment, or to every legislative or judicial operation. It may, however, be always kept in view: and as near as the process actually pursued on these occasions approaches to it, so near will such process approach to the character of an exact one.

VII. The same process is alike applicable to pleasure and pain, in whatever shape they appear: and by whatever denomination they are distinguished: to pleasure, whether it be called *good* (which is properly the cause or instrument of pleasure) or *profit* (which is distant pleasure, or the cause or instrument of distant pleasure,) or *convenience,* or *advantage, benefit, emolument, happiness,* and so forth: to pain, whether it be called *evil,* (which corresponds to *good)* or *mischief,* or *inconvenience,* or *disadvantage,* or *loss,* or *unhappiness,* and so forth.

VIII. Nor is this a novel and unwarranted, any more than it is a useless theory. In all this there is nothing but what the practice of mankind, wheresoever they have a clear view of their own interest, is perfectly conformable to. An article of property, an estate in land, for instance, is valuable, on what account? On account of the pleasures of all kinds which it enables a man to produce, and what comes to the same thing the pains of all kinds which it enables him to avert. But the value of such an article of property is universally understood to rise or fall according to the length or shortness of the time which a man has in it: the certainty or uncertainty of its coming into possession: and the nearness or remoteness of the time at which, if at all, it is to come into possession. As to the *intensity* of the pleasures which a man may derive from it, this is never thought of, because it depends upon the use which each particular person may come to make of it; which cannot be estimated till the particular pleasures he may come to derive from it, or the particular pains he may come to exclude by means of it, are brought to view. For the same reason, neither does he think of the *fecundity* or *purity* of those pleasures.

Thus much for pleasure and pain, happiness and unhappiness, in *general.*

The Deep Beauty of the Golden Rule   R. M. MacIver

Robert M. MacIver (1882–   ) is a prominent sociologist and political theorist who has a strong interest in a number of philosophical issues.

The subject that learned men call ethics is a wasteland on the philosophical map. Thousands of books have been written on this matter, learned books and popular books, books that argue and books that exhort. Most of them are empty and nearly all are vain. Some claim that pleasure is *the* good; some prefer the elusive and more enticing name of happiness; others reject such principles and speak of equally elusive goals such as self-fulfillment. Others claim that *the* good is to be found in looking away from the self, in devotion to the whole—which whole? in the service of God—whose God?—even in the service of the State—who prescribes the service? Here indeed, if anywhere, after listening to the many words of many apostles, one goes out by the same door as one went in.

The reason is simple. You say: "This is the way you should behave." But I say: "No, that is not the way." You say: "This is right." But I say: "No, that is wrong, and this is right." You appeal to experience. I appeal to experience against you. You appeal to authority: it is not mine. What is left? If you are strong, you can punish me for behaving my way. But does that prove anything except that you are stronger than I? Does it prove the absurd dogma that might makes right? Is the slavemaster right because he owns the whip, or Torquemada because he can send his heretics to the flames?

From this impasse no system of ethical rules has been able to deliver itself. How can ethics lay down final principles of behavior that are not your values against mine, your group's values against my group's?

Which, by the way, does not mean that your rules are any less valid for you because they are not valid for me. Only a person of shallow nature and autocratic leanings would draw that conclusion. For the sake of your integrity you must hold to your own values, no matter how much others reject them. Without *your* values you are nothing. True, you should search them and test them and learn by *your* experience and gain wisdom where you can. Your values are your guides through life but you need to use your own eyes. If I have different guides I shall go another way. So far as we diverge, values are relative as between you and me. But your values cannot be relative for you or mine for me.

That is not here the issue. It is that the relativity of values between you and me, between your group and my group, your sect and my sect, makes futile nearly all learned disquisitions about the first principles of ethics.

By ethics I mean the philosophy of how men should behave in their relations to one another. I am talking about philosophy, not about religion. When you have a creed, you can derive from it principles of ethics. Philosophy cannot begin with a creed, but only with reasoning about the nature of things. It cannot therefore presume that the values of other men are less to be regarded than the values of the proponent. If it does, it is not philosophy but dogma, dogma that is the enemy of philosophy, the kind of dogma that has been the source of endless tyranny and repression.

Can it be a philosophy worth the name that makes a universal of your values and thus rules mine out of existence, where they differ from yours?

How can reasoning decide between my values and yours? Values do not claim truth in any scientific sense; instead they claim validity, rightness. They do not declare what is so but what *should* be so. I cling to my values, you to yours. Your values, some of them, do not hold for me; some of them may be repulsive to me; some of them may threaten me. What then? To what court of reason shall we appeal? To what court that you and I both accept is there any appeal?

The lack of any court is the final *fact* about final values. It is a fundamental fact. It is a terrifying fact. It is also a strangely challenging fact. It gives man his lonely autonomy, his true responsibility. If he has anything that partakes of the quality of a God it comes from this fact. Man has more than the choice to obey or disobey. If he accepts authority he also chooses the authority he accepts. He is responsible not only to others but, more deeply, to himself.

Does all this mean that a universal ethical principle, applicable alike to me and you, even where our values diverge, is impossible? That there is no rule to go by, based on reason itself, in this world of irreconcilable valuations?

There is no rule that can prescribe both my values and yours or decide between them. There is one universal rule, and one only, that can be laid down, on ethical grounds—that is, apart from the creeds of particular religions and apart from the ways of the tribe that falsely and arrogantly universalize themselves.

Do to others as you would have others do to you. This is the only rule that stands by itself in the light of its own reason, the only rule that can stand by itself in the naked, warring universe, in the face of the contending values of men and groups.

What makes it so? Let us first observe that the universal herein laid down is one of procedure. It prescribes a mode of behaving, not a goal of action. On the level of goals, of *final* values, there is irreconcilable conflict. One rule prescribes humility, another pride; one prescribes abstinence, another commends the flesh-pots; and so forth through endless variations. All of us wish that *our* principle could be universal; most of us believe that it *should* be, that our *ought* ought to be all men's *ought*, but since we differ there can be, on this level, no possible agreement.

When we want to make our ethical principle prevail we try to persuade others, to "convert" them. Some may freely respond, if their deeper values are near enough to ours. Others will certainly resist and some will seek to persuade us in turn—why shouldn't they? Then we can go no further except by resort to force and fraud. We can, if we are strong, dominate some and we can bribe others. We compromise our own values in doing so and we do not in the end succeed; even if we were masters of the whole world we could never succeed in making our principle universal. We could only make it falsely tyrannous.

So if we look for a principle in the name of which we can appeal to all men, one to which their reason can respond in spite of their differences, we must follow another road. When we try to make our values prevail over those cherished by others, we attack their values, their dynamic of behavior, their living will. If we go far enough we assault their very being. For the will is simply valuation in action. Now the deep beauty of the golden rule is that instead of attacking the will that is in other men, it offers their will a new dimension. "Do as you *would* have others . . ." As *you* would will others to do. It bids you expand your vision, see yourself in new relationships. It bids you transcend your insulation, see yourself in the place of others, see others in your place. It bids you test your values or at least your way of pursuing them. If you would disapprove that another should treat you as you treat him, the situations being reversed, is not that a sign that, by the standard of your own values, you are mistreating him?

This principle obviously makes for a vastly greater harmony in the social scheme. At the same time it is the only universal of ethics that does not take sides with or contend with contending values. It contains no dogma. It bids everyone follow his own rule, as it would apply *apart* from the accident of his particular fortunes. It bids him enlarge his own rule, as it would apply whether he is up or whether he is down. It is an accident that you are up and I am down. In another situation you would be down and I would be up. That accident has nothing to do with my *final* values or with yours. You have numbers and force on your side. In another situation I would have the numbers and the force. All situations of power are temporary and precarious. Imagine then the situations reversed and that you had a more wonderful power than is at the command of the most powerful, the power to make the more powerful act toward you as you would want him to act. If power is your dream, then dream of a yet greater power—and act out the spirit of your dream.

But the conclusive argument is not in the terms of power. It goes far deeper, down to the great truth that power so often ignores and that so often in the end destroys it, the truth that when you maltreat others you detach yourself from them, from the understanding of them, from the understanding of yourself. You insulate yourself, you narrow your own values, you cut yourself off from that which you and they have in common. And this commonness is more enduring and more satisfying than what you possess in insulation. You separate yourself, and for all your power you weaken yourself. Which is why power and fear are such close companions.

This is the reason why the evil you do to another, you do also, in the end, to yourself. While if you and he refrain from doing evil, one to another—not to speak of the yet happier consequences of doing positive good—this reciprocity of restraint from evil will redound to the good of both.

That makes a much longer story and we shall not here enter upon it. Our sole concern is to show that the golden rule is the *only* ethical principle, as already defined, that can have clear right of way everywhere in the kind of world we have inherited. It is the only principle that allows every man to follow his own intrinsic values while nevertheless it transforms the chaos of warring codes into a reasonably well-ordered universe.

Let us explain the last statement. What are a man's intrinsic values? Beyond his mere self-seeking every human being needs, and must find, some attachment to a larger purpose. These attachments, in themselves and apart from the way he pursues them, are his intrinsic values. For some men they are centered in the family, the clan, the "class," the community, the nation, the "race." It is the warfare of their group-attachments that creates the deadliest disturbances of modern society. For some men the focus of attachment is found in the greater "cause," the faith, the creed, the way of life. The conflict of these attachments also unlooses many evils on society and at some historical stages has brought about great devastation.

The greatest evils inflicted by man on man over the face of the earth are wrought not by the self-seekers, the pleasure lovers, or the merely amoral, but by the fervent devotees of ethical principles, those who are bound body and soul to some larger purpose, the nation, the "race," the "masses," the "brethren" whoever they may be. The faith they invoke, whatever it may be, is not large enough when it sets a frontier between the members and the non-members, the believers and the non-believers. In the heat of devotion to that larger but exclusive purpose there is bred the fanaticism that corrodes and finally destroys all that links man to the common humanity. In the name of the cause, they will torture and starve and trample under foot millions on millions of their fellowmen. In its name they will cultivate the blackest treachery. And if their methods fail, as fail in the end they must, they will be ready, as was Hitler, to destroy their own cause or their own people, the chosen ones, rather than accept the reality their blinded purpose denied.

How then can we say that the golden rule does not disqualify the intrinsic values of such people—even of people like Hitler or, say, Torquemada? In the name of his values Torquemada burned at the stake many persons who differed from their fellows mainly by being more courageous, honest, and faithful to their faith. What then were Torquemada's values? He was a servant of the Church and the Church was presumptively a servant of Jesus Christ. It was not the intrinsic values of his creed that moved him and his masters to reject the Christian golden rule. Let us concede they had some kind of devotion to religion. It was the distorted, fanatical way in which they pursued the dimmed values they cherished, it was not the values themselves, to which their inhumanity can be charged.

Let us take the case of Hitler. Apart from his passion for Germany, or the German "folk," he would have been of no account, for evil or for good. That passion of itself, that in his view intrinsic value, might have inspired great constructive service instead of destruction. It was the method he used, and not the values he sought to promote thereby, that led to ruin, his blind trust in the efficacy of ruthless might. Belonging to a "folk" that had been reduced in defeat from strength to humiliation, fed on false notions of history and responsive to grotesque fallacies about a "master race," he conceived the resurgence of Germany in the distorted light of his vindictive imagination. Had Hitler been a member of some small "folk," no more numerous, say, than the population of his native Austria, he might have cherished the same values with no less passion, but his aspirations would have taken a different form and would never have expressed themselves in horror and tragedy.

The golden rule says nothing against Hitler's mystic adoration of the German "race," against any man's intrinsic values. By "intrinsic values" we signify the goals, beyond mere self-seeking, that animate a human being. If your group, your nation, your "race," your church, is for you a primary attachment, continue to cherish it—give it all you have, if you are so minded. But do not use means that are repugnant to the standards according to which you would have others conduct themselves to you and your values. If your nation were a small one, would you not seethe with indignation if some large neighbor destroyed its independence? Where, then, is your personal integrity if, belonging instead to the large nation, you act to destroy the independence of a small one? You falsify your own values, in the longer run you do them injury, when you pursue them in ways that cannot abide the test of the golden rule.

It follows that while this first principle attacks no intrinsic values, no primary attachments of men to goods that reach beyond themselves, it nevertheless purifies every attachment, every creed, of its accidents, its irrelevancies, its excesses, its false reliance on power. It saves every human value from the corruption that comes from the arrogance of detachment and exclusiveness, from the shell of the kind of absolutism that imprisons its vitality.

At this point a word of caution is in order. The golden rule does not solve for us our ethical problems but offers only a way of approach. It does not prescribe our treatment of others but only the spirit in which we should treat them. It has no simple mechanical application and often enough is hard to apply—what general principle is not? It certainly does not bid us treat others as others *want* us to treat them—that would be an absurdity. The convicted criminal wants the judge to set him free. If the judge acts in the spirit of the golden rule, within the limits of the discretion permitted 'him as judge, he might instead reason somewhat as follows: "How would I feel the judge ought to treat *me* were I in this man's place? What could I—the man I am and yet somehow standing where this criminal stands—properly ask the judge to do for me, to me? In this spirit I shall assess his guilt and his punishment. In this spirit I shall give full consideration to the conditions under which he acted. I shall try to understand *him,* to do what I properly can for him, while at the same time I fulfill my judicial duty in protecting society against the dangers that arise if criminals such as he go free."

"Do to others as you would have others do to you." The disease to which all values are subject is the growth of a hard insulation. "I am right: I have the truth. If you differ from me, you are a heretic, you are in error. *Therefore* while you must allow me every liberty when you are in power I need not, in truth I ought not to, show any similar consideration for you." The barb of falsehood has already begun to vitiate the cherished value. While *you* are in power I advocate the equal rights of all creeds: when *I* am in power, I reject any such claim as ridiculous. This is the position taken by various brands of totalitarianism, and the communists in particular have made it a favorite technique in the process of gaining power, clamoring for rights they will use to destroy the rights of those who grant them. Religious groups have followed the same line. Roman Catholics, Calvinists, Lutherans, Presbyterians, and others have on occasion vociferously advocated religious liberty where they were in the minority, often to curb it where in turn they became dominant.

This gross inconsistency on the part of religious groups was flagrantly displayed in earlier centuries, but examples are still not infrequent. Here is one. *La Civilita Catholicâ,* a Jesuit organ published in Rome, has come out as follows:

"The Roman Catholic Church, convinced, through its divine prerogatives, of being the only true church, must demand the right to freedom for herself alone, because such a right can only be possessed by truth, never by error. As to other religions, the Church will certainly never draw the sword, but she will require that by legitimate means they shall not be allowed to propagate false doctrine. Consequently, in a state where the majority of the people are Catholic, the Church will require that legal existence be denied to error. . . . In some countries, Catholics will be obliged to ask full religious freedom for all, resigned at being forced to cohabilitate where they alone should rightly be allowed to live. . . . The Church cannot blush for her own want of tolerance, as she asserts it in principle and applies it in practice."[1]

Since this statement has the merit of honesty it well illustrates the fundamental lack of rationality that lies behind all such violations of the golden rule. The argument runs: "Roman Catholics know they possess the truth; *therefore* they should not permit others to propagate error." By parity of reasoning why should not Protestants say—and indeed they have often said it—"We know we possess the truth; therefore we should

---

[1] Quoted in the *Christian Century* (June, 1948).

not tolerate the errors of Roman Catholics." Why then should not atheists say: "We know we possess the truth; therefore we should not tolerate the errors of dogmatic religion."

No matter what we believe, we are equally convinced that *we* are right. We have to be. That is what belief means, and we must all believe something. The Roman Catholic Church is entitled to declare that all other religious groups are sunk in error. But what follows? That other groups have not the right to believe they are right? That you have the right to repress them while they have no right to repress you? That they should concede to you what you should not concede to them? Such reasoning is mere childishness. Beyond it lies the greater foolishness that truth is advanced by the forceful suppression of those who believe differently from you. Beyond that lies the pernicious distortion of meanings which claims that liberty is only "the liberty to do right"—the "liberty" for me to do what *you* think is right. This perversion of the meaning of liberty has been the delight of all totalitarians. And it might be well to reflect that it was the radical Rousseau who first introduced the doctrine that men could be "forced to be free."

How much do they have truth who think they must guard it within the fortress of their own might? How little that guarding has availed in the past! How often it has kept truth outside while superstition grew moldy within! How often has the false alliance of belief and force led to civil dissension and the futile ruin of war! But if history means nothing to those who call themselves "Christian" and still claim exclusive civil rights for their particular faith, at least they might blush before this word of one they call their Master: "All things therefore whatsoever ye would that men should do unto you, even so do ye also unto them; for this is the law and the prophets."

Contemporary Issues

Civil Disobedience

Civil Disobedience   Henry David Thoreau

Henry David Thoreau (1817–1862), Yankee poet-naturalist and social rebel
published little in his lifetime and hardly even went beyond the limits of
Concord, Massachusetts. Although "Civil Disobedience" went largely unnoticed
in the nineteenth century, its influence has grown steadily in our own century
to include such figures as Mahatma Gandhi, civil rights leaders, and student
revolutionaries.

I heartily accept the motto—"That government is best which governs
least"; and I should like to see it acted up to more rapidly and systematically. Carried out, it finally amounts to this, which also I believe—
"That government is best which governs not at all"; and when men are
prepared for it, that will be the kind of government which they will have.
Government is at best but an expedient; but most governments are usually, and all governments are sometimes, inexpedient. The objections
which have been brought against a standing army, and they are many and
weighty, and deserve to prevail, may also at last be brought against a
standing government. The standing army is only an arm of the standing
government. The government itself, which is only the mode which the
people have chosen to execute their will, is equally liable to be abused and
perverted before the people can act through it. Witness the present Mexican war, the work of comparatively a few individuals using the standing
government as their tool; for, in the outset, the people would not have
consented to this measure.

This American government—what is it but a tradition, though a recent one, endeavoring to transmit itself unimpaired to posterity, but each
instant losing some of its integrity? It has not the vitality and force of a
single living man; for a single man can bend it to his will. It is a sort of
wooden gun to the people themselves. But it is not the less necessary for
this; for the people must have some complicated machinery or other, and
hear its din, to satisfy that idea of government which they have. Governments show thus how successfully men can be imposed on, even impose on
themselves, for their own advantage. It is excellent, we must all allow.
Yet this government never of itself furthered any enterprise, but by the
alacrity with which it got out of its way. *It* does not keep the country free.
It does not settle the West. *It* does not educate. The character inherent in
the American people has done all that has been accomplished; and it

would have done somewhat more, if the government had not sometimes got in its way. For government is an expedient by which men would fain succeed in letting one another alone; and, as has been said, when it is most expedient, the governed are most let alone by it. Trade and commerce, if they were not made of India-rubber, would never manage to bounce over the obstacles which legislators are continually putting in their way; and, if one were to judge these men wholly by the effects of their actions and not partly by their intentions, they would deserve to be classed and punished with those mischievous persons who put obstructions on the railroads.

But, to speak practically and as a citizen, unlike those who call themselves no-government men, I ask for, not at once no government, but *at once* a better government. Let every man make known what kind of government would command his respect, and that will be one step toward obtaining it.

After all, the practical reason why, when the power is once in the hands of the people, a majority are permitted, and for a long period continue, to rule, is not because they are most likely to be in the right, nor because this seems fairest to the minority, but because they are physically the strongest. But a government in which the majority rule in all cases cannot be based on justice, even as far as men understand it. Can there not be a government in which majorities do not virtually decide right and wrong, but conscience?—in which majorities decide only those question to which the rule of expediency is applicable? Must the citizen ever for a moment, or in the least degree, resign his conscience to the legislator? Why has every man a conscience, then? I think that we should be men first, and subjects afterward. It is not desirable to cultivate a respect for the law, so much as for the right. The only obligation which I have a right to assume, is to do at any time what I think right. It is truly enough said, that a corporation has no conscience; but a corporation of conscientious men is a corporation *with* a conscience. Law never made men a whit more just; and, by means of their respect for it, even the well-disposed are daily made the agents of injustice. A common and natural result of an undue respect for law is, that you may see a file of soldiers, colonel, captain, corporal, privates, powder-monkeys, and all, marching in admirable order over hill and dale to the wars, against their wills, ay, against their common sense and consciences, which makes it very steep marching indeed, and produces a palpitation of the heart. They have no doubt that it is a damnable business in which they are concerned; they are all peaceably inclined. Now, what are they? Men at all? or small movable forts and magazines, at the service of some unscrupulous man in power? Visit the Navy-Yard, and behold a marine, such a man as an American government can make, or such as it can make a man with its black arts—a mere shadow and reminiscence of humanity, a man laid out alive and standing, and already, as one may say, buried under arms with funeral accompaniments, though it may be—

> Not a drum was heard, nor a funeral note,
> As his corpse to the rampart we hurried;

> Not a soldier discharged his farewell shot
> O'er the grave where our hero we buried.

The mass of men serve the state thus, not as men mainly, but as machines, with their bodies. They are the standing army, and the militia, jailers, constables, posse comitatus, &c. In most cases there is no free exercise whatever of the judgment or of the moral sense; but they put themselves on a level with wood and earth and stones; and wooden men can perhaps be manufactured that will serve the purpose as well. Such command no more respect than men of straw or a lump of dirt. They have the same sort worthy only as horses and dogs. Yet such as these even are commonly esteemed good citizens. Others—as most legislators, politicians, lawyers, ministers, and officeholders—serve the state chiefly with their heads; and, as they rarely make any moral distinctions, they are as likely to serve the Devil, without *intending* it, as God. A very few, as heroes, patriots, martyrs, reformers in the great sense, and *men,* serve the state with the consciences also, and so necessarily resist it for the most part; and they are commonly treated as enemies by it. A wise man will only be useful as a man, and will not submit to be "clay," and "stop a hole to keep the wind away," but leave that office to his dust at least:

> I am too high-born to be propertied,
> To be a secondary at control,
> Or useful serving-man and instrument
> To any sovereign state throughout the world.

He who gives himself entirely to his fellow-men appears to them useless and selfish; but he who gives himself partially to them is pronounced a benefactor and philanthropist.

How does it become a man to behave toward this American government to-day? I answer, that he cannot without disgrace be associated with it. I cannot for an instant recognize the political organization as *my* government which is the *slave's* government also.

All men recognize the right of revolution; that is, the right to refuse allegiance to, and to resist, the government, when its tyranny or its inefficiency are great and unendurable. But almost all say that such is not the case now. But such was the case, they think, in the Revolution of '75. If one were to tell me that this was a bad government because it taxed certain foreign commodities brought to its ports, it is most probable that I should not make an ado about it, for I can do without them. All machines have their friction; and possibly this does enough good to counterbalance the evil. At any rate, it is a great evil to make a stir about it. But when the friction comes to have its machine, and oppression and robbery are organized, I say, let us not have such a machine any longer. In other words, when a sixth of the population of a nation which has undertaken to be the refuge of liberty are slaves, and a whole country is unjustly overrun and conquered by a foreign army, and subjected to military law, I think that it is not too soon for honest men to rebel and revolutionize. What makes this duty the more urgent is the fact, that the country so overrun is not our own, but ours is the invading army.

Paley, a common authority with many on moral questions, in his chapter on the "Duty of Submission to Civil Government," resolves all civil obligation into expediency; and he proceeds to say, "that so long as the interest of the whole society requires it, that is, so long as the established government cannot be resisted or changed without public inconveniency, it is the will of God that the established government be obeyed, and no longer.... This principle being admitted, the justice of every particular case of resistance is reduced to a computation of the quantity of the danger and grievance on the one side, and of the probability and expense of redressing it on the other." Of this, he says, every man shall judge for himself. But Paley appears never to have contemplated those cases to which the rule of expediency does not apply, in which a people, as well as an individual, must do justice, cost what it may. If I have unjustly wrested a plank from a drowning man, I must restore it to him though I drown myself. This, according to Paley, would be inconvenient. But he that would save his life, in such a case, shall lose it. This people must cease to hold slaves, and to make war on Mexico, though it cost them their existence as a people....

I hear of a convention to be held at Baltimore, or elsewhere, for the selection of a candidate for the Presidency, made up chiefly of editors, and men who are politicians by profession; but I think, what is it to any independent, intelligent, and respectable man what decision they may come to? Shall we not have the advantage of his wisdom and honesty, nevertheless? Can we not count upon some independent votes? Are there not many individuals in the country who do not attend conventions? But no: I find that the respectable man, so called, has immediately drifted from his position, and despairs of his country, when his country has more reason to despair of him. He forthwith adopts one of the candidates thus selected as the only *available* one, thus proving that he is himself *available* for any purposes of the demagogue. His vote is of no more worth than that of any unprincipled foreigner or hireling native, who may have been bought. O for a man who is a *man*, and, as my neighbor says, has a bone in his back which you cannot pass your hand through! Our statistics are at fault: the population has been returned too large. How many *men* are there to a square thousand miles in this country? Hardly one. Does not America offer any inducement for men to settle here? The American has dwindled into an Odd Fellow—one who may be known by the development of his organ of gregariousness, and a manifest lack of intellect and cheerful self-reliance; whose first and chief concern, on coming into the world, is to see that the Almshouses are in good repair; and, before yet he has lawfully donned the virile garb, to collect a fund for the support of the widows and orphans that may be; who, in short, ventures to live only by the aid of the Mutual Insurance Company, which has promised to bury him decently.

It is not a man's duty, as a matter of course, to devote himself to the eradication of any, even the most enormous wrong; he may still properly have other concerns to engage him; but it is his duty, at least, to wash his hands of it, and, if he gives it no thought longer, not to give it practically his support. If I devote myself to other pursuits and contemplations, I must first see, at least, that I do not pursue them sitting upon another man's shoulders. I must get off him first, that he may pursue his contemplations too. See what gross inconsistency is tolerated. I have heard some of my townsmen say, "I should like to have them order me out to help put down an insurrection of the slaves, or to march to Mexico—see if I would go"; and yet these very men have each, directly by their allegiance, and so indirectly, at least, by their money, furnished a substitute. The soldier is applauded who refuses to serve in an unjust war by those who do not refuse to sustain the unjust government which makes the war; is applauded by those whose own act and authority he disregards and sets at naught; as if the State were penitent to that degree that it hired one to scourge it while it sinned, but not to that degree that it left off sinning for a moment. Thus, under the name of Order and Civil Government, we are all made at last to pay homage to and support our own meanness. After the first blush of sin comes its indifference; and from immoral it becomes, as it were, *un*moral, and not quite unnecessary to that life which we have made. . . .

Unjust laws exist: shall we be content to obey them, or shall we endeavor to amend them, and obey them until we have succeeded, or shall we transgress them at once? Men generally, under such a government as this, think that they ought to wait until they have persuaded the majority to alter them. They think that, if they should resist, the remedy would be worse than the evil. But it is the fault of the government itself that the remedy *is* worse than the evil. *It* makes it worse. Why is it not more apt to anticipate and provide for reform? Why does it not cherish its wise minority? Why does it cry and resist before it is hurt? Why does it not encourage its citizens to be on the alert to point out its faults, and *do* better than it would have them? Why does it always crucify Christ, and excommunicate Copernicus and Luther, and pronounce Washington and Franklin rebels?

One would think, that a deliberate and practical denial of its authority was the only offence never contemplated by government; else, why has it not assigned its definite, its suitable and proportionate penalty? If a man who has no property refuses but once to earn nine shillings for the State, he is put in prison for a period unlimited by any law that I know, and determined only by the discretion of those who placed him there; but if he should steal ninety times nine shillings from the State, he is soon permitted to go at large again.

If the injustice is part of the necessary friction of the machine of government, let it go, let it go: perchance it will wear smooth—certainly the machine will wear out. If the injustice has a spring, or a pulley, or a rope, or a crank, exclusively for itself, then perhaps you may consider whether the remedy will not be worse than the evil; but if it is of such a nature that it requires you to be the agent of injustice to another, then, I say, break the law. Let your life be a counter friction to stop the machine. What I have to do is to see, at any rate, that I do not lend myself to the wrong which I condemn.

As for adopting the ways which the State has provided for remedying the evil, I know not of such ways. They take too much time, and a man's life will be gone. I have other affairs to attend to. I came into this world, not chiefly to make this a good place to live in, but to live in it, be it good or bad. A man has not everything to do, but something; and because he cannot do *everything*, it is not necessary that he should do *something* wrong. It is not my business to be petitioning the Governor or the Legislature any more than it is theirs to petition me; and, if they should not hear my petition, what should I do then? But in this case the state has provided no way: its very Constitution is the evil. This may seem to be harsh and stubborn and unconciliatory; but it is to treat with the utmost kindness and consideration the only spirit that can appreciate or deserves it. So is all change for the better, like birth and death, which convulse the body.

I do not hesitate to say, that those who call themselves Abolitionists should at once effectually withdraw their support, both in person and property, from the government of Massachusetts, and not wait till they constitute a majority of one, before they suffer the right to prevail through them. I think that it is enough if they have God on their side, without waiting for that other one. Moreover, any man more right than his neighbors constitutes a majority of one already.

I meet this American government, or its representative, the State government, directly, and face to face, once a year—no more—in the person of its tax-gatherer; this is the only mode in which a man situated as I am necessarily meets it; and it then says distinctly, Recognize me; and the simplest, the most effectual, and, in the present posture of affairs, the indispensablest mode of treating with it on this head, of expressing your little satisfaction with and love for it, is to deny it then. My civil neighbor, the tax-gatherer, is the very man I have to deal with—for it is, after all, with men and not with parchment that I quarrel—and he has voluntarily chosen to be an agent of the government. How shall he ever know well what he is and does as an officer of the government, or as a man, until he is obliged to consider whether he shall treat me, his neighbor, for whom he has respect, as a neighbor and well-disposed man, or as a maniac and disturber of the peace, and see if he can get over this obstruction to his neighborliness without a ruder and more impetuous thought or speech corresponding with his action. I know this well, that if one thousand, if one hundred, if ten men whom I could name—if ten *honest* men only— ay, if *one* HONEST man, in this State of Massachusetts, *ceasing to hold slaves,* were actually to withdraw from this copartnership, and be locked up in the county jail therefor, it would be the abolition of slavery in America. For it matters not how small the beginning may seem to be: what is once well done is done forever. But we love better to talk about it: that we say is our mission. Reform keeps many scores of newspapers in its service, but not one man. If my esteemed neighbor, the State's ambassador, who will devote his days to the settlement of the question of human rights in the Council Chamber, instead of being threatened with the prisons of Carolina, were to sit down the prisoner of Massachusetts, that State which is so anxious to foist the sin of slavery upon her sister—though at present she can discover only an act of inhospitality to be the ground of a quarrel with her—the Legislature would not wholly waive the subject the following winter.

Under a government which imprisons any unjustly, the true place for a just man is also a prison. The proper place to-day, the only place which Massachusetts has provided for her freer and less desponding spirits, is in her prisons, to be put out and locked out of the State by her own act, as they have already put themselves out by their principles. It is there that the fugitive slave, and the Mexican prisoner on parole, and the Indian come to plead the wrongs of his race, should find them; on that separate, but more free and honorable ground, where the State places those who are not *with* her, but *against* her—the only house in a slave State in which a free man can abide with honor. If any think that their influence would be lost there, and their voices no longer afflict the ear of the State, that they would not be as an enemy within its walls, they do not know by how much truth is stronger than error, nor how much more eloquently and effectively he can combat injustice who has experienced a little in his own person. Cast your whole vote, not a strip of paper merely, but your whole influence. A minority is powerless while it conforms to the majority; it is not even a minority then; but it is irresistible when it clogs by its whole weight. If the alternative is to keep all just men in prison, or give up war and slavery, the State will not hesitate which to choose. If a thousand men were not to pay their tax-bills this year, that would not be a violent and bloody measure, as it would be to pay them, and enable the State to commit violence and shed innocent blood. This is, in fact, the definition of a peaceable revolution, if any such is possible. If the tax-gatherer, or any other public officer, asks me, as one has done, "But what shall I do?" my answer is, "If you really wish to do anything, resign your office." When the subject has refused allegiance, and the officer has resigned his office, then the revolution is accomplished. But even suppose blood should flow. Is there not a sort of blood shed when the conscience is wounded? Through this wound a man's real manhood and immortality flow out, and he bleeds to an everlasting death. I see this blood flowing now. . . .

When I converse with the freest of my neighbors, I perceive that, whatever they may say about the magnitude and seriousness of the question, and their regard for the public tranquillity, the long and the short of the matter is, that they cannot spare the protection of the existing government, and they dread the consequences to their property and families of disobedience to it. For my own part, I should not like to think that I ever rely on the protection of the State. But, if I deny the authority of the State when it presents its tax-bill, it will soon take and waste all my property, and so harass me and my children without end. This is hard. This makes it impossible for a man to live honestly, and at the same time comfortably, in outward respects. It will not be worth the while to accumulate property; that would be sure to go again. You must hire or squat somewhere, and raise but a small crop, eat that soon. You must live within yourself, and depend upon yourself always tucked up and ready for a start, and not have many affairs. A man may grow rich in Turkey even, if he will be in all respects a good subject of the Turkish government. Confucius said: "If a state is governed by the principles of reason, poverty and misery are subjects of shame; if a state is not governed by the principles of reason, riches and honors are the subjects of shame." No: until I want the protection of Massachusetts to be extended to me in some distant Southern port, where my liberty is endangered, or until I am bent solely on building up an estate at home by peaceful enterprise, I can afford to refuse allegiance to Massachusetts, and her right to my property and life. It cost me less in every sense to incur the penalty of disobedience to the State, than it would to obey. I should feel as if I were worth less in that case. . . .

I have paid no poll-tax for six years. I was put into a jail once on this account, for one night; and, as I stood considering the walls of solid stone, two or three feet thick, the door of wood and iron, a foot thick, and the iron grating which strained the light, I could not help being struck with the foolishness of that institution which treated me as if I were mere flesh and blood and bones, to be locked up. I wondered that it should have concluded at length that this was the best use it could put me to, and had never thought to avail itself of my services in some way. I saw that, if there was a wall of stone between me and my townsmen, there was a still more difficult one to climb or break through, before they could get to be as free as I was. I did not for a moment feel confined, and the walls seemed a great waste of stone and mortar. I felt as if I alone of all my townsmen had paid my tax. They plainly did not know how to treat me, but behaved like persons who are underbred. In every threat and in every compliment there was a blunder; for they thought that my chief desire was to stand the other side of that stone wall. I could not but smile to see how industriously they locked the door on my meditations, which followed them out again without let or hindrance, and *they* were really all that was dangerous. As they could not reach me, they had resolved to punish my body; just as boys, if they cannot come at some person against whom they have a spite, will abuse his dog. I saw that the State was half-witted, that it was timid as a lone woman with her silver spoons, and that it did not know its friends from its foes, and I lost all my remaining respect for it, and pitied it. . . .

I have never declined paying the highway tax, because I am as desirous of being a good neighbor as I am of being a bad subject; and, as for supporting schools, I am doing my part to educate my fellow-countrymen now. It is for no particular item in the tax-bill that I refuse to pay it. I simply wish to refuse allegiance to the State, to withdraw and stand aloof from it effectually. I do not care to trace the course of my dollar, if I could, till it buys a man or a musket to shoot one with—the dollar is innocent—but I am concerned to trace the effects of my allegiance. In fact, I quietly declare war with the State, after my fashion, though I will still make what use and get what advantage of her I can, as is usual in such cases.

If others pay the tax which is demanded of me, from a sympathy with the State, they do but what they have already done in their own case, or rather they abet injustice to a greater extent than the State requires. If they pay the tax from a mistaken interest in the individual taxed, to save his property, or prevent his going to jail, it is because they have not considered wisely how far they let their private feelings interfere with the public good. . . .

The authority of government, even such as I am willing to submit to —for I will cheerfully obey those who know and can do better than I, and in many things even those who neither know nor can do so well—is still an impure one: to be strictly just, it must have the sanction and consent of the governed. It can have no pure right over my person and property but what I concede to it. The progress from an absolute to a limited monarchy, from a limited monarchy to a democracy, is a progress toward a true respect for the individual. Even the Chinese philosopher was wise enough to regard the individual as the basis of the empire. Is a democracy, such as we know it, the last improvement possible in government? Is it not possible to take a step further toward recognizing and organizing the rights of man? There will never be a really free and enlightened State, until the State comes to recognize the individual as a higher and independent power, from which all its own power and authority are derived, and treats him accordingly. I please myself with imagining a State at last which can afford to be just to all men, and to treat the individual with respect as a neighbor; which even would not think it inconsistent with its own repose, if a few were to live aloof from it, not meddling with it, nor embraced by it, who fulfilled all the duties of neighbors and fellow-men. A State which bore this kind of fruit, and suffered it to drop off as fast as it ripened, would prepare the way for a still more perfect and glorious State, which also I have imagined, but not yet anywhere seen.

Social Protest and Civil Disobedience   Sidney Hook

Sidney Hook (1902–   ), a personal student of John Dewey at Columbia University, New York City, a critical expositor of Karl Marx, and an influential social philosopher, has elaborated and extended the philosophy of John Dewey to contemporary social problems.

In times of moral crisis what has been accepted as commonplace truth sometimes appears questionable and problematic. We have all been nurtured in the humanistic belief that in a democracy, citizens are free to disagree with a law but that so long as it remains in force, they have a *prima facie* obligation to obey it. The belief is justified on the ground that this procedure enables us to escape the twin evils of tyranny and anarchy. Tyranny is avoided by virtue of the freedom and power of dissent to win the uncoerced consent of the community. Anarchy is avoided by reliance on due process, the recognition that there is a right way to correct a wrong, and a wrong way to secure a right. To the extent

This article first appeared in *The Humanist*, Fall 1967, and is reprinted by permission.

that anything is demonstrable in human affairs, we have held that democracy as a political system is not viable if members systematically refused to obey laws whose wisdom or morality they dispute.

Nonetheless, during the past decade of tension and turmoil in American life there has developed a mass phenomenon of civil disobedience even among those who profess devotion to democratic ideals and institutions. This phenomenon has assumed a character similar to a tidal wave which has not yet reached its crest. It has swept from the field of race relations to the campuses of some universities, subtly altering the connotation of the term "academic." It is being systematically developed as an instrument of influencing foreign policy. It is leaving its mark on popular culture. I am told it is not only a theme of comic books but that children in our more sophisticated families no longer resort to tantrums in defying parental discipline—they go limp!

More seriously, in the wake of civil disobedience there has occasionally developed *uncivil* disobedience, sometimes as a natural psychological development, and often because of the failure of law enforcement agencies especially in the South to respect and defend legitimate expressions of social protest. The line between civil and uncivil disobedience is not only an uncertain and wavering one in practice, it has become so in theory. A recent prophet of the philosophy of the absurd in recommending civil disobedience as a form of creative disorder in a democracy cited Shay's Rebellion as an illustration. This Rebellion was uncivil to the point of bloodshed. Indeed, some of the techniques of protesting American involvement in Vietnam have departed so far from traditional ways of civil disobedience as to make it likely that they are inspired by the same confusion between civil and uncivil disobedience.

All this has made focal the perennial problems of the nature and limits of the citizen's obligation to obey the law, of the relation between the authority of conscience and the authority of the state, of the rights and duties of a democratic moral man in an immoral democratic society. The classical writings on these questions have acquired a burning relevance to the political condition of man today. I propose briefly to clarify some of these problems.

To begin with I wish to stress the point that there is no problem concerning "social protest" as such in a democracy. Our Bill of Rights was adopted not only to make protest possible but to encourage it. The political logic, the very ethos of any democracy that professes to rest, no matter how indirectly, upon freely given consent *requires* that social protest be permitted—and not only permitted but *protected* from interference by those opposed to the protest, which means protected by agencies of law enforcement.

Not social protest but *illegal* social protest constitutes our problem. It raises the question: "When, if ever, is illegal protest justified in a democratic society?" It is of the first importance to bear in mind that we are raising the question as principled democrats and humanists in a democratic society. To urge that illegal social protests, motivated by exalted ideals are sanctified in a democratic society by precedents like the Boston Tea Party, is a lapse into political illiteracy. Such actions occurred in societies in which those affected by unjust laws had no power peacefully to change them.

Further, many actions dubbed civilly disobedient by local authorities, strictly speaking, are not such at all. An action launched in violation of a local law or ordinance, and undertaken to test it, on the ground that the law itself violates state or federal law, or launched in violation of a state law in the sincerely held belief that the state law outrages the Constitution, the supreme law of the land, is not civilly disobedient. In large measure the original sympathy with which the original sit-ins were received, especially the Freedom Rides, marches, and demonstrations that flouted local Southern laws, was due to the conviction that they were constitutionally justified, in accordance with the heritage of freedom, enshrined in the Amendments, and enjoyed in other regions of the country. Practically everything the marchers did was sanctioned by the phrase of the First Amendment which upholds "the right of the people peaceably to assemble and to petition the Government for a redress of grievances." Actions of this kind may be wise or unwise, timely or untimely, but they are not civilly disobedient.

They become civilly disobedient when they are in deliberate violation of laws that have been sustained by the highest legislative and judicial bodies of the nation, e.g., income tax laws, conscription laws, laws forbidding segregation in education, and discrimination in public accommodations and employment. Another class of examples consists of illegal social protest against local and state laws that clearly do not conflict with Federal Law.

Once we grasp the proper issue, the question is asked with deceptive clarity: "Are we under an obligation in a democratic community always to obey an unjust law?" To this question Abraham Lincoln is supposed to have made the classic answer in an eloquent address on "The Perpetuation of Our Political Institution," calling for absolute and religious obedience until the unjust law is repealed.

I said that this question is asked with deceptive clarity because Lincoln, judging by his other writings and the pragmatic cast of his basic philosophy, could never have subscribed to this absolutism or meant what he seemed literally to have said. Not only are we under no moral obligation *always* to obey unjust laws, we are under no moral obligation *always* to obey a just law. One can put it more strongly: sometimes it may be necessary in the interests of the greater good to violate a just or sensible law. A man who refused to violate a sensible traffic law if it were necessary to do so to avoid a probably fatal accident would be a moral idiot. There are other values in the world besides legality or even justice, and sometimes they may be of overriding concern and weight. Everyone can imagine some situation in which the violation of some existing law is the lesser moral evil, but this does not invalidate recognition of our obligation to obey just laws.

There is a difference between disobeying a law which one approves of in general but whose application in a specific case seems wrong, and disobeying a law in protest against the injustice of the law itself. In the latter case the disobedience is open and public; in the former, not. But if the grounds of disobedience in both cases are moral considerations, there is only a difference in degree between them. The rejection, therefore, of legal absolutism or the fetishism of legality—that one is never justified in violating any law in any circumstances—is a matter of common sense.

The implications drawn from this moral commonplace by some ritualistic liberals are clearly absurd. For they have substituted for the absolutism of law something very close to the absolutism of individual conscience. Properly rejecting the view that the law, no matter how unjust, must be obeyed in all circumstances, they have taken the view that the law is to be obeyed only when the individual deems it just or when it does not outrage his conscience. Fantastic comparisons are made between those who do not act on the dictates of their conscience and those who accepted and obeyed Hitler's laws. These comparisons completely disregard the systems of law involved, the presence of alternatives of action, the differences in the behavior commanded, in degrees of complicity of guilt, in the moral costs and personal consequences of compliance and other relevant matters.

It is commendable to recognize the primacy of morality to law but unless we recognize the centrality of intelligence to morality, we stumble with blind self-righteousness into moral disaster. Because, Kant to the contrary notwithstanding, it is not wrong sometimes to lie to save a human life; because it is not wrong sometimes to kill in defense to save many from being killed, it does not follow that the moral principles: "Do not lie!" "Do not kill!" are invalid. When more than one valid principle bears on a problem of moral experience, the very fact of their conflict means that not all of them can hold unqualifiedly. One of them must be denied. The point is that such negation or violation entails upon us the obligation of justifying it, and moral justification is a matter of reasons not of conscience. The burden of proof rests on the person violating the rules. Normally, we don't have to justify telling the truth. We do have to justify *not* telling the truth. Similarly, with respect to the moral obligation of a democrat who breaches his political obligation to obey the laws of a democratic community, the resort to conscience is not enough. There must always be reasonable justification.

This is all the more true because just as we can, if challenged, give powerful reasons for the moral principle of truth-telling, so we can offer logically coercive grounds for the obligation of a democrat to obey the laws of a democracy. The grounds are many and they can be amplified beyond the passing mention we give here. It is a matter of fairness, of social utility, of peace, of ordered progress, of redeeming an implicit commitment.

There is one point, however, which has a particular relevance to the claims of those who counterpose to legal absolutism the absolutism of conscience. There is the empirically observable tendency for public disobedience to law to spread from those who occupy high moral ground to those who dwell on low ground, with consequent growth of disorder and insecurity.

Conscience by itself is not the measure of high or low moral ground.

This is the work of reason. Where it functions properly the democratic process permits this resort to reason. If the man of conscience loses in the court of reason, why should he assume that the decision or the law is mistaken rather than the deliverances of his conscience?

The voice of conscience may sound loud and clear. But it may conflict at times not only with the law but with another man's conscience. Every conscientious objector to a law knows that at least one man's conscience is wrong, *viz.*, the conscience of the man who asserts that *his* conscience tells him that he must not tolerate conscientious objectors. From this if he is reasonable he should conclude that when he hears the voice of conscience, he is hearing not the voice of God, but the voice of a finite, limited man in this time and in this place, and that conscience is neither a special nor an infallible organ of apprehending moral truth, that conscience without conscientiousness, conscience which does not cap the process of critical reflective morality, is likely to be prejudice masquerading as a First Principle or a Mandate from Heaven.

The mark of an enlightened democracy is, as far as is possible with its security, to respect the religious commitment of a citizen who believes, on grounds of conscience or any other ground, that his relation to God involves duties superior to those arising from any human relation. It, therefore, exempts him from his duty as a citizen to protect his country. However, the mark of the genuine conscientious objector in a democracy is to respect the democratic process. He does not use his exemption as a political weapon to coerce where he has failed to convince or persuade. Having failed to influence national policy by rational means within the law, in the political processes open to him in a free society, he cannot justifiably try to defeat that policy by resorting to obstructive techniques outside the law and still remain a democrat.

It is one thing on grounds of conscience or religion to plead exemption from the duty of serving one's country when drafted. It is quite another to adopt harassing techniques to prevent others from volunteering or responding to the call of duty. It is one thing to oppose American involvement in Vietnam by teach-ins, petitions, electoral activity. It is quite another to attempt to stop troop trains: to take possession of the premises of draft boards where policies are not made; to urge recruits to sabotage their assignments and feign illness to win discharge. The first class of actions fall within the sphere of legitimate social protest; the second class are implicitly insurrectionary since it is directed against the authority of a democratic government which it seeks to overthrow not by argument and discussion but by resistance—albeit passive resistance.

Nonetheless, since we have rejected legal absolutism we must face the possibility that in protest on ethical grounds individuals may refuse to obey some law which they regard as uncommonly immoral or uncommonly foolish. If they profess to be democrats, their behavior must scrupulously respect the following conditions:

First, it must be nonviolent—peaceful not only in form but in actuality. After all, the protesters are seeking to dramatize a great evil that the community allegedly has been unable to overcome because of complacency or moral weakness. Therefore, they must avoid the guilt of imposing hardship or harm on others who in the nature of the case can hardly be responsible for the situation under protest. Passive resistance should not be utilized merely as a safer or more effective strategy than active resistance of imposing their wills on others.

Secondly, resort to civil disobedience is never morally legitimate where other methods of remedying the evil complained of are available. Existing grievance procedures should be used. No grievance procedures were available to the southern Negroes. The Courts often shared the prejudices of the community and offered no relief, not even minimal protection. But such procedures *are* available in the areas of industry and education. For example, where charges against students are being heard such procedures may result in the dismissal of the charges not the students. Or the faculty on appeal may decide to suspend the rules rather than the students. To jump the gun to civil disobedience in by-passing these procedures is telltale evidence that those who are calling the shots are after other game than preserving the rights of students.

Thirdly, those who resort to civil disobedience are duty bound to accept the legal sanctions and punishments imposed by the laws. Attempts to evade and escape them not only involve a betrayal of the community, but erode the moral foundations of civil disobedience itself. Socrates' argument in the *Crito* is valid only on democratic premises. The rationalé of the protesters is the hope that the pain and hurt and indignity they voluntarily accept will stir their fellow citizens to compassion, open their minds to second thoughts, and move them to undertake the necessary healing action. When, however, we observe the heroics of defiance being followed by the dialectics of legal evasion, we question the sincerity of the action.

Fourth, civil disobedience is unjustified if a major moral issue is not clearly at stake. Differences about negotiable details that can easily be settled with a little patience should not be fanned into a blaze of illegal opposition.

Fifth, where intelligent men of good will and character differ on large and complex moral issues, discussion and agitation are more appropriate than civilly disobedient action. Those who feel strongly about animal rights and regard the consumption of animal flesh as foods as morally evil would have a just cause for civil disobedience if *their* freedom to obtain other food was threatened. They would have no moral right to resort to similar action to prevent their fellow citizens from consuming meat. Similarly with fluoridation.

Sixth, where civil disobedience is undertaken, there must be some rhyme and reason in the time, place, and targets selected. If one is convinced, as I am not, that the Board of Education of New York City is remiss in its policy of desegregation, what is the point of dumping garbage on bridges to produce traffic jams that seriously discomfort commuters who have not the remotest connection with educational policies in New York. Such action can only obstruct the progress of desegregation in the communities of Long Island. Gandhi, who inspired the civil disobedience movement in the twentieth century, was a better

tactician than many who invoke his name but ignore his teachings. When
he organized his campaign of civil disobedience against the Salt Tax,
he marched with his followers to the sea to make salt. He did not hold
up food trains or tie up traffic.

Finally, there is such a thing as historical timing. Democrats who
resort to civil disobedience must ask themselves whether the cumulative
consequences of their action may in the existing climate of opinion
undermine the peace and order on which the effective exercise of other
human rights depend. This is a cost which one may be willing to pay
but which must be taken into the reckoning.

These observations in the eyes of some defenders of the philosophy
of civil disobedience are far from persuasive. They regard them as evad-
ing the political realities. The political realities, it is asserted, do not
provide meaningful channels for the legitimate expression of dissent.
The "Establishment" is too powerful or indifferent to be moved. Ad-
ministrations are voted into office that are not bound by their election
pledges. The right to form minority parties is hampered by unconstitu-
tional voting laws. What does even "the right of the people to present
petitions for the redress of grievances" amount to if it does not carry with
it the right to have those petitions paid attention to, at least to have
them read, if not acted upon?

No, the opposing argument runs on. Genuine progress does not come
by enactment of laws, by appeals to the good will or conscience of one's
fellow citizens, but only by obstructions which interfere with the functioning of the system itself, by actions whose nuisance value is so high that
the Establishment finds it easier to be decent and yield to demands than
to be obdurate and oppose them. The time comes, as one student leader
of the civilly disobedient Berkeley students advised, "when it is necessary
for you to throw your bodies upon the wheels and gears and levers and
bring the machine to a grinding halt." When one objects that such
obstruction, as a principle of political action, is almost sure to produce
chaos, and that it is unnecessary and undesirable in a democracy, the
retort is made: "Amen, if only this were a democracy, how glad we
would be to stop!"

It is characteristic of those who argue this way to define the presence
or absence of the democratic process by whether or not *they* get their
political way, and not by the presence or absence of democratic institu-
tional processes. The rules of the game exist to enable them to win and
if they lose that's sufficient proof the game is rigged and dishonest. The
sincerity with which the position is held is no evidence whatsoever of
its coherence. The right to petition does not carry with it the right to be
heard, if that means influence on those to whom it is addressed. What
would they do if they received incompatible petitions from two different
and hostile groups of petitioning citizens? The right of petition gives one
a chance to persuade, and the persuasion must rest on the power of words,
on the effective appeal to emotion, sympathy, reason, and logic. Petitions
are weapons of criticism, and their failure does not justify appeal to
other kinds of weapons.

It is quite true that some local election laws do hamper minority groups in the organization of political parties; but there is always the right to appeal to the Courts. Even if this fails there is a possibility of influencing other political parties. It is difficult but so long as one is free to publish and speak, it can be done. If a group is unsuccessful in moving a majority by the weapons of criticism, in a democracy it may resort to peaceful measures of obstruction, provided it is willing to accept punishment for its obstructionist behavior. But these objections are usually a preface to some form of elitism or moral snobbery which is incompatible with the very grounds given in defending the right of civil disobedience on the part of democrats in a democracy.

All of the seven considerations listed above are cautionary, not categorical. We have ruled out only two positions—blind obedience to any and all laws in a democracy, and unreflective violation of laws at the behest of individual consciences. Between these two obviously unacceptable extremes, there is a spectrum of views which shade into each other. Intelligent persons can differ on their application to specific situations. These differences will reflect different assessments of the historical mood of a culture, of the proper timing of protest and acquiescence, and of what the most desirable emphasis and direction of our teaching should be in order to extend "the blessing of liberty" as we preserve "domestic tranquility."

Without essaying the role of a prophet, here is my reading of the needs of the present. It seems to me that the Civil Rights Acts of 1964 and the Voting Acts of 1965 mark a watershed in the history of social and civil protest in the U.S. Upon their enforcement a great many things we hold dear depend, especially those causes in behalf of which in the last decade so many movements of social protest were launched. We must recall that it was the emasculation of the 15th Amendment in the South which kept the Southern Negro in a state of virtual peonage. The prospect of enforcement of the new civil rights legislation is a function of many factors—most notably the law-abiding behavior of the hitherto recalcitrant elements in the southern white communities. Their *uncivil*, violent disobedience has proved unavailing. We need not fear this so much as that they will adopt the strategies and techniques of the civil disobedience itself in their opposition to long-delayed and decent legislation to make the ideals of American democracy a greater reality.

On the other hand, I think the movement of civil disobedience, as distinct from legal protest, in regions of the country in which Negroes have made slow but substantial advances are not likely to make new gains commensurate with the risks. Those risks are that what is begun as civil disobedience will be perverted by extremists into uncivil disobedience, and alienate large numbers who have firmly supported the cause of freedom.

One of the unintended consequences of the two World Wars is that in many ways they strengthened the position of the Negroes and all other minorities in American political life. We do not need another, a third World War, to continue the process of liberation. We can do it in peace—without war and without civil war. The Civil Rights and Voting Acts of 1964 and 1965 are far in advance of the actual situation in the country where discrimination is so rife. Our present task is to bring home and reinforce popular consciousness of the fact that those who violate their provisions are violating the highest law of the land, and that their actions are outside the law. Therefore, our goal must *now* be to build up and strengthen a mood of respect for the law, for civil obedience to laws, even by those who deem them unwise or who opposed them in the past. Our hope is that those who abide by the law may learn not only to tolerate them but, in time, as their fruits develop, to accept them. To have the positive law on the side of right and justice is to have a powerful weapon that makes for voluntary compliance—but only if the *reasonableness* of the *prima facie* obligation to obey the law is recognized.

To one observer at least, that reasonableness is being more and more disregarded in this country. The current mood is one of growing indifference to and disregard of even the reasonable legalities. The headlines from New York to California tell the story. I am not referring to the crime rate which has made frightening strides, nor to the fact that some of our metropolitan centers have become dangerous jungles. I refer to a growing mood toward law generally, something comparable to the attitude toward the Volstead Act during the Prohibition era. The mood is more diffuse today. To be law-abiding in some circles is to be "a square."

In part, the community itself has been responsible for the emergence of this mood. This is especially true in those states which have failed to abolish the *unreasonable* legalities, particularly in the fields of marriage, divorce, birth control, sex behavior, therapeutic abortion, voluntary euthanasia, and other intrusions on the right of privacy. The failure to repeal foolish laws, which make morally upright individuals legal offenders, tends to generate skepticism and indifference toward observing the reasonable legalities.

This mood must change if the promise of recent civil rights legislation is to be realized. Respect for law today can give momentum to the liberal upswing of the political and social pendulum in American life. In a democracy we cannot make an absolute of obedience to law or to anything else except "the moral obligation to be intelligent," but more than ever we must stress that dissent and opposition—the oxygen of free society—be combined with civic obedience, and that on moral grounds it express itself as legal dissent and legal opposition.

The Enforcement of Morals

Morals and the Criminal Law   Sir Patrick Devlin

Sir Patrick Arthur Devlin (1905–   ), a former Lord Justice of Appeal and Lord of Appeal in Ordinary and now High Steward of Cambridge University, England, has produced writings in the philosophy of law and punishment which have stimulated discussion on the part of philosophers.

... What is the connexion between crime and sin and to what extent, if at all, should the criminal law of England concern itself with the enforcement of morals and punish sin or immorality as such?

The statements of principle in the Wolfenden Report provide an admirable and modern starting-point for such an inquiry. . . .

Early in the Report the Committee put forward:

> Our own formulation of the function of the criminal law so far as it concerns the subjects of this enquiry. In this field, its function, as we see it, is to preserve public order and decency, to protect the citizen from what is offensive or injurious, and to provide sufficient safeguards against exploitation and corruption of others, particularly those who are specially vulnerable because they are young, weak in body or mind, inexperienced, or in a state of special physical, official or economic dependence.
>
> It is not, in our view, the function of the law to intervene in the private lives of citizens, or to seek to enforce any particular pattern of behaviour, further than is necessary to carry out the purposes we have outlined.

The Committee preface their most important recommendation

> that homosexual behaviour between consenting adults in private should no longer be a criminal offence, [by stating the argument] which we believe to be decisive, namely, the importance which society and the law ought to give to individual freedom of choice and action in matters of private morality. Unless a deliberate attempt is to be made by society, acting through the agency of the law, to equate the sphere of crime with that of sin, there must remain a realm of private morality and immorality which is, in brief and crude terms, not the law's business. To say this is not to condone or encourage private immorality.

Similar statements of principle are set out in the chapters of the Report which deal with prostitution. No case can be sustained, the Report says, for attempting to make prostitution itself illegal. The Committee refer to the general reasons already given and add: 'We are agreed that private immorality should not be the concern of the criminal law except in the special circumstances therein mentioned.' They quote

Edited extract from *The Enforcement of Morals* by Patrick Devlin published by Oxford University Press.

with approval the report of the Street Offences Committee, which says:
'As a general proposition it will be universally accepted that the law is
not concerned with private morals or with ethical sanctions.' It will be
observed that the emphasis is on *private* immorality. By this is meant
immorality which is not offensive or injurious to the public in the ways
defined or described in the first passage which I quoted. In other words,
no act of immorality should be made a criminal offence unless it is
accompanied by some other feature such as indecency, corruption, or
exploitation. This is clearly brought out in relation to prostitution: 'It
is not the duty of the law to concern itself with immorality as such . . .
it should confine itself to those activities which offend against public
order and decency or expose the ordinary citizen to what is offensive or
injurious.'. . .

If this view is sound, it means that the criminal law cannot justify
any of its provisions by reference to the moral law. It cannot say, for
example, that murder and theft are prohibited because they are immoral
or sinful. The State must justify in some other way the punishments
which it imposes on wrongdoers and a function for the criminal law
independent of morals must be found. This is not difficult to do. The
smooth functioning of society and the preservation of order require that
a number of activities should be regulated. The rules that are made for
that purpose and are enforced by the criminal law are often designed
simply to achieve uniformity and convenience and rarely involve any
choice between good and evil. Rules that impose a speed limit or prevent
obstruction on the highway have nothing to do with morals. Since so
much of the criminal law is composed of rules of this sort, why bring
morals into it at all? Why not define the function of the criminal law
in simple terms as the preservation of order and decency and the protection of the lives and property of citizens, and elaborate those terms in
relation to any particular subject in the way in which it is done in the
Wolfenden Report? The criminal law in carrying out these objects will
undoubtedly overlap the moral law. Crimes of violence are morally wrong
and they are also offences against good order; therefore they offend
against both laws. But this is simply because the two laws in pursuit of
different objectives happen to cover the same area. Such is the argument. . . .

I think it is clear that the criminal law as we know it is based upon
moral principle. In a number of crimes its function is simply to enforce
a moral principle and nothing else. The law, both criminal and civil,
claims to be able to speak about morality and immorality generally.
Where does it get its authority to do this and how does it settle the moral
principles which it enforces? Undoubtedly, as a matter of history, it
derived both from Christian teaching. But I think that the strict logician
is right when he says that the law can no longer rely on doctrines in
which citizens are entitled to disbelieve. It is necessary therefore to look
for some other source.

In jurisprudence, as I have said, everything is thrown open to discussion and, in the belief that they cover the whole field, I have framed
three interrogatories addressed to myself to answer:

1. Has society the right to pass judgement at all on matters of morals? Ought there, in other words, to be a public morality, or are morals always a matter for private judgement?
2. If society has the right to pass judgement, has it also the right to use the weapon of the law to enforce it?
3. If so, ought it to use that weapon in all cases or only in some; and if only in some, on what principles should it distinguish?

I shall begin with the first interrogatory and consider what is meant by the right of society to pass a moral judgement, that is, a judgement about what is good and what is evil. The fact that a majority of people may disapprove of a practice does not of itself make it a matter for society as a whole. Nine men out of ten may disapprove of what the tenth man is doing and still say that it is not their business. There is a case for a collective judgement (as distinct from a large number of individual opinions which sensible people may even refrain from pronouncing at all if it is upon somebody else's private affairs) only if society is affected. Without a collective judgement there can be no case at all for intervention. Let me take as an illustration the Englishman's attitude to religion as it is now and as it has been in the past. His attitude now is that a man's religion is his private affair; he may think of another man's religion that it is right or wrong, true or untrue, but not that it is good or bad. In earlier times that was not so; a man was denied the right to practice what was thought of as heresy, and heresy was thought of as destructive of society.

The language used in the passages I have quoted from the Wolfenden Report suggests the view that there ought not to be a collective judgement about immorality *per se*. Is this what is meant by 'private morality' and 'individual freedom of choice and action'? Some people sincerely believe that homosexuality is neither immoral nor unnatural. Is the 'freedom of choice and action' that is offered to the individual, freedom to decide for himself what is moral or immoral, society remaining neutral; or is it freedom to be immoral if he wants to be? The language of the Report may be open to question, but the conclusions at which the Committee arrive answer this question unambiguously. If society is not prepared to say that homosexuality is morally wrong, there would be no basis for a law protecting youth from 'corruption' or punishing a man for living on the 'immoral' earnings of a homosexual prostitute, as the Report recommends. This attitude the Committee make even clearer when they come to deal with prostitution. In truth, the Report takes it for granted that there is in existence a public morality which condemns homosexuality and prostitution. What the Report seems to mean by private morality might perhaps be better described as private behaviour in matters of morals.

This view—that there is such a thing as public morality—can also be justified by *a priori* argument. What makes a society of any sort is community of ideas, not only political ideas but also ideas about the way its members should behave and govern their lives; these latter ideas are its morals. Every society has a moral structure as well as a political one: or rather, since that might suggest two independent systems, I should say that the structure of every society is made up both of politics and morals. Take, for example, the institution of marriage. Whether a man should be allowed to take more than one wife is something about which every society has to make up its mind one way or the other. In England we believe in the Christian idea of marriage and therefore adopt monogamy as a moral principle. Consequently the Christian institution of marriage has become the basis of family life and so part of the structure of our society. It is there not because it is Christian. It has got there because it is Christian, but it remains there because it is built into the house in which we live and could not be removed without bringing it down. The great majority of those who live in this country accept it because it is the Christian idea of marriage and for them the only true one. But a non-Christian is bound by it, not because it is part of Christianity but because, rightly or wrongly, it has been adopted by the society in which he lives. It would be useless for him to stage a debate designed to prove that polygamy was theologically more correct and socially preferable; if he wants to live in the house, he must accept it as built in the way in which it is.

We see this more clearly if we think of ideas or institutions that are purely political. Society cannot tolerate rebellion; it will not allow argument about the rightness of the cause. Historians a century later may say that the rebels were right and the Government was wrong and a percipient and conscientious subject of the State may think so at the time. But it is not a matter which can be left to individual judgement.

The institution of marriage is a good example for my purpose because it bridges the division, if there is one, between politics and morals. Marriage is part of the structure of our society and it is also the basis of a moral code which condemns fornication and adultery. The institution of marriage would be gravely threatened if individual judgements were permitted about the morality of adultery; on these points there must be a public morality. But public morality is not to be confined to those moral principles which support institutions such as marriage. People do not think of monogamy as something which has to be supported because our society has chosen to organize itself upon it; they think of it as something that is good in itself and offering a good way of life and that it is for that reason that our society has adopted it. I return to the statement that I have already made, that society means a community of ideas; without shared ideas on politics, morals, and ethics no society can exist. Each one of us has ideas about what is good and what is evil; they cannot be kept private from the society in which we live. If men and women try to create a society in which there is no fundamental agreement about good and evil they will fail; if, having based it on common agreement, the agreement goes, the society will disintegrate. For society is not something that is kept together physically; it is held by the invisible bonds of common thought. If the bonds were too far relaxed the members would drift apart. A common morality is part of the bondage. The bondage is part of the price of society; and mankind, which needs society, must pay its price. . . .

You may think that I have taken far too long in contending that there is such a thing as public morality, a proposition which most people would readily accept, and may have left myself too little time to discuss the next question which to many minds may cause greater difficulty: to what extent should society use the law to enforce its moral judgements? But I believe that the answer to the first question determines the way in which the second should be approached and may indeed very nearly dictate the answer to the second question. If society has no right to make judgements on morals, the law must find some special justification for entering the field of morality: if homosexuality and prostitution are not in themselves wrong, then the onus is very clearly on the lawgiver who wants to frame a law against certain aspects of them to justify the exceptional treatment. But if society has the right to make a judgement and has it on the basis that a recognized morality it as necessary to society as, say, a recognized government, then society may use the law to preserve morality in the same way as it uses it to safeguard anything else that is essential to its existence. If therefore the first proposition is securely established with all its implications, society has a prima facie right to legislate against immorality as such.

The Wolfenden Report, notwithstanding that it seems to admit the right of society to condemn homosexuality and prostitution as immoral, requires special circumstances to be shown to justify the intervention of the law. I think that this is wrong in principle and that any attempt to approach my second interrogatory on these lines is bound to break down. I think that the attempt by the Committee does break down and that this is shown by the fact that it has to define or describt its special circumstances so widely that they can be supported only if it is accepted that the law *is* concerned with immorality as such.

The widest of the special circumstances are described as the provision of 'sufficient safeguards against exploitation and corruption of others, particularly those who are specially vulnerable because they are young, weak in body or mind, inexperienced, or in a state of special physical, official or economic dependence.' The corruption of youth is a well-recognized ground for intervention by the State and for the purpose of any legislation the young can easily be defined. But if similar protection were to be extended to every other citizen, there would be no limit to the reach of the law. The 'corruption and exploitation of others' is so wide that it could be used to cover any sort of immorality which involves, as most do, the co-operation of another person. Even if the phrase is taken as limited to the categories that are particularized as 'specially vulnerable,' it is so elastic as to be practically no restriction. This is not merely a matter of words. For if the words used are stretched almost beyond breaking-point, they still are not wide enough to cover the recommendations which the Committee make about prostitution.

Prostitution is not in itself illegal and the Committee do not think that it ought to be made so. If prostitution is private immorality and not the law's business, what concern has the law with the ponce or the brothel-keeper or the householder who permits habitual prostitution? The Report recommends that the laws which make these activities criminal offences should be maintained or strengthened and brings them (so far as it goes into principle; with regard to brothels it says simply that the law rightly frowns on them) under the head of exploitation. There may be cases of exploitation in this trade, as there are or used to be in many others, but in general a ponce exploits a prostitute no more than an impressario exploits an actress. The Report finds that 'the great majority of prostitutes are women whose psychological makeup is such that they choose this life because they find in it a style of living which is to them easier, freer and more profitable than would be provided by any other occupation. . . . In the main the association between prostitute and ponce is voluntary and operates to mutual advantage.' The Committee would agree that this could not be called exploitation in the ordinary sense. They say: 'It is in our view an over-simplification to think that those who live on the earnings of prostitution are exploiting the prostitute as such. What they are really exploiting is the whole complex of the relationship between prostitute and customer; they are, in effect, exploiting the human weaknesses which cause the customer to seek the prostitute and the prostitute to meet the demand.'

All sexual immorality involves the exploitation of human weaknesses. The prostitute exploits the lust of her customers and the customer the moral weakness of the prostitute. If the exploitation of human weaknesses is considered to create a special circumstance, there is virtually no field of morality which can be defined in such a way as to exclude the law.

I think, therefore, that it is not possible to set theoretical limits to the power of the State to legislate against immorality. It is not possible to settle in advance exceptions to the general rule or to define inflexibly areas of morality into which the law is in no circumstances to be allowed to enter. Society is entitled by means of its laws to protect itself from dangers, whether from within or without. Here again I think that the political parallel is legitimate. The law of treason is directed against aiding the king's enemies and against sedition from within. The justification for this is that established government is necessary for the existence of society and therefore its safety against violent overthrow must be secured. But an established morality is as necessary as good government to the welfare of society. Societies disintegrate from within more frequently than they are broken up by external pressures. There is disintegration when no common morality is observed and history shows that the loosening of moral bonds is often the first stage of disintegration, so that society is justified in taking the same steps to preserve its moral code as it does to preserve its government and other essential institutions. The suppression of vice is as much the law's business as the suppression of subversive activities; it is no more possible to define a sphere of private morality than it is to define one of private subversive activity. It is wrong to talk of private morality or of the law not being concerned with immorality as such or to try to set rigid bounds to the part which the law may play in the suppression of vice. There are no theoretical limits to the power of the State to legislate against treason and sedition, and likewise I think there can be no theoretical limits to legislation against immorality. You may argue that if a man's sins affect only himself it cannot be the concern of society. If he chooses to get drunk every night in the privacy of his own home, is any one except himself the worse for it? But suppose a quarter or a half of the population got drunk every night, what sort of society would it be? You cannot set a theoretical limit to the number of people who can get drunk before society is entitled to legislate against drunkenness. The same may be said of gambling. The Royal Commission on Betting, Lotteries, and Gaming took as their test the character of the citizen as a member of society. They said: 'Our concern with the ethical significance of gambling is confined to the effect which it may have on the character of the gambler as a member of society. If we were convinced that whatever the degree of gambling this effect must be harmful we should be inclined to think that it was the duty of the state to restrict gambling to the greatest extent practicable.'

In what circumstances the State should exercise its power is the third of the interrogatories I have framed. But before I get to it I must raise a point which might have been brought up in any one of the three. How are the moral judgements of society to be ascertained? By leaving it until now, I can ask it in the more limited form that is now sufficient for my purpose. How is the law-maker to ascertain the moral judgements of society? It is surely not enough that they should be reached by the opinion of the majority; it would be too much to require the individual assent of every citizen. English law has evolved and regularly uses a standard which does not depend on the counting of heads. It is that of the reasonable man. He is not to be confused with the rational man. He is not expected to reason about anything and his judgement may be largely a matter of feeling. It is the viewpoint of the man in the street— or to use an archaism familiar to all lawyers—the man in the Clapham omnibus. He might also be called the right-minded man. For my purpose I should like to call him the man in the jury box, for the moral judge-ment of society must be something about which any twelve men or women drawn at random might after discussion be expected to be unanimous. This was the standard the judges applied in the days be-fore Parliament was as active as it is now and when they laid down rules of public policy. They did not think of themselves as making law but simply as stating principles which every right-minded person would accept as valid. It is what Pollock called 'practical morality,' which is based not on theological or philosophical foundations but 'in the mass of continuous experience half-consciously or unconsciously accumulated and embodied in the morality of common sense.' He called it also 'a certain way of thinking on questions of morality which we expect to find in a reasonable civilized man or a reasonable Englishman, taken at random.'

Immorality then, for the purpose of the law, is what every right-minded person is presumed to consider to be immoral. Any immorality is capable of affecting society injuriously and in effect to a greater or lesser extent it usually does; this is what gives the law its *locus standi*. It cannot be shut out. But—and this brings me to the third question—

the individual has a *locus standi* too; he cannot be expected to surrender to the judgement of society the whole conduct of his life. It is the old and familiar question of striking a balance between the rights and interests of society and those of the individual. This is something which the law is constantly doing in matters large and small. To take a very down-to-earth example, let me consider the right of the individual whose house adjoins the highway to have access to it; that means in these days the right to have vehicles stationary in the highway, sometimes for a considerable time if there is a lot of loading or unloading. There are many cases in which the courts have had to balance the private right of access against the public right to use the highway without obstruction. It cannot be done by carving up the highway into public and private areas. It is done by recognizing that each have rights over the whole; that if each were to exercise their rights to the full, they would come into conflict; and therefore that the rights of each must be curtailed so as to ensure as far as possible that the essential needs of each are safeguarded.

I do not think that one can talk sensibly of a public and private morality any more than one can of a public or private highway. Morality is a sphere in which there is a public interest and a private interest, often in conflict, and the problem is to reconcile the two. This does not mean that it is impossible to put forward any general statements about how in our society the balance ought to be struck. Such statements cannot of their nature be rigid or precise; they would not be designed to circumscribe the operation of the law-making power but to guide those who have to apply it. While every decision which a court of law makes when it balances the public against the private interest is an *ad hoc* decision, the cases contain statements of principle to which the court should have regard when it reaches its decision. In the same way it is possible to make general statements of principle which it may be thought the legislature should bear in mind when it is considering the enactment of laws enforcing morals.

I believe that most people would agree upon the chief of these elastic principles. There must be toleration of the maximum individual freedom that is consistent with the integrity of society. It cannot be said that this is a principle that runs all through the criminal law. Much of the criminal law that is regulatory in character—the part of it that deals with *malum prohibitum* rather than *malum in se*—is based upon the opposite principle, that is, that the choice of the individual must give way to the convenience of the many. But in all matters of conscience the principle I have stated is generally held to prevail. It is not confined to thought and speech; it extends to action, as is shown by the recognition of the right to conscientious objection in war-time; this example shows also that conscience will be respected even in times of national danger. The principle appears to me to be peculiarly appropriate to all questions of morals. Nothing should be punished by the law that does not lie beyond the limits of tolerance. It is not nearly enough to say that a majority dislike a practice; there must be a real feeling of reprobation. Those who are dissatisfied with the present law on homosexuality often say that the opponents of reform are swayed simply by disgust. If that were so it would be wrong, but I do not think one can ignore disgust if it is deeply felt and not manufactured. Its presence is a good indication that the bounds of toleration are being reached. Not everything is to be tolerated. No society can do without intolerance, indignation, and disgust; they are the forces behind the moral law, and indeed it can be argued that if they or something like them are not present, the feelings of society cannot be weighty enough to deprive the individual of freedom of choice. I suppose that there is hardly anyone nowadays who would not be disgusted by the thought of deliberate cruelty to animals. No one proposes to relegate that or any other form of sadism to the realm of private morality or to allow it to be practised in public or in private. It would be possible no doubt to point out that until a comparatively short while ago nobody thought very much of cruelty to animals and also that pity and kindliness and the unwillingness to inflict pain are virtues more generally esteemed now than they have ever been in the past. But matters of this sort are not determined by rational argument. Every moral judgement, unless it claims a divine source, is simply a feeling that no right-minded man could behave in any other way without admitting that he was doing wrong. It is the power of a common sense and not the power of reason that is behind the judgements of society. But before a society can put a practice beyond the limits of tolerance there must be a deliberate judgement that the practice is injurious to society. There is, for example, a general abhorrence of homosexuality. We should ask ourselves in the first instance whether, looking at it calmly and dispassionately, we regard it as a vice so abominable that its mere presence is an offence. If that is the genuine feeling of the society in which we live, I do not see how society can be denied the right to eradicate it. Our feeling may not be so intense as that. We may feel about it that, if confined, it is tolerable, but that if it spread it might be gravely injurious; it is in this way that most societies look upon fornication, seeing it as a natural weakness which must be kept within bounds but which cannot be rooted out. It becomes then a question of balance, the danger to society in one scale and the extent of the restriction in the other. On this sort of point the value of an investigation by such a body as the Wolfenden Committee and of its conclusions is manifest.

The limits of tolerance shift. This is supplementary to what I have been saying but of sufficient importance in itself to deserve statement as a separate principle which law-makers have to bear in mind. I suppose that moral standards do not shift; so far as they come from divine revelation they do not, and I am willing to assume that the moral judgements made by a society always remain good for that society. But the extent to which society will tolerate—I mean tolerate, not approve—departures from moral standards varies from generation to generation. It may be that over-all tolerance is always increasing. The pressure of the human mind, always seeking greater freedom of thought, is outwards against the bonds of society forcing their gradual relaxation. It may be that history is a tale of contraction and expansion and that all developed societies are on their way to dissolution. I must not speak of things I do not know; and anyway as a practical matter no society is willing to make provision for its own decay. I return therefore to the simple and observable fact that in matters of morals the limits of tolerance shift. Laws, especially those which are based on morals, are less easily moved. It follows as another good working principle that in any new matter of morals the law should be slow to act. By the next generation the swell of indignation may have abated and the law be left without the strong backing which it needs. But it is then difficult to alter the law without giving the impression that moral judgement is being weakened. This is now one of the factors that is strongly militating against any alteration to the law on homosexuality.

A third elastic principle must be advanced more tentatively. It is that as far as possible privacy should be respected. This is not an idea that has ever been made explicit in the criminal law. Acts or words done or said in public or private are all brought within its scope without distinction in principle. But there goes with this a strong reluctance on the part of judges and legislators to sanction invasions of privacy in the detection of crime. The police have no more right to trespass than the ordinary citizen has; there is no general right of search; to this extent an Englishman's home is still his castle. The Government is extremely careful in the exercise even of those powers which it claims to be undisputed. Telephone tapping and interference with the mails afford a good illustration of this. A Committee of three Privy Councillors who recently inquired into these activities found that the Home Secretary and his predecessors had already formulated strict rules governing the exercise of these powers and the Committee were able to recommend that they should be continued to be exercised substantially on the same terms. But they reported that the power was 'regarded with general disfavour.'

This indicates a general sentiment that the right to privacy is something to be put in the balance against the enforcement of the law. Ought the same sort of consideration to play any part in the formation of the law? Clearly only in a very limited number of cases. When the help of the law is invoked by an injured citizen, privacy must be irrelevant; the individual cannot ask that his right to privacy should be measured against injury criminally done to another. But when all who are involved in the deed are consenting parties and the injury is done to morals, the public interest in the moral order can be balanced against the claims of privacy. The restriction on police powers of investigation goes further than the affording of a parallel; it means that the detection of crime committed in private and when there is no complaint is bound to be rather haphazard and this is an additional reason for moderation. These considerations do not justify the exclusion of all private immorality from the scope of the law. I think that, as I have already suggested, the test of 'private behaviour' should be substituted for 'private morality' and the influence of the factor should be reduced from that of a definite limitation to that of a matter to be taken into account. Since the gravity of the crime is also a proper consideration, a distinction might well be made in the case of homosexuality between the lesser acts of indecency and the full offence, which on the principles of the Wolfenden Report it would be illogical to do.

The last and the biggest thing to be remembered is that the law is concerned with the minimum and not with the maximum; there is much in the Sermon on the Mount that would be out of place in the Ten Commandments. We all recognize the gap between the moral law and the law of the land. No man is worth much who regulates his conduct with the sole object of escaping punishment, and every worthy society sets for its members standards which are above those of the law. We recognize the existence of such higher standards when we use expressions such as 'moral obligation' and 'morally bound'. The distinction was well put in the judgement of African elders in a family dispute: 'We have power to make you divide the crops, for this is our law, and we will see this is done. But we have not power to make you behave like an upright man.'

It can only be because this point is so obvious that it is so frequently ignored. Discussion among law-makers, both professional and amateur, is too often limited to what is right or wrong and good or bad for society. There is a failure to keep separate the two questions I have earlier posed —the question of society's right to pass a moral judgement and the question of whether the arm of the law should be used to enforce the judgement. The criminal law is not a statement of how people ought to behave; it is a statement of what will happen to them if they do not behave; good citizens are not expected to come within reach of it or to set their sights by it, and every enactment should be framed accordingly.

The arm of the law is an instrument to be used by society, and the decision about what particular cases it should be used in is essentially a practical one. Since it is an instrument, it is wise before deciding to use it to have regard to the tools with which it can be fitted and to the machinery which operates it. Its tools are fines, imprisonment, or lesser forms of supervision (such as Borstal and probation) and—not to be ignored—the degradation that often follows upon the publication of the crime. Are any of these suited to the job of dealing with sexual immorality? The fact that there is so much immorality which has never been brought within the law shows that there can be no general rule. It is a matter for decision in each case; but in the case of homosexuality the Wolfenden Report rightly has regard to the views of those who are experienced in dealing with this sort of crime and to those of the clergy who are the natural guardians of public morals.

The machinery which sets the criminal law in motion ends with the verdict and the sentence; and a verdict is given either by magistrates or by a jury. As a general rule, whenever a crime is sufficiently serious to justify a maximum punishment of more than three months, the accused has the right to the verdict of a jury. The result is that magistrates administer mostly what I have called the regulatory part of the law. They deal extensively with drunkenness, gambling, and prostitution, which are matters of morals or close to them, but not with any of the graver moral offences. They are more responsive than juries to the ideas of the legislature; it may not be accidental that the Wolfenden Report, in recommending increased penalties for solicitation, did not go above the limit of three months. Juries tend to dilute the decrees of Parliament with their own ideas of what should be punishable. Their province of course is fact and not law, and I do not mean that they often deliberately disregard the law. But if they think it is too stringent, they sometimes take a very merciful view of the facts. Let me take one example out of many that could be given. It is an offence to have carnal knowledge of a girl under the age of sixteen years. Consent on her part is no defence; if she did not consent, it would of course amount to rape. The law makes special provision for the situation when a boy and girl are near in age. If a man under twenty-four can prove that he had reasonable cause to believe that the girl was over the age of sixteen years, he has a good defence. The law regards the offence as sufficiently serious to make it one that is triable only by a judge at assizes. 'Reasonable cause' means not merely that the boy honestly believed that the girl was over sixteen but also that he must have had reasonable grounds for his belief. In theory it ought not to be an easy defence to make out but in fact it is extremely rare for anyone who advances it to be convicted. The fact is that the girl is often as much to blame as the boy. The object of the law, as judges repeatedly tell juries, is to protect young girls against themselves; but juries are not impressed.

The part that the jury plays in the enforcement of the criminal law, the fact that no grave offence against morals is punishable without their verdict, these are of great importance in relation to the statements of principle that I have been making. They turn what might otherwise be pure exhortation to the legislature into something like rules that the law-makers cannot safely ignore. The man in the jury box is not just an expression; he is an active reality. It will not in the long run work to make laws about morality that are not acceptable to him.

This then is how I believe my third interrogatory should be answered —not by the formulation of hard and fast rules, but by a judgement in each case taking into account the sort of factors I have been mentioning. The line that divides the criminal law from the moral is not determinable by the application of any clear-cut principle. It is like a line that divides land and sea, a coastline of irregularities and indentations. There are gaps and promontories, such as adultery and fornication, which the law has for centuries left substantially untouched. Adultery of the sort that breaks up marriage seems to me to be just as harmful to the social fabric as homosexuality or bigamy. The only ground for putting it outside the criminal law is that a law which made it a crime would be too difficult to enforce; it is too generally regarded as a human' weakness not suitably punished by imprisonment. All that the law can do with fornication is to act against its worst manifestations; there is a general abhorrence of the commercialization of vice, and that sentiment gives strength to the law against brothels and immoral earnings. There is no logic to be found in this. The boundary between the criminal law and the moral law is fixed by balancing in the case of each particular crime the pros and cons of legal enforcement in accordance with the sort of considerations I have been outlining. The fact that adultery, fornication, and lesbianism are untouched by the criminal law does not prove that homosexuality ought not to be touched. The error of jurisprudence in the Wolfenden Report

is caused by the search for some single principle to explain the division between crime and sin. The Report finds it in the principle that the criminal law exists for the protection of individuals; on this principle fornication in private between consenting adults is outside the law and thus it
becomes logically indefensible to bring homosexuality between consenting adults in private within it. But the true principle is that the law
exists for the protection of society. It does not discharge its function by
protecting the individual from injury, annoyance, corruption, and exploitation; the law must protect also the institutions and the community
of ideas, political and moral, without which people cannot live together.
Society cannot ignore the morality of the individual any more than it
can his loyalty; it flourishes on both and without either it dies. . . .

Society cannot live without morals. Its morals are those standards of
conduct which the reasonable man approves. A rational man, who is also
a good man, may have other standards. If he has no standards at all he
is not a good man and need not be further considered. If he has standards,
they may be very different; he may, for example, not disapprove of homosexuality or abortion. In that case he will not share in the common
morality; but that should not make him deny that it is a social necessity.
A rebel may be rational in thinking that he is right but he is irrational if
he thinks that society can leave him free to rebel. . . .

Immorality and Treason   H. L. A. Hart

Herbert Lionel Adolphus Hart (1907–   ) spent some time as a lawyer in
London and then returned to Oxford University where, in 1952, he became
professor of jurisprudence. The impact of Hart's writings has been felt widely
in contemporary philosophy of law.

The Wolfenden Committee on Homosexual Offences and Prostitution
recommended by a majority of 12 to 1 that homosexual behaviour between
consenting adults in private should no longer be a criminal offence. One
of the Committee's principal grounds for this recommendation was expressed in its report in this way: 'There must remain a realm of private
morality and immorality which in brief and crude terms is not the law's
business.' I shall call this the liberal point of view: for it is a special application of those wider principles of liberal thought which John Stuart
Mill formulated in his essay on Liberty. Mill's most famous words, less
cautious perhaps than the Wolfenden Committee's, were:

> The only purpose for which power can be rightfully exercised over
> any member of a civilized community against his will is to prevent harm to
> others. His own good, either physical or moral, is not a sufficient warrant.
> He cannot rightfully be compelled to do or forbear . . . because in the
> opinion of others to do so would be wise or even right.

Reprinted from *The Listener*, July 30, 1959. Reprinted by permission of the author.

Repudiation of the Liberal Point of View

The liberal point of view has often been attacked, both before and after Mill. I shall discuss here the repudiation of it made by Sir Patrick Devlin, in his recent lecture, which has now been published. This contains an original and interesting argument designed to show that '*prima facie* society has the right to legislate against immorality as such' and that the Wolfenden Committee were mistaken in thinking that there is an area of private immorality which is not the law's business. Sir Patrick's case is a general one, not confined to sexual immorality, and he does not say whether or not he is opposed to the Wolfenden Committee's recommendation on homosexual behaviour. Instead he gives us a hypothetical principle by which to judge this issue. He says: 'If it is the genuine feeling of our society that homosexuality is a vice so abominable that its mere presence is an offence,' society has the right to eradicate it by the use of the criminal law.

The publication by Sir Patrick of this lecture is in itself an interesting event. It is many years since a distinguished English lawyer delivered himself of general reasoned views about the relationship of morality to the criminal law. The last to do so with comparable skill and clarity was, I think, the great Victorian judge James Fitzjames Stephen. It is worth observing that Stephen, like Sir Patrick, repudiated the liberal point of view. Indeed his gloomy but impressive book *Liberty, Equality, Fraternity* was a direct reply to Mill's essay *On Liberty*. The most remarkable feature of Sir Patrick's lecture is his view of the nature of morality—the morality which the criminal law may enforce. Most previous thinkers who have repudiated the liberal point of view have done so because they thought that morality consisted either of divine commands or of rational principles of human conduct discoverable by human reason. Since morality for them had this elevated divine or rational status as the law of God or reason, it seemed obvious that the state should enforce it, and that the function of human law should not be merely to provide men with the opportunity for leading a good life, but actually to see that they led it. Sir Patrick does not rest his repudiation of the liberal point of view on these religious or rationalist conceptions. Indeed much that he writes reads like an abjuration of the notion that reasoning or thinking has much to do with morality. English popular morality has no doubt its historical connection with the Christian religion: 'That,' says Sir Patrick, 'is how it got there.' But it does not owe its present status or social significance to religion any more than to reason.

What, then, is it? According to Sir Patrick it is primarily a matter of feeling. 'Every moral judgment,' he says, 'is a feeling that no right-minded man could act in any other way without admitting that he was doing wrong.' Who then must feel this way if we are to have what Sir Patrick calls a public morality? He tells us that it is 'the man in the street,' 'the man in the jury box,' or (to use the phrase so familiar to English lawyers) 'the man on the Clapham omnibus.' For the moral judgments of society so far as the law is concerned are to be ascertained by the standards of the reasonable man, and he is not to be confused with the rational man.

Indeed, Sir Patrick says 'he is not expected to reason about anything and his judgment may be largely a matter of feeling.'

Intolerance, Indignation, and Disgust

But what precisely are the relevant feelings, the feelings which may justify use of the criminal law? Here the argument becomes a little complex. Widespread dislike of a practice is not enough. There must, says Sir Patrick, be 'a real feeling of reprobation.' Disgust is not enough either. What is crucial is a combination of intolerance, indignation, and disgust. These three are the forces behind the moral law, without which it is not 'weighty enough to deprive the individual of freedom of choice.' Hence there is, in Sir Patrick's outlook, a crucial difference between the mere adverse moral judgment of society and one which is inspired by feeling raised to the concert pitch of intolerance, indignation, and disgust.

This distinction is novel and also very important. For on it depends the weight to be given to the fact that when morality is enforced individual liberty is necessarily cut down. Though Sir Patrick's abstract formulation of his views on this point is hard to follow, his examples make his position fairly clear. We can see it best in the contrasting things he says about fornication and homosexuality. In regard to fornication, public feeling in most societies is not now of the concert-pitch intensity. We may feel that it is tolerable if confined: only its spread might be gravely injurious. In such cases the question whether individual liberty should be restricted is for Sir Patrick a question of balance between the danger to society in the one scale, and the restriction of the individual in the other. But if, as may be the case with homosexuality, public feeling is up to concert pitch, if it expresses a 'deliberate judgment' that a practice as such is injurious to society, if there is 'a genuine feeling that it is a vice so abominable that its mere presence is an offence,' then it is beyond the limits of tolerance, and society may eradicate it. In this case, it seems, no further balancing of the claims of individual liberty is to be done, though as a matter of prudence the legislator should remember that the popular limits of tolerance may shift: the concert-pitch feeling may subside. This may produce a dilemma for the law; for the law may then be left without the full moral backing that it needs, yet it cannot be altered without giving the impression that the moral judgment is being weakened.

A Shared Morality

If this is what morality is—a compound of indignation, intolerance, and disgust—we may well ask what justification there is for taking it, and turning it as such, into criminal law with all the misery which criminal punishment entails. Here Sir Patrick's answer is very clear and simple. A collection of individuals is not a society; what makes them into a society is among other things a shared or public morality. This is as necessary to its existence as an organized government. So society may use the law to preserve its morality like anything else essential to it. 'The suppression of vice is as much the law's business as the suppression of subversive activities.' The liberal point of view which denies this is guilty of 'an error in jurisprudence': for it is no more possible to define an area of private morality than an area of private subversive activity. There can be no 'theoretical limits' to legislation against immorality just as there are no such limits to the power of the state to legislate against treason and sedition.

Surely all this, ingenious as it is, is misleading. Mill's formulation of the liberal point of view may well be too simple. The grounds for interfering with human liberty are more various than the single criterion of 'harm to others' suggests: cruelty to animals or organizing prostitution for gain do not, as Mill himself saw, fall easily under the description of harm to others. Conversely, even where there is harm to others in the most literal sense, there may well be other principles limiting the extent to which he often stresses between theoretical and practical limits. But with criteria, not a single criterion, determining when human liberty may be restricted. Perhaps this is what Sir Patrick means by a curious distinction which he often stresses between theoretical and practical limits. But with all its simplicities the liberal point of view is a better guide than Sir Patrick to clear thought on the proper relation of morality to the criminal law: for it stresses what he obscures—namely, the points at which thought is needed before we turn popular morality into criminal law.

Society and Moral Opinion

No doubt we would all agree that a consensus of moral opinion on certain matters is essential if society is to be worth living in. Laws against murder, theft, and much else would be of little use if they were not supported by a widely diffused conviction that what these laws forbid is also immoral. So much is obvious. But it does not follow that everything to which the moral vetoes of accepted morality attach is of equal importance to society; nor is there the slightest reason for thinking of morality as a seamless web: one which will fall to pieces carrying society with it, unless all its emphatic vetoes are enforced by law. Surely even in the face of the moral feeling that is up to concert pitch—the trio of intolerance, indignation, and disgust—we must pause to think. We must ask a question at two different levels which Sir Patrick never clearly enough identifies or separates. First, we must ask whether a practice which offends moral feeling is harmful, independently of its repercussion on the general moral code. Secondly, what about repercussion on the moral code? Is it really true that failure to translate this item of general morality into criminal law will jeopardize the whole fabric of morality and so of society?

We cannot escape thinking about these two different questions merely by repeating to ourselves the vague nostrum: 'This is part of public morality and public morality must be preserved if society is to exist.' Sometimes Sir Patrick seems to admit this, for he says in words which both Mill and the Wolfenden Report might have used, that there must be the maximum respect for individual liberty consistent with the integrity of society. Yet this, as his contrasting examples of fornication and homosexuality show, turns out to mean only that the immorality which the law may punish must be generally felt to be intolerable. This plainly is no adequate substitute for a reasoned estimate of the damage to the fabric of society likely to ensue if it is not suppressed.

Nothing perhaps shows more clearly the inadequacy of Sir Patrick's approach to this problem than his comparison between the suppression of sexual immorality and the suppression of treason or subversive activity. Private subversive activity is, of course, a contradiction in terms because 'subversion' means over-throwing government, which is a public thing. But it is grotesque, even where moral feeling against homosexuality is up to concert pitch, to think of the homosexual behaviour of two adults in private as in any way like treason or sedition either in intention or effect. We can make it *seem* like treason only if we assume that deviation from a general moral code is bound to affect that code, and to lead not merely to its modification but to its destruction. The analogy could begin to be plausible only if it was clear that offending against this item of morality was likely to jeopardize the whole structure. But we have ample evidence for believing that people will not abandon morality, will not think any better of murder, cruelty and dishonesty, merely because some private sexual practice which they abominate is not punished by the law.

Because this is so the analogy with treason is absurd. Of course 'No man is an island': what one man does in private, if it is known, may affect others in many different ways. Indeed it may be that deviation from general sexual morality by those whose lives, like the lives of many homosexuals, are noble ones and in all other ways exemplary will lead to what Sir Patrick calls the shifting of the limits of tolerance. But if this has any analogy in the sphere of government it is not the overthrow of ordered government, but a peaceful change in its form. So we may listen to the promptings of common sense and of logic, and say that though there could not logically be a sphere of private treason there is a sphere of private morality and immorality.

Sir Patrick's doctrine is also open to a wider, perhaps a deeper, criticism. In his reaction against a rationalist morality and his stress on feeling, he has I think thrown out the baby and kept the bath water; and the bath water may turn out to be very dirty indeed. When Sir Patrick's lecture was first delivered *The Times* greeted it with these words: 'There is a moving and welcome humility in the conception that society should not be asked to give its reason for refusing to tolerate what in its heart it feels intolerable.' This drew from a correspondent in Cambridge the retort: 'I am afraid that we are less humble than we used to be. We once burnt old women because, without giving our reasons, we felt in our hearts that witchcraft was intolerable.'

This retort is a bitter one, yet its bitterness is salutary. We are not, I suppose, likely, in England, to take again to the burning of old women for witchcraft or to punishing people for associating with those of a different race or colour, or to punishing people again for adultery. Yet if these things were viewed with intolerance, indignation, and disgust, as the second of them still is in some countries, it seems that on Sir Patrick's principles no rational criticism could be opposed to the claim that they should be punished by law. We could only pray, in his words, that the limits of tolerance might shift.

Curious Logic

It is impossible to see what curious logic has led Sir Patrick to this result. For him a practice is immoral if the thought of it makes the man on the Clapham omnibus sick. So be it. Still, why should we not summon all the resources of our reason, sympathetic understanding, as well as critical intelligence, and insist that before general moral feeling is turned into criminal law it is submitted to scrutiny of a different kind from Sir Patrick's? Surely, the legislator should ask whether the general morality is based on ignorance, superstition, or misunderstanding; whether there is a false conception that those who practise what it condemns are in other ways dangerous or hostile to society; and whether the misery to many parties, the blackmail and the other evil consequences of criminal punishment, especially for sexual offences, are well understood. It is surely extraordinary that among the things which Sir Patrick says are to be considered before we legislate against immorality these appear nowhere; not even as 'practical considerations,' let alone 'theoretical limits.' To any theory which, like this one, asserts that the criminal law may be used on the vague ground that the preservation of morality is essential to society and yet omits to stress the need for critical scrutiny, our reply should be: 'Morality, what crimes may be committed in thy name!'

As Mill saw, and de Tocqueville showed in detail long ago in his critical but sympathetic study of democracy, it is fatally easy to confuse the democratic principle that power should be in the hands of the majority with the utterly different claim that the majority, with power in their hands, need respect no limits. Certainly there is a special risk in a democracy that the majority may dictate how all should live. This is the risk we run, and should gladly run; for it is the price of all that is so good in democratic rule. But loyalty to democratic principles does not require us to maximize this risk: yet this is what we shall do if we mount the man in the street on the top of the Clapham omnibus and tell him that if only he feels sick enough about what other people do in private to demand its suppression by law no theoretical criticism can be made of his demand.

Suggestions
for Further Reading

Anthologies

Bedau, Hugo (ed.). *Civil Disobedience.* New York: Western Publishing Company, Pegasus Books, 1969. An excellent anthology for the beginning student, which covers issues in both the theory and practice of civil disobedience.

Girvetz, Harry K. (ed.). *Contemporary Moral Issues,* 2nd ed. Belmont, California: Wadsworth, 1968. An anthology of interesting, nontechnical articles on a wide range of frequently debated moral issues.

Taylor, Paul (ed.). *Problems of Moral Philosophy.* Belmont, California: Dickenson Publishing Company, 1967. A good anthology of important writings on a wide range of ethical problems.

Individual Works

Barnes, Hazel E. *An Existentialist Ethics.* New York: Knopf, 1967. A clear presentation of an existentialist approach to ethics, as well as a consideration and rejection of a number of other contemporary ethical views.

Binkley, Luther. *Contemporary Ethical Theories.* New York: Citadel Press, 1961. A clear discussion of the twentieth-century analytic philosophers' approach to ethics.

Brandt, William. *Ethical Theory.* Englewood Cliffs, N.J.: Prentice-Hall, 1959. This is an excellent but somewhat difficult introduction to ethical theory. There are excellent bibliographies on almost all major topics in ethical theory.

Fletcher, Joseph. *Situation Ethics: The New Morality.* Philadelphia: The Westminster Press, 1966. A contemporary Christian view of ethics, which stresses love as the basis for decision-making in ethics.

Frankena, William. *Ethics.* Englewood Cliffs, N.J.: Prentice-Hall, 1963. Provides a clear, concise statement of the major ethical problems and positions.

Hospers, John. *Human Conduct.* New York: Harcourt, 1961. An excellent, clearly written textbook, which is highly recommended for the beginning student.

Russell, Bertrand. *Human Society in Ethics and Politics.* New York: Simon & Schuster, 1952. A clearly written analysis of a variety of ethical issues by a great modern philosopher.

244

Mill, John Stuart. *Utilitarianism.* Indianapolis: Bobbs, 1957. A classic statement of the utilitarian position, which differs from Bentham's version in several important ways.

Olson, Robert G. *The Morality of Self-interest.* New York: Harcourt, 1965. An interesting defense of a version of egoism.

Encyclopedia of Philosophy. Paul Edwards, editor-in-chief. New York: Macmillan, 1967. The student will find many worthwhile articles on the subject treated in this Part, and excellent bibliographies.

Four:
Mind and
Body

Introduction

In Karel Čapek's well-known play *R.U.R.* (Rossum's Universal Robots), scientists have learned to manufacture robots capable of doing all the manual and intellectual activities humans perform. Humans consider the robots to be lacking a soul since they are nothing more than a machine produced by a complex physical process, and use the robots in any way that serves man's needs. The robots, whose manufacture resulted from a new method of organizing matter, look and act very much like humans except that they lack emotions and feelings, which were purposely omitted to increase productivity. Since the robot's insensitivity to pain often leads to accidents, a scientist at Rossum's robot factory experiments with changes in their formula to give them human emotions. His experiments succeed; but the new sensitive robots consider themselves man's equal and, frustrated by their inferior status, rebel and destroy man.

This play raises the question of whether the robots, though only complex machines, differ significantly from the men who created them. The answers to this question can have important effects on man's view of himself and his place in the world. One traditional religious view of man, which gives him special importance, is that he alone, because he possesses an immaterial soul, was made in the image of God. But if man can be shown to be nothing more than a complex machine, this view of his special status must be given up. The doctrine that man is spiritual as well as physical has been thought to be of crucial importance for other reasons. The claim that man is immortal is based on his supposed possession of a soul that can continue in existence after the body's destruction. Some philosophers have argued that since a physical world would be controlled by invariable laws, the doctrine of free will can be maintained only if man has a spiritual aspect, and only if man possesses free will can he be morally responsible. In light of such implications, the philosopher is concerned to determine if man really is more than a complex physical object.

The problem of the nature of man, whether he is wholly physical or not, is called the mind-body problem. One prominent view of reality—*materialism*—holds that man, as is every other object in the universe, is totally a physical being. The universe is considered to consist of the motion of particles of matter in a void or space. Any claim that man has a soul or mind is regarded as a myth. The fact that man can do such things as talk and reason is attributed to his highly developed nervous system and brain. Death

249

occurs when the body ceases to function. Any continuation of life after death is not the disembodied personal immortality defended by various religions, but the continued existence of the molecules that make up the body. This metaphysical materialism should not be confused with a popular use of the term *materialism* to refer to those who have no high ethical aims and who are primarily concerned with acquiring worldly goods and pleasures.

Opposed to the materialist view are those who believe that man is more than a material body; he also has a nonmaterial mind or soul. The idea of a person's being more than his body arose for a number of reasons. One possible reason is that primitive man could not comprehend why some bodies were alive and others dead when they apparently had the same physical parts. They endowed the living body with an invisible spirit or soul which the dead body lacked. The idea of a soul that apparently left the body at the time of death became the foundation for the belief in immortality, i.e., the continued existence of the soul after death.

In speculation about the soul, present-day philosophers generally equate it with the mind, which they claim is that part of us that thinks and has images and sensations. These philosophers posit a nonmaterial mind because, for one reason, the various images and thoughts we have do not have any size, weight, location and so cannot be material. Further, it is often claimed that a mind is necessary to explain purposive behavior. Purposive behavior is behavior that is determined by one's apprehension and desire for some future goal, in contrast to behavior determined by prior physical causes. Philosophers who hold that man has both a physical body and a nonphysical mind are *dualists*.

The most generally held form of dualism and the form that is perhaps closest to our ordinary conception of man is *interactionism*. The interactionists maintain that both mind and body can causally affect each other. Thus events in the mind can produce bodily behavior, and bodily events can produce mental occurrences. An example of events in the mind causing bodily events would be a thought of a girl friend causing one to pick up the phone and call her. An example of a physical event causing mental events would be a case where stubbing one's toe produces a sensation of pain.

Many philosophers have thought the interactionist view unsatisfactory. The major difficulty is that there seems to be no good explanation of how a mental event, such as a thought, can cause physical behavior. We ordinarily think of causation in terms of one physical event producing another. A simple example would be a moving billiard ball's hitting a second and moving it. But how can a thought produce movement in a person's body?

And where does the mind act on the body to cause it to move? One might be inclined to say that the mind affects some portion of the brain, but physiologists have found no place where the brain seems to be stimulated by any invisible cause. Similarly, how can the body produce sensations or images in the mind, which is nonphysical?

Confronted with such difficulties, some philosophers who believe that mental phenomena cannot be reduced to physical ones have given up interactionism in favor of *epiphenomenalism*. This view holds that physical events can cause mental events, but that occurrences in the mind are not able to cause any physical events. Rather than interaction, we have a one-way causal relation from the body to the mind. This view, too, has had its share of critics. This view, like interactionism, needs to explain how a physical event in the body can cause an event to take place in the mind. Another problem is that paradoxical results follow from this theory. One such result is that all thoughts and reasoning are totally without significance in the determination of our behavior. It is certainly hard to believe that the world would be exactly as it is today even though none of men's thoughts about democracy, religion, and morality had ever occurred.

In the first three readings that follow, each of the positions discussed above is defended, and answers to the objections we have mentioned are considered. In "Materialism," Hugh Elliot presents a detailed defense of the materialistic view of man and the world. He maintains that the main principles of materialism are the uniformity of law, the denial of teleology, and the denial of any form of existence other than those envisaged by physics and chemistry. He attempts to answer some of the major difficulties that the materialists face, especially the nature of images and the apparent existence of purposive behavior. In defending an interactionist position, C. E. M. Joad argues that the materialist cannot adequately explain purposive behavior or the way in which meaning is apprehended. He conceives of the mind as an active, creative force, which carries on activities that could not be conceived as resulting from the function of the brain. In opposition to the materialist view, Joad maintains that a perfect knowledge of a person's brain would fail to tell us what he was thinking since different thoughts could result in the same brain state. In "Bodies and Minds," W. F. R. Hardie defends epiphenomenalism. Though he admits that there are problems for the theory, he embraces it because he believes its problems are less serious than those confronting the other two positions. One difficulty Hardie has with epiphenomenalism is that it does not seem to account for our ability to identify our experiences as our own.

Although the development of robots has long been a subject for science-fiction stories and plays, such as *R.U.R.,* it is becoming a subject of increasing interest to philosophers and scientists as a result of the recent development of computers. Some theorists maintain that computers will eventually be developed to the point where they can perform all of the rational processes of human beings. And with the development of computerized robots, we would have a machine that could do everything a human being can do. In fact, it is argued, such a machine would be a human being, and a human being would have been shown to be nothing more than a machine. But is it possible to develop a machine that can perform all of the "mental" feats of a human being? And if such a machine could be developed, would it still lack something that humans possess? If we produce a machine that can do everything a human being can do, then have we shown that humans are really nothing more than physical objects?

In considering whether machines can do everything men can do, John H. Troll argues that machines can never be developed that can perform all of the mental processes of human beings. He contends that the kind of thinking humans do in seeing relations between events and making generalizations is not something that can be programmed into a computer. Dennis Thompson rejects the claim that there are activities performed by human beings that cannot be performed by machines. But he goes further and examines how the acceptance or denial of machines' being conscious affects the three major theories of the mind: materialism, interactionism, and epiphenomenalism. He reaches the surprising conclusion that acceptance of consciousness in a machine would neither establish nor destroy the materialistic position. Rejection of consciousness in machines would, however, tend to disprove interactionism.

A major issue that arises from a discussion of the mind-body problem is that of immortality. Continued existence after physical death would require that man have a nonphysical part of him which can survive without the body. The acceptance of dualism is not, however, by itself sufficient to show that there actually is immortality. It is certainly possible that the mind ceases to function when the body does. So, to have rational grounds for the belief in immortality, one would not only have to show that one has a mind or soul, but also that there is evidence that such continued existence occurs.

Clarence Darrow argues that the widespread belief in immortality has no foundation in fact. He presents a number of arguments against the likelihood of consciousness surviving death as well as arguments against the religious doctrine of the resurrection of the dead. In concluding his article, Darrow states some doubts about the value of a belief in immortality. In opposition to generally held opinions, he believes not only that a satisfactory life can be lived without the belief in immortality, but also that the rejection of a future life will produce a closer kinship with one's fellow man than could otherwise be achieved. In contrast to the views of Darrow,

C. J. Ducasse maintains that the arguments used to show that life after death is impossible are faulty. Against the claim that all the evidence we have shows that the mind ceases to function at the time of death, Ducasse cites possible evidence to the contrary from investigations in psychical phenomena. He is careful to point out, however, that even if such evidence is authentic, it still may not indicate continued existence. Ducasse maintains that the desire to show immortality to be impossible stems from the assumption that materialism is true. Rejection of that assumption at least opens the way for belief in immortality.

Materialism

Materialism Hugh Elliot

Hugh Elliot (1881–1930), editor of the Annual Register, England, was a champion of modern science and materialism, and a student and biographer of Herbert Spencer, the famous nineteenth-century philosopher of evolution.

... The main purpose of the present work is to defend the doctrine of materialism. ...

The outlines of this system are not new; the main features of it, indeed, have been admittedly associated with scientific progress for centuries past. An age of science is necessarily an age of materialism; ours is a scientific age, and it may be said with truth that we are all materialists now. The main principles which I shall endeavour to emphasize are three.

1. The uniformity of law. In early times events appeared to be entirely hazardous and unaccountable, and they still seem so, if we confine attention purely to the passing moment. But as science advances, there is disclosed a uniformity in the procedure of Nature. When the conditions at any one moment are precisely identical with those which prevailed at some previous moment, the results flowing from them will also be identical. It is found, for instance, that a body of given mass attracts some other body of given mass at a given distance with a force of a certain strength. It is found that when the masses, distances, and other conditions are precisely repeated, the attraction between the bodies is always exactly the same. It is found, further, that when the distance between the bodies is increased the force of their attraction is diminished in a fixed proportion, and this again is found to hold true at all distances at which they may be placed. The force of their attraction again varies in a different but still constant proportion to their masses. And hence results the law of gravitation, by which the force of attraction can be precisely estimated from a knowledge of the masses and distances between any two bodies whatever. A uniformity is established which remains absolute within the experience of Man, and to an equivalent extent the haphazard appearance of events is found to be only an appearance. Innumerable other laws of a similar character are gradually discovered, establishing a sort of nexus between every kind of event. If oxygen and hydrogen in the proportion by weight of eight to one are mixed together, and an electric spark is passed through them, water is formed; and on every occasion where precisely the same conditions are realized precisely the same result

From *Modern Science and Materialism* by Hugh Elliot. Published by Longman's, Green and Company, Ltd. Reprinted by permission of the publisher.

ensues. This truth is the basis of the experimental method. If from similar conditions it were possible that dissimilar results should follow on various occasions, then experiments would be useless for advancing knowledge. . . .

2. The denial of teleology. Scientific materialism warmly denies that there exists any such thing as purpose in the Universe, or that events have any ulterior motive or goal to which they are striving. It asserts that all events are due to the interaction of matter and motion acting by blind necessity in accordance with those invariable sequences to which we have given the name of laws. This is an important bond of connection between the materialism of the ancient Greeks and that of modern science. Among all peoples not highly cultivated there reigns a passionate conviction, not only that the Universe as a whole is working out some pre-determined purpose, but that every individual part of it subserves some special need in the fulfilment of this purpose. Needless to say, the purpose has always been regarded as associated with human welfare. The Universe, down to its smallest parts, is regarded by primitive superstition as existing for the special benefit of man. To such extreme lengths has this view been carried that even Bernardin de Saint-Pierre, who only died last century, argued that the reason why melons are ribbed is that they may be eaten more easily by families. . . .

When it is alleged that the Universe is purposive, it is assumed that humanity is intimately connected with the purpose. Without that assumption, none but the most transcendental of philosophers would have any interest in maintaining teleology. As the anthropocentric doctrine falls, therefore, the doctrine of teleology must fall with it. This, at all events, is the position taken up by scientific, as indeed by all materialism; it is the position that I hope I shall have little difficulty in defending in the following pages. Nevertheless, however obvious its truth, we must recognize that it involves a profound alteration in the existing mental point of view of the majority of mankind; for most men have as yet not shaken off the habit, which all men necessarily start from, that they themselves, or their family, nation or kind, are in fact, as in appearance, the very centre of the cosmos.

3. The denial of any form of existence other than those envisaged by physics and chemistry, that is to say, other than existences that have some kind of palpable material characteristics and qualities. It is here that modern materialism begins to part company with ancient materialism, and it is here that I expect the main criticisms of opponents to be directed. The modern doctrine stands in direct opposition to a belief in any of those existences that are vaguely classed as "spiritual." To this category belong not only ghosts, gods, souls, *et hoc genus omne,* for these have long been rejected from the beliefs of most advanced thinkers. The time has now come to include also in the condemned list that further imaginary entity which we call "mind," "consciousness," etc., together with its various subspecies of intellect, will, feeling, etc., in so far as they are supposed to be independent or different from material existences or processes.

. . . It seems to the ordinary observer that nothing can be more remotely and widely separated than some so-called "act of consciousness" and a material object. An act of consciousness or mental process is a thing of which we are immediately and indubitably aware: so much I admit. But that it differs in any sort of way from a material process, that is to say, from the ordinary transformations of matter and energy, is a belief which I very strenuously deny....

The proposition which I here desire to advance is that every event occurring in the Universe, including those events known as mental processes, and all kinds of human action or conduct, are expressible purely in terms of matter and motion. If we assume in the primeval nebula of the solar system no other elementary factors beyond those of matter and energy or motion, we can theoretically, as above remarked, deduce the existing Universe, including mind, consciousness, etc., without the introduction of any new factor whatsoever. The existing Universe and all things and events therein may be theoretically expressed in terms of matter and energy, undergoing continuous redistribution in accordance with the ordinary laws of physics and chemistry. If all manifestations within our experience can be thus expressed, as has for long been believed by men of science, what need is there for the introduction of any new entity of spiritual character, called mind? It has no part to play; it is impotent in causation.... Now there is an ancient logical precept which retains a large validity: *entia non sunt multiplicanda praeter necessitatem*. It is sometimes referred to as William of Occam's razor, which cuts off and rejects from our theories all factors or entities which are superfluous in guiding us to an explanation. "Mind" as a separate entity is just such a superfluity. I will not deny—indeed I cordially affirm—that it is a direct datum of experience; but there is no direct datum of experience to the effect that it is anything different from certain cerebral processes....

The materialism which I shall advocate, therefore, is centred round three salient points: the uniformity of law, the exclusion of purpose, and the assertion of monism; that is to say, that there exists no kind of spiritual substance or entity of a different nature from that of which matter is composed.

The first of these propositions, otherwise called the Law of Universal Causation, affirms that nothing happens without a cause, and that the same causes under the same conditions always produce the same effects. In order to gain a true comprehension of this law, we have to define what we mean by "cause" and "effect," and what is the nature of the nexus between them. The conception of the Universe from which we start is that of a great system of matter and motion undergoing redistribution according to fixed sequences, which in the terminology of science are called laws. The matter is constantly undergoing transformation from one of its forms into another, and the energy is redistributed and transformed in a corresponding manner. From this primary conception alone, we are able to derive a precise definition of what is meant by cause, a problem which is almost insuperable from any other standpoint.... If we regard an event as a momentary phase in the redistribution of matter and motion, then the cause of the event is found in the immediately preceding state of distribution of that same matter and motion.

Let us ask, for instance, what is the cause of the sudden appearance of a new fixed star in the heavens. Supposing that there were previously two extinct suns moving rapidly towards each other and coming into collision, we should be making a statement of events which would be recognized as a possibly true "cause." The second event, or "effect," is represented exclusively in terms of matter and motion by the idea of two coalesced and volatilized bodies giving rise to vast quantities of heat and light. And the cause is given merely by stating the previous distribution of that matter and energy which is concerned in the production of the event. The *matter* concerned in the event consisted of two solid bodies at a rapidly diminishing distance from one another. The *energy* consisted of half the product of their momentum and velocity. By the collision the matter contained in the solid bodies underwent that redistribution involved in passing into a gaseous state, with the decomposition of many of its molecules, that is to say, with a rearrangement or redistribution of its atoms. The energy of motion previously contained in the solid bodies underwent at the same time a transformation into heat and light. The sudden light, therefore, is explained, or derives its cause, merely by furnishing a statement of the previous distribution of the matter and energy concerned in its production. . . .

And this leads me to the second problem which I have here to deal with, the problem of teleology. I have hitherto endeavoured to represent the notion of cause and effect in purely materialistic terms, to the exclusion of all metaphysical transcendentalism; to state the relation of cause and effect in terms of the redistribution of matter and motion. I now have to perform the same task for the conception of purpose, and more particularly of human purpose, in order to show how purposiveness may be translated into purely materialistic and mechanical terms; that is to say, how it, too, may be expressed as a phase of the normal process of redistribution of matter and motion under fixed and invariable laws.

At the outset of this inquiry, we have to notice that the word purpose is involved in the same vagueness of significance that attends almost all words used in popular speech. In general a word in popular use has to be defined and limited to some precise meaning before it is fit for employment in a philosophical discussion. In the present case the word is commonly employed in at least two meanings, which differ greatly from each other; and this duality of meaning leads to a duality in the derivative conceptions of "teleology," "finalism," "end," etc., which has not infrequently given rise to confusion and error. The two significations may be roughly grouped as intelligent purposiveness and unintelligent purposiveness, and the reduction of each of these to mechanistic terms involves two different lines of analysis. I shall deal first with unintelligent purposiveness.

In this case, the word is usually applied to a certain kind of organic reactions that bear an obvious relation to the requirements of the reacting organism. An *Amoeba* in the water throws out pseudopodia at random in all directions. When one of these pseudopodia comes into contact with some substance suitable for food, the protoplasm streams round and encloses the particle, which is thus incorporated in the body of the *Amoeba* and there digested. The reaction is purposive in the sense that a somewhat complicated series of movements is carried out, which leads to the preservation of the active organism.

In just the same way, when we ascend the animal scale, the sea-anemone spreads its tentacles at large under the surface of the water. On contact with any substance suitable for food the tentacles contract around the substance and draw it into the interior of the sea-anemone. This action is similarly purposive in that it procures the continued existence of the animal. In all animals the common movements and reactions are predominantly of this purposive type. If an object suddenly appears close to our eyes, we involuntarily close them for an instant, and this reaction is obviously purposive, as directed towards the protection of the eyes.

All these instinctive actions are purposive in character, yet equally, without doubt, they are all of the nature of reflex action, working blindly and inevitably to their conclusion. On contact with the tentacle of a sea-anemone, the stimulus thus applied to that tentacle sets up by entirely mechanical procedure organic processes which necessarily result in the observed contractions. Similarly, in the case of the human being, the sudden appearance of a near object causes an impulse to be conveyed down the optic nerve, which immediately and mechanically propagates its effect to the efferent nerves which lead to the muscles that close the eyelids. The same kind of reaction is characteristic of the functions in plants. The turning of flowers towards the light, and all the processes of absorption, transpiration, etc., are, on the one hand, subservient to the life and prosperity of the plant, while, on the other hand, they are blind mechanical reactions to stimuli.

Seeing that a single action may thus be at the same time both purposive and mechanical, it is plain that there can be no antithesis between the two; but that the difference between purposive and blind mechanism arises simply from our point of view, and not from any difference of objective character. Purposive reactions are not different from mechanical reactions, but they *are* mechanical reactions of a certain kind. Not all mechanical reactions are purposive, but all purposive reactions are mechanical; and it remains to determine *what* mechanical actions may be correctly described as purposive, and what are simply blind and meaningless. . . .

I now come to the second class of activities to which the name of purpose is applied, that is to say, cases of activity which bear reference to an end consciously and intelligently foreseen, such as the acts inspired by the conscious will in human beings. These activities are commonly regarded as being in a higher degree teleological than the unintelligent reactions hitherto considered; and in many uses of the word "purpose," reference is intended exclusively to these intelligent anticipations of future events, and to the activities carried out in consequence of such anticipations. In this sense purpose is allied to will, and purposive actions are more or less synonymous with voluntary actions. . . .

We are now in a position to appreciate the true meaning of those acts which are described as intelligently purposive. Being deliberate and reasoned activities, they are as far as possible removed from the simple type of reflex action in which response follows immediately on external stimulus. They belong to the category in which the immediate stimulus is in the brain itself, and is to be regarded as consisting of rearrangements of the matter and energy contained in the nervous substance of the brain. The brain during consciousness can never be still, and its unceasing activities supply the stimulus, not only for purposive, but for all actions of an intellectual character. Now this permanent cerebral activity can be divided into a number of different types, known psychologically by such names as memory, imagination, reason, etc. Although nervous physiology has not yet advanced far enough to enable us to say what are the different kinds of material processes in the brain corresponding to these psychical processes, yet there is no doubt that the psychical distinction is based upon some actual distinction in the corresponding activities occurring in the brain. Among these cerebral processes is that which is known psychologically as a desire for some external object or event, a visualization of some external phenomenon as an end or purpose to be attained. This desire may then act upon efferent nerves and give rise to the activities which we know as purposive. The essence of a purposive action, and the standard by which it is distinguished from other kinds of actions, is that the "end" to which the action leads was previously represented in the brain of the agent, and composes the stimulus of action. The compound stimulus arises, as I have said, from the composition of large numbers of elementary stimuli previously received. It consists psychologically of a faint representation of the sensation which would be vividly presented by the realization of some outward occurrence. And when this faint representation actually functions as a stimulus which innervates the muscles whose contraction brings about the external occurrence represented, we have what is called an action of intelligent purpose. . . .

Intelligent purpose, like unintelligent purpose, is then only a name given to a particular kind of incident in the midst of the eternal redistribution of matter and motion under blind mechanical laws. It is in perfect harmony with that materialistic scheme; it can be stated in terms of the purest mechanism. As the matter and motion undergo their invariable and unalterable redistribution, we naturally find ourselves more interested in some phases of it than in others; and in one class of evolving events we are so interested and we have such frequent occasion to refer to them, that we denominate them by a special name—the name of purposive. By this name we designate the majority of those redistributions which issue from the little whirlpools of matter and energy called organisms, and those factors in particular by which the immediate continuance of such whirlpools is ensured.

I have now dealt with the law of universal causation, and with the doctrine of teleology. It remains only to say a few words about the third main pillar of materialism—the assertion of monism, that is, that there are not two kinds of fundamental existences, material and spiritual, but one kind only. . . . For simplifying the discussion, it will be as well at once to dismiss from consideration all those kinds of spiritual entities imagined by religious believers. The Victorian writers said on this subject nearly all that could be said, and interest now attaches only to those problems of matter and spirit which they left unsolved. I shall, therefore, confine myself to an attempt to reduce the last stronghold of dualism; to ascertain the relation between mind and body; to show that mental manifestations and bodily manifestations are not two different things, as generally supposed, but one and the same thing appearing under different aspects. I shall not attempt to deal with any of the so-called "non-material" existences with the exception of mind; for if mind can be identified with matter, all other kinds of non-material entities must lapse, even those described by religious systems. . . .

We reached the conclusion in a previous chapter that the bodily organism is a complex machine. We found that all its processes and activities are attributable to physico-chemical forces, identical with those which are recognized in the inorganic realm. We learnt that there is no "vital force" or other spiritual interference with the normal physical sequences. If, then, there be a mind, it is reduced to the function of inertly and uselessly accompanying the activities of certain neural elements. This is the doctrine of epiphenomenalism, and it is the last word possible to one who accepts the duality of mind and matter. It is a theory which on the face of it is devoid of verisimilitude. What can be the use of such a shadowy and inefficient entity? What parallel can be found in Nature for the existence of so gratuitous a superfluity? Moreover, what mechanism, conceivable or inconceivable, could cause it thus to shadow neural processes, which *ex hypothesi* do not produce it? If one such mental state is the cause of the next, how does it happen that it causes the one which is necessary to accompany the actual neural process at the moment? Epiphenomenalism involves us in a pre-established harmony that is profoundly opposed to the scientific spirit of the twentieth century. The problem, however, is not one that need be discussed on the grounds of *a priori* probability. It is a theory that may be rigidly refuted, and to that task I now turn.

It is a part of the doctrine of epiphenomenalism that a man would to all external appearance be precisely the same whether he was possessed of his epiphenomenal mind or not. Conduct, action, expression, would not in the slightest extent be affected were he completely devoid of mind and consciousness; for all these things depend upon material sequences alone. Men are puppets or automata, and we have no further grounds for supposing them to have minds than the fact that we know we have a mind ourselves, and the argument by analogy from ourselves to them. But arguments from analogy are notoriously insecure, and it seems, therefore, to be quite within the bounds of possibility to the epiphenomenalist that some or all other men may be mindless syntheses of matter. . . .

Now let us assume that such a man actually exists, or, if you prefer, let us assume that physical chemistry has advanced to such a pitch that a man may be synthetized in the laboratory, starting from the elements, carbon, nitrogen, etc., of which protoplasm is composed. Let us assume in any case a "synthetic man" without a mind, yet indistinguishable by the epiphenomenalist hypothesis from another man identically constituted materially but having a mind. Ask the synthetic man whether he has a mind. What will he say? Inevitably he will say yes. For he must say the same thing as the man, identically made, who *has* a mind. Otherwise the same question would set up different responses in the nervous systems of the two, and that is by hypothesis impossible. The sound of the words "have you a mind?" entering the ears of the synthetic man sets up highly complex cerebral associations (which we call grasping their meaning); these associations will, after a short time, culminate in nervous currents to the tongue, lips and larynx, which will be moved in such a way as to produce an audible and intelligent answer. Now this answer must be the same in the case of the man who has a mind as in the case of the mindless man, since their nervous systems are the same. If there was a different vocal response to an identical aural stimulus, then there must in one of them have been some external interference with the physico-chemical sequences. Mind must have broken through the chain of physical causality, and that is contrary to hypothesis.

What can the epiphenomenalist say? That the mindless man is a liar, to say he has a mind? That will not do, for if the two men are objectively identical one cannot be a liar, and the other not; one engaged in deceit, while the other speaks the truth. The epiphenomenalist is thrown back, therefore, on the assumption that the mindless man has made a mistake; that he thinks he has a mind, but really has not one; that his nervous constitution is such as to impel him to the conviction that he has a mind when he really has not, to lead him to talk upon psychical phenomena and their differences from matter, and in general to behave exactly as if he knew all about mind and matter, had considered the subject of their relationship, etc.

The example shows, furthermore, that the condition of "knowing one has a mind" is a condition which can be stated and accounted for in rigidly materialistic terms. When the epiphenomenalist himself asserts that he has a mind, the movements of his vocal cords by which he makes that pronouncement are by his own theory led up to by a chain of purely material sequences. He would make just the same pronouncement if he had no mind at all. His claim to possess a mind, therefore, is wholly irrelevant to the real question whether he actually has a mind or not. The events that make him say he has a mind are not the actual possession of a mind, but those cerebral processes which, in epiphenomenalist language, are said to underlie states of consciousness. It is the cerebral processes alone which make him speak, and his utterance, his belief in a mind, furnish testimony alone to the existence of those cerebral processes. Were the mind truly able to compel a belief and an announcement of its own existence, it could only be by breaking through he chain of material bodily sequences, and this is a vitalistic supposition that is ruled out by physiology. The belief in the possession of a mind is a cerebral condition, due, not to the actual possession of a mind, but to definite pre-existing cerebral conditions on the same material plane.

I do not see how epiphenomenalism could be much more effectively refuted. Yet it is the only respectable dualistic theory that is compatible with physiological mechanism. Let me recapitulate for a moment the facts, now before us, upon which we have to establish a theory of the relationship of mind and body.

Physiology has shown that bodily activity of every kind is a product of purely material sequences, into the course of which there is no irruption of any spiritualistic factor. On the dualistic theory, that doctrine is excessively difficult to understand. You move your arm by an act of will, or what seems to be a non-material cause, and yet it is conclusively established that the movement of the arm is due to definite material changes occurring in the brain, and caused by the fixed laws of physics and chemistry in the most determinist fashion. Now, anchoring ourselves firmly to that fact, we are confronted with the problem of where to put the mind. For every mental state there is some corresponding cerebral state; the one appears to be the exact counterpart of the other down to the smallest discoverable particular. Now on the dualistic assumption, there is only one possible hypothesis, namely, that of epiphenomenalism. Or, rather, it is incorrect to call it an hypothesis; for *if* there are two things, mind and body, epiphenomenalism is no more than a statement of the facts established by physiology and psychology. Dualistic physiologists, therefore, are practically forced to accept it. Yet, as I have shown, it is utterly untenable when properly thought out.

We are faced, therefore, by two possible alternatives: (1) to abandon mechanism, (2) to abandon dualism. Now mechanism is a physiological theory which is proved. We must hold fast to it therefore at any expense to our metaphysical preconceptions. The only remaining alternative, then, is the abandonment of dualism. . . .

When once we have got over the shock which monism carries to those accustomed to think in dualistic terms, we find that the great majority of the difficulties of metaphysics fall away. By an act of will I raise my arm. The plain man insists that his will did it; the physiologist knows that it was physico-chemical processes in the brain. The dilemma is at once overcome when the philosopher points out that the will *is* the physico-chemical processes, and that they both mean the same thing. . . . The difficulty of the epiphenomenalist is also solved. He says he has a mind. What makes him say so is not a transcendental "knowledge of having mind," but a certain cerebral state. When we have affirmed the absolute identity of that knowledge with that cerebral state, all difficulties vanish. The mind is the sum-total of cerebral conditions. He says he has a mind; it is the existence of the cerebral conditions which cause him to say so. He says he has a mind because he has cerebral conditions, and his remark is true and intelligible only on the one hypothesis that the mind *is* the cerebral conditions. . . .

Monism resolves the great biological difficulty as to the origin of consciousness. The biological conclusions as to the origin of life are to the effect that living and organic matter was developed by evolution from non-living and inorganic matter. The evolution of Man from unicellular parentage is a fact. There is little or no reason to doubt that his unicellular ancestor was evolved just as gradually from inorganic matter. Now, says the dualist, we know that the man has a mind. It follows, therefore, either that inorganic matter has a psychical accompaniment, or else that, in the course of evolution, there was a sudden leap: mind was suddenly intruded at some period of Man's past history. Neither of these hypotheses is easy to entertain, or perhaps even practicable to conceive. The doctrine of monism, with its assertion that there are not two ultimate things, but one, causes the difficulty to vanish; for there is then no necessity to introduce a new entity at any period of an organism's evolution. According to our theory, a conscious state is a specific neural functioning. If there is no discontinuity in the evolution of nervous elements from inorganic matter, there is then no discontinuity in the evolution of consciousness.

Interactionism

The Mind as Distinct from the Body   C. E. M. Joad

Cyril Edwin Mitchinson Joad (1891–1953) was a prolific English author, whose books and articles and speeches on philosophy exerted broad public appeal in his lifetime.

The issue between those who endeavour to interpret mind action in terms of body action, and those who contend for the unique, distinct, and in some sense independent status of mind, is not capable of definite settlement.... The most that can be done is to suggest certain objections that can be and have been brought against the materialist position, ... and at the same time to indicate a number of independent considerations which seem to demand a different kind of approach to psychology, and a different interpretation of its problems. This interpretation, to put it briefly, insists that a living organism is something over and above the matter of which its body is composed; that it is, in short, an expression of a principle of life, and that life is a force, stream, entity, spirit, call it what you will, that cannot be described or accounted for in material terms; that in human beings this principle of life expresses itself at the level of what is called mind, that this mind is distinct from both body and brain, and, so far from being a mere register of bodily occurrences, is able, acting on its own volition, to produce such occurrences, and that no account of mind action which is given in terms of brain action, gland activity or bodily responses to external stimuli can, therefore, be completely satisfactory. This is the view which in some form or other is held by those who find a materialist explanation of psychology unsatisfactory, and in this chapter we shall be concerned with the reasons for it.

Biological Considerations

PURPOSIVENESS.   Some of these reasons, and perhaps the most important, are derived in part from regions which lie outside the scope of psychology proper; they belong to biology, and are based on a consideration of the characteristics which all living beings are found to possess in common. With regard to one of these "alleged" characteristics of living organisms it is necessary to say a few words, since it constitutes a starting point for the method of interpretation with which we shall be

From *How Our Minds Work* by C. E. M. Joad. Published by Philosophical Library. Reprinted by permission of the publishers.

concerned in this chapter. The characteristic in question is that to which we give the name of purposiveness, and because of this characteristic it is said that any attempt to interpret the behaviour of living creatures in terms of material response to stimuli must inevitably break down. Purposiveness implies the capacity to be influenced by and to work for a purpose; this in its turn involves the apprehension, whether conscious or unconscious, of some object which lies in the future and which the purpose seeks to achieve; it therefore necessitates the existence of a mind. If, therefore, purposiveness is a true characteristic of living creatures, then we have established a good starting point for our "mental" approach to psychology.

What, therefore, is meant by saying that living creatures are purposive? Primarily, that in addition to those of their movements which may be interpreted as responses to existing situations, they also act in a way which seems to point to the existence of a spontaneous impulse or need to bring about some other situation which does not yet exist. This impulse or need is sometimes known as a conation; a good instance of the sort of thing that is meant is the impulse we feel to maintain the species by obtaining food or seeking a mate. The impulse is chiefly manifested in the efforts a living organism will make to overcome any obstacle which impedes the fulfilment of its instinctive need. It will try first one way of dealing with it and then another, as if it were impelled by some overmastering force which drove it forward to the accomplishment of a particular purpose. Thus the salmon, proceeding up stream, leaping over rocks and breasting the current in order to deposit her spawn in a particular place, is acting in a way which it is difficult to explain in terms of a response to external stimuli. An organism again will seek to preserve the trend of natural growth and development by which alone the purpose of existence will be fulfilled; in its endeavour to reach and to maintain what we may call its natural state or condition, it is capable, if need arises, of changing or modifying its bodily structure. If you take the hydroid plant Antennularia and remove it from the flat surface to which it is accustomed to adhere, it will begin to proliferate long wavy roots or fibers in the effort to find something solid to grip, while everybody has heard of the crab's habit of growing a new leg in place of one that has been knocked off.

Activity of this kind seems difficult to explain on materialist lines as the response to a stimulus; it appears rather to be due to the presence of a living, creative impulse to develop in the face of any obstacle in a certain way. That a living organism works as a machine works, by reacting in the appropriate way to the appropriate stimulus, is admitted; all that is contended is that it acts in other ways as well, that these other activities depend not only upon the quality of stimulus received, but upon the intensity of the creature's conative impulse, and that the existence of the impulse is only explicable on the assumption that the creature is animated by the need to fulfil a purpose.

FORESIGHT AND EXPECTATION. When we apply this conclusion to human psychology, we are immediately struck by the fact that the individual not only exhibits in common with other organisms this characteristic of purposive behaviour, but is in many cases conscious of the nature of the purpose which inspires his behaviour. The man who studies in order to pass an examination is not only impelled by a push from behind; he is drawn forward by a pull from in front. This pull from in front can only become operative if he can be credited with the capacity to conceive the desirability of a certain state of affairs—namely, the passing of the examination, which does not yet exist; he shows, in other words, foresight and expectation. It is activities of this kind which seem most insistently to involve the assumption of a mind to do the foreseeing and expecting. In other words, the capacity to be influenced by events which lie in the future seems inexplicable on the stimulus-response basis; the *thought* of what does not exist may be allowed to influence the mind, but it is difficult to see how the non-existent can stimulate the body. . . .   *reason based on experience!*

The Apprehension of Meaning

An important fact about our mental life is that we are capable of appreciating meaning. A statement of fact written on a piece of paper is, so far as its material content is concerned, merely a number of black marks inscribed on a white background. Considered, then, as a collection of visual, physical stimuli, it is comparatively unimportant; what is important is the meaning which is attached to these marks. If they inform us, for example, that we have received a legacy of ten thousand pounds it is not the black marks on the white background but the meaning they convey that effects a disturbance in our emotional life, sufficiently profound to keep us awake all night. Now the meaning of the marks is obviously not a physical stimulus; it is something immaterial. How, then, is its effect to be explained in terms of bodily responses to physical stimuli, which the mind merely registers? Let us take one or two further examples in order to present the difficulty in a concrete form.

Let us suppose that I am a geometrician and am thinking about the properties of a triangle. As I do not wish at this point to enter into the vexed question of whether *some* physical stimulus is or is not necessary to initiate every chain of reasoning, we will assume that in this case there was a physical stimulus—it may have been a chance remark about Euclid, or the appearance of a red triangular road signpost while I am driving a car—a stimulus which we will call X, which prompted me to embark upon the train of speculations about the triangle. My reasoning proceeds until I arrive at a conclusion, which takes the form of a geometrical proposition expressed in a formula. I carry this formula in my head for a number of days and presently write it down. In due course I write a book, setting forth my formula and giving an account of the reasoning which led me to it. The book is read and understood by A. Presently it is translated into French, and is read and understood by B. Later still I deliver a lecture on the subject which is heard and understood by C. As A, B, and C have each of them understood my formula and the reasoning upon which it is based, we may say that the reasoning process has had for them the same meaning throughout. If it had not, they would not all have reached the same conclusion and understood the same thing by it. Yet in each of the four cases the sensory stimulus was different; for myself it was X, for A it was a number of black marks on a white background, for B a number of different black marks on a white background, and for C a number of vibrations in the atmosphere impinging upon his eardrums. It seems incredible that all these different stimuli should have been able to produce a consciousness of the same meaning, if our respective reactions to them were confined to physical responses (which must in each case have been different) which were subsequently reflected in our minds by a process of mental registration of the different responses. The stimuli being different, the intervention of something possessed of the capacity to grasp the *common* element among these physically different entities alone seems able to account for the facts, but the common element is the meaning, which is immaterial and can be grasped, therefore, only by a mind.

Let us take another example instanced by Professor McDougall:

A man receives a telegram which says "Your son is dead." The visual physical stimulus here is, as before, a collection of black marks on an orange field. The reaction experienced in terms of his bodily behaviour may take the form of a complete cessation of all those symptoms usually associated with life—that is to say, he may faint. When he recovers consciousness his thoughts and actions throughout the whole of the remainder of his life may be completely changed. Now that all these complicated reactions are not constituted by and do not even spring from a response to the *physical* stimulus, may be seen by comparing the reactions of an acquaintance who reads the telegram, and so subjects himself to the same stimulus. Moreover, the omission of a single letter, converting the telegram into "Our son is dead," would cause none of the reactions just described, but might result at most in the writing of a polite letter of condolence.

The independence of the bodily reactions of the physical stimuli actually presented is in these cases very marked, and, unless we are to introduce conceptions such as the intellectual apprehension of the *meaning* of the marks, it seems impossible to explain their effect. Yet such a conception again involves the active intervention of mind.

SYNTHESIZING POWER OF MIND.   This conclusion is reinforced by what we may call the synthesizing power of mind. Synthesizing means putting together, and one of the most remarkable powers that we possess is that of taking a number of isolated sensations and forming them into a whole. We shall have occasion to return to this point at greater length in connection with our account of sensation in the next chapter. For the present we will content ourselves with giving one or two examples of mental synthesis.

Let us consider for a moment the case of aesthetic appreciation. The notes of a symphony considered separately consist merely of vibrations in the atmosphere. Each note may, when sounded in isolation, produce a pleasant sensation, and as one note is struck after another we get a sequence of pleasant sensations. But although this is a sufficient description of the symphony considered as a collection of material events, and of our reactions to these events considered merely in terms of sensations, it is quite clear that we normally think of a symphony as being something more than this. We think of it in fact as a whole, and it is as a whole that it gives what is called aesthetic pleasure. Now in thinking of the symphony in this way our mind is going beyond the mere sequence of pleasant sensations which its individual notes produce, and putting them together into some sort of pattern. If the notes were arranged in a different order, although the actual vibrations which impinged upon our senses would be the same, the pleasurable aesthetic effect would be destroyed.

It seems to follow that our pleasure in a symphony cannot be wholly accounted for, although it may depend upon our physical responses to the stimuli of the individual notes; in order to obtain aesthetic pleasure we must somehow be able to perceive it as more than the sum total of the individual notes—that is, as a whole pattern or arrangement. The pleasure ceases when the *wholeness* of the object perceived is destroyed, as it is, for example, by the transposition of certain notes. We may compare the difference between the physical sensations which are our responses to the visual stimuli of the colours and canvas of which a picture is composed, with our synthesized perception of a picture as a work of art.

We must conclude, then, that we possess the power of realizing external objects not merely as collections of physical stimuli, which of course they are, but as wholes in which the actual sensory elements are combined to form a single object of a higher order. This faculty of combining or putting together seems to involve the existence not only of a mind, but of a mind of an active, creative type which is able to go out beyond the raw material afforded by our bodily sensations, and to apprehend ideal objects as wholes which are more than the collection of physical events which compose their constituent parts.

Summary of Argument

The conclusion to which the arguments of this chapter appear to point is that, in addition to the body and brain, the composition of the living organism includes an immaterial element which we call mind; that this element, although it is in very close association with the brain, is more than a mere glow or halo surrounding the cerebral structure, the function of which is confined to reflecting the events occurring in that structure; that, on the contrary, it is in some sense independent of the brain, and in virtue of its independence is able in part to direct and control the material constituents of the body, using them to carry out its purposes in relation to the external world of objects, much as a driver will make use of the mechanism of his motorcar. Mind so conceived is an active, dynamic, synthesizing force; it goes out beyond the sensations provided by external stimuli and arranges them into patterns, and it seems to be capable on occasion of acting without the provocation of bodily stimuli to set it in motion. It is, in other words, creative, that is, it carries on activities which even the greatest conceivable extension of our physiological knowledge would not enable us to infer from observing the brain. How, then, are we to conceive of the relationship of the mind to the brain?

An actor in a play of Shakespeare not only speaks words, but makes gestures, so that if you were completely deaf you would still be able to infer something of what the play was about from seeing the gestures. It is obvious, however, that there is much more in the play than the pantomime of the players. There are, for example, the words, the characters, the plot, and the poetry. Now to use a simile of the philosopher Bergson, the brain is the organ of pantomime. If you were to observe a man's brain you would know just as much of his thoughts as found vent in gestures. You would know, in other words, all that his thoughts imply in the way of actions or the beginnings of actions,[1] but the thoughts themselves would escape you just as the words and meaning of the play would escape the deaf spectator. This is what is meant by saying that the mind overflows the brain. If our knowledge of both psychology and physiology were perfect, we should be able to describe the movements of the brain without observing it, provided we had complete understanding of a man's state of mind; but we should not from the most minute and thorough inspection of the brain be able to tell what the man was thinking, since just as one gesture of the actor may stand for many different thoughts, so one state of the brain may represent any one of a host of states of mind.

[1] Among the beginnings of actions may be mentioned those movements of the larynx which are involved in talking.

Epiphenomenalism

Bodies and Minds   W. F. R. Hardie

William Francis Ross Hardie (1902–   ), a former fellow and tutor in
philosophy, Corpus Christi College, Oxford, has written a book on Plato and
numerous articles in professional philosophical journals.

The world contains bodies, some of which are alive and some not.
It would, perhaps, sound queer to say that there are minds in the world
as well as bodies. But we can agree that this is so if all that is meant is
that some living bodies are capable of feeling pleasure and pain, being
angry or afraid, asking questions and drawing conclusions. Men have
all these capacities. At least some non-human animals have some of them.
Plants have not; they do not even feel. Hence there is no psychology of
plants. For the processes which occur in a plant are not psychical; they
are all, like growth and decay, physical.

Connection Between the Physical and Psychical

The physical and psychical processes which occur in a man, while
different and distinct from each other, are intimately and variously connected. It will be convenient to enumerate some of these connections
under three heads: the unique position of a man's body in his perceptual
experience; the causal dependence of a man's experiences on his body,
in particular on his sense-organs and his brain; the influence of psychical
processes on physical processes, and especially a man's voluntary control
of his own bodily movements. The facts falling under these heads explain
how a man comes to think of one particular body as his own body and
what is involved in this thought.
A man's perception of his own body differs in two main ways from
his perception of other bodies. First, he has sensations which he locates
in definite parts of his body: pain in his teeth, ears, head, and so on;
tastes in his mouth, tactual feelings on the surface of his skin. Secondly,
his body has a central position in the world as he perceives it by sight
and touch. He sees the world around him from the place where his eyes
are, and, whenever he can see anything, he can see his own body or at
least the clothes he is wearing. Again his own body is the only one which,
if he can touch anything, he can always touch; it is always within reach.
In these ways a man's body is privileged as an object of perception. But

Reprinted with permission of The Macmillan Company from *A Modern Introduction to Philosophy* edited by Paul Edwards and Arthur Pap. Copyright © 1965 by The Free Press, a
Division of The Macmillan Company.

it also has a special position as a causal condition of perception, and of experience generally.

We cannot see when our eyes are shut, or hear when our ears are plugged, or smell without a nose. But in order that a man should see and hear it is not enough that his eyes should be exposed to light rays and his ears to sound waves. Impulses, which are accompanied by electrical effects, must be carried along the optic and auditory nerves to regions at the base of the brain. Moreover, as we are told, "it is only when the impulses have been relayed from the base of the brain to a much more complicated mechanism in the grey matter on the surface of the brain —the central cortex—that a conscious sensation becomes possible."[1] Anatomists and physiologists, using microscopes and electrodes and studying the effects of local injuries to the brain on the working of the mind, are finding it "possible to define in more and more detail the particular anatomical dispositions which appear to be necessary as a basis for mental activity."[2]

A Clear Outline of Knowledge

The broadcast talks by eminent physiologists which are published in the book from which I have quoted give a clear outline of what was then (in 1952) known about processes in the brain. I shall return later to the function of the brain as a "basis for mental activity."

A very important element in a man's thought of a certain body as being his, or as being himself, is the voluntary control he can exercise over some of its movements. When such control extends to tools and implements they too come to feel as if they were parts of his body. Thus, if I poke the ground with a walking stick, I seem to have a feeling of hardness which I actually locate at the end of the stick.

These facts are among those which have led some psychologists and philosophers to say that there is two-way causal "interaction" between minds and bodies. The body acts on the mind when, for example, lack of food causes a pang of hunger or a process in a sense-organ and brain causes the hearing of a noise or the seeing of a view. The mind acts on the body when, for example, a decision to take a walk leads to our going out of the house, or a state of anxiety inhibits digestion, or shame produces a blush. These causal connections are as well supported as any in our experience. It seems obvious to common sense that our bodies and our minds do produce effects on each other. But the word "interaction" suggests something more, namely that mind-body and body-mind causation is comparable with the action of one body on another body, as when a billiard ball causes by impact a movement in another billiard ball, or ice is melted by the sun. We are, however, made uneasy by the suggestion that a man's body is one thing and his mind another thing. There are good reasons for this uneasiness. For there are facts which

[1] Professor Le Gros Clark, in *The Physical Basis of Mind* (Oxford: Basil Blackwell, 1952), p. 14.

[2] *Op. cit.*, p. 24.

suggest that minds lack some of the essential elements in our concept of a thing, that perhaps we ought, if we are not to be misled, to avoid speaking of minds at all but only of mental, or psychical, processes. These facts might be summarized by saying that psychical processes are not continuous and independent, as physical processes are.

Professor Adrian's Views

If we consider the events, physical and psychical, which happen in a man between the time of his birth and the time of his death, we are inclined to say that while in any stretch of time, however short, within this period, physical processes occur, there are stretches of time, within the period, when no psychical processes occur, for example when we are in a state of dreamless sleep. I have said that we are inclined to assert that there are gaps. Some would assert this more confidently. Professor Adrian speaks of "the abrupt departure of the mind in the fainting fit when the blood supply to the brain is suddenly reduced," and remarks that "we have only to be given gas by the dentist to realize that the mind can be turned on and off as abruptly as the B.B.C. news, by agencies which modify the general level of brain activity."[3] This interpretation of the facts is natural, but hardly inevitable. It might be suggested that the apparent gaps are filled by psychical processes of a subdued or dim kind, such as occur in dreams. We certainly forget most of our dreams quickly, and we might have others which we never remember at all. But, while this suggestion cannot be refuted, it would be paradoxical, unless there are positive arguments on its side, to deny that our experience is discontinuous, that our minds come and go, lapsing regularly into nonexistence. Are there any such arguments?

"The mind," Adrian tells us, "can be turned on and off." But, when it is turned on again, it starts roughly where it left off. A man emerging from a fainting fit or sleep is what he was; he has the same ambitions and fears, the same tastes for, and aversions to, particular pursuits, the same tendencies to be interested and happy or bored and sad, the same dispositions to love and hate, like and dislike, the same corpus of knowledge and portfolio of opinions, the same memories. Does this continuity of traits and abilities suggest that the discontinuity of psychical process is apparent rather than real? The question has different aspects. At this stage of the argument I am concerned with its causal aspect. We look for causal explanations of the continuity of a man's dispositions and capacities, including his capacity to remember his own past experiences. The act which contributes to forming a disposition or habit is a causal ancestor of the act or state which manifests the disposition. But physiologists at least tend to assume that the intermediate links are physical and not psychical: they are modifications or "traces," produced by disciplinary or habit-forming acts, in the ten billion or so nerve-cells in the brain.

The hypothesis that mental habits and capacities depend on physical traces in the brain is supported by some evidence; for example, by the

[3] *The Physical Background of Perception*, pp. 6 and 7.

way memory is affected when certain parts of the brain are removed or injured.[4] But the theory is still largely an unverified assumption. Scientists do not claim to be able to show what sort of arrangements in the brain could account for the variety of the mind's abilities; there are many unsolved problems. The nature of traces is largely unknown. Adrian tells us that "we really do not know what sort of change takes place in the brain when a memory is established," that "what actually happens in the nerve cells is still quite uncertain."[5] With these large reservations it is reasonable to accept the assumption of physical traces, and it is very difficult to make sense of any alternative assumption.

If the assumption is made, the answer to our question is plain: the continuity of a man's psychical characteristics is not a reason for denying the discontinuity of his psychical processes. We do not need to suppose, in the gaps between psychical processes, the continuous existence of a soul or mind, if indeed we can conceive such a thing, to be the recipient of the modifications or traces, whatever they would be, which must be assumed to account for the formation of habits and capacities.

There is at the level of common sense no question whether physical processes exist independently of psychical processes. In the universe life is rare, and mind rarer. And it seems obvious that, in the body of an animal or a man, there occur countless processes which have no psychical conditions or accompaniments. On the other hand, there does not seem to be any evidence for the occurrence of any psychical process except in close association with some physical process. Physiologists assume that all sensations and thoughts, and all voluntary activity, are inseparable from contemporaneous processes in the nervous system. The mind, as Professor Adrian puts it, is "anchored to the brain."[6]

The Interactionist

We can now see, in more detail than before, what is true, and what is at least questionable, in the assertion of the interactionist that both body acts on mind and mind acts on body. The interactionist is right when he insists on the apparent absurdity of denying that physical causes have psychical effects and that psychical causes have physical effects. He is wrong, or at least rash, in so far as he ignores or denies the differences and asymmetries which we have been discussing between the physical and the psychical processes which occur in a man. For these differences involve, or include, differences between the way in which body acts on mind and the way in which mind acts on body. So far as I can see, the facts, as we have so far taken them to be, conflict in two main respects with the implications of the interactionist's model of explanation.

First, when the mind acts on the body it produces a change in a preexisting thing; when the body acts on the mind there is, or need be, no such pre-existing mental thing, as when a blow wakes a man from sleep

[4] *The Physical Basis of Mind,* pp. 6 and 7.

[5] *Ibid.*

[6] *The Physical Background of Perception,* p. 6.

and causes a pain. Secondly, when the body acts on the mind it acts, or may act, by itself; when the mind acts on the body it does not act by itself, but with the body; for it never, so far as we know, acts by itself. We might summarize the position, as we have described it, by saying that in body-mind action a physical process brings into existence, or modifies, a psychical process, while in mind-body action a psychical process in conjunction with a physical process causes a process of change in a physical thing. The interactionist does not provide for these asymmetries. He is apt to speak as if a mind and a body, like two billiard balls, were things in the same sense of "thing."

My account so far includes two main assertions. The first is that the processes which occur in a man, and indeed in the world, are of two radically different kinds, physical and psychical, i.e., dualism. The second is that the mind is not a thing but is incidental to the body. I shall refer to this assertion as "epiphenomenalism," although most epiphenomenalists have denied, as I have not, that psychical processes are factors in causes as well as effects.

Some philosophers would like, if they could, to reject dualism. Professor Ryle, for example, says:

> When we read novels, biographies, and reminiscences, we do not find the chapters partitioned into section "A," covering the hero's "bodily" doings, and section "B," covering his "mental" doings. We find unpartitioned accounts of what he did and thought and felt, of what he said to others and to himself, of the mountains he tried to climb and the problems he tried to solve.[7]

Bodily and Mental Transactions

Now it is not, in fact, true that biographical narratives are uniformly unpartitioned. A section or bulletin on the illness of a man may well be couched in purely "bodily" terms. And it is not clear why any "bodily doings" should be included in a section on what he "thought and felt." But it is true that biographical accounts are, for the most part, unpartitioned. They are unpartitioned because so much of the vocabulary employed refers both to bodily and to mental transactions. To say that a statesman developed toothache is to say something about his tooth and also something about his sensations; about his thought as well if the toothache is a diplomatic toothache. When I say that I went for a walk what I report is not exclusively the occurrence of certain bodily movements; seeing sights and having bodily sensations are part of taking a walk. We may say, then, that much of our vocabulary refers jointly both to physical and to psychical processes. That it does so is a natural consequence of the intimate connections between bodies and minds. It is not always obvious whether a word, or a phrase, is thus jointly referent or not. It may straddle in one use but not in another; thus the word "climb" implies experiences if used of a man but not if used of a mechanical toy. The physical reference of "hungry" is clearer than that of "angry." But

[7] *The Physical Basis of Mind,* p. 77.

Aristotle implied that "angry" is jointly referent when he remarked that "to say that it is the soul which is angry is as inexact as it would be to say that the soul weaves webs or builds houses."[8]

Thus words which ostensibly describe mental states and activities often refer also to bodily doings. Conversely words which ostensibly describe bodies often refer also to mental doings. Suppose that Ryle's unpartitioned biographical account states that the mountain climbed by the hero was covered with green vegetation and that its snowy summit glistened in the sun. In this statement "climbed" is jointly referent. But so also are "green" and "glistened." For to mention the color of a thing is to say what it looks like; and to talk about the looks of things is to talk about visual experiences. Hence to speak of green grass and glistening snow is to refer to psychical processes as well as to physical processes. The same can be said of any description of things which refers to the appearances they present, to their so-called secondary qualities.

Epiphenomenalism

We must now consider the epiphenomenalist part of the view which I described as being supported by the facts so far considered. I used "epiphenomenalism" as a term for the doctrine that the mind, being discontinuous and dependent on the body, is not a thing in its own right but is incidental to a body which has a certain degree and kind of complexity. The soul or mind, on this view, is not a permanent and continuously existing owner of experiences, but only a permanent possibility of experiences. No doubt all experiences must and do have owners: my experiences are mine and yours are yours. But what account is the epiphenomenalist to give of what is meant by saying that this experience is mine and that one is yours? He will be tempted to say that my experiences are just those based on one particular body and yours are those based on another particular body. But, if he says this, he will find himself in a difficulty when he considers the question how he comes to know that his experiences are based on his body.

Consider, for example, the fact that we see with our eyes. We have to find out that it is so. I have shut my eyes and cannot see, but I remember that earlier my eyes were open and I was seeing. Any such account presupposes that I can identify past experiences as mine independently of coming to know that they are connected with my body. That they are so connected is an empirical discovery. But if my ownership of experiences were correctly defined in terms of connection with a particular body, it could not be an empirical discovery. For to say that my experiences are connected with a particular body would be to utter the empty tautology that the experiences connected with a particular body are the experiences connected with a particular body. In short, there is a fundamental sense, not definable in terms of connection with a particular body, in which my experiences are mine; the epiphenomenalist would like to evade this but, like everyone else, he has to assume it when he is off his guard.

[8] *De Anima,* A 4, 408b, 11–15.

This argument purports to show that what is meant when it is said that two experiences, occurring at different times, belong to the same person cannot be defined in terms of their connection with the same physical organism. This conclusion is confirmed by reflection on what is involved in a man's concern with his own past and future. We have to ask whether the epiphenomenalist's account of the identity of a person does justice to the familiar, if puzzling, sense in which a man's experiences are his own.

A man looking back at some action of his own in the past may congratulate himself that he did so well or feel sorry that he did so ill. Again he may look forward with pleasure, or with fear, to an experience which he expects to enjoy, or to endure, in the future. The past activities for which a man claims to be responsible, and the future experiences to which he looks forward, certainly were and will be based on the bodily organism which is the basis of his present retrospective and prospective thoughts and feelings. But, if a man is asked why he accepts responsibility for activities connected with his bodily organism, he will reply, if he takes the question seriously, that it is because they are *his* activities. If he is asked why he is especially interested in the experiences which will occur in connection with his bodily organism, he will again answer that it is because they will be *his* experiences; it will be he who enjoys or endures them. In both cases he will seem to himself to be giving a reason for his own exclusive responsibility and concern. He will say that his answer is indeed a truism or platitude, but certainly not that it is an empty tautology. To say that the experiences which were or will be based on my own body were or will be mine is not just to say that they were or will be based on my body.

I can see no convincing way of defending the view which I have called epiphenomenalism against this argument. Unless a defense can be found, it is necessary to give up the view that the persistent owner of a set of experiences which are the experiences of one person is simply the living body on which they are based. It becomes necessary to suggest that the soul or mind of Smith is, after all, something more or other than a permanent possibility of Smithian experiences. When I rehearse the arguments against epiphenomenalism I am tempted to say that the mind is a persisting subject or owner of experiences. But to this temptation there are strong counter-temptations. For, in the first place, I find it difficult to attach any clear meaning to the notion of a persisting non-physical subject of experiences. In the second place the facts that make epiphenomenalism a plausible view remain facts: our experience is dependent on our bodies and is interrupted by gaps. Hence epiphenomenalism continues to attract us even after we have become convinced that what it maintains is in clear conflict with what we all believe about ourselves. In this uncomfortable position I must here leave the problem. I do not know how to answer the questions which I have asked.

Contemporary Issues

Are Men Machines?

The Thinking of Men and Machines   John H. Troll

John Hans Troll (1919–   ), a physicist by training and designer of the
Sidewinder Guidance Missile System, now is president of Ecologic Resources
Corporation. For many years he has worked on thinking machines of various
kinds and has acted as consultant for companies manufacturing electronic
computers.

1

The uneasy, half-embarrassed rivalry between man and machine has
reached a peak with the thinking machine. We have become used to
machines that are more powerful, more durable, more accurate, and faster
than we are, but machines that challenge our intelligence are hard to
take. At this point the competition becomes uncomfortable.

Machines and tools have always been created in the image of man.
The hammer grew from the balled fist, the rake from the hand with
fingers outstretched for scratching, the shovel from the hand hollowed
to scoop. As machines became more than simple tools, outstripping their
creators in performance, demanding and obtaining increasing amounts
of power, and acquiring superhuman speeds and accuracies, their outward
resemblance to the natural model disappeared; only the names of the
machine's parts show vestiges of their human origin. The highly complex
machinery of the modern industrial age has arms that swing, fingers that
fold, legs that support, teeth that grind, and male and female parts that
mate. Machines feed on material, run when things go well, and spit
and cough when they don't.

But the newest machines possess human traits that had always been
considered far beyond mechanization. Here we find not only electric eyes
that see and sensing devices that feel, but also memories that recall and
logic sections that classify, arrange, and select. These machines can
make choices, comparisons, and decisions, learn from past experience, and
reach logical conclusions on the basis of premises. It may no longer be
denied: these machines can really think.

This realization has renewed the furtive rivalry between man and
machine. The battle is being fought underground because even to concede the existence of such a contest would be undignified. Like a small
child jealous of the attention paid a puppy, men do not often admit
openly that this inhuman contrivance of nuts and bolts and evilly gleam-

From *The Atlantic Monthly*, July 1954. Copyright © 1954 by The Atlantic Monthly Company,
Boston, Mass. Reprinted by permission of the author.

ing electron tubes is a threat. But as the child will get even with the puppy by tweaking its tail when no one is looking, so man, consciously or unconsciously, likes to throw monkey wrenches into machines and see them get their comeuppance.

Newspaper editors a few years back felt that there would be interest in a story about a Japanese arithmetician who, with an abacus—a simple device made of a few counting beads—won a race against a mechanical calculating machine. The story was prominently featured in the world press. If the mechanical calculator had won, there would have been no story.

No one likes to depend on a rival. Consequently there is a general desire to distrust and by-pass machines. Pilots during the Second World War preferred to fly by the seat of their pants—a device so notoriously insensitive that it won't tell the pilot when he flies upside down—rather than by their highly precise and reliable instruments. Many posters and disciplinary actions were necessary to make pilots use their instruments.

When Univac, one of the computers used on election night, made an amazingly accurate prediction of the outcome on the basis of very early returns, it was disbelieved by the experts who designed and constructed it. Even when by all rational standards it becomes evident that the machine knows better, man is reluctant to let it have the last word.

An even more telling sign of this half-secret battle of man and the technical monster of his creation is the character of the Utopias of our time. Where Thomas More of the sixteenth century and Edward Bellamy of the nineteenth found ideal, beautifully harmonious societies in their imaginary travels, with satisfactory solutions to the pressing problems of their days, George Orwell and Aldous Huxley in our age see only a nightmarishly heightened outgrowth of the modern world. In their Utopias, standardization, an integral part of the machine culture, extends to the hygienically controlled production of humans; machines take all the major roles in human enjoyment, dominating even sex and simple sports; machines write all novels and plays and newspapers and create all art and entertainment; machines watch and spy day and night, destroying all vestiges of human individuality. Is the arrival of the thinking machine the first sign that these nightmares are about to become a reality? Is man hopelessly outmatched in this bout with the machine?

Take for instance the calculation involved in the design of photographic lenses. Before the arrival of computers, one could design lenses by painstaking pencil and paper work. By this method an experienced lens designer took about six years to design one of the complicated lenses. The desk calculator cut this time to about fifteen weeks, and now a giant computer like the Bureau of Standards SEEAC does the job in a single hour.

2

Let us look at this lens design problem a little closer to learn something about the way such a machine operates. A good optical lens like those used in the best cameras differs from simple lenses or from eyeglasses mainly in that it consists of many glasses of various shapes all cemented together. The designers must prescribe the exact shape of each of these glasses making up a lens so that all rays originating from a point, say from a star we want to photograph, will meet in another point behind the lens, forming an image of the star. Actually, these rays cannot be made to meet in a point, which would be ideal, but will all fall within a circle. The smaller the circle, the better defined the image and the better the lens.

The design procedure is part calculation, part trial and error. There are, of course, an infinite number of angles at which the rays may enter the lens. A good many of these must be traced through the lens. That is, we must find the change in angle for each ray as it enters and leaves each glass. As a result, we know the angle of the ray when it leaves the last glass surface and therefore where it will meet the other rays. Though the arithmetical procedure to find these changes of angles for each ray is not complicated, it requires accuracies to about seven decimals, and many rays have to be considered. After all the required rays are traced we find the diameter of the circle within which they meet. If we find it small enough to suit our requirements, the job is done. But if it appears too large, we must change by a slight amount one of the shapes of the glass surfaces. Now we trace all the rays for the new condition and see whether we have improved the design or made it worse. It used to take a man six years to complete such a job.

How much of this work can the computer take over for us? Almost all of it. It requires only an adequate set of instructions. These must contain a formula which shows what the angle of a ray is when leaving a surface if we know the angle of entrance, some properties of the glass, the shape of the surface, and the color of the ray. In addition, the instructions tell the computer how good a lens it must design and what initial shapes to start with.

Next, we tell the machine how to proceed. Our program may read: "Start with a ray 45° off to the center axis. Figure its entrance and exit angles through each of the eleven surfaces. Note the angle of exit from the last surface; do the same with the ray at 44°, then 43°, and so forth, in intervals of one degree until the ray at 0° has been traced. Compare the resulting circle where the rays meet with the desired one; if it is the same size or smaller, print out the answer; if it is larger, change the shape of the first surface and repeat the ray tracing. If the new answer is better than the old one but still not right, change the surface again in the same direction. If the new answer is worse, change in the opposite direction. When the best answer is still not right, change the second surface the same way, and so through all other surfaces until the answer is right."

The actual instructions to the computer appear not in words but in a mathematical shorthand written on magnetic tape or in the form of punched holes in a paper tape very much like the good old player piano roll—quite a remarkable device in days when no one thought of computers. It could memorize long piano pieces, know which notes to play, when and how loud, and yet no one worried about its being a thinking machine.

Now that the machine has received its instructions, it can go to work. Strangely enough, it performs in an eerie silence. There are no motors whirring, no bells clanging, not even a hum as it races through millions of trial-and-error calculations with a speed that is literally close to that of lightning. Only the even red glow of the tubes shows that anything is going on. When the computer is finished, there is the clacking of an electric typewriter printing out the solution.

If anything goes wrong, the machine stops and types out what is the matter. Often it can tell which of its many tubes has failed or what additional information it requires to complete the problem. Most computers are designed so that they never give wrong answers; if something fails, the machine gives no answer. Once an answer is printed, you can depend upon it. Moreover, computers constantly check their work and will repeat any calculation that appears incorrect.

Can we call such a process thinking? We have seen that it involves remembering, sorting, classifying, and choosing alternatives on the basis of logic. When men do this sort of work, it has always been considered thinking. And so in fairness to the machine we must concede that within the usual meaning of the word it can and does think. And since in the course of its work the machine discards solutions in favor of better ones, acting on past experience, it cannot be denied that it also learns. Since it thinks fast, it learns fast—much faster than man. Moreover, it makes no mistakes and while working on a problem never forgets. Does this mean that the machine is more intelligent than man?

To state it generally, today's thinking machines are in their element and truly superior to men when they draw conclusions about particular cases to which a general rule applies. There are computers in development that can make quick and accurate strategic decisions in air battles, taking into consideration the positions of the friendly and enemy aircraft—provided they are given a basic tactical rule they can follow. And by the same token, there is no reason why tomorrow's computer could not predict the sales volume for an article corrected for season, weather, the general state of prosperity, Mr. Dior's dictates, and the prevailing feminine mood, as long as it has past sales trends that it can use as a rule.

But the unquestioned obedience to the initial rules which makes for the machine's superhuman precision also sets a limit to its general intelligence. For the results of its thinking can only be as good as the rules that it has been taught to follow. If the rules showed themselves to be totally wrong for the situation, the machine would cling to them stubbornly, threatening, like the broom of the sorcerer's apprentice, destruction for its master and itself.

3

There is another kind of thinking—the thinking that sees relations between individual events and forms rules on this basis, and, having formed them, discards or modifies what no longer fits. Men do this kind of thinking so effortlessly that we often do not even consider it thought. If we see a circle, for instance, we immediately recognize it as such regardless of its material or its size. We need not examine each point on the circle separately and compare it with a formula. Moreover, we can tell things that are approximately circular without much strain. Machines cannot sense shapes that are not given point by point or as a mathematical formula.

It is this form of thinking that we use when we recognize someone on the street. We do not, computer fashion, check a lot of details: "5 feet 7 inches tall, size 32 blouse, brown eyes, blond hair, arm length 33 inches, finger lengths 3 inches, 4 inches," and so forth; we can say immediately, "Hello, Mary." It matters little whether Mary has lost or gained weight, has grown taller or dyed her hair. In fact, we need no precise quantitative information about her at all. On a purely statistical basis, the amount of information required to distinguish her definitely among the 75 million females living in this country would be formidable. Yet we need to know astonishingly little to be quite certain that this is Mary. We may recognize her on a cold winter day though she is covered with bulky clothes from head to foot and nothing shows but the tip of a red nose—or we might recognize her from the rear without even this meager clue. People can recognize one another at unexpected meetings after twenty years, when they have last seen one another in grammar school and when they have grown, acquired beards or figures, changed their voices and their clothing—when, in fact, not a particle of their bodies is the same.

Despite the nearly miraculous feat involved in recognition, it requires no outstanding mental ability. Children and even pets are quite good at it. Yet such an activity exceeds the capabilities of the most complex thinking machines. It depends entirely on forming a general picture, an idea—something more than a simple checking off, or adding, or averaging of all the individual parts.

How we form such ideas or generalizations has always been considered one of the most puzzling aspects of the human mind. The ancient Greeks and particularly Plato saw it closely related to the recognition process. He believed that true reality in the form of ideas was stored in a place visited by man's soul before birth, and that the earthly realization of particular objects was a recall of memories acquired during this prenatal experience. Ideas can not only serve in helping us to recognize what we have seen but can be applied to predict the unknown on the basis of similarity. A cab driver in New York told me that he was able to cut his working day to a respectable eight hours while most of his colleagues had to work ten or twelve. Yet he made just as much money and had as many fares as they did. His secret: he learned to recognize the peculiar characteristics of people making up their minds to take a cab. He could spot such people in a crowd or walking out of a building. Before he let me off, he pointed to a man who was just walking along and said, "He wants a cab." He pulled up next to him and the man got in as I got out.

Most good salesmen know who can be called by his first name and slapped on the back after a few minutes' acquaintance and who must always be addressed as "Mr." and treated with formality. Confidence men are very adept at determining what kind of man makes a good "mark," and they don't have at their disposal a set of standardized psychological tests. Their occupation is safe from the intrusion of the thinking machine.

All of us form definite first impressions and adjust our behavior accordingly. We feel whether the new aquaintance is friendly, whether he is a threat or harmless, whether he is bright or dull, and how we may best be able to get along with him. We recognize and adjust to behavior just as we recognize a person, not by the busy examination of many detailed facts but by organizing these facts into a new entity.

A similar process is involved when a doctor makes a diagnosis. There are really an infinite number of possible diseases that a doctor may be faced with, and if he had to proceed entirely on serial examination of all the symptoms, most of his patients would die—most likely of old age —before he was able to make a single diagnosis; yet the good diagnostician often identifies a disease immediately, and at other times requires only relatively few specific tests to come to a conclusion. His mental picture of the disease is a whole, not a collection of many details, and he can therefore recognize it when he sees something that matches this mental picture.

A singular human attribute is not only the formation of ideas but the ability to connect such ideas in a useful fashion. The human memory is a filing system that has a far greater capacity than that of the largest thinking machine built. A mechanical brain that had as many tubes or relays as the human brain has nerve cells (some ten billion) would not fit into the Empire State Building, and would require the entire output of Niagara Falls to supply the power and the Niagara River to cool it. Moreover, such a computer could operate but a fraction of a second at a time before several thousand of its tubes would fail and have to be replaced.

One of the largest of today's computers, the Eniac, has about 10,000 tubes and has therefore about as many brain cells as a flatworm.

The human brain, with one million times as many cells, is unique not only for its ability to store vast amounts of information in a small storage space and for requiring vanishing amounts of operating power, but also for the speed and ease with which any remembered item can be produced. The human filing system is so flexible that it can be reshuffled instantly from an infinity of new viewpoints. The most elaborate filing systems or library catalogues are arranged by author, subject, and sometimes date of publication, with cross references between these files. The human file of ideas, however, classifies each idea in an infinite variety of ways; the word "red" can be connected with "green" or "hot" or "blush" or "Skelton" or "Communist" or "blood" or "herring," to mention only a few. Computers can refer to their memories only in a systematic fashion well planned and explained beforehand but cannot create new cross indexing for themselves.

Yet connection of ideas forms an important aspect of thinking. Without it, Newton could not have associated the apocryphal apple with the motion of the planets because the cross index, "apple falling—*see* rate—*see* square law—*see* planets' motion," had not existed. Nor could Norbert Wiener and Shannon have seen that there is a similarity between the way a message loses intelligibility in transmission and an object loses heat to the surrounding area. Nor could physicists have seen that there are similarities in the ways sound, light, and heat behave, so that picturing them as waves would work for all. Nor could Freud have recognized a connection between accidental slips of the tongue and jokes, dreams, and neuroses.

The sort of thinking that can be called truly creative is such forming and organizing of ideas and the connecting of these ideas into new larger entities. And this is precisely what falls beyond the computer's scope. With its electronics, memories, logic systems, lightning speeds, accuracy, and infallibility, a computer cannot create an idea or ask a question that could form a basis for a new outlook.

Nor does it seem likely that tomorrow's computers will do this. The machines of the future may overcome some of the other handicaps, such as their enormous size and power requirements. There are signs that they may even beget their own kind—but never ideas.

True, a computer could be designed which would randomly and madly connect all sorts of facts and then test them for internal consistencies. It would certainly come up with a million theories. But it would have no criterion for selecting the ones that are meaningful.

For what is meaningful is a function of man's need to survive and to create a world for himself that he can manage physically and mentally.

Thinking machines, more than any other invention in the history of mankind, can aid this creation of a workable and understandable environment by checking man's ideas for validity and internal consistency, by saving him millions of trials and errors, and by speeding up immeasurably the acquisition of new facts and knowledge. But it always takes a human to come up with the approach, the generalization, the idea which furnishes the basis for the machine's lightning checking, applying, and finding of new facts. How such basic ideas are conceived we do not know. Yet only they can be called truly creative thought—a process which must forever remain in the province of the human spirit. The bad dreams of our Utopians will not come true; even the most complex, advanced thinking machines will not replace or dominate this spirit.

Can a Machine Be Conscious?   Dennis Thompson

Dennis F. Thompson (1940–   ) is a member of the Department of Politics at Princeton University. He is the author of *The Democratic Citizen: Social Science and Democratic Theory in the 20th Century* and numerous articles on political theory and philosophy.

'Can machines think?' is a question which in various forms has been the subject of a great deal of speculation in recent years. Yet the question itself has not been precisely stated. Nor have the issues relevant to the problem it raises been carefully sorted out. As a result, many of

From *The British Journal for the Philosophy of Science*, Vol. XVI, No. 61 (May 1965). Reprinted by permission of Cambridge University Press.

the philosophical implications that are supposed to follow from an answer to the question do not follow at all. It is my aim here to indicate just what issues are, and are not, involved in the machine problem, and what consequences for the philosophy of mind follow if the problem is solved. I shall call the view that machines *can* be conscious the 'Machine Theory', and refer to the claim that machines *cannot* be conscious the 'Anti-Machine Theory'. I shall indicate why, contrary to assumptions implicit especially in the writings of the Anti-Machine Theorists, the claim that machines *can* be conscious implies comparatively little for mind-body theories, while the claim that machines *cannot* be conscious does have consequences which most Anti-Machine Theorists would find unpalatable.

First, it is necessary to reformulate the question 'Can machines think?' The fundamental issues at stake in the problem can be brought out more clearly by replacing the term 'think' with the term 'be conscious'. For if we were to demonstrate that a machine could solve a logical problem, recognise dark clouds as a sign of rain, interpret a piece of music or do any other type of thinking, the Anti-Machine Theorist would still ask: 'But can machines *really* think—I mean the way *I* do?' The point of the objection would be that 'thinking' predicates when applied to machines must be used only analogically; human thinking, it would be argued, has a special property which machine 'thinking' does not have, viz. consciouness. Thus the question 'Can machines think?' is appropriately reduced to 'Can a machine be conscious?' In this reformulation there are several possible sources of confusion which must be cleared up.

One possible snare in the question is the term 'conscious'. Since I shall argue that the machine problem becomes clear only if we focus on hypothetical machines which can duplicate all human behaviour, a behaviouristic description of consciousness would allow the question to be decided *ex hypothesi*. A more fruitful approach is to describe consciousness in the way that would be most favourable to the Anti-Machine Theorists. Most of these theorists apparently regard consciousness as somehow a defining attribute of all 'inner' experience. One way of describing what is meant by consciousness in this sense might be to say that it is the total 'inner' difference between being awake and being in a dreamless sleep. Ultimately, however, all that the Anti-Machine Theorist is able to do is to appeal to the reader to examine introspectively his conscious experience. But even on a non-behaviouristic analysis of consciousness, the Machine Theory does not have the consequences that the Anti-Machine Theorists fear. Acceptance or rejection of the Machine Theory does not entail any particular view of consciousness.

The other principal term in the question 'Can a machine be conscious?' is of course 'machine', which like many terms has no precise general definition since there is no one quality common to all machines. The machine which is most relevant to the question is the *robot*, which may be described as a mobile machine, outwardly resembling a human, controlled by a computer unit (the programme of which is independent of subsequent human interference) and capable of performing anything a human can perform.[1] The point of the terms 'can' and 'a' in the question is to focus attention on such machines not yet built.

Here one of the most common and serious mistakes which arise in discussions of the machine problem should be mentioned. Too often the argument about whether machines are conscious degenerates into a technological treasure hunt, which the philosopher would be wise to avoid. If he is interested in the philosophical implications of the Machine Theory, he should assume that it will be possible to construct the sort of machine which some cyberneticians claim to be possible (e.g. a robot), and study the problem from there. (This is not to deny that there may be philosophical problems at various stages in the technological evolution of robots.)

The terms in 'Can a machine be conscious?' should be sufficiently clear now. Anti-Machine Theorists find three barriers to giving an affirmative answer to this question: (1) uncertainty as to what characteristics machines would need to possess in common with humans to be justifiably called conscious; (2) puzzlement about the meaning of 'conscious'; and (3) fear of the philosophical consequences that are thought to follow from the Machine Theory.

The first barrier to acceptance of the Machine Theory should not be too difficult to overcome. It should be clear, irrespective of one's metaphysics, that the only way of deciding whether another person is conscious is by observing his behaviour and his bodily state. If performance is sufficient justification for calling humans conscious, then it is surely sufficient justification for calling machines conscious—even if consciousness is regarded as a property of some sort of 'inner' life. Indeed, this step of the argument is implicitly accepted by Anti-Machine Theorists. This is why the machine debate so often centres around a comparison of what machines and humans can do—the *technological* question.[2]

The technological question usually leads to another objection which Anti-Machine Theorists raise—probably the most common argument in the machine debate. Machines cannot be conscious because no machine can truly create anything or do anything *on its own*, but only what is

---

[1] A fictional portrayal of the sort of machine I have in mind is to be found in Karel Čapek's play, *R.U.R.* However, it is irrelevant to my argument whether a 'robot' is an artefact (i.e. made by man for a purpose) or a natural organism (e.g. a product of evolution).

[2] Machine Theorists have shown that machines can behave adaptively, learn by trial-and-error, show evidence of self-recognition, make mistakes as humans do, exhibit primitive forms of social behaviour, become neurotic, beat their designers in chess, discriminate universal forms and relations, and compose music that is judged by critics to be in some respects better than that produced by human composers. See W. R. Ashby, *Design for a Brain*, New York, 1960; F. H. George, *The Brain as a Computer*, New York, 1961; 'The Machine Closes In', *Time* (February, 1962), 65; D. M. MacKay, 'In Search of Basic Symbols', *Cybernetics—Trans. Eighth Conference*, ed. H. von Foerster, New York, 1952; G. Miller *et al.*, *Plans and Structure of Behaviour*, New York, 1960; C. Shannon, 'A Chess-Playing Machine', *Scientific American* 1950, 48–51; W. Sluckin, *Minds and Machines*, London, 1960; W. G. Walter, *The Living Brain*, New York, 1953.

programmed into it. If all that is meant by this objection is that everything the machine tuns out is a result of its structure, its programme
and stimulation, and the changes it makes in its programme, then the
statement is true enough, but it does not strengthen the Anti-Machine
Theory. For everything a human produces is a result of his structure,
the stimuli he receives, and what he does with that he has learned. If
the objection is supposed to mean that the machine cannot do anything
original because we as humans know everything we programme into it,
it is false. It has been often pointed out that computers, because of
their high speed operations, are able to give results which are in practice
unpredictable.[3] Even W. Grey Walter's simple *Machina speculatrix* has
produced patterns of behaviour that were not predictable even though
the designer had complete knowledge of the parts of the machine and
how they were put together.[4]

The second barrier to accepting the Machine Theory consists of
linguistic confusions. The Anti-Machine Theorist admits that behaviour
and performance generally are necessary conditions for our calling anything conscious, but maintains that they are not sufficient conditions.
It still makes sense, these theorists argue, to ask if a robot, which displays
all the behavioural characteristics of consciousness, is really conscious.
The reason it makes sense is that, in this case, the question expresses
puzzlement about the meaning of 'conscious', rather than a doubt which
further empirical evidence of machines' abilities could settle. In this sense,
'Can a machine be conscious?' comes to mean 'Can the meanings of the
terms "machine" and "conscious" be compatible?'

Incompatibilities may break out anywhere among the meanings of
the terms that make up the network of concepts related to 'machine'
and 'conscious'—in particular, 'living', 'constructed by man', 'made out
of non-living parts', and their contradictories. There is no need here
to examine these incompatibilities in detail. For even if the claim that
it is logically impossible for machines to be conscious is accepted, it is
possble to show that it does not support the Anti-Machine Theory in
the way that it is supposed to.

If 'machine' is now in most contexts incompatible with 'conscious',
it is because machines until recently have failed to display enough of
the characteristics of human behaviour to justify our regarding them as
conscious. 'Machine' once was used to refer only to relatively primitive
devices, such as pulleys and windmills, which no one considered calling
conscious. As technology advances, 'machine' is used to refer also to more
and more complex devices, and genuine disputes about the consciousness
of machines arise. It is a mistake then to suppose that we can determine
whether a machine *can* be conscious by reference only to linguistic usage.
It is true that at any given point in technological development, reference
to linguistic usage is decisive in determining whether the Machine
Theory is true. It is of course also true that if 'machine' is incompatible
with 'conscious' (or if any of the other incompatibilities alluded to above

[3] E.g. N. Wiener, 'Some Moral and Technical Consequences of Automation', *Science*
1960, 131, 1355–1358.

[4] Walter, *The Living Brain*, p. 130.

arise), then it is logically impossible for a machine to be conscious. But this impossibility is based on the present state of technology which has influenced the current usages of 'machine' and 'conscious'. Such a prohibition is a shaky one on which to base a philosophical theory.

Therefore to argue that the ascription of consciousness to a machine results in a logical absurdity, as the Anti-Machine Theorists do, is to beg the question. Such an argument adjudicates by reference to meanings what ultimately can be decided only by reference to facts. Hence, there is no *inherent* logical contradiction involved in calling a machine conscious. Since observation of behaviour is the only way of deciding whether other people are conscious, there is no good reason to suppose the same criterion should not apply to machines.

If we were to convince the Anti-Machine Theorists of all that has been said thus far, they would probably still hesitate to call a robot conscious. The Theorists' reluctance raises the third barrier and reveals what may be the strongest motive for their denunciation of the Machine Theory. If the Anti-Machine Theorists ascribe consciousness to machines, they believe they have committed themselves to a full-blown behaviourism or materialism. (Indeed, Machine Theorists, too, sometimes seem to be motivated to argue for consciousness in machines because they believe their theory *does* entail some sort of behaviourism or materialism.)

Acceptance of the Machine Theory does not commit us to any particular theory of the relation of mind and body. In fact, acceptance of the Theory has fewer implications for mind-body theories than does rejection of it. I shall first examine the consequences on the supposition that the view that machines can be conscious is true. Next, I shall examine the consequences on the supposition that the view is false. For the purpose of this article, it is possible to classify in five categories all theories of the relation of mental events to physical events.[5] Two of the theories, Idealism and Parallelism, need not detain us. Idealism, which holds that all things are really mental, seems to me to be plainly false. But whether true or false, no decision for or against the Machine Theory will have any force for or against Idealism since the Idealist would classify machines themselves as mental in some sense. The second theory, Parallelism, asserts that there is a correlation between mental and physical events, and further that there is no causal connection between the two sorts of events. But this theory is no theory at all, even to the extent that the other mind-body theories are. To explain the correlation of the mental and physical (a fact which no mind-body theory denies), Parallelism says merely that the two kinds of events are correlated. Acceptance or rejection of the Machine Theory could not possibly affect a theory which, in effect, explains or clarifies nothing.

We are left with three categories of mind-body theories which are relevant to the machine problem—Interactionism, Epiphenomenalism, and Materialism. Essentially, Interactionism holds that some mental

[5] By 'mental event', I mean to refer to what has been called at various times in the literature of the mind-body problem 'raw feel qualities' or 'direct experience' or 'the given'. This concept remains vague because the nature of privacy, I believe, has yet to be adequately analysed. By using 'event', I do not intend to decide the question whether the 'mental' is best described as a series of events or as states or as processes.

events cause physical events, and some physical events cause mental events. Epiphenomenalism also admits the existence of mental events. It claims that no mental events cause physical events, no mental events cause mental events, and all mental events are caused by physical events. . . . Materialism asserts that there are no mental events. In this category, I wish to include not only the old-fashioned forms of materialism usually referred to by that term, but also philosophical behaviourism and the various related contemporary linguistic theories that seek to clarify the relation of mental and physical words. Admittedly, these classifications are very rough, and some of the proponents of these theories would object to their classmates. However, for the purpose of showing to what degree mind-body theories are affected by acceptance or rejection of the Machine Theory, I believe this rough classification and the implied distinction between mental and physical events will suffice. Now I shall examine the consequences for mind-body theories, first on the supposition that the Machine Theory is true.

First, we can say, contrary to what is sometimes supposed, that the existence of a conscious machine would not be evidence either for or against Materialism. It is true, as far as we can tell by looking at the parts themselves, there is nothing mental about machines. But neither is there anything mental about other people—if we examine only their constitution. There is nothing special about living matter *as such* that justifies our regarding as conscious whatever is composed of it. The relation of the mental to the physical (or of mental concepts to physical concepts), then, is still a problem even if we accept the Machine Theory. Thus, acceptance of the Machine Theory does not require acceptance of Materialism, unless one has previously accepted it as true on other grounds. Conversely, rejection of the Machine Theory does not entail rejection of Materialism unless one has rejected it on other grounds.

The consequences of the Machine Theory for the two remaining mind-body theories, Interactionism and Epiphenomenalism, are not so easily disposed of. Most Anti-Machine Theorists reject all forms of Materialism and tend to favour Interactionism. Accordingly, it is necessary to see what the consequences for these two theories are.

Both theories agree that physical events cause at least some mental events. The theories disagree about the causal efficacy of mental events. (1) Interactionism holds that some mental events cause physical events, while Epiphenomenalism maintains that no mental events cause physical events; (2) Epiphenomenalism further holds that all mental events are caused by physical events.

Prima facie, the existence of a conscious machine would not favour one or the other of the two theories, any more than does the existence of a conscious human. But perhaps it would be possible to decide these points of disagreement between the two theories by performing some experiments on a robot which we would not be able to perform, for one reason or another, on a human being.

A difference in the structures of machines and humans makes it possible, at least in theory, to obtain some experimental evidence which would bear on the decision between Epiphenomenalism and Interactionism. Although these mind-body theories are not scientific theories, scientific experiments which could be performed on machines but not on humans might give factual evidence which one of the mind-body theories could account for better than the other. Because the human brain is a living organism, each part depends for its *existence as a functioning unit* on many other parts. If we cut or remove one part of the brain, the blood flow to another part may be stopped, and the whole organ might *permanently* cease to function. This complex interdependence on the parts of the brain makes it difficult to carry out experiments of the sort necessary to provide evidence for or against mind-body theories. A second difficulty is that moral attitudes generally prevent tampering with the human brain to the extent necessary in such experiments.

Both of these difficulties are mitigated somewhat in the case of a conscious machine. I am not sure just what our moral attitudes would be toward conscious machines, but I should speculate that we would tend to permit somewhat more tampering with a robot's brain than with a human brain. One reason might be that we would not consider the robot 'one of us'. If our theory of obligation distinguishes human pain from the pain of other conscious beings, then the 'felt' obligation toward robots would not be so strong as toward our fellow humans. Accordingly, perhaps we would be as likely to use robots for experiments as we now use dogs. But it may be that since robots exhibit as high a degree of consciousness as humans, our obligation will be equally strong, in which case the experimental difficulties will remain much the same. On the other hand, it may be that robots will not feel pain from the same sort of experimenting that humans do. But most of these speculations can be substantiated only when we are actually confronted with robots.

The first difficulty would not be totally eliminated either. It would be possible, if we constructed the robot with the experiment in mind, to make the various tubes and wires accessible to disconnection. And in theory we could disconnect one or more at a time in various parts of the computer unit without rendering permanently inoperable the machine's brain. If we disconnected a part from the computer that caused it to cease functioning completely, we could re-connect it and try removing another part. It is problematical whether we could disconnect enough of the right parts in a computer brain to substantiate a particular mind-body theory before the machine ceased to be able to report its mental events or ceased functioning entirely. Again only actual experiments could determine this.

If a conscious machine, because of its structure and because of our moral attitudes toward it, does provide a slight advantage over humans for performing experiments, what experiments might be performed which would help to decide between Interactionism and Epiphenomenalism? There does not seem to be any experiment that would decide the first point of disagreement between the two theories, viz. whether some mental events cause physical events or whether no mental events cause physical events. For in a functioning machine, as in a living human, every physical event is preceded by at least one other physical event; therefore, it would never be correct to infer that a given physical event could not have been caused by a prior physical event.

It seems more likely that an experiment could be designed to help decide the second point of disagreement between Epiphenomenalism and Interactionism. Suppose we systematically disconnect various sets of tubes in the robot. If certain mental events occur, or cease to occur, each time we perform the same physical operation, we can correctly conclude that these mental events are probably caused by the physical events. The more physical causes we discover, the greater the probability of the empirical generalisation that all mental events have physical causes. The probability that Epiphenomenalism is true, in other words, would be increased. It is true that for every step in the disconnecting operation that failed to turn up a physical cause for a mental event, the probability that all mental events are caused by physical events would decrease, thereby weakening Epiphenomenalism and strengthening Interactionism. But since very few of the disconnecting operations could be performed while a given mental event is occurring, the decrease in probability would no doubt be so slight as to be insignificant. Thus, if the results of the experiment tend to favour either theory, they would favour Epiphenomenalism. Epiphenomenalism, in other words, is not likely to lose, though it may never win.

It should be clear now that the consequences of accepting the Machine Theory as true are not as great as the Anti-Machine Theorists suppose. If one has rejected Materialism in the case of human beings, one has just as good (or just as bad) reason to reject it in the case of conscious machines. Moreover, acceptance of the Machine Theory does not require rejection of Interactionism; nor does it require acceptance of Epiphenomenalism. It does give an edge to Epiphenomenalism to the extent that it allows that theory the possibility of more verification than it has if machines are not counted as conscious. But even this consequence may be repugnant to some Anti-Machine Theorists, who generally wish to regard the mind as more than a 'mere epiphenomenon' of the brain and, if they can avoid it, will give no advantage, however slight, to Epiphenomenalism. The price of avoiding it is high, however. For this consequence of accepting the Machine Theory is innocuous compared to the consequences of rejecting it.

If we refuse to regard as conscious a robot which can do everything a human can, we (1) strengthen a certain kind of solipsism, and (2) commit ourselves more fully to Epiphenomenalism than we would if we rejected the Machine Theory. By saying that a robot can do everything a human can do, we imply (as I have shown) that the robot has all the characteristics which justify our calling humans conscious. Thus, if we deny that robots are conscious, as the Anti-Machine Theorists would have us do, we have less reason to say that other humans are conscious. The denial of the Machine Theory thus undermines our justification for the belief in the existence of other minds. What is unfortunate about this consequence is that it amounts to a support of a philosophy which no one holds seriously—least of all Anti-Machine Theorists.

But suppose that Anti-Machine Theorists still believe that other people have minds, despite the fact that their justifications for the belief have been weakened. Still to be faced is the second consequence of rejecting the Machine Theory. By rejecting the Machine Theory we are denying that robots have minds, even though they can do everything a human can do. But if a machine which can do everything a human can do does not have a mind, then there is no reason to suppose that the minds of other people have causal efficacy in the physical world, for it follows on this view that we can account fully for other people's behaviour without reference to a mind. Moreover, if the minds of other people have no causal efficacy, then I have little reason to believe my own does. (If my 'willing my arm to move' causes anything—which is doubtful—it causes a brain event.) This consequence of rejecting the Machine Theory—that minds have no causal efficacy—is what Epiphenomenalism asserts and Interactionism denies. It decides the first point of disagreement between the theories. While we could not decide this disagreement by accepting the Machine Theory, we *do* decide it if we reject the Theory. Of course, we have not thereby shown that all mental events are caused by physical events (the second point of disagreement), but Epiphenomenalism becomes, if the Machine Theory is rejected, more probable by far than Interactionism.

Rejection of the Machine Theory, therefore, turns out to have more drastic consequences for the Anti-Machine Theorists than acceptance of the Theory. Not only does the rejection support a certain kind of solipsism, but it also virtually commits them to Epiphenomenalism. Acceptance of the Machine Theory, it will be remembered, gives not nearly so much support to Epiphenomenalism, nor does it strengthen solipsism. In neither case is Materialism affected.

In this article I have tried to show that refusal to accept the view that a machine *can* be conscious is a result of a number of muddles, the most important of which is a mistake about what philosophical consequences follow from the Machine Theory. Passing in and out of the machine problem are a great number of philosophical issues, but I have had to leave most of these only briefly stated, and certainly not resolved. My chief concerns here have been to eliminate the more troublesome misconceptions concerning the machine problem and to show how and what philosophical problems are related to it. At the same time, I have claimed that machines *can* be conscious, but if I have shown this, I have also shown that it is not such a radical claim after all.

Do We Survive Death?

The Myth of the Soul   Clarence Darrow

There is, perhaps, no more striking example of the credulity of man than the widespread belief in immortality. This idea includes not only the belief that death is not the end of what we call life, but that personal identity involving memory persists beyond the grave. So determined is the ordinary individual to hold fast to this belief that, as a rule, he refuses to read or to think upon the subject lest it cast doubt upon his cherished dream. Of those who may chance to look at this contribution, many will do so with the determination not to be convinced, and will refuse even to consider the manifold reasons that might weaken their faith. I know that this is true, for I know the reluctance with which I long approached the subject and my firm determination not to give up my hope. Thus the myth will stand in the way of a sensible adjustment to facts.

Even many of those who claim to believe in immortality still tell themselves and others that neither side of the question is susceptible of proof. Just what can these hopeful ones believe that the word "proof" involves? The evidence against the persistence of personal consciousness is as strong as the evidence of gravitation, and much more obvious. It is as convincing and unassailable as the proof of the destruction of wood or coal by fire. If it is not certain that death ends personal identity and memory, then almost nothing that man accepts as true is susceptible of proof.

The beliefs of the race and its individuals are relics of the past. Without careful examination, no one can begin to understand how many of man's cherished opinions have no foundation in fact. The common experience of all men should teach them how easy it is to believe what they wish to accept. Experienced psychologists know perfectly well that if they desire to convince a man of some idea, they must first make him *want* to believe it. There are so many hopes, so many strong yearnings and desires attached to the doctrine of immortality that it is practically impossible to create in any mind the wish to be mortal. Still, in spite of strong desires, millions of people are filled with doubts and fears that will not down. After all, is it not better to look the question squarely in the face and find out whether we are harboring a delusion?

It is customary to speak of a "belief in immortality." First, then, let us see what is meant by the word "belief." If I take a train in Chicago at noon, bound for New York, I believe I will reach that city the next morning. I believe it because I have been to New York. I have read about the city, I have known many other people who have been there, and their stories are not inconsistent with any known facts in my own experience. I have even examined the timetables, and I know just how I will go and how long the trip will take. In other words, when I board the train for New York, I believe I will reach that city because I have *reason* to believe it.

But if I am told that next week I shall start on a trip to Goofville; that I shall not take my body with me; that I shall stay for all eternity: can I find a single fact connected with my journey—the way I shall go, the part of me that is to go, the time of the journey, the country I shall reach, its location in space, the way I shall live there—or anything that would lead to a rational belief that I shall really make the trip? Have I ever known anyone who has made the journey and returned? If I am really to believe, I must try to get some information about all these important facts.

But people hesitate to ask questions about life after death. They do not ask, for they know that only silence comes out of the eternal darkness of endless space. If people really believed in a beautiful, happy, glorious land waiting to receive them when they died; if they believed that their friends would be waiting to meet them; if they believed that all pain and suffering would be left behind: why should they live through weeks, months, and even years of pain and torture while a cancer eats its way to the vital parts of the body? Why should one fight off death? Because he does *not* believe in any real sense: he only hopes. Everyone knows that there is no real evidence of any such state of bliss; so we are told not to search for proof. We are to accept through faith alone. But every thinking person knows that faith can only come through belief. Belief implies a condition of mind that accepts a certain idea. This condition can be brought about only by evidence. True, the evidence may be simply the unsupported statement of your grandmother; it may be wholly insufficient for reasoning men; but, good or bad, it must be enough for the believer or he could not believe.

Upon what evidence, then, are we asked to believe in immortality? There is no evidence. One is told to rely on faith, and no doubt this serves the purpose so long as one can believe blindly whatever he is told. But if there is no evidence upon which to build a positive belief in immortality, let us examine the other side of the question. Perhaps evidence can be found to support a positive conviction that immortality is a delusion.

The belief in immortality expresses itself in two different forms. On the one hand, there is a belief in the immortality of the "soul." This is sometimes interpreted to mean simply that the identity, the consciousness, the memory of the individual persists after death. On the other hand, many religious creeds have formulated a belief in "the resurrection of the body"—which is something else again. It will be necessary to examine both forms for this belief in turn.

The idea of continued life after death is very old. It doubtless had its roots back in the childhood of the race. In view of the limited knowledge of primitive man, it was not unreasonable. His dead friends and relatives visited him in dreams and visions and were present in his feeling and imagination until they were forgotten. Therefore the lifeless body did not raise the question of dissolution, but rather of duality. It was thought that man was a dual being possessing a body and a soul as separate entities, and that when a man died, his soul was released from his body to continue its life apart. Consequently, food and drink were placed upon the graves of the dead to be used in the long journey into the unknown. In modified forms, this belief in the duality of man persists to the present day.

But primitive man had no conception of life as having a beginning and an end. In this he was like the rest of the animals. Today, everyone of ordinary intelligence knows how life begins, and to examine the beginnings of life leads to inevitable conclusions about the way life ends. If man has a soul, it must creep in somewhere during the period of gestation and growth.

All the higher forms of animal life grow from a single cell. Before the individual life can begin its development, it must be fertilized by union with another cell; then the cell divides and multiplies until it takes the form and pattern of its kind. At a certain regular time the being emerges into the world. During its term of life millions of cells in its body are born, die, and are replaced until, through age, disease, or some catastrophe, the cells fall apart and the individual life is ended.

It is obvious that but for the fertilization of the cell under right conditions, the being would not have lived. It is idle to say that the initial cell has a soul. In one sense it has life; but even that is precarious and depends for its continued life upon union with another cell of the proper kind. The human mother is the bearer of probably ten thousand of one kind of cell, and the human father of countless billions of the other kind. Only a very small fraction of these result in human life. If the unfertilized cells of the female and the unused cells of the male are human beings possessed of souls, then the population of the world is infinitely greater than has ever been dreamed. Of course no such idea as belief in the immortality of the germ cells could satisfy the yearnings of the individual for a survival of life after death.

If that which is called a "soul" is a separate entity apart from the body, when, then, and where and how was this soul placed in the human structure? The individual began with the union of two cells, neither of which had a soul. How could these two soulless cells produce a soul? I must leave this search to the metaphysicians. When they have found the answer, I hope they will tell me, for I should really like to know.

We know that a baby may live and fully develop in its mother's womb and then, through some shock at birth, may be born without life. In the past, these babies were promptly buried. But now we know that in many cases, where the bodily structure is complete, the machine may be set to work by artificial respiration or electricity. Then it will run like any other human body through its allotted term of years. We also know that in many cases of drowning, or when some mishap virtually destroys life without hopelessly impairing the body, artificial means may set it in motion once more, so that it will complete its term of existence until the final catastrophe comes. Are we to believe that somewhere around the stillborn child and somewhere in the vicinity of the drowned man there hovers a detached soul waiting to be summoned back into the body by a pulmotor? This, too, must be left to the metaphysicians.

The beginnings of life yield no evidence of the beginnings of a soul. It is idle to say that the something in the human being which we call "life" is the soul itself, for the soul is generally taken to distinguish human beings from other forms of life. There is life in all animals and plants, and at least potential life in inorganic matter. This potential life is simply unreleased force and matter—the great storehouse from which all forms of life emerge and are constantly replenished. It is impossible to draw the line between inorganic matter and the simpler forms of plant life, and equally impossible to draw the line between plant life and animal life, or between other forms of animal life and what we human beings are pleased to call the highest form. If the thing which we call "life" is itself the soul, then cows have souls; and, in the very nature of things, we must allow souls to all forms of life and to inorganic matter as well.

Life itself is something very real, as distinguished from the soul. Every man knows that his life had a beginning. Can one imagine an organism that has a beginning and no end? If I did not exist in the infinite past, why should I, or could I, exist in the infinite future? "But," say some, "your consciousness, your memory may exist even after you are dead. This is what we mean by the soul." Let us examine this point a little.

I have no remembrance of the months that I lay in my mother's womb. I cannot recall the day of my birth nor the time when I first opened my eyes to the light of the sun. I cannot remember when I was an infant, or when I began to creep on the floor, or when I was taught to walk, or anything before I was five or six years old. Still, all of these events were important, wonderful, and strange in a new life. What I call my "consciousness," for lack of a better word and a better understanding, developed with my growth and the crowding experiences I met at every turn. I have a hazy recollection of the burial of a boy soldier who was shot toward the end of the Civil War. He was buried near the schoolhouse when I was seven years old. But I have no remembrance of the assassination of Abraham Lincoln, although I must then have been eight years old. I must have known about it at the time, for my family and my community idolized Lincoln, and all America was in mourning at his death. Why do I remember the dead boy soldier who was buried a year before? Perhaps because I knew him well. Perhaps because his family was close to my childish life. Possibly because it came to me as my first knowledge of death. At all events, it made so deep an impression that I recall it now.

"Ah, yes," say the believers in the soul, "what you say confirms our own belief. You certainly existed when these early experiences took place. You were conscious of them at the time, even though you are not aware of it now. In the same way, may not your consciousness persist after you die, even though you are not now aware of the fact?"

On the contrary, my fading memory of the events that filled the early years of my life leads me to the opposite conclusion. So far as these incidents are concerned, the mind and consciousness of the boy are already dead. Even now, am I fully alive? I am seventy-one years old. I often fail to recollect the names of some of those I knew full well. Many events do not make the lasting impression that they once did. I know that it will be only a few years, even if my body still survives decay, when few important matters will even register in my mind. I know how it is with the old. I know that physical life can persist beyond the time when the mind can fully function. I know that if I live to an extreme old age, my mind will fail. I shall eat and drink and go to my bed in an automatic way. Memory—which is all that binds me to the past—will already be dead. All that will remain will be a vegetative existence; I shall sit and doze in the chimney corner, and my body will function in a measure even though the ego will already be practically dead. I am sure that if I die of what is called "old age," my consciousness will gradually slip away with my failing emotions; I shall no more be aware of the near approach of final dissolution than is the dying tree.

In primitive times, before men knew anything about the human body or the universe of which it is a part, it was not unreasonable to believe in spirits, ghosts, and the duality of man. For one thing, celestial geography was much simpler then. Just above the earth was a firmament in which the stars were set, and above the firmament was heaven. The place was easy of access, and in dreams the angels were seen going up and coming down on a ladder. But now we have a slightly more adequate conception of space and the infinite universe of which we are so small a part. Our great telescopes reveal countless worlds and planetary systems which make our own sink into utter insignificance in comparison. We have every reason to think that beyond our sight there is endless space filled with still more planets, so infinite in size and number that no brain has the smallest conception of their extent. Is there any reason to think that in this universe, with its myriads of worlds, there is no other life so important as our own? Is it possible that the inhabitants of the earth have been singled out for special favor and endowed with souls and immortal life? Is it at all reasonable to suppose that any special account is taken of the human atoms that forever come and go upon this planet?

If man has a soul that persists after death, that goes to a heaven of the blessed or to a hell of the damned, where are these places? It is not so easily imagined as it once was. How does the soul make its journey? What does immortal man find when he gets there, and how will he live after he reaches the end of endless space? We know that the atmosphere will be absent; that there will be no light, no heat—only the infinite reaches of darkness and frigidity. In view of modern knowledge, can anyone *really believe* in the persistence of individual life and memory?

There are those who base their hope of a future life upon the resurrection of the body. This is a purely religious doctrine. It is safe to say that few intelligent men who are willing to look obvious facts in the face hold any such belief. Yet we are seriously told that Elijah was carried bodily to heaven in a chariot of fire, and that Jesus arose from the dead and ascended into heaven. The New Testament abounds in passages that support this doctrine. St. Paul states the tenet over and over again. In the fifteenth chapter of First Corinthians he says: "If Christ be preached that he rose from the dead, how say some among you that there is no resurrection of the dead? . . . And if Christ be not risen, then is our preaching vain. . . . For if the dead rise not, then is not Christ raised." The Apostles' Creed says: "I believe in the resurrection of the body." This has been carried into substantially all the orthodox creeds; and while it is more or less minimized by neglect and omission, is still a cardinal doctrine of the orthodox churches.

Two thousand years ago, in Palestine, little was known of man, of the earth, or of the universe. It was then currently believed that the earth was only four thousand years old, that life had begun anew after the deluge about two thousand years before, and that the entire earth was soon to be destroyed. Today it is fairly well established that man has been upon the earth for a million years. During that long stretch of time the world has changed many times; it is changing every moment. At least three or four ice ages have swept across continents, driving death before them, carrying human beings into the sea or burying them deep in the earth. Animals have fed on man and on each other. Every dead body, no matter whether consumed by fire or buried in the earth, has been resolved into its elements, so that the matter and energy that once formed human beings has fed animals and plants and other men. As the great naturalist, Fabre, has said: "At the banquet of life each is in turn a guest and a dish." Thus the body of every man now living is in part made from the bodies of those who have been dead for ages.

Yet we are still asked to believe in the resurrection of the body. By what alchemy, then, are the individual bodies that have successfully fed the generations of men to be separated and restored to their former identities? And if I am to be resurrected, what particular *I* shall be called from the grave, from the animals and plants and the bodies of other men who shall inherit this body I now call my own? My body has been made over and over, piece by piece, as the days went by, and will continue to be so made until the end. It has changed so slowly that each new cell is fitted into the living part, and will go on changing until the final crisis comes. Is it the child in the mother's womb or the tottering frame of the old man that shall be brought back? The mere thought of such a resurrection beggars reason, ignores facts, and enthrones blind faith, wild dreams, hopeless hopes, and cowardly fears as sovereign of the human mind.

Some of those who profess to believe in the immortality of man—whether it be of his soul or his body—have drawn what comfort they could from the modern scientific doctrine of the indestructibility of matter and force. This doctrine, they say, only confirms in scientific language what they have always believed. This, however, is pure sophistry. It is probably true that no matter or force has ever been or ever can be destroyed. But it is likewise true that there is no connection whatever between the notion that personal consciousness and memory persist after death and the scientific theory that matter and force are indestructible. For the scientific theory carries with it a corollary, that the forms of matter and energy are constantly changing through an endless cycle of new combinations. Of what possible use would it be, then, to have a consciousness that was immortal, but which, from the moment of death, was dispersed into new combinations so that no two parts of the original identity could ever be reunited again?

These natural processes of change, which in the human being take the forms of growth, disease, senility, death, and decay, are essentially the same as the process by which a lump of coal is disintegrated in burning. One may watch the lump of coal burning in the grate until nothing but ashes remains. Part of the coal goes up the chimney in the form of smoke; part of it radiates through the house as heat; the residue lies in the ashes on the hearth. So it is with human life. In all forms of life nature is engaged in combining, breaking down, and recombining her store of energy and matter into new forms. The thing we call "life" is nothing other than a state of equilibrium which endures for a short span of years between the two opposing tendencies of nature—the one that builds up, and the one that tears down. In old age, the tearing-down process has already gained the ascendency, and when death intervenes, the equilibrium is finally upset by the complete stoppage of the building-up process, so that nothing remains but complete disintegration. The energy thus released may be converted into grass or trees or animal life; or it may lie dormant until caught up again in the crucible of nature's laboratory. But whatever happens, the man—the *You* and the *I*—like the lump of coal that has been burned, is gone, irrevocably dispersed. All the King's horses and all the King's men cannot restore it to its former unity.

The idea that man is a being set apart, distinct from all the rest of nature, is born of man's emotions, of his loves and hates, of his hopes and fears, and of the primitive conceptions of undeveloped minds. The *You* or the *I* which is known to our friends does not consist of an immaterial something called a "soul" which cannot be conceived. We know perfectly well what we mean when we talk about this *You* and this *Me:* and it is equally plain that the whole fabric that makes up our separate personalities is destroyed, dispersed, disintegrated beyond repair by what we call "death."

Those who refuse to give up the idea of immortality declare that nature never creates a desire without providing the means for its satisfaction. They likewise insist that all people, from the rudest to the most civilized, yearn for another life. As a matter of fact, nature creates many desires which she does not satisfy; most of the wishes of men meet no fruition. But nature does not create any emotion demanding a future life. The only yearning that the individual has is to keep on living—which is a very different thing. This urge is found in every animal, in every plant. It is simply the momentum of a living structure: or, as Schopenhauer put it, "the will to live." What we long for is a continuation of our present state of existence, not an uncertain reincarnation in a mysterious world of which we know nothing.

All men recognize the hopelessness of finding any evidence that the individual will persist beyond the grave. As a last resort, we are told that it is better that the doctrine be believed even if it is not true. We are assured that without this faith, life is only desolation and despair. However that may be, it remains that many of the conclusions of logic are not pleasant to contemplate; still, so long as men think and feel, at least some of them will use their faculties as best they can. For if we are to believe things that are not true, who is to write our creed? Is it safe to leave it to any man or organization to pick out the errors that we must accept? The whole history of the world has answered this question in a way that cannot be mistaken.

And after all, is the belief in immortality necessary or even desirable for man? Millions of men and women have no such faith; they go on with their daily tasks and feel joy and sorrow without the lure of immortal life. The things that really affect the happiness of the individual are the matters of daily living. They are the companionship of friends, the games and contemplations. They are misunderstandings and cruel judgments, false friends and debts, poverty and disease. They are our joys in our living companions and our sorrows over those who die. Whatever our faith, we mainly live in the present—in the here and now. Those who hold the view that man is mortal are never troubled by metaphysical problems. At the end of the day's labor we are glad to lose our consciousness in sleep; and intellectually, at least, we look forward to the long rest from the stresses and storms that are always incidental to existence.

When we fully understand the brevity of life, its fleeting joys and unavoidable pains; when we accept the fact that all men and women are approaching an inevitable doom: the consciousness of it should make us more kindly and considerate of each other. This feeling should make men and women use their best efforts to help their fellow travellers on the road, to make the path brighter and easier as we journey on. It should bring a closer kinship, a better understanding, and a deeper sympathy for the wayfarers who must live a common life and die a common death.

Is Life After Death Possible? C. J. Ducasse

Curt John Ducasse (1881–1969) born in France and educated in the United States, was a distinguished American professor of philosophy, whose interests and writings ranged from philosophy of religion, metaphysics, and aesthetics to psychical research. He was a member of the board of trustees and chairman of the publications committee of the American Society for Psychical Research.

The question whether human personality survives death is sometimes asserted to be one upon which reflection is futile. Only empirical evidence, it is said, can be relevant, since the question is purely one of fact.

But no question is purely one of fact until it is clearly understood; and this one is, on the contrary, ambiguous and replete with tacit assumptions. Until the ambiguities have been removed and the assumptions critically examined, we do not really know just what it is we want to know when we ask whether a life after death is possible. Nor, therefore, can we tell until then what bearing on this question various facts empirically known to us may have.

To clarify its meaning is chiefly what I now propose to attempt. I shall ask first why a future life is so generally desired and believed in. Then I shall state, as convincingly as I can in the time available, the arguments commonly advanced to prove that such a life is impossible. After that, I shall consider the logic of these arguments, and show that they quite fail to establish the impossibility. Next, the tacit but arbitrary assumption, which makes them nevertheless appear convincing, will be

From "Is Life After Death Possible?" The Agnes E. and Constantine E. Foerster Lecture, 1947. Copyright by C. J. Ducasse, 1948. Reprinted by permission of The Regents of the University of California.

pointed out. And finally, I shall consider briefly a number of specific forms which a life after death might take, if there is one.

Let us turn to the first of these tasks.

Why Man Desires Life After Death

To begin with, let us note that each of us here has been alive and conscious at all times in the past which he can remember. It is true that sometimes our bodies are in deep sleep, or made inert by anesthetics or injuries. But even at such times we do not experience unconsciousness in ourselves, for to experience it would mean being conscious of being unconscious, and this is a contradiction. The only experience of unconsciousness in ourselves we ever have is, not experience of total unconsciousness, but of unconsciousness *of this or that;* as when we report: "I am not conscious of any pain," or "of any bell-sound," or "of any difference between those two colors," etc. Nor do we ever experience unconsciousness in another person, but only the fact that, sometimes, some or all of the ordinary activities of his body cease to occur. That consciousness itself is extinguished at such times is thus only a hypothesis which we construct to account for certain changes in the behavior of another person's body or to explain in him or in ourselves the eventual lack of memories relating to the given period.

Being alive and conscious is thus, with all men, a lifelong experience and habit; and conscious life is therefore something they naturally—even if tacitly—expect to continue. As J. B. Pratt has pointed out, the child takes the continuity of life for granted. It is the fact of death that has to be taught him. But when he has learned it, and the idea of a future life is then put explicitly before his mind, it seems to him the most natural thing in the world.[1]

The witnessing of death, however, is a rare experience for most of us, and, because it breaks so sharply into our habits, it forces on us the question whether the mind, which until then was manifested by the body now dead, continues somehow to live on, or, on the contrary, has become totally extinct. This question is commonly phrased as concerning "the immortality of the soul," and immortality, strictly speaking, means survival forever. But assurance of survival for some considerable period—say a thousand, or even a hundred, years—would probably have almost as much present psychological value as would assurance of survival strictly forever. Most men would be troubled very little by the idea of extinction at so distant a time—even less troubled than is now a healthy and happy youth by the idea that he will die in fifty or sixty years. Therefore, it is survival for some time, rather than survival specifically forever, that I shall alone consider.

The craving for continued existence is very widespread. Even persons who believe that death means complete extinction of the individual's consciousness often find comfort in various substitute conceptions of survival. They may, for instance, dwell on the continuity of the indi-

[1] J. B. Pratt, *The Religious Consciousness,* p. 225.

vidual's germ plasm in his descendants. Or they find solace in the thought that, the past being indestructible, their individual life remains eternally an intrinsic part of the history of the world. Also—and more satisfying to one's craving for personal importance—there is the fact that since the acts of one's life have effects, and these in turn further effects, and so on, therefore what one has done goes on forever influencing remotely, and sometimes greatly, the course of future events.

Gratifying to one's vanity, too, is the prospect that, if the achievements of one's life have been great or even only conspicuous, or one's benefactions or evil deeds have been notable, one's name may not only be remembered by acquaintances and relatives for a little while, but may live on in recorded history. But evidently survival in any of these senses is but a consolation prize—but a thin substitute for the continuation of conscious individual life, which may not be a fact, but which most men crave nonetheless.

The roots of this craving are certain desires which death appears to frustrate. For some, the chief of these is for reunion with persons dearly loved. For others, whose lives have been wretched, it is the desire for another chance at the happiness they have missed. For others yet, it is desire for further opportunity to grow in ability, knowledge or character. Often, there is also the desire, already mentioned, to go on counting for something in the affairs of men. And again, a future life for oneself and others is often desired in order that the redressing of the many injustices of this life shall be possible. But it goes without saying that, although desires such as these are often sufficient to cause belief in a future life, they constitute no evidence at all that it is a fact.

In this connection, it may be well to point out that, although both the belief in survival and the belief in the existence of a god or gods are found in most religions, nevertheless there is no necessary connection between the two beliefs. No contradiction would be involved in supposing either that there is a God but no life after death or that there is a life after death but no God. The belief that there is a life after death may be tied to a religion, but it is no more intrinsically religious than would be a belief that there is life on the planet Mars. The after-death world, if it exists, is just another region or dimension of the universe.

But although belief in survival of death is natural and easy and has always been held in one form or another by a large majority of mankind, critical reflection quickly brings forth a number of apparently strong reasons to regard that belief as quite illusory. Let us now review them.

The Arguments Against Survival

There are, first of all, a number of facts which definitely suggest that both the existence and the nature of consciousness wholly depend on the presence of a functioning nervous system. It is pointed out, for example, that wherever consciousness is observed, it is found associated with a living and functioning body. Further, when the body dies, or the head is struck a heavy blow, or some anesthetic is administered, the familiar outward evidences of consciousness terminate, permanently or temporarily.

Again, we know well that drugs of various kinds—alcohol, caffein, opium, heroin, and many others—cause specific changes at the time in the nature of a person's mental states. Also, by stimulating in appropriate ways the body's sense organs, corresponding states of consciousness—namely, the various kinds of sensations—can be caused at will. On the other hand, cutting a sensory nerve immediately eliminates a whole range of sensations.

Again, the contents of consciousness, the mental powers, or even the personality, are modified in characteristic ways when certain regions of the brain are destroyed by disease or injury or are disconnected from the rest by such an operation as prefrontal lobotomy. And that the nervous system is the indispensable basis of mind is further suggested by the fact that, in the evolutionary scale, the degree of intelligence of various species of animals keeps pace closely with the degree of development of their brain.

That continued existence of mind after death is impossible has been argued also on the basis of theoretical considerations. It has been contended, for instance, that what we call states of consciousness—or more particularly, ideas, sensations, volitions, feelings, and the like—are really nothing but the minute physical or chemical events which take place in the tissues of the brain. For, it is urged, it would be absurd to suppose that an idea or a volition, if it is not itself a material thing or process, could cause material effects such as contractions of muscles.

Moreover, it is maintained that the possibility of causation of a material event by an immaterial, mental cause is ruled out *a priori* by the principle of the conservation of energy; for such causation would mean that an additional quantity of energy suddenly pops into the nervous system out of nowhere.

Another conception of consciousness, which is more often met with today than the one just mentioned, but which also implies that consciousness cannot survive death, is that "consciousness" is only the name we give to certain types of behavior, which differentiate the higher animals from all other things in nature. According to this view, to say, for example, that an animal is conscious of a difference between two stimuli means nothing more than that it responds to each by different behavior. That is, the difference of *behavior* is what consciousness of difference between the stimuli *consists in;* and is not, as is commonly assumed, only the behavioral *sign* of something mental and not public, called "consciousness that the stimuli are different."

Or again, consciousness, of the typically human sort called thought, is identified with the typically human sort of behavior called speech; and this, again not in the sense that speech *expresses* or *manifests* something different from itself, called "thought," but in the sense that speech—whether uttered or only whispered—*is* thought itself. And obviously, if thought, or any mental activity, is thus but some mode of behavior of the living body, the mind cannot possibly survive death.

Still another difficulty confronting the hypothesis of survival becomes evident when one imagines in some detail what survival would have to include in order to satisfy the desires which cause man to crave it. It would, of course, have to include persistence not alone of consciousness, but also of personality; that is, of the individual's character, acquired knowledge, cultural skills and interests, memories, and awareness of personal identity. But even this would not be enough, for what man desires is not bare survival, but to go on living in some objective way. And this means to go on meeting new situations and, by exerting himself to deal with them, to broaden and deepen his experience and develop his latent capacities.

But it is hard to imagine this possible without a body and an environment for it, upon which to act and from which to receive impressions. And, if a body and an environment were supposed, but not material and corruptible ones, then it is paradoxical to think that, under such radically different conditions, a given personality could persist.[2]

To take a crude but telling analogy, it is past belief that, if the body of any one of us were suddenly changed into that of a shark or an octopus, and placed in the ocean, his personality could, for more than a very short time, if at all, survive intact so radical a change of environment and of bodily form.

The Arguments Examined

Such, in brief, are the chief reasons commonly advanced for holding that survival is impossible. Scrutiny of them, however, will, I think, reveal that they are not as strong as they first seem and far from strong enough to show that there can be no life after death.

Let us consider first the assertion that "thought," or "consciousness," is but another name for subvocal speech, or for some other form of behavior, or for molecular processes in the tissues of the brain. As Paulsen and others have pointed out,[3] no evidence ever is or can be offered to support that assertion, because it is in fact but a disguised proposal to make the words "thought," "feeling," "sensation," "desire," and so on, denote facts quite different from those which these words are commonly employed to denote. To say that those words are but other names for certain chemical or behavioral events is as grossly arbitrary as it would be to say that "wood" is but another name for glass, or "potato" but another name for cabbage. What thought, desire, sensation, and other mental states are like, each of us can observe directly by introspection; and what introspection reveals is that they do not in the least resemble muscular contraction, or glandular secretion, or any other known bodily events. No tampering with language can alter the observable fact that thinking is one thing and muttering quite another; that the feeling called anger has no resemblance to the bodily behavior which usually goes with it; or that an act of will is not in the least like anything we find when we open the skull and examine the brain. Certain mental events are doubtless connected in some way with certain bodily events, but they are not those bodily events themselves. The connection is not identity.

Epiphenomenal

[2] Cf. Gardner Murphy, "Difficulties Confronting the Survival Hypothesis," _Journal of the American Society for Psychical Research_ for April, 1945, p. 72; Corliss Lamont, "The Illusion of Immortality" (New York, 1935), pp. 26 ff.

[3] F. Paulsen, "Introduction to Philosophy" (trans. by F. Thilly, 2d ed.), pp. 82–83.

This being clear, let us next consider the arguments offered to show that mental processes, although not identical with bodily processes, nevertheless depend on them. We are told, for instance, that some head injuries, or anesthetics, totally extinguish consciousness for the time being. As already pointed out, however, the strict fact is only that the usual bodily signs of consciousness are then absent. But they are also absent when a person is asleep; and, yet, at the same time, dreams, which are states of consciousness, may be occurring.   *DEAD MEN DON'T DREAM*

It is true that when the person concerned awakens, he often remembers his dreams, whereas the person that has been anesthetized or injured has usually no memories relating to the period of apparent blankness. But this could mean that his consciousness was, for the first time, dissociated from its ordinary channels of manifestation, as was reported of the co-conscious personalities of some of the patients of Dr. Morton Prince.[4] Moreover, it sometimes occurs that a person who has been in an accident reports lack of memories not only for the period during which his body was unresponsive but also for a period of several hours *before* the accident, during which he had given to his associates all the ordinary external signs of being conscious as usual.

But, more generally, if absence of memories relating to a given period proved unconsciousness for that period, this would force us to conclude that we were unconscious during the first few years of our lives, and indeed have been so most of the time since; for the fact is that we have no memories whatever of most of our days. That we were alive and conscious on any long past specific date is, with only a few exceptions, not something we actually remember, but only something which we infer must be true.

Evidence from Psychical Research

Another argument advanced against survival was, it will be remembered, that death must extinguish the mind, since all manifestations of it then cease. But to assert that they invariably then cease is to ignore altogether the considerable amount of evidence to the contrary, gathered over many years and carefully checked by the Society for Psychical Research. This evidence, which is of a variety of kinds, has been reviewed by Professor Gardner Murphy in an article published in the Journal of the Society.[5] He mentions first the numerous well-authenticated cases of apparition of a dead person to others as yet unaware that he had died or even been ill or in danger. The more strongly evidential cases of apparition are those in which the apparition conveys to the person who sees it specific facts until then secret. An example would be that of the apparition of a girl to her brother nine years after her death, with a conspicuous scratch on her cheek. Their mother then revealed to him that she herself had made that scratch accidentally while preparing her

[4] "My Life as a Dissociated Personality" (edited by Morton Prince; Boston: Badger).

[5] "An Outline of Survival Evidence," *Journal of the American Society for Psychical Research,* January, 1945.

daughter's body for burial, but that she had then at once covered it with powder and never mentioned it to anyone.

Another famous case is that of a father whose apparition some time after death revealed to one of his sons the existence and location of an unsuspected second will, benefiting him, which was then found as indicated. Still another case would be the report by General Barter, then a subaltern in the British Army in India, of the apparition to him of a lieutenant he had not seen for two or three years. The lieutenant's apparition was riding a brown pony with black mane and tail. He was much stouter than at their last meeting, and, whereas formerly clean-shaven, he now wore a peculiar beard in the form of a fringe encircling his face. On inquiry the next day from a person who had known the lieutenant at the time he died, it turned out that he had indeed become very bloated before his death; that he had grown just such a beard while on the sick list; and that he had some time before bought and eventually ridden to death a pony of that very description.

Other striking instances are those of an apparition seen simultaneously by several persons. It is on record that an apparition of a child was perceived first by a dog, that the animal's rushing at it, loudly barking, interrupted the conversation of the several persons present in the room, thus drawing their attention to the apparition, and that the latter then moved through the room for some fifteen seconds, followed by the barking dog.[6]

Another type of empirical evidence of survival consists of communications, purporting to come from the dead, made through the persons commonly called sensitives, mediums, or automatists. Some of the most remarkable of these communications were given by the celebrated American medium, Mrs. Piper, who for many years was studied by the Society for Psychical Research, London, with the most elaborate precautions against all possibility of fraud. Twice, particularly, the evidences of identity supplied by the dead persons who purportedly were thus communicating with the living were the very kinds, and of the same precision and detail, which would ordinarily satisfy a living person of the identity of another living person with whom he was not able to communicate directly, but only through an intermediary, or by letter or telephone.[7]

Again, sometimes the same mark of identity of a dead person, or the same message from him, or complementary parts of one message, are obtained independently from two mediums in different parts of the world.

Of course, when facts of these kinds are recounted, as I have just done,

[6] The documents obtained by the Society for Psychical Research concerning this case, that of the lieutenant's apparition, and that of the girl with the scratch, are reproduced in Sir Ernest Bennett's "Apparitions and Haunted Houses" (London: Faber and Faber, 1945), pp. 334–337, 28–35, and 145–150 respectively.

[7] A summary of some of the most evidential facts may be found in the book by M. Sage, entitled "Mrs. Piper and the Society for Psychical Research" (New York: Scott-Thaw Co., 1904); others of them are related in some detail in Sir Oliver Lodge's "The Survival of Man," Sec. IV (New York: Moffat, Yard and Co., 1909) and in A. M. Robbins' "Both Sides of the Veil," Part II (Boston: Sherman, French, and Co., 1909). The fullest account is in the *Proceedings of the Society for Psychical Research.*

only in abstract summary, they make little if any impression upon us. And the very word "medium" at once brings to our minds the innumerable instances of demonstrated fraud perpetrated by charlatans to extract money from the credulous bereaved. But the modes of trickery and sources of error, which immediately suggest themselves to us as easy, natural explanations of the seemingly extraordinary facts, suggest themselves just as quickly to the members of the research committees of the Society for Psychical Research. Usually, these men have had a good deal more experience than the rest of us with the tricks of conjurers and fraudulent mediums, and take against them precautions far more strict and ingenious than would occur to the average sceptic.[8]

But when, instead of stopping at summaries, one takes the trouble to study the detailed, original reports, it then becomes evident that they cannot all be just laughed off; for to accept the hypothesis of fraud or malobservation would often require more credulity than to accept the facts reported.

To *explain* those facts, however, is quite another thing. Only two hypotheses at all adequate to do so have yet been advanced. One is that the communications really come, as they purport to do, from persons who have died and have survived death. The other is the hypothesis of telepathy—that is, the supposition, itself startling enough, that the medium is able to gather information directly from the minds of others, and that this is the true source of the information communicated. To account for all the facts, however, this hypothesis has to be stretched very far, for some of them require us to suppose that the medium can tap the minds even of persons far away and quite unknown to him, and can tap even the subconscious parts of their minds.

Diverse highly ingenious attempts have been made to devise conditions that would rule out telepathy as a possible explanation of the communications received; but some of the most critical and best-documented investigators still hold that it has not yet been absolutely excluded. Hence, although some of the facts recorded by psychical research constitute, prima facie, strong empirical evidence of survival, they cannot be said to establish it beyond question. But they do show that we need to revise rather radically in some respects our ordinary ideas of what is and is not possible in nature.

Can Mental States Cause Bodily Events?

Let us now turn to another of the arguments against survival. That states of consciousness entirely depend on bodily processes, and therefore cannot continue when the latter have ceased, is proved, it is argued, by the fact that various states of consciousness—in particular, the several kinds of sensations—can be caused at will by appropriately stimulating the body.

Now, it is very true that sensations and some other mental states can

[8] Cf. H. Carrington, "The Physical Phenomena of Spiritualism, Fraudulent and Genuine" (Boston: Small, Maynard & Co., 1908).

be so caused; but we have just as good and abundant evidence that mental states can cause various bodily events. John Laird mentions, among others, the fact that merely willing to raise one's arm normally suffices to cause it to rise; that a hungry person's mouth is caused to water by the idea of food; that feelings of rage, fear or excitement cause digestion to stop; that anxiety causes changes in the quantity and quality of the milk of a nursing mother; that certain thoughts cause tears, pallor, blushing or fainting; and so on.[9] The evidence we have that the relation is one of cause and effect is exactly the same here as where bodily processes cause mental states.

It is said, of course, that to suppose something non-physical, such as thought, to be capable of causing motion of a physical object, such as the body, is absurd. But I submit that if the heterogeneity of mind and matter makes this absurd, then it makes equally absurd the causation of mental states by stimulation of the body. Yet no absurdity is commonly found in the assertion that cutting the skin causes a feeling of pain, or that alcohol, caffein, bromides, and other drugs, cause characteristic states of consciousness. As David Hume made clear long ago, no kind of causal connection is intrinsically absurd. Anything might cause anything; and only observation can tell us what in fact can cause what.

Somewhat similar remarks would apply to the allegation that the principle of the conservation of energy precludes the possibility of causation of a physical event by a mental event. For if it does, then it equally precludes causation in the converse direction, and this, of course, would leave us totally at a loss to explain the occurrence of sensations. But, as Keeton and others have pointed out,[10] that energy is conserved is not something observation has revealed or could reveal, but only a postulate —a defining postulate for the notion of an "isolated physical system."

That is, conservation of energy is something one has to have if, but only if, one insists on conceiving the physical world as wholly self-contained, independent, isolated. And just because the metaphysics which the natural sciences tacitly assume does insist on so conceiving the physical world, this metaphysics compels them to save conservation by postulations *ad hoc* whenever dissipation of energy is what observation reveals. It postulates, for instance, that something else, which appears at such times but was not until then regarded as energy, is energy too, but it is then said, "in a different form."

Furthermore, as Broad has emphasized, all that the principle of conservation requires is that when a quantity Q of energy disappears at one place in the physical world an equal quanity of it should appear at some other place there. And the supposition that, in some cases, what causes it to disappear here and appear there is some mental event, such perhaps as a volition, does not violate at all the supposition that energy is conserved.[11]

[9] John Laird, "Our Minds and Their Bodies" (London, 1925), pp. 16–19.

[10] M. T. Keeton, "Some Ambiguities in the Theory of the Conservation of Energy," *Philosophy of Science,* Vol. 8, No. 3, July 1941.

[11] C. D. Broad, "The Mind and Its Place in Nature," pp. 103 ff.

A word, next, on the parallelism between the degree of development of the nervous systems of various animals and the degree of their intelligence. This is alleged to prove that the latter is the product of the former. But the facts lend themselves equally well to the supposition that, on the contrary, an obscurely felt need for greater intelligence in the circumstances the animal faced was what brought about the variations which eventually resulted in a more adequate nervous organization.

In the development of the individual, at all events, it seems clear that the specific, highly complex nerve connections which become established in the brain and cerebellum of, for instance, a skilled pianist are the results of his will over many years to acquire the skill.

We must not forget in this context that there is a converse, equally consistent with the facts, for the theory, called epiphenomenalism, that mental states are related to the brain much as the halo is to the saint, that is, as effects but never themselves as causes. The converse theory, which might be called hypophenomenalism, and which is pretty well that of Schopenhauer, is that the instruments which the various mechanisms of the body constitute are the objective products of obscure cravings for the corresponding powers; and, in particular, that the organization of the nervous system is the effect and material isomorph of the variety of mental functions exercised at a given level of animal or human existence. . . .

Suggestions
for Further Reading

Anthologies

Anderson, Alan Ross (ed.). *Minds and Machines.* Englewood Cliffs, N.J.: Prentice-Hall, 1964. A collection of interesting contemporary articles on the question of whether men are machines. The articles are difficult but worthwhile reading.

Flew, Anthony (ed.). *Body, Mind, and Death.* New York: Macmillan, 1966. Some important articles on the mind-body problem from Plato to the present day. The introduction and annotated bibliography are excellent.

Laslett, Peter (ed.). *The Physical Basis of the Mind.* Oxford: Basil Blackwell, 1951. A series of eight radio broadcasts given by British scientists and philosophers. The talks are very clear and interesting.

Individual Works

Adler, Mortimer. *The Difference of Man and the Difference It Makes.* Cleveland: The World Publishing Company, 1967. The relation of the problem of the existence of mind to the issue of how men differ from animals. There is also a good discussion of whether men differ essentially from computing machines.

Beloff, John. *The Existence of Mind.* New York: The Citadel Press, 1964. An examination of the arguments for and against dualism.

Ducasse, C. J. *Nature, Mind, and Death.* LaSalle, Ill.: Open Ct., 1951. A good discussion of the mind-body problem and its relation to the question of immortality.

Hospers, John. *An Introduction to Philosophical Analysis,* 2nd ed. Englewood Cliffs, N.J.: Prentice-Hall, 1967. Chapter 20 contains a very lucid statement of the main arguments and positions.

Lamont, Corliss. *The Illusion of Immortality,* 2nd ed. London: C. A. Watts, 1952. An attack on the belief in immortality. The book is clearly written but the arguments are not very rigorous.

Taylor, Richard. *Metaphysics.* Englewood Cliffs, N.J.: Prentice-Hall, 1963. A very clear analysis of the opposing views and a rejection of dualism.

Encyclopedia of Philosophy. Paul Edwards, editor-in-chief. New York: Macmillan, 1967. The student will find many worthwhile articles on the subject treated in this Part, and excellent bibliographies.

Five:
Knowledge
and Science

Introduction

All men want knowledge, admire it, even revere it. Platitudinous as this statement may appear, it is certainly ambiguous. No doubt this accounts for the fact that so many people think the statement true. For knowledge as something sought, as a value, suggests two quite different things: (1) knowledge as a good or end-in-itself independent of any use to which it may be put; (2) knowledge as a means necessary for the securing of some other value. We call men who dedicate themselves to the disinterested pursuit of knowledge, to the free play of ideas, "intellectuals," "theoreticians." In this sense, philosophers traditionally have seen themselves and have been seen by others as super-intellectuals, as the theoretician's theoretician. Historical legend has it that the first philosopher known to us, Thales of Miletus in Asia Minor (circa 585 B.C.), afflicted with the reproaches of his fellow citizens that he was a man of knowledge but also a poor man (and so what worth did knowledge have?), used his knowledge of nature to predict that the next crop of olives would be a bumper one. Keeping the practical results of his knowledge to himself, as would become a hard-headed businessman, Thales then bought up all of the olive presses in the region, thereby securing a monopoly. When the unusually abundant harvest of olives duly took place, Thales rented out his olive presses at a high price and so made a large amount of money by cornering the market. Philosophers could make money if they wanted to do so, he reportedly declared, but willingly were poor because they valued knowledge above everything else, even wealth. No doubt Thales would never enroll in a business school; however, if he did, he would earn all A's.

Socrates refused to accept money for his teaching, not wishing to be financially dependent on anyone. (No wonder he scorned politicians.) Socrates distrusted wealth; for of what use is wealth but to stimulate and delight the senses, so sapping one's rational energies and distracting one's reason from the pursuit of truth. Refusing to stop asking questions as the price of life and freedom, condemned to death, drinking the hemlock, dying, Socrates has become a symbol of the fearless and unrelenting search for knowledge in spite of the opposition of the ignorant majority. The god Apollo announced that Socrates was the wisest man in Greece. Aristotle, the most influential philosopher in the Western world and the first great biologist, conceived man's highest destiny, because man is the only animal possessing reason, to be the full and unimpeded functioning of that reason, sheer knowing for its own sake. In knowing, man comes closest to being a

313

god. If there are gods, knowing would be the only activity compatible with their exalted status. Practical activities, such as healing broken legs or multiplying loaves and fishes, would be beneath divine dignity. In the seventeenth century, the philosopher Spinoza equated God and Nature. In the glow of his own "intellectual love of God," Spinoza revealed how knowing the unchanging truth for its own sake can elicit all of the traditional religious emotions of devotion to what is greater and worthier than one's self and how knowing for its own sake can satisfy the old religious yearning for triumph over devouring time and for unshakeable peace. The pursuit of knowledge as the ultimate Good thus emits cosmic, religious echoes. The devotees of knowing for its own sake have moved with a priestly mien whether they wore the toga or the white laboratory coat of the modern scientist. In our day, Albert Einstein is the symbol of the philosopher-scientist, the pure Knower, the inspired theoretician—Einstein, with the massive brow, the lined face, the flowing white hair suggesting a symphony conductor or other artist, and the luminous eyes through which the universe gazes into you.

Nevertheless, the pursuit of knowledge for its own sake evokes the supreme allegiance of only a small minority of Americans and people in other countries. The great majority values knowledge as technique, as know-how, as a necessary means to other more important values, such as excitement and amusement. A little over a century ago, a Jewish prophet, who had read Greek and German philosophy, wrote that until his day philosophers had been content to understand the world but that the real task was to change the world. Most Americans and all thoroughly modern people of other countries agree in this with Marx. The great majority of contemporary men and women prize knowledge as power, science as technology, as a kind of magic that works, a cornucopia pouring forth an unending and swelling stream of wealth with its attendant power and luxury. A small minority of intellectuals excepted, most contemporaries know very well what they want—wealth, power, luxury. For them, the problem concerns means: how to produce wealth, power, luxury, and all things dependent on them ever more abundantly. If the cost of that production means a polluted environment, chemically fouled lakes and streams, dying wildlife, and degraded human life, so far we have been willing to pay that cost. And should that cost become exorbitant, even deadly, we are sustained by the faith that the cure for the ills of technology is a bigger and better technology.

Only because science has shown itself so fecund in producing these goods and in progressively eliminating undesirable side effects has it been allowed to develop to its present level. For science, particularly on its theoretical side as a pursuit of knowledge for its own sake, was and is one of the most subversive agents ever invented by man. It is no coincidence that controversy whirls around the figures of Copernicus, Galileo, Darwin, Einstein, and Freud like black clouds rumbling with thunder and flashing with lightning. They symbolize the disturbing fact that science constantly shows us that the world and man really are quite different from what most people thought they were. Hence for most people the value of knowing for its own sake must be subordinated to other values. Millions of Americans drive automobiles and at the same time reject the proposition that man is a mammal. The pursuit of knowledge is splendid but such an enterprise must be compatible with national security. Of course we must hold all of our theories tentatively, but we know that any average American is superior in every way to any foreigner.

No, the great majority of men and women tolerate science, admire it, or revere it only to the degree and extent science is a necessary means to various desired nonscientific ends. When science fails to provide the necessary means, people turn to kinds of "knowledge" other than the scientific. Does scientific psychology look dubiously upon extrasensory perception, does it cast doubt on the claim those messages really came from beloved Uncle Max dead these many years? Then, scientific psychology is dogmatic, materialistic, too narrow, at best merely partial knowledge. Astronomy won't tell us if we will be lucky or unlucky today? Then astrology will. Does science seem to make it difficult to believe God exists? Then our hearts inform us He does exist. Does science fail to prove convincingly that we should all love one another and stop hating? Then mystical insight will.

This ambiguity of knowledge as an end for its own sake and as a means to realizing other values provides the humus out of which philosophical reflection on knowledge and science grows. Hence, philosophers study and discuss what they technically call *epistemology:* the investigation of the origin, nature, methods, and limits of knowledge. Philosophers wonder about and often answer such questions as: What is the nature of knowledge? What criteria distinguish genuine knowledge from the spurious article? Does all knowledge come from sense experience, or can our reason know that certain propositions must be true independently of sense experience? What is science? What is the scientific method? Is there *a* scientific method? Is all knowledge worthy of the name produced by science and science alone? Is there anything science cannot find out? More radically, can we know anything at all or is it all merely a matter of shifting opinions, what we call "knowledge" being merely those illusions, or perhaps even delusions, agreed upon?

Obviously, there is no point in trying to find out something unless we doubt we know everything. Socrates claimed to know only that he did not know. Such doubting of the truth of what is claimed to be known, called *skepticism* in philosophy, can be made systematic and pushed further than

Socrates did. Some philosophers have universalized skepticism to include everything, maintaining that nothing exists; or that, if anything did exist, it cannot be known; or that, if anything can be known, it cannot be communicated. In order to be called a philosophy, skepticism must be defended with arguments. For example, consider the claim that we can never learn anything new. This conclusion follows from the proposition that we cannot find something unless we first know what we are looking for. Unless we know what we are seeking, we won't know when we have found it. Therefore, we only can find out what we already know, or we can never learn what we don't know. It is not recommended that students use this argument in answering examination questions. Add to the argument the observation that all men are born ignorant, and you generate the conclusion that no one can ever learn anything. You say you have learned many things? Then refute the argument of the skeptic, or admit that you have been deceived in thinking you've learned many things. The thoroughgoing skeptic argues that we never can be sure any proposition is true because first we must have reliable criteria to distinguish truth from falsity. But how do we know we can rely on the criteria? First, the criteria must be justified. But how do we know we can rely on the justification of the criteria? First, the justification must be justified. And, before that, we must justify the justification of the justification. An infinite regress is generated—that is, no criteria separating truth from falsehood can ever be justified. There are many variations of this kind of argument. Our senses deceive us. Therefore, we appeal to our reason to tell us when our senses are or are not deceiving us. But first we must know whether or not our reason is deceiving us; and so the infinite regress opens before us. Again, some maintain we should only accept as true those propositions confirmed by observation. But why should we accept the principle that we should only accept as true those propositions confirmed by observation? And then why accept the additional principles used to justify that principle? And so on and on and on.

At first one might suppose naïvely that he could find refuge from the skeptic in Divine revelation, mystical insight, or visions induced by LSD and other drugs. However, many of the revelations, insights, and visions contradict one another, to say nothing of common sense and science; and so the question of truth and falsity cannot be evaded permanently. Therefore, the skeptic patiently waits for our inevitable return.

And yet does there not remain one great practical and theoretical refutation of a universal skepticism? That is, does not the great body of modern science and its successful application nearly everywhere in contemporary life clearly prove that we can distinguish truth from falsehood, can know, and can learn? In the steady light of science, the arguments of the skeptic seem to fade into mere verbal ingenuity, into sleight of hand with language. Indeed, the skeptical arguments, compared with the achievements of science, do not seem worth the trouble needed to expose clearly their logical fallacies. On the contrary, they can simply be dismissed as philosophical curiosities. Or can they?

In the first reading in this Part, Bertrand Russell seeks to prove that skepticism finds renewed vigor and sustenance in the very citadel of science, its supposed conqueror. One of the greatest of recent philosophers, Russell throughout a long life sought knowledge for its own sake; he yearned for the Truth, Certainty. But Russell finds that science fails to supply the indubitable truth he seeks. All science ultimately rests on sense perception, on what we see, hear, smell, taste. All sense perception is a matter of cause and effect. All causes differ from their effects because otherwise all causes would be identical with their effects. Whatever we perceive (colors, sounds, smells, and so on) is an effect. Therefore, we never perceive causes. All causes are postulates, entities inferred by inductive reasoning. But in inductive reasoning (i.e., any attempt to infer a conclusion on the basis of what we perceive), the evidence is never sufficient to prove the conclusion true beyond any doubt. The conclusion of an inductive argument always *may* be false. We can never be sure which scientific theories, if any, are true. Consequently, science does not vanquish skepticism, after all. The common, everyday world we perceive—the world of blue sky, green grass and trees, houses, substantial people, beautiful sunsets—turns out to be a literal illusion whose cause we never can be sure we know. Modern science agrees with Shakespeare's mellow skeptic, Prospero, in *The Tempest:* "We are such stuff as dreams are made on. . . ."

René Descartes, like Bertrand Russell, sought intellectual certainty. To know something is to be unable to doubt its truth. Hence, Descartes searches for a proposition he cannot doubt. If he can discover such a proposition, he can then examine it to learn what characteristics it possesses that make it impervious to any doubt. These characteristics will provide the criteria of certainty. Once we know these criteria of certainty, we can sort out all propositions that satisfy these criteria of certainty from those that do not. Descartes discovers he cannot, in the very act of doubting, doubt the proposition that he is doubting. Since doubting is a kind of thinking, Descartes declares: I think, therefore I am (*Cogito ergo sum.*). Why can't he doubt this? Because it is so clear and distinct to his reason. Clearness and distinctness to one's reason are the criteria of certainty. Descartes soon finds other propositions perfectly clear and distinct, such as: every event has a cause; no cause can be less perfect than its effect; and others. Mathematics, above all, is clear and distinct to our reason. Therefore, mathematical physics must be true. Whatever cannot be treated by mathematical physics must be relegated to the province of faith and subjective opinion. Notice that Descartes' criteria of certainty are clearness and distinctness to reason, not to sense perception. Descartes illustrates a form of philosophical *rationalism* that holds there are some propositions our reason can know to be true independently of sense experience. Given our supply of propositions known to be true, we can then logically deduce still other propositions that must be true until all of human knowledge stands complete in one vast deductive system. Only in this way can the threat of universal skepticism be overcome successfully, the rationalist claims.

The issue is now focused sharply. Are there at least some propositions our reason can know to be true independently of sense experience? The *rationalist* maintains that there are. The *empiricist* denies that there are any such propositions. Arthur E. Murphy defends empiricism by trying to show that sense experience does give us genuine knowledge of the world and ourselves without ultimately succumbing to universal skepticism. The empiricist asks us to surrender absolute certainty as a characteristic of knowledge because it is an impossible and unnecessary ideal. We can make predictions more likely to be fulfilled than one would expect on the basis of chance or intelligent guessing. This is all that is necessary to enable us to do what we desire or to show our desires to be fatuous.

The readings by T. H. Huxley, a biologist and one of the greatest popularizers of science and of the scientific ethos, and Irving M. Copi, an outstanding contemporary logician, provide the student with a clear and authoritative account of the fundamental pattern of that process of inquiry broadly called "scientific" or the "scientific method," which has proven so successful. These selections should help the student to evaluate critically the philosophical positions of *skepticism, rationalism,* and *empiricism* and to clarify and, perhaps in his own mind, to resolve the contemporary issues of the existence or nonexistence of extrasensory perception and of the possibility or impossibility of our creating a society both scientific and humane. The process of scientific inquiry as sketched by Huxley and Copi contains elements of *skepticism, rationalism,* and *empiricism* combined in a working association. A number of questions immediately arise. What elements are retained in this working association and what ones rejected? Is this working association an intellectually durable one, or is it merely a temporary compromise doomed to break apart once the respective implications of *skepticism, rationalism,* and *empiricism* are thoroughly thought out?

The two selections concerning the existence or nonexistence of ESP, whether or not it is possible for some people to communicate by extrasensory perception, provide examples of scientific treatment of a question arousing passionate—in some, even religious—interest. After years of patiently testing the hypothesis of the existence of extrasensory perception, neither dogmatically affirming it nor dogmatically denying it, James C. Crumbaugh has reached a skeptical conclusion of suspension of judgment as a scientist. The experimental results remain too ambiguous and inconclusive. While refuting a number of common objections to the truth of the ESP hypothesis, he finds that parapsychologists so far have failed to meet adequately one criticism: they have not fulfilled the crucial scientific demand for a genuinely repeatable experiment. Any evidence supporting or opposing the existence of extrasensory perception remains unconvincing to Crumbaugh until parapsychologists can devise an experiment that can be repeated again and again by all competent investigators. This position is not due to any prejudice against the reality of ESP on Crumbaugh's part. Indeed, he remarks that he strongly suspects that extrasensory phenomena exist. And for him suspicion quickly gives birth to speculation. Perhaps parapsychological phenomena belong to religion, being by their very nature unsuitable for scientific investigation but rather matters of faith and intuition. However, whether the question of the reality of ESP is capable of being answered by science or not, it must be answered. For on that answer, Crumbaugh feels, depends our conception of the nature of the universe, man, and ultimate human destiny.

C. E. M. Hansel radiates that tough, empirical, no dreamy nonsense aura popularly associated with the experimental scientist. Clearly he will have nothing to do with being unable to know as a justification for faith, for belief. Hansel argues that fraud could account for the positive results of parapsychological experiments. He does not claim to have proven that deception produced evidence appearing to support ESP. It is a possibility, an alternative hypothesis. But as long as it remains, no experimental evidence can be considered as proving conclusively the existence of extrasensory perception. As long as fraud remains an alternative hypothesis, extrasensory perception remains a hypothesis and not a fact.

Today science is not an activity carried on by a few lonely investigators in spite of either total indifference or sporadic persecution on the part of the majority of mankind. On the contrary, it has become a vast collective enterprise directly involving many highly trained people and costing enormous sums of money. Nor is science an activity confined to the academic classroom or the industrial laboratory. As technology, as know-how, as expertise, it sends out rhizomes penetrating all areas of human society. Science has become a social, moral, legal, aesthetic, theological concern for the general populace rather than, as it was in the past, an object of interest to a few professional scientists and a fringe of intellectuals. So revolutionary, so recent, so far-reaching has been technology and so unprepared has been society to assimilate it wisely that to many it seems a threatening monster still best symbolized by Dr. Frankenstein and his abortive creation, which finally destroyed its creator. Erich Fromm, in the selection entitled "The Threat of Scientific Technology," gives expression to this alarm and dread. As technology comes to dominate contemporary society, Fromm sees it exerting a dehumanizing and ultimately disastrous effect on man, squeezing him into an alienated, anxiety-ridden, passive consumer. Superficially, technological man seems rational; on closer examination Fromm diagnoses his rationalism as that of a madman. Fromm is not opposed to all science; he does not bawl for an impossible moratorium on science. Rather, he attacks making technical progress the highest value for which men are willing to sacrifice all other values. This perversion of values must be healed. Scientific certainty has taken the place of religious certainty. Men who are certain soon become fanatical, cruel, destructive. As religious certainty once led men to burn harmless old women as witches, today scientific certainty threatens to lead men to destroy all humanity in a nuclear holocaust. The only way to escape catastrophe is through a willingness on the part of individuals to make their own decisions and assume responsibility for them. To achieve this change in human attitude, Fromm calls for a return to the humanistic religion of the Old Testament prophets and the adoption of a "true scientific rationality," which presents all the alternatives but leaves the decision to man instead of usurping it from him.

Emmanuel G. Mesthene, Director of the Harvard University Program on Technology and Society, views our age as a new and unprecedented one, in which we must think and act in new and unprecedented ways. We constitute the first generation who hope realistically to break the tyranny of physical nature over man. The promise of technology is that there is nothing we cannot do. We can be really "free, free at last" and yet we hang back, vacillating between hope and despair. Why? Because we have never enjoyed such freedom, such godlike power; the unknown puzzles and appalls us. As Mesthene describes the situation, we resemble the prisoner who, after so many years of incarceration he no longer is able to imagine any other kind of life, suddenly finds himself freed. We lack only the will to seize our opportunities. We must exercise the courage of our dreams, conquering the doubts and fears born of a pretechnological age. The real Savior finally has come and his name is Technology.

The Nature of Knowledge

Skepticism

Philosophic Doubts   Bertrand Russell

... Philosophy arises from an unusually obstinate attempt to arrive at real knowledge. What passes for knowledge in ordinary life suffers from three defects: it is cocksure, vague, and self-contradictory. The first step towards philosophy consists in becoming aware of these defects, not in order to rest content with a lazy scepticism, but in order to substitute an amended kind of knowledge which shall be tentative, precise, and self-consistent. There is of course another quality which we wish our knowledge to possess, namely, comprehensiveness: we wish the area of our knowledge to be as wide as possible. But this is the business of science rather than philosophy. A man does not necessarily become a better philosopher through knowing more scientific facts; it is principles and methods and general conceptions that he should learn from science if philosophy is what interests him. ...

I mentioned a moment ago three defects in common beliefs, namely, that they are cocksure, vague, and self-contradictory. It is the business of philosophy to correct these defects so far as it can, without throwing over knowledge altogether. To be a good philosopher, a man must have a strong desire to know, combined with great caution in believing that he knows; he must also have logical acumen and the habit of exact thinking. All these, of course, are a matter of degree. Vagueness, in particular, belongs, in some degree, to all human thinking; we can diminish it indefinitely, but we can never abolish it wholly. Philosophy, accordingly, is a continuing activity, not something in which we can achieve final perfection once for all. In this respect, philosophy has suffered from its association with theology. Theological dogmas are fixed, and are regarded by the orthodox as incapable of improvement. Philosophers have too often tried to produce similarly final systems: they have not been content with the gradual approximations that satisfied men of science. In this they seem to me to have been mistaken. Philosophy should be piecemeal and provisional like science; final truth belongs to heaven, not to this world.

The three defects which I have mentioned are interconnected, and by becoming aware of any one we may be led to recognise the other two. I will illustrate all three by a few examples.

Let us take first the belief in common objects, such as tables and

From *An Outline of Philosophy* by Bertrand Russell. Reprinted by permission of George Allen & Unwin Ltd., London, 1927.

321

chairs and trees. We all feel quite sure about these in ordinary life, and yet our reasons for confidence are really very inadequate. Naïve common sense supposes that they are what they appear to be, but that is impossible, since they do not appear exactly alike to any two simultaneous observers; at least, it is impossible if the object is a single thing, the same for all observers. If we are going to admit that the object is not what we see, we can no longer feel the same assurance that there is an object; this is the first intrusion of doubt. However, we shall speedily recover from this set-back, and say that of course the object is "really" what physics says it is. Now physics says that a table or a chair is "really" an incredibly vast system of electrons and protons in rapid motion, with empty space in between. This is all very well. But the physicist, like the ordinary man, is dependent upon his senses for the existence of the physical world. If you go up to him solemnly and say, "Would you be so kind as to tell me, as a physicist, what a chair really is?" you will get a learned answer. But if you say, without preamble, "Is there a chair there?" he will say, "Of course there is; can't you see it?" To this you ought to reply in the negative. You ought to say, "No, I see certain patches of colour, but I don't see any electrons or protons, and you tell me that they are what a chair consists of". He may reply: "Yes, but a large number of electrons and protons close together look like a patch of colour". "What do you mean by 'look like'?" you will then ask. He is ready with an answer. He means that light-waves start from the electrons and protons (or, more probably, are reflected by them from a source of light), reach the eye, have a series of effects upon the rods and cones, the optic nerve, and the brain, and finally produce a sensation. But he has never seen an eye or an optic nerve or a brain, any more than he has seen a chair: he has only seen patches of colour which, he says, are what eyes "look like". That is to say, he thinks that the sensation you have when (as you think) you see a chair, has a series of causes, physical and psychological, but all of them, on his own showing, lie essentially and forever outside experience. Nevertheless, he pretends to base his science upon observation. Obviously there is here a problem for the logician, a problem belonging not to physics, but to quite another kind of study. This is a first example of the way in which the pursuit of precision destroys certainty.

The physicist believes that he infers his electrons and protons from what he perceives. But the inference is never clearly set forth in a logical chain, and, if it were, it might not look sufficiently plausible to warrant much confidence. In actual fact, the whole development from common-sense objects to electrons and protons has been governed by certain beliefs, seldom conscious, but existing in every natural man. These beliefs are not unalterable, but they grow and develop like a tree. We start by thinking that a chair is as it appears to be, and is still there when we are not looking. But we find, by a little reflection, that these two beliefs are incompatible. If the chair is to persist independently of being seen by us, it must be something other than the patch of colour we see, because this is found to depend upon conditions extraneous to the chair, such as how the light falls, whether we are wearing blue spectacles, and so on. This forces the man of science to regard the "real" chair as the cause (or an indispensable part of the cause) of our sensations when we see the chair. Thus we are committed to causation as an *a priori* belief without which we should have no reason for supposing that there is a "real" chair at all. Also, for the sake of permanence we bring in the notion of substance: the "real" chair is a substance, or collection of substances, possessed of permanence and the power to cause sensations. This metaphysical belief has operated, more or less unconsciously, in the inference from sensations to electrons and protons. The philosopher must drag such beliefs into the light of day, and see whether they still survive. Often it will be found that they die on exposure.

Let us now take up another point. The evidence for a physical law, or for any scientific law, always involves both memory and testimony. We have to rely both upon what we remember to have observed on former occasions, and on what others say they have observed. In the very beginnings of science, it may have been possible sometimes to dispense with testimony; but very soon every scientific investigation began to be built upon previously ascertained results, and thus to depend upon what others had recorded. In fact, without the corroboration of testimony we should hardly have had much confidence in the existence of physical objects. Sometimes people suffer from hallucinations, that is to say, they think they perceive physical objects, but are not confirmed in this belief by the testimony of others. In such cases, we decide that they are mistaken. It is the similarity between the perceptions of different people in similar situations that makes us feel confident of the external causation of our perceptions; but for this, whatever naïve beliefs we might have had in physical objects would have been dissipated long ago. Thus memory and testimony are essential to science. Nevertheless, each of these is open to criticism by the sceptic. Even if we succeed, more or less, in meeting his criticism, we shall, if we are rational, be left with a less complete confidence in our original beliefs than we had before. Once more, we shall become less cocksure as we become more accurate.

Both memory and testimony lead us into the sphere of psychology. I shall not at this stage discuss either beyond the point at which it is clear that there are genuine philosophical problems to be solved. I shall begin with memory.

Memory is a word which has a variety of meanings. The kind that I am concerned with at the moment is the recollection of past occurrences. This is so notoriously fallible that every experimenter makes a record of the result of his experiment at the earliest possible moment: he considers the inference from written words to past events less likely to be mistaken than the direct beliefs which constitute memory. But some time, though perhaps only a few seconds, must elapse between the observation and the making of the record, unless the record is so fragmentary that memory is needed to interpret it. Thus we do not escape from the need of trusting memory to some degree. Moreover, without memory we should not think of interpreting records as applying to the past, because we should not know that there was any past. Now, apart from arguments as to the proved fallibility of memory, there is one awkward consideration which the sceptic may urge. Remembering, which occurs now, cannot possibly—he may say—prove that what is remembered occurred at some other time, because the world might have sprung into being five minutes ago, exactly as it then was, full of acts of remembering which were entirely misleading. Opponents of Darwin, such as Edmund Gosse's father, urged a very similar argument against evolution. The world, they said, was created in 4004 B.C., complete with fossils, which were inserted to try our faith. The world was created suddenly, but was made such as it would have been if it had evolved. There is no logical impossibility about this view. And similarly there is no logical impossibility in the view that the world was created five minutes ago, complete with memories and records. This may seem an improbable hypothesis, but it is not logically refutable.

Apart from this argument, which may be thought fantastic, there are reasons of detail for being more or less distrustful of memory. It is obvious that no *direct* confirmation of a belief about a past occurrence is possible, because we cannot make the past recur. We can find confirmation of an indirect kind in the revelations of others and in contemporary records. The latter, as we have seen, involve some degree of memory, but they may involve very little, for instance when a shorthand report of a conversation or speech has been made at the time. But even then, we do not escape wholly from the need of memory extending over a longer stretch of time. Suppose a wholly imaginary conversation were produced for some criminal purpose, we should depend upon the memories of witnesses to establish its fictitious character in a law-court. And all memory which extends over a long period of time is very apt to be mistaken; this is shown by the errors invariably found in autobiographies. Any man who comes across letters which he wrote many years ago can verify the manner in which his memory has falsified past events. For these reasons, the fact that we cannot free ourselves from dependence upon memory in building up knowledge is, *prima facie,* a reason for regarding what passes for knowledge as not quite certain. . . .

Testimony raises even more awkward problems. What makes them so awkward is the fact that testimony is involved in building up our knowledge of physics, and that, conversely, physics is required in establishing the trustworthiness of testimony. Moreover, testimony raises all the problems connected with the relation of mind and matter. Some eminent philosophers, *e.g.* Leibniz, have constructed systems according to which there would be no such thing as testimony, and yet have accepted as true many things which cannot be known without it. I do not think philosophy has quite done justice to this problem, but a few words will, I think, show its gravity.

For our purposes, we may define testimony as noises heard, or shapes seen, analogous to those which we should make if we wished to convey an assertion, and believed by the hearer or seer to be due to someone else's desire to convey an assertion. Let us take a concrete instance: I ask a policeman the way, and he says, "Fourth to the right, third to the left". That is to say, I hear these sounds, and perhaps I see what I interpret as his lips moving. I assume that he has a mind more or less like my own, and has uttered these sounds with the same intention as I should have had if I had uttered them, namely to convey information. In ordinary life, all this is not, in any proper sense, an inference; it is a belief which arises in us on the appropriate occasion. But if we are challenged, we have to substitute inference for spontaneous belief, and the more the inference is examined the more shaky it looks.

The inference that has to be made has two steps, one physical and one psychological. The physical inference is of the sort we considered a moment ago, in which we pass from a sensation to a physical occurrence. We hear noises, and think they proceed from the policeman's body. We see moving shapes, and interpret them as physical motions of his lips. This inference, as we saw earlier, is in part justified by testimony; yet now we find that it has to be made before we can have reason to believe that there is any such thing as testimony. And this inference is certainly sometimes mistaken. Lunatics hear voices which other people do not hear; instead of crediting them with abnormally acute hearing, we lock them up. But if we sometimes hear sentences which have not proceeded from a body, why should this not always be the case? Perhaps our imagination has conjured up all the things that we think others have said to us. But this is part of the general problem of inferring physical objects from sensations, which, difficult as it is, is not the most difficult part of the logical puzzles concerning testimony. The most difficult part is the inference from the policeman's body to his mind. I do not mean any special insult to policemen; I would say the same of politicians and even of philosophers.

The inference to the policeman's mind certainly *may* be wrong. It is clear that a maker of waxworks could make a life-like policeman and put a gramophone inside him, which would cause him periodically to tell visitors the way to the most interesting part of the exhibition at the entrance to which he would stand. They would have just the sort of evidence of his being alive that is found convincing in the case of other policemen. Descartes believed that animals have no minds, but are merely complicated automata. Eighteenth-century materialists extended this doctrine to men. But I am not now concerned with materialism; my problem is a different one. Even a materialist must admit that, when he talks, he means to convey something, that is to say, he uses words as signs, not as mere noises. It may be difficult to decide exactly what is meant by this statement, but it is clear that it means something, and that it is true of one's own remarks. The question is: Are we sure that it is true of the remarks we hear, as well as of those we make? Or are the remarks we hear perhaps just like other noises, merely meaningless disturbances of the air? The chief argument against this is analogy: the remarks we hear are so like those we make that we think they must have similar causes. But although we cannot dispense with analogy as a form of inference, it is by no means demonstrative, and not infrequently leads us astray. We are therefore left, once more, with a *prima facie* reason for uncertainty and doubt.

This question of what we mean ourselves when we speak brings me to another problem, that of introspection. Many philosophers have held that introspection gave the most indubitable of all knowledge; others have held that there is no such thing as introspection. Descartes, after trying to doubt everything, arrived at "I think, therefore I am", as a basis for the rest of knowledge. Dr. John B. Watson the behaviourist holds, on the contrary, that we do not think, but only talk. Dr. Watson, in real life, gives as much evidence of thinking as anyone does, so, if *he* is not convinced that he thinks, we are all in a bad way. At any rate, the mere existence of such an opinion as his, on the part of a competent philosopher, must suffice to show that introspection is not so certain as some people have thought. But let us examine this question a little more closely.

The difference between introspection and what we call perception of external objects seems to me to be connected, not with what is primary in our knowledge, but with what is inferred. We think, at one time, that we are seeing a chair; at another, that we are thinking about philosophy. The first we call perception of an external object; the second we call introspection. Now we have already found reason to doubt external perception, in the full-blooded sense in which common sense accepts it. . . . [W]hat is indubitable in "seeing a chair" is the occurrence of a certain pattern of colours. But this occurrence, we shall find, is connected with me just as much as with the chair; no one except myself can see exactly the pattern that I see. There is thus something subjective and private about what we take to be external perception, but this is concealed by precarious extensions into the physical world. I think introspection, on the contrary, involves precarious extensions into the mental world: shorn of these, it is not very different from external perception shorn of its extensions. To make this clear, I shall try to show what we know to be occurring when, as we say, we think about philosophy.

Suppose, as the result of introspection, you arrive at a belief which you express in the words: "I am now believing that mind is different from matter". What do you know, apart from inferences, in such a case? First of all, you must cut out the word "I": the person who believes is an inference, not part of what you know immediately. In the second place, you must be careful about the word "believing". I am not now concerned with what this word should mean in logic or theory of knowledge; I am concerned with what it can mean when used to describe a direct experience. In such a case, it would seem that it can only describe a certain kind of feeling. And as for the proposition you think you are believing, namely, "mind is different from matter", it is very difficult to say what is really occurring when you think you believe it. It may be mere words, pronounced, visualised, or in auditory or motor images. It may be images of what the words "mean", but in that case it will not be at all an accurate representation of the logical content of the proposition. You may have an image of a statue of Newton "voyaging through strange seas of thought alone", and another image of a stone rolling downhill, combined with the words "how different!" Or you may think of the difference between composing a lecture and eating your dinner. It is only when you come to expressing your thought in words that you approach logical precision.

Both in introspection and in external perception, we try to express what we know in WORDS.

We come here, as in the question of testimony, upon the social aspect of knowledge. The purpose of words is to give the same kind of publicity to thought as is claimed for physical objects. A number of people can hear a spoken word or see a written word, because each is a physical occurrence. If I say to you, "mind is different from matter", there may be only a very slight resemblance between the thought that I am trying to express and the thought which is aroused in you, but these two thoughts have just this in common, that they can be expressed by the same words. Similarly, there may be great differences between what you and I see when, as we say, we look at the same chair; nevertheless we can both express our perceptions by the same words.

A thought and a perception are thus not so very different in their own nature. If physics is true, they are different in their correlations: when I see a chair, others have more or less similar perceptions, and it is thought that these are all connected with light-waves coming from the chair, whereas, when I think a thought, others may not be thinking anything similar. But this applies also to feeling a toothache, which would not usually be regarded as a case of introspection. On the whole, therefore, there seems no reason to regard introspection as a different *kind* of knowledge from external perception. . . .

As for the *trustworthiness* of introspection, there is again a complete parallelism with the case of external perception. The actual datum, in each case, is unimpeachable, but the extensions which we make instinctively are questionable. Instead of saying, "I am believing that mind is different from matter", you ought to say, "certain images are occurring in a certain relation to each other, accompanied by a certain feeling". No words exist for describing the actual occurrence in all its particularity; all words, even proper names, are general, with the possible exception of "this", which is ambiguous. When you translate the occurrence into words, you are making generalisations and inferences, just as you are when you say "there is a chair". There is really no vital difference between the two cases. In each case, what is really a datum is unutterable, and what can be put into words involves inferences which may be mistaken.

When I say that "inferences" are involved, I am saying something not quite accurate unless carefully interpreted. In "seeing a chair", for instance, we do not first apprehend a coloured pattern, and then proceed to infer a chair: belief in the chair arises spontaneously when we see the coloured pattern. But this belief has causes not only in the present physical stimulus, but also partly in past experience, partly in reflexes. In animals, reflexes play a very large part; in human beings, experience is more important. The infant learns slowly to correlate touch and sight, and to expect others to see what he sees. The habits which are thus formed are essential to our adult notion of an object such as a chair. The perception of a chair by means of sight has a physical stimulus which affects only sight directly, but stimulates ideas of solidity and so on through early experience. The inference might be called "physiological". An inference of this sort is evidence of past correlations, for instance between touch and sight, but may be mistaken in the present instance; you may, for example, mistake a reflection in a large mirror for another room.

Similarly in dreams we make mistaken physiological inferences. We cannot therefore feel certainty in regard to things which are in this sense inferred, because, when we try to accept as many of them as possible, we are nevertheless compelled to reject some for the sake of self-consistency.

We arrived a moment ago at what we called "physiological inference" as an essential ingredient in the common-sense notion of a physical object. Physiological inference, in its simplest form, means this: given a stimulus S, to which, by a reflex, we react by a bodily movement R, and a stimulus S′ with a reaction R′, if the two stimuli are frequently experienced together, S will in time produce R′.[1] That is to say, the body will act as if S′ were present. Physiological inference is important in theory of knowledge, . . . I have mentioned it partly to prevent it from being confused with logical inference, and partly in order to introduce the problem of *induction*, . . .

Induction raises perhaps the most difficult problem in the whole theory of knowledge. Every scientific law is established by its means, and yet it is difficult to see why we should believe it to be a valid logical process. Induction, in its bare essence, consists of the argument that, because A and B have been often found together and never found apart, therefore, when A is found again, B will probably also be found. This exists first as a "physiological inference", and as such is practised by animals. When we first begin to reflect, we find ourselves making inductions in the physiological sense, for instance, expecting the food we see to have a certain kind of taste. Often we only become aware of this expectation through having it disappointed, for instance if we take salt thinking it is sugar. When mankind took to science, they tried to formulate logical principles justifying this kind of inference. . . . [T]hey seem to me very unsuccessful. I am convinced that induction must have validity of some kind in some degree, but the problem of showing how or why it can be valid remains unsolved. Until it is solved, the rational man will doubt whether his food will nourish him, and whether the sun will rise tomorrow. I am not a rational man in this sense, but for the moment I shall pretend to be. And even if we cannot be completely rational, we should probably all be the better for becoming somewhat more rational than we are. At the lowest estimate, it will be an interesting adventure to see whither reason will lead us.

The problems we have been raising are none of them new, but they suffice to show that our everyday views of the world and of our relations to it are unsatisfactory. . . .

[1] *E.g.* if you hear a sharp noise and see a bright light simultaneously often, in time the noise without the light will cause your pupils to contract.

Rationalism

Meditations I and II René Descartes

René Descartes (1596–1650), inventor of analytic geometry and one of the greatest of French philosophers, has affected profoundly the problems, methods, and solutions of modern philosophy.

Meditation I

OF THE THINGS OF WHICH WE MAY DOUBT. Several years have now elapsed since I first became aware that I had accepted, even from my youth, many false opinions for true, and that consequently what I afterwards based on such principles was highly doubtful; and from that time I was convinced of the necessity of undertaking once in my life to rid myself of all the opinions I had adopted, and of commencing anew the work of building from the foundation, if I desired to establish a firm and abiding superstructure in the sciences. But as this enterprise appeared to me to be one of great magnitude, I waited until I had attained an age so mature as to leave me no hope that at any stage of life more advanced I should be better able to execute my design. On this account, I have delayed so long that I should henceforth consider I was doing wrong were I still to consume in deliberation any of the time that now remains for action. Today, then, since I have opportunely freed my mind from all cares, and am happily disturbed by no passions, and since I am in the secure possession of leisure in a peaceable retirement, I will at length apply myself earnestly and freely to the general overthrow of all my former opinions. But, to this end, it will not be necessary for me to show that the whole of these are false—a point, perhaps, which I shall never reach; but as even now my reason convinces me that I ought not the less carefully to withhold belief from what is not entirely certain and indubitable, than from what is manifestly false, it will be sufficient to justify the rejection of the whole if I shall find in each some ground for doubt. Nor for this purpose will it be necessary even to deal with each belief individually, which would be truly an endless labour; but, as the removal from below of the foundation necessarily involves the downfall of the whole edifice, I will at once approach the criticism of the principles on which all my former beliefs rested.

All that I have, up to this moment, accepted as possessed of the highest truth and certainty, I received either from or through the senses. I observed, however, that these sometimes misled us; and it is the part of prudence not to place absolute confidence in that by which we have even once been deceived.

From *The Meditations and Selections from the Principles of René Descartes,* translated by John Veitch, The Open Court Publishing Co., La Salle, Illinois, 1905.

But it may be said, perhaps, that, although the senses occasionally mislead us respecting minute objects, and such as are so far removed from us as to be beyond the reach of close observation, there are yet many other of their informations (presentations), of the truth of which it is manifestly impossible to doubt; as for example, that I am in this place, seated by the fire, clothed in a winter dressing-gown, that I hold in my hands this piece of paper, with other intimations of the same nature. But how could I deny that I possess these hands and this body, and withal escape being classed with persons in a state of insanity, whose brains are so disordered and clouded by dark bilious vapours as to cause them pertinaciously to assert that they are monarchs when they are in the greatest poverty; or clothed in gold and purple when destitute of any covering; or that their head is made of clay, their body of glass, or that they are gourds? I should certainly be not less insane than they, were I to regulate my procedure according to examples so extravagant.

Though this be true, I must nevertheless here consider that I am a man, and that, consequently, I am in the habit of sleeping, and representing to myself in dreams those same things, or even sometimes others less probable, which the insane think are presented to them in their waking moments. How often have I dreamt that I was in these familiar circumstances,—that I was dressed, and occupied this place by the fire, when I was lying undressed in bed? At the present moment, however, I certainly look upon this paper with eyes wide awake; the head which I now move is not asleep; I extend this hand consciously and with express purpose, and I perceive it; the occurrences in sleep are not so distinct as all this. But I cannot forget that, at other times, I have been deceived in sleep by similar illusions; and, attentively considering those cases, I perceive so clearly that there exist no certain marks by which the state of waking can ever be distinguished from sleep, that I feel greatly astonished; and in amazement I almost persuade myself that I am now dreaming.

Let us suppose, then, that we are dreaming, and that all these particulars—namely, the opening of the eyes, the motion of the head, the forth-putting of the hands—are merely illusions; and even that we really possess neither an entire body nor hands such as we see. Nevertheless, it must be admitted at least that the objects which appear to us in sleep are, as it were, painted representations which could not have been formed unless in the likeness of realities; and, therefore, that those general objects, at all events,—namely, eyes, a head, hands, and an entire body— are not simply imaginary, but really existent. For, in truth, painters themselves, even when they study to represent sirens and satyrs by forms the most fantastic and extraordinary, cannot bestow upon them natures absolutely new, but can only make a certain medley of the members of different animals; or if they chance to imagine something so novel that nothing at all similar has ever been seen before, and such as is, therefore, purely fictitious and absolutely false, it is at least certain that the colours of which this is composed are real.

And on the same principle, although these general objects, viz. a body, eyes, a head, hands, and the like, be imaginary, we are nevertheless absolutely necessitated to admit the reality at least of some other objects still more simple and universal than these, of which, just as of certain real colours, all those images of things, whether true and real, or false and fantastic, that are found in our consciousness, are formed.

To this class of objects seem to belong corporeal nature in general and its extension; the figure of extended things, their quantity or magnitude, and their number, as also the place in, and the time during, which they exist, and other things of the same sort. We will not, therefore, perhaps reason illegitimately if we conclude from this that Physics, Astronomy, Medicine, and all the other sciences that have for their end the consideration of composite objects, are indeed of a doubtful character; but that Arithmetic, Geometry, and the other sciences of the same class, which regard merely the simplest and most general objects, and scarcely inquire whether or not these are really existent, contain somewhat that is certain and indubitable; for whether I am awake or dreaming, it remains true that two and three makes five, and that a square has but four sides; nor does it seem possible that truths so apparent can ever fall under a suspicion of falsity or incertitude.

Nevertheless, the belief that there is a God who is all-powerful, and who created me, such as I am, has, for a long time, obtained steady possession of my mind. How, then, do I know that he has not arranged that there should be neither earth, nor sky, nor any extended thing, nor figure, nor magnitude, nor place, providing at the same time, however, for the rise in me of the perceptions of all these objects, and the persuasion that these do not exist otherwise than as I perceive them? And further, as I sometimes think that others are in error respecting matters of which they believe themselves to possess a perfect knowledge, how do I know that I am not also deceived each time I add together two and three, or number the sides of a square, or form some judgment still more simple, if more simple indeed can be imagined? But perhaps Deity has not been willing that I should be thus deceived, for He is said to be supremely good. If, however, it were repugnant to the goodness of Deity to have created me subject to constant deception, it would seem likewise to be contrary to this goodness to allow me to be occasionally deceived; and yet it is clear that this is permitted. Some, indeed, might perhaps be found who would be disposed rather to deny the existence of a Being so powerful than to believe that there is nothing certain. But let us for the present refrain from opposing this opinion, and grant that all which is here said of a Deity is fabulous; nevertheless in whatever way it be supposed that I reached the state in which I exist, whether by fate, or chance, or by an endless series of antecedents and consequents, or by any other means, it is clear (since to be deceived and to err is a certain defect) that the probability of my being so imperfect as to be the constant victim of deception, will be increased exactly in proportion as the power possessed by the cause, to which they assign my origin, is lessened. To these reasonings I have assuredly nothing to reply, but am constrained at last to avow that there is nothing of all that I formerly believed to be true of which it is impossible to doubt, and that not through thoughtlessness or levity, but from cogent and maturely considered reasons; so that henceforward, if I desire to discover anything certain, I ought not the less carefully to refrain from assenting to those same opinions than to what might be shown to be manifestly false.

But it is not sufficient to have made these observations; care must be taken likewise to keep them in remembrance. For those old and customary opinions perpetually recur—long and familiar usage giving them the right of occupying my mind, even almost against my will, and subduing my belief; nor will I lose the habit of deferring to them and confiding in them so long as I shall consider them to be what in truth they are, viz., opinions to some extent doubtful, as I have already shown, but still highly probable, and such as it is much more reasonable to believe than deny. It is for this reason I am persuaded that I shall not be doing wrong, if, taking an opposite judgment of deliberate design, I become my own deceiver, by supposing, for a time, that all those opinions are entirely false and imaginary, until at length, having thus balanced my old by my new prejudices, my judgment shall no longer be turned aside by perverted usage from the path that may conduct to the perception of truth. For I am assured that, meanwhile, there will arise neither peril nor error from this course, and that I cannot for the present yield too much to distrust, since the end I now seek is not action but knowledge.

I will suppose, then, not that Deity, who is sovereignly good and the fountain of truth, but that some malignant demon, who is at once exceedingly potent and deceitful, has employed all his artifice to deceive me; I will suppose that the sky, the air, the earth, colours, figures, sounds, and all external things, are nothing better than the illusions of dreams, by means of which this being has laid snares for my credulity; I will consider myself as without hands, eyes, flesh, blood, or any of the senses, and as falsely believing that I am possessed of these; I will continue resolutely fixed in this belief, and if indeed by this means it be not in my power to arrive at the knowledge of truth, I shall at least do what is in my power, viz., suspend my judgment, and guard with settled purpose against giving my assent to what is false, and being imposed upon by this deceiver, whatever be his power and artifice.

But this undertaking is arduous, and a certain indolence insensibly leads me back to my ordinary course of life; and just as the captive, who, perchance, was enjoying in his dreams an imaginary liberty, when he begins to suspect that it is but a vision, dreads awakening, and conspires with the agreeable illusions that the deception may be prolonged; so I, of my own accord, fall back into the train of my former beliefs, and fear to arouse myself from my slumber, lest the time of laborious wakefulness that would succeed this quiet rest, in place of bringing any light of day, should prove inadequate to dispel the darkness that will arise from the difficulties that have now been raised.

Meditation II

OF THE NATURE OF THE HUMAN MIND; AND THAT IT IS MORE EASILY KNOWN THAN THE BODY. The Meditation of yesterday has filled my mind with so many doubts, that it is no longer in my power to forget them. Nor do I see, meanwhile, any principle on which they can be resolved; and, just as if I had fallen all of a sudden into very deep water, I am so greatly disconcerted as to be unable either to plant my feet firmly on the bottom or sustain myself by swimming on the surface. I will, nevertheless, make an effort, and try anew the same path on which I had entered yesterday, that is, proceed by casting aside all that admits of the slightest doubt, not less than if I had discovered it to be absolutely false; and I will continue always in this track until I shall find something that is certain, or at least, if I can do nothing more, until I shall know with certainty that there is nothing certain. Archimedes, that he might transport the entire globe from the place it occupied to another, demanded only a point that was firm and immoveable; so also, I shall be entitled to entertain the highest expectations, if I am fortunate enough to discover only one thing that is certain and indubitable.

I suppose, accordingly, that all the things which I see are false (fictitious); I believe that none of those objects which my fallacious memory represents ever existed; I suppose that I possess no senses; I believe that body, figure, extension, motion, and place are merely fictions of my mind. What is there, then, that can be esteemed true? Perhaps this only, that there is absolutely nothing certain.

But how do I know that there is not something different altogether from the objects I have now enumerated, of which it is impossible to entertain the slightest doubt? Is there not a God, or some being, by whatever name I may designate him, who causes these thoughts to arise in my mind? But why suppose such a being, for it may be I myself am capable of producing them? Am I, then, at least not something? But I before denied that I possessed senses or a body; I hesitate, however, for what follows from that? Am I so dependent on the body and the senses that without these I cannot exist? But I had the persuasion that there was absolutely nothing in the world, that there was no sky and no earth, neither minds nor bodies; was I not, therefore, at the same time, persuaded that I did not exist? Far from it; I assuredly existed, since I was persuaded. But there is I know not what being, who is possessed at once of the highest power and the deepest cunning, who is constantly employing all his ingenuity in deceiving me. Doubtless, then, I exist, since I am deceived; and, let him deceive me as he may, he can never bring it about that I am nothing, so long as I shall be conscious that I am something. So that it must, in fine, be maintained, all things being maturely and carefully considered, that this proposition, I am, I exist, is necessarily true each time it is expressed by me, or conceived in my mind.

But I do not yet know with sufficient clearness what I am, though assured that I am; and hence, in the next place, I must take care, lest perchance I inconsiderately substitute some other object in room of what is properly myself, and thus wander from truth, even in that knowledge which I hold to be of all others the most certain and evident. For this reason, I will now consider anew what I formerly believed myself to be, before I entered on the present train of thought; and of my previous opinion I will retrench all that can in the least be invalidated by the grounds of doubt I have adduced, in order that there may at length remain nothing but what is certain and indubitable. What then did I formerly think I was? Undoubtedly I judged that I was a man. But what is a man? Shall I say a rational animal? Assuredly not; for it would be necessary forthwith to inquire into what is meant by animal, and what by rational, and thus, from a single question, I should insensibly glide into others, and these more difficult than the first; nor do I now possess enough of leisure to warrant me in wasting my time amid subtleties of this sort. I prefer here to attend to the thoughts that sprung up of themselves in my mind, and were inspired by my own nature alone, when I applied myself to the consideration of what I was. In the first place, then, I thought that I possessed a countenance, hands, arms, and all the fabric of members that appears in a corpse, and which I called by the name of body. It further occurred to me that I was nourished, that I walked, perceived, and thought, and all those actions I referred to the soul; but what the soul itself was I either did not stay to consider, or, if I did, I imagined that it was something extremely rare and subtile, like wind, or flame, or ether, spread through my grosser parts. As regarded the body, I did not even doubt of its nature, but thought I distinctly knew it, and if I had wished to describe it according to the notions I then entertained, I should have explained myself in this manner: By body I understand all that can be terminated by a certain figure; that can be comprised in a certain place, and so fill a certain space as therefrom to exclude every other body; that can be perceived either by touch, sight, hearing, taste, or smell; that can be moved in different ways, not indeed of itself, but by something foreign to it by which it is touched and from which it receives the impression; for the power of self-motion, as likewise that of perceiving and thinking, I held as by no means pertaining to the nature of body; on the contrary, I was somewhat astonished to find such faculties existing in some bodies.

But as to myself, what can I now say that I am, since I suppose there exists an extremely powerful, and, if I may so speak, malignant being, whose whole endeavours are directed towards deceiving me? Can I affirm that I possess any one of all those attributes of which I have lately spoken as belonging to the nature of body? After attentively considering them in my own mind, I find none of them that can properly be said to belong to myself. To recount them were idle and tedious. Let us pass, then, to the attributes of the soul. The first mentioned were the powers of nutrition and walking; but, if it be true that I have no body, it is true likewise that I am capable neither of walking nor of being nourished. Perception is another attribute of the soul; but perception too is impossible without the body: besides, I have frequently during sleep, believed that I perceived objects which I afterwards observed I did not in reality perceive. Thinking is another attribute of the soul; and here I discover what properly belongs to myself. This alone is inseparable from me. I am—I exist: this is certain; but how often? As often as I think; for perhaps it would even happen, if I should wholly cease to think, that I should at the same time altogether cease to be. I now admit nothing that is not necessarily true: I am therefore, precisely speaking, only a thinking thing, that is, a mind, understanding, or reason,—terms whose signification was before unknown to me. I am, however, a real thing, and really existent;

but what thing? The answer was, a thinking thing. The question now arises, am I aught besides? I will stimulate my imagination with a view to discover whether I am not still something more than a thinking being. Now it is plain I am not the assemblage of members called the human body; I am not a thin and penetrating air diffused through all these members, or wind, or flame, or vapour, or breath, or any of all the things I can imagine; for I supposed that all these were not, and, without changing the supposition, I find that I still feel assured of my existence.

But it is true, perhaps, that those very things which I suppose to be nonexistent, because they are unknown to me, are not in truth different from myself whom I know. This is a point I cannot determine, and do not now enter into any dispute regarding it. I can only judge of things that are known to me: I am conscious that I exist, and I who know that I exist inquire into what I am. It is, however, perfectly certain that the knowledge of my existence, thus precisely taken, is not dependent on things, the existence of which is as yet unknown to me: and consequently it is not dependent on any of the things I can feign in imagination. Moreover, the phrase iself, I frame an image, reminds me of my error; for I should in truth frame one if I were to imagine myself to be anything, since to imagine is nothing more than to contemplate the figure or image of a corporeal thing; but I already know that I exist, and that it is possible at the same time that all those images, and in general all that relates to the nature of body, are merely dreams or chimeras. From this I discover that it is not more reasonable to say, I will excite my imagination that I may know more distinctly what I am, than to express myself as follows: I am now awake, and perceive something real; but because my perception is not sufficiently clear, I will of express purpose go to sleep that my dreams may represent to me the object of my perception with more truth and clearness. And, therefore, I know that nothing of all that I can embrace in imagination belongs to the knowledge which I have of myself, and that there is need to recall with the utmost care the mind from this mode of thinking, that it may be able to know its own nature with perfect distinctness.

But what, then, am I? A thinking thing, it has been said. But what is a thinking thing? It is a thing that doubts, understands, conceives, affirms, denies, wills, refuses, that imagines also, and perceives. Assuredly it is not little, if all these properties belong to my nature. But why should they not belong to it? Am I not that very being who now doubts of almost everything; who, for all that, understands and conceives certain things; who affirms one alone as true, and denies the others; who desires to know more of them, and does not wish to be deceived; who imagines many things, sometimes even despite his will; and is likewise percipient of many, as if through the medium of the senses. Is there nothing of all this as true as that I am, even although I should be always dreaming, and although he who gave me being employed all his ingenuity to deceive me? Is there also any one of these attributes that can be properly distinguished from my thought, or that can be said to be separate from myself? For it is of itself so evident that it is I who doubt, I who understand, and I who desire, that it is here unnecessary to add anything by way of rendering it more clear. And I am as certainly the same being who imagines; for, although it may be (as I before supposed) that nothing I imagine is true, still the power of imagination does not cease really to exist in me and to form part of my thought. In fine, I am the same being who perceives, that is, who apprehends certain objects as by the organs of sense, since, in truth, I see light, hear a noise, and feel heat. But it will be said that these presentations are false, and that I am dreaming. Let it be so. At all events it is certain that I seem to see light, hear a noise, and feel heat; this cannot be false, and this is what in me is properly called perceiving, which is nothing else than thinking. From this I begin to know what I am with somewhat greater clearness and distinctness than heretofore.

But, nevertheless, it still seems to me, and I cannot help believing, that corporeal things, whose images are formed by thought, which fall under the senses, and are examined by the same, are known with much greater distinctness than that I know not what part of myself which is not imaginable; although, in truth, it may seem strange to say that I know and comprehend with greater distinctness things whose existence appears to me doubtful, that are unknown, and do not belong to me, than others of whose reality I am persuaded, that are known to me, and appertain to my proper nature; in a word, than myself. But I see clearly what is the state of the case. My mind is apt to wander, and will not yet submit to be restrained within the limits of truth. Let us therefore leave the mind to itself once more, and, according to it every kind of liberty, permit it to consider the objects that appear to it from without, in order that, having afterwards withdrawn it from these gently and opportunely, and fixed it on the consideration of its being and the properties it finds in itself, it may then be the more easily controlled.

Let us now accordingly consider the objects that are commonly thought to be the most easily, and likewise the most distinctly known, viz., the bodies we touch and see; not, indeed, bodies in general, for these general notions are usually somewhat more confused, but one body in particular. Take, for example, this piece of wax; it is quite fresh, having been but recently taken from the bee-hive; it has not yet lost the sweetness of the honey it contained; it still retains somewhat of the odour of the flowers from which it was gathered; its colour, figure, size, are apparent to the sight, it is hard, cold, easily handled; and sounds when struck upon with the finger. In fine, all that contributes to make a body as distinctly known as possible, is found in the one before us. But, while I am speaking, let it be placed near the fire—what remained of the taste exhales, the smell evaporates, the colour changes, its figure is destroyed, its size increases, it becomes liquid, it grows hot, it can hardly be handled, and, although struck upon, it emits no sound. Does the same wax still remain after this change? It must be admitted that it does remain; no one doubts it, or judges otherwise. What, then, was it I knew with so much distinctness in the piece of wax? Assuredly, it could be nothing of all that I observed by means of the senses, since all the things that fell under taste, smell, sight, touch, and hearing are changed, and yet the same wax remains. It was perhaps what I now think, viz., that this wax was neither the sweetness of honey, the pleasant odour of flowers, the whiteness, the figure, nor the sound, but only a body that a little before appeared to me conspicuous under these forms, and which is now perceived under others. But, to speak precisely, what is it that I imagine when I think of it in this way? Let it be attentively considered, and, retrenching all that does not belong to the wax, let us see what remains. There certainly remains nothing, except something extended, flexible, and movable. But what is meant by flexible and movable? Is it not that I imagine that the piece of wax, being round, is capable of becoming square, or of passing from a square into a triangular figure? Assuredly such is not the case, because I conceive that it admits of an infinity of similar changes; and I am, moreover, unable to compass this infinity by imagination, and consequently this conception which I have of the wax is not the product of the faculty of imagination. But what now is this extension? Is it not also unknown? For it becomes greater when the wax is melted, greater when it is boiled, and greater still when the heat increases; and I should not conceive clearly and according to truth, the wax as it is, if I did not suppose that the piece we are considering admitted even of a wider variety of extension than I ever imagined. I must, therefore, admit that I cannot even comprehend by imagination what the piece of wax is, and that it is the mind alone which perceives it. I speak of one piece in particular; for, as to wax in general, this is still more evident. But what is the piece of wax that can be perceived only by the understanding or mind? It is certainly the same which I see, touch, imagine; and, in fine, it is the same which, from the beginning, I believed it to be. But (and this it is of moment to observe) the perception of it is neither an act of sight, of touch, nor of imagination, and never was either of these, though it might formerly seem so, but is simply an intuition of the mind, which may be imperfect and confused, as it formerly was, or very clear and distinct, as it is at present, according as the attention is more or less directed to the elements which it contains, and of which it is composed.

But, meanwhile, I feel greatly astonished when I observe the weakness of my mind, and its proneness to error. For although, without at all giving expression to what I think, I consider all this in my own mind, words yet occasionally impede my progress, and I am almost led into error by the terms of ordinary language. We say, for example, that we see the same wax when it is before us, and not that we judge it to be the same from its retaining the same colour and figure: whence I should forthwith be disposed to conclude that the wax is known by the act of sight, and not by the intuition of the mind alone, were it not for the analogous instance of human beings passing on in the street below, as observed from a window. In this case I do not fail to say that I see the men themselves, just as I say that I see the wax; and yet what do I see from the window beyond hats and cloaks that might cover artificial machines, whose motions might be determined by springs? But I judge that there are human beings from these appearances, and thus I comprehend, by the faculty of judgment alone which is in the mind, what I believed I saw with my eyes.

The man who makes it his aim to rise to knowledge superior to the common, ought to be ashamed to seek occasions of doubting from the vulgar forms of speech: instead, therefore, of doing this, I shall proceed with the matter in hand, and inquire whether I had a clearer and more perfect perception of the piece of wax when I first saw it, and when I thought I knew it by means of the external sense itself, or, at all events, by the common sense, as it is called, that is, by the imaginative faculty; or whether I rather apprehend it more clearly at present, after having examined with greater care, both what it is, and in what way it can be known. It would certainly be ridiculous to entertain any doubt on this point. For what, in that first perception, was there distinct? What did I perceive which any animal might not have perceived? But when I distinguish the wax from its exterior forms, and when, as if I had stripped it of its vestments, I consider it quite naked, it is certain, although some error may still be found in my judgment, that I cannot, nevertheless, thus apprehend it without possessing a human mind.

But, finally, what shall I say of the mind itself, that is, of myself? For as yet I do not admit that I am anything but mind. What, then! I who seem to possess so distinct an apprehension of the piece of wax,—do I not know myself, both with greater truth and certitude, and also much more distinctly and clearly? For if I judge that the wax exists because I see it, it assuredly follows, much more evidently, that I myself am or exist, for the same reason: for it is possible that what I see may not in truth be wax, and that I do not even possess eyes with which to see anything; but it cannot be that when I see, or, which comes to the same thing, when I think I see, I myself who think am nothing. So likewise, if I judge that the wax exists because I touch it, it will still also follow that I am; and if I determine that my imagination, or any other cause, whatever it be, persuades me of the existence of the wax, I will still draw the same conclusion. And what is here remarked of the piece of wax, is applicable to all the other things that are external to me. And further, if the notion or perception of wax appeared to me more precise and distinct, after that not only sight and touch, but many other causes besides, rendered it manifest to my apprehension, with how much greater distinctness must I now know myself, since all the reasons that contribute to the knowledge of the nature of wax, or of any body whatever, manifest still better the nature of my mind? And there are besides so many other things in the mind itself that contribute to the illustration of its nature, that those dependent on the body, to which I have here referred, scarcely merit to be taken into account.

But, in conclusion, I find I have insensibly reverted to the point I desired; for, since it is now manifest to me that bodies themselves are not properly perceived by the senses nor by the faculty of imagination, but by the intellect alone; and since they are not perceived because they are seen and touched, but only because they are understood or rightly comprehended by thought, I readily discover that there is nothing more easily or clearly apprehended than my own mind. But because it is difficult to rid one's self so promptly of an opinion to which one has been long accustomed, it will be desirable to tarry for some time at this stage, that, by long continued meditation, I may more deeply impress upon my memory this new knowledge.

Empiricism

The World We Perceive   Arthur E. Murphy

Arthur Edward Murphy (1901–1962), an American professor of philosophy who taught at many United States universities, defended the moral authority of human reason against the attacks of skepticism and fanaticism.

The World We Perceive. The contrast between mere ideas and their relations on the one hand and substantial matter of fact on the other is central to the common sense notion of a world we find and do not make, a world to which our ideas must conform if they are to be factually true and informationally reliable. And while common sense has had some very hard things said about it by sophisticated critics, it has the advantage, when it is about its own business, of being both common (that is, publicly sharable and testable) and sensible, which is more than can be said of many of the theories that the critics seek to put in its place. We shall do well, therefore, to start our inquiry from its standpoint, and see how far we can go with it. What is the world we find ourselves living in, the world which, to adapt a famous saying of Bishop Berkeley's, we need only open our eyes to see? The full answer to this question would require all the knowledge that men, starting by opening their eyes and looking, and proceeding by using their minds to inquire, and their eyes and hands again to test their ideas, have been able to accumulate, and all they may still accumulate by the further use of their senses and their minds. Fortunately we need not here undertake so full an answer. For whatever else or more this world may prove to be, it is at least the familiar world that we see with our eyes and handle with our hands, the world in which we move about and greet our friends and live and work together. It is also the world in which we do our thinking, and what we can observe of it provides the clue and the test for beliefs about its more remote and perceptually inaccessible areas. We can construct in our minds a more intellectually coherent world, and wish for a more emotionally satisfying one, but in so far as our wishes and our intellectual constructions claim informational accuracy with respect to what is actually going on, or has occurred, or is likely to happen in this world in which, for better or worse, we find ourselves, they must meet the test of truthfulness by agreement with what we find this world to be when and in so far as we are able perceptually to observe it.

From *The Uses of Reason* by Arthur E. Murphy, The Macmillan Company, 1943. Reprinted by permission of the A. E. Murphy Estate.

It is for this reason that the appeal to *experience,* to what we find when we actually observe things at first hand, as distinct from what we might antecedently think or desire them to be, has so important and honorable a place in the history of critical thought. The empiricists have been preeminently the *fact* men, where "fact" is simply something that is found to be so in tested experience, and their function has been to insist on the informational primacy (for reasonable belief) of what is thus discovered, whether we like it or not, and on the primary importance, for such discovery, of accurate observation through the senses, of what is going on around us. So far they have been plainly right, and we shall be on their side in all that follows. Nor is their doctrine a trivial or merely obvious one. There are indeed truths that a man need only open his eyes to see. But to open one's eyes and see what is there to be seen, honestly, accurately and without the bias of preconception, prejudice or tradition, is an intellectual, and not merely a physiological, achievement. The ability to *learn* by experience, that is, to derive ideas from what we observe and to correct beliefs in terms of what is found to be the case, is the most basic factor in our intellectual progress, when such progress actually occurs. And it involves as its precondition the capacity to see and report what happens in just those cases in which what happens does not agree with antecedent ideas, but stands in contrast to them as mere stubborn matter of fact, *to be* taken account of but not, as it stands, either "rational" or pleasant. It is no wonder, then, that modern philosophers have so often stressed the value of experience and tried to make it the standard for all thinking that pretends to informational accuracy concerning the world and ourselves.

But what do we *really* experience? What is the final and ultimate "given" to which our ideas have added nothing and about which, therefore, we cannot possibly be mistaken? In attempting to answer this question the empiricists have often traveled far from the path of fruitful inquiry. . . . "Experience" in epistemological controversy may mean anything or nothing, and there have been appeals to all sorts of experience —"inner" or "outer," scientific, aesthetic or religious, fallible or infallible —for all sorts of purposes. What we propose to ask instead is what we experience, or are aware of, when we are observing the world perceptually, by seeing, hearing, smelling or handling the things in our more immediate bodily environment. This is *one* of the ways, at least, in which we find out, by observation, what is going on around us, and guide and correct our ideas by what we find. If we can see how experience functions in this capacity as a source of reliable information, we shall have a solid basis on which to proceed. Without it, wandering in the mazes of phenomena, sense data, impressions, and their like, we should never even get near to our subject.

There are three things about the process of perceptual observation, critically considered as a source of reliable information about ourselves and our bodily environment, that deserve special attention. First, this process, considered as a source of information, not merely as a physiological event, is fallible. Second, it is corrigible, and it is in the process of correction that the difference between reliable and unreliable information is reasonably made out. Third, it is quite ultimate for us as a source of information about the world, since there is no other or better way of finding out what we learn by its means. And what we learn in this way maintains itself, under philosophical scrutiny, as trustworthy information to which belief in other fields, so far as it refers to the same matters of fact, ought reasonably to conform.

First, perceptual observation is fallible. I use my eyes and my hands in observing objects in my bodily environment, and what I observe in this process is what is going on in the world, not what is going on in my body or in my mind when I observe it. And I observe such objects as they look, or feel or smell, under the conditions in which I can observe them; that is, in the relations in which they stand to me at that time. I can see objects under a variety of conditions, with the aid of a microscope or through blue spectacles or when I am so drunk that I cannot make out what they are. But I shall never see objects when I am not seeing them, or think of them when they are not objects of my thought. It has sometimes—rather oddly—been argued that this is proof that I am not "really" seeing them, or at least not seeing them as they "really" are. On the contrary, however, to see things as they look is evidently and naturally the way to see them, no other or better having yet been devised, and if what they "really" are is at all relevant to what as observable objects they are found to be, then it is through just this process that what they really are must be disclosed. It is quite true, however, that things, as thus observed, are not always what they seem. What looks to be a man may prove on inspection to have been a shadow, and the pink rats of drunken experience and epistemological controversy have no local habitation in my bodily environment, though under some conditions they seem to some people to be there. Hence, I must learn to look carefully, and to look again, and to guide my looking by the lessons of past experience, both my own and that of others as reliably reported to me. There is, however, no mystery about this. What we observe are objects and events in our bodily environment as they appear under the conditions in which we *can* observe them, and what they really are, in this context, is what they reliably prove to be on further perceptual inspection. The "reality" thus achieved is not, of course, thereby certified as a satisfactory object for metaphysics, and it is not in that light that we are here considering it. It is, however, a reliable and quite indispensable source of information concerning our bodies and the world they inhabit, and neither science nor enlightened practice would be able to stir a step without it.

Hence, secondly, perceptual observation is corrigible, and it is in this process of correction through further and more careful observation that the distinction between what is reliable in it, as information about the world, and what is unreliable appearance is reasonably made out. Those who seek to find in a single instance of such observation the infallible certainty in terms of which alone they can distinguish *real* knowledge from mere opinion, will stare fixedly at the object until it becomes transparent, and all they are aware of in it is what they *can* thus be certain about: the shape or color or feel of it which would be there even if they were drunk or dreaming, and about which there is, as they keep on telling themselves, "no reasonably probable shadow of doubt, no possible doubt whatever." The trouble is that while they will then know *something* certainly—unless, as their critics allege, they have been in error even here—what they know will no longer be a material object but only an impression, or sense-datum, which is not itself an object of perceptual observation at all, or a part of the material world. How to get from such disembodied fragments of epistemologically infallible experience to the outdoor world of men and events is a further problem, but for us a quite gratuitous one. The kind of criticism and correction that perceptual observation requires presupposes no such unprofitable quest for certainty. There are other means of correcting the illusion of the drunkard than that of retreating to a world so tenuous that there is nothing left in it that even a drunkard could be mistaken about. There is the process by which the sober man, or the drunkard when he becomes sober, learns, by observation, what sort of world he lives in. No single observation here is infallible; about any one the question can meaningfully be raised as to whether what is observed is, in fact, what it appears to be. Fortunately, however, while the question can be asked, it can also, sometimes, be answered beyond all reasonable doubt. The process of answering it, reasonably, is the process by means of which ideas are used in the pursuit of truth about the nature and behavior of the world of bodies of which our own bodies are a part. The aim of the rational criticism of belief on this subject is not to halt inquiry at the point at which we claim to know so little about the world that no question of error can arise, but to carry it through to a point at which we know enough to distinguish what is permanently reliable in our observations from what is random, superficial and misleading.

And, thirdly, this process of criticism is sufficient to show that, in the rational ordering of our beliefs, perceptual observation, as a self-correcting process, has a quite ultimate and fundamental place. We know that there is a world of bodies, because we perceive it, because we open our eyes and our minds to find ourselves involved in it and capable of learning the lessons it has to teach. If we did not know it in this way, it would be quite futile to try to "construct" it from private sense data, or deduce it from the necessities of speculative reason, or postulate it as the area in which our duty is to be done. Such constructions, postulations and deductions are familiar enough, but all are shamelessly parasitic on the information which perceptual observation provides about the kind of world we actually live in, the world to which, after many wanderings, their speculations somehow bring them back. There may, as we have said, be much more in the "reality" to which they aspire than perceptual observation can disclose, but there cannot be less. Unless this "more" can be understood along with what we find out perceptually, and interpreted in conformity with its veracious and reliable testimony on the subjects with which it is competent to deal, the doctrine that reports it must remain suspect. What can we reason, but from what we know? And *part* of what we know—or have reliable information about—is the observable nature and behavior of objects in our bodily environment. The use of reason in the acquisition of this information, and the use of this information as a criterion for the credibility and authenticity of further beliefs to which it is pertinent are not the end and sum of human wisdom by any means. But they are somewhere near the beginning of it, and no theory, however exalted its pretensions, which ignores or falsifies their findings, can stand the test of rational examination.

The Informational Worth of Scientific Inquiry. We have so far neglected the most serious charge that can be brought against the "reality" of the world we perceive and the veracity of the information derived from perceptual observation concerning it. The sciences, with physics as their leader and model, and mathematics as their method, are alleged to have carried us far beyond the limits of such observation and to have shown in the process that the external world is quite different from what we perceive it to be, and that our perception of it is consequently unreliable. We now have the means of understanding this contention, and discriminating what is true in it from what is confused and misleading. It is true, of course, as every schoolboy is supposed to know, that the world as physics describes it is different in essential respects from what we see when we open our eyes and inspect the objects in our neighborhood. If the schoolboy, or his elders, still lack this information, they are here referred to such classic expositions of the queerness of the world of physics as that provided by Sir Arthur Eddington in *The Nature of the Physical World.* Tables that lose their solidity and prove on analysis to be "mostly empty space," electrons that escape the laws of old-fashioned physics in their indeterminate, or at least unpredictable, pulsations, and space and time of unpicturable complications are among the more striking denizens of this scientific wonderland. If the reader is tempted to exclaim, as did the sensible Alice in a somewhat similar situation, "curiouser and curiouser," we can hardly blame him. And if Sir Arthur's oddities are by this time a little out of date, there will no doubt be others, no less surprising, to take their place. The world does indeed seem to be full of a strange variety of things, and those who have antecedently made their familiar perceptual environment the measure of its possibilities are pretty certain to be surprised at what the scientific explorers have to tell them.

In our discussion of perceptual observation, however, we did not claim that what such observation can tell us is all there is to know about our physical environment. The world, as we said, may well be more than what we see and hear and touch discloses it to be, *but it cannot be less.* It is at that point, and only there, that we need criticize the reports the speculative physicists are pleased to give us. For these reporters seem to suggest that, because what we observe is not the truth they have discovered about objects and processes beyond the range of ordinary observation, it is in consequence not really the truth about the objects we observe and their observable behavior either. They reach this peculiar result not by scientific analysis, but by a familiar and quite wrong-headed sort of philosophy—that which identifies "the external world" with the object of their preferential interest and concludes that whatever is not *this* reality is not "really" what it purports to be at all, that the table on which I rest my weight is, in consequence, not really solid, and that the information I derive from perceptual information concerning it is therefore mistaken. There is a mistake here, surely, but it is not our mistake or that of common sense about its observational business. The solidity of the table that I can handle, rest my weight on, and observe in its physical behavior, when, e.g., it proves substantial enough, used as a battering ram, to break through a door, is not disproved by the fact that when Sir Arthur explores the electrical charges which he takes to be the elements in terms of whose structure and behavior the laws of physics are most simply and usefully stated, he finds no such solidity. It was not about the space between electrons that I was talking when I said the table was solid, and it is not about perceptually observable and verifiable solidity that he is talking when he reports the physical relations of electrical charges to each other. If he supposes that it is—and it is only on that supposition that his theory can be understood as casting doubt on the information supplied by perceptual observation—that does not prove that the world we see is not verifiably what, under reliable conditions, we observe it to be. It only shows that eminent scientists, when they interpret their findings philosophically, do not always know what they are talking about. And while this may be disheartening to the inexperienced, who still regard the physical scientist as a philosophic seer, it is not, for those who survey the history of ideas, any longer surprising.

The point here at issue is important. For it is on the basis of perceptual observation that the scientist proceeds in his own inquiry, and it is in terms of perceptual observation, of what can be seen on a dial, or a photographic plate, or through a telescope or microscope, that the factual veracity of his theories is tested. A laboratory and what goes on in it are as much a part of the world we perceive as any other visible and tangible object, and those who inhabit it have quite as much need as the rest of us for confidence in the reliability of their observations of what goes on in their observable environment. If the theories of physics really did cast doubt on the informational reliability of perceptual observation, they would cast doubt also on their own empirical foundations, and we should then have to ask what good reason there was to suppose that what they said was factually correct, or that Eddington's wonderland has a closer relation to what actually happens in the world than that of Alice. This would not greatly disturb Sir Arthur; for, like other mystics, his philosophic interest is not so much in articulating the rational order of our knowledge as in undermining it for the sake of a faith that not only transcends knowledge but negates its more specific content. But it is disturbing, and rightly so, for those who seek to set their beliefs in order in the light of the best knowledge available, and want good reasons for believing that conclusions advanced as authentic information about the nature and behavior of physical objects are true, i.e., that what they report is in fact the case.

The fact is that a study of the results achieved by scientific inquiry, in the context of research in which that inquiry effectively and reliably proceeds, provides a basis not for doubt of the genuineness of what we perceive but for wonder and delight at the way in which the human mind has been able to use the information thus acquired as a clue to what is going on elsewhere, and to extend its knowledge of the world accordingly. The rational use of ideas in the pursuit of informationally reliable truth is here seen at its best and clearest. There are many critics of many sects who have sought for one reason or another to discredit the findings of the sciences, and to prove that their own more esoteric and inspiring methods provide a better means of access to the world of Reality. There may be some sense in which some of these claims are significant and true; we shall return to them at a later stage. But in so far as they are intended to discredit the informational reliability of the findings of the sciences with respect to what has happened, is happening or is likely to happen in the world around us, they are thoroughly mistaken. One has only to compare what has been found out about the functioning of the human body, or the chemistry of foods, or the nature of light, by scientific inquiry, with what was believed on these matters before the sciences developed or has been contributed to our knowledge of them by other means of inquiry—Bergsonian intuition, say, or authoritarian revelation, or "thinking with the blood"—to see how the cognitive authenticity of scientific inquiry is established. "Science" as metaphysics, religion or social gospel has grave defects, but scientific inquiry, as a means of finding out what is going on beyond the range of direct observation but in the world in which we live and whose order of events we must know if we are to live securely, is a cognitive instrument which has proved its worth beyond all reasonable doubt. It is our clearest example of reason in operation, of ideas at work in the pursuit of knowledge, and those who profess to doubt that "mere human reason" can tell us what the world is like are herewith referred to it for information, not on high metaphysical ground, but because there simply is no better way of finding out what is thus discovered about the world, and no good reason to doubt that much of what has been found out in this way is substantially and reliably correct. If this does not satisfy such doubters, it will not be because the information is unreliable but because they were not looking for information but for something else, for comfort or inspiration or spiritual peace. These are great goods and supremely worth seeking, but they do not take the place of reliable information, nor can they supply it. To condemn one good because it is not another is more petulant than profound. There is a large measure of that kind of petulance in the pseudo-profundities of the rivals and enemies of scientifically ascertainable truth.

It is not my purpose or responsibility to summarize here the content of scientific knowledge, or the procedures by which it is acquired. Its methods of observation, hypothesis and verification have many times been described, and I have nothing to add to them here. The history of the sciences provides the best and most enlightening account we have of the way reason operates in using ideas to extend human knowledge to remoter matters of fact, and in using facts thus discovered to correct and amplify the ideas without the use of which they would not have been found out. In the self-correcting process of inquiry theories guide observation to events that unaided observation had never seen, while observation gives the basis for new theories which mere theorizing could not have established. And therein is the Kantian dictum fulfilled that concepts without percepts are empty, and percepts without concepts are blind, while the effective cooperation of percept and concept, observation and idea, constitutes empirical knowledge. This cooperation, as we have now learned, is not something that happens in the same way always, with predetermined categories stamping on an indeterminate material the form of their own antecedent rationality. What we observe has an obdurate and quite determinate nature of its own which often shows that previously held theories, which constituted in their time the canons of "rational" explanation in the sciences, are limted, biased and defective. The work of reason here has consisted, not in the explaining away of recalcitrant facts so that the ceremonial "rationality" of antecedent preconceptions may be maintained at all cost, but in the development of new theories, frequently shocking to traditional preconceptions, which include the facts discovered in a new, though perhaps more subtle, order and thus advance our intellectual mastery of events. To see this working adjustment clearly gives a better solution to the old puzzle about the respective claims of "fact" and "theory," "reason" and "experience," than much training in epistemology can provide, and the history of the use of rational ideas in the development of the sciences is, in consequence, the best possible foundation for a sound theory of knowledge. For this, though again not the sum and measure of all we claim or desire to know, is what knowledge is like in a case where it can reliably be identified, and to see how reason functions here is to see it as it is, not merely as its defenders or its critics would like it to be. Thus seen, it needs no higher warrant or validation than that which its own further operation in tested inquiry can provide of the informational accuracy and adequacy of the results achieved by its means. Those who participate effectively in this inquiry and those who make its results available in the various activities to which they are pertinent are doing the work of human reason.

The Nature of Science

Method of Scientific Investigation   T. H. Huxley

Thomas Henry Huxley (1825–1895) was an English biologist but won his greatest public fame as a vigorous champion of evolution (He was called "Darwin's Bulldog.") and as a lucid popular lecturer on science, religion, ethics, and education. He was the grandfather of Aldous and Sir Julian Huxley.

... The method of scientific investigation is nothing but the expression of the necessary mode of working of the human mind. It is simply the mode at which all phenomena are reasoned about, rendered precise and exact. There is no more difference, but there is just the same kind of difference, between the mental operations of a man of science and those of an ordinary person, as there is between the operations and methods of a baker or of a butcher weighing out his goods in common scales, and the operations of a chemist in performing a difficult and complex analysis by means of his balance and finely-graduated weights. It is not that the action of the scale in the one case, and the balance in the other, differ in the principles of their construction or manner of working; but the beam of one is set on an infinitely finer axis than the other, and of course turns by the addition of a much smaller weight.

You will understand this better, perhaps, if I give you some familiar example. You have all heard it repeated, I dare say, that men of science work by means of induction and deduction, and that by the help of these operations, they, in a sort of sense, wring from Nature certain other things, which are called natural laws, and causes, and that out of these, by some cunning skill of their own, they build up hypotheses and theories. And it is imagined by many, that the operations of the common mind can be by no means compared with these processes, and that they have to be acquired by a sort of special apprenticeship to the craft. To hear all these large words, you would think that the mind of a man of science must be constituted differently from that of his fellow men; but if you will not be frightened by terms, you will discover that you are quite wrong, and that all these terrible apparatus are being used by yourselves every day and every hour of your lives.

There is a well-known incident in one of Molière's plays, where the author makes the hero express unbounded delight on being told that he had been talking prose during the whole of his life. In the same way, I trust, that you will take comfort, and be delighted with yourselves, on the

From "On Our Knowledge of the Causes of the Phenomena of Organic Nature" by T. H. Huxley in *Darwiniana: Essays,* D. Appleton and Co., New York, 1893.

discovery that you have been acting on the principles of inductive and deductive philosophy during the same period. Probably there is not one here who has not in the course of the day had occasion to set in motion a complex train of reasoning, of the very same kind, though differing of course in degree, as that which a scientific man goes through in tracing the causes of natural phenomena.

A very trivial circumstance will serve to exemplify this. Suppose you go into a fruiterer's shop, wanting an apple,—you take up one, and, on biting it, you find it is sour; you look at it, and see that it is hard and green. You take up another one, and that too is hard, green, and sour. The shopman offers you a third; but, before biting it, you examine it, and find that it is hard and green, and you immediately say that you will not have it, as it must be sour, like those that you have already tried.

Nothing can be more simple than that, you think; but if you will take the trouble to analyse and trace out into its logical elements what has been done by the mind, you will be greatly surprised. In the first place, you have performed the operation of induction. You found that, in two experiences, hardness and greenness in apples went together with sourness. It was so in the first case, and it was confirmed by the second. True, it is a very small basis, but still it is enough to make an induction from; you generalise the facts, and you expect to find sourness in apples where you get hardness and greenness. You found upon that a general law, that all hard and green apples are sour; and that, so far as it goes, is a perfect induction. Well, having got your natural law in this way, when you are offered another apple which you find is hard and green, you say, "All hard and green apples are sour; this apple is hard and green, therefore this apple is sour." That train of reasoning is what logicians call a syllogism, and has all its various parts and terms,—its major premiss, its minor premiss, and its conclusion. And, by the help of further reasoning, which, if drawn out, would have to be exhibited in two or three other syllogisms, you arrive at your final determination, "I will not have that apple." So that, you see, you have, in the first place, established a law by induction, and upon that you have founded a deduction, and reasoned out the special conclusion of the particular case. Well now, suppose, having got your law, that at some time afterwards, you are discussing the qualities of apples with a friend: you will say to him, "It is a very curious thing,—but I find that all hard and green apples are sour!" Your friend says to you, "But how do you know that?" You at once reply, "Oh, because I have tried them over and over again, and have always found them to be so." Well, if we were talking science instead of common sense, we should call that an experimental verification. And, if still opposed, you go further, and say, "I have heard from the people in Somersetshire and Devonshire, where a large number of apples are grown, that they have observed the same thing. It is also found to be the case in Normandy, and in North America. In short, I find it to be the universal experience of mankind wherever attention has been directed to the subject." Whereupon, your friend, unless he is a very unreasonable man, agrees with you, and is convinced that you are quite right in the conclusion you have drawn. He believes, although perhaps he does not know he believes it, that the more extensive verifications are,—that the more frequently experiments have been made, and results of the same kind arrived at,—that the more varied the conditions under which the same results are attained, the more certain is the ultimate conclusion, and he disputes the question no further. He sees that the experiment has been tried under all sorts of conditions, as to time, place, and people, with the same result; and he says with you, therefore, that the law you have laid down must be a good one, and he must believe it.

In science we do the same thing;—the philosopher exercises precisely the same faculties, though in a much more delicate manner. In scientific inquiry it becomes a matter of duty to expose a supposed law to every possible kind of verification, and to take care, moreover, that this is done intentionally, and not left to a mere accident, as in the case of the apples. And in science, as in common life, our confidence in a law is in exact proportion to the absence of variation in the result of our experimental verifications. For instance, if you let go your grasp of an article you may have in your hand, it will immediately fall to the ground. That is a very common verification of one of the best established laws of nature—that of gravitation. The method by which men of science establish the exist-ence of that law is exactly the same as that by which we have established the trivial proposition about the sourness of hard and green apples. But we believe it in such an extensive, thorough, and unhesitating manner because the universal experience of mankind verifies it, and we can verify it ourselves at any time; and that is the strongest possible foundation on which any natural law can rest.

So much, then, by way of proof that the method of establishing laws in science is exactly the same as that pursued in common life. Let us now turn to another matter (though really it is but another phase of the same question), and that is, the method by which, from the relations of certain phenomena, we prove that some stand in the position of causes towards the others.

I want to put the case clearly before you, and I will therefore show you what I mean by another familiar example. I will suppose that one of you, on coming down in the morning to the parlour of your house, finds that a tea-pot and some spoons which had been left in the room on the previous evening are gone,—the window is open, and you observe the mark of a dirty hand on the window-frame, and perhaps, in addition to that, you notice the impression of a hob-nailed shoe on the gravel outside. All these phenomena have struck your attention instantly, and before two seconds have passed you say, "Oh, somebody has broken open the window, entered the room, and run off with the spoons and the tea-pot!" That speech is out of your mouth in a moment. And you will probably add, "I know there has; I am quite sure of it!" You mean to say exactly what you know; but in reality you are giving expression to what is, in all essential particulars, an hypothesis. You do not *know* it at all; it is nothing but an hypothesis rapidly framed in your own mind. And it is an hypothesis founded on a long train of inductions and deductions.

What are those inductions and deductions, and how have you got at this hypothesis? You have observed, in the first place, that the window is open; but by a train of reasoning involving many inductions and deductions, you have probably arrived long before at the general law—and a very good one it is—that windows do not open of themselves; and you therefore conclude that something has opened the window. A second general law that you have arrived at in the same way is, that tea-pots and spoons do not go out of a window spontaneously, and you are satisfied that, as they are not now where you left them, they have been removed. In the third place, you look at the marks on the window-sill, and the shoe-marks outside, and you say that in all previous experience the former kind of mark has never been produced by anything else but the hand of a human being; and the same experience shows that no other animal but man at present wears shoes with hob-nails in them such as would produce the marks in the gravel. I do not know, even if we could discover any of those "missing links" that are talked about, that they would help us to any other conclusion! At any rate the law which states our present experience is strong enough for my present purpose. You next reach the conclusion, that as these kinds of marks have not been left by any other animals than men, or are liable to be formed in any other way than by a man's hand and shoe, the marks in question have been formed by a man in that way. You have, further, a general law, founded on observation and experience, and that, too, is, I am sorry to say, a very universal and unimpeachable one,—that some men are thieves; and you assume at once from all these premises—and that is what constitutes your hypothesis— that the man who made the marks outside and on the window-sill, opened the window, got into the room, and stole your tea-pot and spoons. You have now arrived at a *vera causa;*—you have assumed a cause which, it is plain, is competent to produce all the phenomena you have observed. You can explain all these phenomena only by the hypothesis of a thief. But that is a hypothetical conclusion, of the justice of which you have no absolute proof at all; it is only rendered highly probable by a series of inductive and deductive reasonings.

I suppose your first action, assuming that you are a man of ordinary common sense, and that you have established this hypothesis to your own satisfaction, will very likely be to go off for the police, and set them on the track of the burglar, with the view to the recovery of your property. But just as you are starting with this object, some person comes in, and on learning what you are about says, "My good friend, you are going on a good deal too fast. How do you know that the man who really made the marks took the spoons? It might have been a monkey that took them, and the man may have merely looked in afterwards." You would probably reply, "Well, that is all very well, but you see it is contrary to all experience of the way tea-pots and spoons are abstracted; so that, at any rate, your hypothesis is less probable than mine." While you are talking the thing over in this way, another friend arrives, one of that good kind of people that I was talking of a little while ago. And he might say, "Oh, my dear sir, you are certainly going on a great deal too fast. You are most presumptuous. You admit that all these occurrences took place when you were fast asleep, at a time when you could not possibly have known anything about what was taking place. How do you know that the laws of

Nature are not suspended during the night? It may be that there has been some kind of supernatural interference in this case." In point of fact, he declares that your hypothesis is one of which you cannot at all demonstrate the truth, and that you are by no means sure that the laws of Nature are the same when you are asleep as when you are awake.

Well, now, you cannot at the moment answer that kind of reasoning. You feel that your worthy friend has you somewhat at a disadvantage. You will feel perfectly convinced in your own mind, however, that you are quite right, and you say to him, "My good friend, I can only be guided by the natural probabilities of the case, and if you will be kind enough to stand aside and permit me to pass, I will go and fetch the police." Well, we will suppose that your journey is successful, and that by good luck you meet with a policeman; that eventually the burglar is found with your property on his person, and the marks correspond to his hand and to his boots. Probably any jury would consider those facts a very good experimental verification of your hypothesis, touching the cause of the abnormal phenomena observed in your parlour, and would act accordingly.

Now, in this suppositious case, I have taken phenomena of a very common kind, in order that you might see what are the different steps in an ordinary process of reasoning, if you will only take the trouble to analyse it carefully. All the operations I have described, you will see, are involved in the mind of any man of sense in leading him to a conclusion as to the course he should take in order to make good a robbery and punish the offender. I say that you are led, in that case, to your conclusion by exactly the same train of reasoning as that which a man of science pursues when he is endeavouring to discover the origin and laws of the most occult phenomena. The process is, and always must be, the same; and precisely the same mode of reasoning was employed by Newton and Laplace in their endeavours to discover and define the causes of the movements of the heavenly bodies, as you, with your own common sense, would employ to detect a burglar. The only difference is, that the nature of the inquiry being more abstruse, every step has to be most carefully watched, so that there may not be a single crack or flaw in your hypothesis. A flaw or crack in many of the hypotheses of daily life may be of little or no moment as affecting the general correctness of the conclusions at which we may arrive; but, in a scientific inquiry, a fallacy, great or small, is always of importance, and is sure to be in the long run constantly productive of mischievous, if not fatal results.

Do not allow yourselves to be misled by the common notion that an hypothesis is untrustworthy simply because it is an hypothesis. It is often urged, in respect to some scientific conclusion, that, after all, it is only an hypothesis. But what more have we to guide us in nine-tenths of the most important affairs of daily life than hypotheses, and often very ill-based ones? So that in science, where the evidence of an hypothesis is subjected to the most rigid examination, we may rightly pursue the same course. You may have hypotheses and hypotheses. A man may say, if he likes, that the moon is made of green cheese: that is an hypothesis. But another man, who has devoted a great deal of time and attention to the subject, and availed himself of the most powerful telescopes and the results of the observations of others, declares that in his opinion it is probably composed of materials very similar to those of which our own earth is made up: and that is also only an hypothesis. But I need not tell you that there is an enormous difference in the value of the two hypotheses. That one which is based on sound scientific knowledge is sure to have a corresponding value; and that which is a mere hasty random guess is likely to have but little value. Every great step in our progress in discovering causes has been made in exactly the same way as that which I have detailed to you. A person observing the occurrence of certain facts and phenomena asks, naturally enough, what process, what kind of operation known to occur in Nature applied to the particular case, will unravel and explain the mystery? Hence you have the scientific hypothesis; and its value will be proportionate to the care and completeness with which its basis had been tested and verified. It is in these matters as in the commonest affairs of practical life: the guess of the fool will be folly, while the guess of the wise man will contain wisdom. In all cases, you see that the value of the result depends on the patience and faithfulness with which the investigator applies to his hypothesis every possible kind of verification....

The Detective as Scientist   Irving M. Copi

Irving Marmer Copi (1917–   ), an American professor of philosophy, has written extensively and lucidly on logic, scientific method, and the philosophy of language.

...A perennial favorite in this connection is the detective, whose problem is not quite the same as that of the pure scientist, but whose approach and technique illustrate the method of science very clearly. The classical example of the astute detective who can solve even the most baffling mystery is A. Conan Doyle's immortal creation, Sherlock Holmes. Holmes, his stature undiminished by the passage of time, will be our hero in the following account.

1. The Problem. Some of our most vivid pictures of Holmes are those in which he is busy with magnifying glass and tape measure, searching out and finding essential clues which had escaped the attention of those stupid bunglers, the "experts" of Scotland Yard. Or those of us who are by temperament less vigorous may think back more fondly on Holmes the thinker, "...who, when he had an unsolved problem upon his mind, would go for days, and even for a week, without rest, turning it over, rearranging his facts, looking at it from every point of view until he had either fathomed it or convinced himself that his data were insufficient."[1] At one such time, according to Dr. Watson:

> He took off his coat and waistcoat, put on a large blue dressing-gown, and then wandered about the room collecting pillows from his bed and cushions from the sofa and armchairs. With these he constructed a sort of Eastern divan, upon which he perched himself cross-legged, with an ounce of shag tobacco and a box of matches laid out in front on him. In the dim light of the lamp I saw him sitting there, an old briar pipe between his lips, his eyes fixed vacantly upon the corner of the ceiling, the blue smoke curling up from him, silent, motionless, with the light shining upon his strong-set aquiline features. So he sat as I dropped off to sleep, and so he sat when a sudden ejaculation caused me to wake up, and I found the summer sun shining into the apartment. The pipe was still between his lips, the smoke still curled upward, and the room was full of a dense tobacco haze, but nothing remained of the heap of shag which I had seen upon the previous night.[2]

But such memories are incomplete. Holmes was not always searching for clues or pondering over solutions. We all remember those dark periods—especially in the earlier stories—when, much to the good Watson's annoyance, Holmes would drug himself with morphine or cocaine. That would happen, of course, between cases. For when there is no mystery to be unraveled, no man in his right mind would go out to look for clues. Clues, after all, must be clues for something. Nor could Holmes, or anyone else, for that matter, engage in profound thought unless he had something to think about. Sherlock Holmes was a genius at solving problems, but even a genius must have a problem before he can solve it. All reflective thinking, and this term includes criminal investigation as well as scientific research, is a problem-solving activity, as John Dewey and other pragmatists have rightly insisted. There must be a problem felt before either the detective or the scientist can go to work.

Of course the active mind sees problems where the dullard sees only familiar objects. One Christmas season Dr. Watson visited Holmes to find that the latter had been using a lens and forceps to examine "... a very seedy and disreputable hard-felt hat, much the worse for wear, and cracked in several places."[3] After they had greeted each other, Holmes said of it to Watson, "I beg that you will look upon it not as a battered billycock but as an intellectual problem."[4] It so happened that the hat led them into one of their most interesting adventures, but it could not have done so had Holmes not seen a problem in it from the start. A problem may be characterized as a fact or group of facts for which we have no acceptable explanation, which seem unusual, or which fail to fit in with our expectations or preconceptions. It should be obvious that *some* prior beliefs are required if anything is to appear problematic. If there are no expectations, there can be no surprises.

[1] "The Man with the Twisted Lip."

[2] *Ibid.*

[3] "The Adventure of the Blue Carbuncle."

[4] *Ibid.*

Sometimes, of course, problems came to Holmes already labeled. The very first adventure recounted by Dr. Watson began with the following message from Gregson of Scotland Yard:

My Dear Mr. Sherlock Holmes:

There has been a bad business during the night at 3, Lauriston Gardens, off the Brixton Road. Our man on the beat saw a light there about two in the morning, and as the house was an empty one, suspected that something was amiss. He found the door open, and in the front room, which is bare of furniture, discovered the body of a gentleman, well dressed, and having cards in his pocket bearing the name of 'Enoch J. Drebber, Cleveland, Ohio, U.S.A.' There had been no robbery, nor is there any evidence as to how the man met his death. There are marks of blood in the room, but there is no wound upon his person. We are at a loss as to how he came into the empty house; indeed, the whole affair is a puzzler. If you can come round to the house any time before twelve, you will find me there. I have left everything in statu quo until I hear from you. If you are unable to come, I shall give you fuller details, and would esteem it a great kindness if you would favour me with your opinion.

Yours faithfully,
TOBIAS GREGSON[5]

Here was a problem indeed. A few minutes after receiving the message, Sherlock Holmes and Dr. Watson "were both in a hansom, driving furiously for the Brixton Road."

2. Preliminary Hypotheses. On their ride out Brixton way, Holmes "prattled away about Cremona fiddles and the difference between a Stradivarius and an Amati." Dr. Watson chided Holmes for not giving much thought to the matter at hand, and Holmes replied: "No data yet ... It is a capital mistake to theorize before you have all the evidence. It biases the judgment."[6] This point of view was expressed by Holmes again and again. On one occasion he admonished a younger detective that "The temptation to form premature theories upon insufficient data is the bane of our profession."[7] Yet for all of his confidence about the matter, on this one issue Holmes was completely mistaken. Of course one should not reach a *final judgment* until a great deal of evidence has been considered, but this procedure is quite different from *not theorizing.* As a matter of fact, it is strictly impossible to make any serious attempt to collect evidence unless one *has* theorized beforehand. As Charles Darwin, the great biologist and author of the modern theory of evolution, observed: ". . . all observation must be for or against some view, if it is to be of any service." The point is that there are too many particular facts, too many data in the world, for anyone to try to become acquainted with them all. Everyone, even the most patient and thorough investigator, must pick and choose, deciding which facts to study and which to pass over. He must have some

---

[5] *A Study in Scarlet.*

[6] *Ibid.*

[7] *The Valley of Fear.*

working hypothesis for or against which to collect relevant data. It need not be a *complete* theory, but at least the rough outline must be there. Otherwise how could one decide what facts to select for consideration out of the totality of all facts, which is too vast even to begin to sift?

Holmes' actions were wiser than his words in this connection. After all, the words were spoken in a hansom speeding towards the scene of the crime. If Holmes really had no theory about the matter, why go to Brixton Road? If facts and data were all that he wanted, any old facts and any old data, with no hypotheses to guide him in their selection, why should he have left Baker Street at all? There were plenty of facts in the rooms at 221-B, Baker Street. Holmes might just as well have spent his time counting all the words on all the pages of all the books there, or perhaps making very accurate measurements of the distances between each separate pair of articles of furniture in the house. He could have gathered data to his heart's content and saved himself cab fare into the bargain!

It may be objected that the facts to be gathered at Baker Street have nothing to do with the case, whereas those which awaited Holmes at the scene of the crime were valuable clues for solving the problem. It was, of course, just this consideration which led Holmes to ignore the "data" at Baker Street and hurry away to collect those off Brixton Road. It must be insisted, however, that the greater relevance of the latter could not be *known* beforehand but only conjectured on the basis of previous experience with crimes and clues. It was in fact a *hypothesis* which led Holmes to look in one place rather than another for his facts, the hypothesis that there was a murder, that the crime was committed at the place where the body was found, and that the murderer had left some trace or clue which could lead to his discovery. Some such hypothesis is always required to guide the investigator in his search for relevant data, for in the absence of any preliminary hypothesis, there are simply too many facts in this world to examine. The preliminary hypothesis ought to be highly tentative, and it must be based on previous knowledge. But a preliminary hypothesis is as necessary as the existence of a problem for any serious inquiry to begin.

It must be emphasized that a preliminary hypothesis, as here conceived, need not be a complete solution to the problem. The hypothesis that the man was murdered by someone who had left some clues to his identity on or near the body of his victim was what led Holmes to Brixton Road. This hypothesis is clearly incomplete: it does not say who committed the crime, or how it was done, or why. Such a preliminary hypothesis may be very different from the final solution to the problem. It will never be complete: it may be a tentative explanation of only part of the problem. But however partial and however tentative, a preliminary hypothesis is required for any investigation to proceed.

3. Collecting Additional Facts. Every serious investigation begins with some fact or group of facts which strike the investigator as problematic and which initiate the whole process of inquiry. The initial facts which constitute the problem are usually too meagre to suggest a wholly satisfactory explanation for themselves, but they will suggest—to the competent investigator—some preliminary hypotheses which lead him to search out additional facts. These additional facts, it is hoped, will serve as clues to the final solution. The inexperienced or bungling investigator will overlook or ignore all but the most obvious of them; but the careful worker will aim at completeness in his examination of the additional facts to which his preliminary hypotheses lead him. Holmes, of course, was the most careful and painstaking of investigators.

Holmes insisted on dismounting from the hansom a hundred yards or so from their destination and approached the house on foot, looking carefully at its surroundings and especially at the pathway leading up to it. When Holmes and Watson entered the house, they were shown the body by the two Scotland Yard operatives, Gregson and Lestrade. ("There is no clue," said Gregson. "None at all," chimed in Lestrade.) But Holmes had already started his own search for additional facts, looking first at the body:

> ...his nimble fingers were flying here, there, and everywhere, feeling, pressing, unbuttoning, examining.... So swiftly was the examination made, that one would hardly have guessed the minuteness with which it was conducted. Finally, he sniffed the dead man's lips, and then glanced at the soles of his patent leather boots.[8]

Then turning his attention to the room itself,

> ...he whipped a tape measure and a large round magnifying glass from his pocket. With these two implements he trotted noiselessly about the room, sometimes stopping, occasionally kneeling, and once lying flat upon his face. So engrossed was he with his occupation that he appeared to have forgotten our presence, for he chattered away to himself under his breath the whole time, keeping up a running fire of exclamations, groans, whistles, and little cries suggestive of encouragement and of hope. As I watched him I was irresistibly reminded of a pure-blooded, well-trained foxhound as it dashes backward and forward through the covert, whining in its eagerness, until it comes across the lost scent. For twenty minutes or more he continued his researches, measuring with the most exact care the distance between marks which were entirely invisible to me, and occasionally applying his tape to the walls in an equally incomprehensible manner. In one place he gathered up very carefully a little pile of gray dust from the floor and packed it away in an envelope. Finally he examined with his glass the word upon the wall, going over every letter of it with the most minute exactness. This done, he appeared to be satisfied, for he replaced his tape and his glass in his pocket.
>
> "They say that genius is an infinite capacity for taking pains," he remarked with a smile. "It's a very bad definition, but it does apply to detective work."[9]

One matter deserves to be emphasized very strongly. Steps 2 and 3 are not completely separable but are usually very intimately connected and interdependent. True enough, we require a preliminary hypothesis to begin any intelligent examination of facts, but the additional facts

[8] *A Study in Scarlet.*

[9] *Ibid.*

may themselves suggest new hypotheses, which may lead to new facts, which suggest still other hypotheses, which lead to still other additional facts, and so on. Thus having made his careful examination of the facts available in the house off Brixton Road, Holmes was led to formulate a further hypothesis which required the taking of testimony from the constable who found the body. The man was off duty at the moment, and Lestrade gave Holmes the constable's name and address.

> Holmes took a note of the address.
> "Come along, Doctor," he said: "we shall go and look him up. I'll tell you one thing which may help you in the case," he continued, turning to the two detectives. "There has been murder done, and the murderer was a man. He was more than six feet high, was in the prime of life, had small feet for his height, wore coarse, square-toed boots and smoked a Trichinopoly cigar. He came here with his victim in a four-wheeled cab, which was drawn by a horse with three old shoes and one new one on his off fore-leg. In all probability the murderer had a florid face, and the fingernails of his right hand were remarkably long. These are only a few indications, but they may assist you."
> Lestrade and Gregson glanced at each other with an incredulous smile.
> "If this man was murdered, how was it done?" asked the former.
> "Poison," said Sherlock Holmes curtly, and strode off.[10]

4. Formulating the Hypothesis. At some stage or other of his investigation, any man—whether detective, scientist, or ordinary mortal—will get the feeling that he has all the facts needed for his solution. He has his "2 and 2," so to speak, but the task still remains of "putting them together." At such a time Sherlock Holmes might sit up all night, consuming pipe after pipe of tobacco, trying to think things through. The result or end product of such thinking, if it is successful, is a hypothesis which accounts for all the data, both the original set of facts which constituted the problem, and the additional facts to which the preliminary hypotheses pointed. The actual discovery of such an explanatory hypothesis is a process of creation, in which imagination as well as knowledge is involved. Holmes, who was a genius at inventing hypotheses, described the process as reasoning "backward." As he put it,

> Most people if you describe a train of events to them, will tell you what the result would be. They can put those events together in their minds, and argue from them that something will come to pass. There are few people, however, who, if you told them a result, would be able to evolve from their own inner consciousness what the steps were which led up to that result.[11]

Here is Holmes' description of the process of formulating an explanatory hypothesis. However that may be, when a hypothesis has been proposed, its evaluation must be along the lines that were sketched in Section III [Omitted Here]. Granted its relevance and testability, and its compatibility with other well-attested beliefs, the ultimate criterion for evaluating a hypothesis is its predictive power.

[10] *Ibid.*

[11] *Ibid.*

5. Deducing Further Consequences. A really fruitful hypothesis will not only explain the facts which originally inspired it, but will explain many others in addition. A good hypothesis will point beyond the initial facts in the direction of new ones whose existence might otherwise not have been suspected. And of course the verification of those further consequences will tend to confirm the hypothesis which led to them. Holmes' hypothesis that the murdered man had been poisoned was soon put to such a test. A few days later the murdered man's secretary and traveling companion was also found murdered. Holmes asked Lestrade, who had discovered the second body, whether he had found anything in the room which could furnish a clue to the murderer. Lestrade answered, "Nothing," and went on to mention a few quite ordinary effects. Holmes was not satisfied and pressed him, asking, "And was there nothing else?" Lestrade answered, "Nothing of any importance," and named a few more details, the last of which was "a small chip ointment box containing a couple of pills." At this information,

> Sherlock Holmes sprang from his chair with an exclamation of delight. "The last link," he cried, exultantly. "My case is complete."
> The two detectives stared at him in amazement.
> "I have now in my hands," my companion said, confidently, "all the threads which have formed such a tangle. . . . I will give you a proof of my knowledge. Could you lay your hands upon those pills?"
> "I have them," said Lestrade, producing a small white box . . .[12]

On the basis of his hypothesis about the original crime, Holmes was able to predict that the pills found at the scene of the second crime must contain poison. Here deduction has an essential role in the process of any scientific or inductive inquiry. The ultimate value of any hypothesis lies in its predictive or explanatory power, which means that additional facts must be deducible from an adequate hypothesis. From his theory that the first man was poisoned and that the second victim met his death at the hands of the same murderer, Holmes inferred that the pills found by Lestrade must be poison. His theory, however sure he may have felt about it, was only a theory and needed further confirmation. He obtained that confirmation by testing the consequences deduced from the hypothesis and finding them to be true. Having used deduction to make a prediction, his next step was to test it.

6. Testing the Consequences. The consequences of a hypothesis, that is, the predictions made on the basis of that hypothesis, may require various means for their testing. Some require only observation. In some cases, Holmes needed only to watch and wait—for the bank robbers to break into the vault, in the "Adventure of the Red-headed League," or for Dr. Roylott to slip a venomous snake through a dummy ventilator, in the "Adventure of the Speckled Band." In the present case, however, an experiment had to be performed.

Holmes asked Dr. Watson to fetch the landlady's old and ailing terrier, which she had asked to have put out of its misery the day before.

[12] *Ibid.*

Holmes then cut one of the pills in two, dissolved it in a wineglass of water, added some milk, and

> ...turned the contents of the wineglass into a saucer and placed it in front of the terrier, who speedily licked it dry. Sherlock Holmes's earnest demeanour had so far convinced us that we all sat in silence, watching the animal intently, and expecting some startling effect. None such appeared, however. The dog continued to lie stretched upon the cushion, breathing in a laboured way, but apparently neither the better nor the worse for its draught.
>
> Holmes had taken out his watch, and as minute followed minute without result, an expression of the utmost chagrin and disappointment appeared upon his features. He gnawed his lip, drummed his fingers upon the table, and showed every other symptom of acute impatience. So great was his emotion that I felt sincerely sorry for him, while the two detectives smiled derisively, by no means displeased at this check which he had met.
>
> "It can't be a coincidence," he cried, at last springing from his chair and pacing wildly up and down the room: "it is impossible that it should be a mere coincidence. The very pills which I suspected in the case of Drebber are actually found after the death of Stangerson. And yet they are inert. What can it mean? Surely my whole chain of reasoning cannot have been false. It is impossible! And yet this wretched dog is none the worse. Ah, I have it! I have it!" With a perfect shriek of delight he rushed to the box, cut the other pill in two, dissolved it, added milk, and presented it to the terrier. The unfortunate creature's tongue seemed hardly to have been moistened in it before it gave a convulsive shiver in every limb, and lay as rigid and lifeless as if it had been struck by lightning.
>
> Sherlock Holmes drew a long breath, and wiped the perspiration from his forehead.[13]

By the favorable outcome of his experiment, Holmes' hypothesis had received dramatic and convincing confirmation.

7. *Application.* The detective's concern, after all, is a practical one. Given a crime to solve, he has not merely to explain the facts but to apprehend and arrest the criminal. The latter involves making application of his theory, using it to predict where the criminal can be found and how he may be caught. He must deduce still further consequences from the hypothesis, not for the sake of additional confirmation but for practical use. From his general hypothesis Holmes was able to infer that the murderer was acting the role of a cabman. We have already seen that Holmes had formed a pretty clear description of the man's appearance. He sent out his army of "Baker Street Irregulars," street urchins of the neighborhood, to search out and summon the cab driven by just that man. The successful "application" of this hypothesis can be described again in Dr. Watson's words. A few minutes after the terrier's death,

> ...there was a tap at the door, and the spokesman of the street Arabs, young Wiggins, introduced his insignificant and unsavoury person.
>
> "Please, sir," he said touching his forelock, "I have the cab downstairs."
>
> "Good boy," said Holmes, blandly. "Why don't you introduce this pattern at Scotland Yard?" he continued, taking a pair of steel handcuffs from

[13] *Ibid.*

a drawer. "See how beautifully the spring works. They fasten in an instant."

"The old pattern is good enough," remarked Lestrade, "if we can only find the man to put them on."

"Very good, very good," said Holmes, smiling. "The cabman may as well help me with my boxes. Just ask him to step in, Wiggins."

I was surprised to find my companion speaking as though he were about to set out on a journey, since he had not said anything to me about it. There was a small portmanteau in the room, and this he pulled out and began to strap. He was busily engaged at it when the cabman entered the room.

"Just give me a help with this buckle, cabman," he said, kneeling over his task, and never turning his head.

The fellow came forward with a somewhat sullen, defiant air, and put down his hands to assist. At that instant there was a sharp click, the jangling of metal, and Sherlock Holmes sprang to his feet again.

"Gentlemen," he cried, with flashing eyes, "let me introduce you to Mr. Jefferson Hope, the murderer of Enoch Drebber and of Joseph Stangerson."[14]

Here we have a picture of the detective as scientist, reasoning from observed facts to a testable hypothesis which not only explains the facts but permits of practical application.

[14] *Ibid.*

Contemporary Issues

Science and Extrasensory Perception

A Scientific Critique of Parapsychology   James C. Crumbaugh

James C. Crumbaugh (1912–   ) is a psychologist who is currently Director
of Psychological Services at the Veterans Administration Hospital in Gulfport,
Mississippi. Besides his interest in psychotherapy, he has, for many years,
been interested in the experimental work in extrasensory perception.

Scientific parapsychology is now slightly over a generation old. The
present-day story really begins with the work of J. B. Rhine at Duke in
the early 1930's. To be sure, there were scientific antecedents such as the
French physiologist Charles Richet, who in 1884 anticipated Rhine's basic
methodology: the testing of subjects by having them guess a sequence of
events which is set by chance in known ratios, and statistical evaluation of
the presence of an extrachance factor in the guessing. Richet used playing
cards (which Rhine later replaced with his five "ESP" symbols). The Richet
experiments made little impact, however, save in the circles of the then
newly organized (1882) Society for Psychical Research in London and
among isolated scientists and other individuals already sympathetic to
the claims of psychic (later termed "psi" by R. H. Thoules, English psychologist) phenomena. There were some well-known British figures, such
as physicists Sir William Barrett, Sir William Crookes, Sir Oliver Lodge,
and physician Sir Arthur Conan Doyle (the Sherlock Holmes creator more
oriented toward fiction than science), but in America only a very few
genuine scientists—such as William James, the Harvard physiologist-
philosopher-psychologist who fathered American psychology, and William
McDougall, the English-American physician-psychologist who was Rhine's
mentor at Duke—actually believed in even the possible rare occurrence
of what have now become known as parapsychological phenomena.

While the picture in American science today is by no means so vastly
different as one might expect after a generation of research (if the parapsychological claims are indeed valid), the changes that have occurred
have largely followed the impetus of Rhine's experiments.

The work of the Duke laboratory was introduced in 1935 with Rhine's
monograph, *Extrasensory Perception*, but it was his second book, *New
Frontiers of the Mind* in 1937, which caught the public eye. His studies
were the first to apply the scientific method to the field in a systematic,
consistent, and tenacious attempt to obtain sufficient and adequate data
to gain acceptance by the scientific world. The major phenomena (mental

From *International Journal of Neuropsychiatry*, Vol. 2, September–October, 1966. Reprinted
by permission of *Behavioral Neuropsychiatry*, successor to the *International Journal of
Neuropsychiatry*.

telepathy and clairvoyance) he subsumed under the term extrasensory perception or ESP.

In the early years there was heated controversy, and American scientists divided themselves quickly into "for" and "against" camps. The "unconvinced" platform held 91 per cent of the votes according to a survey of American psychologists by Warner and Clark in 1938. A less extensive questionnaire sent the same year by the present writer suggested that the skeptics constituted about 97 per cent. A second survey by Warner 14 years later indicated that the "ESP is unproven" camp was losing, though it still held some 83 per cent of the chips.

Compared to the British, it was more difficult for American psychologists—dominated as they were by the extreme mechanism of Watsonian behaviorism and its various subsequent afterbirths—to accept the possibility of these phenomena, which have with few exceptions been considerered to represent nonmechanistic or "nonphysical" events in nature.

I entered the parapsychological scene in 1938 with a Master's thesis on extrasensory perception. At the time of performing the experiments involved, I fully expected that they would yield easily all of the final answers. I did not imagine that after 28 years I would still be as much in doubt as when I had begun.

I repeated a number of the then current Duke techniques, but the results of 3,024 runs of the ESP cards—as much work as Rhine reported in his first book—were all negative. In 1940 I utilized further Duke methods with high school students, again with negative findings.

A number of other experimenters had of course repeated Rhine's experiments, some obtaining positive and others negative results. The number of repetitions which failed of verification always seemed, however, to be greater than those that succeeded.

The subsequent literature adequately answered, in my opinion, all of the criticisms leveled at the Duke research except one vital point (to be discussed later).

The *first* and foremost center of early attack was upon Rhine's statistical methods, though these objections came from would-be mathematician-psychologists rather than from professional mathematicians. The latter supported Rhine almost from the first, for he had taken his techniquest directly from their tutorage, and in 1937 this issue was virtually ended by a statement from the American Institute of Mathematical Statistics endorsing the ESP mathematics. It did not, however, change many psychologists' opinions.

And, more important, it did not solve the problem of exactly what interpretive conclusions may properly be drawn concerning the validity of the ESP hypothesis from finding the presence of an extrachance factor in data that have been quite adequately and carefully treated by legitimately applicable statistics. This point will be considered later.

Following the failure of the initial attack (upon Rhine's statistics), a *second* major assault was launched on the grounds of poor experimental control of such extraneous variables as sensory cues, recording errors, and the like. Many of these criticisms were justified in some of the early Duke experiments, but Rhine set about to answer them one by one, and in the course of a few years had produced studies (or could point to the studies of others) which were virtually foolproof in all of these areas.

A third cause of critical rejection of positive ESP results by many scientists was the fact that ESP violated *a priori* the sacred framework of mechanistic science; that is, it could not be logically explained as consistent with natural law. While most experimentalists pay lip service to the importance of evaluating experimental results strictly on the soundness of the experimental procedures involved, they usually feel quite unconsciously that whenever results that cannot be rationalized within the framework of systematic science are obtained, something must be wrong with the experimental work itself. Though this is often correct, the error can also be—and in the history of science often has been—on the other side of the coin: in the theoretical assumptions of the current scientific systems. Such names as Galilei, Pasteur, Mesmer, and Einstein come immediately to mind, and the list could be greatly extended.

In spite of the treacherous and costly fallacy of drawing *a priori* or deductive conclusions from *a posteriori* or inductive data, however, the temptation seems overpowering for many of even the top scientists. Witness the case of D. O. Hebb, one of the most creative names in physiological psychology today, who has chosen by his own admission this route with reference to ESP: "Why do we not accept ESP as a psychological fact? Rhine has offered enough evidence to have convinced us on almost any other issue where one could make some guess as to the mechanics of the disputed process. . . . Personally I do not accept ESP for a moment, because it does not make any sense. . . . I cannot see what other basis my colleagues have for rejecting it. . . . My own rejection of (Rhine's) views is—in a literal sense—prejudice."

That to take this sort of position is to build upon the sands is shown by a more recent Russian opinion which, while remaining utterly mechanistic as required of loyal communists, accepts the existence of ESP and offers a purely physical interpretation of it. Roshchin (the writer) does not specify the actual mechanism involved, but shows that one can postulate such and that many other phenomena for which a physical basis is now known were once rejected because they "could not be true" from a physical standpoint.

If we rejected evidence for any effect which we cannot at the time fit consistently into the picture of current scientific theory, we would still be rejecting the value of aspirin. It seems that physicians do not yet know just how it works, but few would doubt that it does.

This third cause of rejection of ESP—on *a priori* grounds—cannot stand as scientifically valid and need not trouble us further. Rhine has, however, partially brought this criticism upon himself by his refusal to accept the requirements of a *repeatable* experiment as essential to proof of the ESP hypothesis. (This will be discussed later.) Failure here relegates parapsychology to observational rather than experimental science, where Hebb's position is more reasonable.

If one wishes to reject an hypothesis but finds nothing wrong with the evidence for it, he may then turn to an *ad hominem* argument—the dishonesty of the experimenters. So this was the *fourth* line of criticism of the ESP results, though it came, as might be expected, after most other avenues of attack had been exhausted. Price suggested that deliberate fraud on the part of the investigators is the explanation of experiments that cannot be attributed to error or incompetence. And more recently a Russian scientist, Kitaygorodsky, has stated that "there can be only one answer. The successful experiments are simply a matter of dishonest researchers or mediums."

The only immediate rejoinder to this type of argument—an argument which can, of course, always be applied to any scientific findings out of harmony with whatever one wishes to believe—is to point to the number and quality of experimenters who have produced the results in question. In the case of ESP the positive findings come from so large a number of experimenters representing such a variety of disciplines that most critics do not take this kind of criticism seriously. Still there is only one way to rule it out completely, and that is to produce an experimental procedure which can be employed by almost all qualified experimenters with very similar findings.

And that brings us to the *fifth* and last major line of criticism of ESP results, the only criticism not yet adequately met by present data, and the one which I contend is crucial and must be met before the great bulk of scientists will swing over to acceptance of the ESP hypothesis. This is the failure of ESP experimenters to produce a truly *repeatable* experiment—one which can be replicated in almost any laboratory as many times as desired with essentially the same results. Repeatability has long been a cornerstone among the requirements of sound methodology in all *experimental* science.

Rhine has consistently rejected this criterion, admitting that it cannot be met by parapsychologists at present, but arguing that the only type of repeatability necessary is that furnished by the numerous positive experiments.

In addition to Rhine, Murphy has pointed to *observational* sciences like geology and biology, many of whose phenomena cannot be reproduced consistently in an experimental laboratory, One type of example would be the observed phylogenetic relationships upon which the theory of evolution is based. We can easily reproduce the evolutionary process in the laboratory through experiments with *Drosophila Melanogaster,* the common fruit fly. But this does not prove man's evolution, which is an *a priori* inference based on observational rather than experimental data. If this theory were not in logical harmony with the main body of science, we would reject it for the same reason Hebb rejects ESP. So until ESP data become fully repeatable and therefore fully *experimental,* Hebb cannot be criticized too severely. His error is that he apparently accepts ESP data as experimentally adequate yet still refuses them *a priori.*

Since the exact conditions which produce ESP are unknown, experiments that fail are presumed by Rhine to have failed to hit upon these conditions, while those which succeed are presumed to have found them. This argument may, of course, represent the true facts; but on the other hand the real facts may be otherwise: There may be some unknown error in the positive experiments which is just as elusive and subtle as the true conditions for the production of ESP are presumed to be in the negative results. We cannot know which is the true situation until the conditions for the occurrence of ESP can be specified accurately enough to yield a consistently repeatable experiment. Until then the only justifiable scientific position must be one of suspended judgment on the basis of inconclusive evidence.

If one accepts ESP as proven without its having met the criterion of repeatability or of specification of conditions necessary for its control, one is accepting proof based purely on statistical grounds. Now statistics alone can never "prove" the existence of anything, no matter how impressive the statistical results may be. Statistics only state the mathematical odds that an extrachance factor is present in the results. The criterion of any given odds which may be accepted as evidence of this extrachance factor is always arbitrary. The conventional criterion of the "1 per cent level of confidence" means merely that, on the average, if 100 similar samples of data were gathered and if there really is no extrachance factor, one would obtain a chance deviation as great as that actually obtained from the average expected by chance in only one of these 100 samples. If one took 1,000 such samples, he should get by pure chance 10 samples that deviate from chance expectation as much as the deviation actually obtained. But these 10 samples *might* be included in the first 100 samples drawn and there might be none in the remaining 900 samples.

In any given samples of data treated by statistics, we can never be absolutely certain just what did and did not occur by chance. Thus in an ESP experiment the correct hypothesis is *not*, "If odds of 100 to 1 (or any acceptable criterion) are obtained in the experimental results, ESP exists." The correct hypothesis is, "If these odds are obtained *and if* ESP exists, then it probably occurred in this experiment, and the probability is given by the obtained odds."

As the late R. A. Fisher, dean of statisticians, pointed out years ago, "Very long odds . . . are much less relevant to the establishment of the facts of nature than would be a demonstration of the reliable reproducibility of the phenomena." Dr. Malcolm Turner, a statistician formerly on the staff of the Duke Laboratory, once pointed out to me that since the majority of ESP experiments have probably been done by persons predisposed to a belief in ESP, and since many such persons are not scientifically trained and tend to discard and not to report negative results (and, it might be added, since the parapsychological journals have tended to report all positive experiments even where controls are poor but to publish only brief notes of negative studies or to reject them on grounds of methodological errors), it is impossible to evaluate all of the ESP experimentation that has ever been done. But if it were possible to do this, it *might* be that the positive findings represent only the number of spurious or "extra-criterion of chance" deviations to be expected in this amount of data by chance. A similar point has been made by Leuba.

At the time of my own experimentation I was aware of all of this, but it was the following incident which cinched my resolution never to accept the ESP (or any other experimental) hypothesis as *proven* until the criterion of a truly repeatable experiment can be met.

In the summer of 1954, having renewed my ESP experimentation following interruption by World War II, I was on the staff of the Duke Laboratory under a research grant from the Parapsychology Foundation. Even though my own experimentation had continued to yield negative results, I had been impressed almost to the point of conviction by some of the studies in the literature. There were two in particular which, while not among those Rhine considered to be the best advocates of the case for ESP, seemed to me from the written reports as very well done and just about foolproof.

I discussed my reactions to these experiments with other members of the Duke staff and was quite amazed to learn that neither experiment had a good reputation there. In one case there were rumors that the scoring had not been done by the student scorers as the professor believed and reported in the literature; and in the other—a case of phenomenally high ESP scores of one subject in a distance experiment—it was reported that the subject was known to have considerable psychopathology and that she had access to the home of the experimenter where the ESP target cards were kept; and it was suspected that she had gained sensory knowledge from them before making her calls.

Whether the aspersions cast upon either of these experiments were true is beside the point. The reports jolted deeply my confidence in the ability of any experimenter to report with absolute accuracy exactly what he has done. Often what he actually did may deviate in unrecognized ways from what he thinks he has done. Both of the aforementioned experimenters were probably completely honest and believed they reported exactly what happened. But in both there were those close to the experiment who believed the true events occurred—unknown to the experimenters—somewhat differently.

I recalled at this point the words of E. G. Boring in a personal communication to me in response to my 1938 questionnaire on attitudes toward the validity of ESP. In refusing to answer the questionnaire, Boring stated, "I doubt that an evaluative judgment of whether this or that research is valid should ever be sponsored on the basis of published reports alone." The wisdom of this statement was now clear, and from that point on I made my personal criterion of acceptance the production of a genuinely repeatable experiment.

So I set out to find a repeatable experimental design. Nicol and Humphrey and Schmeidler had produced data that suggested a relationship between ESP ability and factors of personality and attitude of belief in ESP. Believers got better scores than disbelievers, and self-confident subjects scored higher than insecure individuals. And Rhine had insisted that the enthusiasm and confident belief of the experimenter was a major factor in stimulating subjects to score significantly.

I reasoned that if *both experimenters and subjects* were fractionated on such variables, self-confident believer experimenters should get far superior results with similar subjects than insecure disbeliever experimenters would get with subjects like themselves. I obtained grants from the Parapsychology Foundation of New York to spend a summer at the Duke

Laboratory studying Rhine's techniques and then to return to the college where at that time I taught psychology and to set up experiments along the above lines.

The first experiment (1955) yielded marginally significant results favorable to ESP, but a repetition (1956) was negative, and the results of the two together were at chance level. I had hoped to interest other laboratories in repeating the same design, but Rhine and others showed an interest in a design of Anderson and White, which, following the lead of van Busschbach, indicated that school children made significantly higher ESP scores when the tests were administered by teachers they liked and who liked them than when given by teachers with whom the children shared a mutual dislike. The design had some successful repetitions.

Therefore, several years later at another institution I interested two of my graduate students in repeating the Anderson and White design. One repetition, that of Deguisne, seemed to support the ESP hypothesis, while the other, that of Goldstone, did not. Since then further repetitions elsewhere have been ambiguous. . . .

Today, as far as I can see, the repeatability issue is left about where it started: Only a portion of repetitions of any ESP experiment is successful, somewhere between 25 per cent and 50 per cent.

Hoping to end this deadlock, I issued a challenge to all parapsychologists to face up to the repeatability issue. I suggested they select a single experimental design that offered promise of becoming repeatable and that at the same time permitted full control of all conditions, and that they enlist the support of all laboratories interested in parapsychology in large-scale mass repetitions of this design. It should be possible, if the ESP hypothesis is valid, to find a design which would yield at least a majority of successful repetitions.

To all of this Rhine dissented, denying as always the necessity of satisfying the criterion of repeatability. So far nothing of consequence has been done on this issue, though some parapsychologists—like Murphy, one of the field's top names—have emphasized its importance.

The result of this situation is that the vast majority of experimental scientists have simply ignored *psi* research. In my opinion the only development which could interest them would be the discovery of a truly repeatable experimental design by which they could obtain reasonably consistent positive ESP results in their own laboratories. And until a far larger share of the best scientific brains are recruited in the study of *psi* capacities (again assuming that they are valid), it is very unlikely that an understanding of their nature and their control will be worked out. . . .

For my part, while scientifically I feel I must suspend judgment on the ESP hypothesis pending the appearance of a repeatable experiment, the evidence to date leads me to a strong suspicion that it is valid. Suspicion is not science; it is nevertheless interesting and often valuable to speculate beyond that which is proven.

And to speculate further, the enigmatic and illusive way in which *psi* capacities avoid being pinned down causes me to suspect that if they do exist as valid phenomena they also bear characteristics which may make it forever impossible to demonstrate them by the criteria of mechanistic science.

While most parapsychologists assume *psi* phenomena are not governed by mechanistic laws, they use the technique of mechanistic science—the experimental or inductive method—to study them. Although this method is the only known means of proof in the usual scientific sense, there may be an inconsistency in its use here: It may turn out that (a) these phenomena exist, (b) they are governed by nonmechanistic laws, (c) nonmechanistic laws can never be discovered by mechanistic methods, and (d) such laws therefore cannot be known with scientific certainty but must be forever inferred by nonrational or intuitive means.

This is a philosophically dignified way of acceding to the religionist's dogma that the ultimate questions of the nature of man and the universe can never be understood by science (a view to which most scientists also subscribe), but must be assumed on the basis of faith rooted in a freely chosen system of values (which, of course, to the religionist are in turn determined by his particular theological system).

In other words, parapsychology may really fall within the province of religion rather than science. If its phenomena are actually nonmechanistic, it would appear likely that this is so. But because the phenomena may in reality be a part of mechanism, as some parapsychologists—and apparently an increasing number—believe, and further because there is a possibility that even if they are nonmechanistic they can still be studied successfully by mechanistic techniques as Rhine seems to assume, there is every good reason to go all out in pressing to the limit the application of the experimental method to their solution. And this is the reason for my insistence on a concerted attack upon the problem of repeatability.

If the latter goal can be achieved, it will change the entire complexion of mechanistic science and the attendant view of the nature of man and probably of the universe. And with this change will come a new birth in philosophy, social and political science and economics—as well as in psychiatry and the mental health professions. Indeed, it will profoundly affect all who deal with man, which includes just about everybody.

We may pause to speculate upon the implications for psychiatry in particular. Eisenbud, Ehrenwald, Ullman, and Meerloo are among the psychiatrists who have led in studying the relationships between *psi* capacities and psychopathology. No one has so far suggested a practical application of *psi* phenomena in the treatment of mental or emotional disorders, but important possibilities for common areas of study are indicated. For example, parapsychologists have concluded that their phenomena operate—exclusively, so far—on the unconscious (though at least partially voluntary) level of awareness. Further, some of the phenomena of psychopathology, such as visual and auditory hallucinations, may be interpreted at least in some instances either as *psi* manifestations or as psychiatric aberrations, or possibly as both. And some psychiatrists feel that patients who have—or think they have—*psi* experiences exhibit particular types of regressive personalities, which means that reports of such phenomena may be valuable in diagnosis. Thus there are many points of common interest between the two disciplines, and therefore very logical reasons for each to be concerned with the phenomena of the other.

And there are still more important reasons why an interest *should* exist on the part of virtually all disciplines in arriving at a satisfactory answer to the question of the validity of *psi* phenomena. Man stands as at no other time in his entire history at the crossroads in his choice between two systems of values based on opposite concepts of the nature of man.

One holds that man is fully reducible to mechanism and Pavlovian reflexiology. This is the thesis of Marxist dialectical materialism and congruent with the entire social and economic thinking of communism, and collectivism.

The other regards man as more than mechanism, as irreducible to its concepts, as existing in a unique dimension of values which transcend the material world. This view is congruent with the concepts of individualism and its socioeconomic correlates, the interpretation of man upon which America was founded.

Between these two diametrically opposed value systems modern man must choose, choose quickly, and bear the responsibility for his choice. Any field of study which offers the hope of clear evidence upon which presently faltering multitudes may base a sound decision is a vital field. Parapsychology is such an area of study.

ESP: Fact or Fraud?   C. E. M. Hansel

C. E. Mark Hansel (1917–   ), holder of the Chair of Psychology at the University College of Swansea, University of Wales, is the author of numerous articles on topics in psychology. He has made a special study of extrasensory perception and has attacked the validity of much of the experimental work in that field.

Is ESP a Fact?

The basic problem of parapsychology is relatively simple when compared with problems in politics or aesthetics. Either it is possible for at least some people to communicate by extrasensory perception, or else ESP does not and cannot exist because the underlying processes necessary for its occurrence do not exist. A great deal of experimental work has failed to provide a clear case for the existence of ESP, but at least two facts have been established: first, subjects when trying to guess card symbols have obtained scores that cannot be attributed to chance; second, some of those taking part in ESP experiments have cheated to produce high scores.

The first fact cannot be disputed. Results such as those obtained by Hubert Pearce or by Riess's high-scoring subject need no statistical analysis for the purpose of establishing that something was happening during the experiments other than pure guesswork. The second fact that those taking part in experiments sometimes cheat is known from admissions of trickery. The first 2 major experiments in Great Britain on the Creery sisters and on Smith and Blackburn in 1882, involved 8 subjects, 7 of whom admitted to cheating, and the other did cheat according to his partner in the act. The last major investigation in Great Britain, on the Welsh schoolboys in 1955–1957, involved 2 subjects, both of whom admitted to cheating after being caught in the act. It would be remarkable if such attempts to assist the natural course of events ceased altogether in parapsychology between the years 1882 and 1956. In fact, close examination of the most spectacular findings in parapsychology invariably points to some form of trickery as an alternative to ESP. To the skeptic, psychical research seems to have been as much a history of the manner in which the artful can mislead the innocent as it is a reflection of any more esoteric activity.

Is ESP a Fraud?

Cheating in one form or another is one of the commonest of human activities. If it never occurred, much of the expense and complication of modern life would be avoided. The paper work involved in accounting and auditing—tickets, bills, counterfoils, invoices—would no longer be necessary. Games, examinations, competitions, and numerous such activities would be simplified. On the other hand, it is unlikely that more than a small number of experiments on ESP are affected by cheating, since the investigator does his best to ensure that his subjects cannot cheat and, no doubt, usually succeeds. The majority of investigators are likely to have sufficient faith in the reality of ESP to believe that it will manifest itself without outside aid. It may then seem strange to the reader that so much space has been given here to the matter of trickery. Why in the case of each of the so-called conclusive experiments should trickery invariably emerge as a likely alternative to ESP?

One reason is that an experiment is not classified as conclusive unless the known causes of experimental error have been eliminated in its design. If a trick is used in an experiment, it might be expected to produce an impressive result having large odds against arising by chance and, if the experiment is of the "conclusive" category, trickery would be the only alternative explanation to ESP. Thus, the process by which conclusive experiments are weeded out will also bring to light experiments in which a trick has been used.

A trick also involves a trickster. The following remarks made by George R. Price are very relevant.

> The wise procedure, when we seek to evaluate probability of fraud, is to try to ignore all vague, psychological criteria and base our reasoning (i) on such evidence as would impress a court and (ii) on purely statistical considerations. And here we must recognise that we usually make a

certain gross statistical error. When we consider the possibility of fraud, almost invariably we think of particular individuals and ask ourselves whether it is possible that this particular man, this Professor X, could be dishonest. The probability seems small, but the procedure is incorrect. The correct procedure is to consider that we very likely would not have heard of Professor X at all except for his psychic findings. Accordingly, the probability of interest to us is the probability of there having been anywhere in the world, among its more than 2 billion inhabitants, a few people with the desire and ability to produce false evidence for the supernatural.[1]

There is one psychological criterion, however, that even a court of law would regard as impressive. That is the question of motive. Why should people go to all the trouble of entering into complicated conspiracies merely to deceive their fellows? It should first be noted that there are many cases of known trickery in science where the motive is not clear. The Piltdown skull discovered in 1912 that at first appeared to be an important piece of evidence in the history of man's development involved the trickster in a lot of work for little apparent gain.

However, in the case of many individuals acting as subjects in parapsychology there is often a very clear motive. Mediums at one time in the United States were said to constitute the second highest paid profession open to women, and where monetary gain is not involved, there may be the desire to impress or to gain prestige. In the case of each of the major experimental investigations to which a chapter has been given in this book, there is a possible monetary or prestige motive for trickery.

In the early 1930's at Duke University, during the Depression, students who acted as subjects in ESP experiments were paid an hourly wage for their services. If Pearce was paid to act as a subject, he had every incentive to continue in that capacity. The Pratt-Woodruff experiment was a continuation of work started by Woodruff constituting part of the requirement for a higher degree. The Soal-Goldney experiment gained Soal his Doctorate of Science at London University. Would that degree have been given for a series of negative experiments? Mrs. Stewart was paid for her services. The Jones boys earned large rewards for high scores.

Parapsychologists are themselves to blame for the emphasis that has to be placed on cheating when considering their work. In science generally it is likely that, at times, investigators indulge in underhanded activities, but their experiments are shown up when other scientists fail to confirm their results. In such cases it may not be necessary to hold a long postmortem on the earlier experiment; it is just forgotten. However, parapsychologists—or at least some of the more vociferous of them—in denying the necessity to confirm experiments by repetition, make it essential to examine every experiment in detail in order to ensure that the result could not have been caused by cheating.

It is often difficult to discuss the possibility of cheating objectively. Parapsychologists tend to present their critics with a *fait accompli*. A similar situation would arise in orthodox science if a chemist reported an

[1] G. R. Price, *Science* (1955), p. 363.

experimental result that contradicted all the previous research findings and theories of his fellow chemists, together with the statement "Either this finding must be accepted as valid or else you must accuse me of being a cheat and a liar. Do you accept it?" In such circumstances, orthodox chemists might feel diffident about openly expressing their doubts. They might, however, repeat the experiment to see whether they got the same result. If they failed to confirm his result, they would not go into a long discussion as to whether the original investigator was a liar or a cheat. They would just take with a grain of salt any further experimental reports from the same source.

The trickster has often been assisted by the investigator's overwhelming confidence in his ability to detect trickery. Observers, however careful, must be prepared to make mistakes. But in psychical research many of the investigators have considered themselves infallible. Soal claimed that boys of the caliber of Glyn and Ieuan could never hope to deceive him.

If a trick is used in an experiment, this fact might be expected to make itself apparent in the course of further research. But parapsychologists have erected a system that aids the trickster and at the same time preserves experimental findings.

Survival Characteristics of ESP

Scientists in general have been little influenced by philosophers who strive to inform them about the methodology and logic of their subject. Science has a basic methodological principle that is self-generating. It was not formulated by anybody, but it has the same empirical basis and underlying logic as the principle of natural selection in evolution. Investigators are continually producing reports of their experimental findings, which may be classified, for convenience, as good and bad. The good ones survive because they are confirmed in further research. The bad ones are forgotten because they cannot be confirmed. Science advances through a process of natural selection. New findings become targets for criticism, and a finding must be confirmed by critics under their own experimental conditions; it then soon becomes clear when it is to be rejected.

If anyone invents a pseudoscience in which this principle ceases to operate, the result soon becomes apparent, for the new "science" fails to have predictive value and leads to more and more findings and theories that are incompatible with orthodox science. This is what has happened in parapsychology. When critics fail to confirm ESP, that is not accepted as a reason for dropping the subject; on the contrary, belief in the reality of ESP is so strong that the principle of repeatability has been rejected or rendered impotent by the invoking of new processes which are claimed as subsidiary characteristics of the phenomenon. Thus, given a high-scoring subject, it would in the normal course of events be only a matter of time before every critic could be silenced, but these subjects cease to score high when tested by critics. Extrasensory perception only manifests itself before uncritical investigators. Again, Rhine and Pratt have observed, "Another major difficulty can be seen in the fact that some experimenters after a period of earlier success in obtaining extra-chance results in psi experiments have proved less effective in their later efforts. In such instances something apparently has been lost that was once a potent factor. The element most likely to change under prolonged testing would seem to be the quality of infectious enthusiasm that accompanies the initial discoveries of the research worker. Those who never succeed at all may, of course, be suspected of not ever having felt such contagious or communicable interest as would help to create a favorable test environment for their subject."[2] In other words, experimenters fail to confirm their own results. And a further subsidiary characteristic emerges: ESP is affected by the mental state of the person investigating it.

If fresh characteristics are postulated in this manner, it is possible to survive almost any form of criticism. An experimental result cannot be confirmed or refuted since ESP does not operate in front of critics. After tightening up his experimental conditions, an investigator cannot disclaim the findings of his earlier work; failure in later work reveals that he has lost his enthusiasm.

Since the chief characteristic of the exploratory stage, according to the statement of Rhine and Pratt . . . , is that the investigator carries out his work without being burdened with too much precautionary concern,"[3] failure to confirm earlier work is likely to arise when the investigator graduates from the exploratory stage to one where he takes more care with his work. After an investigator becomes burdened with concern, his precautions will, presumably, be against error and trickery rather than against ESP. It may be assumed that any change in his experimental results is due to the effectiveness of his precautions.

A Revised Approach

At the present time, there are signs that the arguments put forward to support the work on ESP may be changing. Rhine and Pratt in recent writings imply that the case for ESP does not, after all, depend on conclusive experiments, but on general features that emerge from the whole mass of studies, conclusive or inconclusive; it is as if quantity can make up for quality when the latter has been found lacking. They write:

> The body of fact in parapsychology is like a many-celled organism. Its strength is that of a growth-relationship, consisting not only of the compounding of one cell with another, but also of the many lawful interrelations that emerge in the growing structure. Going back as Hansel has done, with a one-cell perspective, to fix attention on some incomplete stage of development within a single experimental research is hard to understand in terms of healthy scientific motivation.[4]

What is the point of presenting conclusive experiments for the consideration of the scientific world if they cannot be criticized? How can an experiment be criticized until it has first been isolated? If experiments

---

[2] Rhine and Pratt, *Parapsychology*, p. 132.

[3] *Ibid.*, p. 19.

[4] Rhine and Pratt, *Journal of Parapsychology* (1961), p. 94.

are to be considered en masse, will not data be confused with results such as those obtained with the Creery sisters and Smith and Blackburn? But as soon as criteria by means of which experiments are selected or rejected are set up, it becomes necessary to isolate each experiment to see whether it satisfies those criteria.

Moreover, what precisely are the "lawful inter-relationships" within the body of fact in parapsychology to which Rhine refers? To date, not a single lawful inter-relationship appears to have been established. How, for example, does distance affect extrasensory perception? The relationship between scoring rate and distance is completely chaotic, apparently dependent on the investigator, the subject, and the experimental conditions. If it were possible to give a standardized test for ESP to different groups of subjects, systematically varying factors such as age, nationality, intelligence, previous practice, distance, and so on, some lawful inter-relationships might eventually be expected to reveal themselves. But each of the reported investigations yields a result that has little relationship to any of the others.

Extrasensory perception is not a fact but a theory put forward to account for observations consisting of high scores obtained during the course of experiments. Parapsychologists have made such observations under a diversity of research conditions from which a number of facts emerge. If these facts can be related to one another by a theory that enables any one to be deducible from knowledge of the others, that theory has some value and plausibility. By means of it predictions might be made of what will happen in further experiments so that it can be put to further test. However, a theory that fails to account for a variety of facts and that cannot predict what will happen in further tests is of no value.

If some facts gleaned from the literature on ESP are assembled, they might appear as follows:

1. Subjects, when attempting to guess card symbols, have obtained scores that cannot be attributed to chance.

2. Some of those taking part in ESP experiments have indulged in trickery.

3. Subjects who obtain high scores cannot do so on all occasions.

4. Subjects tend to lose their ability to obtain high scores. This loss often coincides with the termination of an experiment.

5. A successful subject is sometimes unable to obtain high scores when tested by a critical investigator.

6. Some investigators often observe high scores in the subjects they test; others invariably fail to observe such scores.

7. A subject may obtain high scores under one set of experimental conditions and fail to do so under other experimental conditions.

8. No subject has ever demonstrated his ability to obtain high scores when the test procedure is completely mechanized.

Fact 1 is directly applicable to an hypothesis of the existence of ESP. Fact 2 is not relevant to such an hypothesis. Facts 3 and 4 are not predictable but could be said to provide further information about ESP; that is, it appears to be spasmodic and temporary. The remaining facts (5–8) are not predictable, and in the case of any other supposed process investigated by psychologists, would throw doubt on its authenticity. These facts can only be explained by invoking subsidiary characteristics of ESP.

Again, fact 1 is directly applicable to an hypothesis predicting trickery. Fact 2 demonstrates that such an hypothesis is correct in the case of certain experiments. The remaining facts (3–4) are all predictable from what is well known about trickery.

Lawful relationships can readily be seen among the facts when they are interpreted in accordance with the hypothesis of trickery. Thus, for example, from fact 7 it might be predicted that those experimental conditions that eliminate the possibility of trickery will also be the ones in which high scores do not arise. This is confirmed by fact 8, and also by examining the experimental conditions under 7 in which high scores have and have not been observed.

Thus the set of facts given above display lawful inter-relationships when interpreted in terms of the hypothesis of trickery, but they are difficult to reconcile with an hypothesis based on the existence of ESP.

A number of other facts could be added to the above list to which neither an hypothesis of ESP nor that of trickery would be applicable. This is to be expected, since a great deal of research both in parapsychology and elsewhere has revealed the manner in which high scores can arise through experimental error.

Summary

During the past 85 years, a large number of investigations have been reported, the majority of which no responsible parapsychologist would claim as having been designed or intended for the purpose of providing conclusive evidence for ESP. Only a small number of studies were begun with the intent to provide such evidence.

The aim of this book has been to isolate the conclusive experiments and then to indicate that other explanations than ESP can account for their results. In the case of each of these conclusive experiments, the result could have arisen through a trick on the part of one or more of those taking part. In addition, closer examination of the experiments to see how far the hypothesis of trickery is consistent with information concerning the experiments in no case invalidates the hypothesis and in some cases strengthens it.

It cannot be stated categorically that trickery was responsible for the results of these experiments, but so long as the possibility is present, the experiments cannot be regarded as satisfying the aims of their originators or as supplying conclusive evidence for ESP. . . .

Technology and Society

The Threat of Scientific Technology   Erich Fromm

Erich Fromm (1900–   ) is professor of psychoanalysis at the Medical School
of the National Autonomous University of Mexico and adjunct professor at
New York University. His writings enjoy a large readership among the
general literate public.

The Present Technological Society

a. Its Principles.   The technetronic society may be the system of the
future, but it is not yet here; it can develop from what is already here,
and it probably will, unless a sufficient number of people see the danger
and redirect our course. In order to do so, it is necessary to understand
in greater detail the operation of the present technological system and
the effect it has on man.

What are the guiding principles of this system as it is today?

It is programed by two principles that direct the efforts and thought
of everyone working in it: The first principle is the maxim that something *ought* to be done because it is technically *possible* to do it. If it is
possible to build nuclear weapons, they must be built even if they might
destroy us all. If it is possible to travel to the moon or to the planets,
it must be done, even if at the expense of many unfulfilled needs here
on earth. This principle means the negation of all values which the
humanist tradition has developed. This tradition said that something
should be done because it is needed for man, for his growth, joy, and
reason, because it is beautiful, good, or true. Once the principle is
accepted that something ought to be done because it is technically possible
to do it, all other values are dethroned, and technological development
becomes the foundation of ethics.

The second principle is that of *maximal efficiency and output*. The
requirement of maximal efficiency leads as a consequence to the requirement of minimal individuality. The social machine works more efficiently,
so it is believed, if individuals are cut down to purely quantifiable units
whose personalities can be expressed on punched cards. These units can
be administered more easily by bureaucratic rules because they do not
make trouble or create friction. In order to reach this result, men must
be de-individualized and taught to find their identity in the corporation
rather than in themselves.

The question of economic efficiency requires careful thought. The
issue of being economically efficient, that is to say, using the smallest
possible amount of resources to obtain maximal effect, should be placed

Abridgment of pp. 32–50 (editor's title, "The Threat of Scientific Technology") in *The
Revolution of Hope* by Erich Fromm. Copyright © 1968 by Erich Fromm. Reprinted by permission of Harper & Row, Publishers, Inc.

in a historical and evolutionary context. The question is obviously more important in a society where real material scarcity is the prime fact of life, and its importance diminishes as the productive powers of a society advance.

A second line of investigation should be a full consideration of the fact that efficiency is only a known element in already existing activities. Since we do not know much about the efficiency or inefficiency of untried approaches, one must be careful in pleading for things as they are on the grounds of efficiency. Furthermore, one must be very careful to think through and specify the area and time period being examined. What may appear efficient by a narrow definition can be highly inefficient if the time and scope of the discussion are broadened. In economics there is increasing awareness of what are called "neighborhood effects"; that is, effects that go beyond the immediate activity and are often neglected in considering benefits and costs. One example would be evaluating the efficiency of a particular industrial project only in terms of the immediate effects on this enterprise—forgetting, for instance, that waste materials deposited in nearby streams and the air represent a costly and a serious inefficiency with regard to the community. We need to clearly develop standards of efficiency that take account of time and society's interest as a whole. Eventually, the human element needs to be taken into account as a basic factor in the system whose efficiency we try to examine.

Dehumanization in the name of efficiency is an all-too-common occurrence; e.g., giant telephone systems employing Brave New World techniques of recording operators' contacts with customers and asking customers to evaluate workers' performance and attitudes, etc.—all aimed at instilling "proper" employee attitude, standardizing service, and increasing efficiency. From the narrow perspective of immediate company purposes, this may yield docile, manageable workers, and thus enhance company efficiency. In terms of the employees, as human beings, the effect is to engender feelings of inadequacy, anxiety, and frustration, which may lead to either indifference or hostility. In broader terms, even efficiency may not be served, since the company and society at large doubtless pay a heavy price for these practices.

Another general practice in organizing work is to constantly remove elements of creativity (involving an element of risk or uncertainty) and group work by dividing and subdividing tasks to the point where no judgment or interpersonal contact remains or is required. Workers and technicians are by no means insensitive to this process. Their frustration is often perceptive and articulate, and comments such as "We are human" and "The work is not fit for human beings" are not uncommon. Again, efficiency in a narrow sense can be demoralizing and costly in individual and social terms.

If we are only concerned with input-output figures, a system may give the impression of efficiency. If we take into account what the given methods do to the human beings in the system, we may discover that they are bored, anxious, depressed, tense, etc. The result would be a twofold one: (1) Their imagination would be hobbled by their psychic pathology, they would be uncreative, their thinking would be routinized and bureaucratic, and hence they would not come up with new ideas and solutions which would contribute to a more productive development of the system; altogether, their energy would be considerably lowered. (2) They would suffer from many physical ills, which are the result of stress and tension; this loss in health is also a loss for the system. Furthermore, if one examines what this tension and anxiety do to them in their relationship to their wives and children, and in their functioning as responsible citizens, it may turn out that for the system as a whole the seemingly efficient method is most inefficient, not only in human terms but also as measured by merely economic criteria.

To sum up: efficiency is desirable in any kind of purposeful activity. But it should be examined in terms of the larger systems, of which the system under study is only a part; it should take account of the human factor within the system. Eventually efficiency as such should not be a *dominant* norm in any kind of enterprise.

The other aspect of the same principle, that of *maximum output,* formulated very simply, maintains that the more we produce of whatever we produce, the better. The success of the economy of the country is measured by its rise of total production. So is the success of a company. Ford may lose several hundred million dollars by the failure of a costly new model, like the Edsel, but this is only a minor mishap as long as the production curve rises. The growth of the economy is visualized in terms of ever-increasing production, and there is no vision of a limit yet where production may be stabilized. The comparison between countries rests upon the same principle. The Soviet Union hopes to surpass the United States by accomplishing a more rapid rise in economic growth.

Not only industrial production is ruled by the principle of continuous and limitless acceleration. The educational system has the same criterion: the more college graduates, the better. The same in sports: every new record is looked upon as progress. Even the attitude toward the weather seems to be determined by the same principle. It is emphasized that this is "the hottest day in the decade," or the coldest, as the case may be, and I suppose some people are comforted for the inconvenience by the proud feeling that they are witnesses to the record temperature. One could go on endlessly giving examples of the concept that constant increase of quantity constitutes the goal of our life; in fact, that it is what is meant by "progress."

Few people raise the question of *quality,* or what all this increase in quantity is good for. This omission is evident in a society which is not centered around man any more, in which one aspect, that of quantity, has choked all others. It is easy to see that the predominance of this principle of "the more the better" leads to an imbalance in the whole system. If all efforts are bent on doing *more,* the quality of living loses all importance and activities that once were means become ends.

If the overriding economic principle is that we produce more and more, the consumer must be prepared to want—that is, to consume—more and more. Industry does not rely on the consumer's spontaneous desires for more and more commodities. By building in obsolescence it often forces him to buy new things when the old ones could last much longer.

By changes in styling of products, dresses, durable goods, and even food, it forces him psychologically to buy more than he might need or want. But industry, in its need for increased production, does not rely on the consumer's needs and wants but to a considerable extent on advertising, which is the most important offensive against the consumer's right to know what he wants. The spending of 16.5 billion dollars on direct advertising in 1966 (in newspapers, magazines, radio, TV) may sound like an irrational and wasteful use of human talents, of paper and print. But it is not irrational in a system that believes that increasing production and hence consumption is a vital feature of our economic system, without which it would collapse. If we add to the cost of advertising the considerable cost for restyling of durable goods, especially cars, and of packaging, which partly is another form of whetting the consumer's appetite, it is clear that industry is willing to pay a high price for the guarantee of the upward production and sales curve. . . .

b. ITS EFFECT ON MAN.   What is the effect of this type of organization on man? It reduces man to an appendage of the machine, ruled by its very rhythm and demands. It transforms him into *Homo consumens,* the total consumer, whose only aim is to *have* more and to *use* more. This society produces many useless things, and to the same degree many useless people. Man, as a cog in the production machine, becomes a thing, and ceases to be human. He spends his time doing things in which he is not interested, with people in whom he is not interested, producing things in which he is not interested; and when he is not producing, he is consuming. He is the eternal suckling with the open mouth, "taking in," without effort and without inner activeness, whatever the boredom-preventing (and boredom-producing) industry forces on him—cigarettes, liquor, movies, television, sports, lectures—limited only by what he can afford. But the boredom-preventing industry, that is to say, the gadget-selling industry, the automobile industry, the movie industry, the television industry, and so on, can only succeed in preventing the boredom from becoming conscious. In fact, they increase the boredom, as a salty drink taken to quench the thirst increases it. However unconscious, boredom remains boredom nevertheless.

The passiveness of man in industrial society today is one of his most characteristic and pathological features. He takes in, he wants to be fed, but he does not move, initiate, he does not digest his food, as it were. He does not reacquire in a productive fashion what he inherited, but he amasses it or consumes it. He suffers from a severe systemic deficiency, not too dissimilar to that which one finds in more extreme forms in depressed people.

Man's passiveness is only one symptom among a total syndrome, which one may call the "syndrome of alienation." Being passive, he does not relate himself to the world actively and is forced to submit to his idols and their demands. Hence, he feels powerless, lonely, and anxious. He has little sense of integrity or self-identity. Conformity seems to be the only way to avoid intolerable anxiety—and even conformity does not always alleviate his anxiety. . . .

Aside from the pathological traits that are rooted in passiveness, there are others which are important for the understanding of today's pathology of normalcy. I am referring to the growing split of cerebral-intellectual function from affective-emotional experience; the split between thought from feeling, mind from the heart, truth from passion.

Logical thought is not rational if it is merely logical[1] and not guided by the concern for life, and by the inquiry into the total process of living in all its concreteness and with all its contradictions. On the other hand, not only thinking but also emotions can be rational. *"Le coeur a ses raisons que la raison ne connaît point,"* as Pascal put it. (The heart has its reasons which reason knows nothing of.) Rationality in emotional life means that the emotions affirm and help the person's psychic structure to maintain a harmonious balance and at the same time to assist its growth. Thus, for instance, irrational love is love which enhances the person's dependency, hence anxiety and hostility. Rational love is a love which relates a person intimately to another, at the same time preserving his independence and integrity.

Reason flows from the blending of rational thought and feeling. If the two functions are torn apart, thinking deteriorates into schizoid intellectual activity, and feeling deteriorates into neurotic life-damaging passions.

The split between thought and affect leads to a sickness, to a low-grade chronic schizophrenia, from which the new man of the technetronic age begins to suffer. In the social sciences it has become fashionable to think about human problems with no reference to the feelings related to these problems. It is assumed that scientific objectivity demands that thoughts and theories concerning man be emptied of all emotional concern with man.

An example of this emotion-free thinking is Herman Kahn's book on thermonuclear warfare. The question is discussed: how many millions of dead Americans are "acceptable" if we use as a criterion the ability to rebuild the economic machine after nuclear war in a reasonably short time so that it is as good as or better than before. Figures for GNP and population increase or decrease are the basic categories in this kind of thinking, while the question of the human results of nuclear war in terms of suffering, pain, brutalization, etc., is left aside.

Kahn's *The Year 2000* is another example of the writing which we may expect in the completely alienated megamachine society. Kahn's concern is that of the figures for production, population increase, and various scenarios for war or peace, as the case may be. He impresses many readers because they mistake the thousands of little data which he combines in ever-changing kaleidoscopic pictures for erudition or profundity. They do not notice the basic superficiality in his reasoning and the lack of the human dimension in his description of the future.

When I speak here of low-grade chronic schizophrenia, a brief expla-

---

[1] Paranoid thinking is characterized by the fact that it can be completely logical, yet lack any guidance by concern or concrete inquiry into reality; in other words, logic does not exclude madness.

nation seems to be needed. Schizophrenia, like any other psychotic state, must be defined not only in psychiatric terms but also in social terms. Schizophrenic experience *beyond* a certain threshold would be considered a sickness in any society, since those suffering from it would be unable to function under any social circumstances (unless the schizophrenic is elevated into the status of a god, shaman, saint, priest, etc.). But there are low-grade chronic forms of psychoses which can be shared by millions of people and which—precisely because they do not go beyond a certain threshold—do not prevent these people from functioning socially. As long as they share their sickness with millions of others, they have the satisfactory feeling of not being alone; in other words, they avoid that sense of complete isolation which is so characteristic of full-fledged psychosis. On the contrary, they look at themselves as normal and at those who have not lost the link between heart and mind as being "crazy." In all low-grade forms of psychoses, the definition of sickness depends on the question as to whether the pathology is shared or not. Just as there is low-grade chronic schizophrenia, so there exist also low-grade chronic paranoia and depression. And there is plenty of evidence that among certain strata of the population, particularly on occasions where a war threatens, the paranoid elements increase but are not felt as pathological as long as they are common.

The tendency to install technical progress as the highest value is linked up not only with our overemphasis on intellect but, most importantly, with a deep emotional attraction to the mechanical, to all that is not alive, to all that is man-made. This attraction to the non-alive, which is in its more extreme form an attraction to death and decay (necrophilia), leads even in its less drastic form to indifference toward life instead of "reverence for life." Those who are attracted to the non-alive are the people who prefer "law and order" to living structure, bureaucratic to spontaneous methods, gadgets to living beings, repetition to originality, neatness to exuberance, hoarding to spending. They want to control life because they are afraid of its uncontrollable spontaneity; they would rather kill it than to expose themselves to it and merge with the world around them. They often gamble with death because they are not rooted in life; their courage is the courage to die and the symbol of their ultimate courage is the Russian roulette. The rate of our automobile accidents and the preparation for thermonuclear war are a testimony to this readiness to gamble with death. And who would not eventually prefer this exciting gamble to the boring unaliveness of the organization man?

One symptom of the attraction of the merely mechanical is the growing popularity, among some scientists and the public, of the idea that it will be possible to construct computers which are no different from man in thinking, feeling, or any other aspect of functioning. The main problem, it seems to me, is not whether such a computer-man can be constructed; it is rather why the idea is becoming so popular in a historical period when nothing seems to be more important than to transform the existing man into a more rational, harmonious, and peace-loving being. One cannot help being suspicious that often the attraction of the computer-man idea is the expression of a flight from life and from humane experience into the mechanical and purely cerebral.

The possibility that we can build robots who are like men belongs, if anywhere, to the future. But the present already shows us men who act like robots. When the majority of men are like robots, then indeed there will be no problem in building robots who are like men. The idea of the manlike computer is a good example of the alternative between the human and the inhuman use of machines. The computer can serve the enhancement of life in many respects. But the idea that it replaces man and life is the manifestation of the pathology of today.

The fascination with the merely mechanical is supplemented by an increasing popularity of conceptions that stress the animal nature of man and the instinctive roots of his emotions or actions. Freud's was such an instinctive psychology; but the importance of his concept of libido is secondary in comparison with his fundamental discovery of the unconscious process in waking life or in sleep. The most popular recent authors who stress instinctual animal heredity, like Konrad Lorenz (*On Aggression*) or Desmond Morris (*The Naked Ape*), have not offered any new or valuable insights into the specific human problem as Freud has done; they satisfy the wish of many to look at themselves as determined by instincts and thus to camouflage their true and bothersome human problems.[2] The dream of many people seems to be to combine the emotions of a primate with a computerlike brain. If this dream could be fulfilled, the problem of human freedom and of responsibility would seem to disappear. Man's feelings would be determined by his instincts, his reason by the computer; man would not have to give an answer to the questions his existence asks him. Whether one likes the dream or not, its realization is impossible; the naked ape with the computer brain would cease to be human, or rather "he" would not *be*.

Among the technological society's pathogenic effects upon man, two more must be mentioned: the disappearance of *privacy* and of *personal human contact*.

"Privacy" is a complex concept. It was and is a privilege of the middle and upper classes, since its very basis, private space, is costly. This privilege, however, can become a common good with other economic privileges. Aside from this economic factor, it was also based on a hoarding tendency in which *my* private life was *mine* and nobody else's, as was *my* house and any other property. It was also a concomitant of *cant*, of the discrepancy between moral appearances and reality. Yet when all these qualifications are made, privacy still seems to be an important condition for a person's productive development. First of all, because privacy is necessary to collect oneself and to free oneself from the constant "noise" of people's chatter and intrusion, which interferes with one's own mental processes. If all private data are transformed into public data, experiences will tend to become more shallow and more alike. People will be afraid

---

[2] This criticism of Lorenz refers only to that part of his work in which he deals by analogy with the psychological problems of man, not with his work in the field of animal behavior and instinct theory.

to feel the "wrong thing"; they will become more accessible to psychological manipulation which, through psychological testing, tries to establish norms for "desirable," "normal," "healthy" attitudes. Considering that these tests are applied in order to help the companies and government agencies to find the people with the "best" attitudes, the use of psychological tests, which is by now an almost general condition for getting a good job, constitutes a severe infringement on the citizen's freedom. Unfortunately, a large number of psychologists devote whatever knowledge of man they have to his manipulation in the interests of what the big organization considers efficiency. Thus, psychologists become an important part of the industrial and governmental system while claiming that their activities serve the optimal development of man. This claim is based on the rationalization that what is best for the corporation is best for man. It is important that the managers understand that much of what they get from psychological testing is based on the very limited picture of man which in fact, management requirements have transmitted to the psychologists, who in turn give it back to management, allegedly as a result of an independent study of man. It hardly needs to be said that the intrusion of privacy may lead to a control of the individual which is more total and could be more devastating than what totalitarian states have demonstrated thus far. Orwell's 1984 will need much assistance from testing, conditioning, and smoothing-out psychologists in order to come true. It is of vital importance to distinguish between a psychology that understands and aims at the well-being of man and a psychology that studies man as an object, with the aim of making him more useful for the technological society.

c. THE NEED FOR CERTAINTY. In our discussion thus far, I have omitted one factor of the greatest importance for the understanding of man's behavior in present society: man's need for *certainty*. Man is not equipped with a set of instincts that regulate his behavior quasi-automatically. He is confronted with choices, and this means in all-important matters with grave risks to his life if his choices are wrong. The doubt that besets him when he must decide—often quickly—causes painful tension and can even seriously endanger his capacity for quick decisions. As a consequence, man has an intense need for certainty; he wants to believe that there is no need to doubt that the method by which he makes his decisions is right. In fact, he would rather make the "wrong" decision and be sure about it than the "right" decision and be tormented with doubt about its validity. This is one of the psychological reasons for man's belief in idols and political leaders. They all take out doubt and risk from his decision making; this does not mean that there is not a risk for his life, freedom, etc., *after* the decision has been made, but that there is no risk that the *method* of his decision making was wrong.

For many centuries certainty was guaranteed by the concept of God. God, omniscient and omnipotent, had not only created the world but also announced the principles of action about which there was no doubt. The church "interpreted" these principles in detail, and the individual, securing his place in the church by following its rules, was certain that, whatever happened, he was on the way to salvation and to eternal life in heaven.

With the beginning of the scientific approach and the corrosion of religious certainty, man was forced into a new search for certainty. At first, science seemed to be capable of giving a new basis for certainty. This was so for the rational man of the last centuries. But with the increasing complexities of life, which lost all human proportions, with the growing feeling of individual powerlessness and isolation, the science-oriented man ceased to be a rational and independent man. He lost the courage to think for himself and to make decisions on the basis of his full intellectual and emotional commitment to life. He wanted to exchange the "uncertain certainty" which rational thought can give for an "absolute certainty": the alleged "scientific" certainty, based on predictability.

This certainty is guaranteed not by man's own unreliable knowledge and emotions but by the computers which permit prediction and become guarantors of certainty. Take as an example the planning of the big' corporation. With the help of computers, it can plan ahead for many years (including the manipulation of man's mind and taste); the manager does not have to rely any more on his individual judgment, but on the "truth" that is pronounced by the computers. The manager's decision may be wrong in its results, but he need not be distrustful of the decision-making processes. He feels that he is free to accept or reject the result of computer prognostication, but for all practical purposes, he is as little free as a pious Christian was to act against God's will. He could do it, but he would have to be out of his mind to take the risk, since there is not a greater source of certainty than God—or the computerized solution.

This need for certainty creates the need of what amounts to blind belief in the efficacy of the method of computerized planning. The managers are relieved from doubt, and so are those who are employed in the organization. It is precisely the fact that man's judgment and emotions allegedly do *not* interfere with the process of decision making that gives the computer-based planning its godlike quality.

In government policy and strategy, the same planning system becomes increasingly popular. The ideal is that foreign policy—and that means today also military planning—are freed from the arbitrariness of the human will and entrusted to a computer system, which tells the "truth" since it is not fallible like men, nor has it any ax to grind. The ideal is that all foreign policy and military strategy are based on computer decision, and this implies that all the facts are known, considered, and made available to the computer. With this method, doubt becomes excluded, although disaster is by no means necessarily avoided. But if disaster does happen after the decisions are made on the basis of unquestionable "facts," it is like an act of God, which one must accept, since man cannot do more than make the best decision he knows how to make.

It seems to me that these considerations are the only terms in which one can answer this puzzling question: How is it possible for our policy and strategy planners to tolerate the idea that at a certain point they may give orders the consequence of which will mean the destruction of their own families, most of Americans, and "at best" most of the industrialized world? If they rely on the decision the facts seem to have made *for them*, their conscience is cleared. However dreadful the consequences of their decisions may be, they need not have qualms about the rightness and legitimacy of the method by which they arrived at their decision. They act on faith, not essentially different from the faith on which the actions of the inquisitors of the Holy Office were based. Like Dostoevsky's Grand Inquisitor, some may even be tragic figures who cannot act differently, because they see no other way of being certain that they do the best they can. The alleged rational character of our planners is basically not different from the religiously based decisions in a prescientific age. There is one qualification that must be made: both the religious decision, which is a blind surrender to God's will, and the computer decision, based on the faith in the logic of "facts," are forms of alienated decisions in which man surrenders his own insight, knowledge, inquiry, and responsibility to an idol, be it God or the computer. The humanist religion of the prophets knew no such surrender; the decision was man's. He had to understand his situation, see the alternatives, and then decide. True scientific rationality is not different. The computer can help man in visualizing several possibilities, but the decision is not made for him, not only in the sense that he can choose between the various models, but also in the sense that he must use his reason, relate to and respond to the reality with which he deals, and elicit from the computer those facts which are relevant from the standpoint of reason, and that means from the standpoint of sustaining and fulfilling man's aliveness....

Technology and Wisdom   Emmanuel G. Mesthene

Emmanuel George Mesthene (1920–   ), a former member of the staff of the Rand Corporation, now Director of the Program on Technology and Society at Harvard University, is also a philosopher professionally trained in America, whose philosophical interests go beyond science and public policy to include metaphysics and aesthetics.

What Is New About Our Age

My objective is to suggest some of the broader implications of what is new about our age. It might be well to start, therefore, by noting what is new about our age.

The fact itself that there is something new is not new. There has been something new about every age, otherwise we would not be able to distin-

Reprinted by permission from *Technology and Social Change* ed. by E. G. Mesthene (New York and Indianapolis: Bobbs-Merrill Co., 1967). The author has made some minor revisions for this reprinting. Adapted from "What Modern Science offers the Church," November 19, 1966, *Saturday Review*, copyright 1966 Saturday Review, Inc.; and "Learning to Live with Science," July 17, 1965, *Saturday Review*, copyright 1965 Saturday Review, Inc. Reprinted by permission of *Saturday Review*.

guish them in history. What we need to examine is what in particular is new about our age, for the new is not less new just because the old was also at one time new.

The mere prominence in our age of science and technology is not strikingly new, either. A veritable explosion of industrial technology gave its name to a whole age two centuries ago, and it is doubtful that any scientific idea will ever again leave an imprint on the world so penetrating and pervasive as did Isaac Newton's a century before that.

It is not clear, finally, that what is new about our age is the rate at which it changes. What partial evidence we have, in the restricted domain of economics, for example, indicates the contrary. The curve of growth, for the hundred years or so that it can be traced, is smooth, and will not support claims of explosive change or discontinuous rise. For the rest, we lack the stability of concept, the precision of intellectual method, and the necessary data to make any reliable statements about the rate of social change in general.

I would therefore hold suspect all argument that purports to show that novelty is new with us, or that major scientific and technological influences are new with us, or that rapidity of social change is new with us. Such assertions, I think, derive more from revolutionary fervor and the wish to persuade than from tested knowledge and the desire to instruct.

Yet there is clearly something new, and its implications are important. I think our age is different from all previous ages in two major respects: first, we dispose, in absolute terms, of a staggering amount of physical power; second, and most important, we are beginning to think and act in conscious realization of that fact. We are therefore the first age who can aspire to be free of the tyranny of physical nature that has plagued man since his beginnings.

The Traditional Tyranny of Matter

The consciousness of physical impossibility has had a long and depressing history. One might speculate that it began with early man's awe of the bruteness and recalcitrance of nature. Earth, air, fire, and water—the eternal, immutable elements of ancient physics—imposed their requirements on men, dwarfed them, outlived them, remained indifferent when not downright hostile to them. The physical world loomed large in the affairs of men, and men were impotent against it. Homer celebrated this fact by investing nature with gods, and the earliest philosophers recognized it by erecting each of the natural elements in turn—water, air, earth, and fire—into fundamental principles of all existence.

From that day to this, only the language has changed as successive ages encountered and tried to come to terms with physical necessity, with the sheer "rock-bottomness" of nature. It was submitted to as fate in the Athenian drama. It was conceptualized as ignorance by Socrates and as metaphysical matter by his pupils. It was labeled evil by the pre-Christians. It has been exorcized as the Devil, damned as flesh, or condemned as illicit by the Church. It has been the principle of nonreason in modern philosophy, in the form of John Locke's Substance, as Immanuel Kant's formless manifold, or as Henri Bergson's pure duration. It has conquered the mystic as nirvana, the psyche as the Id, and recent Frenchmen as the blind object of existential commitment.

What men have been saying in all these different ways is that physical nature has seemed to have a structure, almost a will of its own, that has not yielded easily to the designs and purposes of man. It has been a brute thereness, a residual, a sort of ultimate existential stage that allowed, but also limited, the play of thought and action.

It would be difficult to overestimate the consequences of this recalcitrance of the physical on the thinking and outlook of men. They have learned, for most of history, to plan and act *around* a permanent realm of impossibility. Man could travel on the sea, by sail or oar or breaststroke. But he could not travel *in* the sea. He could cross the land on foot, on horseback, or by wheel, but he could not fly over it. Legends such as those of Daedalus and Poseidon celebrated in art what men could not aspire to in fact.

Thinking was similarly circumscribed. There were myriad possibilities in existence, but they were not unlimited, because they did not include altering the physical structure of existence itself. Man could in principle know all that was possible, once and for all time. What else but this possibility of complete knowledge does Plato name in his Idea of the Good? The task of thought was to discern and compare and select from among this fixed and eternal realm of possibilities. Its options did not extend beyond it, anymore than the chessplayer's options extend beyond those allowed by the board and the pieces of his game. There was a natural law, men said, to which all human law was forever subservient, and which fixed the patterns and habits of what was thinkable.

The Promise of Technology

There was occasionally an invention during all this time that did induce a physical change. It thus made something new possible, like adding a pawn to the chess game. New physical possibilities are the result of invention; of technology, as we call it today. That is what "invention" and "technology" mean. Every invention, from the wheel to the rocket, has created new possibilities that did not exist before. But inventions in the past were few, rare, exceptional, and marvelous. They were unexpected departures from the norm. They were surprises that societies adjusted to after the fact. They were generally infrequent enough, moreover, so that the adjustments could be made slowly and unconsciously, without radical alteration of world views, or of traditional patterns of thought and action. The Industrial Revolution, as we call it, was revolutionary precisely because it ran into attitudes, values, and habits of thought and action that were completely unprepared to understand, accept, absorb, and change with it.

Today, if I may put it paradoxically, technology is becoming less revolutionary, as we recognize and seek after the power that it gives us. Inventions are now many, frequent, planned, and increasingly taken for granted. We were not a bit surprised when we got to the moon. On the contrary, we would have been very surprised if we had not. We are beginning to use invention as a deliberate way to deal with the future, rather than seeing it only as an uncontrolled disrupting of the present. We no longer wait upon invention to occur accidentally. We foster and force it, because we see it as a way out of the heretofore inviolable constraints that physical nature has imposed upon us in the past.

Francis Bacon, in the sixteenth century, was the first to foresee the physical power potential in scientific knowledge. We are the first, I am suggesting, to have enough of that power actually at hand to create new possibilities almost at will. By massive physical changes deliberately induced, we can literally pry new alternatives out of nature. The ancient tyranny of matter has been broken, and we know it. We found, in the seventeenth century, that the physical world was not at all like what Aristotle had thought and Aquinas had taught. We are today coming to the further realization that the physical world need not be as it is. We can change it and shape it to suit our purposes.

Technology, in short, has come of age, not merely as technical capability, but as a social phenomenon. We have the power to create new possibilities, and the will to do so. By creating new possibilities, we give ourselves more choices. With more choices, we have more opportunities. With more opportunities, we can have more freedom, and with more freedom we can be more human. That, I think, is what is new about our age. We are recognizing that our technical prowess literally bursts with the promise of new freedom, enhanced human dignity, and unfettered aspiration. Belatedly, we are also realizing the new opportunities that technological development offers us to make new and potentially big mistakes.

Some Dangers and New Problems

At its best, then, technology is nothing if not liberating. Yet many fear it increasingly as enslaving, degrading, and destructive of man's most cherished values. It is important to note that this is so, and to try to understand why. I can think of four reasons.

First, we must not blink at the fact that technology does indeed destroy some values. It creates a million possibilities heretofore undreamed of, but it also makes impossible some others heretofore enjoyed. The automobile makes real the legendary foreign land, but it also makes legendary the once real values of the ancient market place. Mass production puts Bach and Brueghel in every home, but it also deprives the careful craftsman of a market for the skill and pride he puts into his useful artifact. Modern plumbing destroys the village pump, and modern cities are hostile to the desire to sink roots into and grow upon a piece of land. Some values are unquestionably bygone. To try to restore them is futile, and simply to deplore their loss is sterile. But it is perfectly human to regret them.

Second, technology often reveals what technology has not created: the cost in brutalized human labor, for example, of the few cases of past civilization whose values only a small elite could enjoy. Communications now reveal the hidden and make the secret public. Transportation displays the better to those whose lot has been the worse. Increasing productivity buys more education, so that more people read and learn and compare and hope and are unsatisfied. Thus technology often seems the final straw, when it is only illuminating rather than adding to the human burden.

Third, technology might be deemed an evil, because evil is unquestionably potential in it. We can explore the heavens with it, or destroy the world. We can cure disease, or poison entire populations. We can free enslaved millions, or enslave millions more. Technology spells only possibility, and is in that respect neutral. Its massive power can lead to massive error so efficiently perpetrated as to be well-nigh irreversible. Technology is clearly not synonymous with the good. It *can* lead to evil.

Finally, and in a sense most revealing, technology is upsetting, because it complicates the world. This is a vague concern, hard to pin down, but I think it is a real one. The new alternatives that technology creates require effort to examine, understand, and evaluate them. We are offered more choices, which makes choosing more difficult. We are faced with the need to change, which upsets routines, inhibits reliance on habit, and calls for personal readjustments to more flexible postures. We face dangers that call for constant re-examination of values and a readiness to abandon old commitments for new ones more adequate to changing experience. The whole business of living seems to become harder.

The Mistrust of Technology

This negative face of technology is sometimes confused with the whole of it. It can then cloud the understanding in two respects that are worth noting. It can lead to a generalized distrust of the power and works of the human mind by erecting a false dichotomy between the modern scientific and technological enterprises on the one hand, and some idealized and static prescientific conception of human values on the other. It can also color discussion of some important contemporary issues, that develop from the impact of technology on society, in a way that obscures rather than enhances understanding, and that therefore inhibits rather than facilitates the social action necessary to resolve them.

Because the confusions and discomfort attendant on technology are more immediate and therefore sometimes loom larger than its power and its promise, technology appears to some an alien and hostile trespasser upon the human scene. It thus seems indistinguishable from that other, older alien and hostile trespasser: the ultimate and unbreachable physical necessity of which I have spoken. Then, since habit dies hard, there occurs one of those curious inversions of the imagination that are not unknown to history. Our newfound control over nature is seen as but the latest form of the tyranny of nature. The knowledge and therefore the mastery of the physical world that we have gained, the tools that we have hewed from nature and the human wonders we are building into her, are themselves feared as rampant, uncontrollable, impersonal technique that must surely, we are told, end by robbing us of our livelihood, our freedom, and our humanity.

It is not an unfamiliar syndrome. It is reminiscent of the long-time prisoner who may shrink from the responsibility of freedom in preference for the false security of his accustomed cell. It is reminiscent even more of Socrates, who asked about that other prisoner, in the cave of ignorance, whether his eyes would not ache if he were forced to look upon the light of knowledge, "so that he would try to escape and turn back to the things which he could see distinctly, convinced that they really were clearer than these other objects now being shown to him." Is it so different a form of escapism from that, to ascribe impersonality and hostility to the knowledge and the tools that can free us finally from the age-long impersonality and hostility of a recalcitrant physical nature?

Technology has *two* faces: one that is full of promise, and one that can discourage and defeat us. The freedom that our power implies from the traditional tyranny of matter—from the evil we have known—carries with it the added responsibility and burden of learning to deal with matter and to blunt the evil, along with all the other problems we have always had to deal with. That is another way of saying that more power and more choice and more freedom require more wisdom if they are to add up to more humanity. But that, surely, is a challenge to be wise, not an invitation to despair.

Technology and Work

An attitude of despair can also, as I have suggested, color particular understandings of particular problems, and thus obstruct intelligent action. I think, for example, that it has distorted the public debate about the effects of technology on work and employment.

The problem has persistently taken the form of fear that machines will put people permanently out of work. That fear has prevented recognition of a distinction between two fundamentally different questions. The first is a question of economic analysis and economic and manpower policy about which a great deal is known, which is susceptible to analysis by well-developed and rigorous methods, and on the dimensions and implications of which there is a very high degree of consensus among the professionally competent.

That consensus is that there is not much that is significantly new in the probable consequences of automation on employment. Automation is but the latest form of mechanization, which has been recognized as an important factor in economic change at least since the Industrial Revolution. What *is* new is a heightened social awareness of the implications of machines for men, which derives from the unprecedented scale, prevalence, and visibility of modern technological innovation. That is the second question. It, too, is a question of work, to be sure, but it is not one of employment in the economic connotation of the term. It is a distinct question, that has been too often confused with the economic one because it has been formulated, incorrectly, as a question of automation and employment.

This question is much less a question of whether people will be employed than of what they can most usefully do, given the broader range of choices that technology can make available to them. It is less a technical economic question than a question of the values and quality of work. It is not a question of what to do with increasing leisure, but of how to define new occupations that combine social utility and personal satisfaction.

I see no evidence, in other words, that society will need less work done on some day in the future when machines may be largely satisfying its material needs, or that it will not value and reward that work. But we are, first, a long way still from that day, so long as there remain societies less affluent than the most affluent. Second, there is a work of education, integration, creation, and eradication of disease and discontent to do that is barely tapped so long as most people must labor to produce the goods that we consume. The more machines can take over what we do, the more we can do what machines cannot do. That, too, is liberation: the liberation of history's slaves, finally to be people.

The Fear of Science

Such basically irrational fears of technology have a counterpart in popular fears of science itself. Here, too, anticipatory despair in the face of some genuine problems posed by science and technology can cloud the understanding.

It is admittedly horrible, for example, to contemplate the unintentional evil implicit in the ignorance and fallibility of man as he strives to control his environment and improve his lot. What untoward effects might our grandchildren suffer from the drugs that cure our ills today? What monsters might we breed unwittingly while we are learning to manipulate the genetic code? What are the tensions on the human psyche of a cold and rapid automated world? What political disaster do we court by providing 1984's Big Brother with all the tools he will ever need? Better perhaps, in Hamlet's words, to

> ... bear those ills we have
> Than fly to others that we know not of.

Why not stop it all? Stop automation! Stop tampering with life and heredity! Stop the senseless race into space! The cry is an old one. It was first heard, no doubt, when the wheel was invented. The technologies of the bomb, the automobile, the spinning jenny, gunpowder, printing, all provoked social dislocation accompanied by similar cries of "Stop!" Well, but why not stop now, while there may still be a minute left before the clock strikes twelve?

We do not stop, I think, for three reasons: we do not want to; we cannot, and still be men; and we therefore should not.

It is not at all clear that atom bombs will kill more people than wars have ever done, but energy from the atom might one day erase the frightening gap between the more and less favored peoples of the world.

Was it more tragic to infect a hundred children with a faulty polio vaccine than to have allowed the scourge free reign forever? It is not clear that the monster that the laboratory may create, in searching the secret of life, will be more monstrous than those that nature will produce unaided if its secrets remain forever hidden. Is it really clear that rampant multiplication is a better ultimate fate for man than to suffer, but eventually survive, the mistakes that go with learning? The first reason we do not stop is that I do not think we would decide, on close examination, that we really want to.

The second reason is that we cannot so long as we are men. Aristotle saw a long time ago that "man by nature desires to know." He will probe and learn all that his curiosity prompts him to and his brain allows, so long as there is life within him. The stoppers of the past have always lost in the end, whether it was Socrates, or Christ, or Galileo, or Einstein, or Bonhoeffer, or Boris Pasternak they tried to stop. Their intended victims are the heroes.

We do not stop, finally, because we would not stop being men. I do not believe that even those who decry science the loudest would willingly concede that the race has now been proved incapable of coping with its own creations. That admission would be the ultimate in dehumanization, for it would be to surrender the very qualities of intelligence, courage, vision, and aspiration that make us human. "Stop," in the end, is the last desperate cry of the man who abandons man because he is defeated by the responsibility of being human. It is the final failure of nerve.

The Recovery of Nerve

I am recalling that celebrated phrase, "the failure of nerve," in order to introduce a third and final example of how fear and pessimism can color understanding and confuse our values. It is the example of those who see the sin of pride in man's confident mastery of nature. I have dealt with this theme before, but I permit myself to review it briefly once more, because it points up the real meaning of technology for our age.

The phrase, "the failure of nerve," was first used by the eminent classical scholar, Gilbert Murray, to characterize the change of temper that occurred in Hellenistic civilization at the turn of our era. The Greeks of the fifth and fourth centuries B.C. believed in the ultimate intelligibilty of the universe. There was nothing in the nature of existence or of man that was inherently unknowable. They accordingly believed also in the power of the human intelligence to know all there was to know about the world, and to guide man's career in it.

The wars and mixing of cultures that marked the subsequent period brought with them vicissitude and uncertainty that shook this classic faith in the intelligibility of the world and in the capacity of men to know and to do. There was henceforth to be a realm of knowledge and action available only to God, not subject to reason or to human effort. Men, in other words, more and more turned to God to do for them what they no longer felt confident to do for themselves. That was the failure of nerve.

The burden of what I have been saying is that times are changing. We have the power and will to probe and change physical nature. No longer are God, the human soul, or the mysteries of life improper objects of inquiry. We are ready to examine whatever our imagination prompts us to. We are convinced again, for the first time since the Greeks, of the essential intelligibility of the universe: there is nothing in it that is in principle not knowable. As sociologist Daniel Bell has put it, "Today we feel that there are no inherent secrets in the universe, and this is one of the significant changes in the modern moral temper." That is another way of stating what is new about our age. We are witnessing a widespread recovery of nerve.

Is this confidence a sin? According to Gilbert Murray, most people "are inclined to believe that without some failure and sense of failure, without a contrite heart and conviction of sin, man can hardly attain the religious life." I would suspect that this statement is still true of most people, although it is clear that a number of contemporary theologians are coming to a different view. To see a sense of failure as a condition of religious experience is a historical relic, dating from a time when an indifferent nature and hostile world so overwhelmed men that they gave up thought for consolation. To persist in such a view today, when nature is coming increasingly under control as a result of restored human confidence and power, is both to distort reality and to sell religion short. It surely does no glory to God to rest his power on the impotence of man.

The challenge of our restored faith in knowledge and the power of knowledge is rather a challenge to wisdom—not to God.

Some who have seen farthest and most clearly in recent decades have warned of a growing imbalance between man's capabilities in the physical and in the social realms. John Dewey, for example, said: "We have displayed enough intelligence in the physical field to create the new and powerful instrument of science and technology. We have not as yet had enough intelligence to use this instrument deliberately and systematically to control its social operations and consequences." Dewey said this more than thirty years ago, before television, before atomic power, before electronic computers, before space satellites. He had been saying it, moreover, for at least thirty years before that. He saw early the problems that would arise when man learned to do anything he wanted before he learned what he wanted.

I think the time Dewey warned about is here. My more thoughtful scientific friends tell me that we now have, or know how to acquire, the technical capability to do very nearly anything we want. Can we control our biology and our personality, order the weather that suits us, travel to Mars or to Venus? Of course we can, if not now or in five or ten years, then certainly in twenty-five, or in fifty or a hundred.

But if the answer to the question "What can we do?" is "Anything," then the emphasis shifts far more heavily than before onto the question "What should we do?" The commitment to universal intelligibility entails moral responsibility. Abandonment of the belief in intelligibility 2,000 years ago was justly described as a failure of nerve because it was the prelude to moral surrender. Men gave up the effort to be wise because they found it too hard. Renewed belief in intelligibility 2,000 years later means that men must take up again the hard work of becoming wise. And it is much harder work now, because we have so much more power than the Greeks. On the other hand, the benefits of wisdom are potentially greater, too, because we have the means at hand to *make* the good life, right here and now, rather than just to go on contemplating it in Plato's heaven.

The question "What should we do?" is thus no idle one but challenges each one of us. That, I think, is the principal moral implication of our new world. It is what all the shouting is about in the mounting concern about the relations of science and public policy, and about the impact of technology on society. Our almost total mastery of the physical world entails a challenge to the public intelligence of a degree heretofore unknown in history.

Suggestions for Further Reading

Anthologies

Ammerman, Robert R. and Singer, Marcus G. (eds.). *Belief, Knowledge and Truth.* New York: Scribner, 1970. A rich selection, ranging from elementary to difficult, from philosophical writings on skepticism, empiricism, rationalism, and other issues in the theory of knowledge from ancient Greece to the present. An extensive bibliography of books and articles.

Braybrooke, David (ed.). *Philosophical Problems of the Social Sciences.* New York: Macmillan, Sources in Philosophy Series, 1965. Contains a substantial introductory essay by the editor and a selection of recent philosophical writings treating problems suggested by psychology, history, economics, and the other social sciences. This book of readings is designed for the beginning student.

Burke, John G (ed.). *The New Technology and Human Values.* Belmont, California: Wadsworth, 1966. A useful and introductory collection of readings dealing with various aspects of the impact of scientific technology on contemporary society by philosophers, psychologists, artists, biologists, sociologists, educators, economists, and others. The readings cover such topics as automation and employment, population control, privacy, genetic control, and democracy in a technological society.

Gardner, Martin (ed.). *Great Essays in Science.* New York: Pocket Books, Inc., 1957. A highly readable collection of writings on the nature of science and its social implications by scientists and philosophers. This book is more entertaining than many novels.

Natanson, Maurice (ed.). *Philosophy of the Social Sciences.* New York: Random, 1963. This anthology provides examples of the application of the phenomenological method to the study of human society. Extensive bibliography. For the more advanced student.

Shapere, Dudley (ed.). *Philosophical Problems of Natural Science.* New York: Macmillan, Sources in Philosophy Series, 1965. Contains a substantial introductory essay by the editor and a selection of recent philosophical writings dealing with the structural and historical analyses of science. This book of readings is designed for the beginning student.

Individual Works

Cohen, Morris R. *Reason and Nature,* 2nd ed. New York: Free Press, 1964. A classic work by an American philosopher who was a champion of the supremacy of critical reason in human life. Cohen devotes considerable attention to the ethical, legal, religious, and historic implications of scientific knowledge and method. A scholarly work, yet written so lucidly that the beginning student can read it with pleasure.

Gardner, Martin. *Fads and Fallacies in the Name of Science,* 2nd ed. New York: Dover, 1957. A fascinating examination of extrasensory perception, the hollow earth hypothesis, dianetics, orgone boxes, and other theories and devices which the author criticizes as being pseudo-science.

Huxley, Thomas Henry. *Selections from the Essays of T. H. Huxley,* edited by Alburey Castell. New York: Appleton, 1948. A collection of some of the most famous essays treating such topics as science and education, science and religion, and science and ethics.

Nagel, Ernest. *The Structure of Science.* New York: Harcourt, 1961. A recent comprehensive treatment of the nature of explanation in the natural and social sciences by an outstanding American philosopher of science. A book for the more advanced student.

Otto, Max C. *Science and the Moral Life.* New York: The New American Library, Mentor Book, 1949. An unusually felicitous defense of a scientific humanism in the tradition of William James and John Dewey. With a sophistication developed to the point of simplicity, this book is designed for the layman in philosophy.

Reich, Charles A. *The Greening of America: How the Youth Revolution Is Trying to Make America Livable.* New York: Random, 1970. In this enormously popular book, particularly among students, a professor of law at Yale University supplies a prosecutor's summation to the jury of all the defects of our technological corporate society and points to a new consciousness, a different philosophy emerging out of the alienation and revolutionary turmoil of today's youth. Reich writes with great rhetorical skill.

Russell, Bertrand. *The Scientific Outlook.* New York: Norton, 1962. The first two parts of this book deal with the natures of scientific knowledge and scientific technique. In the third part entitled "The Scientific Society," Russell rewrites and updates Plato's *Republic.* In the course of his philosophic critique of the scientific society, Russell discusses all of the objections to such a society to be found in George Orwell's *1984,* Aldous Huxley's *Brave New World,* and other similar fictional and nonfictional critiques.

Stapledon, Olaf. *Last and First Men and Star Maker.* New York: Dover, 1968. Two science fiction novels by a philosopher which convey the haunting beauty and disturbing strangeness of the world revealed by science better than most abstract treatises. These powerfully imaginative works reveal why many men find the scientific understanding and manipulation of the world and man so fascinating and hopeful and many others find it so appalling and depressing.

Encyclopedia of Philosophy. Paul Edwards, editor-in-chief. New York: Macmillan, 1967. The beginning student will find many worthwhile articles on the subjects treated in this Part, and excellent bibliographies.

Six:
Art and
Society

Introduction

An ancient legend tells of a fabulously wealthy king who, being bored with life, sent into all parts of his kingdom heralds offering the rewards of fame and fortune to any subject who could invent a new pleasure. A quaint, charming, and innocuous fable, you say. However, let us, as artists often do, update this legend by dressing it in contemporary costume. Suppose, then, that the President of the United States were to announce on television his intention of presenting a Freedom Medal at a gala White House ceremony to any American citizen who could invent a new pleasure. What would be the reactions of the President's fellow countrymen and of the other nations of the world? Does anyone really expect that such a promulgation would be discussed seriously, calmly, objectively, logically? No one really does. Everyone knows that in the United States the reaction would be amused puzzlement followed by furious denunciations on the floor of Congress of this moral affront to every decent man and woman in the country, indignant editorials in the mass media bristling with alarm at this additional sign of corruption in high places, thinly veiled hints from the opposition political party of insanity in the national leadership, and a hail of angry resolutions from patriotic and professional organizations vowing to fight the policy to the bitter end. From London, we would hear: "In his television broadcast yesterday, the President of the United States gave what is perhaps the most convincing proof of the crass materialism rampant in our former colony. Being a young country, America has not learned as yet that the old, traditional pleasures are best." From Paris, we would hear: "And you Americans have always called France an immoral country." Moscow and Peking would agree: "The request of the President of the United States for the invention of a new pleasure shows the desperation of the bourgeoisie to escape the reality of inevitable revolution."

The call for an inventor of a new pleasure symbolizes mankind's call for the artist to create new works of art. We desire the pleasure that works of art can give and sometimes reward the artist handsomely. And yet, paradoxically, we fear that pleasure we want so much and distrust the man who provides it. From time to time we see darker tints in the golden wine of art, and suspect it may contain some deadly poison. To some the musical *Hair* represents one of the outstanding artistic works of the last decade. To others it is a blatant encouragement of sexual promiscuity, marijuana smoking, and social anarchy, and to some, the tremendous success of this musical all over the world only supplies further indication of the danger of

401

art. Joseph Stalin allegedly once remarked that Dostoevsky was a great artist but also a terrible reactionary whose writings should be banned. Many people consider Ezra Pound one of the great poets of our century and yet the United States Government charged him with treason. To many people, twentieth-century art in general represents a magnificent period of experimentation, originality, and enduring achievement. To others it reeks of degeneration. This paradoxical relationship of man to art is not unique to our day; we can trace it back to ancient Greece. Plato felt it keenly. It is the kind of problem demanding the philosopher's skill at analysis, criticism, and clarification in order to elucidate the real issues, if any, involved and the direction in which a genuine resolution of them may be found. And so, Socrates-like, the philosopher asks questions. Does art exercise any effect at all on human conduct? If art does influence human conduct, is that influence trivial or significant and how would this be determined rationally? Granted an important impact of art on morality, is it preponderantly for good or for evil? If for evil, is censorship the best way to eliminate or minimize that evil? Or would the disadvantages of censorship outweigh any benefits that might flow from it? We are familiar with the claim of some moral system or ideology to enjoy the unqualified right of judging art. Perhaps a more cogent case can be made for reversing that relationship, setting up art as the arbiter of morality and maintaining that the categories of good and evil are fundamentally aesthetic ones. Should the creation and enjoyment of art be accorded the supreme position in human life and all other human values be subordinated to aesthetic values? Is the attitude of aesthetic detachment an adequate basis for a philosophy of life?

In the dialogue entitled *The Republic,* the Greek philosopher Plato takes up many of these questions. The stated general purpose of *The Republic* is to define *justice* by describing a rational Utopia where the wisest men (i.e., philosophers) rule. Employing the character of Socrates as his mouthpiece, Plato sets forth what he feels to be the proper role of art in a society thoroughly and relentlessly devoted to the promotion of human welfare. Since man is a rational animal, his welfare will be achieved by subordinating all other human values to the complete realization of his intellectual capacity. Of course, in a perfect society the only problem lies in perpetuating it. Plato resolves this problem into one of insuring that the rulers will always be intellectuals by organizing the entire society into a comprehensive educational system, placing each individual in the position for which he is best suited according to his abilities. Education as a placement agency should be familiar to contemporary students. Therefore, for Plato the role of art in society becomes its role in education.

Here it should be pointed out that the meaning of art in Plato is not confined to what today we would call the "fine arts" but includes all human skills from training dogs and building ships to painting pictures and sculpting statues. The highest art, as Plato sees it, is living the good or rational life. Plato evaluates what we refer to as the "fine arts" in terms of the ways in which they help and hinder the making of the good life. Plato is convinced that art in our sense of the "fine arts," appealing primarily to the senses and the desire for pleasure rather than to reason and the desire for knowledge, possesses a tremendous capacity for affecting the molding of human character for good and for evil. Therefore, in *The Republic* Socrates presents the case for an official policy of censorship designed, not to eliminate all of the fine arts, but to deliberately and systematically promote their good effects and prevent them from exercising their harmful powers and thereby advance the highest art of living the rational life.

In the next selection drawn from his *Politics,* Aristotle, Plato's star pupil, presents the case against establishing a censorship of the arts on the grounds that it would be socially unhygienic. Art produces a catharsis, a kind of purging of our emotions, reducing their strength to the point where they can be controlled by reason and thereby preventing them from being socially and individually destructive. Art "imitates" life, not in the sense that it literally copies life, but in the sense that it produces in us emotions evoked by situations encountered in actual life. Since music is the most effective in arousing such emotions, it is the most imitative of the arts. However, art differs from life in that works of art do not incite to action but effect the opposite. Therefore, art is a form of therapy, a sort of safety valve. However, difficult as it may be to settle the issue, both Plato and Aristotle cannot be correct: Art cannot both cause and not cause crime and general moral degeneration.

When philosophers find themselves faced with conflicting theories, neither of which can be easily determined to be true, a common strategy consists in seeking an alternative theory. The theories of both Plato and Aristotle agree on the assumption that art causally affects human conduct; they differ on the general character of that influence, Plato arguing that it is often detrimental to morality and Aristotle that it is on the whole benign. Jean-Paul Sartre, a leading contemporary Existentialist philosopher, rejects this common assumption of Plato and Aristotle, contending that art and morality, Beauty and the Good, are completely independent of each other. The work of art is an autonomous product and should be judged only in terms of aesthetic standards and not in terms of moral, political, theological, or other nonaesthetic ones. Sartre argues that human conduct obviously is an "existential" matter, for human conduct is the making of choices. To choose is to "exist," in the sense in which Sartre employs the concept *existence.* To "exist" is to be real. However, contemplation of a work of art necessitates suspending the making of choices; it means ceasing to act, ignoring past and future and becoming absorbed in the present.

Hence, the work of art does not "exist"; it is a timeless essence, a non-material image—in short, it is purely imaginary. Art belongs to imagination; morality belongs to existence. Art and morality, Beauty and Goodness, occupy distinct and separate planes, and so the problem of whether the influence of art is predominantly for good or for evil is a pseudo-problem. Art is neither moral nor immoral but nonmoral.

Much of the debate concerning art and morality reveals a strong and persistent bias on the part of most participants in favor of the moral man rather than of the aesthetically sensitive man in the general sense of assigning greater dignity, scope, and intrinsic importance to morality in constrast with art. In the selection written by D. W. Prall, the American aesthetician, he seeks to reverse this emphasis, subordinating morality to art. Prall maintains that all moral values derive from aesthetic values. The discrimination of good and evil is ultimately accomplished by the eye of the artist. Aesthetic employment is the only real end-in-itself, all other worthwhile nonaesthetic values being but various means to its attainment.

John Dewey sees the relationship of art and morality in a still different form, not as a relationship of dependence of one on the other or as a relationship of independence of one from the other, but as reciprocal connection. More precisely, the relationship between art and morality *ought* to be one of mutual interdependence if art were not narrowly conceived as the pleasure of an idle moment, as entertainment, and morality crudely seen as the mechanical awarding of praise and blame according to some rigid and over-simplified code. If we construed art and morality more intelligently, neither would be confined artificially to separate compartments, but they would be seen to be elements of all human culture: art imaginatively discerning the ideal and morality being a collective name for all shared human values. Traditional, "academic" art may merely decorate and enhance conventional values. However, new art is new because it makes us sensitive to new values, to novel ideals, and thereby encourages moral innovation. Art as the imaginative discernment of possibilities redeems human life from the damnation of routine and boredom.

The seemingly perennial controversy over art and obscenity focuses the more abstract and general philosophical discussions concerning the relationship between art and morality. On March 21, 1966, the United States Supreme Court handed down its opinion in the case concerning the book entitled *Fanny Hill or Memoirs of a Woman of Pleasure* by John Cleland, long considered by many a classic of pornography. The readings consist of selections from the opinion of Mr. Justice Brennan, announcing the judgment of the Court and joined by Chief Justice Warren and Mr. Justice Fortas, a separate concurring opinion by Mr. Justice Douglas, and dissenting opinions by Mr. Justice Clark and Mr. Justice White. Once again the

Court grappled with the philosophic problem, similar to those attacked by Socrates, of how to define *obscenity* in such a way as to provide a workable set of standards for deciding whether or not something is obscene and so should or should not be illegal. In his opinion, Mr. Justice Brennan devotes himself primarily to elucidating the correct interpretation of the definition of *obscenity* laid down in *Roth v. United States,* 354U.S.476. He argues that it is not enough that a book appeal to prurient interest and be patently offensive in order to legally ban it; the book *also* must be *"utterly without redeeming social value."* Agreeing that a book possessing social value should not be banned, repeating his contention that the First Amendment of the U.S. Constitution forbids any state to rule on the value of a particular expression, Mr. Justice Douglas then launches a witty attack on the claim that censorship is justified because erotically stimulating material causes antisocial sexual conduct. Both Mr. Justice Clark and Mr. Justice White vigorously take issue with the opinions authored by Justices Brennan and Douglas concerning such philosophical questions as the nature of art, the meaning of obscenity, and the relationship between art and morality, thereby illustrating how philosophical conflicts lie at the foundations of our legal and social disputes.

The desirability—indeed, the heroism—of being personally committed, involved, an activist has been urged and exemplified on all sides today by rebels young and old. In order to respond philosophically to this incessant and sometimes strident idealism, one must examine it, take the first steps of finding out what arguments can be marshalled for and against it, and then assess those arguments. In order to make the investigation more manageable and concrete, this Part puts it in terms of whether or not the artist should be morally and politically "committed," of whether or not the ideal of art for art's sake is viable and justifiable. E. M. Forster, one of the great novelists of the twentieth century, argues that the artist must be an outsider, a stranger in the society in which he finds himself because as a social (i.e., moral, political, religious) being, man can express only various parts or fragments of himself, not his whole nature. By nature man yearns for something with what Forster calls *form,* for an object possessing internal harmony. Society has failed to provide this "form." In Forster's estimation, art can bless man with it. Hence, the artist, if he is to be an artist, must to that extent separate and detach himself from society. To become a reformer, a champion of moral, political, and other causes, means not to be an artist. Forster goes on to suggest that the artist's detachment from society constitutes a value important to all nonartists, to all men who seek a fully satisfying life.

The American philosopher Barrows Dunham argues that it is an impossibility for the artist as artist not to be committed, involved. If a work of art possesses any meaning at all, it must have content. Any content, however restricted and seemingly trivial, must be drawn from human experience. Therefore, that content inevitably comes dyed with human feelings and emotions, with political, moral, religious, and other hues. It is impossible to separate some mysterious and elusive "forms" from any content whatsoever. And even were it possible to sever the two, any "pure form" still would have been contaminated by its association with some content. No, the better the art, the more meaningful the work, the more saturated it is with moral, political, and other human values, and the more morally committed and involved its creator. The artist is not an aloof god but human, all too human.

Moral and Immoral Art Plato

Plato (427–347 B.C.), an Athenian aristocrat, was converted by Socrates from poetry to philosophy. With the exception of Aristotle, no philosopher has exerted a greater formative influence on Western culture. In many of the Platonic dialogues, Socrates is made to express ideas doubtless those of Plato. In the following selection, Socrates discusses moral and immoral art with Adeimantus and Glaucon, both young men and brothers of Plato.

Socrates: Come then, and let us pass a leisure hour in story-telling, and our story shall be the education of our heroes.

Adeimantus: By all means.

And what shall be their education? Can we find a better than the traditional sort?—and this has two divisions, gymnastic for the body, and music for the soul.

True.

Shall we begin education with music, and go on to gymnastic afterwards?

By all means.

And when you speak of music, do you include literature or not?

I do.

And literature may be either true or false?

Yes.

And the young should be trained in both kinds, and we begin with the false?

I do not understand your meaning, he said.

You know, I said, that we begin by telling children stories which, though not wholly destitute of truth, are in the main fictitious; and these stories are told them when they are not of an age to learn gymnastics.

Very true.

That was my meaning when I said that we must teach music before gymnastics.

Quite right, he said.

You know also that the beginning is the most important part of any work, especially in the case of a young and tender thing; for that is the time at which the character is being formed and the desired impression is more readily taken.

From "The Republic," by Plato from The Dialogues of Plato, trans. by Benjamin Jowett, 3rd ed., 1892 (as reprinted in the Random House volume, by Raphael Demos, 1937). Reprinted by permission of the Clarendon Press, Oxford.

Quite true.

And shall we just carelessly allow children to hear any casual tales which may be devised by casual persons, and to receive into their minds ideas for the most part the very opposite of those which we should wish them to have when they are grown up?

We cannot.

Then the first thing will be to establish a censorship of the writers of fiction, and let the censors receive any tale of fiction which is good, and reject the bad; and we will desire mothers and nurses to tell their children the authorised ones only. Let them fashion the mind with such tales, even more fondly than they mould the body with their hands; but most of those which are now in use must be discarded.

Of what tales are you speaking? he said.

You may find a model of the lesser in the greater, I said; for they are necessarily of the same type, and there is the same spirit in both of them.

Very likely, he replied; but I do not as yet know what you would term the greater.

Those, I said, which are narrated by Homer and Hesiod, and the rest of the poets, who have ever been the great story-tellers of mankind.

But which stories do you mean, he said; and what fault do you find with them?

A fault which is most serious, I said; the fault of telling a lie, and, what is more, a bad lie.

But when is this fault committed?

Whenever an erroneous representation is made of the nature of gods and heroes,—as when a painter paints a portrait not having the shadow of a likeness to the original.

Yes, he said, that sort of thing is certainly very blameable; but what are the stories which you mean?

First of all, I said, there was that greatest of all lies, in high places, which the poet told about Uranus, and which was a bad lie too,—I mean what Hesiod says that Uranus did, and how Cronus retaliated on him.[1] The doings of Cronus, and the sufferings which in turn his son inflicted upon him, even if they were true, ought certainly not to be lightly told to young and thoughtless persons; if possible, they had better be buried in silence. But if there is an absolute necessity for their mention, a chosen few might hear them in a mystery, and they should sacrifice not a common [Eleusinian] pig, but some huge and unprocurable victim; and then the number of hearers will be very few indeed.

Why, yes, said he, those stories are extremely objectionable.

Yes, Adeimantus, they are stories not to be repeated in our State; the young man should not be told that in committing the worst of crimes he is far from doing anything outrageous; and that even if he chastises his father when he does wrong, in whatever manner, he will only be following the example of the first and greatest among the gods.

I entirely agree with you, he said; in my opinion these stories are quite unfit to be repeated.

[1] Hesiod, Theogony, 154, 459.

Neither, if we mean our future guardians to regard the habit of quarreling among themselves as of all things the basest, should any word be said to them of the wars in heaven, and of the plots and fightings of the gods against one another, for they are not true. No, we shall never mention the battles of the giants, or let them be embroidered on garments; and we shall be silent about the innumerable other quarrels of gods and heroes with their friends and relatives. If they would only believe us we would tell them that quarreling is unholy, and that never up to this time has there been any quarrel between citizens; this is what old men and old women should begin by telling children; and when they grow up, the poets also should be told to compose for them in a similar spirit. But the narrative of Hephaestus binding Here his mother, or how on another occasion Zeus sent him flying for taking her part when she was being beaten, and all the battles of the gods in Homer—these tales must not be admitted into our State, whether they are supposed to have an allegorical meaning or not. For a young person cannot judge what is allegorical and what is literal; anything that he receives into his mind at that age is likely to become indelible and unalterable; and therefore it is most important that the tales which the young first hear should be models of virtuous thoughts. . . .

And if any one asserts that the violation of oaths and treaties, which was really the work of Pandarus,[2] was wrought about by Athene and Zeus, or that the strife and contention of the gods was instigated by Themis and Zeus,[3] he shall not have our approval; neither will we allow our young men to hear the words of Aeschylus, that

> God plants guilt among men when he desires utterly to destroy a house.

And if a poet writes of the sufferings of Niobe—the subject of the tragedy in which these iambic verses occur—or of the house of Pelops, or of the Trojan war or on any similar theme, either we must not permit him to say that these are the works of God, or if they are of God, he must devise some explanation of them such as we are seeking; he must say that God did what was just and right, and they were the better for being punished; but that those who are punished are miserable, and that God is the author of their misery—the poet is not to be permitted to say; though he may say that the wicked are miserable because they require to be punished, and are benefited by receiving punishment from God; but that God being good is the author of evil to any one is to be strenuously denied, and not to be said or sung or heard in verse or prose by any one whether old or young in any well-ordered commonwealth. Such a fiction is suicidal, ruinous, impious.

I agree with you, he replied, and am ready to give my assent to the law.

Let this then be one of our rules and principles concerning the gods, to which our poets and reciters will be expected to conform—that God is not the author of all things, but the good only.

That will do, he said.

[2] Iliad ii. 69.
[3] Ib. xx.

And what do you think of a second principle? Shall I ask you whether God is a magician, and of a nature to appear insidiously now in one shape, and now in another—sometimes himself changing and passing into many forms, sometimes deceiving us with the semblance of such transformations; or is he one and the same immutably fixed in his own proper image?

I cannot answer you, he said, without more thought.

Well, I said; but if we suppose a change in anything, that change must be effected either by the thing itself, or by some other thing?

Most certainly.

And things which are at their best are also least liable to be altered or discomposed; for example, when healthiest and strongest, the human frame is least liable to be affected by meats and drinks, and the plant which is in the fullest vigour also suffers least from winds or the heat of the sun or any similar causes.

Of course.

And will not the bravest and wisest soul be least confused or deranged by any external influence?

True.

And the same principle, as I should suppose, applies to all composite things—furniture, houses, garments: when good and well made, they are least altered by time and circumstances.

Very true.

Then everything which is good, whether made by art or nature, or both, is least liable to suffer change from without?

True.

But surely God and the things of God are in every way perfect?

Of course they are.

Then he can hardly be compelled by external influence to take many shapes?

He cannot.

But may he not change and transform himself?

Clearly, he said, that must be the case if he is changed at all.

And will he then change himself for the better and fairer, or for the worse and more unsightly?

If he change at all he can only change for the worse, for we cannot suppose him to be deficient either in virtue or beauty.

Very true, Adeimantus; but then, would any one, whether God or man, desire to make himself worse?

Impossible.

Then it is impossible that God should ever be willing to change; being, as is supposed, the fairest and best that is conceivable, every God remains absolutely and for ever in his own form.

That necessarily follows, he said, in my judgment.

Then, I said, my dear friend, let none of the poets tell us that

> The gods, taking the disguise of strangers from other lands, walk up and down cities in all sorts of forms,[4]

[4] Hom. Od. xvii. 485.

and let no one slander Proteus and Thetis, neither let any one, either in tragedy or in any other kind of poetry, introduce Here disguised in the likeness of a priestess asking an alms

For the life-giving daughters of Inachus the river of Argos;

—let us have no more lies of that sort. Neither must we have mothers under the influence of the poets scaring their children with a bad version of these myths—telling how certain gods, as they say, 'Go about by night in the likeness of so many strangers and in divers forms;' but let them take heed lest they make cowards of their children, and at the same time speak blasphemy against the gods.

Heaven forbid, he said.

But although the gods are themselves unchangeable, still by witch-craft and deception they may make us think that they appear in various forms?

Perhaps, he replied.

Well, but can you imagine that God be willing to lie, whether in word or deed, or to put forth a phantom of himself?

I cannot say, he replied.

Do you not know, I said, that the true lie, if such an expression may be allowed, is hated of gods and men?

What do you mean? he said.

I mean that no one is willingly deceived in that which is the truest and highest part of himself, or about the truest and highest matters; there, above all, he is most afraid of a lie having possession of him.

Still, he said, I do not comprehend you.

The reason is, I replied, that you attribute some profound meaning to my words; but I am only saying that deception, or being deceived or uninformed about the highest realities in the highest part of themselves, which is the soul, and in that part of them to have and to hold the lie, is what mankind least like;—that, I say, is what they utterly detest.

There is nothing more hateful to them.

And, as I was just now remarking, this ignorance in the soul of him who is deceived may be called the true lie; for the lie in words is only a kind of imitation and shadowy image of a previous affection of the soul, not pure unadulterated falsehood. Am I not right?

Perfectly right.

The true lie is hated not only by the gods, but also by men?

Yes.

Whereas the lie in words is in certain cases useful and not hateful; in dealing with enemies—that would be an instance; or again, when those whom we call our friends in a fit of madness or illusion are going to do some harm, then it is useful and is a sort of medicine or preventive; also in the tales of mythology, of which we were just now speaking—because we do not know the truth about ancient times, we make falsehood as much like truth as we can, and so turn it to account.

Very true, he said.

But can any of these reasons apply to God? Can we suppose that he is ignorant of antiquity, and therefore has recourse to invention?

That would be ridiculous, he said.

Then the lying poet has no place in our idea of God?

I should say not.

Or perhaps he may tell a lie because he is afraid of enemies?

That is inconceivable.

But he may have friends who are senseless or mad?

But no mad or senseless person can be a friend of God.

Then no motive can be imagined why God should lie?

None whatever.

Then the superhuman and divine is absolutely incapable of falsehood?

Yes.

Then is God perfectly simple and true both in word and deed; he changes not; he deceives not, either by sign or word, by dream or waking vision. . . .

And can he be fearless of death, or will he choose death in battle rather than defeat and slavery, who believes the world below to be real and terrible?

Impossible.

Then we must assume a control over the narrators of this class of tales as well as over the others, and beg them not simply to revile, but rather to commend the world below, intimating to them that their descriptions are untrue, and will do harm to our future warriors.

That will be our duty, he said.

Then, I said, we shall have to obliterate many obnoxious passages, beginning with the verses,

> I would rather be a serf on the land of a poor and portionless man than rule over all the dead who have come to nought.[5]

We must also expunge the verse, which tells us how Pluto feared,

> Lest the mansions grim and squalid which the gods abhor should be seen both of mortals and immortals.[6]

And again:—

> O heavens! verily in the house of Hades there is soul and ghostly form but no mind at all![7]

Again of Tiresias:—

> [To him even after death did Persephone grant mind,] that he alone should be wise; but the other souls are flitting shades.[8]

Again:—

> The soul flying from the limbs had gone to Hades, lamenting her fate, leaving manhood and youth.[9]

[5] Od. ix. 489.

[6] Il. xx. 64.

[7] Il. xxiii. 103.

[8] Od. x. 495.

[9] Il. xvi. 856.

Again:—

> And the soul, with shrilling cry, passed like smoke beneath the earth.[10]

And,—

> As bats in hollow of mystic cavern, whenever any of them has dropped out of the string and falls from the rock, fly shrilling and cling to one another, so did they with shrilling cry hold together as they moved.[11]

And we must beg Homer and the other poets not to be angry if we strike out these and similar passages, not because they are unpoetical, or unattractive to the popular ear, but because the greater the poetical charm of them, the less they are meet for the ears of boys and men who are meant to be free, and who should fear slavery more than death.

Undoubtedly.

Also we shall have to reject all the terrible and appalling names which describe the world below—Cocytus and Styx, ghosts under the earth, and sapless shades, and any similar words of which the very mention causes a shudder to pass through the inmost soul of him who hears them. I do not say that these horrible stories may not have a use of some kind; but there is a danger that the nerves of our guardians may be rendered too excitable and effeminate by them. . . .

Again, truth should be highly valued; if, as we were saying, a lie is useless to the gods, and useful only as a medicine to men, then the use of such medicines should be restricted to physicians; private individuals have no business with them.

Clearly not, he said.

Then if any one at all is to have the privilege of lying, the rulers of the State should be the persons; and they, in their dealings either with enemies or with their own citizens, may be allowed to lie for the public good. But nobody else should meddle with anything of the kind; and although the rulers have this privilege, for a private man to lie to them in return is to be deemed a more heinous fault than for the patient or the pupil of a gymnasium not to speak the truth about his own bodily illnesses to the physician or to the trainer, or for a sailor not to tell the captain what is happening about the ship and the rest of the crew, and how things are going with himself or his fellow sailors.

Most true, he said.

If, then, the ruler catches anybody beside himself lying in the State,

> Any of the craftsmen, whether he be priest or physician or carpenter,[12]

he will punish him for introducing a practice which is equally subversive and destructive of ship or State.

Most certainly, he said, if our idea of the State is ever carried out.[13]

In the next place our youth must be temperate?

[10] Ib. xxiii. 100.

[11] Od. xxiv. 6.

[12] Od. xvii. 383 sq.

[13] Or, 'if his words are accompanied by actions.'

Certainly.

Are not the chief elements of temperance, speaking generally, obedience to commanders and self-control in sensual pleasures?

True.

Then we shall approve such language as that of Diomede in Homer,

> Friend, sit still and obey my word,[14]

and the verses which follow,

> The Greeks marched breathing prowess,[15]
> .... in silent awe of their leaders,[16]

and other sentiments of the same kind.

We shall.

What of this line,

> O heavy with wine, who hast the eyes of a dog and the heart of a stag,[17]

and of the words which follow? Would you say that these, or any similar impertinences which private individuals are supposed to address to their rulers, whether in verse or prose, are well or ill spoken?

They are ill spoken.

They may very possibly afford some amusement, but they do not conduce to temperance. And therefore they are likely to do harm to our young men—you would agree with me there?

Yes.

And then, again, to make the wisest of men say that nothing in his opinion is more glorious than

> When the tables are full of bread and meat, and the cup-bearer carries round wine which he draws from the bowl and pours into the cups,[18]

is it fit or conducive to temperance for a young man to hear such words? Or the verse

> The saddest of fates is to die and meet destiny from hunger[19]?

What would you say again to the tale of Zeus, who, like other gods and men were asleep and he the only person awake, lay devising plans, but forgot them all in a moment through his lust, and was so completely overcome at the sight of Here that he would not even go into the hut, but wanted to lie with her on the ground, declaring that he had never been in such a state of rapture before, even when they first met one another

> Without the knowledge of their parents;[20]

[14] Il. iv. 412.

[15] Od. iii. 8.

[16] Ib. iv. 431.

[17] Ib. i. 225.

[18] Ib. ix. 8.

[19] Ib. xii. 342.

[20] Il. xiv. 281.

or that other tale of how Hephaestus, because of similar goings on, cast a chain around Ares and Aphrodite?[21]

Indeed, he said, I am strongly of opinion that they ought not to hear that sort of thing.

But any deeds of endurance which are done or told by famous men, these they ought to see and hear; as, for example, what is said in the verses,

> He smote his breast, and thus reproached his heart,
> Endure, my heart; far worse hast thou endured![22]

Certainly, he said.

In the next place, we must not let them be receivers of gifts or lovers of money.

Certainly not.

Neither must we sing to them of

> Gifts persuading gods, and persuading reverend kings.[23]

Neither is Phoenix, the tutor of Achilles, to be approved or deemed to have given his pupil good counsel when he told him that he should take the gifts of the Greeks and assist them;[24] but that without a gift he should not lay aside his anger. Neither will we believe or acknowledge Achilles himself to have been such a lover of money that he took Agamemnon's gifts, or that when he had received payment he restored the dead body of Hector, but that without payment he was unwilling to do so.[25]

Undoubtedly, he said, these are not sentiments which can be approved.

... [W]e must come to an understanding about the mimetic art,— whether the poets, in narrating their stories, are to be allowed by us to imitate, and if so, whether in whole or in part, and if the latter, in what parts; or should all imitation be prohibited?

You mean, I suspect, to ask whether tragedy and comedy shall be admitted into our State?

Yes, I said; but there may be more than this in questtion: I really do not know as yet, but whither the argument may blow, thither we go.

And go we will, he said.

Then, Adeimantus, let me ask you whether our guardians ought to be imitators; or rather, has not this question been decided by the rule already laid down that one man can only do one thing well, and not many; and that if he attempt many, he will altogether fail of gaining much reputation in any?

Certainly.

And this is equally true of imitation; no one man can imitate many things as well as he would imitate a single one?

He cannot.

[21] Od. viii. 266.

[22] Ib. xx. 17.

[23] Quoted by Suidas as attributed to Hesiod.

[24] Il. ix. 515.

[25] Ib. xxiv. 175.

Then the same person will hardly be able to play a serious part in life, and at the same time to be an imitator and imitate many other parts as well; for even when two species of imitation are nearly allied, the same persons cannot succeed in both, as, for example, the writers of tragedy and comedy—did you not just now call them imitations?

Yes, I did; and you are right in thinking that the same persons cannot succeed in both.

Any more than they can be rhapsodists and actors at once?

True.

Neither are comic and tragic actors the same; yet all these things are but imitations.

They are so.

And human nature, Adeimantus, appears to have been coined into yet smaller pieces, and to be as incapable of imitating many things well, as of performing well the actions of which the imitations are copies.

Quite true, he replied.

If then we adhere to our original notion and bear in mind that our guardians, setting aside every other business, are to dedicate themselves wholly to the maintenance of freedom in the State, making this their craft, and engaging in no work which does not bear on this end, they ought not to practise or imitate anything else; if they imitate at all, they should imitate from youth upward only those characters which are suitable to their profession—the courageous, temperate, holy, free, and the like; but they should not depict or be skilful at imitating any kind of illiberality or baseness, lest from imitation they should come to be what the imitate. Did you never observe how imitations, beginning in early youth and continuing far into life, at length grow into habits and become a second nature, affecting body, voice, and mind?

Yes, certainly, he said.

Then, I said, we will not allow those for whom we profess a care and of whom we say that they ought to be good men, to imitate a woman, whether young or old, quarrelling with her husband, or striving and vaunting against the gods in conceit of her happiness, on when she is in affliction, or sorrow, or weeping; and certainly not one who is in sickness, love or labour.

Very right, he said.

Neither must they represent slaves, male or female, performing the offices of slaves?

They must not.

And surely not bad men, whether cowards or any others, who do the reverse of what we have just been prescribing, who scold or mock or revile one another in drink or out of drink, or who in any other manner sin against themselves and their neighbours in word or deed, as the manner of such is. Neither should they be trained to imitate the action or speech of men or women who are mad or bad; for madness, like vice, is to be known but not to be practised or imitated.

Very true, he replied.

Neither may they imitate smiths or other artificers or oarsmen, or boatswains, or the like?

How can they, he said, when they are not allowed to apply their minds to the callings of any of these?

Nor may they imitate the neighing of horses, the bellowing of bulls, the murmur of rivers and roll of the thunder, and all that sort of thing?

Nay, he said, if madness be forbidden, neither may they copy the behaviour of madmen.

You mean, I said, if I understand you aright, that there is one sort of narrative style which may be employed by a truly good man when he has anything to say, and that another sort will be used by a man of an opposite character and education.

And which are these two sorts? he asked.

Suppose, I answered, that a just and good man in the course of a narration comes on some saying or action of another good man,—I should imagine that he will like to personate him, and will not be ashamed of this sort of imitation: he will be most ready to play the part of the good man when he is acting firmly and wisely; in a less degree when he is overtaken by illness or love or drink, or has met with any other disaster. But when he comes to a character which is unworthy of him, he will not make a study of that; he will disdain such a person, and will assume his likeness, if at all, for a moment only when he is performing some good action; at other times he will be ashamed to play a part which he has never practised, nor will he like to fashion and frame himself after the baser models; he feels the employment of such an art, unless in jest, to be beneath him, and his mind revolts at it. . . .

But shall our superintendence go no further, and are the poets only to be required by us to express the image of the good in their works, on pain, if they do anything else, of expulsion from our State? Or is the same control to be extended to other artists, and are they also to be prohibited from exhibiting the opposite forms of vice and intemperance and meanness and indecency in sculpture and building and the other creative arts; and is he who cannot conform to this rule of ours to be prevented from practising his art in our State, lest the taste of our citizens be corrupted by him? We would not have our guardians grow up amid images of moral deformity, as in some noxious pasture, and there browse and feed upon many a baneful herb and flower day by day, little by little, until they silently gather a festering mass of corruption in their own soul. Let our artists rather be those who are gifted to discern the true nature of the beautiful and graceful; then will our youth dwell in a land of health, amid fair sights and sounds, and receive the good in everything; and beauty, the effluence of fair works, shall flow into the eye and ear, like a health-giving breeze from a purer region, and insensibly draw the soul from earliest years into likeness and sympathy with the beauty of reason.

Glaucon: There can be no nobler training than that, he replied.

And therefore, I said, Glaucon, musical training is a more potent instrument than any other, because rhythm and harmony find their way into the inward places of the soul, on which they mightily fasten, imparting grace, and making the soul of him who is rightly educated graceful, or of him who is ill-educated ungraceful; and also because he who has received this true education of the inner being will most shrewdly per-

ceive omissions or faults in art and nature, and with a true taste, while
he praises and rejoices over and receives into his soul the good, and becomes noble and good, he will justly blame and hate the bad, now in the
days of his youth, even before he is able to know the reason why; and
when reason comes he will recognise and salute the friend with whom
his education has made him long familiar.

Yes, he said, I quite agree with you in thinking that our youth should
be trained in music and on the grounds which you mention.

Just as in learning to read, I said, we were satisfied when we knew the
letters of the alphabet, which are very few, in all their recurring sizes
and combinations; not slighting them as unimportant whether they occupy
a space large or small, but everywhere eager to make them out; and not
thinking ourselves perfect in the art of reading until we recognise them
wherever they are found:

True—

Or, as we recognise the reflection of letters in the water, or in a mirror,
only when we know the letters themselves; the same art and study giving
us the knowledge of both:

Exactly—

Even so, as I maintain, neither we nor our guardians, whom we have
to educate, can ever become musical until we and they know the essential forms, in all their combinations, and can recognise them and their
images wherever they are found, not slighting them either in small
things or great, but believing them all to be within the sphere of one art
and study.

Most assuredly.

And when a beautiful soul harmonizes with a beautiful form, and
the two are cast in one mould, that will be the fairest of sights to him
who has an eye to see it?

The fairest indeed.

And the fairest is also the loveliest?

That may be assumed.

And the man who has the spirit of harmony will be most in love with
the loveliest; but he will not love him who is of an inharmonious soul?

That is true, he replied, if the deficiency be in his soul; but if there
be any merely bodily defect in another he will be patient of it, and will
love all the same. . . .

Art as Social Therapy   Aristotle

Aristotle (384–322 B.C.), son of a Macedonian physician, most famous student of Plato, and tutor of the young Alexander the Great, was called simply "The Philosopher" in medieval universities, so great was his stature. His writings seem to be notes made for or taken from his lectures. His early writings, now lost, are said to have shown great literary skill. Minus the influence of Aristotle's philosophy, Western civilization would not be what it was and is.

No one will doubt that the legislator should direct his attention above all to the education of youth; for the neglect of education does harm to the constitution. The citizen should be moulded to suit the form of government under which he lives. For each government has a peculiar character which originally formed and which continues to preserve it. The character of democracy creates democracy, and the character of oligarchy creates oligarchy; and always the better the character, the better the government.

Again, for the exercise of any faculty or art a previous training and habituation are required; clearly therefore for the practice of virtue. And since the whole city has one end, it is manifest that education should be public, and not private,—not as at present, when every one looks after his own children separately, and gives them separate instruction of the sort which he thinks best; the training in things which are of common interest should be the same for all. Neither must we suppose that any one of the citizens belongs to himself, for they all belong to the state, and are each of them a part of the state, and the care of each part is inseparable from the care of the whole. In this particular as in some others the Lacedaemonians are to be praised, for they take the greatest pains about their children, and make education the business of the state.

That education should be regulated by law and should be an affair of state is not to be denied, but what should be the character of this public education, and how young persons should be educated, are questions which remain to be considered. As things are, there is disagreement about the subjects. For mankind are by no means agreed about the things to be taught, whether we look to virtue or the best life. Neither is it clear whether education is more concerned with intellectual or with moral virtue. The existing practice is perplexing; no one knows on what principle we should proceed—should the useful in life, or should virtue, or should the higher knowledge, be the aim of our training; all three opinions have been entertained. Again, about the means there is no agreement; for different persons, starting with different ideas about the nature of virtue, naturally disagree about the practice of it. There can be no doubt that children should be taught those useful things which are

From 'Politics,' by Aristotle, trans. by Benjamin Jowett from *The Oxford Translation of Aristotle,* ed. by W. D. Ross, Vol. X, 1921. Reprinted by permission of the Clarendon Press, Oxford. Footnotes have been omitted.

really necessary, but not all useful things; for occupations are divided into liberal and illiberal; and to young children should be imparted only such kinds of knowledge as will be useful to them without vulgarizing them. And any occupation, art, or science, which makes the body or soul or mind of the freeman less fit for the practice or exercise of virtue, is vulgar; wherefore we call those arts vulgar which tend to deform the body, and likewise all paid employments, for they absorb and degrade the mind. There are also some liberal arts quite proper for a freeman to acquire, but only in a certain degree, and if he attend them too closely, in order to attain perfection in them, the same evil effects will follow. The object also which a man sets before him makes a great difference; if he does or learns anything for his own sake or for the sake of his friends, or with a view to excellence, the action will not appear illiberal; but if done for the sake of others, the very same action will be thought menial and servile. The received subjects of instruction, as I have already remarked, are partly of a liberal and partly of an illiberal character.

The customary branches of education are in number four; they are—(1) reading and writing, (2) gymnastic exercises, (3) music, to which is sometimes added (4) drawing. Of these, reading and writing and drawing are regarded as useful for the purposes of life in a variety of ways, and gymnastic exercises are thought to infuse courage. Concerning music a doubt may be raised—in our own day most men cultivate it for the sake of pleasure, but originally it was included in education, because nature herself, as has been often said, requires that we should be able, not only to work well, but to use leisure well; for, as I must repeat once again, the first principle of all action is leisure. Both are required, but leisure is better than occupation and is its end; and therefore the question must be asked, what ought we to do when at leisure? Clearly we ought not to be amusing ourselves, for then amusement would be the end of life. But if this is inconceivable, and amusement is needed more amid serious occupations than at other times (for he who is hard at work has need of relaxation, and amusement gives relaxation, whereas occupation is always accompanied with exertion and effort), we should introduce amusements only at suitable times, and they should be our medicines, for the emotion which they create in the soul is a relaxation, and from the pleasure we obtain rest. But leisure of itself gives pleasure and happiness and enjoyment of life, which are experienced, not by the busy man, but by those who have leisure. For he who is occupied has in view some end which he has not attained; but happiness is an end, since all men deem it to be accompanied with pleasure and not with pain. This pleasure, however, is regarded differently by different persons, and varies according to the habit of individuals; the pleasure of the best man is the best, and springs from the noblest sources. It is clear then that there are branches of learning and education which we must study merely with a view to leisure spent in intellectual activity, and these are to be valued for their own sake; whereas those kinds of knowledge which are useful in business are to be deemed necessary, and exist for the sake of other things. And therefore our fathers admitted music into education, not on the ground either of its necessity, or utility, for it is not necessary, nor indeed useful in the same manner as reading and writing, which are useful in money-making, in the management of a household, in the acquisition of knowledge and in political life, nor like drawing, useful for a more correct judgment of the works of artists, nor again like gymnastic, which gives health and strength; for neither of these is to be gained from music. There remains, then, the use of music for intellectual enjoyment in leisure; which is in fact evidently the reason of its introduction, this being one of the ways in which it is thought that a freeman should pass his leisure; as Homer says—

> But he who alone should be called to the pleasant feast,

and afterwards he speaks of others whom he describes as inviting

> The bard who would delight them all.

And in another place Odysseus says there is no better way of passing life than when men's hearts are merry and

> The banqueters in the hall, sitting in order, hear the voice of the minstrel.

It is evident, then, that there is a sort of education in which parents should train their sons, not as being useful or necessary, but because it is liberal or noble. Whether this is of one kind only, or of more than one, and if so, what they are, and how they are to be imparted, must hereafter be determined. Thus much we are now in a position to say, that the ancients witness to us; for their opinion may be gathered from the fact that music is one of the received and traditional branches of education. Further, it is clear that children should be instructed in some useful things,—for example, in reading and writing,—not only for their usefulness, but also because many other sorts of knowledge are acquired through them. With a like view they may be taught drawing, not to prevent their making mistakes in their own purchases, or in order that they may not be imposed upon in the buying or selling of articles, but perhaps rather because it makes them judges of the beauty of the human form. To be always seeking after the useful does not become free and exalted souls. Now it is clear that in education practice must be used before theory, and the body be trained before the mind; and therefore boys should be handed over to the trainer, who creates in them the proper habit of body, and to the wrestling-master, who teaches them their exercises. . . .

Concerning music there are some questions which we have already raised; these we may now resume and carry further; and our remarks will serve as a prelude to this or any other discussion of the subject. It is not easy to determine the nature of music, or why any one should have a knowledge of it. Shall we say, for the sake of amusement and relaxation, like sleep or drinking, which are not good in themselves, but are pleasant, and at the same time 'make care to cease', as Euripides says? And for this end men also appoint music, and make use of all three alike,—sleep, drinking, music,—to which some add dancing. Or shall we argue that music conduces to virtue, on the ground that it can form our minds and habituate us to true pleasures as our bodies are made by gymnastic to be of a certain character? Or shall we say that it contributes to the enjoyment of leisure and mental cultivation, which is a third alternative? Now obviously youths are not to be instructed with a view to their amusement, for learning is no amusement, but is accompanied with pain. Neither is intellectual enjoyment suitable to boys of that age, for it is the end, and that which is imperfect cannot attain the perfect or end. But perhaps it may be said that boys learn music for the sake of the amusement which they will have when they are grown up. If so, why should they learn themselves, and not, like the Persian and Median kings, enjoy the pleasure and instruction which is derived from hearing others? (for surely persons who have made music the business and profession of their lives will be better performers than those who practise only long enough to learn). If they must learn music, on the same principle they should learn cookery, which is absurd. And even granting that music may form the character, the objection still holds: why should we learn ourselves? Why cannot we attain true pleasure and form a correct judgment from hearing others, like the Lacedaemonians?—for they, without learning music, nevertheless can correctly judge, as they say, of good and bad melodies. Or again, if music should be used to promote cheerfulness and refined intellectual enjoyment, the objection still remains—why should we learn ourselves instead of enjoying the performances of others? We may illustrate what we are saying by our conception of the Gods; for in the poets Zeus does not himself sing or play on the lyre. Nay, we call professional performers vulgar; no freeman would play or sing unless he were intoxicated or in jest. But these matters may be left for the present.

The first question is whether music is or is not to be a part of education. Of the three things mentioned in our discussion, which does it produce?—education or amusement or intellectual enjoyment, for it may be reckoned under all three, and seems to share in the nature of all of them. Amusement is for the sake of relaxation, and relaxation is of necessity sweet, for it is the remedy of pain caused by toil; and intellectual enjoyment is universally acknowledged to contain an element not only of the noble but of the pleasant, for happiness is made up of both. All men agree that music is one of the pleasantest things, whether with or without song; as Musaeus says,

> Song is to mortals of all things the sweetest.

Hence and with good reason it is introduced into social gatherings and entertainments, because it makes the hearts of men glad: so that on this ground alone we may assume that the young ought to be trained in it. For innocent pleasures are not only in harmony with the perfect end of life, but they also provide relaxation. And whereas men rarely attain the end, but often rest by the way and amuse themselves, not only with a view to a further end, but also for the pleasure's sake, it may be well at times to let them find a refreshment in music. It sometimes happens that men make amusement the end, for the end probably contains some element of pleasure, though not any ordinary or lower pleasure; but they mistake the lower for the higher, and in seeking for the one find the other, since every pleasure has a likeness to the end of action. For the end is not eligible for the sake of any future good, nor do the pleasures which we have described exist for the sake of any future good but of the past, that is to say, they are the alleviation of past toils and pains. And we may infer this to be the reason why men seek happiness from these pleasures. But music is pursued, not only as an alleviation of past toil, but also as providing recreation. And who can say whether, having this use, it may not also have a nobler one? In addition to this common pleasure, felt and shared in by all (for the pleasure given by music is natural, and therefore adapted to all ages and characters), may it not have also some influence over the character and the soul? It must have such an influence if characters are affected by it. And that they are so affected is proved in many ways, and not least by the power which the songs of Olympus exercise; for beyond question they inspire enthusiasm, and enthusiasm is an emotion of the ethical part of the soul. Besides, when men hear imitations, even apart from the rhythms and tunes themselves, their feelings move in sympathy. Since then music is a pleasure, and virtue consists in rejoicing and loving and hating aright, there is clearly nothing which we are so much concerned to acquire and to cultivate as the power of forming right judgements, and of taking delight in good dispositions and noble actions. Rhythm and melody supply imitations of anger and gentleness, and also of courage and temperance, and of all the qualities contrary to these, and of the other qualities of character, which hardly fall short of the actual affections, as we know from our own experience, for in listening to such strains our souls undergo a change. The habit of feeling pleasure or pain at mere representations is not far removed from the same feeling about realities; for example, if any one delights in the sight of a statue for its beauty alone, it necessarily follows that the sight of the original will be pleasant to him. The objects of no other sense, such as taste or touch, have any resemblance to moral qualities; in visible objects there is only a little, for there are figures which are of a moral character, but only to a slight extent, and all do not participate in the feeling about them. Again, figures and colours are not imitations, but signs, of moral habits, indications which the body gives of states of feeling. The connexion of them with morals is slight, but in so far as there is any, young men should be taught to look, not at the works of Pauson, but at those of Polygnotus, or any other painter or sculptor who expresses moral ideas. On the other hand, even in mere melodies there is an imitation of character, for the musical modes differ essentially from one another, and those who hear them are differently affected by each. Some of them make men sad and grave, like the so-called Mixolydian, others enfeeble the mind, like the relaxed modes, another, again, produces a moderate and settled temper, which appears to be the peculiar effect of the Dorian; the Phrygian inspires enthusiasm. The whole subject has been well treated by philosophical writers on this branch of education, and they confirm their arguments by facts. The same principles apply to rhythms; some have a character of rest, others of motion, and of these latter again, some have a more vulgar, others a nobler movement. Enough has been said to show that music has a power of forming the character, and should therefore be introduced into the education of the young. The study is suited to the stage of youth, for young persons will not, if they can help, endure anything which is not sweetened by pleasure, and music has a natural sweetness. There seems to be in us a sort of affinity to musical modes and rhythms, which makes some philosophers say that the soul is a tuning, others, that it possesses tuning.

And now we have to determine the question which has been already raised, whether children should be themselves taught to sing and play or not. Clearly there is a considerable difference made in the character by the actual practice of the art. It is difficult, if not impossible, for those who do not perform to be good judges of the performance of others. Besides, children should have something to do, and the rattle of Archytas, which people give to their children in order to amuse them and prevent them from breaking anything in the house, was a capital invention, for a young thing cannot be quiet. The rattle is a toy suited to the infant mind, and education is a rattle or toy for children of a larger growth. We conclude then that they should be taught music in such a way as to become not only critics but performers.

The question what is or is not suitable for different ages may be easily answered; nor is there any difficulty in meeting the objection of those who say that the study of music is vulgar. We reply (1) in the first place, that they who are to be judges must also be performers, and that they should begin to practise early, although when they are older they may be spared the execution; they must have learned to appreciate what is good and to delight in it, thanks to the knowledge which they acquired in their youth. As to (2) the vulgarizing effect which music is supposed to exercise, this is a question which we shall have no difficulty in determining, when we have considered to what extent freemen who are being trained to political virtue should pursue the art, what melodies and what rhythms they should be allowed to use, and what instruments should be employed in teaching them to play; for even the instrument makes a difference. The answer to the objection turns upon these distinctions; for it is quite possible that certain methods of teaching and learning music do really have a degrading effect. It is evident then that the learning of music ought not to impede the business of riper years, or to degrade the body or render it unfit for civil or military training, whether for bodily exercises at the time or for later studies.

The right measure will be attained if students of music stop short of the arts which are practised in professional contests, and do not seek to acquire those fantastic marvels of execution which are now the fashion in such contests, and from these have passed into education. Let the young practise even such music as we have prescribed, only until they are able to feel delight in noble melodies and rhythms, and not merely in that common part of music in which every slave or child and even some animals find pleasure.

From these principles we may also infer what instruments should be used. The flute, or any other instrument which requires great skill, as for example the harp, ought not to be admitted into education, but only such as will make intelligent students of music or of the other parts of education. Besides, the flute is not an instrument which is expressive of moral character; it is too exciting. The proper time for using it is when the performance aims not at instruction, but at the relief of the passions. And there is a further objection; the impediment which the flute presents to the use of the voice detracts from its educational value. The ancients therefore were right in forbidding the flute to youths and freemen, although they had once allowed it. For when their wealth gave them a greater inclination to leisure, and they had loftier notions of excellence, being also elated with their success, both before and after the Persian War, with more zeal than discernment they pursued every kind of knowledge, and so they introduced the flute into education. At Lacedaemon there was a choragus who led the chorus with a flute, and at Athens the instrument became so popular that most freemen could play upon it. The popularity is shown by the tablet which Thrasippus dedicated when he furnished the chorus to Ecphantides. Later experience enabled men to judge what was or was not really conducive to virtue, and they rejected both the flute and several other old-fashioned instruments, such as the Lydian harp, the many-stringed lyre, the 'heptagon', 'triangle', 'sambuca', and the like—which are intended only to give pleasure to the hearer, and require extraordinary skill of hand. There is a meaning also in the myth of the ancients, which tells how Athene invented the flute and then threw it away. It was not a bad idea of theirs, that the Goddess disliked the instrument because it made the face ugly; but with still more reason may we say that she rejected it because the acquirement of flute-playing contributes nothing to the mind, since to Athene we ascribe both knowledge and art.

Thus then we reject the professional instruments and also the professional mode of education in music (and by professional we mean that which is adopted in contests), for in this the performer practises the art, not for the sake of his own improvement, but in order to give pleasure, and that of a vulgar sort, to his hearers. For this reason the execution of such music is not the part of a freeman but of a paid performer, and the result is that the performers are vulgarized, for the end at which they aim is bad. The vulgarity of the spectator tends to lower the character of the music and therefore of the performers; they look to him—he makes them what they are, and fashions even their bodies by the movements which he expects them to exhibit.

We have also to consider rhythms and modes, and their use in education. Shall we use them all or make a distinction? and shall the same distinction be made for those who practise music with a view to education, or shall it be some other? Now we see that music is produced by melody and rhythm, and we ought to know what influence these have respectively on education, and whether we should prefer excellence in melody or excellence in rhythm. But as the subject has been very well treated by many musicians of the present day, and also by philosophers who have had considerable experience of musical education, to these we would refer the more exact student of the subject; we shall only speak of it now after the manner of the legislator, stating the general principles.

We accept the division of melodies proposed by certain philosophers into ethical melodies, melodies of action, and passionate or inspiring melodies, each having, as they say, a mode corresponding to it. But we maintain further that music should be studied, not for the sake of one, but of many benefits, that is to say, with a view to (1) education, (2) purgation (the word 'purgation' we use at present without explanation, but when hereafter we speak of poetry, we will treat the subject with more precision); music may also serve (3) for intellectual enjoyment, for relaxation and for recreation after exertion. It is clear, therefore, that all the modes must be employed by us, but not all of them in the same manner. In education the most ethical modes are to be preferred, but in listening to the performances of others we may admit the modes of action and passion also. For feelings such as pity and fear, or, again, enthusiasm, exist very strongly in some souls, and have more or less influence over all. Some persons fall into a religious frenzy, whom we see as a result of the sacred melodies—when they have used the melodies that excite the soul to mystic frenzy—restored as though they had found healing and purgation. Those who are influenced by pity or fear, and every emotional nature, must have a like experience, and others in so far as each is susceptible to such emotions, and all are in a manner purged and their souls lightened and delighted. The purgative melodies likewise give an innocent pleasure to mankind. Such are the modes and the melodies in which those who perform music at the theatre should be invited to compete. But since the spectators are of two kinds—the one free and educated, and the other a vulgar crowd composed of mechanics, labourers, and the like—there ought to be contests and exhibitions instituted for the relaxation of the second class also. And the music will correspond to their minds; for as their minds are perverted from the natural state, so there are perverted modes and highly strung and unnaturally coloured melodies. A man receives pleasure from what is natural to him, and therefore professional musicians may be allowed to practise this lower sort of music before an audience of a lower type. But, for the purposes of education, as I have already said, those modes and melodies should be employed which are ethical, such as the Dorian, as we said before; though we may include any others which are approved by philosophers who have had a musical education. The Socrates of the *Republic* is wrong in retaining only the Phrygian mode along with the Dorian, and the more so because he rejects the flute: for the Phrygian is to the modes what the flute is to musical instruments—both of them are exciting and emotional. Poetry proves this, for Bacchic frenzy and all similar emotions are most suitably expressed by the flute, and are better set to the Phrygian than to any other mode. The dithyramb, for example, is acknowledged to be Phrygian, a fact of which the connoisseurs of music offer many proofs, saying, among other things, that Philoxenus, having attempted to compose his *Mysians* as a dithyramb in the Dorian mode, found it impossible, and fell back by the very nature of things into the more appropriate Phrygian. All men agree that the Dorian music is the gravest and manliest. And whereas we say that the extremes should be avoided and the mean followed, and whereas the Dorian is a mean between the other modes, it is evident that our youth should be taught the Dorian music.

Two principles have to be kept in view, what is possible, what is becoming: at these every man ought to aim. But even these are relative to age; the old, who have lost their powers, cannot very well sing the highstrung modes, and nature herself seems to suggest that their songs should be of the more relaxed kind. Wherefore the musicians likewise blame Socrates, and with justice, for rejecting the relaxed modes in education under the idea that they are intoxicating, not in the ordinary sense of intoxication (for wine rather tends to excite men), but because they have no strength in them. And so, with a view also to the time of life when men begin to grow old, they ought to practise the gentler modes and melodies as well as the others, and, further, any mode, such as the Lydian above all others appears to be, which is suited to children of tender age, and possesses the elements both of order and of education. Thus it is clear that education should be based upon three principles—the mean, the possible, the becoming, these three.

The Autonomy of Art   Jean-Paul Sartre

Jean-Paul Sartre (1905–   ), French existentialist, former professor of philosophy and World War II Resistance leader, is a successful novelist and playwright, as well as philosopher. In 1964, Sartre refused to accept the Nobel Prize for Literature.

. . . We often hear it said, in fact, that the artist first has an idea in the form of an image which he then *realizes* on canvas. This mistaken notion arises from the fact that the painter can, in fact, begin with a mental image which is, as such, incommunicable, and from the fact that at the end of his labors he presents the public with an object which anyone can observe. This leads us to believe that there occurred a transition from the imaginary to the real. But this is in no way true. That which is real, we must not fail to note, are the results of the brush strokes, the stickiness of the canvas, its grain, the polish spread over the colors. But all this does not constitute the object of esthetic appreciation. What is "beautiful" is something which cannot be experienced as a perception and which, by its very nature, is out of the world. We have just shown that it cannot be *brightened,* for instance, by projecting a light beam on the canvas: it is the canvas that is brightened and not the painting. The fact of the matter is that the painer did not *realize* his mental image at all: he has simply constructed a material analogue of such a kind that every-

From *The Psychology of Imagination* by Jean-Paul Sartre, The Philosophical Library, Inc., 1948. Reprinted by permission Literary Masterworks, Inc.

one can grasp the image provided he looks at the analogue. But the image thus provided with an external analogue remains an image. There is no realization of the imaginary, nor can we speak of its *objectification*. Each stroke of the brush was not made *for itself* nor even for the constructing of a coherent real whole (in the sense in which it can be said that a certain lever in a machine was conceived in the interest of the whole and not for itself). It was given together with an unreal synthetic whole and the aim of the artist was to construct a whole of *real* colors which enable this unreal to manifest itself. The painting should then be conceived as a material thing *visited* from time to time (every time that the spectator assumes the imaginative attitude) by an unreal which is precisely the *painted object*. What deceives us here is the real and sensuous pleasure which certain real colors on the canvas give us. Some reds of Matisse, for instance, produce a sensuous enjoyment in those who see them. But we must understand that this sensuous enjoyment, if thought of in isolation —for instance, if aroused by a color in nature—has nothing of the esthetic. It is purely and simply a pleasure of sense. But when the red of the painting is grasped, it is grasped, in spite of everything, as a part of an unreal whole and it is in this whole that it is beautiful. For instance it is the red of a rug by a table. There is, in fact, no such thing as pure color. Even if the artist is concerned solely with the sensory relationships between forms and colors, he chooses for that very reason a rug in order to increase the sensory value of the red: tactile elements, for instance, must be intended through the red, it is a *fleecy* red, because the rug is of a fleecy material. Without this "fleeciness" of the color something would be lost. And surely the rug is painted there *for the red* it justifies and not the red for the rug. If Matisse chose a rug rather than a sheet of dry and glossy paper it is because of the voluptuous mixture of the color, the density and the tactile quality of the wool. Consequently the red can be truly enjoyed only in grasping it as the *red of the rug,* and therefore unreal. And he would have lost his strongest contrast with the green of the wall if the green were not rigid and cold, because it is the green of a wall tapestry. It is therefore in the unreal that the relationship of colors and forms takes on its real meaning. And even when drawn objects have their usual meaning reduced to a minimum, as in the painting of the cubists, the painting is at least not flat. The forms we see are certainly not the forms of a rug, a table, nor anything else we see in the world. They nevertheless do have a density, a material, a depth, they bear a relationship of perspective towards each other. They are *things.* And it is precisely in the measure in which they are things that they are unreal. Cubism has introduced the fashion of claiming that a painting should not *represent* or *imitate* reality but should constitute an object in itself. As an esthetic doctrine such a program is perfectly defensible and we owe many masterpieces to it. But it needs to be understood. To maintain that the painting, although altogether devoid of meaning, nevertheless is a *real* object, would be a grave mistake. It is certainly not an object of nature. The real object no longer functions as an analogue of a bouquet of flowers or a glade. But when I "contemplate" it, I nevertheless am not in a realistic attitude. The painting is still an *analogue.* Only what manifests itself through it is an unreal collection of *new things,* of objects I have never seen or ever will see, but which are not less unreal because of it, objects which do not exist *in the painting,* nor anywhere in the world, but which manifest themselves by means of the canvas, and which have gotten hold of it by some sort of possession. And it is the configuration of these unreal objects that I designate as *beautiful.* The esthetic enjoyment is real but it is not grasped for itself, as if produced by a real color: it is but a manner of apprehending the unreal object and, far from being directed on the real painting, it serves to constitute the imaginary object through the real canvas. This is the source of the celebrated disinterestedness of esthetic experience. This is why Kant was able to say that it does not matter whether the object of beauty, when experienced as beautiful, is or is not objectively real; why Schopenhauer was able to speak of a sort of suspension of the Will. This does not come from some mysterious way of apprehending the real, which we are able to use occasionally. What happens is that the esthetic object is constituted and apprehended by an imaginative consciousness which posits it as unreal.

What we have just shown regarding painting is readily applied to the art of fiction, poetry and drama, as well. It is self-evident that the novelist, the poet and the dramatist construct an unreal object by means of verbal analogues; it is also self-evident that the actor who plays Hamlet makes use of himself, of his whole body, as an analogue of the imaginary person. Even the famous dispute about the paradox of the comedian is enlightened by the view here presented. It is well known that certain amateurs proclaim that the actor *does not believe* in the character he portrays. Others, leaning on many witnesses, claim that the actor becomes identified in some way with the character he is enacting. To us these two views are not exclusive of each other; if by "belief" is meant actually real it is obvious that the actor does not actually consider himself to be Hamlet. But this does not mean that he does not "mobilize" all his powers to make Hamlet real. He uses all his feelings, all his strength, all his gestures as analogues of the feelings and conduct of Hamlet. But by this very fact he takes the reality away from them. *He lives completely in an unreal way.* And it matters little that he is *actually* weeping in enacting the role. These tears, ... he himself experiences—and so does the audience—as the tears of Hamlet, that is as the analogue of unreal tears. The transformation that occurs here is like that we discussed in the dream: the actor is completely caught up, inspired, by the unreal. It is not the character who becomes real in the actor, it is the actor who *becomes unreal* in his character.[1]

But are there not some arts whose objects seem to escape unreality by their very nature? A melody, for instance, refers to nothing but itself. Is a cathedral anything more than a mass of *real* stone which dominates the surrounding house tops? But let us look at this matter more closely. I

---

[1] It is in this sense that a beginner in the theatre can say that stage-fright served her to represent the timidity of Ophelia. If it did so, it is because she suddenly turned it into an unreality, that is, that she ceased to apprehend it for itself and that she grasped it as *analogue* for the timidity of Ophelia.

listen to a symphony orchestra, for instance, playing the Beethoven Seventh Symphony. Let us disregard exceptional cases—which are besides on the margin of esthetic contemplation—as when I go mainly "to hear Toscanini" interpret Beethoven in his own way. As a general rule what draws me to the concert is the desire "to hear the Seventh Symphony." Of course I have some objection to hearing an amateur orchestra, and prefer this or that well-known musical organization. But this is due to my desire to hear the symphony "played perfectly," because the symphony will then be *perfectly itself.* The shortcomings of a poor orchestra which plays "too fast" or "too slow," "in the wrong tempo," etc., seem to me to rob, "betray" the work it is playing. At most the orchestra effaces itself before the work it performs, and, provided I have reasons to trust the performers and their conductor, I am confronted by the symphony itself. This everyone will grant me. But now, what is the Seventh Symphony itself? Obviously it is a *thing,* that is something which is before me, which endures, which lasts. Naturally there is no need to show that that thing is a synthetic whole, which does not consist of tones but of a thematic configuration. But is that "thing" real or unreal? Let us first bear in mind that I am listening to the Seventh Symphony. For me that "Seventh Symphony" does not exist in time, I do not grasp it as a dated event, as an artistic manifestation which is unrolling itself in the Châtelet auditorium on the 17th of November, 1938. If I hear Furtwaengler tomorrow or eight days later conduct another orchestra performing the same symphony, I am in the presence of the same symphony once more. Only it is being played either better or worse. Let us now see *how* I hear the symphony: some persons shut their eyes. In this case they detach themselves from the *visual* and dated event of this particular interpretation: they give themselves up to the pure sounds. Others watch the orchestra or the back of the conductor. But they do not see what they are looking at. This is what Revault d'Allonnes calls reflection with auxiliary fascination. The auditorium, the conductor and even the orchestra have disappeared. I am therefore confronted by the Seventh Symphony, but on the express condition of understanding *nothing about it,* that I do not think of the event as an actuality and dated, and on condition that I listen to the succession of themes as an absolute succession and not as a real succession which is unfolding itself, for instance, on the occasion when Peter paid a visit to this or that friend. In the degree to which I hear the symphony it is *not here,* between these walls, at the tip of the violin bows. Nor is it "in the past" as if I thought: this is the work that matured in the mind of Beethoven on such a date. It is completely beyond the real. It has its own time, that is, it possesses an inner time, which runs from the first tone of the allegro to the last tone of the finale, but this time is not a succession of a preceding time which it continues and which happened "before" the beginning of the allegro; nor is it followed by a time which will come "after" the finale. The Seventh Symphony is in no way *in time.* It is therefore in no way real. It occurs *by itself,* but as absent, as being out of reach. I cannot act upon it, change a single note of it, or slow down its movement. But it depends on the real for its appearance: that the conductor does not faint away, that a fire in the hall does not put an end to the performance.

From this we cannot conclude that *the* Seventh Symphony has come to an end. No, we only think that the *performance* of the symphony has ceased. Does this not show clearly that the performance of the symphony is its *analogue?* It can manifest itself only through analogues which are dated and which unroll in our time. But to experience it on these analogues the imaginative reduction must be functioning, that is, the real sounds must be apprehended as analogues. It therefore occurs as a perpetual elsewhere, a perpetual absence. We must not picture it (as does Spandrell in *Point Counterpoint* by Huxley—as so many platonisms) as existing in another world, in an intelligible heaven. It is not only outside of time and space—as are essences, for instance—it is outside of the real, outside of existence. I do not hear it actually, I listen to it in the imaginary. Here we find the explanation for the considerable difficulty we always experience in passing from the world of the theatre or of music into that of our daily affairs. There is in fact no passing from one world into the other, but only a passing from the imaginative attitude to that of reality. Esthetic contemplation is an induced dream and the passing into the real is an actual waking up. We often speak of the "deception" experienced on returning to reality. But this does not explain that this discomfort also exists, for instance, after having witnessed a realistic and cruel play, in which case reality should be experienced as comforting. This discomfort is simply that of the dreamer on awakening; an entranced consciousness, engulfed in the imaginary, is suddenly freed by the sudden ending of the play, of the symphony, and comes suddenly in contact with existence. Nothing more is needed to arouse the nauseating disgust that characterizes the consciousness of reality.

From these few observations we can already conclude that the real is never beautiful. Beauty is a value applicable only to the imaginary and which means the negation of the world in its essential structure. This is why it is stupid to confuse the moral with the esthetic. The values of the Good presume being-in-the-world, they concern action in the real and are subject from the outset to the basic absurdity of existence. To say that we "assume" an esthetic attitude to life is to constantly confuse the real and the imaginary. It does happen, however, that we do assume the attitude of esthetic contemplation towards real events or objects. But in such cases every one of us can feel in himself a sort of recoil in relation to the object contemplated which slips into nothingness so that, from this moment on, it is no longer *perceived;* it functions as an *analogue* of itself, that is, that an unreal image of what it is appears to us through its actual presence. This image can be purely and simply the object "itself" neutralized, annihilated, as when I contemplate a beautiful woman or death at a bull fight; it can also be the imperfect and confused appearance of *what it could be* through what it is, as when the painter grasps the harmony of two colors as being greater, more vivid, *through* the real blots he finds on a wall. The object at once appears to be *in back of* itself, becomes *untouchable,* it is beyond our reach; and hence arises a sort of sad disinterest in it. It is in this sense that we may say that great beauty in a woman kills the desire for her. In fact we cannot at the same time place ourselves on the plane of the esthetic when this unreal "herself" which we admire appears and on the realistic plane of physical possession. To desire her we must forget she is beautiful, because desire is a plunge into the heart of existence, into what is most contingent and most absurd. Esthetic contemplation of *real* objects is of the same structure as paramnesia, in which the real object functions as analogue of itself in the past. But in one of the cases there is a negating and in the other a placing a thing in the past. Paramnesia differs from the esthetic attitude as memory differs from imagination.

Art in Life and Artists in Society   D. W. Prall

David Wight Prall (1886–1940) was an American professor of philosophy whose work in aesthetics has stimulated artists and critics, as well as philosophers.

... But what ... is this mature and lasting good that art brings into life? The answer is too simple and too obvious to be at all convincing, for all that art brings to life may be put in one word; if it is successful, what art furnishes men's world with is beauty, which a serious-minded people may think of at the best as a pleasant luxury instead of a necessity, an expense, not an investment, if we must put it in our most vulgar terms. This is like condemning art as legislatures condemn universities, whose presidents in answer use the same vulgar terms. Even in these terms it is not hard to make out our case for art. We may do so merely by remarking the traditional and common application of great wealth to the acquiring of works of art, as all that wealth in the end can be spent upon, all that it is good for, if it is to buy immediately and intrinsically valuable objects instead of mere means to further wealth, or more indirect means to the welfare of others, or those expensive evidences of itself that capture the attention of men and give it prestige and power in their eyes. But we may do much better not to rely on such arguments but to seek the evidence of clear thinking, to meditate upon the true satisfactions of life, that is, until beauty comes into its own proper place in our estimation. Persuasion is not the province of aesthetics, and the question here is in any case one of value in general and of relative values in society, not a question of aesthetic theory only. . . . Aesthetic considerations are considerations as to the immediate and often ultimate nature of the actual qualitative world in which we live. When this quality is at its most satisfactory, the world is beautiful; and since the creation of beauty is the aim of art, and since the achievement of artists is the beauty of their works, there is some ground at least for admitting the great actual value of both artists and their works to all men everywhere.

Another consideration enforces this point and carries it much further. It is after all aesthetic criteria that are final in judging the values of all things, including even that of social usages and laws, and of forms of society in general. And it is direct aesthetic attention that most realistically and surely discerns the features of society as it is. The artist as artist is innocent of ulterior purposes and looks upon the world to see it as it actually appears. And such judgments as he gives us as a critic, as well as such accounts of it as his own artistic medium may express and present to us, are likely to upset our habitual notions of its character, constituted as these notions so largely are of social and religious prejudices, pseudo-science, personal inclinations, and dogmatic conceptions, instilled by conventional education and training. It is the artist's very innocence that is so disconcerting here, like that of a child who fails to see reason in an unreasonable order of things, until he is initiated into the mysteries of adult economic fears, religious dogmas, and social superstitions. So the artist fails to see the ugly aspects of our world and our society as beautiful, or its beautiful ones as ugly. But unlike the child, who is gradually tamed into conformity, he fails here permanently, refusing to falsify his own sure, trained perception to suit such esoteric fancies or palpable delusions as are thrust upon him on all sides, refusing to be initiated into a view of life and the world that denies those very appearances that he apprehends so clearly, in the interest of an abstract and often foolish or imaginatively inadequate construction which purports to account for them as merely superficial, and hence somehow unimportant aspects of a reality handed down by the fathers, or built up by patriotic or industrious and ambitious sons.

Radical reformers themselves also often lack the artist's innocent and direct perception of actual beauty and ugliness for the same reason as conservative businessmen or politicians. For their attention is likely to be focussed less on genuine appearances, which are the sole indications of any possible underlying reality, than on their own theoretical explanation of a state of things that does not even exist, but merely exemplifies their theories, and so in actuality needs no remedy, or upon some one, single, objectionable aspect of civilization which can not sanely be removed, unless it has been fully grasped as one aspect of the form and character and quality of the larger complex whole of which it is an element. When such critics and reformers do turn their attention to the form and features of this whole, they succeed in working it over towards a better one, only so far as they have clearly present to mind the content of that better world, a content viewed in the imagination under a structural form, and with a filling which, so far as it is defined at all, is defined in aesthetic data as the vision of a greater perfection. There are obvious, crying evils which men may mitigate without too long hesitating over the further effects of ulterior transformations involved, but once a critic or a prophet or a reformer turns to the future, his dreams themselves are aesthetic structures, made out of such elements as he may have discovered in his discriminating perception of the aesthetic surface of the actually appearing world.

More than this, the society he dreams of and works towards will not be adequate to any full human living, or rationally to be desired by other men, or a satisfactory consummation if achieved, unless the dreamer has dreamt of beauty in it, and of art and artists, the function of art in life and of artists in society being of prime importance to men's happiness in any circumstances.

When we come to the ethical and social standards themselves by which we attempt to measure the satisfactoriness of a society, actual or imagined, these two, like all standards, turn out to be qualities, or degrees of qualities. Obviously, of good qualities and characteristics, the degree is to be heightened; but what are these qualities and characteristics, and what is our test of their goodness? Aesthetic vision again, direct feeling of their intrinsic satisfactoriness, which is so difficult to distinguish from beauty that the great thinkers have named it always in aesthetic terms, justice itself being only a sort of harmony. And in judging specific details these aesthetic categories are equally important. If the rich were forced to look upon the squalor and suffering of the poor, they could not endure it, as the officials of great corporations can not allow themselves to dwell even in imagination on the actually appearing misery or the sordid ugliness of the surroundings of men at the bottom of the great edifices of industry, and still remain content with the scheme that necessitates such sights. It is in their ultimately felt aesthetic quality that men all find such sights revolting and unendurable, and it is this ugliness that tells us unconditionally that they must be removed if any of us are to live even tolerably free from anguish in the world.

Hence the real strength of the democratic principle, which simply reminds us that we live in a world with other men, but with *all* other men, the various aspects of whose lives and surroundings we can not forever conceal, since in our dependence upon them they must come to our attention and finally be exhibited to us as integral aspects of our own life and world. If we are to be happy in a world as it really lies before us and about us in its actual appearance, that appearance can not remain unsatisfactory to contemplate, that is, aesthetically unsatisfactory, —condemned in the bare honesty of recording aesthetic judgments. If poverty and disease bore a pleasant aspect to discriminating perception, if injustice were aesthetically and directly satisfying to experience, and to dwell upon, what would there be to condemn it in any rational creature's eyes? For it is only in the embodiment in concrete aesthetic data of such abstractions as injustice and suffering and poverty, only their appearing in the world as unmistakably marked for aversion in a direct aesthetic view, that makes them unsatisfactory and ugly and bad. Thus it is finally aesthetic criteria that allow us to make those ethical and moral evaluations that we agree upon sooner or later; and it is aesthetic discernment that is required both to see the evils of the world and to picture a better one from which they can be said to have been removed—not merely changed for other or worse evils—just so far as this new world itself is positively valuable in beauty.

But such criticism or such social constructive thinking and imagining as either condemns or rejects or praises and elevates artists and their function in society, will judge artists not only as the makers of art, but as men. In their sensuous and emotional vitality such men as artists almost inevitably are, may do things in life neither aesthetically nor morally praiseworthy. The criticism that this activity calls down upon their heads, whatever their merits or failures, and whatever the competence of the criticism, is not of course criticism of art, nor even of artists as such, nor has it any place in aesthetic theory, though in much purported art criticism it has been dragged in or substituted for aesthetic judgment itself. It would be an absurd mistake to confuse moral shortcomings with aesthetic ones, even though the ultimate criteria both in morals and in scientific theory are themselves aesthetic standards. Beauty is as such a pure good, whatever it is the beauty of, and whoever may be its author; and beauty transforms the surface of what might be in itself merely unclean or unchaste or unholy, into what may be still unlovely in itself, and yet so hold our eyes to its beautiful surface that it seems purified of its evil, as actually happens in a work of art, where it is just this surface that specifies the whole beauty and significance of the object.

The authors of artistic beauty, being men, may also of course be bad men, except in just this authorship, in so much of their activity, that is, as satisfactorily fulfills their artist's function. And what they do here is so absolutely valuable, their function as artists is so precious, that society may perhaps wisely forgive them for their aesthetically irrelevant sins, especially since what we think of as sins in such men are so much oftener the natural and innocent expression of that vitality and power that makes them artists of significance. In a fully civilized society which allowed free rein to the expression of natural human instincts, or at least tried to provide for such expression as the basis of its polity, these so-called sins might turn out to be childlike innocence, or inventive gaiety. Artists need not be allowed to steal or murder; but these are not the crimes of which they are likely to be accused as characteristic failings. In a world where we are just discovering how antiquated and inhuman most of our social institutions are, and how discordant with the necessary or even possible nature of men, and hence how inimical to their happiness, we can afford to be indulgent to any one or anything in the world of which in any sure sense we can affirm great positive human value. This we can do in the case of art and artists, and if society must have high priests at all, we might well substitute great artists as at least better candidates for the temple than the philosophers whom Plato would have made kings.

Art and Civilization   John Dewey

John Dewey (1859–1952) enjoyed a worldwide reputation as one of America's greatest philosophers, writing systematically upon topics in all major fields of philosophy.

... The moral office and human function of art can be intelligently discussed only in the context of culture. A particular work of art may have a definite effect upon a particular person or upon a number of persons. The social effect of the novels of Dickens or of Sinclair Lewis is far from negligible. But a less conscious and more massed constant adjustment of experience proceeds from the total environment that is created by the collective art of a time. Just as physical life cannot exist without the support of a physical environment, so moral life cannot go on without the support of a moral environment. Even technological arts, in their sum total, do something more than provide a number of separate conveniences and facilities. They shape collective occupations and thus determine direction of interest and attention, and hence affect desire and purpose.

The noblest man living in a desert absorbs something of its harshness and sterility, while the nostalgia of the mountain-bred man when cut off from his surroundings is proof how deeply environment has become part of his being. Neither the savage nor the civilized man is what he is by native constitution but by the culture in which he participates. The final measure of the quality of that culture is the arts which flourish. Compared with their influence things directly taught by word and precept are pale and ineffectual. Shelley did not exaggerate when he said that moral science only "arranges the elements that poetry has created," if we extend "poetry" to include all products of imaginative experience. The sum total of the effect of all reflective treatises on morals is insignificant in comparison with the influence of architecture, novel, drama, on life, becoming important when "intellectual" products formulate the tendencies of these arts and provide them with an intellectual base. An "inner" rational check is a sign of withdrawal from reality unless it is a reflection of substantial environing forces. The political and economic arts that may furnish security and competency are no warrants of a rich and abundant human life save as they are attended by the flourishing of the arts that determine culture.

Words furnish a record of what has happened and give direction by request and command to particular future actions. Literature conveys the meaning of the past that is significant in present experience and is prophetic of the larger movement of the future. Only imaginative vision elicits the possibilities that are interwoven within the texture of the actual. The first stirrings of dissatisfaction and the first intimations of a better future are always found in works of art. The impregnation of the characteristically new art of a period with a sense of different values than those that prevail is the reason why the conservative finds such art to be immoral and sordid, and is the reason why he resorts to the products of the past for esthetic satisfaction. Factual science may collect statistics and make charts. But its predictions are, as has been well said, but past history reversed. Change in the climate of the imagination is the precursor of the changes that affect more than the details of life.

The theories that attribute direct moral effect and intent to art fail because they do not take account of the collective civilization that is the context in which works of art are produced and enjoyed. I would not say that they tend to treat works of art as a kind of sublimated Aesop's fables. But they all tend to extract particular works, regarded as

especially edifying, from their milieu and to think of the moral function
of art in terms of a strictly personal relation between the selected works
and a particular individual. Their whole conception of morals is so indi-
vidualistic that they miss a sense of the *way* in which art exercises its
humane function.

Matthew Arnold's dictum that "poetry is criticism of life" is a case in
point. It suggests to the reader a moral intent on the part of the poet and
a moral judgment on the part of the reader. It fails to see or at all events
to state *how* poetry is a criticism of life; namely, not directly, but by
disclosure, through imaginative vision addressed to imaginative experience (not to set judgment) of possibilities that contrast with actual conditions. A sense of possibilities that are unrealized and that might be
realized are when they are put in contrast with actual conditions, the
most penetrating "criticism" of the latter that can be made. It is by a
sense of possibilities opening before us that we become aware of con-
strictions that hem us in and of burdens that oppress.

Mr. Garrod, a follower of Matthew Arnold in more senses than one,
has wittily said that what we resent in didactic poetry is not that it teaches,
but that it does not teach, its incompetency. He added words to the effect
that poetry teaches as friends and life teach, by being, and not by express
intent. He says in another place, "Poetical values are, after all, values in
a human life. You cannot mark them off from other values, as though
the nature of man were built in bulkheads." I do not think that what
Keats has said in one of his letters can be surpassed as to the way in
which poetry acts. He asks what would be the result if every man spun
from his imaginative experience "an airy citadel" like the web the spider
spins, "filling the air with a beautiful circuiting." For, he says, "man
should not dispute or assert, but whisper results to his neighbor, and thus,
by every germ of spirit sucking the sap from mold ethereal, every human
being might become great, and Humanity instead of being a wide heath
of Furze and briars with here and there a remote Pine or Oak, would
become a grand democracy of Forest Trees!"

It is by way of communication that art becomes the incomparable
organ of instruction, but the way is so remote from that usually associated
with the idea of education, it is a way that lifts art so far above what we
are accustomed to think of as instruction, that we are repelled by any
suggestion of teaching and learning in connection with art. But our
revolt is in fact a reflection upon education that proceeds by methods so
literal as to exclude the imagination and one not touching the desires
and emotions of men. Shelley said, "The imagination is the great instrument of moral good, and poetry administers to the effect by acting upon
the causes." Hence it is, he goes on to say, "a poet would do ill to embody
his own conceptions of right and wrong, which are usually those of his
own time and place, in his poetical creations. . . . By the assumption of
this inferior office . . . he would resign participation in the cause"—the
imagination. It is the lesser poets who "have frequently affected a moral
aim, and the effect of their poetry is diminished in exact proportion as
they compel us to advert to this purpose." But the power of imaginative
projection is so great that he calls poets "the founders of civil society."

The problem of the relation of art and morals is too often treated as if the problem existed only on the side of art. It is virtually assumed that morals are satisfactory in idea if not in fact, and that the only question is whether and in what ways art should conform to a moral system already developed. But Shelley's statement goes to the heart of the matter. Imagination is the chief instrument of the good. It is more or less a commonplace to say that a person's ideas and treatment of his fellows are dependent upon his power to put himself imaginatively in their place. But the primacy of the imagination extends far beyond the scope of direct personal relationships. Except where "ideal" is used in conventional deference or as a name for a sentimental reverie, the ideal factors in every moral outlook and human loyalty are imaginative. The historic alliance of religion and art has its roots in this common quality. Hence it is that art is more moral than moralities. For the latter either are, or tend to become, consecrations of the *status quo,* reflections of custom, reënforcements of the established order. The moral prophets of humanity have always been poets even though they spoke in free verse or by parable. Uniformly, however, their vision of possibilities has soon been converted into a proclamation of facts that already exist and hardened into semi-political institutions. Their imaginative presentation of ideals that should command thought and desire have been treated as rules of policy. Art has been the means of keeping alive the sense of purposes that outrun evidence and of meanings that transcend indurated habit.

Morals are assigned a special compartment in theory and practice because they reflect the divisions embodied in economic and political institutions. Wherever social divisions and barriers exist, practices and ideas that correspond to them fix metes and bounds, so that liberal action is placed under restraint. Creative intelligence is looked upon with distrust; the innovations that are the essence of individuality are feared, and generous impulse is put under bonds not to disturb the peace. Were art an acknowledged power in human association and not treated as the pleasuring of an idle moment or as a means of ostentatious display, and were morals understood to be identical with every aspect of value that is shared in experience, the "problem" of the relation of art and morals would not exist.

The idea and the practice of morality are saturated with conceptions that stem from praise and blame, reward and punishment. Mankind is divided into sheep and goats, the vicious and virtuous, the law-abiding and criminal, the good and bad. To be beyond good and evil is an impossibility for man, and yet as long as the good signifies only that which is lauded and rewarded, and the evil that which is currently condemned or outlawed, the ideal factors of morality are always and everywhere beyond good and evil. Because art is wholly innocent of ideas derived from praise and blame, it is looked upon with the eye of suspicion by the guardians of custom, or only the art that is itself so old and "classic" as to receive conventional praise is grudgingly admitted, provided, as with, say, the case of Shakespeare, signs of regard for conventional morality can be ingeniously extracted from his work. Yet this indifference to praise and blame because of preoccupation with imaginative experience constitutes the heart of the moral potency of art. From it proceeds the liberating and uniting power of art.

Shelley said, "The great secret of morals is love, or *a going out of our nature* and the identification of ourselves with the beautiful which exists in thought, action, or person, not our own. A man to be greatly good must imagine intensely and comprehensively." What is true of the individual is true of the whole system of morals in thought and action. While perception of the union of the possible with the actual in a work of art is itself a great good, the good does not terminate with the immediate and particular occasion in which it is had. The union that is presented in perception persists in the remaking of impulsion and thought. The first intimations of wide and large redirections of desire and purpose are of necessity imaginative. Art is a mode of prediction not found in charts and statistics, and it insinuates possibilities of human relations not to be found in rule and precept, admonition and administration. . . .

Contemporary Issues

Art and Pornography:
The U. S. Supreme Court and *Fanny Hill*

The Fanny Hill Case: Majority Opinion   Justice William Brennan

William Joseph Brennan, Jr. (1906–   ), is an associate justice of the U.S. Supreme Court, a position to which he was appointed in 1959 by President Dwight David Eisenhower.

. . . We defined obscenity in *Roth* in the following terms: "Whether to the average persons, applying contemporary community standards, the dominant theme of the material taken as a whole appeals to prurient interest." 354 U. S., at 489. Under this definition, as elaborated in subsequent cases, three elements must coalesce: it must be established that (a) the dominant theme of the material taken as a whole appeals to a prurient interest in sex; (b) the material is patently offensive because it affronts contemporary community standards relating to the description or representation of sexual matters; and (c) the material is utterly without redeeming social value.

The Supreme Judicial Court purported to apply the *Roth* definition of obscenity and held all three criteria satisfied. We need not consider the claim that the court erred in concluding that *Memoirs* satisfied the prurient appeal and patent offensiveness criteria; for reversal is required because the court misinterpreted the social value criterion. The court applied the criterion in this passage:

> It remains to consider whether the book can be said to be "utterly without social importance." We are mindful that there was expert testimony, much of which was strained, to the effect that Memoirs is a structural novel with literary merit; that the book displays a skill in characterization and a gift for comedy; that it plays a part in the history of the development of the English novel; and that it contains a moral, namely, that sex with love is superior to sex in a brothel. But the fact that the testimony may indicate this book has some minimal literary value does not mean it is of any social importance. We do not interpret the "social importance" test as requiring that a book which appeals to prurient interest and is patently offensive must be unqualifiedly worthless before it can be deemed obscene.—Mass., at—, 206 N. E. 2d, at 406.

The Supreme Judicial Court erred in holding that a book need not be "unqualifiedly worthless before it can be deemed obscene." A book can not be proscribed unless it is found to be *utterly* without redeeming social value. This is so even though the book is found to possess the requisite prurient appeal and to be patently offensive. Each of the three

From *A Book Named "John Cleland's Memoirs of a Woman of Pleasure," et al., Appellants, v. Attorney General of the Commonwealth of Massachusetts*, 383 U.S. 413.

federal constitutional criteria is to be applied independently; the social value of the book can neither be weighed against nor canceled by its prurient appeal or patent offensiveness.[1] Hence, even on the view of the court below that *Memoirs* possessed only a modicum of social value, its judgment must be reversed as being founded on an erroneous interpretation of a federal constitutional standard. . . .

The Fanny Hill Case: Concurring Opinion
Justice William O. Douglas

William Orville Douglas (1898–   ) is an associate justice of the U.S. Supreme Court, a position to which he was appointed in 1939 by President Franklin Delano Roosevelt.

Memoirs of a Woman of Pleasure, or, as it is often titled, *Fanny Hill,* concededly is an erotic novel. It was first published in about 1749 and has endured to this date, despite periodic efforts to suppress it.[1] The book relates the adventures of a young girl who becomes a prostitute in London. At the end, she abandons that life and marries her first lover, observing:

> Thus, at length, I got snug into port, where, in the bosom of virtue, I gather'd the only uncorrupt sweets: where, looking back on the course of vice I had run, and comparing its infamous blandishments with the infinitely superior joys of innocence, I could not help pitying, even in point of taste, those who, immers'd in gross sensuality, are insensible to the so delicate charms of VIRTUE, than which even PLEASURE has not a greater friend, nor than VICE a greater enemy. Thus temperance makes men lords over those pleasures that intemperance enslaves them to: the one, parent of health, vigour, fertility, cheerfulness, and every other desirable good of life; the other, of diseases, debility, barrenness, self-loathing, with only every evil incident to human nature.

---

[1] "[M]aterial dealing with sex in a manner that advocates ideas . . . or that has literary or scientific or artistic value or any other form of social importance, may not be branded as obscenity and denied the constitutional protection. Nor may the constitutional status of the material be made to turn on a 'weighing' of its social importance against its prurient appeal, for a work cannot be proscribed unless it is 'utterly' without social importance. See *Zeitlin* v. *Arnebergh,* 59 Cal. 2d 901, 920, 383 P. 2d 152, 165, 31 Cal. Rptr. 800, 813 (1963)." *Jacobellis* v. *Ohio,* 378 U. S. 184, 191 (opinion of Brennan, J.). Followed in, *e. g., People* v. *Bruce,* 31 Ill. 2d 459, 461, 202 N. E. 2d 497, 498 (1964); *Trans-Lux Distributing Corp.* v. *Maryland Bd. of Censors,* 240 Md. 98, 104–105, 213 A. 2d 235, 238–239 (1965).

From *A Book Named "John Cleland's Memoirs of a Woman of Pleasure," et al., Appellants, v. Attorney General of the Commonwealth of Massachusetts,* 383 U.S. 413.

[1] *Memoirs* was the subject of what is generally regarded as the first recorded suppression of a literary work in this country on grounds of obscenity. See *Commonwealth* v. *Holmes,* 17 Mass. 335 (1821). The edition there condemned differed from the present volume in that it contained apparently erotic illustrations.

> ... The paths of Vice are sometimes strew'd with roses, but then they are for ever infamous for many a thorn, for many a cankerworm: those of Virtue are strew'd with roses purely, and those eternally unfading ones.[2]

In 1963, an American publishing house undertook the publication of *Memoirs*. The record indicates that an unusually large number of orders were placed by universities and libraries; the Library of Congress requested the right to translate the book into Braille. But the Commonwealth of Massachusetts instituted the suit that ultimately found its way here, praying that the book be declared obscene so that the citizens of Massachusetts might be spared the necessity of determining for themselves whether or not to read it.

The courts of Massachusetts found the book "obscene" and upheld its suppression. This Court reverses, the prevailing opinion having seized upon language in the opinion of the Massachusetts Supreme Judicial Court in which it is candidly admitted that *Fanny Hill* has at least "some minimal literary value." I do not believe that the Court should decide this case on so disingenuous a basis as this. I base my vote to reverse on my view that the First Amendment does not permit the censorship of expression not brigaded with illegal action. But even applying the prevailing view of the *Roth* test, reversal is compelled by this record which makes clear that *Fanny Hill* is not "obscene." The prosecution made virtually no effort to prove that this book is "utterly without redeeming social importance." The defense, on the other hand, introduce considerable and impressive testimony to the effect that this was a work of literary, historical, and social importance.[3]

We are judges, not literary experts or historians or philosophers. We are not competent to render an independent judgment as to the worth of this or any other book, except as in our capacity as private citizens. ... If there is to be censorship, the wisdom of experts on such matters as literary merit and historical significance must be evaluated. On this record, the Court has no choice but to reverse the judgment of the Massachusetts Supreme Judicial Court, irrespective of whether we would include *Fanny Hill* in our own libraries.

Four of the seven Justices of the Massachusetts Supreme Judicial

---

[2] *Id.*, at pp. 213–214 (Putnam ed. 1963).

[3] The defense drew its witnesses from the various colleges located within the State of Massachusetts. These included: Fred Holly Stocking, Professor of English and Chairman of the English Department, Williams College; John M. Bullitt, Professor of English and Master of Quincy House, Harvard College; Robert H. Sproat, Associate Professor of English Literature, Boston University; Norman N. Holland, Associate Professor of English, Massachusetts Institute of Technology; and Ira Konigsberg, Assistant Professor of English and American Literature, Brandeis University.

In addition, the defense introduced into evidence reviews of impartial literary critics. These are, in my opinion, of particular significance since their publication indicates that the book is of sufficient significance as to warrant serious critical comment. The reviews were by V. S. Pritchett, New York Review of Books, p. 1 (Oct. 31, 1963); Brigid Brophy, New Statesman, p. 710 (Nov. 15, 1963); and J. Donald Adams, New York Times Book Review, p. 2 (July 28, 1963). And the Appendix to this opinion contains another contemporary view.

Court conclude that *Fanny Hill* is obscene.—Mass.—, 206 N. E. 2d 403. Four of the seven Justices of the New York Court of Appeals conclude that it is not obscene. *Larken* v. *Putnam's Sons,* 14 N. Y. 2d 399, 200 N. E. 2d 760. To outlaw the book on such a voting record would be to let majorities rule where minorities were thought to be supreme. The Constitution forbids abridgment of "freedom of speech, or of the press." Censorship is the most notorious form of abridgment. It substitutes majority rule where minority tastes or viewpoints were to be tolerated.

It is to me inexplicable how a book that concededly has social worth can on remand nonetheless be banned because of the manner in which it is advertised and sold. However florid its cover, whatever the pitch of its advertisements, the contents remain the same.

Every time an obscenity case is to be argued here, my office is flooded with letters and postal cards urging me to protect the community or the Nation by striking down the publication. The messages are often identical even down to commas and semicolons. The inference is irresistible that they were all copied from a school or church blackboard. Dozens of postal cards often are mailed from the same precinct. The drives are incessant and the pressures are great. Happily we do not bow to them. I mention them only to emphasize the lack of popular understanding of our constitutional system. Publications and utterances were made immune from majoritarian control by the First Amendment, applicable to the States by reason of the Fourteenth. No exceptions were made, not even for obscenity. The Court's contrary conclusion in *Roth,* where obscenity was found to be "outside" the First Amendment, is without justification.

The extent to which the publication of "obscenity" was a crime at common law is unclear. It is generally agreed that the first reported case involving obscene conduct is *The King* v. *Sir Charles Sedley.*[4] Publication of obscene literature, at first thought to be the exclusive concern of the ecclesiastical courts,[5] was not held to constitute an indictable offense until 1727.[6] A later case involved the publication of an "obscene and impious libel" (a bawdy parody of Pope's "Essay on Man") by a member of the House of Commons.[7] On the basis of these few cases, one cannot say that the common-law doctrines with regard to publication of obscenity

---

[4] There are two reports of the case. The first is captioned *Le Roy* v. *Sr. Charles Sidney,* 1 Sid. 168, pl. 29 (K. B. 1663); the second is titled *Sir Charles Sydlyes Case,* 1 Keble 620 (K. B. 1663). Sir Charles had made a public appearance on a London balcony while nude, intoxicated, and talkative. He delivered a lengthy speech to the assembled crowd, uttered profanity, and hurled bottles containing what was later described as an "offensive liquor" upon the crowd. The proximate source of the "offensive liquor" appears to have been Sir Charles. Alpert, Judicial Censorship of Obscene Literature, 52 Harv. L. Rev. 40–43 (1938).

[5] *The Queen* v. *Read,* 11 Mod. 142 (Q. B. 1708).

[6] *Dominus Rex* v. *Curl,* 2 Strange 789 (K. B. 1727). See Straus, The Unspeakable Curll (1927).

[7] *Rex* v. *Wilkes,* 4 Burr. 2527 (K. B. 1770). The prosecution of Wilkes was a highly political action, for Wilkes was an outspoken critic of the government. See R. W. Postgate, That Devil Wilkes (1929). It has been suggested that the prosecution in this case was a convenient substitute for the less attractive charge of seditious libel. See Alpert, *supra,* at 45.

were anything but uncertain. "There is no definition of the term. There is no basis of identification. There is no unity in describing what is obscene literature, or in prosecuting it. There is little more than the ability to smell it." Alpert, Judicial Censorship of Obscene Literature, 52 Harv. L. Rev. 40, 47 (1938).

But even if the common law had been more fully developed at the time of the adoption of the First Amendment, we would not be justified in assuming that the Amendment left the common law unscathed. In *Bridges* v. *California,* 314 U. S. 252, 264–265, we said:

> [T]o assume that English common law in this field became ours is to deny the generally accepted historical belief that "one of the objects of the Revolution was to get rid of the English common law on liberty of speech and of the press." Schofield, Freedom of the Press in the United States, 9 Publications Amer. Sociol. Soc., 67, 76.
>
> More specifically, it is to forget the environment in which the First Amendment was ratified. In presenting the proposals which were later embodied in the Bill of Rights, James Madison, the leader in the preparation of the First Amendment, said: "Although I know whenever the great rights, the trial by jury, freedom of the press, or liberty of conscience, come in question in that body [Parliament], the invasion of them is resisted by able advocates, yet their Magna Charta does not contain any one provision for the security of those rights, respecting which the people of America are most alarmed. The freedom of the press and rights of conscience, those choicest privileges of the people, are unguarded in the British Constitution."

And see *Grosjean* v. *American Press Co.,* 297 U. S. 233, 248–249.

It is true, as the Court observed in *Roth,* that obscenity laws appeared on the books of a handful of States at the time the First Amendment was adopted.[8] But the First Amendment was, until the adoption of the Fourteenth, a restraint only upon federal power. Moreover, there is an absence of any *federal* cases or laws relative to obscenity in the period immediately after the adoption of the First Amendment. Congress passed no legislation relating to obscenity until the middle of the nineteenth century.[9] Neither reason nor history warrants exclusion of any particular class of expression from the protection of the First Amendment on nothing more than a judgment that it is utterly without merit. We faced the difficult questions the First Amendment poses with regard to libel in *New York Times* v. *Sullivan,* 376 U. S. 254, 269, where we recognized that "libel can claim no talismanic immunity from constitutional limitations."

---

[8] See 354 U. S., at 483 and n. 13. For the most part, however, the early legislation was aimed at blasphemy and profanity. See 354 U. S., at 482–483 and n. 12. The first reported decision involving the publication of obscene literature does not come until 1821. See *Commonwealth* v. *Holmes,* 17 Mass. 335. It was not until after the Civil War that state prosecutions of this sort became commonplace. See Lockhart and McClure, Literature, The Law of Obscenity, and the Constitution, 38 Minn. L. Rev. 295, 324–325 (1954).

[9] Tariff Act of 1842, c. 270, § 28, 5 Stat. 566 (prohibiting importation of obscene "prints"). Other federal legislation followed; the development of federal law is traced in Cairns, Paul, and Wishner, Sex Censorship: The Assumptions of Anti-Obscenity Laws and the Empirical Evidence, 46 Minn. L. Rev. 1009, 1010 n. 2 (1962).

We ought not to permit fictionalized assertions of constitutional history to obscure those questions here. Were the Court to undertake that inquiry, it would be unable, in my opinion, to escape the conclusion that no interest of society with regard to suppression of "obscene" literature could override the First Amendment to justify censorship.

The censor is always quick to justify his function in terms that are protective of society. But the First Amendment, written in terms that are absolute, deprives the State of any power to pass on the value, the propriety, or the morality of a particular expression. Cf. *Kingsley Int. Pictures Corp.* v. *Regents,* 360 U. S. 684, 688–689; *Joseph Burstyn, Inc.* v. *Wilson,* 343 U. S. 495. Perhaps the most frequently assigned justification for censorship is the belief that erotica produces antisocial sexual conduct. But that relationship has yet to be proven.[10] Indeed, if one were to make judgments on the basis of speculation, one might guess that literature of the most pornographic sort would, in many cases, provide a substitute—not a stimulus—for antisocial sexual conduct. See Murphy, The Value of Pornography, 10 Wayne L. Rev. 655, 661 and n. 19 (1964). As I read the First Amendment, judges cannot gear the literary diet of an entire nation to whatever tepid stuff is incapable of triggering the most demented mind. The First Amendment demands more than a horrible example or two of the perpetrator of a crime of sexual violence, in whose pocket is found a pornographic book, before it allows the Nation to be saddled with a regime of censorship.[11]

[10] See Cairns, Paul, and Wishner, Sex Censorship: The Assumptions of Anti-Obscenity Laws and the Empirical Evidence, 46 Minn. L. Rev. 1009, 1034–1041 (1962); Lockhart and McClure, *supra,* at 382–387. And see the summary of Dr. Jahoda's studies prepared by her for Judge Frank, reprinted in *United States* v. *Roth,* 237 F. 2d 796, 815–816 (concurring opinion). Those who are concerned about children and erotic literature would do well to consider the counsel of Judge Bok:

"It will be asked whether one would care to have one's young daughter read these books. I suppose that by the time she is old enough to wish to read them she will have learned the biologic facts of life and the words that go with them. There is something seriously wrong at home if those facts have not been met and faced and sorted by then; it is not children so much as parents that should receive our concern about this. I should prefer that my own three daughters met the facts of life and the literature of the world in my library than behind a neighbor's barn, for I can face the adversary there directly. If the young ladies are appalled by what they read, they can close the book at the bottom of page one; if they read further, they will learn what is in the world and in its people, and no parents who have been discerning with their children need fear the outcome. Nor can they hold it back, for life is a series of little battles and minor issues, and the burden of choice is on us all, every day, young and old." *Commonwealth* v. *Gordon,* 66 Pa. D. & C. 101, 110.

[11] It would be a futile effort even for a censor to attempt to remove all that might possibly stimulate antisocial sexual conduct:

"The majority [of individuals], needless to say, are somewhere in between the over-scrupulous extremes of excitement and frigidity . . . . Within this variety, it is impossible to define 'hard-core' pornography, as if there were some singly lewd concept from which all profane ideas passed by imperceptible degrees into that sexuality called holy. But there is no 'hard core.' Everything, every idea, is capable of being obscene if the personality perceiving it so apprehends it.

"It is for this reason that books, pictures, charades, ritual, the spoken word, *can* and *do* lead to conduct harmful to the self indulging in it and to others. Heinrich Pommerenke, who was a rapist, abuser, and mass slayer of women in Germany, was

Whatever may be the reach of the power to regulate *conduct,* I stand by my view in *Roth* v. *United States, supra,* that the First Amendment leaves no power in government over *expression of ideas.*

The Fanny Hill Case: Dissenting Opinion   Justice Tom C. Clark

Tom Campbell Clark (1899–   ) served as an associate justice of the U.S. Supreme Court, from his appointment in 1949 by President Harry S. Truman until 1967.

. . . Let me first pinpoint the effect of today's holding in the obscenity field. While there is no majority opinion in this case, there are three Justices who import a new test into that laid down in *Roth* v. *United States,* 354 U. S. 476 (1957), namely, that "a book cannot be proscribed unless it is found to be utterly without redeeming social value." I agree with my Brother WHITE that such a condition rejects the basic holding of *Roth* and gives the smut artist free rein to carry on his dirty business. My vote in that case—which was the deciding one for the majority opinion—was cast solely because the Court declared the test of obscenity to be: "whether to the average person, applying contemporary community standards, the dominant theme of the material taken as a whole appeals to prurient interest." I understood that test to include only two constitutional requirements: (1) the book must be judged as a whole, not by its parts; and (2) it must be judged in terms of its appeal to the prurient interest of the average person, applying contemporary community standards.[1] Indeed, obscenity was denoted in *Roth* as having *"such slight social value as a step to truth that any benefit that may be derived . . . is clearly outweighed by the social interest in order and morality. . . .* At 485. Quoting *Chaplinsky* v. *New Hampshire,* 315 U. S. 568, 571–572 (1942). Moreover, in no subsequent decision of this Court has any "utterly without redeeming social value" test been suggested, much less expounded. My Brother HARLAN in *Manual Enterprises, Inc.* v. *Day,* 370 U. S. 478 (1962), made no reference whatever to such a requirement in *Roth.* Rather he interpreted *Roth* as including a test of "patent offensiveness" besides

From *A Book Named "John Cleland's Memoirs of a Woman of Pleasure," et al., Appellants, v. Attorney General of the Commonwealth of Massachusetts,* 383 U.S. 413.

[1] See Lockhart and McClure, Censorship of Obscenity: The Developing Community Standards, 45 Minn. L. Rev. 5, 53–55 (1960).

---

prompted to his series of ghastly deeds by Cecil B. DeMille's *The Ten Commandments.* During the scene of the Jewish women dancing about the Golden Calf, all the doubts of his life came clear: Women were the source of the world's trouble and it was his mission to punish them for this and to execute them. Leaving the theatre, he slew his first victim in a park nearby. John George Haigh, the British vampire who sucked his victims' blood through soda straws and dissolved their drained bodies in acid baths, first had his murder-inciting dreams and vampire-longings from watching the 'voluptuous' procedure of—an Anglican High Church Service!" Murphy, *supra,* at 668.

"prurient appeal." Nor did my Brother BRENNAN in his concurring opinion in *Manual Enterprises* mention any "utterly without redeeming social value" test. The first reference to such a test was made by my Brother BRENNAN in *Jacobellis* v. *Ohio,* 378 U. S. 184, 191 (1964), seven years after *Roth.* In an opinion joined only by Justice Goldberg, he there wrote: "Recognizing that the test enunciated [in *Roth*] is not perfect, we think any substitute would raise equally difficult problems, and we therefore adhere to that standard." Nevertheless, he proceeded to add:

> We would reiterate, however, our recognition in *Roth* that obscenity is excluded from the constitutional protection only because it is "utterly without redeeming social importance," . . . .

This language was then repeated in the converse to announce this *non sequitur:*

> It follows that material dealing with sex in a manner that advocates ideas . . . or that has literary or scientific or artistic value or any other form of social importance, may not be branded as obscenity and denied the constitutional protection.

Significantly no opinion in *Jacobellis,* other than that of my Brother BRENNAN, mentioned the "utterly without redeeming social importance" test which he there introduced into our many and varied previous opinions in obscenity cases. Indeed, rather than recognizing the "utterly without social importance" test, THE CHIEF JUSTICE in his dissent in *Jacobellis,* which I joined, specifically stated:

> In light of the foregoing, I would reiterate my acceptance of the rule of the *Roth* case: *Material is obscene and not constitutionally protected against regulation and proscription* if "to the average person, applying contemporary standards, the dominant theme of the material taken as a whole appeals to prurient interest." (Emphasis added.) At 202.

THE CHIEF JUSTICE and myself further asserted that the enforcement of this rule should be committed to the state and federal courts whose judgments made pursuant to the *Roth* rule we would accept, limiting our review to a consideration of whether there is "sufficient evidence" in the record to support a finding of obscenity. At 202. . . .

Memoirs is nothing more than a series of minutely and vividly described sexual episodes. The book starts with Fanny Hill, a young 15-year-old girl, arriving in London to seek household work. She goes to an employment office where through happenstance she meets the mistress of a bawdy house. This takes 10 pages. The remaining 200 pages of the book detail her initiation to various sexual experiences, from a lesbian encounter with a sister prostitute to all sorts and types of sexual debauchery in bawdy houses and as the mistress of a variety of men. This is presented to the reader through an uninterrupted succession of descriptions by Fanny, either as an observer or participant, of sexual adventures so vile that one of the male expert witnesses in the case was hesitant to repeat any one of them in the courtroom. These scenes run the gamut of possible sexual experience such as lesbianism, female masturbation, homosexuality between young boys, the destruction of a maidenhead with consequent gory descriptions, the seduction of a young virgin boy, the flagellation of male by female, and vice versa, followed by fervid sexual engagement, and other abhorrent acts, including over two dozen separate bizarre descriptions of different sexual intercourses between male and female characters. In one sequence four girls in a bawdy house are required in the presence of one another to relate the lurid details of their loss of virginity and their glorification of it. This is followed the same evening by "publick trials" in which each of the four girls engages in sexual intercourse with a different man while the others witness, with Fanny giving a detailed description of the movement and reaction of each couple.

In each of the sexual scenes the exposed bodies of the participants are described in minute and individual detail. The pubic hair is often used for a background to the most vivid and precise descriptions of the response, condition, size, shape, and color of the sexual organs before, during and after orgasms. There are some short transitory passages between the various sexual episodes, but for the most part they only set the scene and identify the participants for the next orgy, or make smutty reference and comparison to past episodes.

There can be no doubt that the whole purpose of the book is to arouse the prurient interest. Likewise the repetition of sexual episode after episode and the candor with which they are described renders the book "patently offensive." These facts weigh heavily in any appraisal of the book's claims to "redeeming social importance."

Let us now turn to evidence of the book's alleged social value. While unfortunately the state offered little testimony,[2] the defense called several experts to attest that the book has literary merit and historical value. A careful reading of testimony, however, reveals that it has no substance. For example, the first witness testified:

> I think it is a work of art ... it asks for and receives a literary response ... presented in an orderly and organized fashion, with a fictional central character, and with a literary style. ... I think the central character is ... what I call an intellectual ... someone who is exceedingly curious about life and who seeks ... to record with accuracy the details of the external world, physical sensations, psychological responses ... an empiricist. ... I find that this tells me things ... about the 18th Century that I might not otherwise know.

If a book of art is one that asks for and receives a literary response, *Memoirs* is no work of art. The sole response evoked by the book is sensual. Nor does the orderly presentation of *Memoirs* make a difference; it presents nothing but lascivious scenes organized solely to arouse prurient interest and produce sustained erotic tension.[3] Certainly the book's

[2] In a preface to the paperbook edition, "A Note on the American History of *Memoirs of a Woman of Pleasure,* the publisher itself mentions several critics who denied the book had any literary merit and found it totally undistinguished. These critics included Ralph Thompson and Clifton Fadiman. P. xviii.

[3] As one review stated: "Yet all these pangs of defloration are in the service of erotic pleasure—Fanny's and the reader's. Postponing the culmination of Fanny's deflowering is equivalent to postponing the point where the reader has a mental orgasm."

baroque style cannot vitiate the determination of obscenity. From a legal standpoint, we must remember that obscenity is no less obscene though it be expressed in "elaborate language." Indeed, the more meticulous its presentation, the more it appeals to the prurient interest. To say that Fanny is an "intellectual" is an insult to those who travel under that tag. She was nothing but a harlot—a sensualist—exploiting her sexual attractions which she sold for fun, for money, for lodging and keep, for an inheritance, and finally for a husband. If she was curious about life, her curiosity extended only to the pursuit of sexual delight wherever she found it. The book describes nothing in the "external world" except bawdy houses and debaucheries. As an empiricist, Fanny confines her observations and "experiments" to sex, with primary attention to depraved, lewd, and deviant practices.

Other experts produced by the defense testified that the book emphasizes the profound "idea that a sensual passion is only truly experienced when it is associated with the emotion of love" and that the sexual relationship "can be a wholesome, healthy, experience itself," whereas in certain modern novels "the relationship between the sexes is seen as another manifestation of modern decadence, insterility or perversion." In my view this proves nothing as to social value. The state court properly gave such testimony no probative weight. A review offered by the defense noted that "where 'pornography' does not brutalize, it idealizes. The book is, in this sense, an erotic fantasy—and a male fantasy, at that, put into the mind of a woman. The male organ is phenomenal to the point of absurdity." Finally, it saw the book as "a minor fantasy, deluding as a guide to conduct, but respectful of our delight in the body . . . an interesting footnote in the history of the English novel." These unrelated assertions reveal to me nothing whatever of literary, historical, or social value. Another review called the book "a great novel . . . one which turns its conventions upside down. . . ." Admittedly Cleland did not attempt "high art" because he was writing "an erotic novel. He can skip the elevation and get on with the erections." Fanny's "downfall" is seen as "one long delightful swoon into the depths of pleasurable sensation." Rather than indicating social value in the book, this evidence reveals just the contrary. Another item offered by the defense described *Memoirs* as being "widely accredited as the first deliberately dirty novel in English." However, the reviewer found Fanny to be "no common harlot. Her 'Memoirs' combine literary grace with a disarming enthusiasm for an activity which is, after all, only human. What is more, she never uses a dirty word." The short answer to such "expertise" is that none of these so-called attributes have any value to society. On the contrary, they accentuate the prurient appeal.

Another expert described the book as having "detectable literary merit" since it reflects "an effort to interpret a rather complex character . . . going through a number of very different adventures." To illustrate his assertion that the "writing is very skillfully done" this expert pointed to the description of a whore, "Phoebe, who is 'red faced, fat and in her early 50's, who waddles into a room.' She doesn't walk in, she waddles in." Given this standard for "skillful writing," it is not surprising that he found the book to have merit.

The remaining experts testified in the same manner, claiming the book to be a "record of the historical, psychological, and social events of the period." One has but to read the history of the 18th century to disprove this assertion. The story depicts nothing besides the brothels that are present in the metropolitan cities in every period of history. One expert noticed "in this book a tendency away from nakedness during the sexual act which I find an interesting sort of sociological observation" on tastes different from contemporary ones. As additional proof, he marvels that Fanny "refers constantly to the male sexual organ as an engine . . . which is pulling you away from the way these events would be described in the 19th or 20th century." How this adds social value to the book is beyond my comprehension. It only indicates the lengths to which these experts go in their effort to give the book some semblance of value. For example, the ubiquitous descriptions of sexual acts are excused as being necessary in tracing the "moral progress" of the heroine, and the giving of a silver watch to a servant is found to be "an odd and interesting custom that I would like to know more about." This only points up the bankruptcy of *Memoirs* in both purpose and content, adequately justifying the trial court's finding that it had absolutely no social value.

It is, of course, the duty of the judge or the jury to determine the question of obscenity, viewing the book by contemporary community standards. It can accept the appraisal of experts or discount their testimony in the light of the material itself or other relevant testimony. So-called "literary obscenity," *i. e.,* the use of erotic fantasies of the hard-core type clothed in an engaging literary style has no constitutional protection. If a book deals solely with erotic material in a manner calculated to appeal to the prurient interest, it matters not that it may be expressed in beautiful prose. There are obviously dynamic connections between art and sex—the emotional, intellectual, and physical—but where the former is used solely to promote prurient appeal, it cannot claim constitutional immunity. Cleland uses this technique to promote the prurient appeal of *Memoirs*. It is true that Fanny's perverse experiences finally bring from her the observation that "the height of [sexual] enjoyment cannot be achieved until true affection prepares the bed of passion." But this merely emphasizes that sex, wherever and however found, remains the sole theme of *Memoirs*. In my view, the book's repeated and unrelieved appeals to the prurient interest of the average person leave it utterly without redeeming social importance.

In his separate concurrence, my Brother Douglas asserts there is no proof that obscenity produces anti-social conduct. I had thought that this question was foreclosed by the determination in *Roth* that obscenity was not protected by the First Amendment. I find it necessary to comment upon Brother Douglas' views, however, because of the new requirement engrafted upon *Roth* by Brother Brennan, *i. e.,* that material which "appeals to the prurient interest" and which is "patently offensive" may still not be suppressed unless it is "utterly without redeeming social value." The question of anti-social effect thus becomes relevant to the more limited question of social value. Brother Brennan indicates that the social importance criteria encompasses only such things as the artistic, literary, and historical qualities of the material. But the phrasing of the "utterly without redeeming social value" test suggests that other evidence must be considered. To say that social value may "redeem" implies that courts must balance alleged esthetic merit against the harmful consequences that may flow from pornography. Whatever the scope of the social value criterion—which need not be defined with precision here—it at least anticipates that the trier of fact weigh evidence of the material's influence in causing deviant or criminal conduct, particularly sex crimes, as well as its effect upon the mental, moral, and physical health of the average person. Brother DOUGLAS' view as to the lack of proof in this area is not so firmly held among behavioral scientists as he would lead us to believe. For this reason, I should mention that there is a division of thought on the correlation between obscenity and socially deleterious behavior.

Psychological and physiological studies clearly indicate that many persons become sexually aroused from reading obscene material.[4] While erotic stimulation caused by pornography may be legally insignificant in itself, there are medical experts who believe that such stimulation frequently manifests itself in criminal sexual behavior or other anti-social conduct.[5] For example, Dr. George W. Henry of Cornell University has expressed the opinion that obscenity, with its exaggerated and morbid emphasis on sex, particularly abnormal and perverted practices, and its unrealistic presentation of sexual behavior and attitudes, may induce anti-social conduct by the average person.[6] A number of sociologists think that this material may have adverse effects upon individual mental health, with potentially disruptive consequences for the community.[7]

In addition, there is persuasive evidence from criminologists and police officials. Inspector Herbert Case of the Detroit Police Department contends that sex murder cases are invariably tied to some form of obscene literature.[8] And the Director of the Federal Bureau of Investigation, J. Edgar Hoover, has repeatedly emphasized that pornography is associated with an overwhelmingly large number of sex crimes. Again, while the correlation between possession of obscenity and deviant behavior has not been conclusively established, the files of our law enforcement agencies contain many reports of persons who patterned their criminal conduct after behavior depicted in obscene material.[9]

[4] For a summary of experiments with various sexual stimuli see Cairns, Paul, and Wishner, Sex Censorship: The Assumptions of Anti-Obscenity Laws and the Empirical Evidence, 46 Minn. L. Rev. 1009 (1962). The authors cite research by Kinsey disclosing that obscene literature stimulated a definite sexual response in a majority of the male and female subjects tested.

[5] E. g., Wertham, Seduction of the Innocent (1954), p. 164.

[6] Testimony before the Subcommittee of the Judiciary Committee to Investigate Juvenile Delinquency, S. Rep. No. 2381, 84th Cong., 2d Sess., pp. 8–12 (1956).

[7] Sorokin, The American Sex Revolution (1956).

[8] Testimony before the House Select Committee on Current Pornographic Materials, H. R. Rep. No. 2510, 82d Cong., 2d Sess., p. 62 (1952).

[9] See, e.g., Hoover, Combating Merchants of Filth: The Role of the FBI, 25 U. Pitt. L. Rev. 469 (1964); Hoover, The Fight Against Filth, The American Legion Magazine (May 1961).

The clergy are also outspoken in their belief that pornography encourages violence, degeneracy and sexual misconduct. In a speech reported by the *New York Journal-American,* August 7, 1964, Cardinal Spellman particularly stressed the direct influence obscenity has on immature persons. These and related views have been confirmed by practical experience. After years of service with the West London Mission, Rev. Donald Soper found that pornography was a primary cause of prostitution. Rolph, Does Pornography Matter? (1961), pp. 47–48.[10]

Congress and the legislatures of every State have enacted measures to restrict the distribution of erotic and pornographic material,[11] justifying these controls by reference to evidence that anti-social behavior may result in part from reading obscenity.[12] Likewise, upon another trial, the parties may offer this sort of evidence along with other "social value" characteristics that they attribute to the book.

But this is not all that Massachusetts courts might consider. I believe it can be established that the book "was commercially exploited for the sake of prurient appeal, to the exclusion of all other values" and should therefore be declared obscene under the test of commercial exploitation announced today in *Ginzburg* and *Mishkin.*

As I have stated, my study of *Memoirs* leads me to think that it has no conceivable "social importance." The author's obsession with sex, his minute descriptions of phalli, and his repetitious accounts of bawdy sexual experiences and deviant sexual behavior indicate the book was designed solely to appeal to prurient interests. In addition, the record before the Court contains extrinsic evidence tending to show that the publisher was fully aware that the book attracted readers desirous of vicarious sexual pleasure, and sought to profit solely from its prurient appeal. The publisher's "Introduction" recites that Cleland, a "never-do-well bohemian," wrote the book in 1749 to make a quick 20 guineas. Thereafter, various publications of the book, often "embellished with fresh inflammatory details" and "highly exaggerated illustrations," appeared in "surreptitious circulation." Indeed, the cover of *Memoirs* tempts the reader with the announcement that the sale of the book has finally been permitted "after 214 years of suppression." Although written in a sophisticated tone, the "Introduction" repeatedly informs the reader that he may expect graphic descriptions of genitals and sexual exploits. For instance, it states:

> Here and there, Cleland's descriptions of lovemaking are marred by what perhaps could be best described as his adherence to the "longitudinal fallacy"—the formidable bodily equipment of his most accomplished lovers is apt to be described with quite unnecessary relish . . . .

[10] For a general discussion see Murphy, Censorship: Government and Obscenity (1963), pp. 131–151.

[11] The statutes are compiled in S. Rep. No. 2381, 84th Cong., 2d Sess., pp. 17–23 (1956). While New Mexico itself does not prohibit the distribution of obscenity, it has a statute giving municipalities the right to suppress "obscene" publications. N. M. Stat. § 14–17–14 (1965 Supp.).

[12] See Report of the New York State Joint Legislative Committee Studying the Publication and Dissemination of Offensive and Obscene Material (1958), pp. 141–166.

Many other passages in the "Introduction" similarly reflect the publisher's "own evaluation" of the book's nature. The excerpt printed on the jacket of the hard-cover edition is typical:

> *Memoirs of a Woman of Pleasure* is the product of a luxurious and licentious, but not a commercially degraded, era. . . . For all its abounding improprieties, his priapic novel is not a vulgar book. It treats of pleasure as the aim and end of existence, and of sexual satisfaction as the epitome of pleasure, but does so in a style that despite its inflammatory subject, never stoops to a gross or unbecoming word.

Cleland apparently wrote only one other book, a sequel called *Memoirs of a Coxcomb,* published by Lancer Books, Inc. The "Introduction" to that book labels *Memoirs of a Woman of Pleasure* as "the most sensational piece of erotica in English literature." I dare say that this fact alone explains why G. P. Putnam's Sons published this obscenity—preying upon prurient and carnal proclivities for its own pecuniary advantage. I would affirm the judgment.

The Fanny Hill Case: Dissenting Opinion Justice Byron R. White

Byron Raymond ("Whizzer") White (1917–   ) is an associate justice of the U.S. Supreme Court, a position to which he was appointed in 1962 by President John Fitzgerald Kennedy.

In *Roth* v. *United States,* 354 U. S. 476, the Court held a publication to be obscene if its predominant theme appeals to the prurient interest in a manner exceeding customary limits of candor. Material of this kind, the Court said, is "utterly without redeeming social importance" and is therefore unprotected by the First Amendment.

To say that material within the *Roth* definition of obscenity is nevertheless not obscene if it has some redeeming social value is to reject one of the basic propositions of the *Roth* case—that such material is not protected *because* it is inherently and utterly without social value.

If "social importance" is to be used as the prevailing opinion uses it today, obscene material, however far beyond customary limits of candor, is immune if it has any literary style, if it contains any historical references or language characteristic of a bygone day, or even if it is printed or bound in an interesting way. Well written, especially effective obscenity is protected; the poorly written is vulnerable. And why shouldn't the fact that some people buy and read such material prove its "social value"?

A fortiori, if the predominant theme of the book appeals to the prurient interest as stated in *Roth* but the book nevertheless contains here and there a passage descriptive of character, geography or architecture, the

From *A Book Named "John Cleland's Memoirs of a Woman of Pleasure," et al., Appellants, v. Attorney General of the Commonwealth of Massachusetts,* 383 U.S. 413.

book would not be "obscene" under the social importance test. I had thought that *Roth* counseled the contrary: That the character of the book is fixed by its predominant theme and is not altered by the presence of minor themes of a different nature. The *Roth* Court's emphatic reliance on the quotation from *Chaplinsky* v. *New Hampshire,* 315 U. S. 568, means nothing less:

> "... There are certain well-defined and narrowly limited classes of speech, the prevention and punishment of which have never been thought to raise any Constitutional problem. *These include the lewd and obscene ....It has been well observed that such utterances are no essential part of any exposition of ideas, and are of such slight social value as a step to truth that any benefit that may be derived from them is clearly outweighed by the social interest in order and morality....*" (Emphasis added.) 354 U. S., at 485.

In my view, "social importance" is not an independent test of obscenity but is relevant only to determining the predominant prurient interest of the material, a determination which the court or the jury will make based on the material itself and all the evidence in the case, expert or otherwise.

Application of the *Roth* test, as I understand it, necessarily involves the exercise of judgment by legislatures, courts and juries. But this does not mean that there are no limits to what may be done in the name of *Roth.* Cf. *Jacobellis* v. *Ohio,* 378 U. S. 184. *Roth* does not mean that a legislature is free to ban books simply because they deal with sex or because they appeal to the prurient interest. Nor does it mean that if books like *Fanny Hill* are unprotected, their nonprurient appeal is necessarily lost to the world. Literary style, history, teachings about sex, character description (even of a prostitute) or moral lessons need not come wrapped in such packages. The fact that they do impeaches their claims to immunity from legislative censure.

Finally, it should be remembered that if the publication and sale of *Fanny Hill* and like books are proscribed, it is not the Constitution that imposes the ban. Censure stems from a legislative act, and legislatures are constitutionally free to embrace such books whenever they wish to do so. But if a State insists on treating *Fanny Hill* as obscene and forbidding its sale, the First Amendment does not prevent it from doing so.

I would affirm the judgment below.

Art and a Better Society

Art for Art's Sake   E. M. Forster

Edward Morgan Forster (1879–1970), an English writer, was not only one of the outstanding novelists of the first half of the twentieth century, but also an effective essayist on art and social questions.

I believe in art for art's sake. It is an unfashionable belief, and some of my statements must be of the nature of an apology. Fifty years ago I should have faced you with more confidence. A writer or a speaker who chose "Art for Art's Sake" for his theme fifty years ago could be sure of being in the swim, and could feel so confident of success that he sometimes dressed himself in esthetic costumes suitable to the occasion—in an embroidered dressing-gown, perhaps, or a blue velvet suit with a Lord Fauntleroy collar; or a toga, or a kimono, and carried a poppy or a lily or a long peacock's feather in his mediaeval hand. Times have changed. Not thus can I present either myself or my theme today. My aim rather is to ask you quietly to reconsider for a few minutes a phrase which has been much misused and much abused, but which has, I believe, great importance for us—has, indeed, eternal importance.

Now we can easily dismiss those peacock's feathers and other affectations—they are but trifles—but I want also to dismiss a more dangerous heresy, namely the silly idea that only art matters, an idea which has somehow got mixed up with the idea of art for art's sake, and has helped to discredit it. Many things, besides art, matter. It is merely one of the things that matter, and high though the claims are that I make for it, I want to keep them in proportion. No one can spend his or her life entirely in the creation or the appreciation of masterpieces. Man lives, and ought to live, in a complex world, full of conflicting claims, and if we simplified them down into the esthetic he would be sterilised. Art for art's sake does not mean that only art matters, and I would also like to rule out such phrases as "The Life of Art," "Living for Art," and "Art's High Mission." They confuse and mislead.

What does the phrase mean? Instead of generalising, let us take a specific instance—Shakespeare's *Macbeth,* for example, and pronounce the words, "*Macbeth* for *Macbeth's* sake." What does that mean? Well, the play has several aspects—it is educational, it teaches us something about legendary Scotland, something about Jacobean England, and a good deal about human nature and its perils. We can study its origins, and study and enjoy its dramatic technique and the music of its diction. All that is true. But *Macbeth* is furthermore a world of its own, created by Shakespeare and existing in virtue of its own poetry. It is in this aspect *Macbeth* for *Macbeth's* sake, and that is what I intend by the phrase "art for art's sake." A work of art—whatever else it may be—is a self-contained entity, with a life of its own imposed on it by its creator. It has internal order. It may have external form. That is how we recognise it.

Take for another example that picture of Seurat's which I saw two years ago in Chicago—"*La Grande Jatte.*" Here again there is much to study and to enjoy: the pointillism, the charming face of the seated girl, the nineteenth-century Parisian Sunday sunlight, the sense of motion in immobility. But here again there is something more; "*La Grande Jatte*" forms a world of its own, created by Seurat and existing by virtue of its own poetry: "*La Grande Jatte*" *pour* "*La Grande Jatte*": *l'art pour l'art.* Like *Macbeth* it has internal order and internal life.

It is to the conception of order that I would now turn. This is important to my argument, and I want to make a digression, and glance at order in daily life, before I come to order in art.

In the world of daily life, the world which we perforce inhabit, there is much talk about order, particularly from statesmen and politicians. They tend, however, to confuse order with orders, just as they confuse creation with regulations. Order, I suggest, is something evolved from within, not something imposed from without; it is an internal stability, a vital harmony, and in the social and political category it has never existed except for the convenience of historians. Viewed realistically, the past is really a series of *dis*orders, succeeding one another by discoverable laws, no doubt, and certainly marked by an increasing growth of human interference, but disorders all the same. So that, speaking as a writer, what I hope for today is a disorder which will be more favourable to artists than is the present one, and which will provide them with fuller inspirations and better material conditions. It will not last—nothing lasts—but there have been some advantageous disorders in the past—for instance, in ancient Athens, in Renaissance Italy, eighteenth-century France, periods in China and Persia—and we may do something to accelerate the next one. But let us not again fix our hearts where true joys are not to be found. We were promised a new order after the first world war through the League of Nations. It did not come, nor have I faith in present promises, by whomsoever endorsed. The implacable offensive of Science forbids. We cannot reach social and political stability for the reason that we continue to make scientific discoveries and to apply them, and thus to destroy the arrangements which were based on more elementary discoveries. If Science would discover rather than apply—if, in other words, men were more interested in knowledge than in power—mankind would be in a far safer position, the stability statesmen talk about would be a possibility, there could be a new order based on vital harmony, and the earthly millennium might approach. But Science shows no signs of doing this: she gave us the internal combustion engine, and before we had digested and assimilated it with terrible pains into our social system, she harnessed the atom, and destroyed any new order that seemed to be evolving. How can man get into harmony with his surroundings when he is constantly altering them? The future of our race is, in this direction, more unpleasant than we care to admit, and it has sometimes seemed to me that its best chance lies through apathy, uninventiveness, and inertia. Universal exhaustion might promote that Change of Heart which is at present so briskly recommended from a thousand pulpits. Universal exhaustion would certainly be a new experience. The human race has never undergone it, and is still too perky to admit that it may be coming and might result in a sprouting of new growth through the decay.

I must not pursue these speculations any further—they lead me too far from my terms of reference and maybe from yours. But I do want to emphasise that order in daily life and in history, order in the social and political category, is unattainable under our present psychology.

Where is it attainable? Not in the astronomical category, where it was for many years enthroned. The heavens and the earth have become terribly alike since Einstein. No longer can we find a reassuring contrast to chaos in the night sky and look up with George Meredith to the stars, the army of unalterable law, or listen for the music of the spheres. Order is not there. In the entire universe there seem to be only two possibilities for it. The first of them—which again lies outside my terms of reference—is the divine order, the mystic harmony, which according to all religions is available for those who can contemplate it. We must admit its possibility, on the evidence of the adepts, and we must believe them when they say that it is attained, if attainable, by prayer. "O thou who changest not, abide with me," said one of its poets. *"Ordina questo amor, o tu che m'ami,"* said another: "Set love in order, thou who lovest me." The existence of a divine order, though it cannot be tested, has never been disproved.

The second possibility for order lies in the esthetic category, which is my subject here: the order which an artist can create in his own work, and to that we must now return. A work of art, we are all agreed, is a unique product. But why? It is unique not because it is clever or noble or beautiful or enlightened or original or sincere or idealistic or useful or educational—it may embody any of those qualities—but because it is the only material object in the universe which may possess internal harmony. All the others have been pressed into shape from outside, and when their mould is removed they collapse. The work of art stands up by itself, and nothing else does. It achieves something which has often been promised by society, but always delusively. Ancient Athens made a mess—but the *Antigone* stands up. Renaissance Rome made a mess—but the ceiling of the Sistine got painted. James I made a mess—but there was *Macbeth*. Louis XIV—but there was *Phèdre*. Art for art's sake? I should just think so, and more so than ever at the present time. It is the one orderly product which our muddling race has produced. It is the cry of a thousand sentinels, the echo from a thousand labyrinths; it is the lighthouse which cannot be hidden: *c'est le meilleur témoignage que nous puissions donner de notre dignité.** *Antigone* for *Antigone's* sake, *Macbeth* for *Macbeth's*, *"La Grande Jatte" pour "La Grande Jatte."*

If this line of argument is correct, it follows that the artist will tend to

---

* ["It is the best witness we could give of our dignity."—ed.]

be an outsider in the society to which he has been born, and that the nineteenth-century conception of him as a Bohemian was not inaccurate. The conception erred in three particulars: it postulated an economic system where art could be a full-time job, it introduced the fallacy that only art matters, and it overstressed idiosyncrasy and waywardness—the peacock-feather aspect—rather than order. But it is a truer conception than the one which prevails in official circles on my side of the Atlantic—I don't know about yours: the conception which treats the artist as if he were a particularly bright government advertiser and encourages him to be friendly and matey with his fellow citizens, and not to give himself airs.

Estimable is mateyness, and the man who achieves it gives many a pleasant little drink to himself and to others. But it has no traceable connection with the creative impulse, and probably acts as an inhibition on it. The artist who is seduced by mateyness may stop himself from doing the one thing which he, and he alone, can do—the making of something out of words or sounds or paint or clay or marble or steel or film which has internal harmony and presents order to a permanently disarranged planet. This seems worth doing, even at the risk of being called uppish by journalists. I have in mind an article which was published some years ago in the London *Times,* an article called "The Eclipse of the Highbrow," in which the "Average Man" was exalted, and all contemporary literature was censured if it did not toe the line, the precise position of the line being naturally known to the writer of the article. Sir Kenneth Clark, who was at that time director of our National Gallery, commented on this pernicious doctrine in a letter which cannot be too often quoted. "The poet and the artist," wrote Clark, "are important precisely because they are not average men; because in sensibility, intelligence, and power of invention they far exceed the average." These memorable words, and particularly the words "power of invention," are the Bohemian's passport. Furnished with it, he slinks about society, saluted now by a brickbat and now by a penny, and accepting either of them with equanimity. He does not consider too anxiously what his relations with society may be, for he is aware of something more important than that—namely the invitation to invent, to create order, and he believes he will be better placed for doing this if he attempts detachment. So round and round he slouches, with his hat pulled over his eyes, and maybe with a louse in his beard, and—if he really wants one—with a peacock's feather in his hand.

If our present society should disintegrate—and who dare prophesy that it won't?—this old-fashioned and démodé figure will become clearer: the Bohemian, the outsider, the parasite, the rat—one of those figures which have at present no function either in a warring or a peaceful world. It may not be dignified to be a rat, but many of the ships are sinking, which is not dignified either—the officials did not build them properly. Myself, I would sooner be a swimming rat than a sinking ship—at all events I can look around me for a little longer—and I remember how one of us, a rat with particularly bright eyes called Shelley, squeaked out, "Poets are the unacknowledged legislators of the world," before he vanished into the waters of the Mediterranean.

What laws did Shelley propose to pass? None. The legislation of the artist is never formulated at the time, though it is sometimes discerned by future generations. He legislates through creating. And he creates through his sensitiveness and his power to impose form. Without form the sensitiveness vanishes. And form is as important today, when the human race is trying to ride the whirlwind, as it ever was in those less agitating days of the past, when the earth seemed solid and the stars fixed, and the discoveries of science were made slowly, slowly. Form is not tradition. It alters from generation to generation. Artists always seek a new technique, and will continue to do so as long as their work excites them. But form of some kind is imperative. It is the surface crust of the internal harmony, it is the outward evidence of order.

My remarks about society may have seemed too pessimistic, but I believe that society can only represent a fragment of the human spirit, and that another fragment can only get expressed through art. And I wanted to take this opportunity, this vantage ground, to assert not only the existence of art, but its pertinacity. Looking back into the past, it seems to me that that is all there has ever been: vantage grounds for discussion and creation, little vantage grounds in the changing chaos, where bubbles have been blown and webs spun, and the desire to create order has found temporary gratification, and the sentinels have managed to utter their challenges, and the huntsmen, though lost individually, have heard each other's calls through the impenetrable wood, and the lighthouses have never ceased sweeping the thankless seas. In this pertinacity there seems to me, as I grow older, something more and more profound, something which does in fact concern people who do not care about art at all.

In conclusion, let me summarise the various categories that have laid claim to the possession of Order.

(1) The social and political category. Claim disallowed on the evidence of history and of our own experience. If man altered psychologically, order here might be attainable; not otherwise.

(2) The astronomical category. Claim allowed up to the present century, but now disallowed on the evidence of the physicists.

(3) The religious category. Claim allowed on the evidence of the mystics.

(4) The esthetic category. Claim allowed on the evidence of various works of art, and on the evidence of our own creative impulses, however weak these may be, or however imperfectly they may function. Words of art, in my opinion, are the only objects in the material universe to possess internal order, and that is why, though I don't believe that only art matters, I do believe in Art for Art's Sake.

Art for Man's Sake   Barrows Dunham

Barrows Dunham (1905–   ) is a philosopher professionally trained in America, whose writings in social philosophy and intellectual history have attracted many readers from the general literate public.

... "I cannot take part in politics." The words reminded me at once of a painter I had met some years ago under the double heat of conversation and whisky. "I am an artist," he said, asserting perhaps more than was true, "and I think it enough if I save a few flowers to hand over to posterity." At that time Spain was going under, the long shadow was deepening over Europe, and it did seem that an artist might do more than gather flowers. For a successful defense of the Spanish Republic would have saved the lives of millions since dead, the anguish of yet other millions, and the captivity of peoples. To assert that all these things are "politics," with which art has nothing to do, is to assert that art does not concern itself with humanity.

Who should profit from such illusions? Not my friend the painter, for, in ignoring Spain, he ignored the cause of human freedom, with all the vast fertility which such a theme can give to art. Not you and I, for we needed to be stirred out of the deadly quiet of those years. Not the people of Europe, who faced enemies abroad and collaborators at home. Only the fascists could profit; only the would-be conquerors, who thus gained a self-imposed silence upon the part of their natural foes. The assassin steals close, the dagger is lifted; but the victim murmurs, "I am an artist: I have no comment to make."

Thus the belief that art and politics are incompatible has its social uses. The primary purpose is to silence and disarm. Everyone knows that ideas, when transmitted in the excitement of esthetic experience, have a powerful effect upon the mind. Not only are they then more readily accepted, but they are more readily acted upon. The flame lit in contemplation becomes a holocaust. If you have an *Uncle Tom's Cabin,* you may have a Civil War. Reactionaries therefore take no chances. So far as they can manage it, there will not be any novels or plays or paintings expressive of human suffering and the means of remedy.

While democracy persists, it is difficult to prevent such works by the use of governmental machinery. Suppression must be subtler. There can be no suppression more subtle and at the same time more effective than to persuade novelists, playwrights, and painters that their true vocation lies elsewhere. Once social themes are abandoned by the very men who could most passionately treat them, little need to be feared from the imperfect performers who remain.

The primary use is thus preventive. A secondary, though valuable, use is as a weapon of attack against those works which, despite all cajolery and enticement, continue to plead the hopes of mankind. To say that these are "propaganda but not art" is to say that the creator either has no knowledge of his craft or has sacrificed it to purposes beyond his legitimate reach. In this manner the novel is made to lose its readers, the play its audiences, and the painting its spectators. The superstition achieves all this without once hinting that the real object of attack was not the work itself but the social ideas it contained.

If, lastly, the superstition, having fully concealed its origin and purpose, sets up as an independent esthetic theory, it will have an almost limitless capacity for harm. Creative genius, the mightiest of human faculties, must then confess itself a shorn Samson and humbly put its body to the wheel. Betrayed by a faithless Delilah and blinded by shrewd Philistines, it will have neither the thought nor the wish to pull down temples.

Is It Possible to Say Nothing?

There must be some irony in the spectacle of artists striving to avoid politics on behalf of a doctrine whose purpose is political. Yet sincere artists are sincere craftsmen. Their various skills are as painfully acquired as they are brilliant when achieved. It is perfectly natural for writers and musicians and painters to be somewhat more concerned with the means to an effect than they are with the effect itself. And we, for whom their creations are made, come also to prize technique as the ultimate manifestation of their talents. The mark of connoisseurship lies, we begin to think, in observing not what has been done, but how it was done.

This separation of form from content, of technique from result, arises simply from our being interested rather more in the one than in the other. The preference itself is one which has not always existed and doubtless will not always exist. All thought of such a separation vanishes when we inquire how far an artist can detach himself and his works from the life around him. To attain complete detachment, what would he have to do?

Well, take a writer, for example. His medium is words. Now, words have meanings and, with those meanings, emotional associations. Despite all cynical doubts, it is very difficult for a writer not to say something whenever he assembles words, and he likewise cannot avoid stirring in some measure the emotions of his readers. But so far as he does these things, he is intimately bound to life and to the world about him. He could be completely detached only if he treated words as sounds which have no sense, and this he would have to do in such a way as not to suggest any meaning through the very absence of it. This technique has been attempted by some writers, notably by Miss Gertrude Stein, but it cannot be said to have caught on.

The painter has a wider area in which to practice detachment. He does not have to represent on canvas the forms and movements of ordinary life. He may, if he likes, paint "non-objectively"; that is to say, he can assemble colors into patterns of his own choosing without any resemblance to objects as they are seen. There can be no objection to this procedure so long as it remains one among many possible choices for painters to make: we do not require literal representation upon rugs or drapery, and there seems to be no reason why we should specifically require it of painting. Yet even here, if complete detachment were to be attained, the painter would have to annul any possible suggestion which might lie in the painting's emotional appeal. Kandinsky, for example, copies nothing; but the magnificence of his composition suggests harmony and movement, which in turn can suggest other concepts to the very boundary of an observer's thought.

The composer seems, at first sight, more detached from life than any other artist. Unlike the writer, he actually does deal with sounds that have no fixed meanings. Yet he is bound to life by emotional association fully as much as writers are. No one can take Tchaikovsky to have been an optimist; no one can imagine Beethoven to have been a man of small ideas. For his part, the old giant maintained that in every work he expressed some portion of his philosophy. The apparent meaninglessness of musical composition is in fact an invitation to listeners to supply it with meanings as their minds roam free. Probably the only way to cancel all possible meanings would be to make the work so dull as to be no invitation.

It seems unlikely, then, that there can be many works of art which have no reference to life and the problems of living. For most artists it must remain insuperably difficult to negate the very humanity which is the source of their own skills. Try as one may to empty art of content, there will remain some hint, some whisper, which shall set in motion the minds of other men. I recall how often, during the rise of fascism, I used to repeat to myself the lines of MacLeish's lovely poem "You, Andrew Marvell":

> And Spain go under and the shore
> Of Africa the gilded sand
> And evening vanish and no more
> The low pale light across that land
>
> Nor now the long light on the sea—
>
> And here face downward in the sun
> To feel how swift how secretly
> The shadow of the night comes on . . .*

The poet intended no more than a description of approaching night, but his lines became irresistibly symbolic.

These things being true, one may look with justifiable doubt upon works of art which expressly assert their detachment from life. We shall certainly feel that the artist is likely to be mistaken about this, and we may feel, in addition, that he is being disingenuous. For if, as is probable, the work does have a reference to life, though he says it has none, this condition may be due to his having missed the reference or to his having concealed it. There are thus two possibilities: an illusory detachment in which the work contains unconscious comment, and a hypocritical detachment in which there is comment deliberately hidden.

* [From Archibald MacLeish, "You, Andrew Marvell," *Collected Poems 1917–1952*. Reprinted by permission of Houghton Mifflin Company, the publisher.]

It may be difficult to tell into which of these categories a given work will fall, but the membership of both is surely large. Lately, for example, a kind of neo-Victorianism has begun to set in. Art exhibits now display new versions of the old farms, water mills, and Mississippi steamboats which one used to see on the ancestral wall. Mr. Eliot has edited the poems of Kipling, and Mr. Auden those of Tennyson. I am not sure why two of the most abstruse poets should turn toward two of the most plain-spoken, but I don't suppose they turn thither in order to recapture the morality of Galahad. Wittingly or unwittingly, they are commenting upon our present world—and commenting, I think, unfavorably.

But these are limited examples, and we need a larger view. It seems to be a fact that the more a work of art is directed to mass audiences, the greater the amount of surreptitious comment it contains. Best-selling novels present themselves as pure narratives, that is to say, as chronicles of speedy and exciting events, without the least commentary. Yet the sufferings of Scarlett O'Hara would almost persuade us to love those wayward and exquisite slaveowners who refused to pass peacefully out of power. And if we love the owners of human flesh, how shall we learn to love the men whose flesh was owned? Even for reactionaries, grief over a lost tyranny is a waste of tears.

A more humble art form is the comic strip, but the public which it reaches is now so enormous that one can exclude oneself from it only by a violent exercise of will. In my boyhood, comic strips contained one joke per day, with no attempt at continuity. Even then, however, *Bringing Up Father* was a spirited expression of democratic revolt against parvenus and aristocrats. I do not know whether Mr. McManus drew all this consciously, but I acknowledge that I am in his debt.

Beneath the extravagant narratives of contemporary strips one can discern all sorts of ideologies, among which the antilabor philosophy of *Little Orphan Annie* can hardly be unintentional. Superman, who (as we are told) is not a bird or a plane, clearly compensates by his incredible powers for the impotence of common man. We readers, thwarted on every side by a social system which we do not control, find pleasure in the imaginary existence of a man whose powers are limitless and whose purposes are sublime. Unfortunately, he acts as a substitute, not an inspiration. He leads us to rely on intervention from outside us and to forget how massive our strength can be, if we but organize it. *Superman,* I am afraid, is founded upon a retrograde social theory. At any rate, it is certainly not mere narrative.

The greatest of all mass arts is the cinema, and nowhere else does the belief more ardently prevail that entertainment is the goal, not propaganda. "Entertainment" has acquired the power of a shibboleth. It appears to mean, primarily, escape from tedium or anxiety, from ugliness or defeat. It means, also, the sublimation of frustrated desire, as when the screen exhibits rooms we would like to live in and cannot, men or women we would like to love and cannot. It means, perhaps, the mere holding of attention, by which a few moments can be made to slip by.

Does the cinema "teach?" Obviously—one may say, notoriously—it does. No protestations about "entertainment" can long conceal the fact that movie audiences over a period of years have been absorbing an entire philosophy. They have been learning that no woman over twenty-five can be handsome or attractive, though men can be both to a fairly ancient age; that the feminine landscape should be as visible as possible without being actually seen; that the most interesting people are those who are well-dressed, well-loved, and acquainted with cabarets. Above all, they have been learning that there is nothing fundamentally wrong with our society.

The existence of censorship puts the fact beyond doubt, for all censorship is indoctrination. The fate which overtook Donald Ogden Stewart's script for *Keeper of the Flame* will show what kind of censorship we have. This movie had to do with a woman who discovered that her husband was plotting to become the American *Führer*. She permitted him to be killed in an automobile accident, by failing to telephone him that a certain bridge had been washed away. After his death, the fascist plot was discovered and destroyed.

Mr. Stewart had intended to close the story with Miss Hepburn and Mr. Tracy where we like to see them, in one another's arms. But at this point censorship intervened. The wife had been guilty of a mortal sin in the accident which befell her husband. The penalty of mortal sin is death. Therefore Miss Hepburn had to die, while Mr. Tracy, an engaging newspaperman, lived on to the partial satisfaction of the audience.

We need not discuss the moral casuistry which is able to rate the struggle against fascism lower than the prescriptions of a special code. It suffices to perceive that movie-goers were being told (1) that things ought to happen in a certain way, and (2) more remarkable yet, that they do happen that way. In this particular case, I think the lessons were lost on the audience. Generally, however, the lessons strike home. One can only guess to what extent American racism is sustained by film stereotypes of the amusing, lazy Negro and the insidious Oriental, the latter of which completely frustrates any clear understanding of Japanese fascism.

Cinema comment is plainly the kind which enforces a certain set of values, and therefore influences action. It is, consciously or unconsciously, propaganda in any reasonable sense of the term. Movie-goers may think they are being merely entertained, but actually they are being instructed. And not always well. . . .

Beauty, Content, and Utility

Let us see what fortifications a man might erect who, for fear of comment obnoxious to himself, wished to defend the view that art should have no social comment at all. The word "should" is, of course, somewhat ambiguous. In all probability, our antagonist would not mean anything ethical by it; that is to say, he wouldn't mean that such a work of art is immoral. He would probably mean that such a work is esthetically unsuccessful, that its beauty has been impaired by the comment or removed altogether. How could he defend this view?

First, he could wall in the entire area, after the manner of Bell and Fry, by saying that form alone is the source of esthetic merit, content being a distracting irrelevance. Apart from the great difficulty of deciding what, in any work of art, is form and what is content, this argument must assume that form and content are in fact separable. And they must be separable to such an extent that either (1) there can be works of art which have form but no content whatever, or (2) in works which have both, but are nevertheless esthetically successful, attention can be restricted to the form (the source of excellence) without any influence from the content.

Now, as for assumption (1), we have already observed how rare such achievements must be. For, in order to do this, an artist must be at pains not only to say nothing overtly, but also to make sure that his saying nothing overtly does not itself suggest some genuine comment. For if a man says nothing, when everybody is expecting him to say something, then his silence (or at any rate, his meaninglessness) will be bound to seem significant. I do not know how many modern painters have done their abstracts with the intent of avoiding comment; but it seems clear to me that they have been teaching us new ways in which to look at the physical world, and have thus been commenting all the time. In some of them, like Léger and Picasso, the comment has been perfectly conscious and extremely persuasive, so that it is now part of the natural life of men in the western world. It is one of the things you would think of, if you undertook to answer the question, "What does life, as we now live it, signify?"

Assumption (2) covers certainly most of the works of painting, sculpture, literature, and music as men have produced these in the past, before there arose any conviction that comment should be avoided. The effect of the assumption seems to be to take the soliloquies out of Shakespeare, the Franciscan narratives out of Giotto, the chorales out of Bach. For in these works the commentary which forms their content is an essential part of their esthetic effect. Otherwise, you would have to suppose that Hamlet merely utters lovely syllables, whose meaning is accidental and irrelevant. You would have to suppose that Giotto's admiration for St. Francis had no effect upon the frescoes and found no expression in them. In general, you would have to suppose that ideas as such have no esthetic appeal. This view is so fantastic, so contradicted by the great works of the past, that one is led to suspect in the men who hold it some special and curious hostility to thought. It must be that they are misologists, "haters of reason," such as Plato used to denounce.

Having thus breached the outer wall, we should find that our antagonist had built an inner defense. He would by this time concede that works of art may have thought content without being spoiled by it; but he would perhaps say that, if the thought content is intended to influence our action later on, then the work of art had a utilitarian purpose in addition to that of merely being beautiful. He would say, dimly remembering Emerson, that "Beauty is its own excuse for being," and that beautiful things lose their beauty as soon as they are put to some use. In short, the beautiful and the useful are incompatible with each other.

Such a view is far easier to disprove than to support. If it were true that nothing utilitarian can be a work of art, then architecture would disappear immediately as a source of esthetic experience. One can think of hardly any building which has been erected for no useful purpose but for the sake of its beauty alone. All the architectural marvels which spring to mind are tombs or temples or churches or houses or office buildings, all of which bear the obvious mark of utility. It is an interesting commentary upon the influence of economics on art that even the most conspicuous spendthrifts decline to lavish money upon buildings that have no purpose at all.

Furthermore, the beautiful is so far from being incompatible with the useful that some products clearly gain in beauty in proportion as their form reveals the uses they are to serve. According to the Functionalists, who have certainly demonstrated their theory by convincing practice, the architecture of a home, for example, ought plainly to show that the building is intended to be lived in; it ought not to conceal the fact behind Spanish, Dutch, or English Tudor façades. Hence the new style of the modern home, which gets rid of irrelevancies, and makes the form expressive of the use.

Evidently it cannot be maintained that utility necessarily corrupts beauty. There remains, however, the chance that a work of art which is useful in the sense of influencing later action will be damaged on that account. If, for example, the work of art were a play which describes some social injustice and calls for action against it, one might hold that the "message" (*i.e.* the call to action) was an intrusion which destroyed the esthetic effect. People do in fact hold this view, and it is precisely what they mean when they say that you cannot mix art and politics. They like to point out that Shakespeare (an excellent dramatist) discusses many problems, but seems never to advocate anything. In saying this, they have certainly forgotten the patriotic fervor of the Histories. And they have forgotten Ibsen altogether.

To understand the error of this view, we shall have to remember that esthetic experience is spread out in time. It begins, it continues, and it ends. The *esthetic* success of the experience relates to that extent of time which is encompassed by the beginning and the ending. The *utilitarian* success of the experience, however, relates to a period of time after the experience has ceased. There is no apparent reason why these two kinds of success should conflict with each other, as they might conceivably do if they related to the same period of time. For all one knows, an object which is beautiful to us *within* esthetic experience may, without damage to its beauty, have effects upon our actions later on.

Everyone can test this by his own experience. During the long crisis of the last fifteen years, when mankind has lived in exceptional torment, I have returned more and more frequently to the reading of Milton's *Lycidas*. When my blood seems turned to water and my bones to jelly, I find in *Lycidas* that vertebrate strength which enables men to walk erect and lay hands upon the future. Evidently in all this I have been putting the poem to use. Strength in the midst of adversity is a practical aim, and poetry has long been recognized as one of the means to it. What is the effect of such a purpose upon the beauty of *Lycidas*.

Well, I cannot find that the beauty is in any way impaired. A pleasure which even repetition will not dull is likely to be proof against irrelevancies. But I learn this fact also: *Lycidas* is not beautiful because it gives me strength; on the contrary, *Lycidas* gives me strength because it is beautiful. One could pick up a score of volumes entitled "Poems of Inspiration" or "Cantos of Courage" with the desperate foreknowledge that they will contain nothing which can encourage or inspire. True beauty, however, has precisely this power. It is what Shelley meant when he said, rather extravagantly, that "poets are the unacknowledged legislators of the world." The conclusion is, then, that to decide the beauty of a work of art is one thing, and to decide what effects it will have, because it is beautiful, is quite another. Social comment can be art, provided it is *art*. If it remains merely comment, it will not be art certainly, and probably not successful persuasion either.

This, too, can be verified from personal experience. I, for one, can testify that a conviction of truth is not enough. My first realization, some years ago, of what was really wrong with the world touched off in me an explosion of versifying. "I lisped in numbers, for the numbers came." As they came, they seemed good; at any rate, they were remarkable in quantity. A kindly editor to whom I sent them replied that their good stuff had to be "quarried out, more or less." He was perfectly right, and I am by now accustomed to the despair of being no poet. Yet it troubles me that I (having of course the right ideas) can never be a poet, while T. S. Eliot (having of course the wrong ideas) indubitably is. Facts are facts, nonetheless.

Except for reservations like these, social comment is fully capable of reappearing in art. When the comment is obviously biased, or paid for, or altogether mendacious, there will be much greater difficulty. At the best it will appear an attempt to "put something over," and at the worst it will arouse such distaste for lying as to kill any esthetic experience in decent people. But artists should have the benefit of every doubt. For our part, we ought never to let a fear of being propagandized prevent us from learning the minds of other men.

The best refutation, however, is one which I cannot give, for it remains to be given by artists themselves. Arguments like mine may prove whatever they prove; but the superstition will die, when it does die, under the skill with which artists treat the problems of their day. A contemporary Milton might (and would) be traduced as a subversive influence, but even the Hearst press would hardly venture to call him an incompetent poet. I can imagine a time, not perhaps far distant, when the belief that you cannot mix art and politics will crumble before a battery of works too powerful for resistance and too magnificent for reproach.

When such expectations have been fulfilled, let the content of these pages be laid, unremembered, by. There will then be no need to persuade artists that they are full of speech, and that their speech can have fair meaning for mankind. As there is no creator who is not in some degree a man, so there is no man who is not in some degree a creator. Without surrendering any of the admiration we feel for the insuperable achievements of genius, we may nevertheless hope for a narrowing of the distance between ourselves and them, for the awakening of a universal interest in art *and* in life. When artists have fully recovered their humanity, humanity at last will have recovered art.

Suggestions
for Further Reading

Anthologies

Ellmann, Richard and Feidelson, Jr., Charles (eds.). *The Modern Tradition: Backgrounds of Modern Literature.* New York: Oxford U. P., 1965. Although this hefty volume contains numerous selections from philosophers, it is particularly rich in selections from artists revealing the attitudes and ideas so influential in the development of modern art. The relationships of the artist to morality and to science constitute pervasive themes of this anthology.

Hofstadter, Albert and Kuhns, Richard (eds.). *Philosophies of Art and Beauty.* New York: Random, A Modern Library Giant, 1964. A collection of lengthy selections from comprehensive and systematic philosophies of art ranging from Plato to Martin Heidegger.

Philipson, Morris (ed.). *Aesthetics Today.* New York: The World Publishing Company, Meridian Books, 1961. Contains writings by contemporary philosophers, historians, and critics on such topics as art and cultural purposes, style, expression and communication, art and knowledge, and psychology and aesthetics. This book includes material on Marxism and art, Asian art, and existentialism and art, areas often neglected in American anthologies. A brief, very selective bibliography. The beginning student will find this anthology a good place to start explorations.

Weitz, Morris (ed.). *Problems in Aesthetics,* 2nd ed. New York: Macmillan, 1970. A large selection of writings on the nature of art, the nature of tragedy, the character of the aesthetic response, and other aesthetic problems by Western philosophers from ancient Greece to the present. An example of a standard American textbook in aesthetics with selective bibliographies at the end of each section.

Individual Works

Beardsley, Monroe C. *Aesthetics.* New York: Harcourt, 1958. A clear, stimulating, and critical discussion of various subjects in the field of aesthetics. Chapter XII, "The Arts in the Life of Man," deals with such topics as art for art's sake and art and obscenity. The close of each chapter is followed by a large and annotated bibliography.

Bell, Clive. *Art.* New York: Capricorn Books, 1958. A famous and relatively recent statement of a nearly pure Aestheticist view of art as form and only form.

Gotshalk, D. W. *Art and the Social Order,* 2nd ed. New York: Dover, 1962. A lively, easily read book, in which the author develops his own theory of art and emphasizes the relations of art and society. A good example of recent American philosophical thinking on the social context of art.

The Report of the Commission on Obscenity and Pornography. Introduction by Clive Barnes. New York: A New York Times Book, Bantam Books, 1970. (Hardback edition published by Random House.) The highly controversial report of the commission established by President Lyndon Baines Johnson. Also contains separate statements by the commission members dissenting from the majority report.

Santayana, George. *Reason in Art.* (*The Life of Reason,* Vol. IV.) New York: Scribner, 1933. A classic work on the role of art in human life and human life as an art by a great American philosopher and poet.

Sartre, Jean-Paul. *Essays in Aesthetics.* Translated by Wade Baskin. New York: The Citadel Press, 1963.

————. *Literary and Philosophical Essays.* Translated by Annette Michelson. New York: Collier Books, 1962.

————. *Saint Genet.* Translated by Bernard Frechtman. New York: The New American Library, A Mentor Book, 1964.

————. *Situations.* Translated by Benita Eisler. New York: Fawcett World Library, A Fawcett Crest Book, 1966. A leading French existentialist and artist uses his philosophical system to analyze and illuminate the art of Gide, Camus, Faulkner, Giacometti, Dos Passos, Genet, and other novelists, painters, and playwrights. Perhaps the best approach to Sartre for the beginning student.

Tolstoy, Leo N. *What Is Art?* Translated by Almyer Maude. Indianapolis: Bobbs, The Library of Liberal Arts, 1960. A great artist's defense of the subordination of art to morality and religion.

Encyclopedia of Philosophy. Paul Edwards, editor-in-chief. New York: Macmillan, 1967. The beginning student will find many worthwhile articles on the subjects treated in this Part, and excellent bibliographies.

Epilogue

In 1918, Clarence Darrow delivered a high school commencement address remarkable for its brevity and Socratic wisdom. While waiting to speak, Darrow suffered through a verbose and preposterously flattering introduction depicting him as a perfect model whom young people should emulate. Finally the introductory speech came to an end, and Darrow ambled to the lectern, smiled, and gave probably one of the shortest commencement addresses ever given.

> That was as fine a lot of bunk as I ever heard in my life and I know darned well you youngsters didn't believe a word of it. You're no more fit to go forth and serve than the man in the moon. You're just a bunch of ignorant kids, full of the devil, and you've learned practically nothing to show for the years you spent here. You can't fool me, for I once spent four years in such a place.

If, after reading this book and reflecting on what he has read, the student now knows he is ignorant he will be a true friend of Socrates.